D0002661

HUMAN GENETICS
FOR THE SOCIAL SCIENCES

GREGORY CAREY

INSTITUTE FOR BEHAVIORAL GENETICS
UNIVERSITY OF COLORADO

SAGE Publications
International Educational and Professional Publisher
Thousand Oaks ▪ London ▪ New Delhi

Copyright © 2003 by Sage Publications, Inc.

All rights reserved. No part of this book may be reproduced or utilized in any form or by any means, electronic or mechanical, including photocopying, recording, or by any information storage and retrieval system, without permission in writing from the publisher.

For information:

Sage Publications, Inc.
2455 Teller Road
Thousand Oaks, California 91320
E-mail: order@sagepub.com

Sage Publications Ltd.
6 Bonhill Street
London EC2A 4PU
United Kingdom

Sage Publications India Pvt. Ltd.
M-32 Market
Greater Kailash I
New Delhi 110 048 India

Printed in the United States of America

Library of Congress Cataloging-in-Publication Data

Carey, Gregory.
  Human genetics for the social sciences / by Gregory Carey.
    p. cm.
Includes bibliographical references and index.
  ISBN 0-7619-2345-4
  1. Human genetics. 2. Behavior genetics. 3. Social sciences. I. Title.
  QH431 .C243 2002
  599.93'5—dc211

                                      2002005571

This book is printed on acid-free paper.

02 03 04 05 06 10 9 8 7 6 5 4 3 2 1

Acquisitions Editor:	Jim Brace-Thompson
Editorial Assistant:	Karen Ehrmann
Copy Editor:	A. J. Sobczak
Typesetter:	C&M Digitals (P) Ltd.
Indexer:	Cynthia D. Bertelsen
Cover Designer:	Michelle Lee

BRIEF CONTENTS

CONTENTS

PREFACE

Sage Publications and I embarked on this enterprise with the understanding that the text is not conventional. It is not a textbook (although it may be marketed in some quarters as such). Neither is it a professional book (although marketing, again, may target it as such). Instead, it is written for social scientists—from the advanced undergraduate to the professional—who want to learn about genetics and how the science of genetics informs us regarding human behavior.

Later sections of this preface apply to different audiences for this book. No matter what you want this text to be, be mindful of the following:

1. This is not a conventional textbook.

2. I use footnotes liberally. They explain technical terms and elaborate on issues in the text that are not germane for straightforward reading. Skip them unless you are interested in learning more about a topic.

3. The level of discourse is variable. The tone of the initial chapters may appear obsequious for those of you with a solid background in molecular biology, but later chapters may prove difficult for those of you with the same background. Similarly, the level of explanation in some of the later chapters may challenge even the astute social scientist. I offer no apologies. Some material is indeed difficult, and I refused to sacrifice the explanation of difficult empirical findings to the altar of ease of understanding.

4. This is not a comprehensive book. I take isolated behaviors (such as schizophrenia) to represent a whole class of behaviors (such as psychopathology). Consult the professional literature for results on more specific information on phenotypes such as manic-depressive disorder or anxiety disorders.

5. I deliberately oversimplify some biological and molecular genetic material for the sake of understanding. For example, I ignore the implications of the 5´ to 3´ direction of the synthesis of single-stranded DNA

complement, and hence oversimplify the description and depiction (see Figure 3.2) of DNA replication. I hope that the small errors in such presentations of material are compensated for by the ease of understanding on the part of the social scientist.

6. There is a Web site for the course at http://psych.colorado.edu/hgss.

● FOR COURSE INSTRUCTORS

This is not a conventional textbook. It contains much more than you can teach in a single semester, so be selective, ignore whole chapters (or whole sections of chapters), and reorganize material according to your needs.

The organization of material in this book (i.e., ordering of chapters) is content driven. It is *not* meant to be an organic organization of a course that should start at Chapter 1 and end at the last chapter. Consider the students in your course, their level of background knowledge, and the purpose of the course. Then organize the material accordingly. Maybe you will teach Chapter 9 (Mendelian genetics) first and Chapter 10 at the end of the course. In my upper division undergraduate course on behavioral genetics, I no longer lecture on Mendelian genetics (Chapter 9) because most students already have sufficient knowledge of the material. Instead, I give the students a series of problems on the subject and then deal personally with the small minority who have trouble mastering this topic.

Current research on the disorders covered in this text, as well as discourse and opinions on many topics in this book, can be researched on informative Web sites. Because these sites change so quickly, I have not included them in the body of the text. If you and your students are interested in topics such as the effect of diet in phenylketonuria or the XYY syndrome and antisocial behavior, then logon and do searches on MEDLINE or PSYCHINFO on these topics.

This book has a dedicated Web site that is currently evolving. Please go to http://psych.colorado.edu/hgss for the latest material. The materials on the Web site have been funded by (in order of dollar amounts) (a) myself and my family, (b) the University of Colorado, and (c) Sage Publications. These materials are copyrighted by the author of this text and may be used freely for educational purposes. Any commercial use of the materials on this Web site must be approved by the author of this text, the University of Colorado, and Sage Publications.

FOR STUDENTS ●

This is not a conventional textbook. It lacks the "glitter" common in most textbooks. You will not find color figures, photographs, and a plethora of text boxes to distract your attention from the major story about genetics and human behavior. Sage Publications and I deliberately embarked on this course of action for one major reason—$$$. To save you some of these, everything is in black and white. Go to the Web site for the book, http://psych.colorado.edu/hgss, to view the illustrations in this book in color and to experience the learning exercises, practice tests, and other material that can help you master the domain of genetics and human behavior. Be forewarned: The Web site is under development even as you read this preface. Check with your instructor on the requirements (if any) for your course.

FOR PROFESSIONALS ●

This is not a conventional textbook. It is not a text on genetics, it is not a text on evolution and evolutionary psychology, and it is not a text on behavioral genetics. It is a book intended to help the social scientist understand the science of genetics and its implications for explaining human behavior.

There are major gaps in this book. Chiefly, you will not find a discussion of animal models of (fill in your favorite topic—Alzheimer's disease, schizophrenia, or attention-deficit hyperactive disorder). It is not that animal models are unimportant. Indeed, they are quite the opposite—they may be the best research agendas to uncover neurobiological mechanisms for these phenotypes.

Instead, the field of genetics and behavior is simply too large to allow one single book to encompass everything. Hence, I concentrate solely and exclusively on human genetics, with the hope that someone eventually will write a companion volume on genetic animal models of human behavior.

You also will not find extended discussion of philosophical and political implications of studying the genetics of human behavior. Again, this topic is far from unimportant, but I cannot cram all issues about human genetics and behavior into a single volume. In this book, I concentrate on the empirical results of the research rather than on the moral import of the endeavor. Many other authors can fill this gap.

● FOR ALL OF YOU WHO HAVE HELPED ME

Finally, the acknowledgments. I thank Sage Publications, Lyle Bourne, and Jim Brace-Thompson for letting me write the book that I wanted to write.

Nikki Erlenmeyer-Kimling sparked my interest in genetics. From this initial tinder, I experienced the intense intellectual climate at the University of Minnesota and the Institute of Psychiatry in London, fueled by my mentors—Irv Gottesman, Jerry Shields, and Eliot Slater. Many others at these institutions contributed to the knowledge and modes of thought that (right or wrong—I accept all mistakes) appear in this volume—Paul Meehl, David Lykken, Auke Tellegen, Tom Bouchard, Isaac Marks, and David Fulker. The comradeship of outstanding graduate student and postdoctoral colleagues during this period also must be acknowledged—Hill Goldsmith, Dan Hansen, Matt McGue, Bill Iacono, Ann Lumry, Dante Chichetti, Francie Gabbay, Sheri Berenbaum, Nancy Segal, John Hewitt, and many others. Also to be acknowledged are other scholars I encountered through my postdoctoral and professorial years who provided a "cultural inheritance" to the thoughts in this volume—Eli and Lee Robins, John Rice, Brian Suarez, Barry Hong, Lindon Eaves, Andrew Heath, Mick Martin, Jeff Long, Hilary Coon, Dave DiLalla, and Liz DiLalla. Finally, I thank those who have given feedback on earlier drafts or helped to develop themes in this book—Irv Gottesman (again), Michelle Sauter, Bert Covert, Bob Spencer, Steve Maier, Mike Miller, David Rowe, Laura Baker, Jinks Cooper, Henry Harpending, Herb Gintis, the lunch crowd at the University of Colorado (Peter Polson, Alice Healy, Serge Campeau, Heidi Day, Dick Olson, Gary McClelland, and Jerry Rudy), and several anonymous referees for this text. Lastly, I thank those who managed to help convert the words and information contained herein into modern information technology (Debbie Aguiar, Jon Roberts, May Anne Tucker, Ernie Mross, Linda Lund, and A. J. Sobczak).

Ad familiam meam

CHAPTER 1

LEMONADE

INTRODUCTION ●

Like ancient Gaul, this book is divided into three parts, or *modules*, as they will be referred to herein. The first module—Chapters 2 through 11—explains, to the biologically impaired, what genes are. I intend no personal slight here. I wrote this book for college-level academics whose main intellectual pursuits focus on social science. If you already know about biochemistry, cell biology, and molecular genetics, then the first module will bore you. Few of us social scientists have that background.

The second module—and the skimpiest one—deals with evolution and evolutionary psychology. The skimpiness should not be taken to underplay the importance of the topic. We have gained—and are still gaining—a considerable amount of knowledge about evolution, but our knowledge of how this pertains to human behavior is much more nebulous than the hard science overviewed in the first module. Several topics, most notably anthropological genetics, cannot be presented in detail because of space limitations.

The third module deals with the traditional behavioral genetics of individual differences. From our day-to-day interactions with relatives, friends, and acquaintances, it is obvious that some people are more outgoing than others. To what extent do genes contribute to these individual differences? This is the type of question to be discussed in this module. The largest fault in this module is its lack of integration with the first module. I offer no apologies for this shortcoming because the body of empirical data demands it: Although there has been considerable research on the molecular genetics of human behavior, it is hard to find a body of consistent, replicable results to report. Rather than survey the most recent findings in this area and report that results have failed to replicate or that there are no data from other laboratories to assess replication, I have deliberately ignored this research. I hope that a body of well-replicated data emerges on the molecular genetics of, say, intelligence or schizophrenia, one that can be carved into the stone of textbooks, much like the physical structure of DNA has been.

In the interim, we are left with one consistent theme that spans all three modules—lemonade. Let's discuss that for a minute.

● LEMONADE

Imagine that you are taking one of those standardized, multiple-choice, computer-scored tests that are part of the process of getting into college (e.g., the SAT), medical school (e.g., MCAT), or law school (e.g., LSAT). The following item appears in the test booklet:

> Lemonade is:
> (a) lemon juice.
> (b) water.
> (c) sugar.

According to the test instructions, you must fill in one and only one of the bubbles on the answer sheet. You have two options. First, you could respond to the pragmatics of the test situation—to compete with all others taking the test, you must pick one and only one answer and hope that your choice matches the one on the scoring key. The second option requires more chutzpah: you recognize that the question is phenomenally stupid and protest the question to the test constructors. Lemonade is a compound, a solution, and an inextricable combination of lemon juice, water, and sweetener. It is something more than any one of its parts.

One can construct analogous multiple-choice questions on human behavior. For example:

Intelligence [or extraversion, or antisocial behavior] is:
- (a) genetic.
- (b) cultural.
- (c) familial.
- (d) due to all your idiosyncratic learning experiences.

According to all the empirical scientific evidence on genes, and on environment, and on behavior, this question is as stupid as the one on lemonade.

A HISTORICAL PERSPECTIVE ON LEMONADE ●

In 1957, Anne Anastasi initiated her presidential address to the American Psychological Association by stating:

> Two or three decades ago, the so-called heredity-environment question was the center of a lively controversy. Today, on the other hand, many psychologists look upon it as a dead issue. It is now generally conceded that both hereditary and environmental factors enter into all behavior. The reacting organism is a product of its genes and its past environment, while present environment provides the immediate stimulus for current behavior. (Anastasi, 1958, p. 197)

Carefully note the date of this quotation—1958, more than 40 years ago. Anastasi tried her best to drive a stake through the heart of the nature versus nurture debate, nail it securely into its coffin, and bury it so deep that it would never resurface. Despite her good intentions, the debate, like the evil vampire in a B movie, continually resurrects itself and intrudes upon rational discourse to an extent far beyond its true merit.

Lemonade is not a philosophical statement. It is a concept about the relationship between genes and the environment that has—since Anastasi's time—been proved again and again in the empirical literature. I restate Anastasi's conclusion in terms of two fundamental laws about genes and behavior that have yet to be disproved. These are not new laws—Anastasi stated them. Almost 20 years later, they were repeated by Loehlin and Nichols (1976), and they have recently been reiterated by Turkheimer (2000). The first law states that

> *Environmental factors always contribute to individual differences in human behavior.*

Again, this law is not a philosophical position: It is a generalization from almost 100 years of empirical research on identical twins. For all behavioral traits studied thus far, identical twins are never identical in behavior. As a group, they may be very *similar* to each other, but the two members of every twin pair do not behave *identically* to each other. To say the same thing in statistical parlance, the correlation for identical twins on every behavioral measure studied thus far has always been less than 1.0.

The second conclusion of the empirical data is that

Genes contribute to individual differences in almost every dimension of human behavior that has been studied thus far.

Once again, this is not a philosophical postulate but a generalization from decades of research. The dimensions of human behavior include intelligence (Bouchard, 1998; Bouchard & McGue, 1981); the personality traits of extraversion, emotionality, openness to experience, agreeableness, cultural pursuits, and many others too numerous to name here (Eaves, Eysenck, & Martin, 1989; Jang, Livesley, & Vernon, 1996; Loehlin, 1992; Loehlin & Nichols, 1976, Tellegen et al., 1988); almost all patterns of vocational interests (Loehlin & Nichols, 1976); divorce (McGue & Lykken, 1992), amount of TV watched (Plomin, Corley, DeFries, & Fulker, 1990), age at first sexual intercourse (Dunne et al., 1997), and combat exposure in Vietnam (Lyons et al., 1993).

In short, during the 40 or so years since Anastasi's original overview of the area, the empirical data have verified her conclusions. In fact, the growing knowledge of biology of the gene within neuroscience confirms her conclusions far more than any number of twin or adoption studies—the only types of data available to her at the time—could ever do. In terms of genes and environment, behavior is lemonade.

● THE IMPLICATIONS OF LEMONADE

One may wax eloquent about the lemonade analogy, but the best way to illustrate lemonade is to take published media accounts—and sadly, some academic publications as well—and answer their rhetorical headlines in terms of the empirical evidence.

Is intelligence genetic? Stupid question—intelligence is lemonade. Do genes determine your personality? A completely idiotic thing to ask because personality is lemonade. Is alcoholism a genetic disease? Balderdash! Alcoholism is lemonade. Do males cheat on their spouses because of their genes? Bull. All male behavior—as well as all female behavior—is lemonade. Is language genetic? Absurd! Language is lemonade because it needs environmental inputs and feedback to develop. In short, generic questions of the form "Is this genetic?" should never be asked for any t type of behavior. Claims by any researcher that this or that behavior is "genetically determined" are false or, at best, pejorative to the meaning of the word "determined."

At the opposite end of the spectrum, assertions by opponents to genetic research that geneticists have attempted to propose some form of "genetic determinism" for behavior are equally ludicrous. Genetic determinism for any behavior implies that the correlation for identical twins on that behavior will be 1.0, but such a correlation has never been reported for any substantive human behavior. If there is any "genetic determinism" for a human behavior, it has yet to be reported. All human behaviors studied thus far are lemonade.

Perhaps more insidious are tacit assumptions that individual differences in many human behaviors are environmental in origin simply because one or two environmental reasons explain some of those individual differences. The fact that environmental factors explain *some* portion of individual differences cannot be used to conclude that environmental factors must explain *all* of the individual differences. Almost all—not 100%, but pretty close—human individual differences show some heritable influence.

LEMONADE AND THIS TEXT ●

A century of research suggests that human behavior is lemonade. It is an inextricable combination of genes, culture, family, and personal learning experiences—a compound, a solution. So what does one do now?

Anne Anastasi's suggestion is to focus research on the question of *how* genes and environment produce a phenotype. Indeed, much of the focus of this text will be placed on the *how* issue. Genes are biological entities. They are strands of DNA that are the blueprint for important chemicals in every cell of our bodies. To understand the *how*, we must first understand the gene and its biology. This is the topic of Chapters 2 through 8. Known mechanisms of the "how" are portrayed in the chapter on Mendelian traits (Chapter 5), for which the relationship between genes and behavior can be viewed unequivocally.

The transmission of genes follows certain mathematical rules that were first outlined by Gregor Mendel in 1864 and later elaborated by Thomas Hunt Morgan and others shortly after the turn of the 20th century. These transmission rules permit scientists to calculate risk for genetic diseases in relatives as well as quantify the magnitude of the genetic influence on a trait from the correlations among different types of relatives. This line of genetics is covered in Chapters 9 through 11.

Genes not only influence individual differences among us humans but also help to define the very nature of our species. Genes decide that we humans have four appendages instead of six or eight, that we walk upright instead of on all fours, and that we have a cerebral cortex that is very large relative to our body size. These types of influences are evolutionary in nature and are discussed in Chapters 12 through 16.

Finally, a selected sample of the empirical literature on behavioral genetics is reviewed in Chapters 17 through 24. The emphasis in these chapters is less on raising a flag toting "Genetic influence on intelligence discovered" than it is on tackling the major ways in which genes for intelligence relate to society today. Sadly, the "how" in these chapters is lacking, but not because of any desire of this author or the efforts of researchers in the field. The lack of "how" studies derives simply from the nascent nature of the research on this question. One cannot explore the mysterious ocean about the "how" of genes and environment concerning issues of personality, intelligence, schizophrenia, and antisocial behavior when such research is at the stage of placing one's toes into the water to test its temperature.

● REFERENCES

Anastasi, A. (1958). Heredity, environment, and the question "How?" *Psychological Review, 65,* 197-208.

Bouchard, T. J., Jr. (1998). Genetic and environmental influences on adult intelligence and special mental abilities. *Human Biology, 70,* 257-279.

Bouchard, T. J., Jr., & McGue, M. (1981). Familial studies of intelligence: A review. *Science, 212,* 1055-1059.

Dunne, M. P., Martin, N. G., Statham, D. J., Slutske, W. S., Dinwiddie, S. H., Bucholz, K. K., et al. (1997). Genetic and environmental contributions to variance in age at first sexual intercourse. *Psychological Science, 8,* 211-216.

Eaves, L. J., Eysenck, H. J., & Martin, N. G. (1989). *Genes, culture, and personality: An empirical approach.* San Diego: Academic Press.

Jang, K. L., Livesley, W. J., & Vernon, P. A. (1996). Heritability of the big five personality dimensions and their facets: A twin study. *Journal of Personality, 64,* 577-591.

Loehlin, J. C. (1992). *Genes and environment in personality development.* Newbury Park, CA: Sage.

Loehlin, J. C., & Nichols, R. C. (1976). *Heredity, environment, and personality.* Austin: University of Texas Press.

Lyons, M. J., Goldberg, J., Eisen, S. A., True, W., Tsuang, M. T., Meyer, J. M., et al. (1993). Do genes influence exposure to trauma? A twin study of combat. *Am J Med Genet, 48,* 22-27.

McGue, M., & Lykken, D. T. (1992). Genetic influence on risk of divorce. *Psychological Science, 3,* 368-373.

Plomin, R., Corley, R., DeFries, J. C., & Fulker, D. W. (1990). Individual differences in television viewing in early childhood: Nature as well as nurture. *Psychological Science, 1,* 371-377.

Tellegen, A., Lykken, D. T., Bouchard, T. J., Jr., Wilcox, K. J., Segal, N. L., & Rich, S. (1988). Personality similarity in twins reared apart and together. *Journal of Personality and Social Psychology, 54,* 1031-1039.

Turkheimer, E. (2000). Three laws of behavioral genetics and what they mean. *Current Directions in Psychological Science, 9,* 160-164.

MODULE I

WHAT GENES ARE

CHAPTER 2

THE CELL

INTRODUCTION ●

You and I began life as single cells. Now, both of us are composed of several trillion cells. If and when one of us conceives a child, one of these trillion cells, either a sperm or an egg, will join with one of the trillion cells, again a sperm or an egg, of our partner. This cell, now a fertilized egg, will divide into two cells, these two into four, and so on, until another trillion-celled organism develops. This organism, our offspring, will contribute a single cell to a union with his or her partner's single cell. This fertilized egg divides, and the next trillion-celled organism is our grandchild.

Cells beget cells, which beget cells. Cells have always begotten cells, ever since the first viable cells capable of begetting cells developed on our planet several billion years ago. Looking backwards, you and I began as single fertilized eggs that were the union of two single cells, each coming from the trillion-celled organisms that were our parents. Each of our parents began as a single cell formed from a sperm and an egg from our grandparents. And so on, and so on. The trillions of cells that are you and the trillions that are me are the result of a chain of cellular transmission unbroken over billions of years. You and I share great-great-great-to-a-very-high-power grandparents in some long-lost primordial soup. We have also shared grandparents continuously on the way. Sixty million years ago, we had a grandfather who was one of the first mammals, and shortly thereafter, a grandmother who was the direct ancestor of the first primates. Possibly as recently as 200,000 years ago, our grandfather and grandmother gazed at a sunset on the African savanna and spoke about their love for each other.

Because cells beget cells, not only are you and I related, but we are also cousins to chimpanzees, orangutans, cows, snakes, frogs, mosquitoes, and oak trees. Why? Because we all share DNA, because DNA instructs a cell on how to make another cell, and because cells beget cells. To understand genetics, we must first understand the cell.

● CELL STRUCTURE

Although cells can have quite complicated structures, certain features common to all cells are important for understanding genetics. A schematic of such a cell is given in Figure 2.1.[1]

The first—and very important—structure in the cell is the cell wall, referred to in "biologicalese" as the *plasma membrane*. It is very much incorrect to think of the cell wall as merely a physical structure to keep the insides from spilling out, much as a sealed plastic bag might contain a cup of clam chowder. The cell wall has dynamic properties in addition to its structural properties. Embedded in the cell wall is a wide range of molecules called *receptors*. Receptors on the cell surface act as sentinels, permitting some substances to enter the cell, refusing entry to others, and signaling to the inside of the cell that something is knocking at the gate. Likewise, receptors regulate which substances inside the cell can exit the cell.

The nucleus is much like a cell within a cell, having its own "wall." The most important structures within the nucleus are the *chromosomes*. These are packages of DNA and other molecules. They are the physical structures for genetic information and for transmitting that genetic information when the cell divides.

The material outside the nucleus is termed the *cytoplasm*. Of the various structures in the cytoplasm, three are important here. The first of these is the *endoplasmic reticulum*. This is a series of convoluted, wall-like structures connected like a large network snaking throughout the cytoplasm. The endoplasmic reticulum is less noteworthy in its own right than it is for being the location of the second important cytoplasmic structure, the *ribosome*.

A ribosome is a protein factory. Think of a ribosome as a building that contains all the tools and some of the raw materials for making proteins but lacks a blueprint. Without instructions, such a structure is incapable of manufacturing a protein. It is the DNA that provides the blueprint to a ribosome. After the blueprint is provided, the ribosome can manufacture a

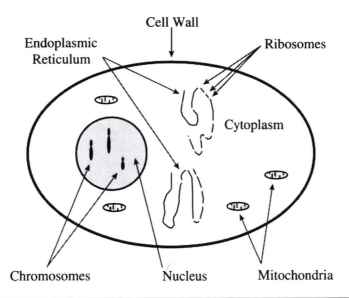

Figure 2.1   A Schematic Diagram of the Cell.

protein. There are thousands of ribosomes in the cytoplasm, so there are literally thousands of protein factories in each cell.

The third cytoplasmic structure is the *mitochondrion* (plural = *mitochondria*). Mitochondria are little energy packets that help the cell to convert chemicals efficiently.[2] Of equal importance is the fact that mitochondria contain DNA. This mitochondrial DNA is abbreviated as mtDNA and is minuscule compared to the amount of DNA in the nucleus. Mitochondrial DNA is maternally transmitted via the egg; sperm have mitochondria in their tails but not in their nucleus. Consequently, all siblings in a family receive their mitochondrial DNA from their mother. The fact of maternal transmission for mtDNA makes it an excellent system with which to study evolutionary trees.

Before leaving cell structure, we note an interesting hypothesis about the origin of mitochondria. It is speculated that billions of years ago, the ancestors of mitochondria were their own individual life-forms that had a leg up on most other single-celled organisms because of their efficient metabolism. The other, much larger organisms would tend to engulf and then feed on the smaller mitochondria. During evolution, some of these large unicellular organisms began to devour the ancient mitochondria. Instead of digesting the primitive grandparents of mitochondria, the large cells evolved to enslave them. The mitochondria then provided their host with efficient metabolism while the host saved the mitochondria from being eaten to extinction. If this hypothesis is true, then all of us modern life-forms owe our existence to an ancient form of slavery.[3]

● LIFE IN THE BIG CELL: INTRACELLULAR PROCESSES

Metabolism

Life inside a cell can be hell. It is a continual and never-ending process of chemical reactions, termed *metabolism*. Few molecules within the cell have the luxury of sitting back and relaxing. There is always some chemical ready to chop the molecule up, grab it and attach it to some other molecule, or kidnap it by moving it to some other section of the cell or, sometimes, entirely out of the cell. A very important class of molecules in this turbulent scene is the *enzyme*, a particular type of protein that is responsible for a chemical reaction. The suffix "-ase" is conventionally used to denote an enzyme (e.g., hydroxylase, decarboxylase, tyrosinase).

Both a language and a model exist for the action of enzymes, as depicted in Figure 2.2. A molecule termed the *substrate* physically binds with a specific enzyme, forming a substrate-enzyme complex. The analogy of a lock and key is used to describe this process. Not every substrate can bind to a particular enzyme, and not every enzyme can bind to a specific substrate. The substrate and enzyme must physically fit together, in the same way that a particular key opens a specific lock. Thus, one encounters such lingo as "binding site" to refer to that portion of the enzyme that the substrate recognizes and binds to.

Once a substrate-enzyme complex is formed, a chemical reaction occurs. For example, a hydrogen atom might get lopped off of the substrate, or a hydroxyl group (a combination of hydrogen and oxygen atoms) may be added. The altered substrate is now called a *product*. The product and the enzyme dissociate. The enzyme goes its merry way, hoping to encounter another substrate molecule to mutilate, and the product usually becomes the substrate for a different enzyme. In this way, a chain of chemical reactions occurs until something of importance is made. This chain of reactions is called a *metabolic pathway*.

Figure 2.3 illustrates the metabolic pathway in the synthesis of norepinephrine, an important *neurotransmitter* (a chemical that communicates between nerve cells). The process begins with a molecule called tyrosine that acts as a substrate for the enzyme tyrosine hydroxylase. Tyrosine binds to tyrosine hydroxylase that converts it into the product dihydroxyphenylalanine, better known as DOPA. DOPA is then converted into dopamine (DA) by the action of the enzyme DOPA decarboxylase. At this point, one of two things can happen to dopamine, depending on the type of nerve cell in which the metabolic path is operating. In some nerve cells, no further chemical conversions will take place, and the DA will be used as a neurotransmitter. In other cells, the enzyme dopamine β-hydroxylase converts dopamine into norepinephrine (NE), which will be used as the neurotransmitter.

We can now begin to glimpse the important role of genes in this process. DNA contains the blueprint for proteins, and enzymes are a particular class

1. Substrate and enzyme...

2. bind together, forming a
substrate-enzyme complex.

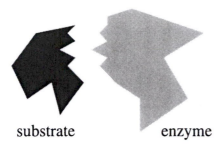

substrate   enzyme

3. A chemical reaction occurs...

4. leaving a product when the
enzyme dissociates.

product

Figure 2.2   A Model for Enzyme Action.

of proteins. Consequently, DNA has the instructions for the enzymes that are responsible for the chemical reactions in hundreds of metabolic pathways occurring in each one of our cells.

Transportation

DNA contains the blueprint for making a protein or an enzyme. The actual manufacture of the protein, however, takes place at a ribosome that could be on the endoplasmic reticulum almost anywhere in the cell. Many proteins, however, have to be at a specific place in the cell in order to perform their appropriate cellular duties. It is very inefficient—although it occurs at times—for the protein to be left alone to bang into this molecule and collide with that substance until, by dumb luck, it gets to where it belongs. More often, mechanisms and structures exist within the cell to transport the protein to its appropriate location.

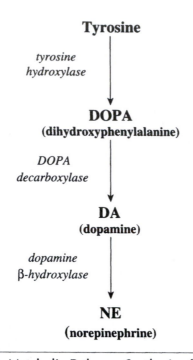

Figure 2.3   An Example of a Metabolic Pathway: Synthesis of the Neurotransmitters Dopamine (DA) and Norepinephrine (NE).

Transportation is not limited only to proteins and enzymes. Many other substances, especially the end products of a metabolic path, are actively transported.

Storage

Much as you and I might have a special location in the refrigerator for the butter dish, many cells have storage units for certain molecules. These storage units, called *vesicles*, usually serve two purposes. First, vesicles can store large amounts of a molecule in a strategic location so that these molecules can be released en masse at a critical time. Second, storage in vesicles can prevent the molecules from being *degraded*—a fancy term for maiming and mutilation by roving gangs of psychopathic enzymes.

For example, consider the molecule CRH (corticotropin releasing hormone). It is manufactured in the cells of a particular area of the hypothalamus (a structure in our brains) called the paraventricular nucleus. Newly made CRH is transported to a vesicle in these cells until the number of vesicles and amount of CRH are large enough to inhibit the manufacture of new CRH. Within the vesicle, a molecule of CRH has a happy and placid existence, relaxing with its neighboring CRH molecules—that is, until something dreadful occurs. If a person encounters something that provokes anxiety, stress, or fear, the nerves in the brain that lie next to the CRH storage cells fire, the CRH-containing cells fire in response, and the CRH is released to enter the blood-stream, which carries it to other cells. There, CRH initiates a cascade of physiological responses. (We will learn more about this process in Chapter 4.)

Cell Division

Cell division is important and must be carried on with a high degree of fidelity to ensure that all the genetic material is present in both daughter cells. The intricacies of the cell cycle and cell division need not concern us here, but two terms are important. *Mitosis* is the ordinary form of cell division that occurs for all of our cells, save sperm and egg. It is depicted in Figure 2.4. The chromosomes duplicate, each one making an exact replica of itself, and the two copies (called sister chromatids) are joined together in a region called the *centromere*. During this stage, the chromosomes coil and condense, giving a characteristic X-like shape that is visible under the microscope, and the wall separating the nucleus from the cytoplasm begins to degrade. In a complicated series of steps, two sets of spindles are constructed, one each on the right-hand and left-hand sides of the cell. The spindles then attach themselves to the chromosomes and pull apart the joined chromosomes, with one pulled in one direction while its carbon copy is pulled in the opposite direction. This eventually gives two complete sets of chromosomes, one on the right and the other on the left of the cell. Nuclear membranes form around the two sets of chromosomes and a cell wall is constructed down the middle of the cytoplasm. When this process is completed, there are now two cells.

The second major type of cell division is *meiosis* (the adjectival form is *meiotic*), the specialized cell division that produces sperm and eggs (see Figure 2.5). Obviously, ordinary mitosis cannot be used for these important cells—if it were, the number of chromosomes would double each generation. Meiosis begins with the replication and condensing of the chromosomes that takes place in ordinary cell division. But then an important difference occurs: There is a physical pairing of the chromosome from the father with its counterpart from the mother. At this point, a very important phenomenon, termed *recombination* or *crossing over*, often occurs. In recombination, the maternal and the paternal chromosomes exchange DNA with each other. More information about recombination is given in Chapter 10. For now, it is important to recognize that there are four strands of DNA physically connected to one another—the "maternal" chromosome and its "carbon copy" and the "paternal" chromosome and its "carbon copy." (I use quotation marks here to signify that the terms "maternal" and "paternal" are used loosely, because the two already will have exchanged DNA. Hence, the "maternal" chromosome contains one or more sections of the original paternal chromosome and the

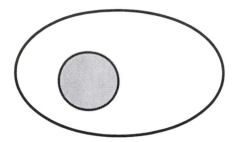

I. Chromosomes are expanded into long structures in the nucleus and are invisible under the light microscope.

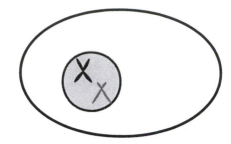

II. Chromosomes replicate and condense. With appropriate staining, they can now be seen under a microscope.

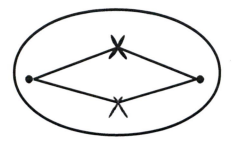

III. The nuclear wall degrades, spindles form and attach themselves to the chromosomes.

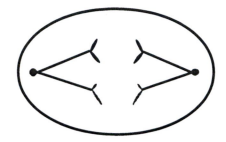

IV. Spindles pull the chromosome pairs apart, pulling them to opposite poles of the cell.

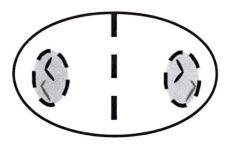

V. Nucleus develops around each set of chromosomes and the cell wall starts to form, splitting the cell into two parts.

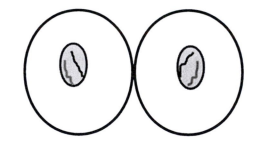

VI. Nucleus and cell wall complete development and chromosomes expand, giving two daughter cells.

Figure 2.4   Mitosis, the Process of Cell Division in All Cells Except Sperm and Egg.

I. As in mitosis, chromosomes replicate and condense.

II. Unlike mitosis, the maternal (solid) and paternal (dotted) chromosomes pair up and exchange genetic material.

III. Spindles form, attach themselves, and pull the chromosomes to the poles of the cell.

IV. The cell divides.

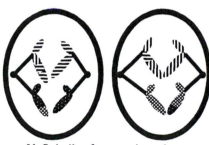

V. Spindles form again and pull each chromosome away from its partner.

VI. Each cell divides again, reducing the number of chromosomes to half that of the original cell.

Figure 2.5   Meiosis, Cell Division That Generates a Sperm or an Egg.

"paternal" chromosome contains maternal DNA. The same applies to the "carbon copies" because they too will have exchanged genetic material.)

Spindles appear and separate the "maternal" chromosome and its "carbon copy" from the "paternal" chromosome and its "carbon copy." Ordinary cell division then takes place, generating two cells each with the complete chromosome complement. That is, each of us humans has 23 pairs of chromosomes, so the two cells will also have 23 pairs of chromosomes.

The next stage of cell division is called *reduction division*, and it is essentially mitosis in the two pre-germ cells. Here, spindles appear just as they do in mitosis and attach themselves to the chromosomes and their "carbon copies." The spindles then pull the chromosomes into the two poles of the cell and the cell divides. Now each cell will contain 23 chromosomes instead of 23 *pairs* of chromosomes. Hence, the necessary reduction in the number of chromosomes is accomplished.

● CELL TALK: HOW CELLS COMMUNICATE

Cells must communicate—and not merely to their immediate neighbors. When my bladder is full, the appropriate cells in my lower gut must get the message to my eyeballs to look around for a restroom. By far the most frequently used mechanism for cell talk is chemical communication.

The mechanism for chemical communication is analogous to the binding lock and key model of enzyme action. One cell sends out a chemical message. Another cell contains a molecule called a *receptor*. Just as the physical conformation of an enzyme is specific for its substrate, so is the physical conformation of the receptor specific to the chemical messenger. The messenger and receptor bind together in the same way that a substrate binds to an enzyme. Just what happens after the messenger-receptor binding depends on the particular system—there is a wide array of mechanisms. The result, however, is always the same. Some chemical reaction or binding with yet other molecules occurs, informing the cell what has happened and how to respond.

Receptors can reside on the cell wall, in which case they are called cell *surface* or *membrane receptors*, or within the cytoplasm and the nucleus of the cell (*intracellular receptors*). All receptors are proteins or have a protein somewhere within their structure.

Cell talk can happen between very different types of cells quite far away from each other. The chemical communicators in this case are called *hormones*. For example, certain cells in the pituitary gland, located just underneath the brain, send a messenger hormone called ACTH to cells in the adrenal gland, located on the top of the kidney. The mode for this type of distance communication is to send the message through the blood.

Another type of cell talk occurs between nerve cells. Let us first explore the anatomy of nerve cells and then discuss how they talk to one another.

THE NERVE CELL ●

One of the most important types of cells for behavior is the nerve cell or *neuron*. Popular similes and metaphors for the nervous system often invoke electricity and electrical engineering. A psychotic person may be described as having a short circuit in the brain, but who ever refers to an incontinent person as having a short-circuited kidney? It is indeed true that nerve cells generate electrical impulses, but it is equally true that they, just like all other cells, are organized bundles of chemical reactions. Furthermore, genes play just as important a role in the chemical reactions of the nerve cell as they do in the kidney cell.

Nerve cells have the same logical structure as other cells. Neurons have a cell wall, and a host of chemical sentinels and gatekeepers embedded in the plasma membrane perform the same function as the receptors on other cells. They announce to the neuron that some messenger is knocking at the gate, let other messengers in, keep certain ones out, and see to it that the appropriate molecules inside the neuron either stay inside or exit the neuron as needed. Neurons have mitochondria, an endoplasmic reticulum, and thousands of ribosomes busily making proteins and enzymes from the DNA blueprint. Also just like other cells, neurons have a nucleus with chromosomes. Like the DNA in your bone marrow, muscles, skin, and lungs, the DNA in the nerves of your brain is actively telling your neurons which proteins and enzymes to make and which proteins and enzymes not to make.

What then, besides the ability to generate an electrical impulse (i.e., *depolarize*) distinguishes a nerve cell from other cells? The answer is nothing, really. It is just that most nerve cells look funny.

The Neuron

Although neurons come in all shapes and sizes, the typical neuron, depicted in Figure 2.6, resembles a regular elliptoid cell, looking like something extruded from a pasta machine that was having a bad day. Suppose that you intend to make vermicelli. Instead of a long, very thin cylinder, the pasta dough starts coming out as a frizzled mess, followed by the desired structure for a strand of spaghetti, but ending with a big irregular blob with frizzy ends. That is a neuron. It looks like an octopus with a neck the size of a giraffe.

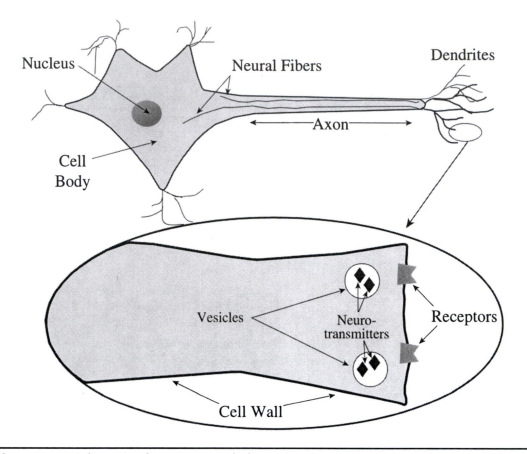

Figure 2.6   Schematic of a Neuron, Including a Synaptic Button.

There is a very good reason for this structure and for the electrical nature of the impulse in neurons. Imagine that you mistakenly sat on an anthill, and the little critters, resenting the intrusion, declared war on your posterior. How long would it take your body to react if those assaulted cells in your gluteus maximus had to chemically communicate this fact to their neighboring cells, those cells to their own neighbors, and so on, until the message finally got to your brain? Then the brain cells would have to chemically communicate the message "Ouch! Get off this stupid anthill!" back down the millions of cells, one cell at a time, until the message prompted movement of the appropriate muscles.

The speed of electrical transmission is on the order of turning on a switch and watching a bulb light up. That is why nerves use electricity. But why the funny structure? The answer is that one nerve uses chemistry, not electricity, to communicate with the next nerve. If nerves were just like other cells, there could be a million very tiny neurons between your butt and your brain. The chemical transmission between neurons would be painfully slow, even if each individual neuron fired an electrical burst. But with that very long, thin, spaghetti-like structure in Figure 2.6, only a few neurons are needed to connect your seat to your central processing unit. The chain of chemical transmission to electrical impulse to chemical transmission to electrical impulse becomes a very efficient way to send messages rapidly. In the case of the anthill, electric impulses sent along very elongated cells permit a speedy retreat and allow you to live to sit another day.

Naturally, scientists must come up with fancier names than "spaghetti-like structure" to refer to the anatomy of the neuron. The large blob that contains the nucleus is called the *cell body*; the long, vermicelli portion, along which the electrical impulse is carried, is termed the *axon*; and the frizzled ends that resemble the finer and finer branching of tree limbs are called *dendrites*. Finally, the series of railways and superhighways that transport molecules from the cell body along the axon to the dendrites are referred to as *neurofilaments* and *neurotubules*.

Do not imagine any of these structures, especially the dendrites, as being like a copper wire. They are parts of *cells* and thus have cytoplasm, cell walls, vesicles, proteins, enzymes, and a host of other chemical molecules. This is highlighted in the bottom portion of Figure 2.6, which shows an exploded view of the end of one dendrite. An important structure in the dendrites of most neurons is the vesicle that contains many molecules of neurotransmitter—the chemical that transmits a message to the next nerve.

Cell Talk Between Nerve Cells: Neuronal Transmission

It is important to place the chemical transmission of neurons under a microscope to examine the process in more detail. Not only will this closer examination give us a better appreciation for cell talk, but it also will help us to understand an important focus of today's genetic research on behavior, especially for psychiatric disorders.

The process of neural cell talk is outlined in Figure 2.7. Pictured here are portions of two neurons—the one that fires (the *presynaptic neuron*) and the one that responds to the firing of the first one (the *postsynaptic neuron*). Usually, the two neurons do not physically touch each other. Instead, there is a physical gap between neurons called the *synapse* (aka *synaptic cleft* or *synaptic junction*). The adjectival form of this word—*synaptic*—is used as a suffix for a number of biological terms (e.g., a presynaptic receptor is a receptor on the presynaptic neuron, and a postsynaptic receptor is a receptor on the postsynaptic neuron).

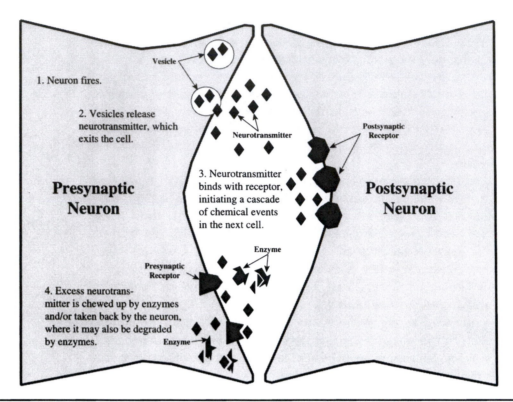

Figure 2.7   The Process of Neurotransmission.

When the first neuron fires, vesicles containing the chemical messenger (aka *neurotransmitter*) move to the cell wall and release the messenger into the synapse. This process occurs very rapidly. With a large number of vesicles and thousands of neurotransmitter molecules, release resembles a flash flood more than a trickling stream.

The physical force behind the release pushes the neurotransmitter across the synapse. Sitting on the plasma membrane of the postsynaptic neuron are a host of receptors. The neurotransmitter and receptor bind together in the same lock-and-key way that substrate and enzyme bind. The binding between neurotransmitter and receptor sparks a chemical reaction in the postsynaptic neuron that, in turn, initiates a whole cascade of chemical events that alters the whole chemical state of the neuron. In some cases, this change of state is excitatory and makes the postsynaptic neuron more likely to fire. In other cases, the change is inhibitory and decreases the probability of firing.

The final step in the process is really an exercise in tidy housekeeping. It is important not to let the large mass of neurotransmitter stay in the synapse. Otherwise, the constant binding, unbinding, and rebinding of the neurotransmitter with the postsynaptic receptor would keep the postsynaptic neuron in a state of perpetual change. Two major mechanisms take care of the excess neurotransmitter. The first is called *reuptake*. Here, the neurotransmitter binds to a protein called a *transporter* on the presynaptic neuron and gets "reabsorbed" back into the cell. The second mechanism is enzymatic degradation. One set of enzymes lurks around the synapse, ready to pounce on any wayward neurotransmitter. Another set lies low in the presynaptic neuron, waiting to ambush any neurotransmitter that went through the reuptake process but has not made it back to the safety of a vesicle.

Cell Talk Between Nerve Cells: The Results of the Message

The fact that thousands of molecules of neurotransmitters flood the synaptic cleft and bind to their receptors does not end the story of communication among neurons. A number of salient events then happen in the postsynaptic neuron. To understand this clearly, we must first realize that neurons are not connected to each other like links in a chain. Hundreds—even thousands—of neurons connect to that single postsynaptic neuron depicted in Figure 2.7. Hence, the state of the postsynaptic neuron depends less on what happens in any single presynaptic neuron and more on the cacophony of events occurring in all the presynaptic neurons.

To understand the end result of a neuronal chemical message, it is useful to consider the influence of one and only one presynaptic neuron. For didactic purposes, we can distinguish two types of effects of neurotransmitter binding—immediate, short-term influences and eventual long-term effects. The immediate effects are illustrated in Figure 2.8. The postsynaptic receptor molecule is often linked to a series of other molecules, one being a protein or enzyme that influences channels in the postsynaptic neuron that permit *ions* (electrically charged atoms) to enter or exit the neuron. Figure 2.8 illustrates the specific case where the binding of a neurotransmitter with its receptor changes the conformation of an enzyme that changes the channel to permit ions to flow into the postsynaptic neuron.

The effect of the transfer of ions into (or out of) the postsynaptic neuron is to change the electrical potential of that neuron. That is, it makes it easier for the neuron to fire (an excitatory effect) or more difficult for the neuron to fire (an inhibitory effect), a phenomenon that neuroscientists refer to as *neuromodulation*. To understand the workings of the nervous system, it is crucial to recognize that neuronal talk does not always happen according to a simple relay system like the old pony express, in which a signal (i.e., message) is passed along intact from one station to the next. Instead, the firing of a neuron influences the *state* of the next neuron, making it easier for a postsynaptic neuron to fire or more difficult for it to fire. Whether the

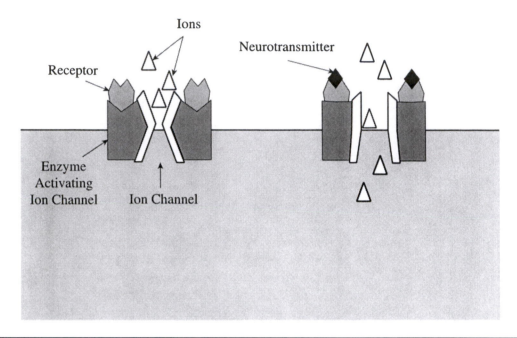

Figure 2.8   The Immediate Effects of Neurotransmission: Opening (or Closing) Ion Channels That Alter the Electrical Potential of the Postsynaptic Neuron.

postsynaptic neuron fires or not depends on the inputs from the thousands of other neurons impinging on it.

For our purposes here, the long-term effects of neurotransmitter binding are more important than the short-term effects, although they are much less understood. An example of the favored model is illustrated in Figure 2.9. The receptor is physically connected to a series of molecules that form a scaffold. When the neurotransmitter binds with the receptor, it alters the conformation of several of the proteins in the scaffold, permitting them to bind with other molecules (the complex on the right-hand side of Figure 2.9). The binding induces a cascade of chemical reactions that result in a *second messenger system* in the postsynaptic neuron. As opposed to the short-term effects of binding, which alter the immediate electrical state of the next neuron, the long-term effects change the *chemical* state of the neuron.

The most important influence of the second messenger system is that it instructs the DNA in the postsynaptic neuron to start making more blueprints for certain types of proteins and enzymes and to cease making blueprints for other proteins and enzymes. This is a phenomenon called *gene regulation* or *gene expression*, the details of which will be explicated in Chapter 4. The important lesson is to recognize the lemonade quality of

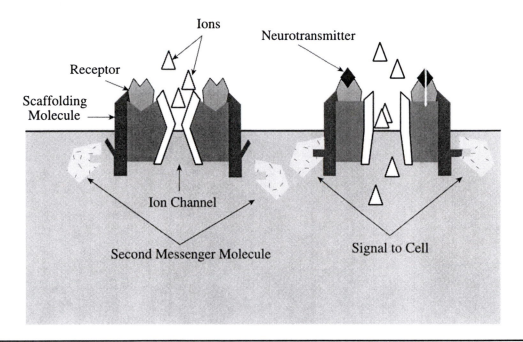

Ions

Neurotransmitter

Receptor

Scaffolding
Molecule

Ion Channel

Second Messenger Molecule

Signal to Cell

Figure 2.9   The Long-Term Effects of Neurotransmission: Altering the Chemical State
of the Postsynaptic Neuron Via Second Messenger Systems.

neuronal cell talk. Environmental stimuli that impinge on, say, your visual system initiate a whole cascade of events in your neurons that effectively turn some genes on and shut other genes down in your brain cells. The mere fact of looking at something influences the genes in your central nervous system.

Neurotransmitters, Receptors, and Genes

How do genes fit into neuronal transmission? There are several different ways. In the previous discussion of metabolic pathways, we saw how DNA contains the blueprint for the enzymes that synthesize neurotransmitters (review Figure 2.2). The receptors for neurotransmitters, both on the firing neuron and its recipient, do not appear from anywhere. DNA contains the code for these receptor proteins and/or the enzymes that synthesize them. DNA also holds the information for making the enzymes that metabolize the extra neurotransmitter that gets released and for the transporter proteins that carry the neurotransmitter back into the presynaptic neuron. Many steps in the second messenger system are also influenced by proteins and enzymes, the blueprints for which are encoded in the DNA. Finally, the long-term result of cell talk among neurons is to "turn on" certain genes in the postsynaptic neuron and to "turn off" other genes.

Not only does DNA have the blueprint for these important proteins and enzymes, but it may also play a role in the numbers of protein or enzyme molecules that are synthesized and their distribution throughout the neuron. Scientific knowledge on this is skimpy, but it is likely that genes may influence such factors as the number and size of vesicles containing neurotransmitters, the number of receptor molecules, and perhaps even the density at which these receptors cluster at various places on the neuronal wall. Much research is needed to clarify the role of DNA in the human nervous system, but there is no doubt that without DNA in each and every neuron, we humans would have no nervous system at all.

The importance of the genetic blueprint for proteins, enzymes, receptors, and so on has not gone unnoticed in the business world. The potential for using the genetic blueprint to uncover causes of disease and to find treatments for the same disorders has led to large investments in biotechnology (see Text Box 2.1).

Text Box 2.1

GENES, MEDICINE, AND THE BIOTECHNOLOGY INDUSTRY

Even though we have yet to learn in this text about the molecular biology of the gene, knowledge about the cell lets us appreciate the reasons that attract medical research and private industry to genes. Let us focus on receptors because all receptors have their blueprints in genes. Because receptors act as gatekeepers and sentinels to the cell, they are major factors in how the world outside a cell communicates with that cell. There is often a very intricate symphony between the inner workings of a cell and the communication that the cell receives. For example, many cells produce their own cholesterol but reduce the rate of cholesterol production when there is high cholesterol in the diet. Here, some proteins that carry cholesterol in the blood "communicate" with receptors in the cell to ratchet down the cell's production of cholesterol.

Many drugs used in medicine operate by binding with and blocking a receptor so that the natural "messenger" molecule cannot bind with the receptor and hence cannot communicate to the cell. Other drugs may bind with a receptor and simulate the natural messenger molecule so that the cell receives the message even though a natural messenger is not present. A worthwhile research goal would be to isolate the receptors (as well as other proteins) involved in the feedback loop between dietary and cell-produced cholesterol. A drug that would block a particular receptor might enhance the feedback so that cells produce even less cholesterol than they ordinarily would for a given level of dietary cholesterol.

To develop such a drug, one needs to know something about the physical structure of the receptor proteins. Knowing the gene for a receptor means that we have the basic blueprint for that protein and provides an important head start in figuring out the receptor's physical structure. This, in turn, eases the development of drugs that can specifically target that receptor.

Naturally, such a technology will be very attractive to pharmaceutical firms. Because they operate in a competitive market system, many pharmaceutical firms (along with other biotechnology companies) are spending considerable amounts of money to patent genes and the proprietary drugs that can come from knowledge of such genes. Today, considerable debate about genes stretches far beyond the science of genetics and into areas of law and biomedical ethics. We will return to this issue of gene patenting in the next chapter, after we learn more about the biology of the gene.

THREE DISCLAIMERS ABOUT THE NERVOUS SYSTEM ●

1. If it has not already been done, I hope that one day a historian of the English language will trace the evolution of the word "nervous." The Latin word "nervus," from which the English word derives, means a sinew, and the word apparently was taken up by anatomists to refer to the tendon-like structure of the axons of some nerves. Somehow along the way, the word developed connotations of worry and apprehension, on one hand, and jitteriness and agitation on the other. This is very curious, because our nervous system plays just as important a role when we are calm and relaxed as it does when we are tense and anxious.

2. Although the nervous system plays a crucial role in behavior, one should not conclude that genes influencing behavior must do so by acting directly in the nervous system. All of us large, multicellular life-forms are conglomerations of many different systems that talk to one another and can influence behavior. Later on, we will see how a gene for an enzyme in the liver can reduce the risk of alcoholism.

3. Finally, a disclaimer is needed for the simplicity with which the nervous system has been described. From a scientific view, almost every statement made above requires qualifications because the nervous system is a *very, very, very* complicated structure in which virtually every rule has its exception. For example, a few neurons do communicate electrically and not chemically, and not every neuro-transmitter is synthesized from enzymes. We will soon see that with genes and their physiological effects, complexity and perplexity are the rule instead of the exception.

● NOTES

1.   This figure depicts what biologists call a eukaryotic cell (a cell that has a nucleus). Some organisms such as bacteria are prokaryotic and do not contain a nucleus.

2.   Technically, mitochondria are responsible for oxidative metabolism, the process of using oxygen as an energy source to break down or synthesize chemical compounds within a cell. Anaerobic metabolism (i.e., metabolism without oxygen) is a much slower and less efficient process.

3.   Of course, a different scenario is possible. Perhaps the mitochondria developed their own mechanism that allowed them to be engulfed, but not digested, by other species in order to escape predation. Like much evolutionary speculation, the true answer may be lost in history.

CHAPTER 3

DNA AND THE GENETIC CODE

INTRODUCTION ●

Life's genetic code is written in the DNA molecule (aka deoxyribonucleic acid).[1] From the perspective of design, no human language can match the simplicity and elegance of DNA. But from the perspective of implementation—how it is actually written and spoken in practice—DNA is a linguist's worst nightmare. DNA has four major functions:

1. It contains the blueprint for making proteins and enzymes.

2. It plays a role in regulating when the proteins and enzymes are made and when they are not made.

3. It carries this information when cells divide.

4. It transmits this information from parental organisms to their offspring.

In this chapter, we will explore the structure of DNA, its language, and how the DNA blueprint becomes translated into a physical protein.

● PHYSICAL STRUCTURE OF DNA

You probably have encountered a pictorial representation of DNA; few people in literate societies can avoid seeing one. Physically, DNA resembles a spiral staircase. For our purposes here, imagine that we twist the staircase to remove the spiral so that we are left with the ladder-like structure depicted in Figure 3.1. The two backbones to this ladder are composed of sugars (S) and phosphates (P); they need not concern us further. The whole action of DNA is in the rungs.

Each rung of the ladder is composed of two chemicals, called *nucleotides* or *base pairs*, that are chemically bonded to each other. DNA has four nucleotides: adenine, thymine, guanine, and cytosine, usually abbreviated by the first letter of their names—A, T, G, and C. These four nucleotides are very important, so their names should be committed to memory.

Inspection of Figure 3.1 reveals that the nucleotides do not pair randomly with one another. Instead, A always pairs with T, and G always pairs with C. This is the principle of *complementary base pairing* that is critical for understanding many aspects of DNA functioning.

Because of complementary base pairing, if we know one strand (i.e., helix) of the DNA, we will always know the other helix. Imagine that we sawed apart the DNA ladder in Figure 3.1 through the middle of each rung and threw away the entire right-hand side of the ladder. We would still be able to know the sequence of nucleotides on this missing piece because of the complementary base pairing. The sequence on the remaining left-hand piece starts with ATGCTC, so the missing right-hand side must begin with the sequence TACGAG.

DNA also has a particular orientation in space, so that the "top" of a DNA sequence differs from its "bottom." The reasons for this are too complicated to consider here, but the lingo used by geneticists to denote the orientation is important. The "top" of a DNA sequence is called the 5′ end (read "five prime"), and the bottom is the 3′ ("three prime") end.[2] If DNA nucleotide sequence number 1 lies between DNA sequence number 2 and the "top," then it is referred to as being *upstream* from DNA sequence 2. If it lies between sequence 2 and the 3′ end, then it is *downstream* from locus 2.

● DNA REPLICATION

Complementary base pairing also assists in the faithful reproduction of the DNA sequence, a process geneticists call DNA *replication* (see Figure 3.2). When a cell divides, both the daughter cells must contain the same genetic

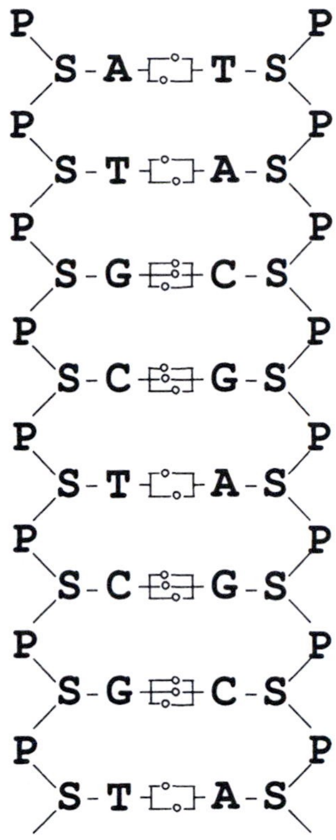

Figure 3.1 The Physical Structure of DNA (P = phosphate, S = sugar, A = adenine, T = thymine, C = cytosine, and G = guanine).

instructions. Consequently, DNA must be duplicated so that one copy ends up in one cell and the other in the second cell. Not only does the replication process have to be carried out, but it must be carried out with a high degree of fidelity. Most cells in our bodies—neurons being a notable exception—are constantly dying and being replenished with new cells. For example, the average life span of some skin cells is on the order of 1 to 2 days, so the skin that you and I had last month is not the same skin that we have today. By living into our eighties, we will have experienced more than 10,000 generations of skin cells! If this book were to be copied sequentially by 10,000 secretaries, one copying the output of another, the results would contain quite a lot of gibberish—through the accumulation of small, infrequent errors—by the time the task was completed. DNA replication must be much more accurate than that.[3]

The first step in DNA replication occurs when an enzyme (can't get away from those enzymes, can we?) separates the rungs, much as our mythical saw

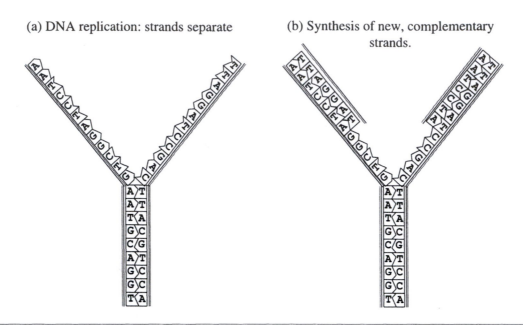

(a) DNA replication: strands separate

(b) Synthesis of new, complementary strands.

Figure 3.2 DNA Replication. (a) Enzymes separate the strands. (b) Other enzymes attach to the single-stranded DNA and attach free nucleotides according to complementary base pairing.

cut them right down the middle. The two strands of the DNA separate. Enzymes then grab on to nucleotides floating free in the cell, glue them onto their appropriate partners on the separated strands, and synthesize a new backbone. The situation is analogous to opening the zipper of a coat, but as the teeth of the zipper separate, new teeth appear. One set of new teeth binds to the freed teeth on the left-hand side of the original zipper, while another set bind to the teeth on the original right-hand side. When you get to the bottom, you are left with two completely closed zippers, one on the left and the other on the right of your jacket front.

● DNA PACKAGING

To appreciate the way that DNA is packaged, we should first think of three types of objects—a very long piece of twine, several million jelly donuts, and the Eiffel Tower. Taking the twine in one hand and a donut in the other, wrap the twine twice around the donut in the manner shown in panel (a) of Figure 3.3. Leaving a few inches of twine free, grab another donut and loop the twine around it twice. Repeat this process until you have about six donuts with twine wrapped around them, giving a structure similar to that in panel (b). Arrange these donuts in a circle on the ground, right next to the bottom

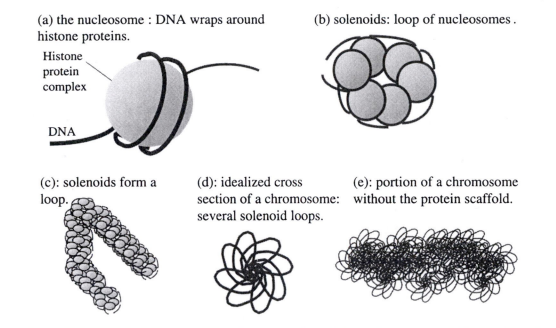

(a) the nucleosome : DNA wraps around histone proteins.

Histone protein complex

DNA

(b) solenoids: loop of nucleosomes .

(c): solenoids form a loop.

(d): idealized cross section of a chromosome: several solenoid loops.

(e): portion of a chromosome without the protein scaffold.

Figure 3.3   How DNA and Protein Scaffolding Create Chromosomes.

of the Eiffel Tower. Repeat this with another six donuts and place them, again in a circle, almost on top of the first six donuts. Repeat this process until there is a loop of these twine-donut complexes as depicted in panel (c).

Eventually, the pile of twine and donuts will become high enough to make it unstable and in danger of toppling over. To prevent this, have a few helpers take the pile of donuts and start circling it around a leg of the Eiffel Tower to give it support, gluing it to the tower if necessary. Proceed with this strategy of looping twine around donuts, arranging circles of donuts, and snaking these piles in and around all the rigid structure of the tower. When you finally run out of string, jelly donuts, and tower space, you will have created a chromosome.

The twine in this procedure is the DNA molecule, and the donuts are composed of small proteins called *histones*. Geneticists give special names to the twine-donut complex and to the loops of these complexes. Although the names are given in Figure 3.3, do not waste precious neuronal space memorizing them, except for one important term. Geneticists call this complicated, looping structure of DNA and proteins *chromatin*. The important thing to recognize is that DNA (or chromatin) is packaged as spirals within spirals within spirals.

The rigid structure of the Eiffel Tower serves as a scaffold for the DNA-protein structures. To be truthful, the scaffold in the chromosomes is composed of proteins, not iron, and any physical resemblance between these proteins and the Parisian landmark is coincidental. Nevertheless, the

DNA-protein spirals and loops bind with these scaffold proteins, albeit in ways that are not well understood. In addition to physically supporting and organizing DNA, proteins, especially the histones, may play a role in gene expression, a topic covered in the next chapter.

Chromosomes are discussed at length in a latter chapter, but some preparatory words about them are necessary here. *It is the chromosome, not the gene, that is literally the physical unit of genetic inheritance.* Genes are sequences of DNA that contain the blueprint for the stuff that makes up proteins and enzymes, and thousands of genes can be physically located within a single chromosome. Cells do not carry the genes as physically independent snippets of DNA. Rather, when cells beget cells, even in the sperm and egg that carry the genetic material to the next generation, they do so with the DNA packaged into chromosomes.

● RNA: RIBONUCLEIC ACID

Before discussing the major role of DNA, it is important to discuss DNA's first cousin, *ribonucleic acid* or RNA. Besides its chemical composition, RNA has important similarities to as well as differences from DNA. First, like DNA, RNA has four and only four nucleotides, but unlike DNA, RNA uses the nucleotide *uracil* (abbreviated as U) in place of thymine (T). Thus, the four RNA nucleotides are adenine (A), cytosine (C), guanine (G), and uracil (U).

Second, the nucleotides in RNA also exhibit complementary base pairing. The RNA nucleotides may pair with either DNA or other RNA molecules. When RNA pairs with DNA, G always pairs with C, and T in DNA always pairs with A in RNA, but A in DNA pairs with U in RNA. When RNA pairs with RNA, then G pairs with C and A pairs with U.

Third, RNA is single-stranded while DNA is double-stranded. That is, RNA does not have the ladder-like structure of the DNA in Figure 3.1. Instead, RNA would look like Figure 3.1 after the ladder was sawed down the middle and half of it discarded (with, of course, the added proviso that U would substitute for T in the remaining half).

Fourth, although there is one type of DNA, there are several different types of RNA, each of which performs different duties in the cell. Think of DNA as the monarch of the cell, giving all the orders. Unlike human monarchs, however, king DNA is unable to leave the throne room (i.e., the cell's nucleus) and hence can never execute his own orders. The different types of RNA correspond to the various types of henchmen who carry out the king's orders. Some occupy buildings in outlying districts (ribosomal RNA), others transport material to strategic locations (transfer RNA), and still others act as messengers to give instructions on what to build (messenger RNA). As we will see, the common language of the realm is the genetic code, and it is communicated by the way of complementary base pairing.

THE GENETIC CODE: A GENERAL PERSPECTIVE ●

DNA is a blueprint. It does not physically construct anything. Before discussing how the information in the DNA results in the manufacture of a molecule, it is it important to obtain an overall perspective on the genetic code.

It is convenient to view the genome for any species as a book, with the genetic code as the language common to the books of all life-forms. The "alphabet" for this language has four and only four letters, given by four nucleotides in DNA (A, T, C, and G) or RNA (A, U, G, and C). In contrast to human language, in which a word is composed of any number of letters, a genetic "word" consists of three and only three letters. Each genetic word symbolizes an amino acid. (We will define an amino acid later.) For example, the nucleotide sequence AAG is "DNAese" for the amino acid phenylalanine, the sequence GTC denotes the amino acid glutamine, and the sequence AGT stands for the amino acid serine. Like natural language, DNA has synonyms; that is, there is more than one triplet nucleotide sequence symbolizing the same amino acid. For example, ATA and ATG both denote the amino acid tyrosine. Table 3.1 gives the genetic code in terms of the DNA triplet words.

The "sentence" in the DNA language is a series of words that gives a sequence of amino acids. For example, the DNA sentence AACGTATCGCAT would be read as a polypeptide chain composed of the amino acids leucine-histidine-serine-valine. Because of the triplet nature of the DNA language, it is not necessary to put spaces between the words. Given the correct starting position, the language will translate with 100% fidelity.

Like natural written language, part of the DNA language consists of punctuation marks. For example, the nucleotide DNA triplets ATT, ATC, and ACT are analogous to a period (.) in ending a sentence—all three signal the end of a polypeptide chain. Other punctuation marks denote the start of the amino acid sequence for the peptide. Unlike the triplet nature of the DNA words for amino acids, some DNA punctuation marks may be more or less than three nucleotides.

Finally, DNA, just like a book, is organized into chapters. The chapters correspond to the chromosomes, so their number will vary from one species to the next. The book for humans consists of 23 different chapters, one for each chromosome. The book for other species may contain fewer or more

Table 3.1   The Genetic Code

First Letter	Second Letter				Third Letter
	U	**C**	**A**	**G**	
	F Phe	S Ser	Y Tyr	C Cys	U
	F Phe	S Ser	Y Tyr	C Cys	C
U	L Leu	S Ser	Stop[b]	Stop[b]	A
	L Leu	S Ser	Stop[b]	W Trp	G
	L Leu	P Pro	H His	R Arg	U
	L Leu	P Pro	H His	R Arg	C
	L Leu	P Pro	Q Gln	R Arg	A
C	L Leu	P Pro	Q Gln	R Arg	G
	I Ile	T Thr	N Asn	S Ser	U
	I Ile	T Thr	N Asn	S Ser	C
	I Ile	T Thr	K Lys	R Arg	A
A	M Met[a]	T Thr	K Lys	R Arg	G
	V Val	A Ala	D Asp	G Gly	U
	V Val	A Ala	D Asp	G Gly	C
	V Val	A Ala	E Glu	G Gly	A
G	V Val	A Ala	E Glu	G Gly	G

NOTE: The three letters constitute a codon in mRNA. The letter before the three-letter code is the conventional abbreviation for the amino acid used in the Human Genome Project. Ala = Alanine, Arg = Arginine, Asn = Asparagine, Asp = Aspartic acid, Cys = Cysteine, Glu = Glutamic acid, Gln = Glutamine, Gly = Glycine, His = Histidine, Ile = Isoleucine, Leu = Leucine, Lys = Lysine, Met = Methionine, Phe = Phenylalanine, Pro = Proline, Ser = Serine, Thr = Threonine, Trp = Tryptophan, Tyr = Tyrosine, and Val = Valine.

a. Start codon for synthesizing the polypeptide chain.
b. The stop codon terminates the synthesis of a polypeptide chain.

chapters, with little correlation between the number of chapters and the complexity of the life-form.

The differences between natural human language and DNAese are as important as the similarities. All differences reduce to the fact that human language is coherent, whereas DNA is the most muddled and disorganized communication system ever developed.

First, the chapters in a human language book are arranged to tell a coherent story. There is no such ordering to chromosomes. Second, sentences in English physically follow one another, with one sentence qualifying, embellishing, or adding information to another so as to complete a coherent line of thought. The genetic language rarely, if ever, has a logical sequence. Metaphorically, one DNA sentence might describe the weather, the next might give two ingredients for a chili recipe, and the third could be a political aphorism.

Third, whereas it is absurd to write an English compound sentence with a paragraph or two interspersed between the two independent clauses, DNA frequently places independent clauses of the same sentence in entirely different chapters. Fourth, it is extremely unlikely that a book written in English would be published if most of its sentences were interrupted with what appeared to be the musings of a chimpanzee randomly striking a keyboard. A single DNA sentence may be perforated with more than a dozen long sequences of such apparent nonsense.

Fifth, in natural language it is considered bad rhetoric to repeat a thought in adjacent sentences, let alone using the same words. With DNA, repetition is the norm, not the exception. Not only does DNA continuously stutter, stammer, and hem and haw, but it also contains numerous nonsensical passages that are repeated thousands of times, sometimes in the same chapter.

Finally, the size of the DNA "book" for any mammalian species far exceeds that of any book written by a human. With 80 or so characters per line and perhaps 30 or so lines on a page of a paperback, a 500-page book contains about 1,500,000 English letters. It would take more than 2,000 such books to contain the DNA book of *homo sapiens*. And almost 90% of the characters in these 2,000 volumes would have no apparent meaning!

PROTEIN SYNTHESIS ●

Proteins and Enzymes Revisited

We now examine the specifics of how the blueprint in the DNA guides the manufacture of a protein. Although we have already spoken of proteins and enzymes, we must now take a closer look at these molecules. The basic building block for any protein or enzyme is the *amino acid*.[4] There are 20 amino acids used in constructing proteins, most of which contain the suffix "ine" (e.g., phenylalanine, serine, tyrosine). Amino acids frequently are abbreviated by three letters, usually the first three letters of the name—for example, "phe" for phenylalanine and "tyr" for tyrosine.

There are three major sources for the amino acids in our bodies. First, the cells in our bodies can manufacture amino acids from other, more basic compounds (or, as the case may be, from other amino acids). Second, proteins and enzymes within a cell are constantly being broken down into amino acids. Finally, we can obtain amino acids from our diet. When we eat a juicy steak, the protein in the meat is broken down into its amino acids by enzymes in our stomach and intestine. These amino acids are then transported by the blood to other cells in the body.

A series of amino acids physically linked together is called a *polypeptide chain*. For now, think of a polypeptide chain as a linear series of boxcars coupled together. The boxcars are the amino acids, and their couplings are the chemical bonds holding them together. The series is linear in the sense that it does not branch into a Y-like structure. The notion of a polypeptide chain is absolutely crucial for proper understanding of genes, so permit some latitude for a digression into terminology.

Unfortunately, there are no written conventions for the language used to describe polypeptide chains, so terminology can be confusing to the novice. Typically, the word *peptide* is used to describe a chain of linked amino acids when the number of amino acids is small—say, a few hundred or less. The word *peptide* is also used as an adjective and suffix to describe a substance that is composed of amino acids. For example, a *peptide hormone* is a hormone that is made up of linked amino acids, and a *neuropeptide* is a series of linked amino acids in a neuron. The phrases *polypeptide chain*, *polypeptide*, or *peptide chain* usually refer to a longer series of coupled amino acids, sometimes numbering in the thousands. Be wary, however. One can always find exceptions to this usage.

We are now ready to define our old friend the protein. A *protein* is a polypeptide chain or more than one polypeptide chain physically joined together and taking on a three-dimensional configuration. The polypeptide chain(s) constituting a protein will bend, fold back upon themselves, and bond at various spots to give a molecule that is no longer a simple linear structure. An example is hemoglobin, a protein in the red blood cells that carries oxygen. It is composed of four polypeptide chains that bend and bond and join together.

Some proteins contain chemicals other than amino acids. For example, a *lipoprotein* contains a lipid (i.e., fat) in addition to the amino acid chain. A particularly important class of proteins is the receptor protein that resides on the cell membrane (but sometimes within the cell) and is responsible for "communication" between the cell and extracellular "messengers."

Finally, we must recall the definition of an enzyme. An *enzyme* is a particular class of protein responsible for metabolism.

With these definitions in mind, we can now present one definition of a gene. *A gene is a sequence of DNA that contains the blueprint for the manufacture of a peptide or a polypeptide chain.* Such genes are sometimes qualified by calling them *structural genes* or *coding regions*. A synonym for gene is *locus* (plural = *loci*), the Latin word meaning site, place, or location.

Table 3.2   The Five Steps in Protein Synthesis

Step	Name	Process
1	Photocopying (*transcription*)	An RNA chain is synthesized that is a "mirror image" of the DNA.
2	Editing (*posttranscriptional modification*)	Sections of junk (*introns*) are cut out, and sections of message (exons) are spliced together.
3	Transportation	Messenger RNA (*mRNA*) leaves the nucleus, enters the cytoplasm, and attaches to a ribosome.
4	Translation	A triplet (*codon*) of mRNA enters a "reading frame" in the ribosome. A molecule of transfer RNA (*tRNA*) with the complementary triplet (anticodon) binds to the codon. The amino acid carried by the tRNA attaches to the growing polypeptide chain.
5	Final assembly (*post-translational modification*)	The polypeptide chain bends and folds on itself, taking on a three-dimensional form. A number of other modifications (e.g., adding another folded polypeptide chain) also may occur.

NOTE: Italicized names in parentheses are terms used in genetics.

Protein Synthesis: The Process

We can now look at the actual "manufacturing process" whereby the information on the DNA blueprint eventually becomes translated into a physical molecule. There are five steps in this process: (a) photocopying (or *transcription*), (b) editing (or *post transcriptional modification*), (c) transportation, (d) translation, and (e) final assembly (or *post translational modification*). Table 3.2 summarizes these steps.

Photocopying (or transcription). Depicted in Figure 3.4, transcription is the processes whereby a section of DNA gets "read" and chemically "photocopied" into a molecule of RNA. In the first step of transcription, the bonds joining the two nucleotides that constitute a rung of the DNA ladder are broken by an enzyme. Then, a chain of RNA is synthesized from one strand of the DNA using the principles of the complementary pairing of nucleotides. For example, if the DNA sequence is GCTAGA, then the RNA sequence that is synthesized will read CGAUCU. In this way, the information in the DNA is faithfully preserved in the RNA, albeit in the genetic equivalent of a"mirror image."

The process of transcription does not occur everywhere on the DNA. Instead, a DNA sequence called a *promoter region* is located upstream of the DNA that has the blueprint for the polypeptide chain. A series of proteins and

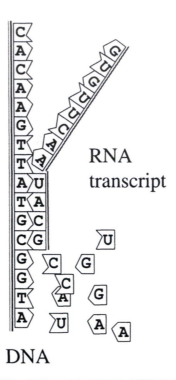

Figure 3.4   The Process of Transcription. Enzymes attach to DNA, cut the hydrogen bonds, and make the DNA single-stranded. Other enzymes attach to the DNA strand and synthesize a chain of RNA using free nucleotides and complementary base pairing.

enzymes (called herein the "transcription stuff") binds to the promoter region and starts the transcription process. Other punctuation marks act as stop signs to terminate transcription. Later on, we will see how these sites play an important role in genetic regulation. For now, let us just recognize that only 10% to 15% of human DNA ever becomes transcribed into RNA. Of the rest, about 1% consists of punctuation marks, and the remaining 99% has no discernible function.

Editing (or posttranscriptional modification). After transcription, the RNA contains three different types of information. The first of these is, of course, the information about the amino acid sequence for the peptide chain. These sections of RNA are called *exons* and contain the actual blueprint for peptide synthesis. The second type of information is the punctuation mark. These marks are the biological equivalents of saying "the information on making this polypeptide starts here" or . . . "stops here." The third type is called an *intron*. In terms of blueprint information, introns are literally junk. That is, they do not contain code for the

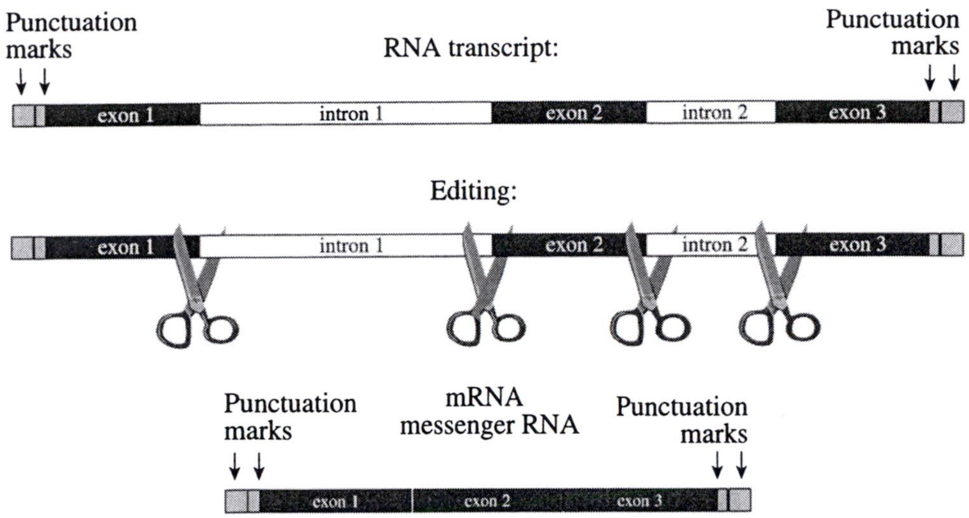

Figure 3.5   Editing: Enzymes Cut Out the Junk (Introns) and Splice the Message (Exons) Together.

amino acid sequence of the polypeptide, although on occasion introns may play a role in gene expression (see Chapter 4). Although all RNA that is transcribed from DNA begins with a series of punctuation marks, there can be many different exons and introns in a single molecule of transcribed RNA.

Editing is a cut-and-paste process in which the junk is eliminated from the RNA, leaving only the important punctuation marks and the message. In more precise terms, the introns are physically cut out of the RNA transcript and the exons are spliced together. Figure 3.5 gives an example of this process. The resulting RNA is termed *messenger RNA* and is abbreviated as *mRNA*.

One important term related to mRNA is the *codon*. A codon is a series of three adjacent mRNA nucleotides that contain the message for a specific amino acid. (Sometimes the term *codon* is also used to refer to the triplet in DNA that gives rise to the mRNA.)

Transportation. King DNA is imprisoned in the nucleus of the cell, but the actual synthesis of a polypeptide chain takes place in the cytoplasm. In transportation, the mRNA exits the nucleus, enters the cytoplasm, and attaches to an almost forgotten old friend, a ribosome. Recall that the ribosome is a "protein factory," in the sense that it is the physical location where the polypeptide chain is created. Ribosomes are composed of RNA (to which the mRNA attaches) and various proteins and enzymes that are the tools used in the manufacturing process.

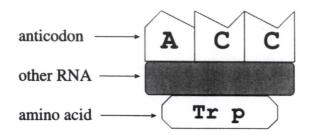

anticodon

other RNA

amino acid

Figure 3.6   Schematic of a Transfer RNA (tRNA) Molecule. The anticodon acts as a "bar code" signaling the specific amino acid that the molecule is carrying.

Translation. In translation, the message on the mRNA is read and a peptide chain is synthesized. To examine this step, let us begin with another class of RNA called transfer RNA or tRNA, depicted in Figure 3.6. In addition to ribonucleic acid, one molecule of tRNA carries one amino acid. Each tRNA also contains an *anticodon*—a series of three nucleotides that acts as a label identifying the specific amino acid attached to the tRNA. For example, the anticodon AAG means that the tRNA carries phenylalanine, and the anticodon ACG, shown in Figure 3.6, denotes that the tRNA molecule carries tryptophan.

The process of translation is illustrated in Figure 3.7. The mRNA molecule moves through the ribosome until a punctuation mark is encountered that signifies "the next three nucleotides constitute the first codon, so start the synthesis of the polypeptide chain here." The first codon on mRNA then moves through the ribosome, and a tRNA molecule that has the appropriate anticodon to the codon is attached to the mRNA. In Figure 3.7, the first mRNA codon is UUU (denoting phenylalanine or "phe"), so only a tRNA molecule with the anticodon AAA (and, hence, carrying phenylalanine) will pair with it. Consequently, the first amino acid for the polypeptide chain will be "phe" or phenylalanine.

The second codon is then "read," the appropriate tRNA binds to it, and the amino acid carried by the tRNA is physically bound to the first amino acid. In Figure 3.6, the second codon is ACG, so the tRNA molecule that binds with it will be UGC, carrying the amino acid threonine ("thr"). The nascent polypeptide chain now consists of the amino acid sequence "phe-thr."

The mRNA then moves through the ribosome, the next codon is "read," the appropriate tRNA molecule is attached, and the amino acid that it carries is physically joined to the previous amino acid. This is depicted on the right-hand side of Figure 3.7. The codon is CGG, and the tRNA molecule has the anticodon GCC. Hence, the amino acid "arg" (arginine) is added to the polypeptide chain. (Note how the tRNA molecule associated with the first amino acid has now dissociated from it.) This process continues—one codon

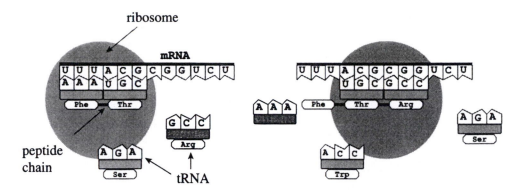

Figure 3.7 The Process of Translation. The mRNA strand attaches to a ribosome. In the left panel, two codons then attract their complementary anticodons using the principles of base pairing; enzymes cleave off the two amino acids from the tRNA molecules and join them together. In the right panel, the mRNA moves through the ribosome like a ticker tape. The next tRNA molecule binds with the mRNA codon, and the amino acid is released and then attached to the growing polypeptide chain.

moving through the ribosome, having a tRNA molecule attach to it, and then having the amino acid cleaved and joined to the polypeptide chain—until a punctuation mark on the mRNA signifies termination of the message.

Final assembly (or posttranslational modification). In some cases, the polypeptide produced after translation is a perfectly fine biological molecule. Here, the polypeptide chain folds, bends, and binds upon itself to take on a three-dimensional configuration, and the protein or enzyme is complete. In other cases, the polypeptide is a raw product that requires further processing at the finishing table. Sometimes the polypeptide chain may be cleaved in one or more places to give a smaller, but biologically functional, peptide—the bio- logical equivalent to removing spurs from a metal casting. More often, two or more polypeptide chains are joined together to make a functioning protein or enzyme. The process of assembly is too complicated and protein-specific to describe here, so we merely state that intracellular processes will join two or more polypeptide chains together to form the final protein. An important twist on the assembly process is that some molecules other than polypeptide chains may be added to generate a protein complex. For example, a chain of lipids (i.e., fat) may be added, giving a lipoprotein complex, or a sugar may be added to give a glycoprotein.

● HEMOGLOBIN: AN EXAMPLE OF THE GENETIC CODE AND ITS ORGANIZATION

The hemoglobin protein will figure prominently in several different sections of this book, so it will be used here to illustrate the genetic code and the organization of the genome. It will also help us to practice the genetic lingo we have learned in this chapter.

When we breathe in air, a series of chemical reactions in our lungs extracts oxygen atoms and implants them into the hemoglobin protein in our red blood cells. The red blood cells pulse through our arteries and eventually reach tiny capillaries in body tissues (e.g., liver cells, pancreas cells, muscle cells, neurons, etc.) where the hemoglobin releases the oxygen atoms. In humans 5 months of age or older, hemoglobin is composed of four polypeptide chains, two α chains and two β chains.[5]

Figure 3.8 depicts the DNA segment containing the gene for the β polypeptide. This long section of DNA is located on chromosome 11 and is more than 60,000 nucleotides long (or 60 kb, where kb denotes a kilobase or 1,000 base pairs). Only the tiny box with the label β contains the blueprint for the β peptide chain. (For the moment, ignore the boxes labeled ε, Gγ, Aγ, and δ.[6]) The boxes labeled $\psi\beta_1$ and $\psi\beta_2$ are called *pseudogenes* for the β locus. A pseudogene is a nucleotide sequence highly similar to a functional gene, but its DNA is not transcribed and/or translated.

The middle section of Figure 3.8 gives the structure of the β locus, including the "punctuation marks." Note the promoter regions and recall that this is the area that the transcription stuff binds to and begins the transcription process. There are also two punctuation marks downstream of the promoter. The first indicates where transcription is to begin, and the second marks the first codon for translation.

The β locus is roughly 1,600 base pairs long and includes three exons. The first exon is composed of the 90 nucleotides that have the code for the first 30 amino acids in the peptide chain. The second exon contains codes for the 31st through 104th amino acids, and the last for the remaining 40. Hence, of the 1,600 base pairs, only 438 contain blueprint material. If we add to these about 60 nucleotides worth of punctuation marks, then less than a third of the whole β locus contains the actual blueprint and processing information for the polypeptide chain. The final section of Figure 3.8 gives the actual nucleotide sequence for the beginning of exon 1.

Figure 3.9 depicts the DNA region for the α chains. This is located on an entirely different chromosome from the β cluster, chromosome 16, and is roughly 30 kb in length. The boxes labeled α_1 and α_2 both contain the blueprint for the α peptide chain. This is an example of *gene duplication*—the

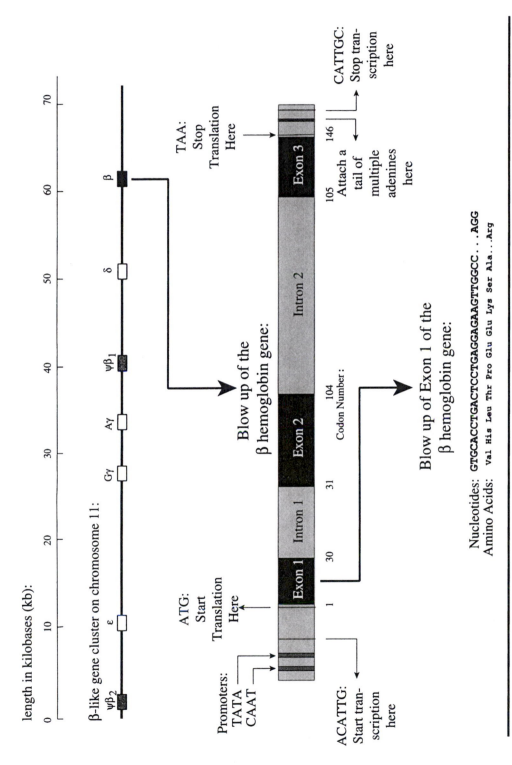

Figure 3.8 Schematic of the DNA Sequence That Codes for the β Polypeptide Chain of the Hemoglobin Protein.

45

length in kilobases (kb):

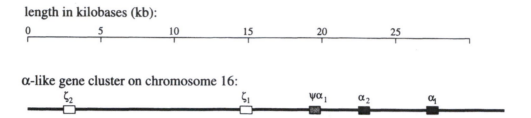

α-like gene cluster on chromosome 16:

Figure 3.9   The Structure of the DNA Sequence Coding for the α Polypeptide Chain of the Hemoglobin.

DNA for both of these loci is transcribed, edited, and translated into the same α chains. Like the β chain, there is also a pseudogene for the α locus, denoted in Figure 3.9 by the box labeled ψα₁. (Once again, ignore the boxes labeled ζ₁ and ζ₂.⁷) The actual structure for the two α loci is very similar to that of the β locus—they too have three exons—and is not depicted in Figure 3.9.

Adult hemoglobin is composed of two polypeptide chains coded for by the α loci as well as two chains coded for by the β locus. These are joined together in the assembly stage of protein synthesis. Two heme groups are added to the protein. (A heme group contains an iron atom that permits oxygen to bind when the hemoglobin is carried through the lungs.)

Hemoglobin is a good example of the capricious organization of our human genome. Only about 10% of the DNA in both clusters is actually used, and the two clusters are on entirely different chromosomes! In addition, the fact that there are two α loci but only one β locus requires an elaborate genetic control mechanism to ensure that an equal number of α and β polypeptide chains is manufactured. A human engineer would clearly arrange things quite differently by, for example, placing the α and β loci close together so they are transcribed as a unit. This would ensure that an equal number of α and β chains is produced, avoiding the mess of regulatory mechanisms. If any intelligent being created the human genome, then he or she must have had a few beers before starting the project and considerably more than a few while removing the bugs!

● GENE PATENTING AGAIN

In the previous chapter, we gained an appreciation for why industry and capital are moving into biotechnology. With our knowledge of what a gene is and how protein synthesis takes place, it is timely to revisit the issue to see exactly what is involved in patenting genes. Text boxes 3.1 and 3.2, respectively,

(Text continues on page 50)

Text Box 3.1

HUMAN GENE PATENTING: WHAT IS IT?

Now that we have seen what a gene is and examined the process of protein synthesis, we can revisit the controversy surrounding gene patents. As an example, let us consider the BRCA1 gene (breast cancer gene 1). We all have this gene, but a few rare individuals have mutant alleles (i.e., "spelling" variations in the nucleotide sequence of the BRCA1 gene) that place them at very high risk for developing breast cancer. In 1995, Myriad Genetics Inc. received a patent on this gene from the U.S. Patent and Trademark Office. In the patent application, Myriad Genetics specified the normal nucleotide sequence of the BRCA1 gene and the spelling for the mutant alleles, provided a technique for detecting the mutant allele, and demonstrated the utility of the patent (i.e., screening for breast cancer). Since 1995, Myriad has spent millions of dollars in research and has obtained other patents on the BRCA1 gene.

How does a gene get patented, and what does the patent mean? After all, you and I both have the BRCA1 gene in our bodies. Does that mean that Myriad "owns" our BRCA1 genes? No. One cannot patent something that exists in nature. This means that you cannot patent your children or the oak tree in your backyard. As a result, both you and I can logon to the Internet, go to a genetic database such as Online Mendelian Inheritance in Man (or OMIM, currently at www.ncbi. nlm.nih.gov/Omim), search on BRCA1, download the nucleotide sequence for this gene and the mutant alleles, photocopy that sequence, and hand it out for free.

So what is Myriad's patent about? According to John Doll, director of biotechnology at the U.S. Patent and Trademark Office (*Scientific American*, August 2001), a successful patent meets four criteria. First, the patent must involve something that is nonobvious to a person working in the field. Second, the patented process or product must not have been done, published, or created before. Third, it must have some direct utility: One cannot simply patent knowledge. Finally, the patent application must be written in such a manner that others working in the field can use the invention.

The third and fourth criteria—utility and use—allowed Myriad to patent the gene. The nucleotide sequence that we downloaded is simply knowledge. It does not tell us the importance of the sequence of As, Ts, Cs, and Gs, nor does it provide a method to test for that sequence. Myriad's patent showed a practical effect for knowing the sequence (i.e., predicting breast cancer risk) and presented a technology for detecting the mutant allele that others in the field of medical genetics could use.

Once a patent is awarded, all information in the patent becomes public knowledge. Hence, Myriad's patents give the nucleotide sequences of the normal and mutant BRCA1 alleles as well as methods for detecting those sequences. In return, Myriad is granted exclusive rights to use those methods for detecting BRCA1 alleles for a specified amount of time (currently 20 years in the United States).

This is the logic behind patenting a human gene. A very different question is whether human genes *should* be patented. Patents involving the genetics of some types of organisms have been in place for decades (e.g., patenting a new hybrid strain of corn). But should we permit an individual human gene to be patented? That is the topic of Text Box 3.2.

Text Box 3.2

HUMAN GENE PATENTING: SHOULD WE DO IT?

There is both extensive and acrimonious debate over gene patenting. Naturally, proprietors and stockholders of privately financed biotech firms argue that the protection received from patenting allows them to recoup their investments and make a profit. Without the possibility of earning a profit, what would be the incentive to develop a test for the mutant BRCA1 alleles? Advocates also stress that they do not "own" the gene. Instead, they have found a nonobvious way of isolating a specific DNA sequence from its natural state that has a practical significance in medicine or some other field.

Many others who support the patent system in principle, however, see a fundamental difference between patenting a gene and patenting a better mousetrap. Some oppose patents for genes or other biological materials for reasons that are largely philosophical and ethical. After all, the majority of the technology that allowed Myriad to detect the BRCA1 gene in the first place and then develop a test for it was funded by tax dollars. Does not the public deserve a return on its investment?

Others who favor gene patenting question the limits to which intellectual property rights should apply. Suppose that another firm developed a test for BRCA1 through a completely different technology. Can this firm get its own patent? Or does Myriad own all the property rights to the BRCA1 gene and thus all the rights for all potential tests for that gene? The argument gets complicated when we consider the "mouse-trap" involved in this example. Many consider a nucleotide sequence much as a mouse in the sense that both occur in nature. Hence, "gene patents" should be restricted to specific *tests* for genes and not for genes themselves. After all, does the award of a patent for a new mousetrap include the concept of "mouse-catching" and prevent others from developing novel devices?

Further clouding the situation is the financial consequence of granting patents for human genes. In October 2001, the cost of one of Myriad's test kits was $2,680. Granted, the kit tests for a large number of mutant alleles at BRCA1 and also at another gene, BRCA2, that contribute to breast cancer risk. But many health agencies in Canada and Europe have rebelled against incurring the costs of Myriad's kit when their own labs can test for the same alleles at a much lower cost (see "Europe's Patent Rebellion" in *Fortune*, October 1, 2001).

Sadly, the types of organization that can settle such thorny issues—groups of elected public officials—apparently consider the topic so politically charged that they have avoided legislation regulating gene patenting. Hence, the issues are likely to be resolved only through costly litigation and eventually will be decided by court rulings. Even here, it is not clear that the court rulings in one country will agree with those in another.

For those interested in further information on the topic, the best way to research opinions and current news on this topic is to do a Web search on the phrase "gene patents."

present a description of patenting and the arguments for and against patenting human genes.

● NOTES

1. Several types of viruses, of which HIV is an important example, are exceptions. Their code is written into a molecule called RNA (aka ribonucleic acid), DNA's "first cousin."

2. The terms 5′ and 3′ refer to the position of carbon atoms that link a nucleotide to the DNA backbone.

3. Of course, DNA does not replicate with 100% accuracy, and problems in replication may cause irregularities and even disease in cells. Organisms do, however, have the equivalent of DNA proofreading mechanisms that serve two purposes—helping to ensure that DNA is copied accurately and preventing DNA from becoming too damaged from environmental factors. A genetic defect in one proofreading mechanism, as an example, leads to the disorder xeroderma pigmentosum, which eventually results in death from skin cancer.

4. Although proteins are composed of amino acids, amino acids can perform other functions than simply being chained together to make a protein or an enzyme. Some are used as substrates from which important substances are synthesized. For example, in Chapter 2, we saw how the amino acid tyrosine was used to manufacture the neurotransmitters dopamine and norepinephrine. Several amino acids also operate as neurotransmitters in their own right.

5. I am lying here. There is another chain called the δ chain, but only 3% of hemoglobin molecules contain this chain, so we can safely ignore it in order to make things simple.

6. Three of the other four genes—ϵ, Gγ, and Aγ—are expressed in the embryo, fetus, and neonate. The δ gene produces a δ hemoglobin chain that also forms functional adult hemoglobin with the α chain. However, this locus is not strongly expressed, so only about 3% of adult hemoglobin is composed of δ chains.

7. Loci ζ_1 and ζ_2 are expressed in the early embryo.

CHAPTER 4

EPIGENESIS AND GENETIC REGULATION

Virtually every cell in your body contains all the genetic information that would be needed to make a complete human being that would be your identical twin. This fact makes cloning you a theoretical possibility. A "mad geneticist" could try this by extracting the DNA from one of your cells, placing it into the nucleus of a human egg from which the DNA has been removed, inducing the egg to start dividing, and then inserting it into the uterus of a woman. If the resulting zygote were viable, the organism would be your identical twin, albeit in a different phase of the life cycle. This theoretical possibility raises an interesting question: If every cell has the same genetic code, then why are some cells liver cells, for example, and others are neurons?

Another question arises from the consideration of cell division. You and I each began as a single fertilized egg. A human egg divides into two cells that contain the same genetic material. These two genetically identical cells each divide, giving four genetically identical cells; these four divide, giving eight, and so on. Why were our parents not rewarded for 9 months of pregnancy by bouncing, 7-pound blobs of identical cells?

Although the answers to these questions are complicated and not well understood even by experts, some understanding can be found in the knowledge that genes are differentially expressed in some tissues and are also regulated over time even within the same tissue. To oversimplify, even though a liver cell has all the genetic information to make a neuron, only "liver cell" genes are working in the liver, and the "neuron cell" genes in the liver are in some way shut down. This process of differential gene expression is called *genetic regulation, gene expression, epigenesis,* or *epigenetic control.*

Progress in unraveling the mechanisms of epigenesis is occurring at a blistering pace. Researchers discover more about the mechanisms on almost a daily basis, and much of what was state-of-the-art knowledge recently has been superseded. Hence, only a few of these mechanisms will be discussed.

● LYONIZATION: X-CHROMOSOME INACTIVATION

Females have two X chromosomes, and males have only one. Thus, one might expect that females should have twice the level of X-chromosome proteins and enzymes as males. Empirically, however, this is not true—the levels are equal in men and women.

The reason is that in the cells of a human female, one and only one X chromosome is active. The other X chromosome coils and condenses into a small ellipsoid structure called a Barr body and is functionally deactivated—the genes on that chromosome are not transcribed.[1] Geneticist Mary Lyon hypothesized this almost 40 years ago, so the phenomenon is often called Lyonization.

During the very early embryonic development of a female, both her maternal and paternal X chromosomes are active. After 12 days of development, when the embryo has about 5,000 cells, one of these chromosomes is randomly deactivated in all the cells. Once a given cell has an inactive chromosome, all its daughter cells will have the same chromosome deactivated. That is, if "cell number 23" has the paternal X deactivated, then all descendants of cell 23 will also have the paternal X deactivated. The particular X chromosome deactivated in the original cell is random. Consequently, half of a female's cells will express her paternal X chromosome while the other half will express her maternal X. Thus, females are genetic mosaics.

Fur color in the calico cat is a classic example of Lyonization. A gene on one X chromosome of the calico contains the instructions for black pigment, while a gene on the other X codes for an orangish brown pigment. Hence, the black fur comes from cells in which the "black chromosome" is active and the "orange chromosome" is Lyonized, whereas the orange fur is generated by cells in which the reverse occurs. (White fur derives from another gene that determines whether any pigment at all will be expressed.) This is the reason why all calicos are females.

The gene responsible for X chromosome inactivation, the XIST locus, has recently been localized to the long arm of the X, but the precise mechanism for achieving inactivation is not totally understood. Certain data suggest that the major reason for Lyonization is "dosage compensation"—making certain that the same levels of proteins and enzymes are expressed in males and females. Females with Turner's syndrome (only one X chromosome) do not have Barr bodies, females with three X chromosomes have two Barr bodies in each cell, and males with Klinefelter's syndrome (two X chromosomes and one Y chromosome) have one Barr body. It appears that the process evolved to guarantee that one and only one X chromosome is active in any given cell.

DIFFERENTIAL RNA SPLICING ●

The editing step of protein synthesis removes introns and splices exons together. Ordinarily, the same introns are removed and the same exons are joined together, so that the same mRNA results from all transcription events. For some genes, however, different exons are spliced together, resulting in different mRNA nucleotide sequences after transcription. This phenomenon is termed *differential RNA splicing* (or simply *RNA splicing*) and is a major epigenetic event in regulating the amino acid sequence that can result from a single gene.

The molecular mechanisms responsible for differential RNA splicing are not well understood. Once considered a curiosity, more and more examples of RNA splicing are being discovered, so the phenomenon appears to be common. The percentage of genes in which RNA splicing occurs is unknown, but we do know that in several important genes, RNA splicing does influence the amino acid sequence of the polypeptide. One example is the amyloid precursor protein gene (APP), which is receiving considerable research attention because of its possible role in the pathology of Alzheimer's disease.

● GENOMIC IMPRINTING

Genomic imprinting (aka *parental imprinting*) is a recently discovered phenomenon that is not well understood (Mannens & Alders, 1999). It relates to the fact that the expression of a gene depends on whether it is inherited from the mother or the father. Imprinting is a functional change— the actual DNA is not altered in any way; it is just that the expression of the gene product is changed. The imprinting occurs before or soon after conception, and once it occurs, all daughter cells seem to be imprinted in the same way.

The textbook example of imprinting concerns a genetic syndrome that arises when a small section of chromosome 15 is deleted. If the chromosome deletion is inherited from the father, then the offspring will have the Prader-Willi syndrome, characterized by an insatiable appetite, obesity, and mental retardation. When the deletion is inherited from the mother, then the child will exhibit the Angelman syndrome, involving severe mental retardation, loss of motor coordination (ataxia), lack of speech, and seizures. It is suspected that some of the mother's genes are imprinted in the section of the deletion; that is, they are turned off. With the father's genes deleted, the fact that some of the mother's genes "don't work" causes Prader-Willi syndrome. The opposite occurs in Angelman's syndrome.

Very few genes are known to be susceptible to imprinting, so it may not turn out to be a major mechanism for genetic regulation. On the other hand, some evidence from animal models and Turner's syndrome (discussed in Chapter 8) is being interpreted as suggesting that imprinting may occur for some aspects of sociality (Skuse et al., 1997) and cognition (Isles & Wilkinson, 2000).

● TRANSCRIPTIONAL CONTROL

Many different mechanisms regulate gene expression by influencing whether messenger RNA is or is not transcribed from DNA. These mechanisms all fall into the generic category of transcriptional control. There are several different ways to achieve this control.

Methylation

Methylation of certain DNA nucleotide sequences is a mechanism receiving considerable attention. In methylation, a methyl group (one carbon atom and three hydrogen atoms) is attached to cytosine nucleotides in the DNA. Methylation typically inhibits the transcription of DNA. Certain areas of the inactive X chromosome in a Barr body are methylated, and the administration of demethylating agents to cell cultures can activate these regions. Methylation also plays an important part in Fragile X syndrome and will be discussed further in Chapter 5.

Regulatory Molecules

A second mechanism of control is the *regulatory molecule*. This mechanism is the major force behind gene regulation and expression. Transcription usually is initiated at a "punctuation mark" in the DNA termed a *promoter region*—a nucleotide sequence that signals the transcription stuff to "bind to the DNA here and get ready to start transcription." Many genes also have another punctuation mark, often called an *operator region*, that, in some organisms like bacteria, is in close proximity to the promoter region. The operator region contains a nucleotide sequence that acts as a recognition site for the regulatory molecule. The molecule can then bind to the DNA at that recognition site. Because the regulatory molecule is physically quite large with respect to the DNA, when it binds to the DNA there is no longer any room for the transcription enzyme to bind to the promoter region and start transcription. The gene is effectively "shut off."

The classic example of such control is the regulation of the genes for enzymes controlling lactose metabolism in the bacterium *E. coli*. During millions of years of evolution, *E. coli* and mammals have developed a cozy, symbiotic relationship with each other. *E. coli* physically reside in the intestines of mammals and obtain nourishment from the food ingested by the organisms. The *E. coli* graciously return the favor by helping us mammals to digest our food.

Mammals, however, present an interesting problem for *E. coli* because, for a significant time after birth, most mammals live on milk and milk alone. Lactose is the primary sugar in mammals' milk, but for it to be used as an energy source, a series of enzymes must convert it into two other sugars, galactose and glucose. Consequently, for the *E. coli* to survive in the gut of an infant mammal, they must produce large amounts of these enzymes to metabolize the lactose in milk. After a mammal is weaned, however, there is no more milk—and no more lactose—for the *E. coli* to live on. Producing large amounts of lactose-metabolizing enzymes during this phase of a mammal's life cycle is a waste of precious resources and energy for the tiny bacteria.

E. coli have evolved an elegant solution to this problem by transcribing the genes for lactose-metabolizing enzymes when lactose is present, but blocking the transcription of the same genes when lactose is absent. The situation is depicted in Figure 4.1. When lactose is absent (left panel of Figure 4.1), a protein, called a regulatory protein, binds to the bacterial DNA at the operator region. The regulatory protein is large enough, and the operator region is close enough to the promoter region, that the transcription enzymes have no room to bind to the DNA and transcribe the code for the lactose-metabolizing enzymes. The lactose system is shut down, and the little *E. coli* do not have to use their precious amino acids to build these enzymes.

The presence of lactose, however, turns the system on (right panel of Figure 4.1). As large amounts of lactose enter the gut, they also enter into the *E. coli*. There, some of the lactose molecules bind to the regulatory protein, changing its physical structure so that it can no longer bind to the DNA. The transcription enzymes are now free to bind to the promoter region and begin transcription of the genes coding for the lactose-metabolizing enzymes. The lactose system is now "switched on."

What happens next is simply a matter of logic. The enzymes that are produced eventually will chew up all the lactose. Thus, there is no more lactose to bind to the regulatory protein, and the regulatory protein can once again bind to the DNA. This prevents the transcription enzyme from binding to the promoter region, so no more messenger RNA for the lactose-metabolizing enzymes is produced. The system shuts down, and we return to the situation depicted in the left panel of Figure 4.1.

Hormones

Hormones are a major class of regulatory molecules in large, multicellular animals such as humans. A *hormone* is defined as a substance excreted from a cell into the bloodstream that carries it to other cells, where it initiates a physiological response. The two major types of hormones are based on the chemical substances from which they are composed. The first is *steroid hormones*, which include cortisol and the sex hormones (e.g., testosterone and estrogen). Steroid hormones are not made directly from genes. Instead, genes usually code for the enzymes in the metabolic pathway that synthesizes the steroid. The second type of hormone is the *peptide hormone*. These are composed of amino acids, so they are coded for directly in the DNA.

Many hormones influence transcription, although they do not always physically bind to the DNA as the regulatory molecule does in the lac operon. When hormones do not bind directly to DNA, they spark a series of chemical events in the cell that eventually result in some genes being turned on (i.e., transcription is started or enhanced) and in other genes being turned off (i.e., transcription is inhibited or stopped). A good analogy is to think of the

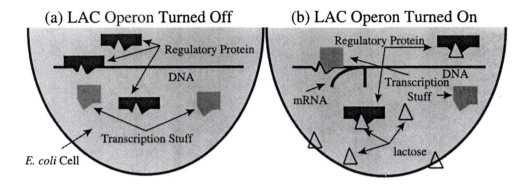

Figure 4.1   The Lac Operon in Bacteria. (a) When lactose is absent, the regulatory protein binds with the DNA and prevents the transcription enzymes from attaching themselves and transcribing RNA; all genes downstream of the regulatory binding (i.e., to the right of the regulatory protein) are shut off. (b) When lactose is present, it binds to the regulatory protein and prevents it from attaching itself to the DNA; the transcription enzymes cannot bind with the DNA and produce the RNA for the enzymes that metabolize lactose. After all the lactose is metabolized, the system reverts to panel (a) and shuts down.

hormone as a messenger molecule that is produced in one type of cell and then sent to the cells of other organs to tell them to "turn these genes on and turn those genes off."

Which genes are turned on or turned off by a particular hormone is a hot topic in the research world.

Transcriptional Control and Behavior: Stress, Anxiety, and Genes

This section will describe what is known about one physiological response to stress, the excretion of cortisol, and how this response influences gene regulation. We will explore this in considerable detail—and risk losing the reader in the process—to illustrate an important phenomenon about genes, physiological systems, and behavior.

Imagine that a good friend convinces you to try a parachute jump. You pay the money, go through the ground training, and receive considerable reinforcement from your friend, your instructor, and your fellow virgin parachutists about how thrilling and exciting this experience will be. After donning the appropriate regalia and entering the airplane, you are flown to a point more than a mile above the solid earth. The green light flashes, the instructor points to you, and you move to the door. You look down and ask

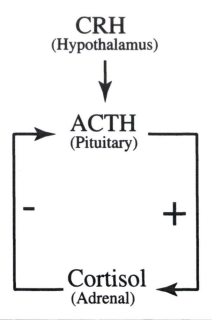

Figure 4.2   The Hypothalamic-Pituitary-Adrenal (HPA) Axis. The excretion of cortisol from the hypothalamus stimulates release of ACTH from the pituitary gland. ACTH enters the blood and eventually is taken up by the adrenal gland, on top of the kidney, where it stimulates the production and release of cortisol. As cortisol builds up in the blood, it inhibits the release of ACTH and shuts down the system.

yourself the proverbial question, "Why am I jumping out of a perfectly good airplane?"

It is easy for the social scientist to focus on the obvious—and very important—environmental circumstances that produce stress in this situation. But this clear environmental stressor also has a genetic side, albeit a poorly understood one. A generic view of the process begins with the endocrine (i.e., hormonal) system referred to as the hypothalamic-pituitary-adrenal (HPA) axis that is depected in Figure 4.2. The stress and anxiety of your parachute jump are accompanied by the release of corticotropin releasing hormone (CRH). CRH stimulates the production of another hormone, adrenocorticotropin hormone (ACTH), which in turn initiates production of cortisol. The cortisol response is now engaged. As cortisol builds up and plays its part in informing cells that stress is present, it also inhibits the production of ACTH. As ACTH levels drop, so does cortisol, and the system shuts down. This is a classic case of negative feedback. Let us now put this process under a more powerful microscope to see how genes play a role in it.

Everyone has a structure in the hypothalamus of the brain called the paraventricular nucleus; it contains nerve inputs from other parts of the brain. Within the cells of this nucleus are a large number of vesicles that contain the hormone CRH. At various stages in your jump, the neurons from the central nervous system that impinge on the paraventricular nucleus fire. In response, the cells release CRH into the surrounding extracellular fluid. The stress response has just begun.

CRH soon encounters the cells of the anterior pituitary gland, located below the hypothalamus. There, it binds to a receptor molecule and starts a series of reactions that have two important consequences. The first and most immediate consequence is stimulation of release of ACTH that is stored in vesicles in the cell. This ACTH leaves the cell and enters the bloodstream.

The second consequence of CRH is initiation of the synthesis of more ACTH to replace the ACTH that was released. This process begins with transcription of the pro-opiomelanocortin (POMC) gene. The POMC polypeptide chain synthesized after translation undergoes an important posttranslational process. Enzymes literally cut out a section of the POMC polypeptide. This section of amino acids cleaved from POMC is the peptide hormone ACTH. The newly manufactured ACTH is transported and stored in vesicles in the cells of the anterior pituitary.

Our attention now switches away from the head and to the adrenal gland, located on the top of the kidney. Like most cells, adrenal cells both manufacture cholesterol and "import" it from the blood. Unlike other cells, the adrenal gland contains receptors specific for ACTH within its plasma membrane. The ACTH that is circulating in your blood as a result of the stress of your first parachute jump binds to this receptor. There, the resulting ACTH-receptor complex initiates a cascade of events that activates a series of enzymes. These enzymes begin the metabolism of cholesterol within the cell. After five different enzymatic steps, the hormone cortisol is produced from the cholesterol.

The newly manufactured cortisol is excreted from the adrenal cells, enters the bloodstream, and is diffused throughout the body. Cortisol enters the cells of a wide variety of organs and cells—pancreas, liver, kidney, neurons, and many immune cells. There, it binds to its receptors and the cortisol-receptor complex influences the transcription of mRNA from what may turn out to be a large number of genes. In some cases, the cortisol-receptor complex initiates transcription, while in other cases it inhibits transcription.

The stress and anxiety of your parachute jump are now turning some of your genes on and turning some of them off!

Among all the cells that cortisol enters are those of the anterior pituitary, the very cells that released ACTH and sparked the production of cortisol in the first place. There, cortisol binds with another receptor, and this cortisol-receptor complex stops transcription of the POMC locus. With no more POMC polypeptides, there is no more ACTH being produced. With no more ACTH, the enzymes that synthesize cortisol from cholesterol are no longer activated, so cortisol production stops. The system is now shut down.

The HPA axis illustrates two major points. First, gene regulation can occur in response to environmental cues and circumstances. Although regulation occurs within the cell, it is not some closed, endogenous, biological process immune to events that physically occur outside the organism. In the case of cortisol, a wide variety of environmental cues can influence gene regulation. Such cues range from the anticipation of taking a final exam to downright, life-threatening events.[2]

The second major point is the sheer stupidity and inefficiency of this system. From an engineering standpoint, the cortisol response resembles a nightmarish Rube Goldberg mousetrap. The ultimate goal is to produce cortisol when nerves in the brain signal that something important is happening and cortisol is needed. However, both the neurons in your central nervous system and those in the paraventricular nucleus of your hypothalamus contain cholesterol and the genes for the enzymes necessary to metabolize the cholesterol into cortisol. One highly efficient system would be for these neurons to produce the cortisol once the neurons fire. Just think of the waste of the precious biological resources that this system would overcome: (a) There would be no need to make and store CRH and its receptors; (b) there would be no need to transcribe the POMC gene and produce POMC polypeptide, only to throw much of it away to get ACTH; (c) there would be no need to store ACTH; (d) and there would be no need to release ACTH and diffuse it throughout your blood, only to have it influence only one small organ. The HPA axis makes as much engineering sense as plugging a monitor into a computer with a cord that passes through each room in the building. We will return to this topic after discussing development.

● DEVELOPMENTAL GENETICS

Homeotic Genes

To appreciate development, it is helpful to reflect on the problems faced by individual cells. Imagine that you are a cell within an undifferentiated blob of embryonic cells several days after fertilization. Should you become a "head" cell, so that your descendants might become the eyes of the organism? Or should you become a "tail" cell? What would happen if you chose the head path but the cell to your right picked the tail? Obviously, there must be some way to synchronize cell development. If you had to answer the hypothetical question about your cellular fate, you would likely respond, "I will do as I am told to do." But who will tell you what to do? If the instructions come from some kind of "master cell," then who told that cell to become a master cell in the first place? The basic problem in development is that there are millions of clones (cells) but no centralized control. The embryonic development of a single human is akin to cloning millions of humans and then having them form an ordered society without any government.

Multicellular life-forms evolved an answer to this problem hundreds of millions of years ago. Probably because the plan worked so well, it has been handed down to contemporary life-forms with only minor modifications. As a result, many of the basic genetic mechanisms for development in us humans are also found in birds, reptiles, insects, and fish. Genes that influence development in this way are called *homeotic* genes, and they have two fundamental functions. First, they act as a "global positioning system" for the developing embryo by allowing a cell to "know" where it is located with respect to other cells. Second, they assist in the differentiation of the cell.

A classic example of the "global positioning" role of homeotic loci is the series of Hox gene clusters. Each Hox cluster contains a series of genes, located one right after the other, that have similar nucleotide sequences. One cluster influences the anterior-posterior developmental axis (i.e., the head-to-tail axis). By recognizing which gene in this cluster is turned on, an embryonic cell recognizes its relative position in the head-to-tail axis of development. In fruit flies, the first Hox gene is expressed in cells destined to become the mouth. The second gene is turned on in cells that will form the face. The third gene is expressed in cells responsible for the back part of the head. The next gene is expressed in cells joining the head and thorax, and so on until the last Hox gene in the cluster is expressed in the posterior. In short, the expression of these genes in the head-to-tail axis conforms perfectly to their ordering along the chromosome.

The similarity of nucleotide sequence in the Hox genes comes from the facts that these genes all code for proteins that bind to the DNA and that the DNA binding region of the protein has the same genetic code from one gene to the next. (The general name for this DNA binding region in homeotic genes is a *homeobox*.) Hence, Hox genes, like all other homeotic genes, are thought to produce transcription factors that will turn on or turn off other genes in the cell. The similarity over species of the homeobox regions and the homeotic genes is remarkable. Geneticists who have knocked out a particular homeotic gene in a fruit fly and then replaced it with its human equivalent can produce a developmentally normal fruit fly (e.g., Sharman & Brand, 1998).

Hence, the result of the global positioning homeotic genes is to "chemically compartmentalize" the embryo. Each compartment is then further specialized by other homeotic loci. For example, consider those cells in a developing fruit fly designated as "head parts" by their Hox gene. A second series of genes will be expressed to define a front-to-back (technically, a ventral-to-dorsal) axis, giving front and back compartments to the head.

Eventually, other genes that get turned on or off from homeotic transcription factors result in cell differentiation. Geneticists studying this process have developed quite bizarre experimental organisms. For example, if one transplanted tissue destined to become a leg into the eye of a fruit fly embryo, then one might create an unfortunate fly with a perfectly formed leg reaching out of its eyeball.

For obvious ethical reasons, research on homeotic genes is performed in experimental organisms. Hence, human genetic examples are few. Still, there is one classic example of development in mammals and humans that deserves comment—the epigenesis of sex.

Sexual Development

Sexual differentiation is the textbook example for developmental genetics. The typical course of human sexual development is female. Males are, metaphorically, masculinized females. Masculinization begins with the SRY locus (for sex-determining region of the Y) on the Y chromosome that codes for a protein that binds to DNA. It is thought that this protein initiates a cascade of events that regulates other loci on both the autosomal chromosomes and the X chromosome. Individuals who are chromosomally XY but have a deletion in the SRY gene develop as females with normal female external genitalia but malfunctioning ovaries.[3]

Other loci responsible for sex development have been identified because of mutations. Androgens (masculinizing hormones such as testosterone and dihydroxytestosterone) exert their influence by binding with an androgen receptor. The gene for this receptor is located on the X chromosome. Chromosomally XY individuals with a mutation at this locus may not produce any androgen receptors at all or may produce receptors that do not bind appropriately with the androgens. The result can range from undermasculinization and ambiguous external genitalia to completely normal female genitalia. It is not unusual for an XY woman with complete androgen sensitivity to be diagnosed only as an adult, after seeking consultation for fertility problems.

The masculinizing nature of androgens is demonstrated by the genetic syndrome of congenital adrenal hyperplasia (CAH), also called the adrenogenital syndrome. CAH results from a defect in any one of the five different genes containing the blueprints for the enzymes that convert cholesterol into cortisol. Because cortisol production is blocked, substances that chemically resemble androgens or androgens themselves build up in the system. CAH individuals who are chromosomally XX will be masculinized, to a degree dependent upon which locus is affected and other factors. CAH is discussed in more detail in Chapter 5.

WHY SUCH COMPLEXITY? ●

At this point, let us postpone discussion of genetic regulation and development and return to the statement made earlier about how the HPA axis is, from an engineer's perspective, a complicated and inefficient system. A moment's reflection on the genetic code, the organization of the human genome, and the process of protein synthesis reveals that they also are quite disorganized. Each of us humans has more than a trillion cells, and each cell contains more than 12 billion nucleotides. Thus, we each have a minimum of 12,000,000,000,000,000,000,000 nucleotides, the majority of them unneeded. Why should bone marrow cells spend energy and resources maintaining all those nucleotides for enzymes that produce skin pigment, fingernails, or hair? Clearly, any bioengineer who designed a protein synthesis system by placing introns into the blueprint would quickly lose his or her job. So would a chip designer who insisted that the manufacturer keep the nonfunctioning β hemoglobin pseudochip in the computer along with its perfectly functioning counterpart.

As knowledge of genetics expands, some mechanisms currently suspected as junk undoubtedly will turn out to be important. But it defies reason to imagine that human DNA, and each and every anatomical and physiological entity influenced by the DNA, is perfectly optimized in terms of simplicity, elegance, efficiency, and reliability of design. Otherwise, we would all look and act the same. The intriguing question is, "Why is the genome so complicated and inefficient?"

Truthfully, the reason is unknown, but the answer that first comes to the geneticist's mind is evolution. Evolution never anticipates or thinks ahead.[4] There is never any ultimate or teleological goal that evolution strives for when it alters an organism's DNA. Instead, evolution is the ultimate pragmatist. Evolution cares—actually demands—that a problem *gets solved*. It does not care *how* the problem gets solved. When there is a difficulty, evolution solves it in the here and now. It will tinker with and adopt any ad hoc solution, with no consideration as to how elegantly the solution is designed and no forethought about whether that solution will be beneficial or detrimental to the organism after the problem is solved.

Evolution's motto is "If it ain't broke, don't fix it." As long as we humans reproduce at an acceptable rate, evolution does not care if we all waste extra energy and nucleotides carrying around a β hemoglobin pseudogene that does nothing. The only reason for evolution to be concerned about simplicity and efficiency is when the lack of them interferes with reproduction. Even then, evolution retains its pragmatism. If an inefficient and complex system impedes reproduction, evolution could actually make the organism more complicated with a series of "string and bubble gum" patches, as long as those patches overcome the problems with reproduction.

The purpose for this digression into evolution is not merely to point out the complexity of the genome. It is crucial to recognize that our human behavior has gone through the same pragmatic process of evolution as our DNA. It is likely that many aspects of human behavior are not simple, logical, efficient, and parsimonious, or for that matter, even "nice" from a moral standpoint. Perhaps much of our behavior is illogical, inefficient, and complicated when viewed through the faculty of reason. Perhaps we all harbor Rube Goldberg contraptions and processes extending far beyond our DNA and hypothalamic-pituitary-adrenal axes.

● NOTES

1. Inactivation of the X chromosome is not complete. A few loci of the chromosome comprising a Barr body remain active, most notably those loci homologous to the pseudoautosomal region of the Y chromosome. The pseudoautosomal region is a series of genes that occurs on both the X and the Y chromosomes.

2. Neither do events have to be stress related. There is a daily rhythm to cortisol production, with high levels being produced soon after waking in the morning.

3. A similar syndrome, Turner's syndrome, is described in Chapter 8.

4. For rhetorical reasons, I deliberately portray evolution in almost anthropomorphic terms. In reality, evolution has no such qualities as force, direction, intent, and so on. It is a descriptive term for a complex biological process of change.

REFERENCES ●

Isles, A. R., & Wilkinson, L. S. (2000). Imprinted genes, cognition and behaviour. *Trends in Cognitive Science, 4*, 309-318.

Mannens, M., & Alders, M. (1999). Genomic imprinting: Concept and clinical consequences. *Annals of Medicine, 31*, 4-11.

Sharman, A. C., & Brand, M. (1998). Evolution and homology of the nervous system: Cross-phylum rescues of *otd/Otx* genes. *Trends in Genetics, 14*, 211-214.

Skuse, D. H., James, R. S., Bishop, D. V, Coppin, B., Dalton, P., Aamodt-Leeper, G., et al. (1997). Evidence from Turner's syndrome of an imprinted X-linked locus affecting cognitive function. *Nature, 387*, 705-708.

CHAPTER 5

MENDELIAN TRAITS AND BEHAVIOR

INTRODUCTION ●

According to geneticists, a Mendelian trait is the result of a single gene that follows classic Mendelian transmission. Likewise, a Mendelian disorder is one influenced by a single locus. In this chapter, we examine several Mendelian traits and disorders to illustrate the basic principles of how genes and gene products relate to behavior. The lessons will be broad. They begin with the genetic disorder of phenylketonuria, which illustrates basic principles of metabolic pathways, and conclude with sickle-cell anemia, a disorder that illustrates the relationship between genes, ecology, and ethnicity. Before beginning, however, we must provide some terminology.

Terminology

One does not inherit genes per se. Instead, at conception we all inherit several distinct strands of DNA that are "packaged" within a complex system of proteins. Hence, it is the *chromosome* and not the gene that is truly the physical unit of inheritance. A *gene* is usually defined as a section of DNA that contains the blueprint for a polypeptide chain. The term *locus* (plural = *loci*) is a synonym for gene; it carries with it the implication that a gene has a fixed location on a chromosome. A single human chromosome contains several thousand genes.

The term *allele* may be defined as a "spelling variation" at a gene (i.e., a difference in the positioning and ordering of the A, T, C, and G along that stretch of DNA. Unfortunately, many geneticists also use the term *gene* to refer to an allele, sowing untold confusion among beginning genetics students. Let us examine a specific case to explain the technical difference between a gene and an allele.

The ABO gene (or ABO locus) is a stretch of DNA close to the bottom of human chromosome 9 that contains the blueprint for an enzyme that manufactures a molecule that sits within the plasma membrane of red blood cells. Not all of us, however, have the identical sequence of A, T, G, and C nucleotides along this DNA sequence. Spelling variations or alleles exist in the human gene pool at the ABO locus. The three most common alleles are the A allele, the B allele, and the O allele.

Because we all inherit two number nine chromosomes—one from Mom and the other from Dad—we all have two copies of the ABO locus. By chance, the spelling variation at the ABO stretch of DNA on Dad's chromosome may be the same as the spelling variation at this region on Mom's chromosome. An organism like this is called a *homozygote* (*homo* for "same" and *zygote* for "fertilized egg"). The strict definition of a homozygote is *an organism that has the same two alleles at a gene*. For the ABO locus, those who inherit two A alleles are homozygotes, as are those who inherit two B alleles or two O alleles. A *heterozygote* is *an organism with different alleles at a locus*. For example, someone who inherits an A allele from Mom but a B allele from Dad is a heterozygote.

The *genotype* is defined as the genetic constitution of an individual. A genotype may refer to only one locus, or it may refer in an abstract sense to many loci. At the ABO locus, the genotypes are AA, AB, AO, BB, BO, and OO. (There is a tacit understanding that the heterozygotes AO and OA are the same genotype.)

A *phenotype* is defined as the *observed characteristic or trait*. Height, weight, extraversion, intelligence, interest in blood sports, memory, and shoe size are all phenotypes. *There is not always a simple, one-to-one correspondence between a genotype and a phenotype*. For example, there are four phenotypes at the ABO blood group—A, B, AB, and O. These phenotypes come about when a drop of blood is exposed to a chemical that reacts to the molecule produced from the A enzyme and then to another chemical that reacts specifically to the enzyme produced from a B allele. (The O allele produces no polypeptide chain, so there is no reaction.) If someone takes a drop of your blood, adds the A chemical to it, and observes a reaction, then it is clear that you must have at least one A allele and possibly two. If your blood reacts to the A chemical and if another drop of blood reacts to the B chemical, then you must have phenotype AB. In this case, your genotype must be AB. If a reaction occurs to the A chemical but not to the B chemical, then you have phenotype A but could be genotype AA or genotype AO: The test cannot distinguish one of these genotypes from the other. Similarly, if your blood fails to react to the A chemical but reacts to the B chemical, then you are phenotype B, although it is uncertain whether your genotype is BB or BO. When there is no reaction to either the A or the B chemical, then the phenotype is O and the genotype is OO.

Finally, several terms are used to describe allele action in terms of the phenotype that is observed in a heterozygote. When the phenotype of a heterozygote is the same as the phenotype of one of the two homozygotes, then the allele in the homozygote is said to be *dominant* and the allele that is "not observed" is termed *recessive*. Because the heterozygote with the genotype AO has the same phenotype as the homozygote AA, then allele A is dominant and O is recessive. Similarly, allele B is dominant to O, or in different words, allele O is recessive to B. When the phenotype of the heterozygote takes on a value somewhere between the two homozygotes, then allele action is said to be *partially dominant, incompletely dominant, additive,* or *codominant*. Because the genotype AB gives a phenotype different from both genotypes AA and BB, one would say that alleles A and B are codominant with respect to each other. (The term *additive* would apply equally as well, but this phrase is usually used when the phenotypes are numbers and not qualities.) Note carefully that allele action is a *relative* and not an *absolute* concept. For example, the allele action of A depends entirely on the other allele—it is dominant to O but codominant with B.

Relationship Between Genotypes and Phenotypes

Let us now examine three central terms that describe the relationship between a single gene and a phenotype. The first of these is *penetrance* of a genotype. Penetrance is defined as *the probability that a person exhibits a phenotype given that the person has the genotype for that phenotype.* When applied to a disease, penetrance refers to the probability that a person will develop the disorder given that the person has the genotype for the disorder. Penetrance is a conditional probability and therefore is a number that can logically range from 0 to 1.0. *Complete penetrance* refers to disorders and traits where the probability is very close to 1.0. Thus, if a person has the genotype, he or she will almost always develop the disorder. Huntington's disease and cystic fibrosis are two examples of disorders with complete penetrance.[1] *Incomplete penetrance* occurs when the probability is significantly less than 1.0. Marfan's syndrome is a classic example of a disorder with incomplete penetrance. About half of the people with the gene for Marfan's syndrome actually develop the full syndrome.

The second phenomenon relating genotype to phenotype is *pleiotropism* or *pleiotropy*. Pleiotropy refers to the phenomenon that a single gene can influence more than a single phenotype. For example, the Huntington's disease gene can influence several different phenotypes. Two phenotypes—intellect and movement—will be used here to demonstrate pleiotropism. Huntington's disease (HD) usually has an onset in midlife, around age 40, and is initially indicated by increasing clumsiness. As the disorder progresses, the person gradually develops involuntary motor movements in the head and limbs.[2] The loss of voluntary motor control worsens, and the person eventually loses the ability to walk and feed himself or herself. Even before these motoric problems are noticeable enough to diagnose HD, there is often a decline in intellectual functioning that is imperceptible to the person or family members. As HD progresses, the decline accelerates and becomes noticeable. Eventually dementia (the progressive and irreversible loss of cognitive functioning) occurs. Hence, one aspect of pleiotropy for the HD gene is its influence on both cognitive processes and motoric behavior.

The third phenomenon relating genotype to phenotype is *variable expressivity*. Variable expressivity occurs when *a single gene results in a range of phenotypic values for a single trait*. A classic example is the relationship between intelligence and phenylketonuria (PKU). When untreated, PKU reduces the *average* cognitive ability of affected individuals; however, PKU exhibits variable expressivity because it results in a significant range of IQ scores. Some children with untreated PKU are severely mentally retarded, whereas other untreated children are in the low normal range of IQ.

As you read about Mendelian traits and disorders in the following pages, keep in mind these three basic phenomena—penetrance, pleiotropy, and variable expressivity.

● PHENYLKETONURIA (PKU)

Phenylketonuria (PKU) is the poster child for behavioral genetics because an effective environmental intervention can ameliorate the damaging effects of the disorder. Clinically, untreated PKU babies are physically normal at birth but develop symptoms within the first year of life. These symptoms include mousy-smelling urine and sweat; small head size (microcephaly); motoric abnormalities in posture, stance, and gait; light-colored skin, blond hair, and blue eyes (hypopigmentation); eczema; seizures; mental retardation; irritability; and hyperactivity.

The genetic defect underlying PKU is an abnormality in the enzyme phenylalanine hydroxylase (PAH), the gene for which is located on the long

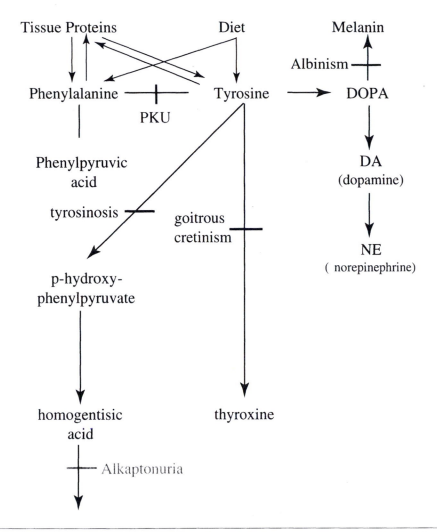

Figure 5.1 The Metabolic Pathway From Phenylalanine to Tyrosine. Metabolic blocks at a number of steps can produce disorders.

(i.e., *q*) arm of chromosome 12. Part of the metabolic pathway that involves this enzyme is depicted in Figure 5.1. Let us spend some time going through this figure so that we can learn about the pathways from gene to behavior.

Phenylalanine is an amino acid and, hence, a constituent of peptides, proteins, and enzymes. The two major sources of phenylalanine are diet and the breakdown of cellular proteins and enzymes into their basic amino acids; hence, arrows are drawn from diet and tissue proteins into phenylalanine in the figure. Three things occur to the phenylalanine in our system: (a) It is used to build peptide chains, depicted in the figure by the arrow from phenylalanine to tissue proteins; (b) it acts as a substrate for the construction of another amino acid, tyrosine; and (c) it is degraded into phenylpyruvic acid. The enzyme PAH is responsible for the second of these—the conversion of phenylalanine into tyrosine. When PAH is defective, then it acts as a metabolic block. The term *metabolic block* is very important in genetics because it describes the mechanism for a large number of Mendelian disorders. Generally, it refers to a defective enzyme that results in the buildup of precursor substances in a metabolic pathway. In PKU, phenylalanine and phenylpyruvic acid build up in the body, and the amount of tyrosine is reduced. By some unknown mechanism, damage occurs to the nervous system, leading to mental retardation and some of the neurological symptoms noted above.

At this stage, let us postpone discussion of the metabolic pathway to focus on the first major lesson from PKU—an effective environmental therapy. Because something associated with excess phenylalanine is responsible for PKU and because diet is a major source of phenylalanine, restricting the dietary intake of phenylalanine sounds as if it might prevent the harmful symptoms of PKU. Indeed, this is the case. Currently, accepted U.S. medical practice is for newborns to be pricked on a heel and a small quantity of blood taken and tested for excessive levels of phenylalanine and phenylpyruvic acid. If this test is positive, a more sensitive test is performed to confirm the diagnosis. If it is confirmed, the parents are informed and the infant is placed on a special formula. The infant cannot have mother's milk, cow milk, or standard formula, and after weaning, the child must avoid all foods with high levels of protein and be maintained on special dietary supplements. In typical medical practice, the diet is individualized. Blood levels of phenylalanine are constantly monitored and the diet is adjusted to keep the levels within safe limits. Many PKU children eventually are able to tolerate certain fruits, vegetables, and grains that are low in phenylalanine. The biggest limiting factor is the child's adherence to the dietary recommendations.

If the diet is adhered to, then the mean IQ of children with PKU does not differ markedly from that of normal children. Many finer issues about the diet are still debated—for example, the levels of blood phenylalanine that are considered safe (Diamond, 1994); the age at which the diet may be discontinued (Azen, Koch, Friedman, Wenz, & Fishler, 1996; Burgard, Schmidt, Rupp, Schneider, & Bremer, 1996; Griffiths, Paterson, & Harvie, 1995); and the importance of supplementing the diet with tyrosine (Diamond, 1996).[3] There is an active research agenda into predicting when and for whom the diet may be safely discontinued. Despite such uncertainties, PKU is a clear indication that a genetic influence on a disorder is no cause for therapeutic nihilism. Even if something is 100% genetic, the environment may still present an effective way of dealing with it.

We can now return to the metabolic pathway. Because the enzyme PAH is damaged, the amount of tyrosine is reduced in PKU. Tyrosine itself is converted to DOPA, which, in skin cells, eventually produces pigment (melanin). The reduction in tyrosine, and hence pigment, apparently is the reason why the skin, hair, and eye colors of individuals with PKU are lighter than those of their normal sibs.

Tyrosine also acts as a precursor to DOPA, which eventually is synthesized into the neurotransmitters dopamine and norepinephrine. It is possible—although not really known—that some behavioral consequences of PKU may be associated with deficits in these neurotransmitters, especially dopamine (Diamond, 1996).

We have now encountered the second major lesson that PKU has for the genetics of behavior—*pleiotropism*, or the phenomenon of a single gene influencing more than one phenotype. The PAH locus, for example, affects anatomy (small head size and undermyelinization of the nerve cells) and physiology (reduced melanin production) as well as several domains of behavior—cognition, personality, and motor functioning. Pleiotropism is far from rare among genetic disorders. Indeed, eminent geneticist Sewall Wright stated that *all* genes are pleiotropic.

A moment's reflection on the metabolic pathway in Figure 5.1 gives a convincing illustration of Wright's concept of universal pleiotropism. The biochemical systems mediated by enzymes and receptors (and thus by the genes that code for these enzymes and receptors) are highly interconnected with feedback loops and other regulatory mechanisms to ensure that the system does not capriciously shut down or turn into a runaway process that damages the organism. If a monkey wrench is thrown into such an interdependent system—just like the defective PAH enzyme is thrown into the metabolic pathway in Figure 5.1—then there will be a large number of consequences both upstream and downstream from the point that the monkey wrench does its damage. With this in mind, it would be very surprising to find that a major defect in a single gene would influence one and only one phenotype.

Our previous consideration of evolutionary principles is also consistent with universal pleiotropism. Evolution is a pragmatic tinkerer with no forethought beyond fixing something so that organisms can reproduce at an acceptable rate. Hence, it is likely to alter something that already exists in an organism's biochemistry rather than design a system *de novo* to solve a reproductive problem. If an organism with pigment needs a specialized neurotransmitter, then evolution is more likely to tinker with the enzymes that act on tyrosine to let it eventually produce dopamine than to start out with a brand new substrate and construct a novel metabolic path for it. Hence, it is not unreasonable for the evolutionist to find that the production of skin pigment has something to do with neurotransmission even though there is no logical connection between the two.

PKU is a recessive disorder—the disorder is expressed only when two deleterious alleles come together in the same individual. People who inherit one normal allele and one deleterious allele are phenotypically normal but are often referred to as *carriers*. A recessive mode of inheritance is common for disorders involving metabolic blocks; hence, as a general rule, the mRNA transcripts and the translated enzymes from only one DNA segment (i.e., allele) are sufficient to maintain metabolism.

PKU exhibits the phenomenon of *allelic heterogeneity*—the fact that many different alleles at a single locus can produce the same syndrome. Again, this is a logical consequence of what we have learned about the biological nature of the gene. There are many ways in which the DNA blueprint for the PAH enzyme can go awry, and if any one of them happens, then the translated product of that DNA will not work correctly. Well over a hundred different alleles at the PAH locus have been identified; if any two of these hundred or so alleles come together, then PKU will result. Because there are so many different alleles, most people with PKU do not have the same nucleotide sequence at both of their PAH genes. Again, there is an active research agenda examining the correlation between the genotype and the phenotypic consequences from this allelic variation (Koch, Fishler, Azen, Guldberg, & Guttler, 1997; Ramus, Forrest, Pitt, Saleeba, & Cotton, 1993; Trefz et al., 1993).

The fourth lesson from PKU comes from examining the IQ distribution in untreated cases. Here, we must go back several generations to examine the relevant data because virtually all PKU cases in modern industrialized countries are now detected and treated at birth. Hence, untreated cases are rare.

When definitive tests for PKU were first developed, it was noted that some siblings of a PKU individual tested positive for PKU but did not suffer from severe mental retardation. Although few had IQ levels above the average in the general population, a significant number fell into the low normal range. Why? The reason for this is a mystery and is likely to remain a mystery for some time. It would be unethical and cruel to withhold the dietary intervention in order to identify those whose eventual IQs fall into the normal range. Still, this fact underscores the variable expressivity that can occur with PKU and IQ.

● CONGENITAL ADRENAL HYPERPLASIA

Congenital adrenal hyperplasia[4] (CAH) is a medical syndrome that illustrates *genetic heterogeneity*. In genetic heterogeneity, the same syndrome (or very similar syndromes) can appear from *defects (or differences) at more than a single locus*. A defect in any one of the loci can produce the syndrome. Albinism is another example of a genetically heterogeneous syndrome.

In CAH, there is a metabolic block somewhere in the synthesis of cortisol from cholesterol in the adrenal gland. Figure 5.2 illustrates the metabolic pathway. There are five different steps in cortisol synthesis, and if any one of these steps is blocked, some form of CAH can result. There is a reduction of cortisol and a buildup of the precursors to cortisol synthesis. Like most metabolic blocks, the genes for CAH are recessive. That is, to exhibit the syndrome, a person must have two defective alleles at a single locus. Because CAH is genetically heterogeneous, a block at any one of the five enzymes listed in Figure 5.2 will result in the syndrome.

CAH also influences sexual differentiation. The adrenal gland plays an important part in the early masculinization of the fetus before the testes are fully developed. Not only is cholesterol the precursor to cortisol, but it is also a precursor to the important androgen[5] testosterone (see Figure 5.2). When the metabolic block occurs after the branch point between androgen production and the synthesis of 17-hydroxyprogesterone, then there is a buildup of the precursors to testosterone and the fetus can be masculinized, even when the fetus has two X chromosomes. When the metabolic block occurs before this branch, there is little precursor to testosterone, so the fetus will not undergo normal sexual development.[6]

Having established that CAH is genetically heterogeneous, let us focus on the most common form of CAH, 21-hydroxylase deficiency. Because this is an autosomal recessive disorder, it will occur in XY and XX individuals with equal frequency. XY individuals have normal external genitalia but often have problems such as high blood pressure (hypertension) and salt loss that require medical intervention.

The situation is quite different in the fetus who is chromosomally XX. Initial sex development proceeds normally, so the tissues develop into the usual internal sex organs—ovaries, fallopian tubes, etc. However, the high dose of male hormones alters the development of the external genitalia toward a male direction. The extent of virilization (i.e., masculinization) of external genitalia is variable. Differences can range from clitoral enlargement through ambiguous genitalia to genitalia that so closely resemble those of a male that they go unrecognized at birth. The typical medical intervention for virilized girls is to surgically correct the genitalia to agree with chromosomal sex. They are then raised as girls.

The feature of virilization that is intriguing for the study of behavior is the effect of the early dose of androgens on brain development. Prenatal androgens have been shown to influence early rough-and-tumble play, aggression, and copulatory behavior in both rodents and primates. Could the same be true of humans?

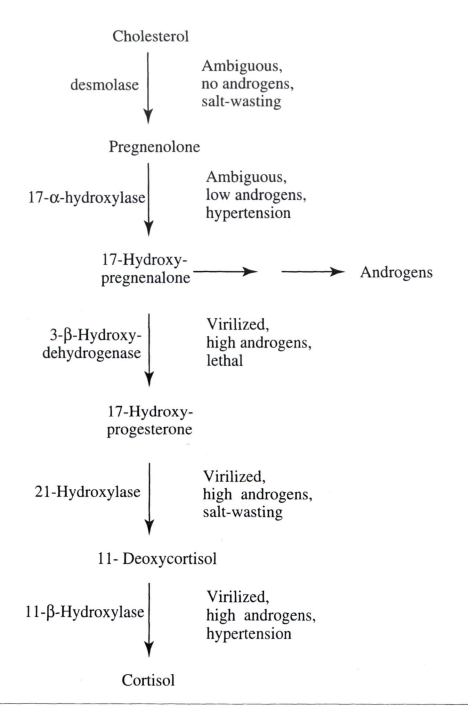

Figure 5.2 The Metabolic Pathway for the Synthesis of Cortisol From Cholesterol. Metabolic blocks at any one of these steps can produce a form of congenital adrenal hyperplasia (CAH). Shown to the right of the metabolic step are the aberrations in the genitalia, androgen level, and major medical complications of the syndrome.

Sheri Berenbaum and her colleagues have begun systematic research into children with CAH. In one study (Berenbaum & Hines, 1992), they tested CAH boys and girls and their unaffected siblings in a toy preference situation. The experimental paradigm, used extensively in past research on child development, involves placing a child into a room with toys that are stereotypically "boyish" (e.g., a fire engine), stereotypically "girlish" (e.g., dolls), or neutral (e.g., a book). The child can freely play with any toy that he or she chooses, and an assistant records the toys that are played with and the amount of time played with each toy. There is considerable individual variability in children in which toys they play with, but on average boys spend more time with the trucks while girls spend more time on the dolls. The control boys and girls in this study showed exactly this play pattern.

The CAH boys were no different from the control boys. This suggests that the extra prenatal androgen does not "supermasculinize" a boy, at least with respect to toy preferences. The CAH girls, on the other hand, exhibited a preference that more closely resembled that of the control boys more than of the control girls. Berenbaum and Hines were unable to find that parental treatment or degree of childhood illness could account for this and suggested that the masculinization of phenotypic toy preferences in these girls may have been due to the prenatal effects of androgens.

Other research suggests that CAH girls show more aggression (Berenbaum & Resnick, 1997) or at least more masculinized forms of aggression (Helleday, Edman, Ritzen, & Siwers, 1993) than their normal sisters and cousins. They often show more masculine-related social behavior and activity levels (Dittmann, Kappes, Kappes, Borger, Meyer-Bahlburg et al., 1990a; Dittmann, Kappes, Kappes, Borger, Stegner, et al., 1990b). However, CAH girls are far from being boys in girls' bodies. Although their psychosexual orientation differs slightly from that of normal girls and women, both Dittmann, Kappes, and Kappes (1992) and Zucker, Bradley, Oliver, and Blake (1996) report that as a group, they are heterosexually oriented and well adjusted.

CAH illustrates how a Mendelian trait can be used as a quasi-experiment to examine hormonal influences on behavior. Like all work on substantive human behaviors, the CAH story is not a clean and neat laboratory experiment, and there are important confounding factors. Virilized girls undergo surgery, and many also have hormone replacement therapy to counter the effects of low cortisol levels. The data on virilized CAH girls nevertheless agree with the experimental manipulation of prenatal hormones in birds, rodents, and primates. There appears to be a sensitive period during which hormones exert an influence on later sex-typed behaviors. How prenatal hormones do this work is a topic of intense research.

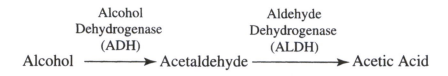

Figure 5.3   The Major Pathway for the Metabolism of Alcohol in the Liver

● ALDEHYDE DEHYDROGENASE, ALCOHOL USE, AND ALCOHOL ABUSE

After alcohol is ingested, it enters the stomach and small intestine, where it is absorbed into the bloodstream and carried throughout the body. The major organ that metabolizes alcohol is the liver. There, alcohol is converted into acetaldehyde by the enzyme alcohol dehydrogenase (ADH), and acetaldehyde is then converted into acetic acid by the enzyme aldehyde dehydrogenase (ALDH; see Figure 5.3). Several genes have blueprints for ALDH, and each of these genes makes different forms of this enzyme in different tissues of the body. One gene, ALDH-2, codes for the major form of this enzyme located in liver mitochondria, where most ingested alcohol is metabolized.

As many as 50% of people of Asian descent possess an allele at the ALDH-2 locus[7] that results in an ALDH-2 enzyme molecule that has either greatly reduced activity or no activity at all (Goedde, Agarwal, & Harada, 1983; Yoshida, 1992). Consequently, when individuals with this allele drink alcohol, the pathway from acetaldehyde to acetic acid is blocked (or greatly diminished in activity), and acetaldehyde accumulates in the blood and tissue. The result is often a "flushing" response in which the person may turn red and experience uncomfortable side effects such as dizziness and nausea. Disulfiram (Antabuse®) produces a similar reaction because it inhibits the same enzyme.

Both the ALDH-2 allele and the flushing response are associated with alcohol metabolism and elimination (Steinmetz, Xie, Weiner, & Hurley, 1997; Yin, 1994), drinking habits (Higuchi, Matsushita, Muramatsu, Murayama, & Hayashida, 1996; Muramatsu et al., 1995; Nakawatase, Yamamoto, & Sasao, 1993; Takeshita, Maruyama, & Morimoto, 1998; Tu & Israel, 1995), alcoholism (Murayama, Matsushita, Muramatsu, & Higuchi, 1998; Thomasson et al., 1991; Yoshida, 1992), and alcoholic liver diseases (Tanaka et al., 1997; Yoshida, 1992). Individuals with this allele are more often abstainers, and those who do drink imbibe lower quantities of alcohol and engage in less binge drinking than those without the allele (Tu & Israel, 1995). Thus, the allele appears to lower the risk for the development of alcohol-related problems.

Because the allele is present among different Asian populations but is either missing or extremely rare among Caucasoids and Africans, it has been postulated as one of the factors that contribute to lower rates of drinking and, hence, lowered rates of alcohol abuse and dependence among Asians. Tu and Israel (1995) go so far as to claim that this gene is the major predictor of the difference in drinking habits between Asians and other ethnic groups in North America.

The ALDH-2 polymorphism is a classic example of how a gene can influence behavior. The mechanism of its action can be traced all the way from the DNA to the substantive behavior. First, at the DNA level, a single nucleotide substitution at the ALDH-2 locus results in an altered polypeptide chain.[8] Four of these chains are joined together to get this form of the ALDH enzyme. If a person has one normal allele and one deficient allele, then the only active ALDH enzyme molecules in the person's liver will be formed when, by dumb luck, four of the peptide chains from the good allele get joined together. This is likely the reason why ALDH-2 deficiency shows some degree of dominance.

When a person drinks alcohol, the enzyme ADH converts the alcohol into acetaldehyde. When that person has ALDH-2 deficiency, then the acetaldehyde cannot be readily converted into acetic acid and builds up in the system. The amount of buildup depends, of course, on the amount of alcohol ingested and the time course of ingestion. When the buildup of acetaldehyde occurs, the person may show the symptoms of a flushing response. The response and its severity vary from one person to another, but in some individuals it is associated with unpleasant effects. Many of these individuals may develop mild conditioned food aversions to alcohol, and some reduce the amount of drinking to avoid the unpleasant symptoms. Because these individuals abstain or are temperate drinkers, the risk for developing alcohol abuse and alcohol dependence is reduced.

The ALDH-2 story contains other very important lessons. First, it has been demonstrated repeatedly that people with the deficiency can still become alcoholic. For example, Thomasson et al. (1991) reported that 12% of Chinese alcoholics in Taipei were heterozygotes for this gene. Thus, the gene influences risk, but in the heterozygote, it does not guarantee a life free of alcohol problems. Many geneticists refer to this type of locus as a *susceptibility* gene—depending upon background, genotype, and environmental factors, it increases or decreases the *probability* of alcohol problems but does not rigidly determine alcohol use.

Second, the enzyme defect does its work in the liver, not in the central nervous system. There is a natural tendency to suspect that genetic effects on behavior operate on development of the nervous system and on the enzymes and proteins responsible for communication among neurons. The ALDH-2 story is a sober reminder that genes operating elsewhere in the body can influence behavior. Could some forms of schizophrenia turn out to be liver disorders?

● FRAGILE X SYNDROME

In contrast to most clinical presentations, let us first consider the genetics of the Fragile X syndrome[9] and then discuss its clinical manifestations. The gene responsible for the syndrome is called the FMR-1 locus and is located on the X chromosome. The complete role of the FMR-1 protein is still not clear, but it is well established that the protein binds with RNA and probably plays a role in the functioning of ribosomes. The genetic problem causing Fragile X is *an abnormal number of trinucleotide repeats* inside the promoter region of the FMR-1 gene (Hagerman & Hagerman, 2001). Within the area of the DNA that is initially transcribed from this gene, all humans have a series of CGG repeats. Normally, the number of CGG repeats ranges between 6 and 50 to 54. However, when the number of CGG repeats reaches a critical value (usually taken as 200), the DNA becomes methylated, transcription of the gene is inhibited, levels of the FMR-1 protein decline, and some form of Fragile X results. The degree of impairment in Fragile X is moderately correlated with the number of CGG repeats (the larger the number, the greater the impairment) and the degree of methylation of the DNA. The best predictor of impairment, however, is the amount of FMR-1 protein that is produced—the lower the amount of protein, the higher the impairment (Hagerman & Hagerman, 2001).[10]

To recapitulate, 6 to 50 or so CGG repeats is normal, but 200 or more repeats is associated with pathology. What about repeats in the 50 to 200 range? Within this range, a curious phenomenon occurs. Individuals who carry 50 to 200 repeats are phenotypically within normal limits, but when they transmit the gene, it stands a higher probability of mutating to a greater length (i.e., it is *hypermutable*). Hence, individuals with 50 to 200 CGG repeats stand a high risk of transmitting an FMR-1 allele with more than 200 repeats to their offspring. This creates a phenomenon known as *anticipation*—an increase in the clinical severity of a syndrome in more recent generations of the pedigree (Sherman et al., 1985; Sherman, Morton, Jacobs, & Turner, 1984). As the gene travels "down" in a pedigree, it has a tendency to elongate the repeat even further, thus creating more severe cases of Fragile X.

Because males have only one X chromosome, inheritance of a single abnormal allele creates impairment. The vast majority of females who carry the abnormal allele are heterozygotes. For them, the allele action may be described as having incomplete penetrance or incomplete dominance because about half of them will show measurable impairment, albeit quite minor impairment in a significant number of cases (Bennetto, Pennington, Porter, Taylor, & Hagerman, 2001). The rare homozygous female can exhibit the same syndrome as a male.

The number of CGG repeats and the concomitant loss of FMR-1 protein influence several different phenotypes, illustrating once again the phenomenon of pleiotropy (de Vries, Halley, Oostra, & Niermeijer, 1998; Hagerman & Hagerman, 2001; Hoogeveen & Oostra, 1997). The physical features of Fragile X male children blend well into the normal distribution, but as they mature, these children often develop elongated faces, large and protuberant ears, prominent foreheads and jaws, and enlarged testicles (macroorchidism). Often, the development of connective tissue is influenced, giving Fragile X individuals double-jointed fingers and toes. Cognition and cognitive abilities also are affected. A significant number of Fragile X cases exhibit enough difficulties with concentration and attention and a sufficient number of hyperactivity problems to qualify for a diagnosis of attention deficit-hyperactivity disorder, or ADHD. As a group, Fragile X individuals have low scores on IQ tests; however, the range of IQ scores is quite broad, with many cases scoring in the low normal range while others suffer from significant mental retardation (Bailey, Hatton, & Skinner, 1998). Indeed, Fragile X syndrome is the most frequent Mendelian disorder associated with mental retardation. Severe cases may also shows signs and symptoms similar to those of autism—poor eye contact, failure to attend to social cues, and a general lack of responsiveness to human interaction—although the extent to which these behaviors represent classic autism is a matter of debate. Irregularities in language development, speech patterns, cognitive styles, and mood also have been noted.

Perhaps the most striking feature of Fragile X syndrome is its variable expressivity. Individuals with the full mutation (i.e., more than 200 CGG repeats) can have social behavior that ranges anywhere between social hyper-exuberance and abnormal overdetachment. Although mean IQ is somewhere between 60 and 70, the standard deviation of IQ scores is not remarkably different from that in the normal population. Hence, some Fragile X individuals are within the low normal limits and can profit from standard public education, whereas others require special interventions for their cognitive impairment and learning problems. Some cases may exhibit socially engaging behavior; others may be characterized by inappropriate aggression.

Figure 5.4 presents a hypothetical pedigree that illustrates both the genetics and the variable expressivity of the Fragile X phenotype. The progenitor is the X chromosome carried by the male parent at the top of the pedigree. This chromosome has 29 CGG repeats, so he is normal. It is passed

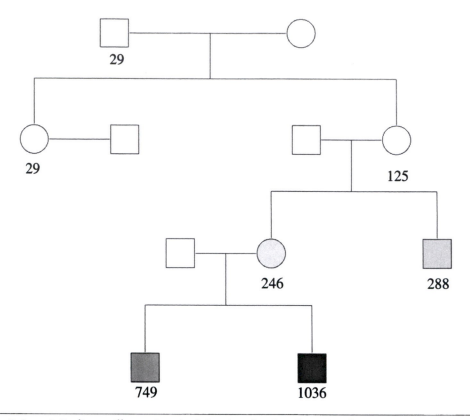

Figure 5.4 A Pedigree Illustrating Anticipation for Fragile X Syndrome.

NOTE: A number below an individual is the number of trinucleotide repeats, and the shading shows the degree to which the phenotype is affected.

along intact to the first daughter, but in the genesis of the sperm that results in the second daughter, a mutation occurs that expands the CGG sequence from 29 to 125 repeats. The number of repeats in this daughter is now within the 50 to 200 range, which means that the FMR-1 locus on this chromosome is now "hypermutable," or at a very high risk of mutating to longer CGG repeats in future generations.

Because the X chromosome for this woman has 125 CGG repeats (and also because her other chromosome has a normal number of repeats), she is unaffected. However, when she generates her eggs, they have an increased probability of mutating to a longer series of repeats. (Actually, hypermutability is much more common in sperm than in eggs, so this woman is the exception rather than the rule.) A mutation occurs in one of her eggs, and a sequence of 246 CGG repeats is passed to her firstborn, a daughter. This passes the critical level of 200 repeats, so this daughter may show mild signs of the syndrome but would probably be well within the normal range of behavior because she is "buffered" or protected by the good FMR-1 locus on her other X chromosome. For example, she may have an IQ that is lower than that predicted by her family history, and she may show minor difficulties with attention, but these symptoms may not be noticeable enough to have her referred to a school psychologist.

The mutation also occurs in the X chromosome transmitted to her brother, who receives 288 CGG repeats. The difference between these 288 CGG repeats and the 246 repeats in his sister is relatively minor, but because the male lacks an extra X chromosome, he is not protected from the deleterious effects. He is likely to show features of the Fragile X phenotype, although they will be on the less severe side. For example, he may have learning difficulties at school, be diagnosed as mildly mentally retarded, and exhibit enough attention problems and hyperactivity to qualify for a possible or probable diagnosis of ADHD.

His sister marries and has two children, both boys. The hypermutability of the locus is evident in the number of CGG repeats inherited by both of her sons. The first inherits a FMR-1 locus with 749 repeats. He is likely to show a full-blown syndrome with some irregularity in facial features, moderate mental retardation, marked attention difficulties, and other behavioral problems. He may be placed in a special education program for the developmentally disabled and also be given medication for ADHD. By bad luck, his brother also inherits the hypermutable X chromosome, but the repeats in his case number 1,036. He shows severe Fragile X. In addition to mental retardation, he could have the physical irregularities of facial appearance that make him appear "unusual" in a very amorphous and inarticulable sense to casual observers. He could have serious learning disabilities and problems with attention and concentration. In addition, his social behavior may be awkward enough that some psychologists might consider him as having autistic features.

Fragile X has many lessons for behavior. It has a great similarity to a classic "metabolic block" that acts as a dam misplaced in the flow of a mountain stream, so that water backs up and floods surrounding areas. In the classic metabolic blocks such as PKU and CAH, the problem is in the genetic blueprint for a protein or enzyme. In Fragile X, however, the blueprint for the FMR-1 protein is perfectly fine. The defect is in the *regulation of the protein's production*. In most Fragile X cases, the abnormal number of CGG repeats effectively "turns the FMR-1 gene off," and the lack of gene product plays havoc within the cell. In other cases, transcription may take place, but other problems, perhaps with translation, may occur (Chiang et al., 2001). Hence, we must always be alert to the possibility that various proteins, enzymes, receptors, transporters, etc. might be perfectly normal in a person with a disorder such as schizophrenia; instead, it may be the timing of production and the amount of such proteins, enzymes, etc., that could lead to psychopathology.

A second lesson from Fragile X is the mechanism of an abnormal number of trinucleotide repeats. This is not unique to Fragile X. Indeed, an abnormal number of trinucleotide repeats at various loci is responsible for several Mendelian disorders, most notably Huntington's disease and several forms of muscular dystrophy. The fact has led to research that is now searching for trinucleotide repeats in schizophrenia, bipolar disorder, and other forms of psychopathology. It is much too early to assess the merit of these approaches, but the efforts may uncover a major model for some complex disorders associated with behavior.

Finally, the variable expressivity of Fragile X convincingly demonstrates the futility of a "one size fits all" approach to the clinical management of some genetic disorders. Although there is no cure for Fragile X, various combinations of pharmacotherapy (i.e., drugs), educational regimens, and behavioral and cognitive therapy can improve the day-to-day functioning of individuals with the syndrome (Hagerman, 1997). The precise combination of these therapeutic techniques depends on the idiosyncratic expression of signs and symptoms in the individual case. As is the case with many behavioral problems, the optimal combination of therapies for Fragile X is determined more by rational guesswork and clinical experience than by empirical research results.

● SICKLE-CELL ANEMIA

Sickle-cell disease is a recessive disorder resulting from alleles that influence the β chain of the hemoglobin molecule. Several different alleles at the β hemoglobin locus can cause sickle-cell disease, but the most common allele in U.S. populations causes *sickle-cell anemia*. The sickle-cell anemia allele is a point mutation (i.e., the substitution of just one nucleotide for another) that results in a different amino acid being substituted into the β polypeptide.[11]

The effect of this amino acid substitution is profound. After the hemoglobin molecule transfers oxygen to the target organ, the hemoglobin molecules often line up in a side-to-side fashion to create a long, thin string. The abnormal hemoglobin from the sickle-cell allele causes these strings to form into rigid bundles that change the shape of the red blood cell from a platelet into an elongated form (Mirchev & Ferrone, 1997). Viewed under the microscope, an elongated red blood cell often resembles the blade of a sickle, giving the disorder its name.

The altered shape of the red blood cells has two major consequences. First, it makes it easier for them to be destroyed, contributing to anemia (low red blood cell count). Second, the sickle shape makes it much easier for the red blood cells to clog up the small capillaries. This impedes circulation and ultimately deprives target organs of blood and oxygen. If matters do not return to normal, the person can enter a "sickling crisis" in which she or he experiences profound weakness, pain, and cramps. The medical complications from the anemia and the slow necrosis (cell death) of the organs lead to early death. Although a minority of sufferers have a benign course (Thomas, Higgs, & Serjeant, 1997), most people with sickle-cell anemia do not survive until adulthood (variable expressivity again). As is the case for many lethal genetic disorders, however, medical advances are increasing both the length and quality of life of people with sickle-cell anemia (Reed & Vichinsky, 1998).

Apart from the medical symptoms, people with sickle-cell anemia have normal behavior. They have the same prevalence of psychiatric disorders as members of the general community (Hilton, Osborn, Knight, Singhal, & Serjeant, 1997). Intellect and cognitive functioning are normal, apart from the disruptive and momentary influence of a sickling crisis and the long-term effects of medical complications such as infarcts (Armstrong et al., 1996). The major lesson from sickle-cell anemia resides in its population genetics and not in any behavioral sequelae of the syndrome.

In the past, it was known that the allele for sickle-cell anemia was found in high frequency in areas of Africa, the Saudi Arabian peninsula, and the Indian subcontinent. Originally, it was speculated that the mutation for sickle-cell anemia originated several thousand years ago among the Bantu-speaking peoples of Africa and diffused to other areas, but current evidence supports the idea that independent mutations occurred in the different geographical locales (Mears et al., 1981; Solomon & Bodmer, 1979; Wainscoat et al., 1983). At least three independent mutations occurred in Africa and one in India.

After the original mutations, the allele for sickle-cell anemia underwent a unique evolutionary history that corresponded to the presence or absence of a particular form of malaria[12] in the differing ecologies. It turns out that heterozygote carriers (those with one normal and one sickle-cell allele) were resistant to malaria, especially its lethal consequences such as cerebral malaria. In the heterozygote, the red blood cells that carried the malarial parasite would tend to sickle themselves and be readily destroyed. This prevented the infection from running amok in a heterozygote and increased her survival rate.

Hence, the frequency of the allele among the various populations evolved as a function of a malarial ecology. In regions free of malaria, there was no advantage to the heterozygote, so the sickle-cell allele diminished in frequency. Indeed, the allele is quite rare in many populations of eastern Africa, especially around Cape Horn, and southern Africa. In the Saudi peninsula, its prevalence is high in oasis populations where mosquitoes are encountered but quite rare among neighboring desert nomads (el-Hazmi, Warsy, al-Swailem, al-Swailem, & Bahakim, 1996). In malarial regions, the allele encountered two opposing selective pressures—the lethality of the allele in the recessive homozygotes worked to remove it from the population, but the advantage conferred by the allele to the heterozygote worked to increase its frequency. These two opposing forces eventually arrived at an equilibrium in which the frequency of the sickle-cell allele remained much higher than in nonmalarial areas. To give some figures, the frequency of the sickle-cell allele is 1% or less in some South African populations but exceeds 25% in some areas of western Africa where malaria could at times reach epidemic proportions.

The major lesson of sickle-cell disorder is the complex relationship between genes, race-ethnicity, and ecology. Somewhere between 5% and 9% of African Americans carry the sickle-cell allele, and in the United States it is often perceived of as a "black" disorder (Lorey, Arnopp, & Cunningham, 1996). There is an element of truth to this, but the mere association of a gene with what we socially define as race and ethnicity is a gross understatement compared to the rich biology behind sickle-cell anemia. The statistical association that we observe is the visible part of an iceberg fashioned by millennia of the actions and effects of environmental adaptation, ecology, evolutionary fitness, and a big dash of just dumb luck.

The first part of dumb luck is the multiple origins of the mutation. These origins could just as well have occurred in other malarial regions such as the Mediterranean or Southeast Asia,[13] but they just happened to occur in Africa and in India. The second instance of chance is that the mutation was beneficial to some of—but certainly not all—the people who carried it. The reason that it increased in frequency had everything to do with the biology and the ecology of malaria and absolutely nothing to do with the external morphology that we use as cues to ethnicity. This is why it spread outside of Africa into the Middle East and Asia.

The last piece of dumb luck is the location of the slave trade into the New World. The majority of embarkation ports were on the West and West-Central coast of Africa, and a majority of those captured as slaves came from the neighboring indigenous populations—precisely those areas where malaria occurred in high frequency and the sickle-cell allele was most prevalent. Had the slave trade originated from ports in South Africa, we would never consider sickle-cell anemia as an "African American" disease. Had the slave trade originated in some parts of India instead of western Africa, we might consider it an "Indian American" disease.

It is time to reflect once again on the relationship between correlation and causality: Correlations do not necessarily imply causality. The correlation—or the statistical association, if you prefer that term—between sickle-cell anemia and African American heritage does not imply any direct causality between a section of DNA coding for hemoglobin and any index of African Americans. The causes are dumb luck, evolution, and historical accident.

CONCLUSION ●

This chapter has presented several mechanisms for disorders. Classic metabolic blocks cause phenylketonuria and congenital adrenal hyperplasia. In PKU, the deleterious alleles occur at a single locus (that for the enzyme phenylalanine hydroxylase), while for CAH, the faulty alleles could occur at five different loci. Errors in genetic regulation can also influence phenotypic irregularity—the abnormal methylation of the FMR-1 locus is responsible for the Fragile X syndrome.

Genes, however, can act as protective factors that diminish susceptibility toward disorders. The ALDH-2 polymorphism is a classic example because the presence of the less frequent allele diminishes the probability of alcohol abuse and alcohol dependence. This trait also illustrates one biochemical mechanism for genetic dominance (partial dominance, to be exact). The heterozygote will produce two types of mRNA that result in two types of translated polypeptide chains—one functional and the other nonfunctional. Because four of these polypeptide chains must join together to give the ALDH-2 enzyme, only 1 in 16 ALDH-2 molecules in the heterozygote will be functional.

Sickle-cell anemia illustrates how an allele can be beneficial in one circumstance (i.e., in the heterozygote) but harmful in another (the recessive homozygote). Hence, the influence of an allele or a gene must always be judged against the genetic background in which it occurs. Sickle-cell also demonstrates how human genetic diversity can be caused by ecological factors, giving secondary correlations with what we socially define as race and ethnicity.

For all these traits, one cannot help but marvel at the degree of penetrance, pleiotropism, and variable expressivity when the phenotypes are "molar" behaviors such as cognitive ability, attentional processes, personality, and psychopathology. It is very likely that the same principles may apply to the genes that underlie more common phenotypes. Perhaps a single gene may have a large effect on schizophrenia when it occurs along with a certain genetic background but only a small influence when present in another background. Any particular locus for, say, intelligence is bound to have considerable variable expressivity. And the effects of other loci may be to buffer an individual against developing agoraphobia.

● NOTES

1. You may have noted the cautionary phrases "close to 1.0" and "almost always" develop the disorder. In the past, cystic fibrosis (CF) was regarded as having a penetrance of 1.0, but with the advent of genotyping at the locus, several cases were discovered that had the genotype for CF but did not show the complete syndrome. The same may be true of other disorders previously considered to be fully penetrant.

2. Some people with HD develop a rigid, akinetic (i.e., absence of movement) form.

3. In some cases, dietary restrictions may be continued throughout life. Another special case involves women with PKU who desire to have children; to avoid damage to the fetus, they are urged to go on a phenylalanine restricted diet before conception.

4. Hyperplasia refers to an abnormal number of cells in a tissue or organ. Hence, CAH is the name for a congenital syndrome involving an abnormal number of cells in the adrenal glands located on the top of the kidneys.

5. An *androgen* is a member of a class of hormones that masculinizes a fetus.

6. In these cases, CAH can also influence estrogen levels and sexual development in XX individuals.

7. The allele causing the deficiency is called the ALDH-2*2 allele; ALDH-2*1 is the normal allele.

8. The normal mRNA codon for the 487th amino acid in the polypeptide chain is GAA, which codes for glutamic acid; in the ALDH-2 deficiency, an A replaces the G, giving the codon AAA, which places a lysine into the polypeptide sequence.

9. Fragile X syndrome is so named because it was first described by cytogeneticists who noted that the X chromosome appeared to almost or completely break apart at a particular location in certain karyotype preparations. The localization of the disorder to a specific locus on the X chromosome occurred after the syndrome was described.

10. For a while, geneticists have known that impairment in Fragile X is not perfectly predicted by transcriptional silencing because a number of cases with impairment show little methylation and almost normal levels of mRNA for FMR-1 (Tassone, Hagerman, Chamberlain, & Hagerman, 2000). It was reported recently that the CGG repeats may also impair the ability of the mRNA to attach to and enter the ribosome to prepare for translation (Chiang, Carpenter, & Hagerman, 2001).

11. The point mutation for sickle-cell anemia occurs in the sixth codon of the chain. The normal DNA codon is CTC, which places the amino acid glutamate in the peptide chain. The allele for sickle-cell anemia substitutes adenine for thymine, giving the DNA codon CAC that results in the amino acid valine being placed into the chain instead of glutamate.

12. *Plasmodium falciparum.*

13. Instead, other genetic mutations occurred in these regions and increased in frequency because they protected against the harmful effects of malaria. These mutations are the thalassemia allele in the Mediterranean area and the hemoglobin E allele in Southeast Asia.

REFERENCES ●

Armstrong, F. D., Thompson, R. J., Jr., Wang, W., Zimmerman, R., Pegelow, C. H., Miller, S., Moser, F., Bello, J., Hurtig, A., & Vass, K., for the Neuropsychology Committee of the Cooperative Study of Sickle Cell Disease. (1996). Cognitive functioning and brain magnetic resonance imaging in children with sickle cell disease. *Pediatrics, 97,* 864-870.

Azen, C., Koch, R., Friedman, E., Wenz, E., & Fishler, K. (1996). Summary of findings from the United States Collaborative Study of children treated for phenylketonuria. *European Journal of Pediatrics, 155*(Suppl. 1), S29-S32.

Bailey, D. B., Jr., Hatton, D. D., & Skinner, M. (1998). Early developmental trajectories of males with fragile X syndrome. *American Journal on Mental Retardation, 103,* 29-39.

Bennetto, L., Pennington, B. F., Porter, D., Taylor, A. K., & Hagerman, R. J. (2001). Profile of cognitive functioning in women with the fragile X mutation. *Neuropsychology, 15,* 290-299.

Berenbaum, S. A., & Hines, M. (1992). Early androgens are related to childhood sex-typed toy preferences. *Psychological Science, 3,* 203-206.

Berenbaum, S. A., & Resnick, S. M. (1997). Early androgen effects on aggression in children and adults with congenital adrenal hyperplasia. *Psychoneuroendocrinology, 22,* 505-515.

Burgard, P., Schmidt, E., Rupp, A., Schneider, W., & Bremer, H. J. (1996). Intellectual development of the patients of the German Collaborative Study of children treated for phenylketonuria. *European Journal of Pediatrics, 155*(Suppl. 1), S33-S38.

Chiang, P. W., Carpenter, L. E., & Hagerman, P. J. (2001). The 5´-untranslated region of the FMR1 message facilitates translation by internal ribosome entry. *Journal of Biological Chemistry, 276,* 37916-37921.

de Vries, B. B., Halley, D. J., Oostra, B. A., & Niermeijer, M. F. (1998). The fragile X syndrome. *Journal of Medical Genetics, 35,* 579-589.

Diamond, A. (1994). Phenylalanine levels of 6-10 mg/dl may not be as benign as once thought. *Acta Paediatrica, 83* (Suppl. 407), 89-91.

Diamond, A. (1996). Evidence for the importance of dopamine for prefrontal cortex functions early in life. *Philosophical Transactions of the Royal Society of London. Series B: Biological Sciences, 351,* 1483-1493.

Dittmann, R. W., Kappes, M. E., & Kappes, M. H. (1992). Sexual behavior in adolescent and adult females with congenital adrenal hyperplasia. *Psychoneuroendocrinology, 17,* 153-170.

Dittmann, R. W., Kappes, M. H., Kappes, M. E., Borger, D., Meyer-Bahlburg, H. F., Stegner, H., Willig, R. H., & Wallis, H. (1990a). Congenital adrenal hyperplasia. II: Gender-related behavior and attitudes in female salt-wasting and simple-virilizing patients. *Psychoneuroendocrinology, 15,* 421-434.

Dittmann, R. W., Kappes, M. H., Kappes, M. E., Borger, D., Stegner, H., Willig, R. H., & Wallis, H. (1990b). Congenital adrenal hyperplasia. I: Gender-related behavior and attitudes in female patients and sisters. *Psychoneuroendocrinology, 15,* 401-420. (Published erratum appears in *Psychoneuroendocrinology, 16,* 369-371)

el-Hazmi, M. A., Warsy, A. S., al-Swailem, A. R., al-Swailem, A. M., & Bahakim, H. M. (1996). Sickle cell gene in the population of Saudi Arabia. *Hemoglobin, 20,* 187-198.

Goedde, H. W., Agarwal, D. P., & Harada, S. (1983). Pharmacogenetics of alcohol sensitivity. *Pharmacology, Biochemistry and Behavior, 18,* 161-166.

Griffiths, P., Paterson, L., & Harvie, A. (1995). Neuropsychological effect of subsequent exposure to phenylalanine in adolescents and young adults with early-treated phenylketonuria. *Journal of Intellectual Disability Research, 39*, 365-372.

Hagerman, R. (1997). Fragile X: Treatment of hyperactivity. *Pediatrics, 99*, 753.

Hagerman, R. J., & Hagerman, P. J. (2001). Fragile X syndrome: A model of gene-brain-behavior relationships. *Molecular Genetics and Metabolism, 74*, 89-97.

Helleday, J., Edman, G., Ritzen, E. M., & Siwers, B. (1993). Personality characteristics and platelet MAO activity in women with congenital adrenal hyperplasia (CAH). *Psychoneuroendocrinology, 18*, 343-354.

Higuchi, S., Matsushita, S., Muramatsu, T., Murayama, M., & Hayashida, M. (1996). Alcohol and aldehyde dehydrogenase genotypes and drinking behavior in Japanese. *Alcoholism: Clinical and Experimental Research, 20*, 493-497.

Hilton, C., Osborn, M., Knight, S., Singhal, A., & Serjeant, G. (1997). Psychiatric complications of homozygous sickle cell disease among young adults in the Jamaican Cohort Study. *British Journal of Psychiatry, 170*, 69-76.

Hoogeveen, A. T., & Oostra, B. A. (1997). The fragile X syndrome. *Journal of Inherited Metabolic Disease, 20*, 139-151.

Koch, R., Fishler, K., Azen, C., Guldberg, P., & Guttler, F. (1997). The relationship of genotype to phenotype in phenylalanine hydroxylase deficiency. *Biochemical and Molecular Medicine, 60*, 92-101.

Lorey, F. W., Arnopp, J., & Cunningham, G. C. (1996). Distribution of hemoglobinopathy variants by ethnicity in a multiethnic state. *Genetic Epidemiology, 13*, 501-512.

Mears, J. G., Lachman, H. M., Cabannes, R., Amegnizin, K. P., Labie, D., & Nagel, R. L. (1981). Sickle gene: Its origin and diffusion from West Africa. *Journal of Clinical Investigation, 68*, 606-610.

Mirchev, R., & Ferrone, F. A. (1997). The structural link between polymerization and sickle cell disease. *Journal of Molecular Biology, 265*, 475-479.

Muramatsu, T., Wang, Z. C., Fang, Y. R., Hu, K. B., Yan, H., Yamada, K., Higuchi, S., Harada, S., & Kono, H. (1995). Alcohol and aldehyde dehydrogenase genotypes and drinking behavior of Chinese living in Shanghai. *Human Genetics, 96*, 151-154.

Murayama, M., Matsushita, S., Muramatsu, T., & Higuchi, S. (1998). Clinical characteristics and disease course of alcoholics with inactive aldehyde dehydrogenase-2. *Alcoholism: Clinical and Experimental Research, 22*, 524-527.

Nakawatase, T. V., Yamamoto, J., & Sasao, T. (1993). The association between fast-flushing response and alcohol use among Japanese Americans. *Journal of Studies on Alcohol, 54*, 48-53.

Ramus, S. J., Forrest, S. M., Pitt, D. B., Saleeba, J. A., & Cotton, R. G. (1993). Comparison of genotype and intellectual phenotype in untreated PKU patients. *Journal of Medical Genetics, 30*, 401-405.

Reed, W., & Vichinsky, E. P. (1998). New considerations in the treatment of sickle cell disease. *Annual Review of Medicine, 49*, 461-474.

Sherman, S. L., Jacobs, P. A., Morton, N. E., Froster-Iskenius, U., Howard-Peebles, P. N., Nielsen, K. B., Partington, M. W., Sutherland, G. R., Turner, G., & Watson, M. (1985). Further segregation analysis of the fragile X syndrome with special reference to transmitting males. *Human Genetics, 69*, 289-299.

Sherman, S. L., Morton, N. E., Jacobs, P. A., & Turner, G. (1984). The marker (X) syndrome: A cytogenetic and genetic analysis. *Annals of Human Genetics, 48*, 21-37.

Solomon, E., & Bodmer, W. F. (1979). Evolution of sickle variant gene. *Lancet, 1*, 923.

Steinmetz, C. G., Xie, P., Weiner, H., & Hurley, T. D. (1997). Structure of mitochondrial aldehyde dehydrogenase: The genetic component of ethanol aversion. *Structure, 5*, 701-711.

Takeshita, T., Maruyama, S., & Morimoto, K. (1998). Relevance of both daily hassles and the ALDH2 genotype to problem drinking among Japanese male workers. *Alcoholism: Clinical and Experimental Research, 22*, 115-120.

Tanaka, F., Shiratori, Y., Yokosuka, O., Imazeki, F., Tsukada, Y., & Omata, M. (1997). Polymorphism of alcohol-metabolizing genes affects drinking behavior and alcoholic liver disease in Japanese men. *Alcoholism: Clinical and Experimental Research, 21*, 596-601.

Tassone, F., Hagerman, R. J., Chamberlain, W. D., & Hagerman, P. J. (2000). Transcription of the FMR1 gene in individuals with fragile X syndrome. *American Journal of Medical Genetics, 97*, 195-203.

Thomas, P. W., Higgs, D. R., & Serjeant, G. R. (1997). Benign clinical course in homozygous sickle cell disease: A search for predictors. *Journal of Clinical Epidemiology, 50*, 121-126.

Thomasson, H. R., Edenberg, H. J., Crabb, D. W., Mai, X. L., Jerome, R. E., Li, T. K., Wang, S. P., Lin, Y. T., Lu, R. B., & Yin, S. J. (1991). Alcohol and aldehyde dehydrogenase genotypes and alcoholism in Chinese men. *American Journal of Human Genetics, 48*, 677-681.

Trefz, F. K., Burgard, P., Konig, T., Goebel-Schreiner, B., Lichter-Konecki, U., Konecki, D., Schmidt, E., Schmidt, H., & Bickel, H. (1993). Genotype-phenotype correlations in phenylketonuria. *Clinica Chimica Acta, 217*, 15-21.

Tu, G.-C., & Israel, Y. (1995). Alcohol consumption by Orientals in North America is predicted largely by a single gene. *Behavior Genetics, 25*, 59-65.

Wainscoat, J. S., Bell, J. I., Thein, S. L., Higgs, D. R., Sarjeant, G. R., Peto, T. E., & Weatherall, D. J. (1983). Multiple origins of the sickle mutation: Evidence from beta S globin gene cluster polymorphisms. *Molecular Biology and Medicine, 1*, 191-197.

Yin, S. J. (1994). Alcohol dehydrogenase: Enzymology and metabolism. *Alcohol and Alcoholism, 2*, 113-119.

Yoshida, A. (1992). Molecular genetics of human aldehyde dehydrogenase. *Pharmacogenetics, 2*, 139-147.

Zucker, K. J., Bradley, S. J., Oliver, G., & Blake, J. (1996). Psychosexual development of women with congenital adrenal hyperplasia. *Hormones & Behavior, 30*, 300-318.

CHAPTER 6

DCG

Disorders With Complex Genetics

INTRODUCTION: COMPLEX GENETIC DISORDERS ● AND DISORDERS WITH COMPLEX GENETICS

In medicine and medical genetics, one often encounters the phrase *complex genetic disorder* in reference to many common syndromes such as diabetes, cancers, and hypertension. The definition of a complex genetic disorder is quite simple—it is a disorder that has something genetic going on behind it, but no one has a clue as to what the genetics are. The term *complex genetic disorder* is a misnomer because it implies that the disorder is genetic, whereas empirical research usually shows that the environment can play a large etiological role. To ensure that we do not neglect the environment, the term *disorder(s) with complex genetics* (DCG) will be used in this text.

One central epidemiological variable correlates very highly with DCG—the prevalence of the disorder. The frequency of Mendelian disorders is one in several thousands of births. (Sickle-cell anemia is a rare exception.) The frequency of DCG is one to two orders of magnitude higher. Indeed, if a disorder has a prevalence of 0.1% or above, it is certain to be a DCG.

In terms of human behavior, all forms of psychopathology (schizophrenia, affective disorder, the anxiety disorders, etc.) are DCGs. Indeed, all forms of psychopathology have important—albeit largely unknown—environmental factors intimately tied up in their etiologies.

Do not let the term DCG engender pessimism about ever finding the causes and effective treatments for psychopathology (or any medical DCG, for that matter). Indeed, research into DCG, although it is very difficult, is one of the exciting challenges to both the genetic and the epidemiological communities. Finding and cloning the gene for a Mendelian disorder is much akin to following the Oregon Trail after a generation of pioneers have charted the land and founded communities along the way—just follow the road signs and you will get there. Research into DCG explores virgin territory.

● ALZHEIMER'S DISEASE: A MODEL DCG

There are many model DCG, among them breast cancer, diabetes, hypercholesterolemia, and atherosclerosis. Unfortunately, no forms of psychopathology can be used as a model DCG because our knowledge about their genetics is too embryonic at this stage. Perhaps the best model with behavioral sequelae is Alzheimer's disease (AD), so we will use that to illustrate how DCG is being researched.

AD: The Phenotype

AD is a progressive and irreversible disorder that involves damage and the eventual death of neurons in the central nervous system. The first sign of AD is usually memory loss for recent events—one may have trouble recalling the name of the current president but have no difficulty remembering who the president was when one was born. In normals, memory abilities begin a slow decline starting in the mid-20s[1] and become noticeable in middle age—that familiar experience of recognizing a face but failing to recall the name just becomes more common with age. Indeed, it is quite difficult to distinguish the very early stages of AD from normal forgetfulness, and many family members fail to recognize that someone is having significant problems with memory.

As AD progresses, cognitive functioning and judgment deteriorate, and the *dementia* (a progressive and irreversible loss of intellectual functioning) becomes evident. It is not uncommon at this stage to see changes in personality—someone with a lifelong tendency to be patient and forbearing may become hostile and irritable, or a reserved person may become outgoing and fatuous. Depression is also encountered. Eventually, all forms of reasoning are impaired, the person becomes unable to perform routine tasks such as getting washed and dressed, and in the last stages the person is incapable of communication. The course of the illness can range anywhere between 2 and 20 years, but on average people with AD survive around 8 to 10 years after the first diagnosis. AD does not appear to be fatal per se. Instead, in the final stages, people become bedridden and physically weak, permitting opportunistic infections to occur. Most people with AD die from pneumonia.

AD is an adult disorder with an age of onset as early as 30 to 40. The risk for developing AD increases with age and roughly doubles every 5 years after the age of 65. Advances in medicine and public recognition of healthy diets and lifestyles have dramatically increased life expectancy over the past century, greatly increasing the overall prevalence of AD, placing heavy economic burdens on the health care system, and creating heavy personal, emotional, and financial problems for family members and caregivers. For these reasons, AD is being heavily researched.

Although AD can be diagnosed using psychometric tests of memory and cognition, the only sure diagnosis is made on autopsy, when the brain is examined under the microscope. AD brains show characteristic plaques and neurofibrillary tangles. Plaques are dense deposits of protein (especially β-amyloid[2]) and non-nerve cells that build up outside the neuron. Neurofibrillary tangles occur when the neurofibers[3] lose their structure and twist together.

AD: Classification

AD is classified along two different dimensions—family history and age of onset. It has long been recognized that AD can run in some families, and early family studies suggested that a minority of families had transmission patterns consistent with a dominant gene. Today, family history is used to classify AD into two types, although the boundary between the two types is often quite fuzzy. The first type is called *familial AD* or FAD and is diagnosed when the pedigree is consistent with dominant transmission. The second, and by far more common, type is usually referred to as *nonfamilial AD* or *sporadic AD* and is diagnosed when there is no clear pattern of familial transmission.[4]

Although age of onset is a continuous and quantitative variable, it is often dichotomized, giving the two classes of *early-onset AD* and *late-onset AD*. The age of onset distinguishing the two is usually taken as 60 to 65 years. The vast majority of AD patients are late-onset cases.

Familial AD (FAD) is strongly correlated with age of onset. Most FAD cases are early onset and also have a quickly deteriorating course. Not all early-onset cases are FAD. Most late-onset cases are sporadic.

AD: Genetics of Familial Alzheimer's Disease

The fact that cases of Down's syndrome (which involves the inheritance of extra material from chromosome 21) eventually show the AD-like pathology of plaques and tangles led to a focus in early linkage and association studies on chromosome 21. Soon it was found that a small minority of FAD cases was due to mutations in the gene for the amyloid precursor protein (APP) on this chromosome. Shortly afterwards, other positive linkage results were found, with suggestions of a link to a gene on chromosome 14. The gene has since been located and is called the presenilin 1 locus. Recently, a third locus, on chromosome 1—the presenilin 2 gene—has been implicated in AD in a group of German pedigrees originating from the Volga Valley in Russia (Blacker & Tanzi, 1998; Pericak-Vance et al., 2000; St. George-Hyslop, 2000).

The three loci—APP and presenilins 1 and 2—all show dominant transmission, so the risk to an offspring is .50. Together, these three loci account for almost half of the families with FAD, but because FAD accounts for no more than 10% of all Alzheimer's cases, the three genes are responsible for roughly 5% of all AD. This is an important lesson from AD and is an emerging pattern in the study of DCG—Mendelizing forms occur, but they are rare and account for only a few percent of all cases.[5]

A second lesson—actually, a problem—from AD is the possibility of predicting who will develop a Mendelizing form of AD. A person with AD in a pedigree for FAD could be tested to find if he or she has a deleterious locus at one of the three genes. Under current medical genetic practice, decisions about whether or not to test reside with the patient. Thorny ethical issues emerge nevertheless. Suppose that the grandfather in an FAD pedigree tests positive for the presenilin 1 mutation, but his son Fred and his granddaughter Sally—Fred's daughter—are unaffected. Fred is adamant that he not be tested or given any other information about whether he carries the gene. Sally, on the other hand, is equally adamant about being tested so that she can plan her life according to the results. If Sally is tested and tests negative, there is no problem—the probability that her father, Fred, has the gene remains at .50. However, if Sally tests positive, then Fred must have the gene, because that is the only way Sally could have gotten it. If Sally's test results in this case become known within the family, Fred's desire to remain uninformed is violated. In short, testing some people within a pedigree could violate issues of doctor-patient confidentiality of other people in the pedigree.

A third lesson of AD concerns the importance of finding a gene. You may quite rightly question the importance of isolating these three genes when they account for less than 1 in 20 Alzheimer's cases. The major importance may actually be in the ability to learn more about the neurobiology and the disease process (also known as the *pathophysiology*) of AD than in shouting to the world "Researcher Finds AD Gene." It is helpful to digress here for a moment to see how the gene discoveries have assisted in the understanding of AD. Again, the details are unimportant—it is the logic of the scientific quest that requires careful attention.

The locus for APP on chromosome 21 codes for a polypeptide[6] that eventually gets cleaved into certain sections. One of the longer fragments[7] is chemically "sticky," so these fragments bind together (i.e., form *multimers*) and join with other chemicals. The long fragments were found to be heavily concentrated in the plaques and tangles of AD brains. Several of the mutations in the APP locus result in an increased proportion of the longer fragment. In addition, the effects of the two presenilin genes appeared to be associated with increased production of amyloid, especially the longer fragment. These findings (along with many others not reviewed here) have coalesced into the "amyloid cascade hypothesis" that holds that AD (or at least certain cases of AD) is due to some combination of amyloid overproduction and failure to appropriately break down and get rid of the longer beta-amyloid fragments (Fine, 1999; Neve & Robakis, 1998; Small, 1998).

This working hypothesis has guided research in many different directions, three of which will be mentioned here. The first is in the area of therapeutics. Scientists are now exploring ways to interfere in the normal process of amyloid degradation so that the longer, "sticky" fragment can get broken down more easily. They are also investigating ways to have the amyloid deposits digested in the plaques. A second area of research is into the genetics and the enzymology of those enzymes (called *proteases*) that cleave APP. Finally, researchers have placed a mutant human APP allele and mutant presenilin alleles into mice and found that these transgenic mice strains show plaques and tangles similar to that exhibited in AD. This is an especially exciting development because an animal model permits research and drug testing that cannot be done with humans (Janus & Westaway, 2001).

At the same time, work on basic neurobiology is guiding genetic research. The neurofibers that become tangled in AD may be viewed as flexible railroad tracks that are prevented from tangling because they are spiked into a series of railroad ties. In the neuron, the chemical equivalents of the railroad ties are tau proteins, so the genes for tau proteins are being screened to see if mutations here may play a role in AD.

AD: The Apolipoprotein E Locus

The three dominant genes for FAD account for a small fraction of cases of AD. What is responsible for all the other cases—that half of FAD that is not a result of the three loci, and all of sporadic Alzheimer's? It turns out that there is another gene, the APOE locus (for *apolipoprotein E*), that contributes to AD, especially the late-onset form. It is expressed in a different fashion than the three Mendelizing forms. The three dominant loci appear to be fully penetrant—if a person has the deleterious allele at any one of these three loci, then the probability of developing AD is close to 1.0. In contrast, the APOE locus is viewed as a *susceptibility locus*—that is, it increases the *likelihood* of developing AD but in no way guarantees that AD will occur.

The APOE locus codes for a protein that assists in the transportation of cholesterol throughout the body. It has long been of great interest to cardiology because of its role in heart disease, but the discovery of its association with AD was largely fortuitous. There are three alleles at the locus that are formally designated as ε2 (i.e., epsilon 2), ε3, and ε4 but will be called E2, E3, and E4 herein. E3 is the most frequent allele and E2 is the rarest, but the frequencies vary across populations. Among populations of European ancestry, the rounded-off frequencies are around .10 for E2, .75 for E3, and .15 for E4 (Gerdes, Klausen, Sihm, & Faergeman, 1992).

The E2 allele acts as a protective factor against AD, whereas the E4 allele increases the risk for AD in a dose-dependent way—that is, the E4 homozygote is at higher risk than the E4 heterozygote (Farrer et al., 1997; Rubinsztein & Easton, 1999). The E4 heterozygote has about twice to three times the risk, and the E4 homozygote around 10 times the risk, of developing Alzheimer's disease,[8] but actual risk figures may vary according to ethnicity. The deleterious influence of E4 appears to be more pronounced in some Asian, Indian, and white populations than in African Americans (Farrer et al., 1997; Ganguli et al., 2000; Tang et al., 1996). The E4 allele may also be associated with an earlier onset and more rapid course of illness. However, not everybody with the E4 allele develops AD, and many people without an E4 allele do develop AD. This is the reason why the APOE locus is referred to as a susceptibility or risk factor gene.

Testing for APOE is useful in research settings and in some clinical settings where a diagnosis of AD is already suspected. But should there be general population screening for APOE? This is a controversial issue. Unlike many medical test results, knowledge of the APOE genotype in an otherwise healthy person is neither diagnostic nor prognostic. All statements about APOE are probabilistic, so the most a clinician could tell a person about his or her risk for AD is something akin to "maybe or maybe not." Enthusiasm for general testing is also dampened by the fact that there are no known ways to prevent AD. If an effective but costly prevention were developed, then it would make sense to genotype healthy individuals and devote scarce resources to those at highest risk of developing AD. A further issue muddling the debate is confidentiality. If accepted medical practice were to screen, then insurance carriers could know the results, with untoward consequences for those at risk for AD. Hence, although there are no laws preventing a person from getting genotyped, most public policy statements by medical groups and patient-advocacy associations do not recommend screening at the present time. The same public policy statements also recognize, however, that screening eventually may be useful as science progresses and issues of confidentiality and insurability are resolved.

AD: The Great Unknown

To summarize, there are four genes known to be involved in AD. Together, however, they account for only a small percentage of AD cases. The etiology of the majority of cases is obscure, so the models for these are more on the theoretical than the empirical level. Hence, we embark into the great unknown to discuss phenocopies, polygenic transmission, and the multifactorial threshold model.

Phenocopies

Technically defined, a *phenocopy* is an environmentally produced phenotype that resembles a genetic syndrome. For classic Mendelian disorders, several intrauterine effects can produce a neonate with physical features resembling a known Mendelian disorder. For example, an autosomal dominant mutation can lead to Holt-Oram syndrome, which results in incomplete and deformed limb development. The drug thalidomide, if taken during a sensitive period of pregnancy, will produce similar malformations.

The term *phenocopy* is chauvinistic. One could just as well invent the word "genocopy" to denote a genetic abnormality that results in the same phenotype as a well-described environmental syndrome. Holt-Oram syndrome might be regarded as a genocopy of thalidomide toxicity. The terminology becomes even more confusing when the concept of a phenocopy is applied to a DCG. Ingestion of large amounts of lead and other heavy metals during infancy and childhood will lead to mental retardation in an otherwise normal person. Calling this a "phenocopy" carries with it a tacit assumption that mental retardation is a genetic syndrome.

To avoid a useless, hair-splitting discussion about terminology, the following is suggested. The definition of a phenocopy given above is the one encountered in all textbooks on human and medical genetics. In practice, however, most researchers who work with DCGs that involve behavioral phenotypes (learning disabilities, psychopathology) use the term in a much looser sense to refer to a person who may have any type of genetic vulnerability toward the disorder but in whom the etiology is clearly traced to a significant environmental event (or events) of very large effect. According to this definition, a psychosis resulting from prolonged amphetamine abuse may be regarded as a phenocopy of schizophrenia or brief reactive psychosis without any implication that either of the disorders are 100% genetic syndromes. It is this loose definition that will be used herein.

In terms of Alzheimer's disease, there are no firmly documented phenocopies; however, several types of environmental factors are being researched as potential candidates. These include severe head trauma, stroke, and other forms of brain damage.

Multifactorial Transmission: Genetics

Many traits are the result of the combined effects of several different gene products (peptides, proteins, and/or enzymes), where each product is the result of the DNA blueprint at a different locus. When the effects of several different genes add and/or interact together to produce a phenotype, then the mode of transmission is called *oligogenic* (when the number of genes is on the small side) or *polygenic* (when the number of genes is large). There is not an exact number that separates oligogenic from polygenic transmission; researchers rely on a rough order of magnitude—6 genes are clearly oligogenic and 60 genes are obviously polygenic, but 16 genes could be either oligo- or polygenic. There should really be no debate about the extent to which DCG are oligogenic or polygenic. At present, we lack the technology to determine the number of loci that contribute to, say, schizophrenia or major depression. Speculation as to that number is more akin to medieval scholastic arguments about angels and pinheads than to contemporary science. In the remainder of this text, *polygenic* will be used to avoid the awkward phrase "oligogenic or polygenic," with the tacit implication that the number of genes involved need not be large.

It is helpful to give a hypothetical illustration of polygenic inheritance. Consider a continuous phenotype such as height and assume that three different genes contribute to individual differences in height. Denote the three loci as A, B, and C, and let there be two alleles, denoted by an uppercase letter and a lowercase letter, at each locus. At the A locus, assume that

Table 6.1   Hypothetical Effects of Genotypes on Height

Genotype	Amount[a]	Genotype	Amount[a]	Genotype	Amount[a]
AABBCC	+5.6	AaBBCC	+1.8	aaBBCC	−2.0
AABBCc	+5.0	AaBBCc	+1.2	aaBBCc	−2.6
AABBcc	+4.4	AaBBcc	+0.6	aaBBcc	−3.2
AABbCC	+4.4	AaBbCC	+0.6	aaBbCC	−3.2
AABbCc	+3.8	AaBbCc	+0.0	aaBbCc	−3.8
AABbcc	+3.2	AaBbcc	−0.6	aaBbcc	−4.4
AAbbCC	+3.2	AabbCC	−0.6	aabbCC	−4.4
AAbbCc	+2.6	AabbCc	−1.2	aabbCc	−5.0
AAbbcc	+2.0	Aabbcc	−1.8	aabbcc	−5.6

a. The extent to which the genotype deviates from the population mean.

allele *A* adds 1.9 cm to height while allele *a* subtracts 1.9 cm from height.[9] Hence, genotype *AA*, having two *A* alleles, will add 3.8 cm to height; genotype *Aa* adds 0 cm to height; and genotype *aa* subtracts 3.8 cm from height. Assume that allele B adds 0.6 cm to height and *b* subtracts 0.6 cm, and allele C adds 0.3 cm while *c* subtracts 0.3 cm.

The genotypes in the population will contain all combinations of the alleles at these loci—*AABbCc, AaBBcc*, and so on. There will be 27 different genotypes. Assume that the influences of each locus are additive. Then the individual differences in height resulting from these three loci are given in Table 6.1. To find the predicted height of a person, take the average height in the population and then add the amount in Table 6.1 corresponding to the person's genotype. For example, if mean height were 176.2 cm, then a person with genotype *AABbCC* would be predicted to be 176.2 + 4.4 = 180.6 cm tall.

Now it is time to learn some terminology from this example. Note that the three loci do not have equal effects. The ultimate influence of locus A on height is greatest, and the influence of locus C is least. This would be called a *weighted polygenic system*. The alternative, an unweighted polygenic system, assumes that each locus contributes the same amount to the phenotype. The unweighted model is important for theoretical genetics but is implausible in nature.[10]

In the weighted system, locus A would be called a *major gene* or *major locus* in the sense that it has a large influence on the phenotype. It would appear natural to refer to locus B and locus C as minor loci, but in the twisted logic of scientific language, the term *modifying genes, modifying loci,* or even *background genes* is preferred. These are loci that have a relatively small quantitative effect on the phenotype.

Note how the effects of the alleles and the loci added together. For example, consider genotype *AABbcc*. There are two *A* alleles, each contributing +1.9 cm, one *B* allele (adding 0.6 cm) and one *b* allele (subtracting 0.6 cm), and two *c* alleles, each of which subtracts 0.3 cm. Hence, the deviation for this genotype is $2 \times 1.9 + (0.6 - 0.6) + 2 \times (-.3) = +3.2$ cm. Hence, this is called an *additive model*. Once again, the additive model is an *assumption* and not a necessary consequence of nature. Departures from the strictly additive model occur when there is any degree of dominance or *epistasis* (i.e., statistical interaction among several genes) and will be discussed in Chapter 18.

Multifactorial Transmission: Environmental Factors

Recall that the phrase "predicted height" was used to describe the expected height of someone with a particular genotype. For example, someone with genotype *AABbCC* is predicted to be 108.6 cm. An actual person with this genotype may not be exactly 108.6 cm tall because various environmental factors could influence the phenotype. It is often assumed that several different environmental factors may contribute to the phenotype, so not only are there multiple genes, but there are also multiple environmental factors that contribute to disorder. A classic example of multiple environmental factors influencing a DCG would be the role of smoking, exercise, and diet on cardiovascular disease.

When there are several genes and several different environmental factors contributing to a trait, then the model is usually referred to as *multifactorial*. The phrase *polygenic* is also used instead of multifactorial, with the tacit assumption that environment may play a role in addition to that of genes.

The Multifactorial Threshold Model

The multifactorial threshold model applies polygenic transmission and several etiological environmental factors to a *discrete* or *dichotomous* phenotype. A discrete or dichotomous phenotype is one that can be classified into two or more groups, with no intermediate phenotypes between the groups. Pregnancy is a classic discrete phenotype—women are either pregnant or not pregnant, and it is impossible to be in between. Note that a discrete phenotype may still have sub-phenotypes that are graded continuums. For example, length of pregnancy is an important continuous variable among the category of pregnant women.

Polydactyly (i.e., having an extra toe on a foot) in mice is a classic example of the multifactorial threshold model. Ordinarily, mice have four digits on a paw, but under some circumstances, a fifth digit may appear. The extra digit may be poorly formed and nonfunctional, but in terms of phenotypic classification, it is an all-or-none trait. Both genes and environment (especially prenatal stress) contribute to this phenomenon, but there is more than a single locus involved in the trait.

Originally developed by Falconer (1965), the multifactorial threshold model was first applied to human behavior by Gottesman and Shields (1967, 1972) in their classic twin study of schizophrenia. It has since become a popular model of the transmission of psychiatric disorders and psychopathology. A version of it is depicted in Figure 6.1. The key concept of this model is *liability* (aka *susceptibility*, *vulnerability*, or *predisposition*). Liability is not the disorder per se. Instead, liability is defined as an *unmeasured (i.e., latent) continuous variable that probabilistically relates to the disorder*. The higher one is in liability, the greater the chances of developing the disorder.

Genes contribute to the *genetic liability*. For example, genotype *AABbccDd* might contribute +1.3 units to genetic liability while genotype *aabbCcdd* might contribute –2.3 units to genetic liability. Because genetic liability is unmeasured, any "units" are completely arbitrary. It is customary, however, to let 0 denote the mean liability and to let positive numbers denote risk (i.e., a greater propensity to develop the disorder) and negative numbers denote protection (a lower probability of developing the problem).

Environmental factors contribute to *environmental liability*, which has an analogous interpretation and measurement scale to that of genetic liability but applies to environments instead of genes. Together, genetic and environmental liability contribute to *total liability*. It is the total liability that relates directly to the disorder. Once the total liability reaches a certain point (the *threshold*), then the phenotype changes and a disorder results. Note how only the total liability correlates perfectly with the phenotype. Knowing a person's genetic liability permits *probabilistic* statements of the form "Joe is at high risk for bipolar disorder" or "Susie is at reduced risk for agoraphobia" but does not allow one to predict with certainty that Joe will become bipolar and that Susie will never develop agoraphobia. Similarly, knowing a person's environmental liability permits only probabilistic statements about the development of a disorder.

The threshold model is developed in more detail in a later chapter. Here we note that the important fact is that the model is once again *a set of assumptions about how nature works*. It is not the case that all the genetic and environmental factors for a number of disorders have been clearly elucidated and that the multifactorial threshold model emerged as a parsimonious mathematical explanation for the empirical data.

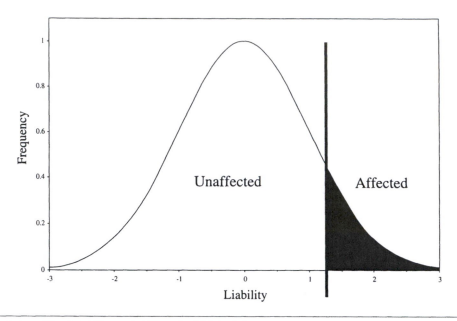

Figure 6.1   The Multifactorial Threshold Model.

● OVERALL PERSPECTIVE OF DCG

If we join the empirical evidence about the genetics of AD with the speculations about polygenic transmission and the multifactorial threshold model, we arrive at the overall model proposed by Gottesman (1991) about the mode of genetic transmission for schizophrenia. Figure 6.2 presents an adaptation of this model but will be discussed here in terms of AD.

The figure partitions the etiology of AD according to its major (but not necessarily exclusive) causes. There are three Mendelian forms of the disorder, corresponding to the APP, presenilin 1, and presenilin 2 mutations. Although these three forms have high penetrance, they account for only a small percentage (4% in Figure 6.2) of all AD.

Two major loci contribute to AD. The first might be the APOE locus that is responsible for 8% of cases. This figure means that in 8% of AD, the APOE locus is the major cause for the disorder even though there may be many other genes and environmental factors that also contribute to the onset among this 8%. Note well that the 8% figure is completely hypothetical—we do not know how many AD cases have APOE as their major cause. In the future, a second major locus may be uncovered that also contributes to susceptibility. This eventuality is portrayed in Figure 6.2 as Major Locus 2, the major cause for 15% of cases.

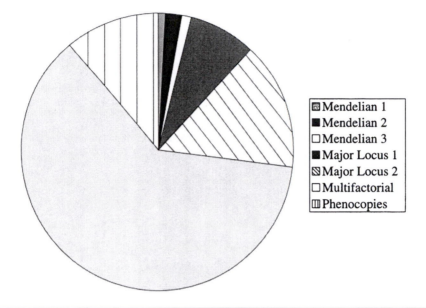

Figure 6.2   Principal Etiological Causes of a DCG.

The majority of cases—62% in Figure 6.2—may be due to the effects of many different loci and a variety of environmental factors that combine and influence risk. This is the multifactorial threshold model that was discussed earlier and is denoted simply as "Multifactorial" in the figure. Once again, the estimate of 62% is fictitious. Most contemporary geneticists suspect that multifactorial transmission eventually will account for the bulk of any DCG, but no one really knows that for certain.

Lastly, phenocopies account for the remaining 11%. Gross insults to the brain through trauma, viral infections, or a number of yet-unknown environmental factors might produce AD in people who are otherwise at low risk for AD. Again, the percentage used here is an uneducated guess.

Taken together, this model implies that there is no single "cause" of AD. Rather, a number of different events, some large and some small, lead to the same process or very similar processes. Just as many roads lead to Rome, there are different pathways to AD, and the road traveled by one person may be very different from that taken by another. Some roads are superhighways (e.g., the three Mendelizing forms) that get one there in a hurry, but the majority are minor streets with twists, turns, detours, and dead ends. But everyone who enters Rome develops AD. As a result, the causative factors in one person could be quite distinct from the etiological events in someone else.

This overall model has long been applied to complex behavioral phenotypes such as mental retardation, specific learning disabilities, and every form
of psychopathology. In every case, however, empirical knowledge about the
relative contributions of Mendelizing forms, major loci, multifactorial transmission, and phenocopies is rudimentary. For mental retardation, there are
indeed many documented Mendelizing forms—PKU and Fragile X syndrome
are but 2 of more than 100—and several recognized phenocopies such as
severe lead toxicity. The ALDH-2 polymorphism illustrates the role of a major
locus, at least in some Asian populations. However, slicing the rest of the pie
is primarily guesswork. To complicate matters, the division of the pie for one
DCG may be quite different from that of another disorder.

● THE FINAL LESSON FOR DCG: GENETICS IS A TOOL, NOT A GOAL

The progress being made in AD research should reinforce a major lesson
from our study of Mendelian traits. Finding a gene or genes for any disorder
or behavior is not the goal or holy grail of science. Instead, it must be looked
upon as reaching a milestone in a long journey, the majority of which is still
in front of us. All of us have had the experience of being on a long road trip
and spending hours passing cornfield after cornfield, desert and more
desert, or town after town. When we arrive at a salient point—whether it be
the halfway mark, an important geographical landmark, or a major city—our
lethargy gives way to a momentary sense of excitement and renewal. But do
we stop and consider the journey complete? Of course not! We trudge on
until we arrive at the intended destination.

So it is with finding a gene for a disorder like AD or any other human
behavior or characteristic. It is an important accomplishment. It should be
celebrated, and kudos should be bestowed on the discoverers. But finding a
gene for schizophrenia, intelligence, or extraversion is not the raison d'être
of genetics. It is an important step in the long journey toward unraveling the
biology behind a phenotype.

The importance of the Alzheimer's story is the interplay between genetics and basic neurosciences. Genetics has led to the development of transgenic animal strains that are exceptionally important for basic neuroscience
research. In turn, the results of neurobiology will aid in the search for other
genes that may influence the disorder. In short, for DCG, genetics is a tool,
not an end in itself.

NOTES ●

1. The decline in the 20s can be documented with psychometric tests but is virtually imperceptible and has no practical consequences.

2. Amyloid is a generic name for proteins or protein fragments that aggregate and form an insoluble mass.

3. Neurofibers are long, thin, threadlike bodies that give structure to the neuron and act as transportation highways for neuronal chemicals.

4. In classical genetics, the term *sporadic* refers to a person with a Mendelian disorder (or more generally, a person with a certain Mendelizing phenotype) that appears unexpectedly in an otherwise normal pedigree. Sporadics may be due to new mutations, to environmental factors, or to some complex interplay between unknown genetic and environmental factors.

5. Breast cancer is another example. The two dominant loci for this syndrome, BRCA1 and BRCA2, account for about 3% of all cases. One must be wary, however, of overgeneralization of this principle. The search for genes is in the early stages, so more Mendelizing forms for AD may be discovered in the future.

6. The APP locus is actually more complicated than this simple statement implies. There are 19 exons in this gene, and different mRNA sequences are made by gene splicing—linking together different exons in the editing process. For example, the most frequent APP polypeptide in the brain (APP695) results from the splicing of exons 1 to 6, 9 to 13, and the last 5 exons, whereas APP751, the most prevalent form elsewhere, inserts exon 7 into this sequence.

7. A-β 1-42.

8. The risk figures have been developed mostly from case-control types of studies in which allele frequencies are calculated from a group of patients with AD and community controls. The results of prospective studies now under way may change the numbers somewhat.

9. The phrase "subtracts 1.9 cm" should not be taken literally. It is purely a mathematical convenience that should be translated as "all things being equal, individuals with one *a* allele are 1.9 cm shorter than people without an *a* allele." It does not imply that allele *a* physically shrinks a person.

10. The critical mathematical issue is not the weighted versus unweighted model but the differences in the weights. When the differences among the weights are on the small side, then the mathematics of an unweighted polygenic model give a very close approximation to the real state. At present, we do not have any empirical evidence as to the distribution of weights for behavioral phenotypes; the distribution may well depend upon the specific phenotype.

REFERENCES ●

Blacker, D., & Tanzi, R. E. (1998). The genetics of Alzheimer disease: Current status and future prospects. *Archives of Neurology, 55*, 294-296.

Falconer, D. S. (1965). The inheritance of liability to certain diseases, estimated from the incidence among relatives. *Annals of Human Genetics, 31*, 1-20.

Farrer, L. A., Cupples, L. A., Haines, J. L., Hyman, B., Kukull, W. A., Mayeux, R., et al. (1997). Effects of age, sex, and ethnicity on the association between apolipoprotein E genotype and Alzheimer disease. A meta-analysis. *JAMA, 278,* 1349-1356.

Fine, R. E. (1999). The biochemistry of Alzheimer disease. *Alzheimer Disease and Associated Disorders, 13*(Suppl. 1), S82-S87.

Ganguli, M., Chandra, V., Kamboh, M. I., Johnston, J. M., Dodge, H. H., Thelma, B. K., et al. (2000). Apolipoprotein E polymorphism and Alzheimer disease: The Indo-US Cross-National Dementia Study. *Archives of Neurology, 57,* 824-830.

Gerdes, L. U., Klausen, I. C., Sihm, I., & Faergeman, O. (1992). Apolipoprotein E polymorphism in a Danish population compared to findings in 45 other study populations around the world. *Genetic Epidemiology, 9,* 155-167.

Gottesman, I. I. (1991). *Schizophrenia genesis: The origins of madness.* San Francisco: W. H. Freeman.

Gottesman, I. I., & Shields, J. (1967). A polygenic theory of schizophrenia. *Proceedings of the National Academy of Sciences of the United States of America, 58,* 199-205.

Gottesman, I. I., & Shields, J. (1972). *Schizophrenia and genetics: A twin study vantage point.* New York: Academic Press.

Janus, C., & Westaway, D. (2001). Transgenic mouse models of Alzheimer's disease. *Physiology and Behavior, 73,* 873-886.

Neve, R. L., & Robakis, N. K. (1998). Alzheimer's disease: A re-examination of the amyloid hypothesis. *Trends in Neurosciences, 21,* 15-19.

Pericak-Vance, M. A., Grubber, J., Bailey, L. R., Hedges, D., West, S., Santoro, L., et al. (2000). Identification of novel genes in late-onset Alzheimer's disease. *Experimental Gerontology, 35,* 1343-1352.

Rubinsztein, D. C., & Easton, D. F. (1999). Apolipoprotein E genetic variation and Alzheimer's disease: A meta-analysis. *Dementia and Geriatric Cognitive Disorders, 10,* 199-209.

Small, G. W. (1998). The pathogenesis of Alzheimer's disease. *Journal of Clinical Psychiatry, 59,* 7-14.

St. George-Hyslop, P. H. (2000). Molecular genetics of Alzheimer's disease. *Biological Psychiatry, 47,* 183-199.

Tang, M. X., Maestre, G., Tsai, W. Y., Liu, X. H., Feng, L., Chung, W. Y., et al. (1996). Effect of age, ethnicity, and head injury on the association between APOE genotypes and Alzheimer's disease. *Annals of the New York Academy of Sciences, 802,* 6-15.

CHAPTER 7

THE NEW GENETICS

Techniques for DNA Analysis

INTRODUCTION ●

Before the 1980s, finding the genotype of an individual usually involved various laboratory assays for a gene product—the protein or enzyme. The cases of the ABO and Rhesus blood groups are classic examples of how one infers genotypes from the reaction of gene products with certain chemicals. In the mid-1980s, genetic technology took a great leap forward with the ability to genotype DNA itself. The geneticist could now examine DNA directly, without going through the laborious process of developing assays to detect individual differences in proteins and enzymes. Direct DNA analysis had the further advantage of being able to identify alleles in sections of DNA that did not code for polypeptide chains. As a result of these advances, the number of genetic loci that could be detected increased exponentially, soon leading to the identification of the genes for disorders like Huntington's disease and cystic fibrosis that had remained a mystery for the better part of the 20th century.

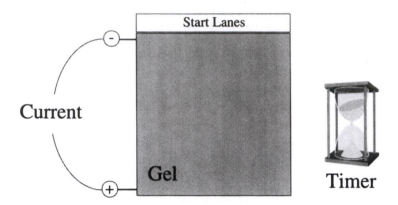

Figure 7.1   Gel Electrophoresis. Biological material (DNA, proteins, etc.) is placed in the start lane and an electric current is turned on for a specified amount of time. Molecules will migrate toward the opposite end of the gel according to their molecular weights. Smaller molecules will move farther than larger molecules.

In this chapter, the major molecular techniques are outlined. The purpose is to provide a quick and understandable reference for the social scientist. The content of this chapter is not something that is required to understand genetics, what genes are, or how they relate to human behavior. Indeed, this chapter may be skipped without any great loss of continuity. Hence, only the essentials are given, and the reader interested in the laboratory science behind the techniques is referred to contemporary textbooks on molecular genetics. We begin by defining a series of basic tools and techniques.

● BASIC TOOLS AND TECHNIQUES

Basic Tools: Electrophoresis

Electrophoresis is a technique that separates small biological molecules by their molecular weight. It may be applied to molecules as large as proteins and enzymes as well as to small snippets of DNA and RNA. One begins the procedure by constructing a "gel"—a highly viscous material the actual chemistry of which need not concern us. Purified copies of the biological specimen are then injected into a "starting lane" at one end of the gel. Finally, a weak electric current is passed through the gel for a specified amount of time. Gravity and the electric current cause the biological molecules to migrate toward the opposite end of the gel. The extent to which any molecule moves depends on its electrical charge, its molecular weight, the viscosity of the gel, the strength of the current, and the amount of time that the current is applied. With constant charge, viscosity, current, and time, smaller molecules will migrate farther through the gel than will larger molecules.

Basic Tools: Cloning

In the popular imagination, the term *cloning* is associated with Aldous Huxley's 1936 novel *Brave New World*, science fiction, and a famous sheep named Dolly. To the molecular geneticist, however, the term *cloning* simply means the copying of a desired section of DNA. Historically, cloning began by isolating a small (i.e., several thousand base pairs) section of human DNA and then, after an elaborate series of steps, incorporating this segment into the DNA of another organism. The "other" organism is called a *vector*, and of course, not any type of vector will do. To make many copies of the human DNA segment, one desires a vector that can reproduce rapidly; hence, the most common vectors are small organisms with dramatic reproductive potential—plasmids, virus, bacteria, and yeast.[1]

Among the several major reasons for cloning human DNA, one is to obtain large amounts of a human DNA sequence that can then be used as a *probe* in other types of molecular genetic techniques. A second reason is to construct DNA libraries, a topic discussed later in this chapter. Finally, cloning is also used for therapeutic genetic engineering. In that application, the hope is that the vector with a cloned copy of the "good" gene missing in a patient might be incorporated into the patient's cells and produce the missing protein or enzyme.[2]

Basic Tools: Probes and Primers

Probes and primers each consist of a segment of single-stranded DNA or RNA with a known nucleotide sequence. The primer or probe is either synthesized in the lab or cloned in very large amounts and is then placed into physical contact with human DNA that has been treated to become single-stranded.[3] Because of complementary base pairing, the primer or probe will bind to the DNA segment that contains the specific nucleotide sequence that complements the probe's sequence.[4]

The difference between a primer and a probe is the purpose of the nucleotide chain. A primer is used to initiate a process (e.g., the synthesis of double-stranded DNA used in the polymerase chain reaction, a process that is discussed later). A probe carries a "light bulb," usually a fluorescent tag, and is meant to illuminate the location of the strand of DNA to which the probe binds. An example of a probe is given in Figure 7.2.

Figure 7.2   An Example of a Probe. Probes are manufactured segments of single-stranded DNA that carry a "light bulb," usually a fluorescent tag, and that bind to a complementary single-stranded DNA (or RNA) sequence.

Basic Tools: Light Bulbs

Purified DNA and RNA resemble viscous water. If many small sections of single-stranded DNA are subjected to gel electrophoresis, the sections will migrate to the opposite side of the gel according to their size, but they will be invisible. If probes are added, these will bind to the appropriate complementary snippets of the single-stranded DNA, forming a double strand. But the probes, being composed of nucleotides, also will be invisible.

To locate the probe after it binds to the DNA, it is necessary to engineer the probe so that it carries the biological equivalent of a light bulb. Two major types of light bulbs are used in molecular genetics. The first type is constructed by labeling the probe with radioactive isotopes.[5] The second type of probe uses special fluorescent dyes that allow the probe to be visualized and photographed under specialized lighting conditions. For many types of DNA analyses, radioactive probes are still the method of choice, but fluorescent technology is quickly replacing that method.

Basic Tools: Restriction Enzymes

A restriction enzyme (also known as restriction endonuclease) is an enzyme that recognizes a specific nucleotide sequence and cuts DNA at the sequence. For example, the restriction enzyme EcoRI (for *E. coli* Restriction enzyme number I)[6] recognizes the sequence GAATTC and slices the DNA right after the G.

Restriction enzymes are used in a wide variety of techniques. One major advantage is that they can cut DNA (or "digest" DNA, as the microbiologists prefer to call it) into fragments of manageable lengths. Without digestion using restriction enzymes, human DNA segments would simply be too long to allow them to be cloned or subject to many kinds of electrophoresis. Restriction enzymes also play an important role in detecting human polymorphisms.

Basic Tools: The Polymerase Chain Reaction (PCR)

The polymerase chain reaction or PCR is a technique used to "amplify" DNA—that is, make a sufficient number of copies of a DNA segment to permit it to be used for other types of techniques. Many people are familiar with the forensic application of PCR. When only a tiny drop of blood, semen, or other biological specimen is available at a crime scene, PCR is used to make a sufficient amount of DNA to permit genotyping.

PCR methodology makes use of many of the concepts outlined above, so it will be explained in some detail (see Figure 7.3). The procedure begins with purifying DNA from a biological specimen and then heating it almost to the boiling point of water. The heat separates the double-stranded DNA into two single strands. Once the DNA has become single-stranded, large amounts of primer[7] are added to the mixture along with an enzyme[8] and a large number of free nucleotides. The probe binds to the DNA, and then the enzyme synthesizes a complementary strand to the DNA beginning with the end of the probe and continuing to the end of the DNA segment. If we began with a single copy of DNA, then the end of this process will result in two copies of the DNA molecule. By repeating the process of heating, bathing the DNA with probes, and adding the enzyme and nucleotides, we create a total of four molecules of the desired DNA segment. Continuous repetition results in a geometric progression of DNA copies—8, then 16, then 32—until a sufficient amount of DNA is available for genotyping.

Today, PRC is machine automated and is often done in conjunction with a robot that automatically sequences the amplified DNA. The advantage here is that PCR avoids the complicated laboratory procedures necessary to harvest enough DNA required for other types of genotyping.[9] Automation also reduces the time and cost of genotyping. The biggest disadvantage of PCR is that the technique is so sensitive that it is susceptible to contamination from other DNA. Hence, careful laboratory protocol must be followed.

TYPES OF POLYMORPHISMS ●

Polymorphisms 1: Blood Groups

In the early days of human genetics, the majority of polymorphisms were those associated with proteins and enzymes in blood. When your blood is typed, you are informed that you are blood group O+, AB–, A+, or a similar type with a letter and a sign. The letter in the blood group gives your phenotype at the ABO locus, and the plus (+) or minus (–) sign denotes your

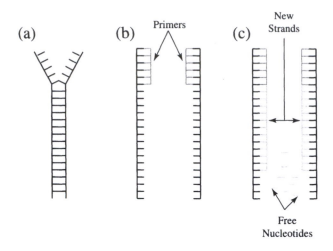

Figure 7.3   The Polymerase Chain Reaction (PCR). (a) With heating, DNA becomes single-stranded. (b) A primer section of DNA is added; it will bind with its complementary base pairs on the original DNA. (c) Free nucleotides and enzymes are added that will synthesize a new chain starting at the end of the primer.

phenotype at the Rhesus locus. A number of other loci, such as Kell, Duffy, MN, and Kidd, also can be phenotyped from blood. These polymorphisms are still used today to assess suitability of donors and recipients for blood transfusions (ABO locus) and to assess Rhesus incompatibility between a mother and her fetus. However, blood group polymorphisms have given way to other, more sophisticated techniques in modern human genetic research.

Polymorphisms 2: Restriction Fragment Length Polymorphism (RFLP)

At this point, it is helpful to describe a genotyping technique that will use all the tools outlined above, even though it is not the preferred method for today's research. *The restriction fragment length polymorphism or RFLP* began the dramatic explosion in genetic technology by allowing the field to locate genes for Mendelian disorders like Huntington's disease and cystic fibrosis. The procedure is illustrated in Figure 7.4. First, a probe must be constructed that will bind with a known sequence of DNA. The sequence is the gene that we want to examine. The probe for this example was shown in Figure 7.2.

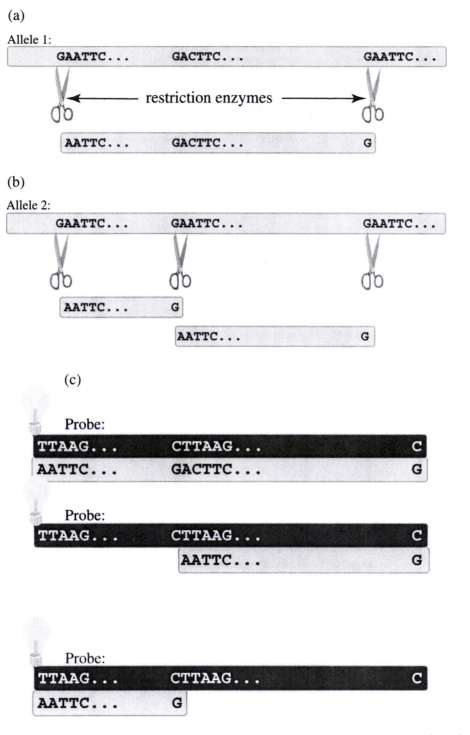

(a)

Allele 1:

(b)

Allele 2:

(c)

Probe:

restriction enzymes

(continued)

(d)

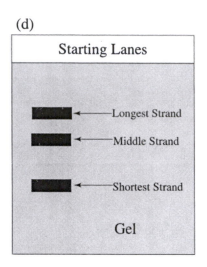

Figure 7.4   The Restriction Fragment Length Polymorphism (RFLP). (a) Allele 1 has two restriction sites, so incubating this allele in the restriction enzyme will result in one long fragment. (b) Allele 2 has three restriction sites, so incubating this allele with the restriction enzyme results in two fragments. (c) After the restriction enzyme cuts the DNA, the DNA is subjected to electrophoresis that separates the fragments according to size. A probe is then added to bind to the gene of interest. The binding of the probe after electrophoresis is illustrated in this panel. (d) The gel is then viewed under special lighting, (if the probe's light bulb is fluorescent) or special photographic film is placed on it (if the probe is radioactive). The result will be the characteristic bands illustrated in this panel.

The DNA of an individual—I will use myself as the example—is then purified, and the bonds connecting the two strands of the DNA molecule are cut, making the DNA single-stranded. I happen to be a heterozygote at the locus at which the probe will bind. The difference in the alleles is subtle, but it appears in the middle nucleotide sequence for alleles 1 and 2 in Figure 7.3. Allele 1 contains the sequence GACTTC, whereas allele 2 contains the sequence GAATTC. The third nucleotide in this series differs. But this sequence is an important one because it is the one that is recognized by the EcoRI restriction enzyme.

Suppose now that we take my DNA and place it into a solution with this restriction enzyme. Panels (b) and (c) show this for my alleles. Allele 2 contains the necessary sequence for the restriction enzyme to cut the gene in the middle (in addition, of course, to cutting it at the beginning and end of the gene). This allele will now have two fragments. The first will begin with the sequence AATTC and will end with the G close to the middle. The second will begin with the AATTC near the middle and will end with the terminal G. For allele 1, on the other hand, the EcoRI enzyme recognizes the initial sequence GAATTC and cuts the DNA between the G and the A. EcoRI will also recognize the last (rightmost) nucleotide sequence and cut the DNA after the G. EcoRI does not recognize the middle sequence, so it will not cut it there. Hence, allele 1 will contain one very long DNA fragment.

Now let us subject these fragments to electrophoresis. Allele 1, being quite long, will not move much from the start lane. The two fragments from allele 2, however, are considerably shorter than the single one for allele 1. These two fragments will move much farther along the gel, the smaller of the two migrating more than the larger.

We now have to "light up" the invisible DNA strands by bathing everything in the probe.[10] The single-stranded probe will bind to all three of my DNA fragments—the long one from allele 1 and two shorter ones from allele 2. When the probe "lights up," all three strands will be revealed—see panel (d) of Figure 7.4. The laboratory now knows my genotype at this locus.

Polymorphisms 3: Tandem Repeat Polymorphisms

Although RFLPs were the first of the modern molecular methods used to detect polymorphisms, they have given ground to other, more discerning techniques. One generic class of polymorphisms has their origin in DNA nucleotide sequences that are repeated a certain number of times, one right after the other. These "tandem repeats" are highly polymorphic in the sense that a large number of alleles may be found at any given locus. For example, one allele at a locus may have the sequence CAG repeated 4 times, another may have it repeated 8 times, and yet a third may have it repeated 20 times. Unfortunately, even though the concept of the tandem repeat is quite simple, the terminology for referring to these polymorphisms is quite confusing to the uninitiated.[11] For simplicity's sake, we will lump all these fine distinctions together into the single category of tandem repeat polymorphisms.

Figure 7.5 illustrates this type of polymorphism. The repetitive nucleotide sequence is GAAC, which is contained eight times in allele 1 but only four times in allele 2. The probe in this case contains the repetitive complement CTTG.

There are several different ways to genotype for tandem repeats. When the number of nucleotides in a sequence is fairly large (e.g., a series of 25 nucleotides is repeated over and over), then separating alleles by electrophoresis is often done. When the number is small (e.g., repeats of two to four nucleotides), then PCR is commonly used. Here, a special probe for the gene of interest is constructed for the area before the repeated sequence. PCR is then done to amplify the DNA that is then placed into a special sequencing machine that counts the number of repeats.

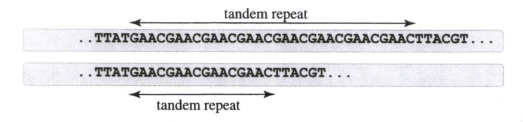

Figure 7.5   A Tandem Repeat Polymorphism. The polymorphism consists in the number of times that a nucleotide sequence (in this case, GAAC) is repeated. The upper allele has eight repeats, whereas the lower one has five repeats.

Polymorphisms 4: Single Nucleotide Polymorphisms (SNPs)

A single nucleotide polymorphism or SNP is a sequence of DNA on which humans vary by one and only one nucleotide. Because humans differ by one nucleotide per every thousand or so nucleotides, there are millions of SNPs scattered throughout the human genome.

The major advantage of using SNPs lies in the fact that they can be detected in a highly automated way using DNA chips. This avoids the laborious process of using gel electrophoresis, so many more people and many more loci can be genotyped within a given amount of time.

Genotyping begins with PCR to amplify the region containing an SNP. The resulting DNA is then heated to make it single-stranded and placed onto a special chip that contains single-stranded DNA and microcircuitry. Specialized computer software can then "read" the specific polymorphism.[12] The potential of SNPs is so great that the Human Genome Project has established a special group, the SNP Consortium, to develop the technology and to locate SNPs. To date, the consortium has characterized more than one million SNPs in the human genome.

Polymorphisms 5: Gene Sequencing

Nothing surpasses finding the ordering of the nucleotide sequence for a gene, a technique known as *sequencing*, for the detection of polymorphisms. Although this is the ultimate knowledge for the geneticist and will in time overshadow all other types of polymorphism detection, it is too time-consuming and expensive to be used anywhere but in the more advanced research centers.

Here, we eschew explanation of sequencing procedures for one major reason: The Human Genome Project is devoting large amounts of its resources to automating the process of sequencing, so it is difficult to predict what will be the methods of choice by the time these words hit print. Suffice it to say that within the next few decades, the computerized laboratory robots now available to well-funded genetics laboratories will encounter the dramatic price decreases witnessed by the electronic calculator and, later, the personal computer. Every hospital—as well as many laboratories researching individual differences in human behavior—eventually will have a "DNAnalyzer" sitting in the corner of a room spurting out sequence information about genotypes.

OTHER MOLECULAR TECHNIQUES ●

In Situ Hybridization

In situ (Latin for "on site") hybridization is a technique used with whole chromosomes to (a) find which chromosome a gene of known nucleotide sequence is located on or (b) determine if a section of chromosome has been deleted or duplicated. The technique begins by preparing chromosomes much in the same way that is done for a karyotype (see Chapter 8). The chromosomes are then placed into a solution with a large amount of either radioactively labeled or fluorescent probe.[13] Combinations of chemicals and heat are used to split the double-stranded DNA in the chromosomes into single-stranded DNA, permitting the probe to bind with the DNA. Excess probe is washed away, and the chromosomes are then stained. If a section of a chromosome "lights up," then we know that it has the nucleotide sequence complementary to that of the probe.

Mutational Screening

Once a probe for a section of a protein-coding gene is identified, the curious geneticist can hardly resist the temptation to see if patients with a particular disorder have an irregularity at the locus. A classic example would be schizophrenia and the genes for dopamine receptors. For a long time, it was known that many drugs that diminish the florid hallucinations and delusions of the schizophrenic had important influences on dopamine receptors. Hence, when the gene for a dopamine receptor was first cloned, it was a natural matter to question if schizophrenics differed from nonschizophrenics in this gene.

Except for direct sequencing, many of the techniques outlined above are not suitable for screening the genotypes of patients. For example, RFLPs will detect DNA differences only at a restriction site, and the chances are quite remote that the aberration in the schizophrenic dopamine receptor allele happens to be at just this site. Several other techniques, collectively known as mutational screening, are preferred in this circumstance.

The two most widely developed mutational screens use souped-up versions of electrophoresis to find small and subtle differences in DNA. One technique uses a gel that varies in temperature from the top to the bottom of the gel.[14] As the DNA moves through the gel, the increased temperature will cause it to denature into its single strands, and the resolution of the procedure permits detection of small sequence differences between a patient and a control. Once such a difference is detected, then the patient's DNA is sequenced to find the exact nucleotide variation(s).

The second technique is conceptually identical, with the exception that the gel does not have a temperature gradient.[15] It relies on the fact that small differences in the nucleotide sequence between two strands of DNA can be resolved in different bands on a specialized gel. Again, the patient's DNA is sequenced after a difference is found.

DNA Microarrays

You have probably heard of DNA chips, or "microarrays" as they are termed in the profession. A microarray, which is about the size of a credit card, can be thought of as a glass structure with thousands of tiny "wells" embedded in them. A single-stranded nucleotide sequence of DNA (or RNA) unique to a specific gene is inserted in each well, where it dries against the glass. The chip now has thousands of wells, each one devoted to its own locus.

Now imagine that a neuroscientist removes the hippocampus (a region in the brain) from a number of rats and extracts the mRNA from those neurons. The scientist then bathes the chip in this mRNA. The mRNA from a specific gene will bind to the complementary nucleotide sequence. Hence, if a gene is expressed in the hippocampus, its "well" will have double-stranded nucleotide sequences. If a gene is not expressed in that region of the brain, then its "well" will have only the single-stranded sequence that was initially placed there. Using sophisticated procedures that need not concern us, the research "lights up" those wells with double-stranded nucleotides, leaving the single-stranded wells dark. A special optical scanner then reads the chip. In this way, the researcher can determine which genes are being expressed in the hippocampus.

Now that their cost has diminished, DNA microarrays are being used heavily in medicine. The technique holds considerable promise, but like most novel strategies, it will take time to gather a large body of empirical evidence to evaluate the microarray's usefulness. It is hoped that the technology used to develop and to manufacture these microarrays may also be used to create different types of DNA chips that could greatly simplify other lab techniques, such as detecting polymorphisms.

FINDING THE GENE FOR A TRAIT ●

Having surveyed the various tools and techniques of modern DNA genotyping, we now present the logic of going about the labor-intensive task of actually finding a gene for a trait. The first task is to make certain that the trait has some genetic influence on it. In the case of simple Mendelian disorders, the rarity of the disorder and the risk to different classes of relatives usually are sufficient to implicate a single gene. More complicated methods must be used for complex phenotypes. These complications are treated in later chapters. Here, to keep matters simple, let us assume that we want to locate the gene for a dominant disorder.

The first challenge is to identify the chromosome on which the gene is located. Without knowing either the gene or its product, it is necessary to use a statistical procedure called *linkage analysis* to achieve this goal. Linkage begins with a host of genetic loci called *markers* or *marker loci*. A marker locus is a polymorphic locus with a known location on a chromosome. Linkage does not try to locate the precise position of the disease gene; rather, it tries to identify which marker loci are close to the disease gene. In this way, a rough area of a particular chromosome will be targeted for further analysis. With current linkage maps, a disease gene can be located to anywhere within 1Mb (million base pairs) to 2Mb of its exact location. The major advantage of new technology is that it has greatly expanded the number of polymorphic loci that can be used as markers in a linkage study. Linkage is treated in greater detail in Chapter 10.

Before the human genome was fully sequenced, positive linkage findings were followed up by a procedure called *positional cloning* or *gene walking* to identify the location of the disease gene.[16] Because the actual DNA sequence is now known, contemporary researchers power up their computers and download the nucleotide sequence for the region with the positive linkage. They then try to locate genes within this region by looking for promoter regions, initiation codons, stop codons, etc.

ADVANCED TOPICS: HOW THE ●
HUMAN GENOME WAS SEQUENCED

The descriptions of molecular genetic techniques given above liberally omitted many important steps in order to focus on conceptual issues. In this section, the major technique for sequencing DNA in the Human Genome Project is described in some detail. It can help to give you an appreciation of the laboratory techniques used in modern molecular genetics.

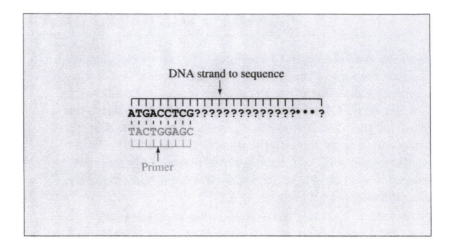

Figure 7.6   Dideoxy Sequencing. The procedure begins with a large number of single-stranded DNA molecules that we want to sequence. A primer (a short, single-stranded sequence of nucleotides) is added to the "soup." To do this, we must already know the beginning nucleotide sequence of the DNA strand that we want to sequence. The primer will bind with the beginning of the DNA molecule that we wish to sequence.

As with all human molecular techniques, sequencing begins with biological material, almost always blood. Through a series of steps that need not concern us, the DNA from the blood cells is extracted and purified. A very small sample of this DNA is then used for analysis.

The physical process of extraction and purification breaks the DNA at large numbers of random places. Even though many breaks are made, very long fragments of DNA—too long to work with—still remain. Hence, the DNA is often bathed with a restriction enzyme to cut it into fragments of more manageable size. PCR is then used to obtain a large amount of DNA for the region to be sequenced.

The first steps in sequencing are the same as those in PCR (see Figure 7.6). The DNA is heated so that the double-stranded helix breaks apart into two single strands (a process called *denaturing*). Then a primer—the identical one used in the PCR—is added. This primer is a small section of single-stranded nucleotides that will bind with its complementary section of DNA that was previously amplified in the PCR.

The next step is to synthesize the rest of the double-stranded DNA, starting with the primer. Essentially, this is the same process as DNA replication, but here it is performed in the test tube instead of the cell nucleus. The two

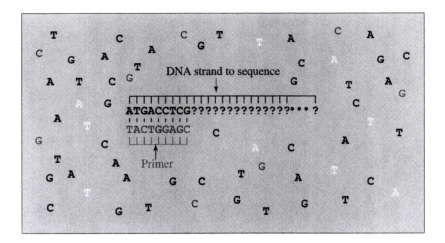

Figure 7.7   Addition of Nucleotide "Alphabet Soup." Next, add nucleotide "alphabet soup." Two types of nucleotides are in the soup. The first type consists of ordinary nucleotides, depicted in this figure as the dark letters A, T, C, and G. The second type is composed of special nucleotides called *dideoxy nucleotides* that have two important properties. First, they will halt the synthesis of the DNA strand whenever they are incorporated into it. Second, they will fluoresce when viewed under appropriate lighting conditions, but each nucleotide is "color-coded." Although the dideoxy nucleotides are shaded in this figure, dideoxy adenine (A) will fluoresce as green, thymine (T) as yellow, cytosine (C) as blue, and guanine (G) as red.

major ingredients for replication are (a) a large number of free nucleotides and (b) a polymerase enzyme that will build the chain.

Figure 7.7 shows the DNA with its nucleotide "soup." The majority of nucleotides in the soup have the same chemical composition as the nucleotides in ordinary DNA—these are the dark letters in Figure 7.7. The clever trick in this step of the process is the addition of a small amount of specially engineered nucleotides (called *dideoxy nucleotides*) that have two key features. The first is that these nucleotides are chain terminating. That is, whenever one of these special nucleotides gets entered into the chain, the process of building the double helix stops dead in its tracks. The second important property is that each special nucleotide is "color-coded" through a chemical tag so that it will fluoresce into a specific color when exposed to the appropriate light conditions. Each type of these special nucleotides is given a different color— for example, green for adenine, yellow for thymine, and so on.

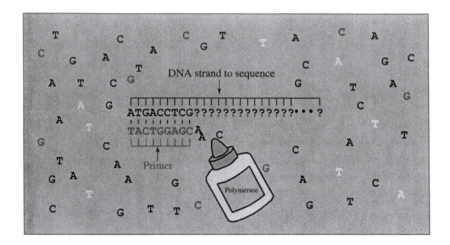

Figure 7.8   Addition of the Enzyme DNA Polymerase to the Soup. This enzyme will "grab" free nucleotides—either regular nucleotides or dideoxy nucleotides—and add them to the left-hand side of the primer strand.

Next, a large number of polymerase molecules are added (Figure 7.8). The polymerase is a complicated enzyme that ordinarily acts to replicate DNA in the cell after the hydrogen bonds are split and the double helix is separated into two single strands. To imbue polymerase with a sentience that it really lacks, one could say that the molecule grabs free nucleotides, inspects the next nucleotide in the single-stranded chain, and then "glues" the appropriate nucleotide partner into the other DNA strand. For example, if the next nucleotide on the single strand is A, then the polymerase will place a T on the growing strand.

The next step is simply to wait and let nature take its course. Because there are millions of single-stranded DNA fragments with primer attached to them, millions of polymerase molecules, and several gazillion nucleotides, many thousands of double-stranded DNA molecules will be synthesized. However, these complementary DNA strands will be of different lengths because of the chance incorporation of the special, dideoxy nucleotides. Whenever one of these special nucleotides is placed into the chain, further synthesis of the DNA strand stops. The net result is many millions of copies of double-stranded DNA, but all of different lengths (Figure 7.9).

If the DNA mixture is now heated, the double-stranded DNA will break down into its single strands, giving a large number of single-stranded DNA molecules of various lengths (Figure 7.10). The next step is to load the

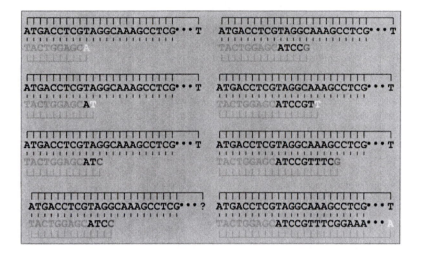

Figure 7.9 Synthesized Strands of Different Lengths. Note that all complementary strands end with a dideoxy nucleotide. A large number of complementary strands will be synthesized by this procedure, but they will be of different lengths. Why? Simple—whenever one of the dideoxy nucleotides (i.e., a shaded letter in this figure) is added, the strand stops dead in its tracks. Hence, the complementary strands of DNA will be of different lengths. This figure gives some examples. Note that all complementary strands end with a dideoxy (shaded) nucleotide.

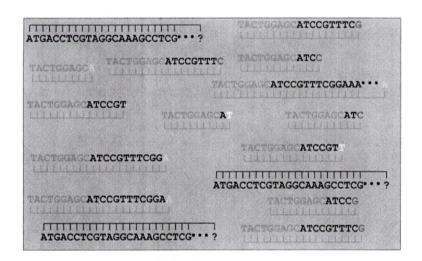

Figure 7.10 The "Soup" After Heating to Denature the DNA. Next, heat the soup to denature the DNA (i.e., make the DNA single-stranded). Note that there will be a large number of strands of different lengths. The longest strands will consist of the DNA that we initially wanted to sequence. The shorter strands will consist of the complementary strands that have a dideoxy nucleotide (i.e., a shaded letter in this figure) incorporated into them.

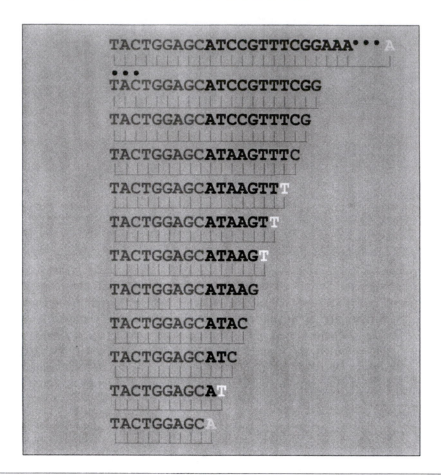

Figure 7.11   A Sample of the "Soup" in an Electrophoretic Gel. Grab a sample of the "soup" and put it into an electrophoretic gel. The electrophoresis will separate the DNA strands according to their size. Long strands (especially the DNA strands that we wanted to sequence in the first place) will not move very far and will remain at the "top" of the gel. The shorter strands that are terminated with a dideoxy nucleotide will migrate toward the bottom of the gel.

single-stranded DNA onto an electrophoretic gel. The new forms of electrophoresis are so sensitive that they can detect the difference between two DNA strands that differ in length by only one nucleotide. The result after electrophoresis is completed is depicted in Figure 7.11, where the fragments would have been loaded at the top of the figure.

When the gel is viewed under the appropriate lighting, the bands will fluoresce. Because the special nucleotides are color-coded, simply reading the sequence of colors gives the nucleotide sequence of the DNA (Figure 7.12).

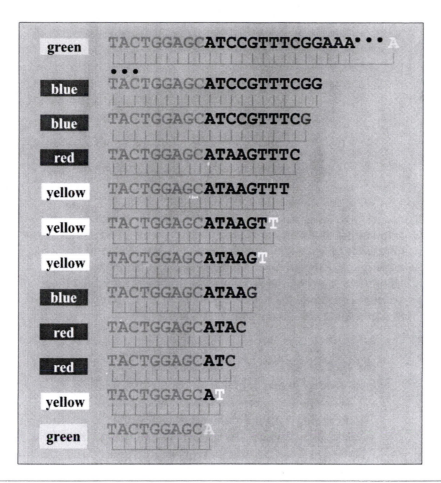

Figure 7.12   A Special Laser Detects Differences in the Spectrum of Ordinary Light Within the Gel to Identify Dideoxy Nucleotides and Interpret the Nucleotide. Place the gel under a special laser that can detect differences in the spectrum of ordinary light. Recall that the dideoxy nucleotides are "color coded." A special optical scanner reads the color of the band on the electrophoretic gel and interprets the nucleotide. Starting at the bottom of this figure, the scanner reads green (and hence, nucleotide A), yellow (T), then red (C), red again (C), then blue (G), and so on.

This type of sequencing procedure is now highly automated. Specialized sequencing machines that are essentially computerized robots perform the automated tasks of timing, heating and cooling, and pipetting mixtures. The newer models also contain a special capillary tube that permits the electrophoresis to be done automatically. Laser lighting and optical scanning allow the colors to be read by a computer instead of a human observer. All

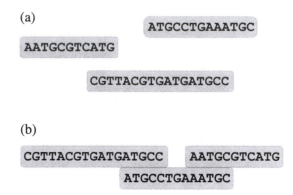

Figure 7.13 Sequencing of the Human Genome by Matching Nucleotide Sequences. Many thousands of individual sequences were generated, and each was entered into a computer. Panel (a) shows three sequences. Sophisticated computer algorithms searched the sequences to find pairs for which the end of one sequence matched the beginning of the other sequence. The result, illustrated in panel (b), gives the nucleotide sequence for very long stretches of DNA.

the data are processed by specialized software that analyzes the sequence, flags areas of uncertainty, and stores the data.

At this point, we now have thousands of small sections of DNA sequenced. The next step is to put these sections together to get the sequence for the whole human genome. The key here reverts back to the original splitting of the DNA into manageable sizes for sequencing. Think of using many different types of restriction enzymes to cut the DNA. Because one type will cut the DNA at one nucleotide sequence but another will cut the DNA at a different sequence, the resulting sections will have some overlap. By testing which sequences overlap with others, one can reconstruct the whole sequence.

Figure 7.13 illustrates the process. Three separate sections of DNA are depicted in panel (a). Two of the sections contain the nucleotide sequence ATGCC, one at the end of its sequence and the other at the beginning of its sequence. Hence, these two must overlap. Two of the sections also contain the nucleotide sequence AATGC, again one at the beginning and the other at the end. These two sections must also overlap. The result of placing these sections together gives panel (b) in Figure 7.13. The problem, then, is analogous to solving a very large, one-dimensional jigsaw puzzle.

In reality, the DNA segments are much larger and the number of overlapping nucleotides is greater than those depicted in Figure 7.13. The DNA nucleotide sequences for the segments are stored in a computer, and powerful search algorithms are used to piece them together.

NOTES ●

1. A plasmid is a very small, circular section of DNA that lives inside a bacterium. Generally, the size of the vector places limits on the length of the DNA segment that can be cloned. Plasmids and viruses, being the smallest, can be used for segments up to 20 kb. Yeast, the largest, can clone vectors of more than one million bases. The procedure for cloning human DNA and inserting the segments into vectors is called *recombinant DNA technology*.

2. The logic of such genetic engineering is straightforward, but there are huge technical issues to surmount before this technique makes it into clinical practice.

3. The process of making double-stranded DNA into single-stranded DNA is termed *denaturing*, and the resultant single-stranded DNA is called *denatured* DNA. The simplest method of denaturing DNA is to heat it.

4. The process of a single-stranded probe binding to its complementary single-stranded DNA sequence is termed *hybridization* or *annealing*.

5. The generic name for this procedure is *autoradiography*. Through a complicated series of steps, the molecules in the gel are transferred onto a special paper that is then placed upon X-ray film. The radioactive probe will expose the X-ray film, revealing its location.

6. The peculiar naming of restriction enzymes can be traced to their initial discovery in bacteria. Hence, the enzymes are named after the species in which they were found and numbered roughly in order of their discovery.

7. The primer for PCR is a short sequence of nucleotides that is specific to the section of DNA to be amplified in the PCR. First, two primers are added. The first will bind to the "right-hand" section of the DNA, while the second, an exact complement to the first, binds to the "left-hand" section. In this way, both single strands of DNA will have the primer binding in the same place. The other specialized feature of the primer is that one side of it is "open ended" in the sense that it is ready to act as a starting point for the synthesis of another strand of DNA.

8. The enzyme is called a *polymerase*, hence the name *polymerase chain reaction*.

9. Before PCR, cells called lymphocytes were extracted from blood and then infected with a specialized virus that would, in essence, immortalize the cells. The cells would then be grown in a culture, and when enough of them were available, DNA would be extracted to do a genotype.

10. Here, I omit several steps to keep the explanation simple. In actuality, after electrophoresis is done, the molecules in the gel are blotted onto a nitrocellulose filter and the filter is then bathed in a solution containing the probe. Excess probe is washed away, and the filter is then placed on top of a sheet of X-ray film. After a suitable time, the radioactive label in the probe will expose the film, revealing the locations of its binding. This whole procedure is called a *Southern blot*.

11. The terms *microsatellite DNA, simple sequence repeat polymorphism (SSR or SSRP)*, and *short tandem repeat polymorphism (STRP)* refer to two, three, or four nucleotides repeated in tandem—e.g., CACACA. The number of repeats is highly variable, and some tandem repeats such as the CA repeat may occur at several thousand different areas in human DNA. *Minisatellite DNA* refers to a sequence of 20 or more nucleotides that may be repeated up to 100 times. The *variable number of tandem repeats (VNTR)* is a technique for detecting minisatellite DNA repeats that are flanked

on either end by restriction sites. Historically, VNTRs were used to construct genetic fingerprints, but in reality any polymorphisms may be used for that purpose.

12. The situation is actually more complicated and involves extension of the DNA strand that hybridizes to the chip using special color-coded nucleotides that stop DNA synthesis.

13. When a fluorescent probe is used, the procedure is called FISH, for fluorescence in situ hybridization. FISH is rapidly becoming the method of choice for in situ hybridization.

14. This procedure is called denaturing gradient gel electrophoresis (DGGE).

15. This technique is known as single-strand conformation polymorphism (SSCP).

16. The term *reverse genetics* was used in the past to refer to positional cloning.

● REFERENCE

Huxley, A. (1936). *Brave new world*. Garden City, NY: Sun Dial Press.

CHAPTER 8

CHROMOSOMES AND CHROMOSOMAL ANOMALIES

INTRODUCTION AND A HISTORICAL CURIOSITY ●

The word *chromosome* is derived from the Greek words *chromos*, meaning color, and *soma*, meaning body. Chromosomes were discovered in the latter half of the 19th century when early cell biologists were busily staining cell preparations and examining them under microscopes. It was soon recognized that the number of chromosomes in the sperm and the egg was half that in an adult organism, and by the 1880s it was conjectured that the chromosomes carried the genetic material. Theorizing about genetics and chromosomes abounded and generated one of the more interesting curiosities in the history of science. Despite the ability to actually see genetic material under the microscope, for more than 20 years early cell biologists were unable to derive the simple laws of segregation and independent assortment postulated by an obscure Austrian monk, Gregor Mendel, who to the best of our knowledge never even saw a chromosome!

131

● THE KARYOTYPE

Over the past century, the technology for staining chromosomes and viewing them under a microscope has dramatically improved and has led to the development of a subfield of genetics called *cytogenetics*—the study of chromosomes and chromosomal aberrations. This science begins with the construction of a *karyotype*, which is literally a picture of stained chromosomes. Construction of a typical karyotype begins with living tissue, usually a particular type of white blood cell called a *lymphocyte*[1], obtained from a blood sample. Lymphocytes are kept alive, undergoing their process of division, in a culture. Then, in a series of complicated steps,[2] they are stained and examined under a microscope. Pictures are taken of the chromosomes under a microscope. The chromosomes are then cut out of the photographs and pasted onto paper in a certain order. Today, the process is greatly aided by computer imaging technology, reducing the need for the tedious photographic and cut-and-paste steps.

Some sections of chromosomes absorb the stain better than others, leading to a characteristic banding pattern for every chromosome. Several different staining techniques are used to generate a karyotype, each one having its advantages and limitations. In clinical cytogenetics, it is not unusual to perform more than one karyotype to determine whether someone has a chromosomal abnormality.

● THE NOMENCLATURE OF CHROMOSOMES

There is a standard terminology (the ISCN, or International System for Human Cytogenetic Nomenclature) used among cytogeneticists for ordering and numbering chromosomes, referring to the bands of a chromosome, and describing any chromosomal abnormalities. Humans have 23 pairs of chromosomes. They are divided into the sex chromosomes (i.e., the X and Y chromosome) and the *autosomes* (i.e., the other 22 pairs). The term *autosomal* frequently is encountered in genetics to refer to a gene or chromosomal anomaly involving an autosome. The autosomes are ordered by length, position of the *centromere* (the region separating the two arms of the chromosome), and banding patterns.

Figure 8.1 provides a schematic for the banding pattern of chromosome 18. The short arm, always placed at the top, is called the *p* arm and the long arm, the *q* arm. Numbering of the bands begins at the centromere and progresses to the terminal of an arm. The number of bands depends upon the type of staining and the particular stage of cell division at which the cells are

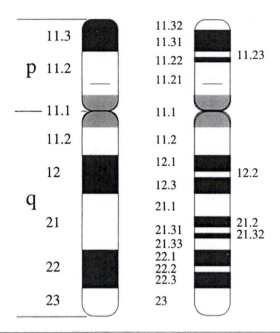

Figure 8.1   A Schematic of Banding Patterns for Human Chromosome 18.

arrested in culture. The high-resolution bands, shown in the chromosome on the right-hand side of Figure 8.1, are derived from cells where the chromosome is more elongated.[3] As the process of cell division progresses, the chromosomes become more compacted and dense, leading to the banding pattern on the left-hand chromosome in Figure 8.1.[4]

Karyotypes are abbreviated by the total number of chromosomes, a comma, and the sex chromosomes of an individual. Thus, the notation 46,XX denotes a normal female; 46,XY, a normal male; and 45,X (or sometimes 45,XO) an individual who has only one X chromosome, a condition that produces Turner's syndrome. Karyotypes followed by a plus sign and then a number indicate *trisomy*, the inheritance of a whole extra chromosome. For example, 47,XX,+21 denotes a female with a trisomy of chromosome 21 that results in Down's syndrome. Similarly, a minus sign followed by a number denotes *monosomy*, or the loss of an entire chromosome.

Bands are denoted by the chromosome number, arm, and band number(s). For example, 15q11-13 denotes bands 11 through 13 of the long arm of chromosome 15. Deletions in this region can result in Prader-Willi syndrome or Angelman syndrome. (See Chapter 4 on parental imprinting.)

There are many other notational devices for chromosomal anomalies, but they are too detailed for our purposes here. The interested reader should consult a standard textbook on medical genetics.

● CHROMOSOMAL ABERRATIONS

Because chromosomal anomalies involve inheritance of extra genetic material or the deletion of important genetic material, the vast majority of them are lethal and result in spontaneous abortion. Nevertheless, conceptions that involve chromosomal anomalies are surprisingly common. About 15% of all recognized pregnancies terminate in a spontaneous abortion, and more than half of these involve identifiable chromosomal abnormalities. The percentage of aberrations in unrecognized pregnancies (i.e., those involving spontaneous abortion before pregnancy testing) is thought to be even higher. Clearly, chromosomal aberrations recognized at or shortly after birth represent the tip of an iceberg from the perspective of all human conceptions.

Three chromosomal aberrations, illustrative for their consequences, are discussed in the following sections.

Down's Syndrome

Down's syndrome involves inheritance of extra chromosomal 21 material. Of the three forms of Down's syndrome, the most common, accounting for more than 95% of cases, is trisomy 21 (the inheritance of a whole extra copy of chromosome 21). The trisomy is an accident of birth and results from one of the gametes—the sperm or the egg, but usually the egg—accidentally getting two copies of chromosome 21 instead of one.[5] Hence, this form of Down's syndrome, like the overwhelming number of chromosomal abnormalities, does not run in families. The second most common form comes from translocation, a phenomenon that occurs when a chromosome breaks and then one of the fragments becomes attached to another chromosome. In Down's syndrome, a section of chromosome 21 breaks and attaches itself to another chromosome, often chromosome 14. The Down's child will then inherit that chromosome with the extra piece of chromosome 21. The third, and least common, form of Down's syndrome is *mosaicism*, accounting for about 1% of cases. In this form, some of the person's cells carry the normal chromosome complement while others carry extra chromosome 21 material. The extent of medical and psychological problems in a person with the mosaic form depends on the percentage of cells with the extra genes from chromosome 21.

The critical region on chromosome 21 that results in Down's syndrome is thought to be on the long arm (i.e., q arm), specifically band 22. Considerable research is being conducted to narrow the region suspected to be problematic and locate the gene(s) responsible for the disorder.

About 1 in 600 to 700 births has Down's syndrome, although the prevalence among pregnancies is much higher. The large number of physical features associated with Down's syndrome include flattening of the nasal bridge; epicanthal folds that give the eyes an Asian appearance;[6] protruding tongue; small ears; simian crease (the "lifeline" on the palm of the hand extends all the way across the palm); unusual fingerprints and toeprints (aka *dermatoglyphics*); and short stature. It is crucially important to recognize that few people with Down's syndrome exhibit all the physical aberrations, and no single physical characteristic is present in all Down's cases. Affected individuals are at high risk for heart defects, leukemia, and problems with immune functioning. Down's cases also have delayed physical development—the Down's child often begins walking 3 to 24 months later than typical for normal children.

The brains of those affected by Down's syndrome also show the typical pathology of Alzheimer's disease,[7] a fact that led researchers to concentrate on chromosome 21 in their search for Alzheimer's genes. About half of Down's cases over 50 years of age show demonstrable signs of dementia (Chapman & Hesketh, 2000). Males are invariably infertile, but there have been cases of females bearing children. Because medical technology can relieve many of the medical complications, people with Down's syndrome can now live into their 50s and 60s, whereas as recently as the 1930s, most died before their 10th birthday.

The major risk factor for having a Down's child is maternal age. Women pregnant in their teens and early twenties have a risk for a Down's child of roughly 1 per 1,000 to 2,000 births. Risk increases gradually, so that by the early thirties it is about 1 in 750. Thereafter, there is a marked increase in risk per year of age, so that by age 45 the risk is almost 1 in 15 births. Many obstetricians now counsel clients who are having children later in life about the risk of conceiving a Down's child. As is true for many issues of reproductive choice, there are sharp differences in opinion among prospective parents. Those not wishing to bear a Down's child usually elect to have amniocentesis or chorion villus sampling performed early in the pregnancy[8] and, if the results are positive, choose to abort the fetus. As a result of elective abortion, the prevalence of Down's syndrome has decreased in the past 25 years.

With few exceptions, Down's cases have mental retardation and learning disabilities (Kessler & Moos, 1973). On average, the degree of mental retardation is moderate, but the extent of cognitive impairment is remarkably variable. A rare Down's case may require institutionalization, but many can be mainstreamed in schools. Outcomes in Down's cases are clearly associated with education and family-background variables (Hauser-Cram et al., 2001; Hay, 1985), and there is some evidence that behavioral problems are less severe in Down's cases than in those not affected by the syndrome but with similar levels of cognitive disability (Chapman & Hesketh, 2000).

With specialized education and training, a significant proportion of Down's cases would be able to hold jobs and be productive members of society. They might not be the neurosurgeons or the appellate judges of our society, but they, like a large number of people with mental retardation, could function well in such jobs as stocking shelves, cleaning up stores after hours, and running errands. The fact that few actually perform such work says more about our society's willingness to train and employ these people than it does about their cognitive capabilities.

Down's cases are real human beings. They do have differences from those born with 46 chromosomes, but they laugh, socialize, and love affection just the same. You and I have acquaintances with rough edges who can be disruptive and overbearing at times. So too can some individuals with Down's syndrome. But you and I also know sweet, disarming people whose pleasantness so impresses us that we silently wonder to ourselves why we cannot be more like that person. You and I will also encounter such people among those with Down's syndrome.

The largest lesson for the behavioral scientist lies in the variability of Down's cases. This lesson will be reinforced time and time again as we examine genetic disorders. The inheritance of a whole extra chromosome 21 can result in a wide range of intellectual abilities, developmental potential, and personality (Cicchetti, 1988).

Turner's Syndrome

Turner's syndrome (TS) involves loss of X chromosomal material in a person with another X chromosome. The most common karyotype, accounting for slightly more than half the cases, is 45,X (also written as 45,XO); the nomenclature signifies that an entire sex chromosome is missing. About two thirds of 45,XO cases inherit their single X chromosome from their mothers (Jacobs, Betts, et al., 1990). Individuals with only part of an X chromosome, those with certain structural alteration in an X, and mosaics make up the remaining TS cases. Although the prevalence of TS is about 1 in 2,500 to 5,000 births, it is the largest detectable chromosomal abnormality among spontaneous abortions. Some authors estimate that more than 99% of Turner conceptions fail to make it to term. About 80% of the Turner's cases with a 45,XO karyotype fail to inherit a chromosome from their fathers.

All Turner's people are phenotypic females.[9] Physically, almost all Turner's women have short stature. Otherwise, the physical characteristics of many Turner's cases are so subtle and blend so well into the normal range that they are indistinguishable to anyone but an experienced professional. These characteristics include obesity (often mild), puffiness (lymphedema) of the hands and feet, unusual shape and positioning of the ears, a broad chest with widely spaced nipples, and a thick, webbed neck.

Like all chromosomal anomalies, TS women are at risk for a variety of medical complications. The most notable of these is irregular development of the ovaries (gonadal dysgenesis). As a result, a girl with Turner's syndrome fails to develop secondary sex characteristics (menstruation, breast development, and pubic hair). Fortunately, TS can be treated with hormone replacement therapy to promote adolescent growth and the development of secondary sex characteristics. The irregular development of the ovaries can also result in infertility. Many people affected by TS elect to have their ovaries surgically removed because they are at high risk for the development of ovarian cancer.

Behaviorally, the most notable feature of TS is its normality. A significant proportion of cases first came to medical attention because of concern over the absence of sexual maturation in the teenage years. This fact alone suggests that behavioral differences between TS and normal girls are not very large.

In terms of personality, there are indeed detectable differences between TS cases and normal girls in levels of maturity, social skills, and self-esteem (McCauley, Ross, Kushner, & Cutler, 1995; Ross, Zinn, & McCauley, 2000), but these differences are small relative to the overlap between the two groups. The differences do not come close to the magnitude of the behavioral differences found between normals and those with Mendelian disorders. In addition, these differences appear to diminish after growth hormone therapy increases the stature of girls affected by TS (Huisman et al., 1993; Siegel, Clopper, & Stabler, 1998).

Cognitively, TS cases have notably lower means than controls on spatial-perceptual tasks (e.g., the ability to mentally rotate a three-dimensional image) and slightly lower averages on quantitative skills. Verbal intelligence is normal. Once again, the magnitude of these differences is small.

Many early clinical descriptions portray women affected by TS as having stereotypically feminine interest patterns (Money, 1970). As children, they preferred frilly dresses to jeans and enjoyed playing with dolls more than climbing trees. However, few systematic data have been gathered on this issue, and it would be unwise to generalize these clinical impressions to the present day, when gender roles have changed.

Despite the lack of an entire chromosome, TS cases grow up to be largely well-adjusted women with a range of academic and occupational outcomes typical of normal women (Aran et al., 1992; Delooz, Van den Berghe, Swillen, Kleczkowska, & Fryns, 1993). Once again, adult TS cases express problems with self-confidence and insecurity, but the differences between them and normal people are very small compared to the marked differences that occur in most genetic syndromes.

The intriguing feature of TS is why it occurs in the first place. In the discussion of Lyonization, we learned that all women are mosaics: One X chromosome is inactivated in every cell of the body. In TS, the single X chromosome is active in every cell. Why, then, should TS women be any different from women with two Xs? At present, speculation rests on those few genes on the X that are still active in the Barr body, but to date no one isolated which of those loci may contribute to TS.

A final—and also controversial—feature of TS is its interplay with genomic imprinting. After the phenomenon of genomic imprinting was described, it was natural to ask if any of the features of TS are associated with the maternal or paternal transmission of the single X chromosome. Some physical features, most notably height, cardiovascular anomalies, and neck-webbing, are associated with maternal inheritance of the X (Chu et al., 1994). The controversial issue arose when Skuse et al. (1997) reported that inheritance of the paternal X in TS was associated with increased cognitive skills and social adjustment. The researchers argued that there might be an imprinted gene on the X chromosome that contributes to social cognition. This locus would be silenced when inherited from the mother but activated when transmitted by the father. This is an exciting development in behavioral genetics, but the initial finding awaits replication in other labs.

XYY Syndrome

In the propagation of a sperm, nondisjunction may occur, so that one gamete inherits two Y chromosomes while the other gamete inherits no sex chromosomes. If the gamete with no sex chromosomes fertilizes an egg, the resulting zygote will be nonviable and will die *in utero* (i.e., within the mother's womb). The gamete with the two Y chromosomes, however, may actually fertilize the egg and produce a viable offspring. The resulting zygote will have the XYY syndrome.

The most striking feature of the XYY syndrome—as indeed is characteristic of most chromosomal anomalies involving the sex chromosomes—is the overwhelming normality of the phenotype. Because XYY individuals have a Y chromosome, they are always males. As a group, they tend to be tall and have several ill-defined learning disabilities as children, but in most other regards they would pass as completely normal individuals throughout life. Their faces are not irregular (as in Down's syndrome), they are not mentally retarded (as in most cases of Fragile X), they do not have peculiar smelling urine (as in phenylketonuria), and they do not have characteristic medical complications.

From a scientific viewpoint, the XYY genotype is remarkable more because of its history in the sociology of science rather than because of any physical or psychological deficits suffered by the individuals with this genotype. Jacobs and colleagues (Jacobs, Brunton et al., 1965) reported an increased frequency of XYY individuals in an institution for dangerous criminal offenders. A number of other research groups reported similar results in other institutions (see Hook, 1973, for a review of the literature of that time). A flurry of speculation following these empirical reports suggested, either overtly or between the lines, that the inheritance of an extra Y chromosome "overmasculinized" XYY individuals and led to a heightening of sex- and gender-stereotypical behavior. In the extreme, the XYY male was characterized as being something of a hypermasculinized sexual psychopath particularly prone to violence and rape.

More sober minds of that era—including several of the researchers who reported the initial association between XYY and institutionalization—recognized that prospective longitudinal designs were required to fully characterize the syndrome. Studies of institutional populations fail to sample those XYY males who develop normally. Only the identification of XYY males at birth and longitudinal study of these individuals could resolve the issue.

Several research groups were ready to embark on such an endeavor, but they encountered a strong backlash from other scientists. Because of fears that identifying these boys at birth and labeling them as antisocial might create a self-fulfilling prophecy, research in the United States was effectively stopped in its tracks.

This controversy influenced research in the United States but left the question open for scientists in other countries. Paramount among them was a group in Denmark (Witkin et al., 1976). Because the military draft is compulsory for males in Denmark, these researchers were able to identify virtually the entire male cohort in Denmark by examining draft records. They selected individuals from this cohort who were taller than average (to increase the potential yield of XYY males) and genotyped a random sample of 4,139 of them. Of these, they found 12 XYY men. The researchers then searched the centralized Danish records to find all those of the 4,139 males who were registered for committing a crime. Of the normal men, 9% were so registered, but 5 of the 12 XYY males (42%) were registered. This difference was significant and suggests that XYY males do, in fact, get into trouble with the law more often than do normal males.

A search for the reasons *why* these XYY males were more prone to law-breaking behavior was especially illuminating. They had not been arrested for crimes of murder, rape, and general mayhem that a stereotypic impression of "overtestosteronized" males might imply. Instead, their arrests and convictions were largely due to petty crimes. The authors of the study suggested that this result might be due to a slight depression in the average IQ score of XYY individuals.

Other research on much smaller samples of XYY individuals agrees with this opinion (Gotz, Johnstone, & Ratcliffe, 1999; Robinson, Bender, & Linden, 1990; Theilgaard, 1984). The emerging view is that XYY boys have mild learning problems and mild behavioral problems that might predispose them to act impulsively in certain situations and hence get into contact with law enforcement authorities. It is certainly the case that the picture of the XYY male as a hypervirilized, oversexed, aggressive sociopath has not been confirmed.

In summary, then, two myths about the XYY syndrome must be disputed. The first is that these individuals have some unknown hormonal balance that makes them superaggressive and hypersexual. Although there may be mean differences between XYY and XY males in aggressiveness and sexuality, those mean differences are likely to be small.

The second myth is that XYY males are entirely unremarkable and do not differ in any way from XY males. The available evidence suggests that there are important differences between these groups. The differences are not particularly large, nor are they specific to interpersonal violence, aggression, and rape. Still, some XYY males have mild learning disabilities and may eventually come to the attention of the legal system.

● CHROMOSOMAL MICRODELETIONS

Prader-Willi syndrome, Angelman syndrome, and Williams syndrome are three disorders with behavioral consequences that are caused in most cases by small deletions in a chromosome. In many cases, the deletions are too small to be seen in a karyotype, so in situ hybridization is used for diagnostic purposes. (See Chapter 7 for an explanation of in situ hybridization.) Although these syndromes are discussed as chromosomal anomalies, some may turn out to be single-gene, Mendelian disorders—it is just that the deletion of a large section of DNA is effectively knocking out a critical gene.

Prader-Willi syndrome (PWS) and the Angelman syndrome (AS) illustrate the intriguing phenomenon of genomic imprinting. Both syndromes are caused by a deletion of DNA in the same region of chromosome 15.[10] When the deletion comes from the sperm, PWS results, but when it is inherited maternally, then AS occurs. As you read the descriptions of the syndromes, pay close attention to the striking behavioral differences.

Prader-Willi Syndrome

As for all chromosomal disorders, a number of physical features are associated with PWS.[11] However, the behavioral features associated with PWS are by far more interesting (Dykens & Kasari, 1997; van Lieshout, De Meyer, Curfs, & Fryns, 1998a; van Lieshout, De Meyer, Curfs, Koot, et al., 1998b). By age 3 to 7, PWS children usually develop insatiable appetites (*hyperphagia*) and are doubly disadvantaged because they require fewer calories than normal to gain weight. PWS individuals often spend considerable time foraging for food and sequestering large amounts of it. As a result, life-threatening obesity can result. The customary intervention is to institute an exercise regimen and strict environmental controls to reduce food availability and intake.

Cognitive development is delayed. The average IQ is around 65, and the variance in IQ is reduced—but not markedly so—from that of normals. As a result, PWS can result in anything from severe mental retardation to an IQ well within the low normal range. Other frequent features include *perseveration* (the repeated and often uncontrolled repetition of a phrase or gestures), mild obsessive-compulsive rituals, intolerance of a change in daily routine, and sleep problems (PWS people often require several naps during the day). Although the PWS child is often talkative and friendly, he is especially prone to stubbornness, argumentativeness, irritability, and verbal and physical aggression. Short but very intense tantrums and temper outbursts are common. Although the unruly behavior is sometimes a response to the withholding of food, it can frequently occur without provocation. Many of these behavioral characteristics extend into adulthood (Clarke, Boer, Chung, Sturmey, & Webb, 1996).

Angelman Syndrome

Although there are striking physical symptoms characteristic of AS,[12] the behavioral abnormalities are the most intriguing. The temper, eating disorder, and obesity found in those affected by PWS do not characterize those with Angelman syndrome. Instead, AS cases are marked by hyperactivity, attention problems, unusual happiness, and a failure to speak (Penner, Johnston, Faircloth, Irish, & Williams, 1993; Zori et al., 1992). Like all syndromes, AS differs from normal behavior mostly in mean levels but much less in variance. Hence, there is a wide amount of variability in AS. AS infants often express persistent social smiling as early as the first trimester after birth. Soon they begin to laugh, often uncontrollably, at the proverbial drop of a hat and, in many cases, for no discernible reason.

AS cases exhibit a striking disparity in their understanding versus expression of language. Even as adults, few people with AS have a vocabulary exceeding 10 words, and they often use their few words indiscriminately and without symbolic meaning. For example, the word "mama" may be uttered without any reference to a mother. Higher-functioning people with AS may develop nonverbal communication skills such as pointing, gesturing, and signing, but even here communication is rudimentary. Although formalized IQ and developmental testing usually suggest severe mental retardation, many clinicians are convinced that the communication deficits of AS lead to invalid results on standard tests and underestimate the cognitive ability of people with AS. High-functioning adults with AS enjoy socializing and participate in the daily activities of their families.

Why do laughter and language deficits occur when maternal DNA is missing, whereas obesity and temper present when paternal DNA is missing? No one is certain at present, although remarkable progress in being made in identifying the genes responsible for these syndromes. Converging evidence is implicating the UBE3A[13] gene on chromosome 15 as the source for AS. This gene is turned off when inherited from the father, so when the gene and its surrounding area are deleted in a mutant maternal chromosome, AS results. Evidence for this view comes from some rare AS cases in which the UBE3A gene is completely normal but a mutation in a prompter region effectively turns the gene off.

● CONCLUSION

The brief overview given here does little justice to the large number of different chromosomal aberrations and syndromes that researchers have described. The interested reader is referred to current textbooks on medical genetics as well as to the increasing number of Web sites devoted to these syndromes.

NOTES ●

1. Lymphocytes are actually colorless cells formed in the lymph nodes, in the spleen, and in a few other organs. The two major types of lymphocytes, B cells and T cells, play an important role in the immune response.

2. The cells are kept in a culture that promotes cell division. After 48 to 72 hours, a chemical such as colchicine or colcemid is added to arrest cell division at a crucial stage (prophase or metaphase), when the chromosomes are especially condensed. The cells are placed onto a slide, and a low salt (hypotonic) solution is added to swell and eventually rupture the cells. They are then stained and photographed.

3. Here the cells are in the prophase stage of cell division.

4. Denser banding comes from chromosomes in the metaphase stage.

5. This is called nondisjunction—the phenomenon whereby a pair of chromosomes fails to segregate, each into its own gamete.

6. In earlier times, the term *Mongolism* was used to describe Down's syndrome because of the appearance of the eyes of afflicted people.

7. Neurofibrillary tangles (i.e., the neurofibers that assist in transporting molecules from the cell body to the dendrites become tangled) and plaques (small, disk-shaped formations in the neurons).

8. Usually performed between week 15 and week 17 of pregnancy, amniocentesis involves the insertion of a needle into the sac surrounding the fetus and extraction of a fluid sample (amniotic fluid from the amniotic sac). A karyotype is then done on the fetal cells harvested from the fluid. Chorion villus sampling is quite similar but involves a biopsy of the developing placenta and can be performed earlier than amniocentesis, usually between week 9 and week 12 of pregnancy.

9. The natural course of sex development in humans is female. It takes the presence of a Y chromosome to masculinize a developing fetus.

10. The precise area of deletion is 15q11-13 and consists of about 3.5 million nucleotides. Chromosomal rearrangements and certain gene mutations in this area may also result in these syndromes (Nichols & Knepper, 2001; Repetto, 2001).

11. PWS is characterized by a lack of muscle tone (*hypotonia* or "floppy baby"), incomplete sex development at birth (*hypogonadism*, or small penis and undescended testes in males and small clitoris and labial folds in females), almond-shaped eyes, downturned mouth, thin upper lip, small chin, and short stature. The hypotonia is present at birth and is often associated with suckling problems that can necessitate tube feeding. It typically improves after 1 or 2 years but seldom reaches normal levels.

12. AS cases often appear normal at birth, with the disorder being diagnosed after the child fails to develop appropriately. The physical characteristics include small head circumference (*microcephaly*), inability to focus the eyes properly (*strabismus*), and wide mouth with widely spaced teeth. Pigmentation in both PWS and AS is underdeveloped (*hypopigmentation*), often resulting in fair colored hair and eyes.

13. UBE3A is the ubiquitin-protein ligase E3A gene.

● REFERENCES

Aran, O., Galatzer, A., Kauli, R., Nagelberg, N., Robicsek, Y., & Laron, Z. (1992). Social, educational and vocational status of 48 young adult females with gonadal dysgenesis. *Clinical Endocrinology, 36*, 405-410.

Chapman, R. S., & Hesketh, L. J. (2000). Behavioral phenotype of individuals with Down syndrome. *Mental Retardation and Developmental Disability Research Reviews, 6*, 84-95.

Chu, C. E., Donaldson, M. D., Kelnar, C. J., Smail, P. J., Greene, S. A., Paterson, W. F., et al. (1994). Possible role of imprinting in the Turner phenotype. *Journal of Medical Genetics, 31*, 840-842.

Cicchetti, D. (1988). The organization and coherence of socioemotional, cognitive, and representational development: Illustrations through a developmental psychopathology perspective on Down syndrome and child maltreatment. *Nebraska Symposium on Motivation, 36*, 259-366.

Clarke, D. J., Boer, H., Chung, M. C., Sturmey, P., & Webb, T. (1996). Maladaptive behaviour in Prader-Willi syndrome in adult life. *Journal of Intellectual Disability Research, 40*, 159-165.

Delooz, J., Van den Berghe, H., Swillen, A., Kleczkowska, A., & Fryns, J. P. (1993). Turner syndrome patients as adults: A study of their cognitive profile, psychosocial functioning and psychopathological findings. *Genetic Counseling, 4*, 169-179.

Dykens, E. M., & Kasari, C. (1997). Maladaptive behavior in children with Prader-Willi syndrome, Down syndrome, and nonspecific mental retardation. *American Journal of Mental Retardation, 102*, 228-237.

Gotz, M. J., Johnstone, E. C., & Ratcliffe, S. G. (1999). Criminality and antisocial behaviour in unselected men with sex chromosome abnormalities. *Psychological Medicine, 29*, 953-962.

Hauser-Cram, P., Warfield, M. E., Shonkoff, J. P., Krauss, M. W., Sayer, A., & Upshur, C. C. (2001). Children with disabilities: A longitudinal study of child development and parent well-being. *Monographs of the Society for Research in Child Development, 66*, 1-114.

Hay, D. A. (1985). *Essentials of behavior genetics*. London: Blackwell.

Hook, E. B. (1973). Behavioral implications of the human XYY genotype. *Science, 179*, 139-150.

Huisman, J., Slijper, F. M., Sinnema, G., Akkerhuis, G. W., Brugman-Boezeman, A., Feenstra, J., et al. (1993). Psychosocial effects of two years of human growth hormone treatment in Turner syndrome. *Hormone Research, 39*, 56-59.

Jacobs, P. A., Betts, P. R., Cockwell, A. E., Crolla, J. A., Mackenzie, M. J., Robinson, D. O., et al. (1990). A cytogenetic and molecular reappraisal of a series of patients with Turner's syndrome. *Annals of Human Genetics, 54*, 209-223.

Jacobs, P. A., Brunton, M., Melville, M. M., Brittain, R. P., & McClemont, W. F. (1965). Aggressive behavior, mental sub-normality and the XYY male. *Nature, 208*, 1351-1352.

Kessler, S., & Moos, R. H. (1973). Behavioral aspects of chromosomal disorders. *Annual Review of Medicine, 24*, 89-102.

McCauley, E., Ross, J. L., Kushner, H., & Cutler, G., Jr. (1995). Self-esteem and behavior in girls with Turner syndrome. *Journal of Developmental and Behavioral Pediatrics, 16*, 82-88.

Money, J. (1970). Behavior genetics: Principles, methods and examples from XO, XXY and XYY syndromes. *Seminars in Psychiatry, 2*, 11-29.

Nichols, R. D., & Knepper, J. L. (2001). Genome organization, function, and imprinting in Prader-Willi and Angelman syndromes. *Annual Review of Genomics and Human Genetics, 2*, 153-175.

Penner, K. A., Johnston, J., Faircloth, B. H., Irish, P., & Williams, C. A. (1993). Communication, cognition, and social interaction in the Angelman syndrome. *American Journal of Medical Genetics, 46*, 34-39.

Repetto, G. M. (2001). Genomic imprinting and human chromosome 15. *Biological Research, 34*, 141-145.

Robinson, A., Bender, B. G., & Linden, M. G. (1990). Summary of clinical findings in children and young adults with sex chromosome anomalies. *Birth Defects Original Article Series, 26*, 225-228.

Ross, J., Zinn, A., & McCauley, E. (2000). Neurodevelopmental and psychosocial aspects of Turner syndrome. *Mental Retardation and Developmental Disabilities Research Reviews, 6*, 135-141.

Siegel, P. T., Clopper, R., & Stabler, B. (1998). The psychological consequences of Turner syndrome and review of the National Cooperative Growth Study psychological substudy. *Pediatrics, 102*, 488-491.

Skuse, D. H., James, R. S., Bishop, D. V., Coppin, B., Dalton, P., Aamodt-Leeper, G., et al. (1997). Evidence from Turner's syndrome of an imprinted X-linked locus affecting cognitive function. *Nature, 387*, 705-708.

Theilgaard, A. (1984). A psychological study of the personalities of XYY- and XXY-men. *Acta Psychiatrica Scandinavica, 315*(Suppl.), 1-133.

van Lieshout, C. F., De Meyer, R. E., Curfs, L. M., & Fryns, J. P. (1998a). Family contexts, parental behaviour, and personality profiles of children and adolescents with Prader-Willi, Fragile-X, or Williams syndrome. *Journal of Child Psychology and Psychiatry and Allied Disciplines, 39*, 699-710.

van Lieshout, C. F., De Meyer, R. E., Curfs, L. M., Koot, H. M., & Fryns, J. P. (1998b). Problem behaviors and personality of children and adolescents with Prader-Willi syndrome. *Journal of Pediatric Psychology, 23*, 111-120.

Witkin, H. A., Mednick, S. A., Schulsinger, F., Bakkestrom, E., Christiansen, K. O., Goodenough, D. R., et al. (1976). Criminality in XYY and XXY men. *Science, 193*, 547-555.

Zori, R. T., Hendrickson, J., Woolven, S., Whidden, E. M., Gray, B., & Williams, C. A. (1992). Angelman syndrome: Clinical profile. *Journal of Child Neurology, 7*, 270-280.

CHAPTER 9

MENDEL

In the next three chapters, we examine the *quantitative* and the *statistical* impact of genes on observable phenotypes. The impact of this influence on genetics cannot be underestimated. Indeed, almost 100 years before the DNA molecule was characterized by James Watson and Francis Crick, the quantitative implications of the impact of genes were inferred by an obscure Austrian monk. The mathematical regularities of the transmission of these "hereditary factors" (the word "gene" was not coined at that time) allowed this long-ignored monk to create a paradigm shift in science. In essence, he said, hereditary factors did not blend, as the prevailing thought of the day said they did. Instead of taking a dab of yellow here and a dab of green there to produce blue, the hereditary factors were discrete. We inherit the hereditary factor of yellow and the hereditary factor of green. Even though we appear blue, we pass one of these discrete factors—yellow or blue—to our offspring.

Table 9.1   Mendel's Three Laws of Heredity

Law	Explanation
1. Dominance	When two different hereditary factors are present, one will be dominant and the other will be recessive
2. Segregation	Hereditary factors are discrete. Each organism has two discrete hereditary factors and passes one of these, at random, to an offspring
3. Independent assortment	The discrete hereditary factors for one trait (e.g., color of pea) are transmitted independently of the hereditary factors for another trait (e.g., shape of pea).

● GREGOR MENDEL

In the middle of the 19th century, an Austrian monk, Gregor Mendel, toiled for almost 10 years systematically breeding pea plants and recording his results. Like many of his contemporaries, Mendel was intrigued with heredity and wanted to uncover the laws behind it. In 1864, just 5 years after the publication of Charles Darwin's *Origin of Species*, Mendel presented his results to the local natural history society in Brunn,[1] which published his paper in its proceedings 1 year later.

To be honest, many historians surmise that Mendel's presentation and his paper were quite boring. They were crammed with numbers and percentages related to green versus yellow peas, round versus wrinkled peas, axial versus terminal inflorescences, yellow versus green pods, red-brown versus white seed coats, and so on. To make matters worse, many of these traits were cross-tabulated. Hence, his audience had to listen to or read numbers concerning round and yellow versus wrinkled and yellow versus round and green versus wrinkled and green pea plants. Perhaps as a consequence of this, no one paid attention to Mendel, and the basic principles of genetics that he elucidated in his presentation and subsequent paper went unrecognized until shortly after the turn of the 20th century.

Mendel postulated three laws: (a) dominance, (b) segregation, and (c) independent assortment. Table 9.1 presents these laws and their definitions. The following sections examine some of Mendel's actual data and try to deduce how Mendel may have arrived at them.

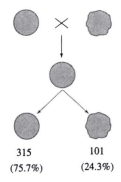

Figure 9.1   Mendel's Data From a Cross of Round and Wrinkled Peas.

MENDEL'S LAWS: DOMINANCE ●

Figure 9.1 presents the results of one of Mendel's breeding experiments.[2] Mendel began with two lines of yellow peas that always bred true.[3] One line consistently gave round peas, whereas the second always gave wrinkled peas. Mendel cross bred these two strains by fertilizing the round strain with pollen from the wrinkled strain and fertilizing the wrinkled strain with pollen from the round plants. The seeds from the next generation were all round. At this point, Mendel probably asked himself, "Whatever happened to the hereditary information about making a wrinkled pea?"

Mendel did not stop at this point. He cross-fertilized all the pea plants in this generation with pollen from other plants in the same generation. When their progeny matured, he noticed a very curious phenomenon—wrinkled peas reappeared! How could this happen when all the parents of these plants had round seeds? Obviously, the middle generation in Figure 9.1, despite being all round, still possessed the hereditary information for making a wrinkled pea, but somehow that information was not being expressed. Hence, Mendel surmised, some hereditary factors are dominant to other hereditary factors. In this case, a round shape is dominant to a wrinkled shape.

MENDEL'S LAWS: SEGREGATION ●

Figure 9.1 gives the number and percentage of round and wrinkled peas in the third generation. There were just about three round seeds for every wrinkled seed. This ratio of three plants with the dominant hereditary factor to

Table 9.2   Illustration of Mendel's Law of Segregation for Round (R) and Wrinkled (W) Hereditary Factors in Peas

Male Parent		Female Parent			
		R Information ½		W information ½	
R information	½	RR	¼	RW	¼
W information	½	WR	¼	WW	¼

every one plant with the recessive factor kept coming up time and time again in Mendel's breeding program. There were 3.01 yellow seeds for every green seed; 3.15 colored flowers to every white flower; and 2.95 inflated pods to every constricted pod. Mendel must have spent considerable time cogitating over a sound, logical reason why this 3:1 ratio should always appear.

To answer this question, let us return to Figure 9.1 and consider the middle generation in the light of the law of dominance. Obviously, because they are themselves round, these plants must have the hereditary information to make a round pea. They must also have the hereditary information to make a wrinkled pea because one quarter of their progeny are wrinkled. Mendel's stroke of genius lay in applying elementary probability theory to this generation—what would one expect if these two types of hereditary information were discrete and combined at random in the next generation?

The situation for this is depicted in Table 9.2, where R denotes the hereditary information for making a round pea and W, the information for a wrinkled pea. The probability that a plant in the middle generation transmits the R information is simply the probability of a heads on the flip of a coin or ½. Thus, the probability of transmitting the W information is also ½. Hence, the probability that the male parent transmits the R information and the female parent also transmits the R information is ½ × ½ = ¼. All the progeny that receive two Rs will be round. Similarly, the probability that the male transmits R while the female transmits W is also ¼, as is the probability that the male transmits W and the female, R. Thus, ¼ × ¼ = ½ of the offspring will have both the R and the W information. They, however, will all be round because R dominates W. Thus far, ¾ of all the offspring will be round.

The only other possibility is that of both the male and female plant transmitting W. The probability of this is also ½ × ½ = ¼; thus, the remaining ¼ of the progeny will receive only the hereditary information on making a wrinkled pea and consequently will be wrinkled themselves. "Voila!" Mendel must have thought, "The hereditary factors are *discrete*. Every plant has two hereditary factors and passes only one, at random, to an offspring."

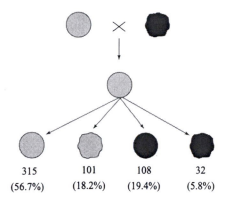

315
(56.7%)

101
(18.2%)

108
(19.4%)

32
(5.8%)

Figure 9.2   Mendel's Data for Two Traits Simultaneously Analyzed—Pea Shape (Round Versus Wrinkled) and Pea Color (Yellow [Light] Versus Green [Dark]). The type of design is called a dihybrid cross.

MENDEL'S LAWS: INDEPENDENT ASSORTMENT ●

A scientist who achieves success using one particular technique nearly always uses that technique in the initial phase of solving the next similar problem. Mendel probably was no exception. His success in using the mathematics of probability to develop the law of segregation undoubtedly influenced his approach to his next problem, that of dealing with two different traits at once.

Figure 9.2 gives the results of his breeding round, yellow plants with wrinkled green plants and keeping track of both color and shape in the subsequent generations. The middle generation is all yellow and round. Hence, yellow is the dominant hereditary factor for color; and round, as we have seen, is the dominant for shape. The next generation is both confirmatory and troubling. First, there are a total of 423 round and 133 wrinkled peas, giving a ratio of 3.18 to 1, very close to the 3:1 ratio expected from the laws of dominance and segregation. Also confirming these predictions is the 2.97 to 1 ratio of yellow to green peas.

This generation, however, has combinations of traits not seen in either of the previous generations—wrinkled, yellow peas and round, green peas. What can explain this? Once again, the mathematics of probability gave a solution. Mendel's hypothesis was that the hereditary factors for pea color are independent of the hereditary factors for pea shape. The mathematical calculations for deriving the expected number of plants of each type in the third generation are more complicated than those for deriving the law of segregation, but they follow the same basic principles of probability theory.

Table 9.3   The Four Types of Gametes From the Middle Generation of Figure 9.2 if the Hereditary Factors for Shape Assort Independently of Those for Color

Shape Information		*Color Information*			
		Y	*½*	*G*	*½*
R	*½*	*RY*	¼	*RG*	¼
W	*½*	*WY*	¼	*WG*	¼

Table 9.4   Expected Frequencies of Peas in the Third Generation if Pea Shape and Pea Color Assort Independently

	Female Gametes			
Male Gametes	*RY* = ¼	*WY* = ¼	*RG* = ¼	*WG* = ¼
RY = ¼	*RR,YY* (round, yellow)	*RW,YY* (round, yellow)	*RR,YG* (round, yellow)	*RW,YG* (round, yellow)
WY = ¼	*WR,YY* (round, yellow)	*WW,YY* (wrinkled, yellow)	*WR,YG* (round, yellow)	*WW,YG* (wrinkled, yellow)
RG = ¼	*RR,GY* (round, yellow)	*RW,GY* (round, yellow)	*RW,GG* (round, green)	*RW,GG* (round, green)
WG = ¼	*WR,GY* (round, yellow)	*WW,GY* (wrinkled, yellow)	*WR,GG* (round, green)	*WW,GG* (wrinkled, green)

NOTE: Each cell has a probability of occurrence of 1/16.

The middle generation will have four discrete hereditary factors, the *R* and *W* factors that we have already discussed and the *Y* (for yellow) and *G* (for green) factors that determine color. If the hereditary factors for shape are independent of those for color, then the plants in the second generation can give any of four different combinations to their offspring. The combinations are *RY*, *RG*, *WY*, and *WG*, and the probability of passing on any single combination is ¼ (see Table 9.3).

Table 9.4 gives the results of these four types of gametes, as we now call them, coming together in the offspring in the third generation. Nine sixteenths of the offspring are expected to be round and yellow, three sixteenths will be round and green, another three sixteenths will be wrinkled and yellow, and the remaining one sixteenth should be wrinkled and green. Indeed, this expected 9:3:3:1 ratio is very close to that observed by Mendel. Were this to happen today, Mendel would have high-fived all the assistants who helped him to plant and to count the peas (and probably to harvest and dine on them as well) and dashed off a paper to *Science* or *Nature*. Instead, he patiently tabulated his results and embarked on the journey to Brunn.

MENDEL'S LAWS: EXCEPTIONS ●

The majority of seminal scientific discoveries never get things completely right. Instead, they turn science in a different direction and make us think about problems in a different way. It often takes years of effort to fill in the fine points and find the exceptions to the rule. Mendel's laws follow this pattern. None of the three laws is completely correct. We know now that some hereditary factors are codominant, not completely dominant, to others; one can cross red with white petunias and get pink offspring, not red or white offspring, as Mendel would have predicted. We also know that the law of segregation is not always true in its literal sense. In humans, the X and the Y chromosomes are indeed discrete, but they are not passed along entirely at random from a father— slightly more boys than girls are conceived. We also know that not all hereditary factors assort independently. Those that are located close together on the same chromosome tend to be inherited as a unit, not as independent entities.

These exceptions are individual trees within the forest. Mendel's great accomplishment was to orient science toward the correct forest. Hereditary factors do not "blend," as Darwin thought; they are discrete and particulate, as Mendel postulated. As Mendel conjectured, we have two hereditary factors, one of which we received from our father and the other from our mother. We do not have 23 hereditary factors, one on each chromosome, as early cell biologist August Weissman theorized. Furthermore, two different hereditary factors, provided that they are far enough away on the same chromosome or located on entirely different chromosomes, are transmitted independently of each other. Mendel's basic concepts provided a paradigm shift and sparked the nascent science of genetics at the turn of the 20th century, an achievement for which the humble monk was never recognized during his life.

APPLICATION OF MENDEL'S LAWS: ●
THE PUNNETT RECTANGLE

In high school biology, many of you were exposed to a Punnett square. Indeed, we have seen examples of the Punnett square in Tables 9.2, 9.3, and 9.4. High school has also taught us that a square is a specific case of a more

Table 9.5   Steps in Constructing a Punnett Rectangle

Step	Operation
1.	Write down the genotypes of the mother's gametes along with their associated probabilities. These will label the rows of the rectangle.
2.	Write down the genotypes of the father's gametes along with their associated probabilities. These will label the columns of the rectangle. (Naturally, it is possible to switch the steps—mother's gametes forming the columns and father's gametes, forming the rows—without any loss of generality.)
3.	The genotype for each cell within the rectangle is the genotype of the row gamete united with the genotype of the column gamete. Enter these for all cells in the rectangle.
4.	The probability for each cell within the rectangle equals the probability of the row gamete multiplied by the probability of the column gamete. Enter these for all cells in the rectangle.
5.	Make a table of the unique genotypes of the offspring and their probabilities. If a genotype occurs more than once within the cells of the Punnett rectangle, then add the cell probabilities together to get the probability of that genotype.
6.	If needed, make a table of the unique phenotypes and their probabilities from the table of genotypes. If two or more genotypes in the genotypic table give the same phenotype, then add the probabilities of those genotypes to get the probability of the phenotype.

general geometric form, the rectangle. We can now generalize and develop the concept of a Punnett rectangle to apply Mendel's concepts of heredity to calculating the genotypes and phenotypes of offspring from a given mating type. The formal rules for constructing a Punnett rectangle are given in Table 9.5. They should be studied carefully.

The Punnett Rectangle: An Example

As an example of this technique, consider the mating of a woman who has genotype AO at the ABO blood group locus and a man who also has genotype AO. From Step 1, the mother's egg can contain either allele A (with a probability of ½) or allele O (also with a probability of ½). From Step 2, the father's sperm may contain either A or O, each with a probability of ½. The row and column labels for this Punnett rectangle are given in Table 9.6.

Step 3 requires entry of the offspring genotypes into the cells of the rectangle. The upper left cell represents the fertilization of mother's A egg by

Table 9.6   Setting Up the Row and Column Labels for a Punnett Rectangle for a Mating Between an *AO* Mother and an *AO* Father

	Father's Gametes and Probabilities	
Mother's Gametes and Probabilities	*A* = ½	*O* = ½
A = ½ *O* = ½		

Table 9.7   Punnett Rectangle for a Mating Between an *AO* Mother and an *AO* Father

	Father's Gametes and Probabilities	
Mother's Gametes and Probabilities	*A* = ½	*O* = ½
A = ½ *O* = ½	AA = ¼ OA = ¼	AO = ¼ OO = ¼

father's *A* sperm, so the genotypic entry is *AA*. The upper right cell represents the fertilization of mother's *A* egg by father's *O* sperm, giving genotype *AO*. Following these rules, the genotypes for the lower left and lower right cells are, respectively, *OA* and *OO*.

The probabilities for Step 4 require us to multiply the row probability by the column probability. For the upper left cell, the row probability is ½ and the column probability is also ½ , so the cell probability is ½ × ½ = ¼. It is obvious that each cell for this example will have a probability of ¼. The completed Punnett rectangle is given in Table 9.7.

In Steps 5 and 6, we must complete a table of genotypes and, if needed, phenotypes. To complete Step 5, we note that there are three unique genotypes in the cells of the Punnett rectangle—*AA*, *AO*, and *OO*. Genotypes *AA* and *OO* occur only once, so the probability of each of these genotypes is ¼. Genotype *AO*, on the other hand, occurs twice, once in the upper right cell and again in the lower left. Consequently, the probability of the heterozygote *AO* is the sum of these two cell probabilities or ¼ + ¼ = ½. Table 9.8 gives the genotypes and their frequencies.

Step 6 requires calculation of the phenotypes from the genotypes. Because allele *A* is dominant in the ABO blood system, both genotypes *AA* and *AO* will have phenotype *A*. The probability of phenotype *A* will be the

Table 9.8 Expected Offspring Genotypes and Their Probabilities From an *AO* by *AO* Mating

Genotype	Probability
AA	¼
AO	½
OO	¼

Table 9.9 Expected Offspring Genotypes and Their Probabilities From an *AO* by *AO* Mating

Genotype	Probability	Phenotype	Probability
AA	¼	A	¾
AO	½	O	¼
OO	¼		
	Sum = 1.0		Sum = 1.0

sum of the probabilities for these two genotypes, or ¼ + ½ = ¾. Genotype *OO* will have phenotype *O*. Because genotype *OO* occurs only once, the probability of phenotype *O* is simply ¼. The complete table of genotypic and phenotypic frequencies is given in Table 9.9.

The column probabilities should always sum to 1.0. Although this is visually obvious for the present example, it is recommended that the sums be calculated to avoid errors, especially for more complicated problems.

The Punnett Rectangle: A Two-Locus Example

The logic of the Punnett rectangle may be applied to genotypes at more than one locus. The only requirement is that all the loci are unlinked, that is, no two loci are located close together on the same chromosome. (Later, we deal with the case of Punnett rectangles with linked loci.) The Punnett rectangle for two loci will be illustrated by calculating traditional blood types.

Traditional blood-typing for transfusions uses phenotypes at two genetic loci. The first is the ABO locus, and the second is the Rhesus locus. Although the genetics of the Rhesus locus are actually quite complicated, we will assume that there are only two alleles, a "plus" or + allele and a "minus" or – allele.[4] The + allele is dominant to the – allele, so the two Rhesus phenotypes are + and –. The blood types used for transfusions and blood donations

Table 9.10 Maternal Gametes From a Mother Who Is *OO/+−*

	Rhesus Allele and Probability	
ABO Allele and Probability	+ = ½	− = ½
O = 1.0	*O*+ = ½	*O*− = ½

concatenate the ABO phenotype with the Rhesus phenotype, giving phenotypes such as *A*+, *B*−, and *AB*+. What are the expected frequencies for the offspring of a father with genotype *AO/+−* (read "genotype *AO* at the ABO locus and genotype +− at the Rhesus locus") and a mother who is genotype *OO/+−*?

The trick to the problem of two unlinked loci is to go through the Punnett rectangle steps three times. In the first pass, the Punnett rectangle is used to obtain the genotypes for the maternal gametes. The second pass calculates the paternal gametes, and the third and final pass uses the results from the first two passes to get the offspring genotypes.

The mother in this problem has genotype *OO+−*. Because the ABO and Rhesus loci are unlinked, the probabilities for the ABO locus are independent of those for the Rhesus locus. This permits us to use a Punnett rectangle to derive the maternal gametes. The rows of the rectangle are labeled by the contribution to the maternal egg from mother's ABO alleles and their probabilities. Here, mother can give only an *O*. Consequently there will be only one row to the rectangle, and it will be labeled *O* and have a probability of 1.0. The columns are labeled by the contribution of mother's Rhesus alleles and their probabilities. In the present case, the columns will be labeled + and −, each with probability ½. The completed Punnett rectangle needed to get the maternal gametes and their probabilities is given in Table 9.10.

From this table, we see that there are two possible maternal gametes, each with a probability of ½. The first has one of mother's *O* alleles at the ABO locus and the + allele at the Rhesus locus, giving gamete *O*+. The second gamete, *O*−, contains one of mother's *O* alleles but her − allele at Rhesus.

The second pass through the Punnett rectangle is used to calculate the father's gametes. His contribution to the gamete from his alleles at the ABO locus may be either allele *A*, with probability ½, or *O*, also with probability ½. Thus, there will be two rows to the father's Punnett rectangle, one labeled *A* and the other labeled *O*, each with probability ½. Like the mother, the father is a heterozygote at Rhesus; hence, the columns for his table will equal those for the maternal table. The Punnett rectangle for the paternal gametes is given in Table 9.11.

Table 9.11 Paternal Gametes From a Father Who Is *AO*/+

	Rhesus Allele and Probability	
ABO Allele and Probability	+ = ½	– = ½
A = ½ *O* = ½		

Table 9.12 ABO Allele and Probabilities

	Father's Gametes and Probabilities			
Mother's Gametes and Probabilities	*A*+ = ¼	*A*– = ¼	*O*+ = ¼	*O*– = ¼
O+ = ½	*AO*/++ = •	*AO*/+– = •	*OO*/++ = •	*OO*/+– = •
O– = ½	*OA*/ –+ = •	*OA*/– – = •	*OO*/–+ = •	*OO*/–– = •

The father has four different paternal gametes, each with a probability of ¼. The first possible gamete carries father's *A* allele at the ABO locus and father's + allele at the Rhesus locus (*A*+). Analogous interpretations apply to the remaining three gametes—*A*–, *O*+, and *O*–.

We may now construct the last Punnett rectangle to find the offspring genotypes and their frequencies. In this rectangle, the rows are labeled by the maternal gametes and their probabilities, whereas the columns are labeled by the paternal gametes and their probabilities. This will give a rectangle with two rows and four columns. The completed rectangle is given in Table 9.12.

From this Punnett rectangle, we can construct the table of expected genotypes, expected phenotypes, and their frequencies. This is given as Table 9.13.

Hence, ⅜ or 37.5% of the offspring are expected to have blood type *A*+, ⅛ or 12.5% will have blood type *A*–, ⅜ or 37.5% will have blood type *O*+, and ⅛ or 12.5% will have blood type *O*–.

The Punnett Rectangle: X-Linked Loci

Genetic females, of course, have two X chromosomes, whereas genetic males have one X chromosome and one Y chromosome. The Y chromosome is much smaller than the X chromosome and contains many

Table 9.13 Expected Offspring Genotypes, Phenotypes, and Probabilities From a Mating of Genotypes *OO/+−* and *AO/+−*

Genotypes	Probability	Phenotypes	Probability
AO/++	●	*A+*	●
AO/+−	¼	*A−*	●
AO/−−	●	*O+*	●
OO/++	●	*O−*	●
OO/+−	¼		
OO/−−	●		

Table 9.14 Punnett Rectangle for a Mating Between an *Aa* Woman and an *a* Man for a Sex-Linked Locus

	Father's Gametes and Probabilities	
Mother's Gametes and Probabilities	**X-a = ½**	**Y = ½**
X-A = ½	*XX-Aa* = ¼	*XY-A* = ¼
X-a = ½	*XX-aa* = ¼	*XY-a* = ¼

fewer loci than the X. Thus, many genes on the X chromosome—in fact, an overwhelming number of genes—do not have counterparts on the Y.[5] Such loci are called X-linked genes. For X-linked genes, females have two alleles, one on each X, whereas males have only one allele, the one on their single X chromosome.

The trick to dealing with this situation in a Punnett square is to include the chromosome when writing a gamete. Hence, if a mother is genotype *Aa* for a locus on the X chromosome, we will write her gametes as *X-A* and *X-a* instead of just *A* and *a*. A father who is genotype *A*, for example, will have his gametes written as *X-A* and *Y*. Note that the father's gamete containing the Y chromosome does *not* have an allele associated with it because the locus does not exist on the Y. To illustrate this technique, consider the offspring from a mating between an *Aa* female and an *a* male where allele *a* causes hemophilia, a locus located on the X chromosome but not on the Y chromosome. Hemophilia is a recessive disorder, so in phenotypic terms, this mating is between a hemophiliac male and a normal, but carrier, female. The Punnett rectangle appears in Table 9.14. Table 9.15 shows expected genotypes, phenotypes, and probabilities.

Table 9.15 Expected Genotypes, Phenotypes, and Probabilities for the Offspring of a Male Hemophiliac and a Female Carrier for Hemophilia

Genotype	Probability	Phenotype	Probability
XX-Aa	¼	Female, carrier	¼
XX-aa	¼	Female, hemophiliac	¼
XY-A	¼	Male, normal	¼
XY-a	¼	Male, hemophiliac	¼

● CONCLUSION

This chapter introduced the principles of Mendelian genetics. As was stated in the text, these principles introduced a paradigm shift that was not entirely correct. Mendel's law of dominance does not apply universally to all hereditary factors. This is not a major problem because we can always amend his laws to allow for "partial dominance" or "codominance."

On the other hand, Mendel's law of independent assortment has been demonstrated to be incorrect in a significant number of cases. The reason is that "hereditary factors," as Mendel called them, are not a "flood" on individual discrete particles within a cell. Instead, many of them appear to be linearly arranged on the physical molecules of inheritance, the chromosomes.

The concept of the linear arrangement of hereditary factors is the topic of the next exposition of quantitative genetics—linkage.

● NOTES

1. Brunn currently is located in the Czech Republic.

2. The actual breeding design was Mendel's dihybrid cross of round versus wrinkled and yellow versus green peas.

3. Indeed, Mendel's discoveries, like many important scientific breakthroughs, were partly the result of dumb luck. Without knowing the actual genetics behind what they were doing, people had been inbreeding peas for many years, creating what are now known as *inbred strains*. An inbred strain is a strain that is homozygous at all loci. These inbred strains formed the starting point of Mendel's breeding designs.

4. In reality, there are more than two alleles for the Rhesus locus, just as there are more than three alleles for the ABO locus. We used the outdated Rhesus and ABO systems because treating all the alleles for both blood groups introduces unneeded complexity for the introductory student.

5. A few regions of the Y chromosome contain loci found on the X chromosome. These genes are called *pseudoautosoma*.

CHAPTER 10

MORGAN AND LINKAGE

INTRODUCTION: THOMAS HUNT MORGAN ●

Thomas Hunt Morgan was a famous geneticist who, in the initial years of the 20th century, studied *Drosophila*, the fruit fly, in his lab at New York City's Columbia University. Morgan's choice of *Drosophila* was both fortuitous and prescient, not only for his own historic findings but also for introducing a model organism that has evolved to become a major workhorse in the science of genetics. These tiny flies reproduce quickly and leave a large number of progeny. Whereas Mendel had to wait months to plant and harvest two generations of peas, Morgan could study half a dozen generations in the same time. Moreover, *Drosophila* have only three chromosomes.

Two of Morgan's many findings stand out. Despite all the complicated looping of the DNA around chromosomal proteins, Morgan found that the genes on a chromosome have a remarkable statistical property—namely, in mathematical terms, genes appear as if they are linearly arranged along the chromosome. Thus, one can draw a schematic of a chromosome as a single straight line, with the genes in linear order along that straight line, even though the actual physical construction of the chromosome is a series of looped and folded DNA. Morgan's second finding was no less important. He discovered that chromosomes recombine and exchange genetic material.

Morgan's finding set the stage for what has evolved into *linkage analysis*. The purpose of linkage analysis is to find the *approximate location of a gene for a trait*. Usually the trait is a disease, but in other circumstances the trait could be a continuously distributed variable like height or IQ scores. The importance of linkage analysis in modern human genetics cannot be underestimated. Searching through the whole 3.2 billion base pairs of the human genome for a few nucleotides that may cause a Mendelian disorder is akin to searching through the whole state of Iowa (the largest corn producer in the United States) for a specific abnormal corn plant or two. Linkage analysis allows us to narrow the search to a specific county or township in Iowa. Even though linkage analysis may not detect the specific corn plant(s), it saves a tremendous amount of time and effort in the search for the mutant plant(s).

To understand linkage analysis, we must first have a firm knowledge of several basic terms. They are *homologous chromosomes*, *recombination*, *haplotypes*, *marker genes*, and the *recombination fraction*. Let us examine each in turn.

● BASIC DEFINITIONS

Homologous Chromosomes

We humans are *diploid* organisms. That means that we have two copies of every gene, except for those genes on the X and the Y chromosomes.[1] We inherit one gene from our mother and the other from our father. Because the chromosome (and not the gene) is the physical unit of inheritance, it is more appropriate to say that we inherit one maternal chromosome (that happens to have that gene on it) and one paternal chromosome (that also happens to have a sequence of DNA that codes for the same kind of polypeptide as the gene on the maternal chromosome). Those two chromosomes that have the same ordering of genes on them are termed *homologous* chromosomes and are illustrated in Figure 10.1.

Homologous chromosomes have the same ordering of genes, but they do not always have the same *alleles* (i.e., DNA spelling variations) at the gene. For example, the homologous chromosomes depicted in Figure 10.1 have four different genes—the A locus, the B locus, the C locus, and the D locus. At the A locus, however, one chromosome has the *A* allele, whereas the other has the *a* allele.

Figure 10.1   An Example of Homologous Chromosomes. One homologue is transmitted from the mother and the other from the father, but both chromosomes have the same ordering of genes.

Recombination

Recombination, or *crossing over*, as it is also called, refers to the fact that in the genesis of a sperm or an egg, the maternal chromosome pairs with its counterpart paternal chromosome and the two chromosomes exchange genetic material. We have already discussed recombination in Chapter 2, under the topic of meiosis. Here, we will deal with the statistical implications of crossing over. The process is diagrammed in Figure 10.2.

In this figure, we begin with the same homologous chromosomes depicted in Figure 10.1 (the left-hand pair of chromosomes). In the genesis of a sperm or an egg, these chromosomes pair up and exchange genetic material. In Figure 10.2 (middle panel), the exchange occurs between the B and the C locus. As a result, the chromosome that is transmitted by a sperm or an egg is a combination of the original paternal and maternal chromosomes (right-hand pair of chromosomes in the figure).

The most important fact to recognize about crossing over is that *the probability that a recombination event occurs between two loci is a function of the distance between the two loci*. The alleles at two loci that are *far apart* on a chromosome are *more likely* to encounter a recombination event than are the alleles for two loci that are *close together* on the chromosome.

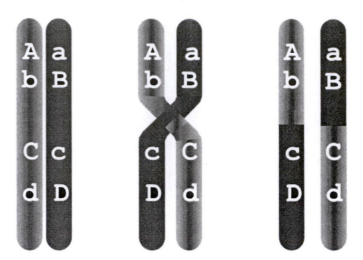

Figure 10.2   An Example of Recombination, or Crossing Over.

A convenient mnemonic to remember this principle is a dart game. Imagine that the target for a dart contest consisted of the two chromosomes in Figure 10.1. The place where a dart hits one of these chromosomes signifies a recombination event at that spot. What is the probability of placing a dart somewhere between the A and the B loci as compared to the probability of hitting somewhere between the A and the D loci? The probability of hitting somewhere between the A and the B loci is much lower than the probability of placing a dart between the A and the D loci. Hence, recombination is less likely for two genes located close together on the same chromosome than it is for two genes that are far apart on the same chromosome.

Haplotypes

In genetics, a *haplotype* is defined as *the alleles that exist on a short chromosomal segment*. As in many cases of terminology, examples can be more informative than abstract definitions. Examine Figure 10.3, which depicts a short segment of the paternal and maternal chromosomes for two hypothetical individuals, Abernathy Smith and Zebulon Jones. Three loci occur in this segment, the A, D, and B loci. Both Abernathy and Zebulon have the same genotypes at these loci: Both have genotype *Aa* at the A locus, *Dd* at the D locus, and *Bb* at the B locus.

But Abernathy and Zebulon have different haplotypes. Abernathy has haplotype *ADb* on his maternal chromosome and *adB* on his paternal chromosome. Hence, one would denote Abernathy's haplotypes as *ADb/adB*. Despite having the same genotypes as Abernathy, Zebulon's haplotypes are *aDB and Adb*. The two have the same genotypes but different haplotypes because the ordering of the alleles on their chromosomes is different.

Marker Genes

Previously, a gene was defined as a section of DNA that contains the blueprint for a polypeptide chain or a protein. This is the definition used in molecular biology. In linkage analysis, however, this definition is expanded to include *marker genes*. A marker gene is *a polymorphic locus that has a known chromosomal location*. Hence, the two key aspects of a marker locus (or gene) are that it (a) is polymorphic and (b) has a known location on the 23 human chromosomes. Marker genes may code for polypeptide chains, but they do not necessarily *have to* code for polypeptides. Indeed, the vast majority of marker genes are DNA spelling variations that occur in what geneticists suspect is the "junk" DNA.

The Recombination Fraction (θ)

With the basic definitions at hand, we can now begin to understand linkage analysis. Reconsider Abernathy Smith in Figure 10.3. To make matters simple, let us (a) ignore the B locus, (b) assume that gene A is a marker gene, and (c) let locus D be responsible for a rare dominant disorder (allele *D* causes the disorder, while allele *d* is the normal allele). Obviously, Abernathy has the disorder, because he has genotype *Dd* at the disease gene.

One of Abernathy's chromosomes has the *AD* haplotype, whereas the other has the *ad* haplotype. Now imagine the 300 million sperm that Abernathy produced when he impregnated his partner and fathered his first child. Half of his sperm would have marker allele *A*, while the other half would have marker allele *a*. But those gametes that have marker *A* are more likely to also have allele *D* than those gametes that have allele *a*. The reason for this is that loci A and D are linked (i.e., are close together on the same chromosome) and one of Abernathy's haplotypes is *AD*. Because the *A* and *D* alleles are close together on the same chromosome, they will tend to be inherited as a unit and will seldom be broken apart by recombination.

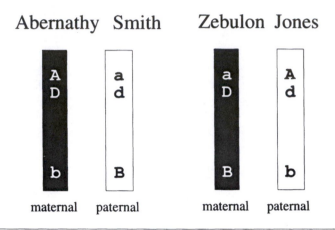

Figure 10.3 Illustration of Haplotypes (Linked Alleles in a Short Section of One Chromosome) in Two Hypothetical Individuals.

By similar logic, Abernathy's gametes that have the marker *a* allele will also tend to have the *d* allele at the disease gene. Why? Because Abernathy has haplotype *ad*, so the *a* and the *d* alleles will tend to be inherited as a unit. Hence, Abernathy's children who receive his *A* marker allele will more often have the disease than those who have his *a* marker allele.

The *recombination fraction* is a statistical measure of the distance between loci. Strictly speaking, the recombination fraction is the probability that a two-locus haplotype is *not* transmitted intact. In different words, the recombination fraction is the probability that Abernathy's gamete will have disease allele *d* given that the gamete has marker allele *A*. It is also the conditional probability that Abernathy's gamete will have disease allele *D* given that the gamete has marker allele *a*.

It is customary to denote the recombination fraction as the lower case Greek letter theta (θ). The quantity $(1 - \theta)$ gives the probability that the two alleles forming a haplotype will be transmitted together. Thus, if Abernathy's gamete contains the *A* marker allele, the probability that the gamete also contains the *D* allele is $(1 - \theta)$. Similarly, if Abernathy's gamete contains the *A* marker allele, the probability that recombination has occurred so that the gamete has the *d* allele from the other chromosome is θ. Mathematically, θ has a lower bound of 0 and an upper bound of .5. When θ is so small that it is effectively 0, then there is no recombination, and the two-gene haplotype will always be transmitted intact. When $\theta = .5$, then the two loci are either very far apart or on different chromosomes. Mendel's law of independent assortment applies when $\theta = .5$.

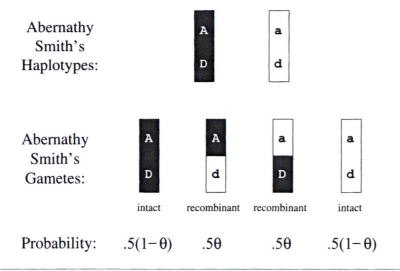

Figure 10.4 An Illustration of Gametes and Their Probabilities for Two Linked Loci.

THE PROBABILITY OF GAMETES ● AND OFFSPRING UNDER LINKAGE

Gametes

With the basic concepts at hand, we can now explore how to calculate the probability of gametes under linkage. Figure 10.4 presents a general template for performing such calculations using Abernathy Smith's haplotypes on the A and D loci from Figure 10.3. The probabilities given at the bottom are derived from simple probability theory. For example, the probability that a gamete has marker allele A is .5. Also, given that a gamete has marker allele A, the probability that the gamete also has D is $(1 - \theta)$. Hence, the probability that a gamete contains both A and D is the product of these two probabilities, or $.5(1 - \theta)$.

To calculate gametes under linkage, just use Figure 10.4 as a template. Draw the two haplotypes of an individual and then draw the four different gametes. Finally, plug in the value of θ. (You must be given a numerical value for θ in order to arrive at numerical results.) As an example, let us calculate the probability of Zebulon Jones's gametes (see Figure 10.3) when $\theta = .12$. Zebulon has haplotypes aD and Ad. The four gametes that Zeb can produce are aD (intact), ad (recombinant), AD (recombinant), and Ad (intact). The probability of intact gamete aD is $.5(1 - \theta) = .5(1 - .12) = .44$. This is also the

Table 10.1 The Probability of Gametes From a Person Who Has Haplotypes aD and Ad Under Different Values of the Recombination Fraction (θ)

	Gametes			
θ:	**aD Intact .5(1 − θ)**	**ad Recombinant .5θ**	**AD Recombinant .5(1 − θ)**	**Ad Intact .5θ**
.00	.50	.00	.00	.50
.10	.45	.05	.05	.45
.20	.40	.10	.10	.40
.30	.35	.15	.15	.35
.40	.30	.20	.20	.30
.50	.25	.25	.25	.25

probability of intact gamete Ad. The probability of recombinant gamete ad is $.5\theta = .5(.12) = .06$, which is also the probability for recombinant gamete AD.

Table 10.1 presents the probability of Zebulon's gametes under different values of θ. Notice that when θ is small, there is a high probability of transmitting the intact haplotype. When θ reaches its maximum value of .5, then each of the four gametes is equally likely.

Offspring

It is very simple to calculate the genotypes and phenotypes (and their frequencies) of offspring under linkage. First, calculate the gametes and their probabilities of the first parent using the algorithm described for Figure 10.4. Next, calculate the gametes and probabilities for the other parent using the same algorithm. Finally, follow the rules for creating a Punnett rectangle as described in Chapter 9.

To illustrate, suppose that Zebulon marries a woman with haplotypes Ad and Ad and that the recombination fraction (θ) is .04. Using the template in Figure 10.4, Zebulon's gametes and their probabilities are aD (.48), ad (.02), AD (.02), and Ad (.48). These gametes and their probabilities will form the columns of our Punnett rectangle, as illustrated in Table 10.2.

The mother's gametes are very easy to calculate. Irrespective of recombination, she can only transmit Ad because she is homozygous at both genes. Hence, she has only one type of gamete, Ad, which is transmitted with a probability of 1.0. The mother's gamete and probability label the row of the Punnett rectangle in Table 10.2.

Finally, the inner cells of the Punnett rectangle are derived by joining the mother's gamete with the column gamete. The probabilities are calculated by

Table 10.2 Probability of Offspring From a Mating of a Father With Haplotypes *aD* and *Ad* and a mother with haplotypes *Ad* and *Ad* With a Recombination Fraction (θ) of .04

	Paternal Gametes and Probabilities			
Maternal Gametes	**aD = .48**	**ad = .02**	**AD = .02**	**Ad = .48**
Ad = 1.0	*Ad/aD* = .48	*Ad/ad* = .02	*Ad/AD* = .02	*Ad/Ad* = .48

multiplying the row probability with the column probability. These are also shown in Table 10.2. Recall that allele *D* causes a rare dominant disorder. Hence, the table also gives the affected or unaffected status of the children for this disorder.

Note how linkage allows us to predict which of Zeb's children are likely to have the disorder with only knowledge of the marker allele that they received from their father. For example, half of his offspring will receive Zeb's *a* allele. Of this half, .48 will get the disorder and .02 will be unaffected. Hence, the probability of an offspring having the disorder given that he or she inherits Zeb's *a* allele is .48/.50 = .96. This is considerably higher than the .50 probability that we would have guessed if we did not know the marker information. Similarly, 96% of the children who received Zeb's *A* allele will be unaffected. The ability to predict who will and will not be affected on the basis of marker information is the rationale behind linkage analysis, our next topic.

LINKAGE ANALYSIS ●

Introduction to the Logic Behind Linkage Analysis

We have placed the cart before the horse in the sense that real world genetics first knows that a disorder is dominant, recessive, or complex and then tries to find the approximate location of the gene(s) for that disorder. Above, we pretended that we knew the location of the gene for a dominant disorder and then examined the transmission of a marker close to that gene.

Linkage analysis typically starts with *pedigrees*. There is a conventional notation used to denote individuals and their relationships to one another in a family. The major conventions are reviewed in Text Box 10.1.

Linkage analysis is a statistical technique that *traces the cosegregation of one or more marker alleles with a trait allele within pedigrees*. There are three crucial parts to this definition. The first is the term *cosegregation*, which

Text Box 10.1

NOTATIONS FOR PEDIGREES

Pedigrees in publications on genetics follow certain conventions. Please refer to Figure 10.5, which gives a hypothetical pedigree of Zebulon Jones and his wife as discussed in the main text. Squares denote males and circles denote females. Roman numerals designate a generation, and an Arabic numeral modifying a Roman numeral signifies the individual in the generation. For example I.1 in Figure 10.5 is Zebulon, the first person in generation 1; II.3 is the third person in generation 2, and so on. A diagonal slash through a person denotes that the person is deceased. So poor old Zeb has expired (God bless).

Filled-in squares or circles denote an affected individual. A square or circle that is half filled in may signify a partly affected individual or a "spectrum case." For example, schizophrenics may be completely filled in, whereas those with a diagnosis of schizotypal personality disorder may be partly filled in. In Figure 10.5, Zeb was affected while his son II.4 was partly affected.

Horizontal lines joining a male and female denote a mating. The horizontal line between I.1 (Zeb Jones) and I.2 (his wife, Mrs. Jones) denotes their mating. Vertical lines "dropped" from this horizontal line denote the offspring from this mating. In Figure 10.5, Zeb and his wife had eight children. (Another God bless to Mrs. Jones.)

Finally, an arrow pointing to an individual denotes that that person is a *proband*, the person through whom the pedigree was ascertained. Usually, the proband is the person with the disorder who enters a clinic or hospital and initially enrolls in the research project.

In linkage studies, it is also customary to give the genotypes at the marker locus (or loci) for the individuals in the pedigree. Hence, the Aa for individual II.2 denotes that that person is a heterozygote at the marker locus.

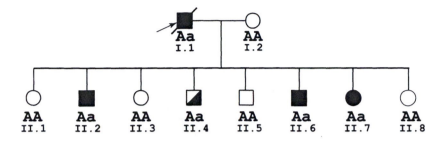

Figure 10.5 Hypothetical Pedigree of Zebulon Jones, Illustrating Conventions Used in Drawing Pedigrees.

refers to the fact that when two loci are linked, the alleles at those loci will tend to *segregate together*. The second major phrase is *trait allele*. Usually, the trait is a disorder and individuals are phenotypes that are either affected or unaffected (and, in some cases, partly affected). Earlier, we illustrated the principles behind linkage analysis using the gene for a rare dominant disorder as the trait locus. Linkage analysis, however, is much more flexible and can also be used to locate the approximate position of genes for continuously distributed traits, a topic that we will consider later. The last crucial phrase is *within pedigrees*. Linkage starts with a single pedigree, say, the Jones pedigree, and tests whether marker alleles cosegregate with trait alleles in the Jones family. The analysis then goes to the next pedigree—the Smiths, for example—and tests whether a marker allele cosegregates with the trait allele within the Smith family. If the empirical data provide a sufficient number of pedigrees in which the marker cosegregates with the trait allele, then we conclude that the trait gene is located somewhere near the marker.

To illustrate the principles behind linkage analysis, consider a hypothetical pedigree from our friends Zeb Jones and his wife, depicted in Figure 10.5. (The Jones offspring are depicted under the special case where $\theta = 0$.) The data in this figure would form the starting point of a linkage analysis. Everyone has been phenotyped for both the marker allele and for the trait (the rare dominant disorder).

We can infer some genotypes for the disorder, even though we do not know how to genotype directly for that gene. For example, Zeb's wife, Mrs. Jones, is unaffected. Therefore, she must be genotype *dd* at the disease locus. Similarly, all the unaffected Jones children must also be *dd*. Very few people with a rare dominant disorder will be *DD* homozygotes, so it is reasonable to conclude that Zeb's genotype for the disorder is *Dd*. Hence, to test for cosegregation, we want to ask whether one of Zeb's marker alleles, *A* or *a*, is transmitted with Zeb's *D* allele and the other marker allele is transmitted with his *d* allele.

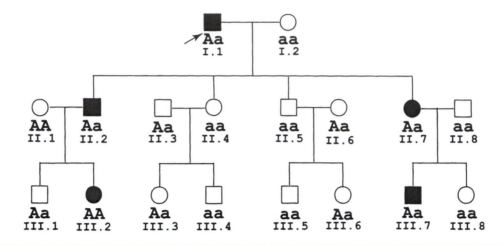

Figure 10.6   Hypothetical Pedigree of Abernathy Smith in Conventional Notation.

This is a rather simple procedure for a rare dominant and the mating type in this pedigree. Because Mrs. Jones must transmit an *A* allele, cross off one *A* allele in each of the offspring. The remaining marker allele in the offspring must have come from Zeb. Now examine whether the affected offspring tend to have inherited the same marker allele from Zeb. They do—all four of the affected offspring received allele *a* from Zeb. Next, ask whether the unaffected offspring tend to have received the *other* allele from Zeb. Indeed, all four unaffected children inherited Zeb's *A* allele. We would conclude that the Jones pedigree is consistent with linkage and that Zeb's allele for the disease is being transmitted with his *a* allele.

We would now proceed to the next pedigree. Here, we resurrect our friend Abernathy Smith (see Figure 10.3) and give him a spouse with haplotypes *ad* and *ad*. The hypothetical pedigree is presented in Figure 10.6. Because tracing cosegregation in three-generation pedigrees borders on a sadistic brain teaser, the chromosomal picture of transmission is depicted in Figure 10.7.

We test for cosegregation in the Smith pedigree in a similar way. Mrs. Smith must give an *a* marker allele to all her children. Hence, cross off one *a* allele in each of her four children. The remaining marker allele must have come from Abernathy. Do the affected children have the marker from Abernathy? Yes. Both of the affected offspring received Abernathy's *A* allele. Did the unaffected children receive his other allele? Once again, the answer is yes—both II.4 and II.5 inherited their father's *a* allele. Thus far, the pedigree is consistent for linkage and suggests that the disease allele, *D*, is being transmitted with Abernathy's *A* allele at the marker.

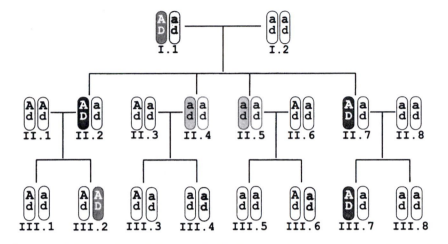

Figure 10.7 Hypothetical Pedigree of Abernathy Smith Showing Chromosomes.

The grandchildren in the Smith pedigree may also be examined for consistency for linkage. For example, consider the children of II.1 and II.2. Their mother can give only an *A*, so cross off one *A* allele in each of the two children. The other allele must have come from their father, II.2, who in turn inherited it from either Abernathy or his wife. II.2's *a* allele must come from unaffected Grandma Smith; hence, any of II.2's children who received his *a* allele should be unaffected. Indeed, his son, III.1, inherited this *a* allele and is unaffected. II.2 got his *A* allele and also the disease from Abernathy. Hence, if the pedigree is consistent, II.2's affected offspring should have the *A* marker. His affected daughter, III.2, does indeed have the *A* allele.

Similar logic shows that grandchildren III.7 and III.8 are also consistent with linkage. Cross off one *a* allele in each of these two children because their father can only contribute an *a*. The other allele must come from their mother and hence from either Abernathy or Grandma Smith. The one who received Grandma Smith's *a* is unaffected (III.8), while her brother, who received Abernathy's *A*, is affected. Hence, the grandchildren are consistent with the disease allele cosegregating with Abernathy's *A* allele.

Do not despair if you are bewildered in trying to follow this explanation because you are in good company. Trying to trace cosegregation, particularly in large multigenerational pedigrees, can be the ultimate in mind puzzlers and will challenge even the most knowledgeable geneticist. For this reason, actual linkage analysis is performed by highly sophisticated computer algorithms that can trace cosegregation much faster and with a higher degree of accuracy than any human. The important point is to recognize the logic behind linkage analysis. If we can predict, from the marker information in pedigrees, who does and does not have the trait allele, then the trait gene must be located somewhere on the marker locus.

● SOME FURTHER ISSUES IN LINKAGE ANALYSIS

Disease Genes and Marker Genes

One of the biggest obstacles to understanding linkage analysis is confusing the marker alleles with disease alleles. Physiologically and biochemically, the marker alleles *have nothing to do with the development of a disorder*. The marker alleles are simply spelling variations in a section of DNA that is physically *close* to the gene that causes a disorder or other trait. Think of the relationship between marker and trait as correlations that are not causal. Within a single pedigree, markers *predict* who will and will not be affected, but the markers *do not cause* the disorder. A clear example of this fallacy can be seen if we compare the Jones to the Smith pedigree. In both families, the affected children had genotype *Aa*. In fact, this is a total coincidence, and we should not conclude that somehow genotype *Aa* contributes to the disease. The genotypes of the affected offspring depend on which chromosome carries the *D* allele *and* the genotype of the spouse.

Linkage: Mendelian Disorders Versus DCG

Linkage analysis has had spectacular success in limiting the areas on a chromosome that one should search for a Mendelian trait. Huntington's disease (HD) was first described in 1872 by American physician George Huntington and was recognized as following Mendelian transmission as a dominant disorder early in the 20th century. After that, many attempts were made to locate the HD gene, but it was not until 1984 that they met with success. The same is true of many other Mendelian disorders such as phenylketonuria and cystic fibrosis. The reason for the recent successes was not improvements in the logic of linkage analysis. Indeed, the basic principles were firmly established in Morgan's time. Instead, the technology revolution that allowed linkage to achieve its successes was the *ability to detect polymorphisms and map them to chromosomal locations*. For most of the 20th century, only several dozen polymorphisms, largely related to blood groups, were known. Today, with the SNP (single nucleotide polymorphism) technology, more than a million polymorphisms have been characterized and placed on chromosomes.

Compared to progress on Mendelian traits, linkage analysis of DCG (disorders with complex genetics) has met with only modest success. The main accomplishments have come about by isolating a few large pedigrees in which transmission of the DCG appears to follow that of a Mendelian disorder. Examples of such DCG include breast cancer, diabetes, and Alzheimer's disease. These known Mendelian forms of the disorder account for only a small percentage of all cases of the DCG.

Linkage and Statistics

The vast majority of linkage analyses are what scientists call "shotgun" techniques, in the sense that one blindly fires a shotgun in a random direction hoping to hit something. (The opposite type of research occurs when a well-defined hypothesis dictates the design of the study so that only one or two outcomes of the study are possible.) When geneticists try to locate a gene for a disorder, they gather a large number of families in which the disorder runs and obtain some biological specimen (usually blood, but sometimes cheek scrapings) from each member. DNA is extracted from the biological specimen and then genotyped on a large number of the marker loci. Ideally, marker loci are selected so that they are evenly spaced but cover each and every chromosome. The linkage analysis is then done on one set of markers, then another set, and then another until some positive results are found. This type of procedure in which one tests a set of markers scattered throughout the genome is called a *whole genome scan*.

As the reader probably suspects, this approach is prone to false positive errors in which a chance finding reaches statistical significance. To guard against this error, geneticists use a more stringent statistical criterion than that used in typical social science research. Social scientists typically use the ".05 level" of significance, implying that there is a 5% chance that a statistically significant result will be a false positive. In linkage analysis for Mendelian traits, geneticists use a significance level of .001 (1 in 1,000 chance of a false positive). For DCG, the criterion is usually more conservative and may approach .00001 (1 in 100,000).

Linkage in a Single Pedigree

Although linkage was discussed in terms of pedigrees in the plural, it is possible, under favorable circumstances, to detect linkage in a single pedigree. The best scenario here is a large, multigenerational pedigree in which a disorder runs according to Mendelian transmission. A classic example with behavioral overtones is what I will call Brunner syndrome, in honor of the geneticist who first described it.

An Brunner, a Dutch physician, was approached by members of a local family who were concerned about the behavior of several male relatives. Brunner and his colleagues studied these men and characterized the phenotype as having moderate mental retardation, mild aggression, impulsivity, and inappropriate sexual behavior. Because the pattern of inheritance followed that of an X-linked recessive, they started linkage analysis with the X chromosome and soon found positive evidence of linkage to a small area on the X (Brunner et al., 1993, Brunner, Nelen, Breakefield, Ropers, & van Oost, 1993). The team followed up this lead and soon located the mutant gene—a chain terminating mutation in the blueprint for the enzyme monoamine oxidase A, which breaks down some neurotransmitters. (A chain terminating mutation is one that prematurely stops the chain of amino acids in the translation step of protein synthesis; the shortened polypeptide chain does not have biological function).

One interesting feature of Brunner syndrome is that many other attempts to detect it in other families have failed (Xandra Breakfield, personal communication; David Goldman, personal communication). It appears that it is an "orphan" disorder. That is, a *recent* mutation occurred in this one pedigree, and it was passed on to other members of the family. The recency of the mutation means that it has not had time to spread beyond the immediate pedigree, so that other families with the same mutation are exceedingly rare.

Linkage: Parametric and Nonparametric Techniques

Finally, there are two major types of linkage analysis, *parametric* and *nonparametric*. Parametric linkage analysis estimates population parameters and then tests whether the estimated values of those parameters differ from their theoretical values under the null hypothesis of no linkage. For example, a parametric approach might estimate the recombination fraction, θ, and then test whether the estimated θ differs significantly from its theoretical value of .50 if there is no linkage. Nonparametric linkage analysis does not estimate population parameters. Instead, it develops a test that can reject the null hypothesis of no linkage.

An example of a nonparametric strategy is the *affected sib-pair* method. Here, the geneticist gathers data on a large number of sibships in which both members of the pair are affected with the disorder (or have the trait). These affected sib-pairs are then genotyped at the marker locus and the sib-pairs are placed into one of two mutually exclusive categories based on their genotypes at the marker. The first category includes all sib-pairs who have the same genotype at the marker; we can term these the *marker-concordant* pairs. The second category is for the *marker-discordant* pairs (i.e., those sib-pairs who have different genotypes at the marker).

If the marker is not linked to the gene for the disorder, then we should expect the same number in both categories.[2] However, if the marker is linked to the disease locus, then there should be more marker-concordant pairs than marker-discordant pairs. Hence, one simply performs a statistical test to see whether the number of marker-concordant pairs is significantly larger than the number of marker-discordant pairs.

Parametric linkage analysis is usually favored when the trait is a known Mendelian disorder. For DCG and other complex phenotypes, most linkage specialists are shifting to nonparametric techniques because they are more robust against the violations of assumptions required for parametric methods.

LINKAGE AND QTLs ●

With the exception of some forms of psychopathology, most traits of interest to social science are continuously distributed or quantitative traits. In a quantitative trait like height, everyone *has* the trait but possesses *different values* of it. Examples include IQ scores and all personality traits. A gene that contributes to variation in a quantitative trait is called a QTL, for *quantitative trait locus*.

Methods for detecting QTLs were initially developed by Haseman and Elston (1972) and have been elaborated on by many different groups (e.g., Cardon et al., 1994; Carey & Williamson, 1991; Nance & Neale, 1989). Similarly, there are several different strategies for studying linkage and QTL. All methods and strategies, however, share the common logic that relatives who inherit the same marker allele should be more similar to each other on the quantitative trait than relatives who inherit different markers.

Let us examine one simple method for QTL linkage. We will assume a highly polymorphic marker locus with a large number of alleles and will examine only those families where the parents have four different alleles. For example, let mother have alleles A_1 and A_2 at the marker, where the subscripts refer to the allele. Let father have alleles A_3 and A_4. This type of mating will produce four types of marker genotypes in the offspring—A_1A_3, A_1A_4, A_2A_3, and A_2A_4. Now consider a sib-pair with this mating type as parents. Any sib-pair can have both marker alleles in common, have one common and one different marker allele, or have no common and two different marker alleles.

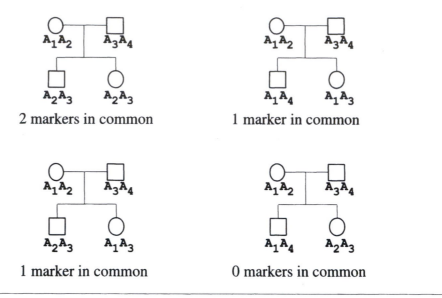

2 markers in common   1 marker in common

1 marker in common   0 markers in common

Figure 10.8 Pedigrees Illustrating Sib-Pairs That Share Two, One, or No Alleles Identical by Descent.

Figure 10.8 gives four pedigrees that illustrate the categories into which sib-pairs will fall.

Having separated each sib-pair into one of the three categories, we would now enter their trait scores into a table such as Table 10.3. The scores in this table are hypothetical.

If there is a QTL that is closely linked to the marker, then sib-pairs with two common markers should also tend to have the same alleles at the QTL. Those sib-pairs who have no common marker alleles should tend to have different alleles at the QTL. Finally, those with only one common marker allele should tend to have one QTL allele in common and one different QTL allele. Hence, when there is linkage, the trait scores for sib-pairs with two markers in common should be more similar than the scores for pairs with one marker in common, which, in turn, should be more similar than those who have no markers in common. The best statistical index of similarity for sib-pairs' trait scores is the correlation coefficient. If there is linkage, then the correlation for pairs with two common markers should be higher than those for pairs with one common marker, which, in turn, should be higher than for those with no common markers. When there is no QTL close to the marker, then the correlations for the three types of sib-pairs should be equal. Illustrative values for the correlations under linkage and under no linkage are given at the bottom of Table 10.3.

Table 10.3   Hypothetical Sib-Pair Data Illustrating the Principles for Detecting a Quantitative Trait Locus (QTL) Using Linkage

	Number of Marker Alleles in Common					
	2		*1*		*0*	
	Sib 1	*Sib 2*	*Sib 1*	*Sib 2*	*Sib 1*	*Sib 2*
	21	17	35	19	30	14
	38	44	24	13	26	42
	12	23	21	46	45	19
	.	.	.	.	.	.
	29	36	37	14	25	39
Correlation	.38		.26		.19	

WHAT NEXT? ●

If linkage analysis can locate the approximate position of a gene, it is logical to ask the next steps that must be taken to identify the actual locus. In years past, this involved a laborious process termed positional cloning that began by finding markers on both sides of the trait locus and then searching for polymorphisms in between the two flanking markers. In the case of Huntington's disease, it took 10 years of constant effort until the actual gene was located after the first positive linkage was reported.

The sequencing of the human genome has given us so much information that the post-linkage phase of finding genes has been shortened. First, those parts of the Human Genome Project directed at detecting polymorphisms have found so many of them that there is little need to detect them in an individual lab. Second, the number of known genes that code for proteins has skyrocketed, and it will not be long before genetics has characterized more than 90% of all human genes. Hence, there is a wide body of published knowledge on many of the spelling differences in DNA that occur between flanking markers.

NOTES ●

1.   Not all life-forms are diploid. Many single-cell organisms such as bacteria and viruses are *haploid* and hence have only one copy of a gene. Some plants are *polyploid* and have more than two copies of a gene.

2.   Strictly speaking, when there is no linkage, the ratio of marker concordant to marker discordant pairs is a complicated function of the frequencies of the marker alleles. The example in the text assumes that there is a very large number of alleles, so that the frequency of any single allele is always quite small.

● REFERENCES

Brunner, H. G., Nelen, M. R., van Zandvoort, P., Abeling, N. G., van Gennip, A. H., Wolters, E. C., et al. (1993). X-linked borderline mental retardation with prominent behavioral disturbance: Phenotype, genetic localization, and evidence for disturbed monoamine metabolism. *American Journal of Human Genetics, 52,* 1032-1039.

Brunner, H. G., Nelen, M., Breakefield, X. O., Ropers, H. H., & van Oost, B. A. (1993). Abnormal behavior associated with a point mutation in the structural gene for monoamine oxidase A. *Science, 262,* 578-580.

Cardon, L. R., Smith, S. D., Fulker, D. W., Kimberling, W. J., Pennington, B. F., & DeFries, J. C. (1994). Quantitative trait locus for reading disability on chromosome 6. *Science, 266,* 276-279.

Carey, G., & Williamson, J. (1991). Linkage analysis of quantitative traits: Increased power by using selected samples. *American Journal of Human Genetics, 49,* 786-796.

Haseman, J. K., & Elston, R. C. (1972). The investigation of linkage between a quantitative trait and a marker locus. *Behavior Genetics, 2,* 3-19.

Nance, W. E., & Neale, M. C. (1989). Partitioned twin analysis: A power study. *Behavior Genetics, 19,* 143-150.

CHAPTER **11**

THE ASSOCIATION STUDY

INTRODUCTION: USE OF THE ASSOCIATION DESIGN ●

Linkage performs tests for cosegregation using a number of markers that "hitchhike" with a trait locus but do not contribute to the trait. Association designs, on the other hand, test actual genes that either empirically or theoretically have a probability of contributing to the disorder. The association study is used in two different situations. First, it is used as a follow-up to successful linkage results to isolate the gene. Second, it is used when there are good theoretical reasons to suspect that a gene may contribute to a trait.

Linkage and Association

Recall that linkage finds the *approximate* location of a gene for a trait. The typical linkage strategy in what is called a *whole genome scan* is to geno-type pedigrees on a large number of markers that are evenly spaced throughout the genome, say at 5 to 10 centiMorgans or cM. (Five to 10 cM is a distance equal to a recombination fraction of .05 to .10.) After statistical analyses, those markers that are suggestive of linkage are isolated and the pedigrees are genotyped at additional markers around 1 to 2 cM from the suggestive markers. Such a procedure has its limits. At the end of the day, one is usually left with an area of at least five or more cM in which the trait gene is likely to be located. This area could correspond to several million nucleotides and may contain several different genes.

In the past, rather complicated techniques such as positional cloning were used to pinpoint the gene, but such tasks were very labor-intensive and took a long time. For example, the first linkage for Huntington's disease was reported in Gusella et al. (1983), but it took until 1994 (Huntington's Disease Colla-borative Research Group, 1993) to actually locate the HD gene. Today, with the human genome sequenced and with the promise of identifying and locating all human genes within the next few years, it appears that the association design eventually will supplant these older techniques. In the future, after a positive linkage result, geneticists will consult a genetic database to find the protein-coding genes close to the markers and then test for those genes directly.

Association and Genes of Theoretical Interest

The association design is used in a second way when there is a polymor-phism in a protein-coding gene that has theoretical relevance to the trait being studied. Let us take some time to provide an example that will be used later for other purposes in this chapter.

Dopamine is a major neurotransmitter in the central nervous system and has five known neuroreceptors, abbreviated as DRD1 (for dopamine receptor D1) through DRD5. Although dopamine plays a role in many behaviors, it has been long known that stimulants such as amphetamines and cocaine influ-ence dopaminergic transmission. Because methylphenidate (Ritalin®) is an amphetamine derivative and has demonstrable effects on attention deficit-hyperactivity disorder (ADHD), it is quite logical to ask whether the genes for proteins and enzymes that influence dopamine play a role in ADHD.

In the early 1990s, several groups reported a polymorphism in the D4 receptor for dopamine (Lichter et al., 1993; Van Tol et al., 1992). The poly-morphism is a tandem repeat of 48 base pairs (bp) that occurs in the third exon of the DRD4 gene. This 48 bp sequence may be repeated anywhere between 2 and 10 times, resulting in DRD4 proteins of different length. The most frequent alleles have either four or seven repeats.

Three years later, LaHoste et al. (1996) reported that children with ADHD had the seven-repeat allele more often than the other alleles. Since that time, more than 14 different groups have examined the association between the seven-repeat allele and ADHD (e.g., Kotler et al., 2000; Rowe et al., 1998; Smalley et al., 1998). In this use of association, one begins with a polymorphic gene (DRD4) that has clear relevance for a trait (ADHD) and then tests individuals on the gene.

ASSOCIATION STUDIES: TWO MAJOR DESIGNS ●

There are two major research designs used for association studies. The first of these is the *population-based* association study, and the second is the *family-based* association design. Let us discuss each in turn.

Population-Based Association Designs

Population-based designs are so named because the controls are sampled from the *general population*. The logic of the design is simple and straightforward. In the case of DRD4 and ADHD, one would take a certain number of cases diagnosed with ADHD and a control group from the general population and then genotype all the participants on the DRD4 locus. Illustrative data, based on the meta-analysis of Faraone, Doyle, Mick, and Biederman (2001) are presented in Table 11.1.

In the hypothetical study used to construct Table 11.1, 100 cases of ADHD were ascertained and a like number of controls, who do not have ADHD, were sampled from the general population. Because there are a number of alleles at the DRD4 locus, it has become conventional to categorize the genotypes at this locus as having at least one long allele (i.e., a seven, eight, or ten repeat) or no long alleles.

In this table, 35% of ADHD but only 20% of controls had at least one long allele. Hence, the odds of having a long allele are 1.75 greater (.35/.20 = 1.75) if a person has ADHD than if a person does not have ADHD. A statistical test is also performed on the table to test the null hypothesis of no association between genotype and trait. For Table 11.1, one test (a χ^2 that equals 6.42) is significant, suggesting that the longer DRD4 alleles do in fact increase risk for ADHD.

The two main advantages of the population-based association design are its ease of execution and its simplicity. Hospitals and clinics can be used to ascertain affected individuals, and sampling from the general population is quite easy. Similarly, the tables generated by a population-based design are simple to interpret.

Table 11.1   Example of a Population-Based Association Design

	Genotype at DRD4 Locus		
Group	No Seven Repeat	At Least One Seven Repeat	Total
ADHD	65	35	100
Controls	80	20	100
Total	145	55	200

The big disadvantage of population-based association designs is a phenomenon called *population stratification*. Let us take some time to explore this important issue.

Population Stratification

Population stratification comes about because allele frequencies are not evenly distributed across human populations. Hence, when people with a disorder and the control group are not carefully matched in terms of ethnicity, erroneous conclusions can be drawn about the causal role of genes. This is a difficult concept in the abstract, so let us consider a simple example.

Assume that science has identified a gene that influenced the rate of and amount of melanin production in the skin. Let allele *A* denote high production while allele *a* is associated with low production. Genotype *AA* would be darkly pigmented, genotype *aa* would be lightly pigmented, and genotype *Aa* would have intermediate pigmentation. Suppose that the disease that we wished to study was sickle-cell anemia and that we did a straightforward association design. From a clinic in the United States, we select 50 patients with sickle-cell anemia and then pick 50 random controls; we then genotype all 100 individuals on the melanin locus. The design is given in Table 11.2.

Mentally try to fill in numbers for this table. The majority of sickle-cell cases in the United States will be the descendants of Africans. Hence, there will be a high frequency of allele *A* among those with sickle cell. In a random sample of the United States, however, the majority will be white. Hence, there will be a high frequency of allele *a* among controls. This would give a positive statistic. Should one then conclude that there is an association between the hypothetical melanin locus and sickle-cell anemia?

The answer to this question lies in the relationship between correlation and causality that should be well recognized by even the beginning social science student. There is a real statistical association—or correlation, if you prefer that term—between pigmentation and sickle-cell anemia in the United

Table 11.2   A Hypothetical Association Study Between a Melanin Production Locus and Sickle-Cell Anemia

| | Genotype | | | |
Disease Status	aa	Aa	AA	Total
Control				50
Sickle cell				50
Total				100

States. That association, however, is *not* causal. For obvious reasons, genes for melanin production have nothing to do with the β hemoglobin chain that causes sickle-cell anemia.

The biggest problem with population stratification is that we do not know how much of a problem it really is. The example given above is extreme and, of course, no reasonable person would ever conduct such a study. The simplest solution to stratification is to use a case-control strategy. Instead of randomly sampling controls from the general population, each control is selected to be an ethnic match for the case. The difficulty here is that we do not know how fine-grained the matching needs to be. Is it sufficient to match on broadly defined categories like "European ancestry," moderately sized subdivisions like Irish or German, or even more refined categories? Imagine someone with ADHD who is one fourth Italian, one fourth English, and half Swedish. If we must locate an unaffected person from the general population who is an exact ethnic match, then the major advantage of the population-based design—its simplicity—is lost. To reiterate, the problem of population stratification is that we do not know how much of a problem it really is.

For this reason, many geneticists consider family-based association designs the "gold standard" in genetics. Why? Because family-based designs give perfect control for population stratification.

Family-Based Association Designs

There are many varieties of family-based association designs, but they all have the common philosophy of testing for a *disturbance in segregation within families*. That phrase—albeit technically correct—is quite a mouthful, so let us simplify the situation by dividing family-based designs into two categories, those that use genetic relatives as controls and those that test for transmission disequilibrium. Each will be explained in turn.

Table 11.3   A Family-Based Association Design Using Unaffected Siblings as Controls

	Number of Long DRD4 Alleles		
Family	ADHD Sib	Unaffected Sib	Difference
Smith	2	1	1
Jones	0	1	−1
Williams	0	0	0

Genetic Relatives as Controls

By definition, siblings always share the same ethnicity. Hence, the best control subject for a case is not an ethnically matched person from the general population but an unaffected sibling. Using unaffected siblings as controls perfectly matches the case and the control on ethnicity and hence perfectly controls for population stratification. The unit of analysis in this design is the *sibship*, not the individual. Any row in the data matrix consists of a sibship, with separate columns for the affected and unaffected sib in the pair.[1] The hypothetical data in Table 11.3 illustrate how the design would be implemented for the ADHD example.

Because the longer DRD4 alleles are thought to be associated with ADHD, siblings who have ADHD should on average have more long DRD4 alleles than their unaffected brothers or sisters. Hence, one would genotype all the participants and tabulate the number of long alleles in the manner illustrated in Table 11.3. The column labeled "Difference" is simply the arithmetic difference between the ADHD sibling and the unaffected sibling. Under the null hypothesis of no association between the DRD4 alleles and ADHD, the mean of this column should be close to 0. If the long allele confers risk for ADHD, then the mean should be greater than 0. (Likewise, if the long allele were a protective factor against ADHD, then the unaffected sibs should have more long alleles than the affected sibs and the mean of the difference should be lower than 0.) Hence, testing whether the mean of the column labeled "Difference" in Table 11.3 is approximately zero provides a test for an association that controls perfectly for population stratification.

The only problem with using genetic relatives like siblings as controls is that the designs are more expensive and difficult to execute than simply taking controls from the general population. A case of ADHD must have a sibling to begin with, the sibling must be unaffected, and the sib must be of a sufficient age that he or she is not likely to develop the disorder in the

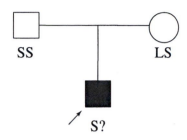

Figure 11.1 A Type of Pedigree Used in the Transmission Disequilibrium Test. The pedigree is ascertained through the affected offspring, and the test consists of the allele transmitted by mother. Is it *L* or *S*?

future. With adult-onset disorders, one faces the additional problem that the unaffected sib may not be living close to the proband. These difficulties are far from insurmountable, but they will add to the cost and time of a research project. On the other hand, when the association study is used as a follow-up to positive linkage results, then one already has data on cases and their relatives. Hence, the difficult part of the fieldwork already has been done.

A Transmission Disequilibrium Test

Falk and Rubenstein (1987) developed the haplotype relative risk from which the transmission disequilibrium test (TDT) evolved. Since then, many variants of the test have been published. The logic of the TDT can be seen by referring to Figure 11.1, which shows a simple pedigree in which the single offspring has ADHD and the offspring and both parents are genotyped at the DRD4 locus. (The offspring's genotype at DRD4 is not shown for the purpose of exposition.) The father can transmit only a short (*S*) allele because he is a homozygote. The mother in this case is the informative parent. Under the null hypothesis of no association between DRD4 and ADHD, Mendel's law of segregation dictates that the probability that the offspring received her long allele (*L*) is .50, the flip of a coin. In different words, the transmission of the short and long alleles would be in "equilibrium." On the other hand, if the long allele confers risk for ADHD, then there is a slightly greater than 50/50 chance that the mother transmitted her long allele—after all, her son does have ADHD. In other words, there is a "disequilibrium" in transmission.

Now suppose that the researcher collected 100 pedigrees just like the one illustrated in Figure 11.1. (Of course, this is implausible because many

Table 11.4   Hypothetical Data From a Transmission Disequilibrium Test

	DRD4 Allele Transmitted From Mother		
	S (Short)	L (Long)	Total
Expected[a]	50	50	100
Observed	35	65	100

a. Expected numbers are those from the null hypothesis of no association
between ADHD and DRD4.

other genotypic combinations for mother and father would be found in real practice; the hypothetical situation, however, makes it much easier to understand the logic behind the TDT.) If there is no association between DRD4 and ADHD, then we expect that 50 of the children should have received the S allele and the other 50 the L allele from the mother. On the other hand, if the L alleles are risk factors for ADHD, then more than 50% of the offspring should have received the L allele from the mother. Hence, one just tabulates the number of offspring who received the L versus the S allele from the mother and then performs a statistical test on whether the observed frequencies differ significantly from a 50/50 split. Sample data are given in Table 11.4.

A statistical test would be performed on these data to check whether the observed frequencies differ from their expected values. In this case, the result (a χ^2 of 9.0 with 1 degree of freedom) is significant, so we would conclude that there is indeed a difference in transmission and that the long allele (L) is associated with increased risk.

In practice, TDTs deal with pedigrees more complicated than the one depicted in Figure 11.1. For example, consider the pedigree in Figure 11.2, in which there is an unaffected offspring. If DRD4 long alleles confer risk for ADHD and short alleles give protection from the disorder, then the mother should be more likely to transmit her long allele to her affected firstborn child but her short allele to her unaffected second-born child. Similar logic applies for larger sibships. The mathematics become more difficult in testing whether transmission departs from an even 50/50 split, but the logic of the design remains the same. Again, because alleles always segregate regardless of the ethnicity of the family, the TDT requires no control for population stratification.

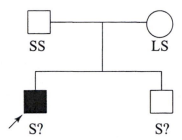

Figure 11.2   Another Type of Pedigree Used in the Transmission Disequilibrium Test. If *L* contributes susceptibility to the disorder, then the mother should tend to transmit *L* to the affected child but *S* to the unaffected child.

ADVANTAGES AND DISADVANTAGES ●
OF THE ASSOCIATION STUDY

Several years ago, there was considerable debate over the relative merits of linkage versus association strategies, but today there is widespread recognition that each strategy has its advantages and disadvantages. The two major advantages of the association study are statistical power[2] and knowledge. In terms of statistical power, it is much easier to find a gene contributing to a disease with an association design than with linkage. When several genes contribute to liability, then even very large linkage studies may not have sufficient statistical power to detect a gene. Much smaller samples are required to detect an effect in an association design. Similarly, association studies can detect genes of small effect, making them ideal for finding genes for multifactorial traits.

The second advantage is the increase in knowledge. Linkage studies find the approximate location of a gene but cannot locate the gene itself or provide information about what the gene does. With an association study, on the other hand, one can begin to develop hypotheses about the pathophysiology of and treatment of the disorder from knowledge about the locus and what it does. For example, in the DRD4 case, isolating the physiological differences between the "short-form" and "long-form" receptors could aid in understanding some of the causes for ADHD. Such knowledge may also promote more effective interventions.

A potential disadvantage of association studies is the large number of known loci that could potentially be tested. Although the number of human genes (i.e., protein-coding loci) is not known exactly, it is certainly in the tens of thousands. Many of these genes will have polymorphisms, if not in the exons then in regions close by. If researchers proceed in a shotgun fashion and try to associate a disorder with each and every known gene, then a large number of false positive findings could arise just by chance.[3] This is not a problem when association is used to follow up positive linkage results because the number of polymorphisms may be several dozen or so.

A further problem with association studies is that they rely on a gene that is already known. What happens if a major locus that contributes to a disease has yet to be described by molecular geneticists? Here, the advantage is to linkage because it can detect effects in regions of DNA where the actual genes are not known. That advantage, however, will be short-lived because in coming years the majority of human loci should be known and cataloged.

The final difficulty with association designs is a phenomenon called linkage disequilibrium. This is an important but difficult topic, so we devote a section to it.

The Problem of Linkage Disequilibrium

Suppose that there were a point mutation (a change in one and only one nucleotide) in the third exon to the DRD4 gene and the point mutation results in an amino acid substitution in the D4 receptor. (Recall that the third exon also contains the tandem repeat polymorphism that we have been discussing.) Let A denote the normal allele and a the allele with the point mutation.[4] There would be four different haplotypes at the DRD4 locus—AS, AL, aS, and aL. A phenomenon termed *linkage equilibrium* occurs when the frequency of every haplotype equals the product of the frequencies of the two alleles involved in the haplotype. For example, if the frequency of the A allele were .80 and the frequency of the S allele were .70, then the predicted frequency of haplotype AS under linkage equilibrium would be $.80 \times .70 = .56$. When some haplotypes are more frequent and, by necessity, other haplotypes are less frequent than their expected values, then the alleles are said to be in *linkage disequilibrium*.

A full treatise on linkage disequilibrium is beyond the scope of this text, but we can immediately see the problem for an association study. Suppose that the point mutation, a, occurred more frequently with the long allele, L, than would be predicted by chance. If ADHD cases have L more often than S, then they will also have allele a more often than chance. So which allele is etiologically involved in ADHD? Is it the point mutation, the tandem repeat, or perhaps both?

Hence, when there is a positive and replicated association between a gene and a trait, then the actual polymorphic alleles may be involved, or other alleles in linkage disequilibrium with the tested allele may be causal agents for the trait. This is not a fatal problem with the association design because refinements of research design can sometimes overcome the problem. In addition, studies of the physiology of the proteins themselves can assist in distinguishing which of two alleles in disequilibrium is the real culprit.

CONCLUSION ●

In the near future, linkage and association studies will be used in tandem to search for genes contributing to liability in DCG and normal traits. In fact, the large pedigrees collected in linkage studies are very suitable for within-family segregation designs used to test for associations. For DCG, especially those involving behavior, there should be no argument as to which strategy is superior—both are currently needed. As the human genome becomes better characterized by dense marker loci, it will be easier to detect the influence of genes of moderate effect size with linkage. On the other hand, as more and more polymorphisms are identified that influence protein structure and/or production, then association designs, with their greater statistical power, will become increasingly important.

In the future, more insight will be gained into the problem of population stratification. Perhaps (and we can hope) there will be little difficulty as long as one uses common sense in matching for ethnicity. On the other hand, future data might show that stratification is a real problem and within-family segregation designs are the only way to achieve satisfactory scientific control. It is simply too early to tell.

NOTES ●

1.   It is also possible to deal with sibships greater than size two; however, the mathematics of doing so is beyond the scope of this text.

2.   Statistical power is the probability that a statistical test can reject a hypothesis when, in fact, the hypothesis is false.

3.   The more statistical tests that are performed, the greater is the probability that at least one of them will be significant just by chance. Given that the number of polypeptide coding genes may approach 50,000, shotgun approaches to association will definitely uncover many false leads. One can, of course, adjust the statistical method to minimize the false positives, but this strategy robs the association design of its major advantage—statistical power.

4.   Although the short and long DRD4 polymorphism is real, the point mutation example is fictitious and is used only to illustrate the phenomenon of linkage disequilibrium.

● REFERENCES

Falk, C. T., & Rubenstein, P. (1987). Haplotype relative risk: An easy reliable way to construct a proper control sample for risk calculations. *Annals of Human Genetics, 51*, 227-233.

Faraone, S. V., Doyle, A. E., Mick, E., & Biederman, J. (2001). Meta-analysis of the association between the 7-repeat allele of the dopamine D(4) receptor gene and attention deficit hyperactivity disorder. *American Journal of Psychiatry, 158*, 1052-1057.

Gusella, J. F., Wexler, N. S., Conneally, P. M., Naylor, S. L., Anderson, M. A., Tanzi, R. E., et al. (1983). A polymorphic DNA marker genetically linked to Huntington's disease. *Nature, 306*, 234-238.

Huntington's Disease Collaborative Research Group. (1993). A novel gene containing a trinucleotide repeat that is expanded and unstable on Huntington's disease chromosomes. *Cell, 72*, 971-983.

Kotler, M., Manor, I., Sever, Y., Eisenberg, J., Cohen, H., Ebstein, R. P., et al. (2000). Failure to replicate an excess of the long dopamine D4 exon III repeat polymorphism in ADHD in a family-based study. *American Journal of Medical Genetics, 96*, 278-281.

LaHoste, G. J., Swanson, J. M., Wigal, S. B., Glabe, C., Wigal, T., King, N., et al. (1996). Dopamine D4 receptor gene polymorphism is associated with attention deficit hyperactivity disorder. *Molecular Psychiatry, 1*, 121-124.

Lichter, J. B., Barr, C. L., Kennedy, J. L., Van Tol, H. H., Kidd, K. K., & Livak, K. J. (1993). A hypervariable segment in the human dopamine receptor D4 (DRD4) gene. *Human Molecular Genetics, 2*, 767-773.

Rowe, D. C., Stever, C., Giedinghagen, L. N., Gard, J. M., Cleveland, H. H., Terris, S. T., et al. (1998). Dopamine DRD4 receptor polymorphism and attention deficit hyperactivity disorder. *Molecular Psychiatry, 3*, 419-426.

Smalley, S. L., Bailey, J. N., Palmer, C. G., Cantwell, D. P., McGough, J. J., Del'Homme, M. A., et al. (1998). Evidence that the dopamine D4 receptor is a susceptibility gene in attention deficit hyperactivity disorder. *Molecular Psychiatry, 3*, 427-430.

Van Tol, H. H. M., Wu, C. M., Guan, H.-C., Ohara, K., Bunzow, J. R., Civelli, O., et al. (1992). Multiple dopamine D4 receptor variants in the human population. *Nature, 358*, 149-152.

MODULE II

EVOLUTION AND EVOLUTIONARY PSYCHOLOGY

CHAPTER **12**

INTRODUCTION TO MODULE II

Evolution

FRUIT FLIES AND BANANAS ●

You and I have two eyes. They are located in the front of our face, point outward, and are slightly recessed into the skull. Each of our eyes has one lens and one retina. We do not have eyes like a fruit fly (*Drosophila*)—large, multilensed, bulbous structures protruding far outside the head and occupying almost a quarter of the head's space. In many ways, we would be better off having the eyes of a fly. Except for the obstruction imposed by the head and body, we would have a completely unencumbered, 360° view of the world. We would not have to move our heads around—or, for that matter, our whole bodies—to see what was behind us, and there would be no need to turn our heads to look both ways before crossing a street.

I eat bananas. Most of you reading this probably do too. Fruit flies also like bananas, a fact that many of us are aware of from having left our bananas too long in their brown paper bag.

What do eyeballs and bananas have in common? And why do I keep talking about fruit flies? The reason is genes. Our genes determined the format of human photography, film, and video. They also determined the whole production, distribution, and sales schedules for getting bananas from trees onto our breakfast cereal. We can see how human genes play this role by looking at fruit flies.

Imagine for a moment that fruit flies had evolved incredible intelligence and technology that permitted them to develop their own brand of photography and agriculture. What would a *Drosophila* photo look like? It certainly would not be the typical two-dimensional image that you and I get back from Kodak. Any self-respecting fruit fly would find such an image quite disturbing and would immediately ask, "Where are the top, the two sides, the back, and the bottom?" Their perception of such an image would be as whimsical to a fly as yours and mine would be to an Ansel Adams photograph that contained only the 3-inch-square central part, with the outer section thrown away.

A *Drosophila* television set would be the antithesis of the "flat screen" touted by advertisers for higher-end human consumption. It would be a spherical object into which the tiny fruit fly could insert its head. The inside of the sphere would be the TV screen, and the image would be projected along the whole 360° of the inside, so the viewer could appreciate what was happening simultaneously in the front, back, sides, top, and bottom. Just as us humans appreciate surround sound, the discerning *Drosophila* videophile would tolerate nothing less than surround sight.

And bananas?[1] We humans all know the developmental life cycle of a banana. In "adolescence," the banana has yet to reach even the green stage that most of us find unpalatable; it has such exceptional hardness that some liberal-minded states would ban it as a lethal weapon except for the fact that we never get to see it in such a condition. We encounter bananas in the supermarket only when they reach "early adulthood." Here, they are green, hard, and, to many of us, indigestible. If the fruit section contains only these types of bananas, we have three choices: (a) check out the raspberries instead, (b) go to another store, or (c) buy them, keep them in a brown paper bag, and wait until they reach complete "maturity and ripeness" when they turn bright yellow and soften. By choosing the third option, we always run the risk that neglected bananas will enter the "over the hill" stage where the skins turn black and the actual fruit is useful only for making banana bread.

The *Drosophila* who just read the above paragraph would be so incensed that it would fly to the nearest lawyer and press civil rights charges against me for "speciesism." Although the little critter might not take offense with the terms "adolescence" and "early adulthood," it would rightly be offended by the stages that I describe as "maturity" and "over the hill." The *Drosophila* supermarket would never offer green or yellow bananas. Instead, it would display only bananas that have turned black, and the blacker the banana, the better. Whereas many humans would feel squeamish even handling a black banana with insides the consistency of yogurt, the *Drosophila* would find such a fruit the epitome of haute cuisine.

The reason, according to psychologist David Barash (1982), is in our genes. We primates have an efficient metabolic system for the sugars in fruit. To obtain optimal nutritional content from fruit, we should eat it when the sugar content is high. Evolution has effectively tricked us into doing this by giving us taste buds and central brain mechanisms that respond to sugar as "pleasurable."[2] As Barash puts it, that is why we find sugar sweet, while an anteater might take equal delight experiencing a horde of termites biting its tongue.

Fruit flies, on the other hand, have a wonderful metabolic system for the digestion of alcohols. As fruit becomes "overripe," as we humans would have it, the sugars ferment into alcohol. As the alcohol content increases, the fruit becomes more nutritional for the *Drosophila*. If *Drosophila* have pleasure centers in their tiny brains, then a completely mushy, semi-fermented banana is as delectable to them as a sweet, ripe strawberry is to us.

To understand human behavior, we must understand evolution. So argue the proponents of a growing field of the social sciences called evolutionary psychology. The above example illustrates what have come to be known as *biological constraints* on human behavior. Generally defined, biological predispositions and constraints are mechanisms that have evolved over time to make it more likely that we behave in one way rather than other ways. Of all the possible ways of enjoying a banana, our evolutionary history has shaped us to enjoy the fruit only at a certain stage in its development. Because of similar evolutionary constraints, our forward-facing, binocular vision makes us quite content to enjoy flat, two-dimensional visual images. Module II, "Evolution and Evolutionary Psychology," highlights the *sameness* of humans and asks questions such as "Why do all humans use spoken language?" "Why can't humans smell odors as well as most other species?" and "Why are humans social?"

DESCRIPTION, ETIOLOGY, AND EVALUATION ●

The generic issue of genes, evolution, and behavior is politically and philosophically charged. To appreciate this module of the book, it is essential to distinguish among *descriptive*, *etiological*, and *evaluative* statements. "The sky is blue" is a descriptive statement. "Why is the sky blue?" is an etiological question. "Should the sky be blue?" is an evaluative issue. Too often, students who are wedded to a particular etiological cause or evaluative judgment erroneously deny the validity of a descriptive statement because it conflicts with their idea of what "caused this" or what "should be." Be careful of this error.

The issue will be most pressing in the discussion of evolutionary psychology. To illustrate the problem, consider two descriptive statements: (a) "Humans eat and enjoy fruit when its sugar content is close to maximum" and (b) "Men report a higher premium on physical attractiveness in a potential mate than women, while women say they want resources and security in a mate more often than men do." Few, if any, of you readers would experience an emotional reaction to the first statement, but a significant number will have a negative, visceral response to the second because it smacks of sexism. There is absolutely nothing wrong with a negative reaction to the statement on mate preferences—that, after all, is part of an evaluative judgment. The error is to let this negative evaluation call the validity of the descriptive statement into question.

Consider the process by which this statement was constructed. Researchers administer the same forms with the same instructions to men and women. Men and women then fill out the forms differently, and the researchers report this fact. The statement on mate preferences is a simple descriptive statement of what happened in the research. It is as true as the statement "the sky is blue."

Students frequently attack these descriptive statements, along with the researchers who made them, because the descriptive statements contradict their views of what "should be." According to them, researchers who report that men place a higher emphasis on physical attractiveness in a mate than women do are "sexist" because men and women *should* have the same values in mate preferences. In fact, the researchers are not making this conclusion. The men and women who filled out the forms simply differed in their responses, and the researchers are accurately reporting this difference. The researchers are making a simple descriptive statement. There may be very legitimate disagreements about the *etiology* of the sex difference in mate preferences and about the "should be" of these differences; however, these disagreements should never obfuscate the simple, declarative reporting of the sex difference in the first place.

The real area of debate should target *etiological explanations* of descriptive statements, not the descriptive statements themselves. "*Why* do men and women differ in these aspects of mate preferences?" is quite a different issue than reporting the observation in the first place. Here, evaluative judgments actually play an important role in the process of scientific inquiry. They force researchers to confront methodological problems, they encourage the scientist to develop different strategies for looking at the problem, and they ultimately result in a greater amount of knowledge.

THE NATURALISTIC FALLACY ●

The naturalistic fallacy attributes a moral rectitude or correctness to a phenotype developed through evolution. This is one of the most important myths to guard against because it is often misused in the science of genetics and human behavior. We humans engage in many morally opprobrious behaviors that may be influenced in some way or another by our evolutionary history. Extreme jealousy is a mild example; murder and warfare are extreme cases. If there is an evolutionary backdrop for human violence, then the naturalistic fallacy would state that violence is morally justified because we humans have some type of biological underpinning for violence.

Philosopher G. E. Moore explicated the naturalistic fallacy in 1903.[3] In its simplest form, it equates "what actually is" with "what actually ought to be" and confuses a descriptive statement ("The sky is blue") with an evaluative statement ("The sky ought to be blue"). It is very easy to follow the fallacious reasoning when applied to the color of the sky. The fallacy becomes much more seductive and tempting once human behavior becomes the content of discussion.

Once again, evolution is a process that follows certain rules but lacks insight, intentions, and morals. Observing that young adult males are at high risk for committing violence is a descriptive statement. Attributing young adult violence to an evolutionary mechanism is an etiological hypothesis. Permitting young adult violence to occur is a moral decision. We humans are the ones that must make the moral decisions and take responsibility for the outcomes of our decisions.

NOTES ●

1. The banana example was inspired from a passage by David Barash (1982) on why we humans find that sugar is sweet.
2. Once again, I warn the reader that evolution has no forethought or design. The "trickery" that I attribute to it is a literary convention.
3. See Wright (1994, pp. 330 ff) for a brief but excellent summary of the historical problem.

REFERENCES ●

Barash, D. P. (1982). *Sociobiology and behavior* (2nd ed.). New York: Elsevier.
Wright, R. (1994). *The moral animal*. New York: Pantheon.

CHAPTER 13

THE FIVE FORCES BEHIND HUMAN EVOLUTION

INTRODUCTION ●

Five different forces have influenced human evolution: *natural selection*, *random genetic drift*, *mutation*, *population mating structure*, and *culture*. All evolutionary biologists agree on the first three of these forces, although there have been disputes at times about the relative importance of each force. The fourth and fifth forces are new in the sense that they are not explicated in more traditional texts. The introduction of these forces is not an attempt to develop a "new" theory of human evolution. Instead, the forces of population mating structure and culture are arbitrary categorizations used to *organize* several different phenomena of human evolution. Scientists agree on the phenomena themselves, although they do not always organize them the same way.

Each of the five forces will be explained in turn. This is a risky approach because it can lead to the false impression that the five operate quite distinctly and differently from one another. In fact, there are important interactions among these forces, a topic that will be discussed at the end of this chapter.

● NATURAL SELECTION

Natural selection is defined as *the differential reproduction of organisms as a function of heritable traits that influence adaptation to the environment.* There are three essential components to this definition—(a) differential reproduction, (b) heritable traits, and (c) adaptation to the environment.

Charles Darwin noted that most species reproduce at a rate that, if unchecked, would lead to exponential population growth. Such growth is seldom realized in nature, however, because many organisms fail to reproduce. Darwin reasoned that if this differential reproduction was associated with adaptation to an environmental niche and if the adaptive traits were transmitted to a subsequent generation, then the physical and behavioral traits of a species would change over time in the direction of better adaptation.

Genetic variation fuels natural selection, and genetic inheritance transmits adaptive traits from one generation to the next. If all the members of a species were genetically identical, then there would be no genetic variation and hence no natural selection. The organisms in this species could still differentially reproduce as a function of their adaptation, but they would transmit the same genes as those who failed to reproduce.

Biologists index natural selection by *reproductive fitness*, often abbreviated as just *fitness*. Reproductive fitness can be measured in one of two ways. *Absolute reproductive fitness* may be defined as the raw number of gene copies or raw number of offspring transmitted to the subsequent generation. It may be expressed in terms of individuals (e.g., George has three children), phenotypes (e.g., on average, the red birds produce 3.2 fledglings), or genotypes (e.g., on average, genotype *Aa* has 2.4 offspring). For sexually reproducing diploid[1] species like humans, a convenient way to calculate absolute fitness is to count the number of children and divide by 2. For example, someone with two children would have an absolute fitness of 1.0, indicating that the person has left one copy of his genotype to the next generation.

The second way of measuring reproductive fitness is *relative reproductive fitness*. Relative fitness is simply the absolute fitness of an individual, phenotype, or genotype divided by the absolute fitness of a reference individual, phenotype, or genotype. For example, suppose that the absolute finesses of genotypes *aa*, *Aa*, and *AA* are, respectively, 1.8, 2.4, and 2.5. If *AA* is the reference genotype, then the relative fitness of *aa* is 1.8/2.5 = .72, the relative fitness of *Aa* is 2.4/2.5 = .96, and the relative fitness of *AA* is 2.5/2.5 = 1.0. It is customary, but not necessary, to express the relative fitness of genotypes in terms of the most fit genotype.

It is crucial to distinguish reproductive fitness from desirability. The fastest, the most agile, the longest-lived, and the most intelligent do not need to be the "fittest" in a reproductive sense. Fitness is defined solely and exclusively in terms of gene copies left to the subsequent generations. There is no mention of social values in this definition. A genotype that promotes longevity is more fit than one leading to a shorter lifespan only if it leaves more copies of itself.

Similarly, fitness is correlated with survival, but it is not synonymous with survival. Unfortunately, popular culture has equated natural selection with the term "survival of the fittest,"[2] implying a tooth and nail struggle in the jungle. Natural selection often involves subtle mechanisms, some of which may actually end in the organism's death! After a perilous journey from saltwater to the headwaters of a stream, salmon reproduce and then die. The male praying mantis is literally devoured by the female while in the very act of copulation.

An important part of fitness and natural selection is competition with other *conspecifics* (other members of the same species). The environment for an organism is much more than physical surroundings. It also includes the behavior of conspecifics. Hence, reproductive fitness for many organisms is defined less in terms of their physical capacity to reproduce and more in terms of being able to outreproduce other conspecifics. A male gorilla, for example, can survive, be healthy, and be physiologically capable of producing many offspring. His main problem with reproductive fitness lies with other males. Unless he can entice fertile females away from an established male, his reproductive fitness will be low.

The Three Modes of Natural Selection

For continuous traits, there are three modes of natural selection—*directional*, *stabilizing*, and *disruptive*. In directional selection, fitness increases with trait value. An example of directional selection is presented in Figure 13.1.

Here, the phenotype has a normal distribution (solid line). The dashed line gives the fitness function (aka selection function), and the relative fitness is expressed on the right-hand vertical scale. Fitness is lower for low values of the phenotype and becomes progressively larger for larger phenotypic values. After several generations of selection, the mean of the distribution will shift toward the right, in the direction of increased fitness.

Most human evolutionists suspect that human brain size underwent directional selection. About 4 million years ago (mya), the brain size of our

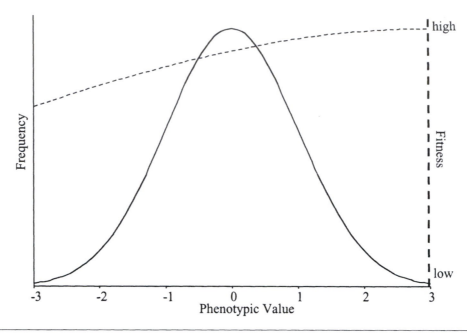

Figure 13.1   An Example of Directional Selection. The solid, bell-shaped curve plots the frequency of a phenotypic value (vertical axis on the left) as a function of the phenotypic value (horizontal axis). The dashed line plots the fitness for a phenotypic value (right-hand vertical axis) as a function of the phenotypic value.

probable ancestors, the *Australopithecines*, was around 450 cc (cubic centimeters), only slightly larger than that of a contemporary chimpanzee. Around 2 mya, brain size almost doubled with the emergence of *Homo habilis* and later *Homo erectus*. Brain size increased so that modern humans average between 1,300 and 1,400 cc.

The second mode of natural selection is *stabilizing selection*. Here, trait values that are close to average have the highest fitness, and fitness decreases as one moves away from the mean (Figure 13.2). In the popular mind, natural selection is almost always equated with directional selection, but most biologists suspect that stabilizing selection is the most frequent mode of natural selection. Most species are well adapted to their ecological niches—otherwise, they would have gone extinct many eons ago—so being somewhere around the average is more likely to be beneficial than having an extreme phenotype. Stabilizing selection will not change the mean of a distribution, but it may reduce the genetic variance over time.

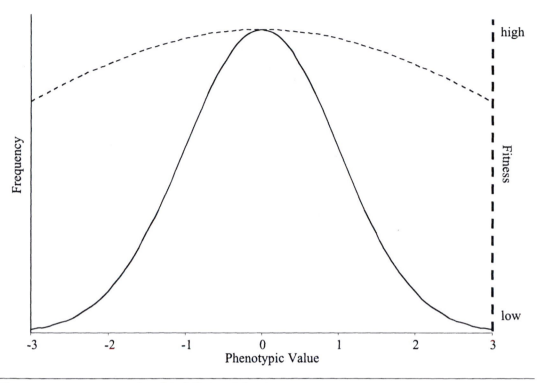

Figure 13.2   An Example of Stabilizing Selection.

NOTE: See the caption to Figure 13.1.

Human birth weight is a classic example of stabilizing selection. Before modern medical interventions, low birth weight neonates had high mortality. Similarly, neonates much larger than average posed serious problems for their mothers and themselves. In terms of infant survival, it was preferable to be near the mean rather than at one of the extremes.

The third mode of natural selection is *disruptive selection* (Figure 13.3). Here, phenotypes close to the average have reduced fitness compared to phenotypes at the extremes. Disruptive selection appears to be the rarest form of natural selection, and there are few well-documented cases of it. There does not appear to be a good example of disruptive selection in human evolution. Despite its rarity, however, disruptive selection may be very important for the emergence of species. After a suitable time, disruptive selection can lead to bimodal distributions that might eventually lead to different species.

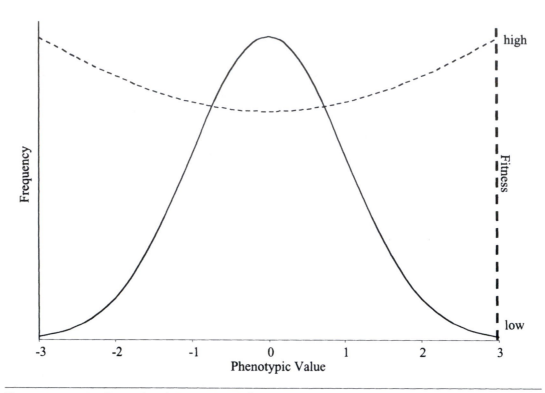

Figure 13.3 An Example of Disruptive Selection

NOTE: See the caption to Figure 13.1.

The Effects of Natural Selection

The ultimate effect of natural selection is to *change allele frequencies*. It operates only on what is already present in the genome of a species, making some alleles (and combinations of alleles) more frequent and others less frequent. Nevertheless, the appearance, anatomy, and physiology of a species may change over time simply because some alleles become rare after lengthy natural selection. Programs in artificial selection where humans control the selection process are the best illustrations of the tremendous genetic variability hidden in a species's genome. All contemporary strains of dogs had their origin in the wolf. The fact that dogs come in all sizes (from chihuahua to wolfhounds), color patterns (Dalmatians to golden retrievers), and temperaments (high-strung terriers to phlegmatic basset hounds) is due to deliberate selection of rare allelic combinations in the wolf genome.[3] Despite these differences, dogs can still reproduce with wolves.

GENETIC DRIFT •

Genetic drift is defined as *the change in allele frequencies over time due to chance and chance alone*. To illustrate drift, imagine the change over time in allele *A* in a small, isolated population of 10 individuals. Suppose that the frequency of *A* is .50 and the frequency of the other allele, *a*, is also .50. Hence, with 10 individuals, there will be 20 alleles—10 *A* alleles and 10 *a* alleles. In transmitting alleles to the next generation, the probability of transmitting *A* is the same probability as flipping a fair coin 20 times and getting 10 heads and 10 tails. This is the most likely of all possible outcomes, but the probability of this outcome is only .17; the probability of an outcome *other than* an even 50/50 split is 1 − .17 = .83.[4]

Suppose that we actually flipped the fair coin and ended up with 12 heads (or *A* alleles) and 8 tails (or *a* alleles). The frequency of *A* is now .60. The probability of transmitting allele *A* to the next generation now is equal to flipping a *biased* coin that has a 60% chance of heads and a 40% chance of tails. In 20 flips of this biased coin, the most likely outcome is 12 heads and 8 tails, but once again the probability of this single event is only .18. Again, we are more likely to experience an outcome *other than* a 60/40 split.

Suppose that we flipped this biased coin and ended up with 13 heads and 7 tails. In this generation, the frequency of *A* is .65. In the next generation, the probability of transmitting *A* is equal to the flip of yet another biased coin, but one that has a probability of heads being .65.

You can see how chance changes in allele frequencies in one generation alter the probability of transmitting the allele to the next generation. The process of genetic drift is equivalent to tossing biased coins in each generation. The degree of bias is determined by the allele frequency in that generation. As a result, a plot of the frequency of allele *A* by generation should show that *A* usually changes in frequency from one generation to the next.

Figure 13.4 illustrates the principle of genetic drift in three populations—one of size 10, one of size 100, and one of size 1,000. This figure illustrates two salient issues about drift. First, note how the line for the smallest population "bounces around" more than that for the population of size 100, which in turn is more variable than the line for the largest population. This phenomenon is due to the fact that *the most important factor influencing genetic drift is population size*. Drift will be greater in smaller populations. As population size increases, the effects of drift diminish.

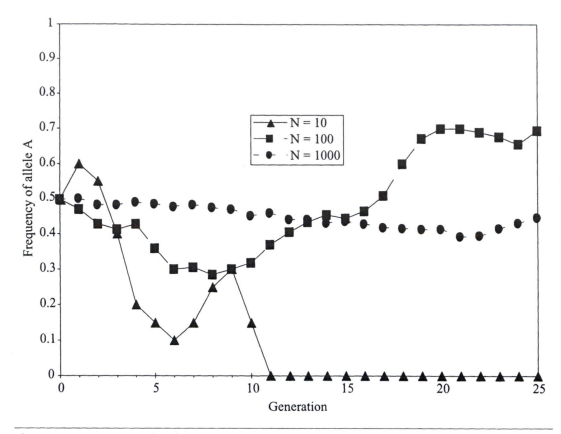

Figure 13.4   An Example of Genetic Drift in Three Populations of Different Sizes.

The second important issue in Figure 13.4 involves the line for the smallest population. At generation 10, there were only 3 *A* alleles with 17 *a* alleles, so the probability of transmitting an *A* allele is 3/20 = .15. By dumb luck, no *A* alleles were transmitted to the 11th generation. Once this occurs, allele *A* is lost from the population. Geneticists call this phenomenon *fixation*. In this case, allele *a* is fixed in the population. The only ways to get allele *A* back are by mutation or by immigration of an individual with *A* into the population.

Whenever the population size is small, the ultimate effect of drift will be to fix alleles. That is, if the process of drift continues over a large number of generations, then eventually one of the two alleles, *A* or *a*, will become fixed. Which of the alleles becomes fixed is a matter of chance.

The role of drift in evolution has been hotly debated. If we find a polymorphism in a gene among contemporary humans, does that polymorphism reflect the effects of drift, the effects of natural selection, or some combination of drift and natural selection?

Because we lack a time machine to travel back and sample DNA, there is no easy answer to the question. Geneticists weigh substantive issues ("What is the gene product for?") and educated guesswork about early human evolution ("How useful was this gene product in the millennia when humans were hunter-gatherers?") to arrive at a commonsense solution. Clearly, the genes responsible for the development of the eye and for the neural circuitry and mental computations that result in vision were heavily influenced by natural selection. The same may not apply to those polymorphisms that influence contemporary myopia (nearsightedness).

Geneticists capitalize on the phenomenon of genetic drift by studying polymorphisms in the junk DNA. Because these genes are not influenced by natural selection, these polymorphisms can act as a molecular "clock" that assists anthropologists in determining when groups of peoples split apart, migrated, and so on. More will be said of this in the next section, in the discussion of neutral genes.

MUTATION ●

Mutation is defined as *an error in copying the DNA*. Although geneticists use a bewildering array of terms to classify mutations, we consider only two different classifications, the first depending on the type of cell affected by mutation and the second on the amount of DNA that is mutated. In terms of the type of human cells affected by mutation, geneticists distinguish *somatic mutations* from *germinal mutations*. Somatic mutations influence somatic cells—that is, all cells of the body other than those that directly produce the gametes (sperm and egg). Germinal mutations affect the cells that directly turn into the gametes.

Because there are many more somatic than germinal cells in humans, the overwhelming majority of detectable mutations are somatic. Somatic mutations may have no discernible effect on an organism; for example, they may take place in an unused section of DNA, or they can influence the physiology of the cell (and the cell's daughter cells) when they occur in a coding region or a regulatory region of DNA. In some cases, somatic mutations result in abnormal cell growth, ranging from benign moles to malignant carcinomas. Although somatic mutations can affect the reproductive fitness of the organism experiencing them, they cannot be passed to offspring.

Germinal mutations, on the other hand, are the life force behind evolution. The ultimate effect of germinal mutations is to *introduce new genetic material*. Without germinal mutation, there would be no genetic variation, no natural selection, no genetic drift, and hence, no evolution. According to contemporary evolutionary theory and modern reproductive biology, germinal mutations are the only method of introducing *new* alleles and *new* arrangements of DNA into a species. All the other forces of evolution change allele and/or genotypic frequencies; they do not introduce new genetic material.

The amount of genetic material affected by mutation can range from a single nucleotide (as in the sickle-cell allele for β hemoglobin) to a whole chromosome (as in most cases of Down's syndrome). Mutations that influence a single nucleotide are called *point mutations* and have generated an important class of polymorphisms termed SNPs (for *S*ingle *N*ucleotide *P*olymorphisms), which were discussed in Chapter 7. Here, we will lump all mutations that influence more than a single nucleotide into a single category and term them *gross mutations*. Gross mutations can take many forms, including the deletion of a series of nucleotides, duplication of a large number of nucleotides, or insertion of a nucleic sequence. A classic example of a gross mutation in human evolution is the number of human chromosomes. Chimps and other great apes have 24 pairs of chromosomes, whereas we humans have 23 pairs. Somewhere in human evolution, two chromosomes fused together to give human chromosome number 2.

The effect of a mutation depends on where the mutation occurs in the genome. If the mutation occurs in a section of DNA that does not contain code for a peptide chain, does not regulate the production of a peptide chain, and does not influence subsequent replication of the DNA molecule, then it may have no influence on the organism or the organism's progeny. Some mutations that do occur in coding regions may also have no effect. For example, a point mutation that changes the DNA codon from AAA to AAG will still result in the amino acid phenylalanine being placed in the peptide chain. Mutations that do not influence the ultimate reproductive fitness of an organism are called *neutral mutations* and give rise to what are called *neutral genes* and *neutral alleles*. Although neutral alleles may not be important for evolutionary change, they are of extreme importance to geneticists tracing the evolution of populations and species. For example, if two human populations diverged recently, the frequency of the neutral alleles should be similar in the two groups, but if they separated a long time ago, then the allelic frequencies of neutral alleles should differ. Similarly, older human populations should have accumulated more neutral mutations than populations that have more recently fissioned from one another. Hence, genetic similarity as well as genetic variation on neutral alleles can assist in reconstructing human evolutionary trees.

The most likely effect of a mutation that actually has an effect on a phenotype is to reduce fitness. Proteins and enzymes have been honed and shaped by generations of natural selection to make sure that they work appropriately for the organism. An abrupt, random change to a protein or enzyme is akin to tossing an extra gear into a finely tuned motor or capriciously rearranging a circuit on a computer chip. Most such random acts harm rather than help functioning. If the affected allele is recessive, the loss of functioning is not critical. In all likelihood, the other allele will produce a functioning protein or enzyme. Consequently, deleterious mutations can build up for recessive alleles. This is probably the reason why several hundred different deleterious alleles have been identified for any single recessive disorder.

Occasionally, however, mutations can be beneficial and increase fitness. On the primate X chromosome, the gene for green retinal cone pigment is located quite close to the locus for red cone pigment. It is suspected that at one time, very long ago in mammalian evolution, there was only one gene, but a gross mutation resulted in its duplication. Further mutations altered the gene product in the duplicated locus (or perhaps the original one) so that it responded to light of a different wavelength. Natural selection favored the resulting increase in color discrimination and ultimately gave us the color vision that we primates have today.

Mutations are both rare and common depending on the type of mutation. We have seen that gross chromosomal mutations are quite common in human fertilizations, but the majority of embryos die *in utero*. Mutation rates for a single allele are very difficult to quantify. Those that occur in coding regions for dominant alleles that influence an organism's prenatal development may suffer much the same fate as chromosomal anomalies and hence be undercounted. Most geneticists, however, agree that mutation for an allele is rare and is on the order of one mutation for several thousand or several tens of thousands of gametes.

POPULATION MATING STRUCTURE ● (AKA POPULATION STRUCTURE)

Although the concept of population mating structure is implied in all texts on evolution, the actual term *population mating structure* is seldom encountered. Here, population mating structure is defined as all those factors—physical, temporal, anatomical/physiological, and behavioral—that result in nonrandom mating among members of a species. To understand this concept, we must first understand the meaning of a population. A population is *a group of individuals who belong to the same species, have a characteristic set of allele frequencies, usually reside in the same geographic area, and have a history of mating among themselves.* Some examples may help to clarify the concept of a population and how population structure influences evolution.

Marmots are a genus of rodent, and several species are found only in alpine (i.e., areas far above sea level) ecologies. Imagine two populations of marmots in the Rocky Mountains, one group inhabiting the alpine region of Long's Peak in Rocky Mountain National Park, the other group residing on neighboring Meeker's Peak. For a marmot born on Long's Peak to mate with a marmot living on Meeker's Peak, the first marmot must leave the alpine region of Long's Peak, traverse a valley, and then climb into the alpine region of Meeker's Peak. Although this may occur, it happens infrequently. Most Long's Peak marmots are born on Long's Peak, live their whole lives on Long's Peak, and mate with marmots who have been born and raised on Long's Peak. The same occurs with marmots on Meeker's Peak. In short, the marmots on Long's Peak are one population, and the marmots on Meeker's Peak are another population. Hence, *geographical separation* of populations is a major factor influencing the population structure of a species.

In some cases, different populations may reside in the same geographical area. Mayflies spend 2 years living as nymphs in the bottom of lakes and streams before they metamorphose into winged insects, reproduce, and die. Imagine mayfly nymph Elmer who has just met the love of his life, mayfly nymph Esmeralda. Elmer could be the persistent suitor who wines and dines Esmeralda every night for a year, but if Elmer is scheduled to metamorphose in an odd year and Esmeralda is programmed to change in an even year, the two will never be able to mate. Consequently, even-year mayflies are one population and odd-year mayflies are another population, even though the two may physically reside next to each other or in the same geographic region.

Physical and temporal separation permits different populations to evolve in different ways. Imagine that an unusually large avalanche on Long's Peak decimates the local marmot population. With lowered population size, genetic drift may be accentuated for a few generations and alter allele frequencies. Similarly, a drought in one year may deplete the number of hatching mayflies, again intensifying natural selection and accentuating the effects of drift.

Another factor in population structure is the *founder effect* that occurs when only a few members of a species colonize a new territory. The South American finches that originally colonized the Galapagos Islands (and provided Charles Darwin with an excellent example of natural selection) were probably few in number. Genetic drift, the effects of natural selection in adapting to a new environment, and their geographical isolation contributed to their evolution.

The amount of *immigration* and *emigration* among populations also influences allele and genotypic frequencies—large amounts of immigration/emigration reduce the differences between local populations, while small amounts of immigration/emigration permit the populations to diverge.

The evolution of human populations has been dramatically influenced by physical population structure. Even today, the physical separation of human populations maintains genetic diversity that otherwise would be absent. For example, people born and raised in the tropical rain forests of the Amazon basin are more likely to mate with other people born and raised in the same geographical area than they are with, say, North American Eskimos. Even within national boundaries, there are local populations. Someone living in Nebraska is more likely to mate with a fellow cornhusker than with a Yankee from Maine.

One of the major variables that influence population mating structure is behavior. Because behavior is central for social science, let us discuss it in some detail.

Behavioral Effects on Population Mating Structure

One of the clearest examples of psychological influences on population structure is the phenomenon of *mate preference*. Mate preference occurs when members of one sex prefer to mate with individuals who have certain phenotypes. Evolution occurs when these preferences result in *actual* differences in fitness—the preferred phenotype does, in fact, leave more gene copies than the less preferred phenotypes. One account of how the peacock's tail evolved invokes mate preferences. We have all witnessed the display of a male peacock during which he fans his long tail out into a semicircle of brightly colored "eyes." The reason for the display, however, has nothing to do with human aesthetics—the male simply uses this display to attract a female and mate with her. The story says that at some point in time, female peacocks developed a preference for males with large and colorful displays. Hence, they preferentially mated with males of these phenotypes. The males passed on their genes for large, colorful displays, and the females passed on their own genes for *preference* for large, colorful displays. The process in which mate preferences in one sex result in differences in fitness for phenotypes of the opposite sex is called *sexual selection*.[5]

We humans also have mate preferences, most of which show strong cross-cultural agreement, as demonstrated by the work of evolutionary psychologist David Buss (1994). When people from different cultures are asked to rate or rank traits in terms of preference in a potential spouse, almost all place a "nice person" as the number one quality; kindness, sincerity, and compassion consistently rate high. Intelligence is second. Not all traits, however, show cross-cultural uniformity. The desirability for premarital chastity in a spouse varies considerably from one culture to another.

Buss's research clearly demonstrates that, on average, different cultures agree on the traits that are desirable, neutral, or not desirable in a mate. But do people actually *do* what they *say*? And do (or did in the past) mate preferences result in *real* differences in fitness?

Here, the evidence is mixed. If males and females have similar mate preferences, if these preferences are strong, and if they are actually acted upon, then there should be strong spousal correlations for preferred traits. For example, if a woman—let us call her Diane—is a very nice person, highly intelligent, and physically attractive, she should be highly sought after as a potential spouse. Because many different men are pursuing Diane, she can have her choice of a partner. Because Diane has her own mate preferences and has a choice of Tom, Dick, and Harry, she is likely to select a male who is also nice, smart, and good-looking. A woman lacking Diane's attributes is less likely to attract someone like Diane's husband and is more likely to mate with a guy of her own level of mate desirability. As a consequence, we should find positive correlations among spouses for niceness, intelligence, and physical attractiveness.

Empirically, we do find significant spousal correlations for intelligence and cognitive ability[6] (about .40) and for physical attraction (about .30). The problem comes with niceness. Virtually all the empirical data on spouses show that they are completely uncorrelated on the majority of personality traits! Consequently, contemporary personality inventories fail to tap the construct of "niceness," and/or there really is no spousal correlation in the first place. Other evidence suggests that there is no spousal correlation.

When people are asked about mate preferences, almost all agree that "personality" is the most important issue, before even intelligence and physical attractiveness. In addition to niceness, people also express preference for a mate who is happy, outgoing, active, and talkative. These are attributes of the dimension called extraversion or positive affect. No studies have reported significant spousal correlations for this trait. People also express preferences against having a mate who is anxious, high strung, and worrying. These attributes comprise the dimension of emotional stability, negative affect, or neuroticism. Once again, there is no spousal similarity for this trait. In addition, few people report that social and political attitudes have any importance on mate selection, yet spousal correlations for social and political attitudes are higher than those for intelligence.

Hence, some aspects of mate preference might reflect discrepancies between self-report and actual behavior. People may think and even genuinely feel that an outgoing mate is more desirable than a shy one, but in the actual, day-to-day encounters with a specific person, the overt and concrete behaviors that constitute extroversion do not matter much in choosing a mate. Similarly, the failure to rate social and political attitudes highly may be due to our own underappreciation of these traits. We may think and even genuinely feel that they are arbitrary behaviors of little consequence, but when faced with a person whose attitudes are very different from our own, attitudes become an issue in mate choice.

CULTURE ●

Culture is not unique to humans. Species of monkeys and apes—and quite possibly other mammals and some birds—can transmit information and behavior from one generation to the next. Examples include termite fishing in chimps, potato washing among macaques, and even swimming. But culture has influenced human evolution to a degree unprecedented in any other species.[7]

Medicine is a clear example. Our contemporary knowledge about public sanitation and antibiotics has dramatically reduced death and disability from infection, and it is ludicrous to believe that the engineering plans for an urban sewer or the chemical formula for erythromycin are encoded directly in our DNA. Instead, clever people developed new insights into the causes of infection and then transmitted this information horizontally to their colleagues and vertically to the next generation. The result, in all likelihood, has been a reduction in the pressure from natural selection for genes that confer resistance to cholera, typhus, and a number of other infectious diseases.

There are many other examples of culture's effect on human evolution. The social and religious attitudes that are a part of culture influence allele frequencies. Feelings and beliefs concerning population growth, birth control, and abortion clearly influence reproductive fitness, and social and religious attitudes, like virtually all behavior, have a moderate heritability. Similarly, social attitudes about whom to marry and whom not to marry influence mating structure. Military culture obviously has influenced the reproductive fitness of individuals continually since recorded history began. Travel technology has made it possible for people in different parts of the world to meet and mate, diminishing the reproductive isolation of human populations. Domestication of the horse and camel intensified population migrations, and developments in oceanic transportation removed the reproductive isolation between Native Americans and Europeans. Even our new information age affects evolution: People on different continents can now meet over the Internet.

The prospect of genetic engineering is a developing cultural event that may have profound consequences for human evolution. It is still much too early to predict the long-term outcome of genetic engineering. For some traits, genetic engineering, even if it is technologically feasible, may not be the option of choice. For example, suppose that you had a child with a growth hormone deficiency. Would you pay $100,000 for genetic engineering or pay $2,000 to give your child injections of growth hormone at important stages of development?

Other aspects of genetic engineering inspire awe and dread. In the past, the overwhelming effect of human culture on humans has been to alter allele and genotypic frequencies.[8] Genetic engineering could open what may be Pandora's box by allowing science to create new alleles, thus changing mutation from a random phenomenon into a deliberate, scientifically guided enterprise. Suppose, for example, that altering the regulatory region of a few genes could allow them to operate for a longer time during fetal development and increase the number of neurons in the brain and human cranial capacity? We would have the potential for creating humans with *new* and *novel* genotypes that do not currently exist in the human genome. Prognosticating on the long-term future is best left to science-fiction writers, astrologers, and crystal ball–gazers, so there is no immediate urgency to act. If history is any judge, then some parts of contemporary science fiction will turn into science, while others remain fiction. In the case of genetic engineering, it is impossible at present to distinguish the two.

● THE FIVE FORCES: INTEGRATION

The five forces of evolution do not operate in five individual vacuums, with each force doing its own thing independently of the other four. Instead, the five forces have dynamic interactions, making it difficult for us humans to conceptualize the evolutionary process. (We humans have problems visualizing with five-dimensional space!) The most elaborate attempt to combine the forces is called *shifting balance theory* and was developed by the famous geneticist Sewall Wright (1968-1978).

Wright's synthesis of shifting balance theory was presented in no less than four volumes, but he offered a simple analogy for understanding it. Imagine a three-dimensional map of a mountainous region that has been flipped 180 degrees, so that the peaks of mountains become deep pits and the original valleys turn into ridges. This three-dimensional terrain represents the adaptive landscape of a species—the pits are regions of strong adaptation to the environment, while the ridges are areas of poor adaptation.

A species is represented as a blob—not a rigid and firm structure like a pinball, but a heavily viscous blob like a dollop of heavy grease, with all types of dust and dirt particles in it. Natural selection is the force of gravity.

When a species is well adapted to its environmental niche, the species (blob) resides in a pit. As the environment for the species changes, the landscape itself alters. When the environmental changes are small, the pit changes only slightly, rising a bit here or sinking a bit there. Some movement is imparted to the blob, so that it appears to rock back and forth a bit, but the overall change in terrain is too modest to expel the blob from its pit. This is a situation known as *stasis*, in which a species remains the same for a long period of geological time.

However, the environment can change in a big way, sometimes physically (e.g., an ice age), sometimes physiologically (e.g., development of a new pathogen), but often from competition from other species. When this happens, there is uplift in the adaptive pit, so that the terrain changes from a deep pit to a shallow bowl to, eventually, a ridge. In such circumstances, natural selection influences fecundity so that population size decreases. The decrease in population size permits random genetic drift to come into play. In this scenario, drift is equal to shaking the whole landscape in an unpredictable way, and population size equals a change in the size of the blob.

As the uplift changes the pit into a ridge, the blob—much smaller and lighter than it used to be—begins rolling downhill (i.e., natural selection is moving it toward a point of adaptation). The effect of genetic drift, however—in shaking the landscape—is unpredictable. If the population is on a ridge, drift may bounce it to the left or to the right. If the population is in a shallow depression where gravity would otherwise keep it, drift might be large enough to eject it from this potential adaptive pit. Eventually, the blob will be rolled and jostled into deeper and deeper pits. The species is adapting to the environmental changes. It will grow in size, reducing the effect of drift. As the shaking subsides and as the environment stabilizes, the blob will remain in the pit and another period of stasis will occur.

The blob, however, is no longer the same. During the period of intense change, the blob will have lost some particles of dirt and dust, while other particles of dirt and dust have replicated themselves. This represents allele loss and the increase in frequency of rare advantageous mutations. Effectively, the blob has changed, perhaps enough to become a new species. In some cases, the blob may have split into two different parts, each eventually settling into its own adaptive pit.

The effects of population structure and culture may be incorporated into Wright's model by imagining that we place the adaptive pit under a powerful microscope. Magnification shows that what appeared to be a single blob is in fact a large series of "bloblettes" that have settled into the tiny crevices among the boulders in the deep pit. Small bloblettes are connected to their neighbors through small crevices, while others are isolated from a partner by a pile of rubble. This denotes the spatial and temporal aspects of population structure. Mate preferences may be represented as different forms of magnetism that attract certain dust particles to others. When the landscape changes, the appearance from far away is that of a single, large blob moving, when in fact it is the movement of a large number of these bloblettes, all responding to gravity.

Culture changes the bloblettes from inanimate matter into things that can move and act on their own accord. They can now dig downward by themselves, becoming better adapted and allowing the population size to increase. As population size increases, bloblettes grow larger and merge.

Like all analogies, this account of shifting balance is not perfect, but it does demonstrate the important interactions of the various forces of evolution. When selection pressure is intense, population size decreases, allowing a greater role for drift. Viewed from a distance, the blob may appear to split apart, but under the microscope, the fission is really an isolated bloblette going its own way. The ultimate fate for most isolated bloblettes is extinction—they get trapped in small local pits where the decrease in population size is too rapid to permit them to slide into deeper adaptive areas. But occasionally, one bloblette makes it into one adaptive pit while another ends up in a second pit, and both increase in size until another upheaval takes place. In this case, speciation has occurred.

● COMMON MISTAKES IN EVOLUTIONARY THINKING

As we discuss human evolution and then evolutionary psychology, it is crucial to keep in mind the interactive nature of the forces of evolution. Amateur evolutionists, as well as many of their critics, often fall into certain errors that can color and even invalidate conclusions derived from data. This section will point out several of the common mistakes.

Evolution Has a Goal

Evolution is a *description of a process* that lacks consciousness, intentions, morals, and goals. Tigers do not have stripes because evolution wanted them to blend in against a forested background where the sun highlights one area but leaves an adjacent area in deep shade. Instead, tigers have stripes because at some point in their past striped tigers outreproduced other tigers. If things had gone differently, tigers may well have had spots, like leopards and jaguars. Writers speak of evolution as "working towards this" or "acting against that" because it is difficult to speak about a process without attributing some sense of agency to it. "The sun warms the earth" is a descriptive statement; it does not mean that the sun consciously changes its physics in order to keep the earth warm. Similarly, "evolution made humans smart" is also a descriptive statement. Evolution did not "intend" for that to happen—it just happened.

Evolution Works for the Good of the Species

Older writings and TV documentaries often spoke of evolution as working "for the good of the species." Lacking sentience, evolution does not work for the good of anything, even individuals. Species are a necessary consequence of evolution because of genetic transmission and, in sexual species, because of the requirement that one have the anatomy, physiology, and behavior to allow successful mating with conspecifics.

In *The Selfish Gene*, Richard Dawkins (1989) argues that evolution is really a case of some forms of DNA being able to outreplicate other forms of DNA. A chicken's egg did not evolve for the good of the chicken species. Instead, the chicken is an egg's way of making another egg. In the process, DNA can develop *any* type of mechanism that assists in its own replication, even when the mechanism involves inhibiting other conspecifics from reproducing. A classic example is the mechanism of the copulatory plug that occurs in some insect and reptilian species. After a male mates with a female, he secretes a thick, viscous "glue" into the female that inhibits—and in some cases even prevents—other males from having successful intercourse with her. This clearly works against the good of the species. To ensure the female's maximal reproduction, she should mate with many different males, to ensure that each and every one of her eggs is fertilized. Instead, the mechanism evolved because males with the genes for the anatomy and physiology for secreting a copulatory plug outreproduced males without those genes.

Natural Selection Explains Everything

Few humans can visualize more than three dimensions at one time, so when systems involve a number of different interacting forces, we cannot simply close our eyes and picture the landscape. In such cases, there is a temptation to keep everything else constant and allow only one dimension to vary. In general, there is nothing wrong with this approach, but one may run into problems in a highly interactive and complex system like evolution. The most common dimension to vary is natural selection.

There is a tendency to take aspects of human anatomy, physiology, and behavior and explain them in terms of natural selection having acted *directly* upon them. In the long run, it *may* turn out that the direct effects of natural selection explain most everything, but our knowledge of human evolution is so embryonic that we cannot make that claim today. Indeed, contemporary knowledge of genetics encourages a skeptical wait-and-see attitude.

Wright (1968–1978) argued for the principle of *universal pleiotropism*— the idea that any single gene influences several different phenotypes. Even if this principle is not universal, it certainly applies to a large number of loci. Consequently, if natural selection operates on one trait, changes probably will occur in several other traits. Deliberate and controlled experiments on selection in plants and animals bear this out. For example, John DeFries (DeFries, Gervais, & Thomas, 1978) derived two lines of mice, one selected for high activity, the other for low activity. It turned out that the two lines also differed in defecation rates, even though there was no direct selection for defecation. We humans defecate about once a day, not many times a day like many other mammals. Undoubtedly, one can concoct some selective advantage for our behavior, imagining for example that it reduced the scent trail left by a group of protohumans moving through the savanna. But historically, once-a-day defecation may have been a by-product from selection on an entirely different trait.

Similarly, many traits exhibited today may be secondary by-products of evolution, a phenomenon that Darwin referred to as *pre-adaptation*. It is unlikely that early hunter-gatherer populations experienced direct selection for operatic talent or the ability to memorize long lists of nonsense syllables. Instead, the evolution of cognitive abilities and a sophisticated vocal system opened the door for these behaviors to emerge as secondary consequences of natural selection.

The effect that genetic drift had on human evolution is impossible to establish at present because drift is a random and chance process. Some anatomical differences among contemporary human populations may have arisen simply by dumb luck because the populations were initially established by a small number of migrants. We may be able to piece the answer together at some time in the far future, when the genes for these traits are identified and the biological pathways of their effects are characterized. For the present, however, we must remain cautious.

Evolution and Optimization

Herons, pelicans, osprey, and loons all catch fish for a living, but they do so in quite different ways. A heron stands motionless in shallow water patiently waiting for a fish to swim by. When this happens, the heron swiftly grabs the fish with its long, extended beak. Pelicans fly over water looking for fish near the surface. When the pelican spots a fish or a school of small fishes, it goes into an abrupt dive and crashes into the water, attempting to scoop up the prey in its pouch. Ospreys soar high above water. When the osprey locates a fish near the surface, it goes into a deep dive and grabs the fish with its talons. Loons paddle on the surface like ducks. When the loon spots a fish swimming underneath, it dives and swims after the fish.

The different strategies for fishing illustrate that evolution does not find the *global* optimum. Instead, it finds *solutions*, some of which may be *local* optima. To use the shifting balance landscape, evolution has resulted in the heron, pelican, osprey, and loon living in their own adaptive pits. It does *not* guarantee that all four species *must* end up in the deepest pit in the whole landscape. There is no "best" solution for a bird to catch fish. Instead, there are several different solutions, and as long as a species develops *one* of them, it is perfectly okay.

To complete the analogy, when there is upheaval in the adaptive landscape, a blob is more likely to end up in a pit close to the one in which it started rather than in a deeper pit at the opposite end of the landscape. This reflects the fact that natural selection is constrained by the genes and the phenotypes that already exist in a species. If ospreys have to become better at fishing, then natural selection is likely to work in the direction of better eyesight, stronger talons, and more fluid aerodynamic design. It is not likely to reengineer the osprey to make it look and behave like a pelican.

Confusing Relative With Absolute Fitness

The confusion between relative and absolute fitness can lead to false inferences about evolution. When there is continuous selection against a genotype over time, then that genotype will decrease relative to the more fit genotypes. However, this *does not necessarily imply that the less fit genotypes eventually will be removed from the population*. That *may* be the case, but it is *not necessarily* the case. Why? Because the extinction of an allele or of a genotype depends on population size and absolute fitness, not on relative fitness.

To illustrate this principle, consider the data on relative fitness presented in Table 13.1. Here, allele *A* confers more fitness than allele *a*. In the current generation, it is assumed that the frequency of *A* is .60. With the relative fitnesses

Table 13.1   Response to Selection Using Relative Fitness

Genotype	Relative Fitness	Genotypic Frequencies		
		Current Generation	Next Generation	After 100 Generations
AA	1.00	.36	.366	.845
Aa	.98	.48	.478	.158
aa	.96	.16	.156	.006

Table 13.2   Response to Selection Using Absolute Fitness

Genotype	Absolute Fitness	Number of Genotypes		
		Current Generation	Next Generation	After 100 Generations
AA	1.050	36.0	38.4	11,116.1
Aa	1.029	48.0	50.2	1,948.6
aa	1.008	16.0	16.4	85.4

given in Table 13.1, the frequency of A in the next generation will increase to .605. After 100 generations of such selection, the frequency of A would be .92.

Now consider the same data expressed in terms of absolute fitness (see Table 13.2). Here, it is assumed that there was an initial population size of 100 and that individuals in this population transmitted, on average, 1.05 copies of their genes to the next generation. Hence, the absolute fitness of a genotype equals the relative fitness multiplied by 1.05. Notice how genotype *aa* increases in absolute numbers over time. After 100 generations, *aa* is quite rare *relative* to AA, but its actual numbers have quintupled.

As you might guess, the critical variable in all of this is *the rate of population growth*. When this rate is high relative to the relative fitness of genotypes, then less-fit genotypes can increase in absolute numbers. Once their numbers increase sufficiently to overcome the effects of drift, then the alleles for less-fit genotypes can remain in the population. When the rate of population growth is low relative to the relative fitness of the genotypes (or, of course, when population size is stable or decreasing), then the less-fit alleles are likely to be removed from the population.

Since the beginning of recorded history—and probably before that—the pattern of human evolution has been one of high population growth. Although natural disasters, famines, epidemics, and warfare act to the contrary, reductions in population are local and temporary—they are irregular blips compared to the long-term trend. Hence, the human genome may contain a number of alleles that would have been eliminated had not the population been growing.

The Naturalistic Fallacy

The naturalistic fallacy was described in Chapter 12. It is a fallacy so important to avoid that it merits reiteration here. It states that any predispositions that we have evolved give no moral justification for us humans to engage in those predispositions. Evolution is the ultimate pragmatist. It is a description of a process that has no goals, no purpose, and no morals. Yet we humans have evolved into moral animals. Our genes have provided brains that can remember what we have been taught and can anticipate the consequences of the actions that we are about to perform. Our cultures have imbued these brains with many different guidelines, along with a sense of moral opprobrium for violating them.

Many or most other species lack the moral sense that evolution has allowed us humans to acquire. House cats will torture a poor mouse for an hour or more before killing and devouring it. Wolves in northern Canada will isolate a bison from the herd, chase it until it succumbs from fatigue, and then eat it alive. Some humans do torture animals, although no one has ever been charged with extracting a rib roast from a living cow. Cats and wolves do not know any better. We humans do. Evolution may have worked to make us act selfish, devious, and iniquitous in certain situations, but evolution provides no moral justification for those selfish, devious, and iniquitous acts.

NOTES ●

1.   "Diploid" refers to a species that has two gene copies in its genome. Some plants are tetraploid, meaning that they have four gene copies.

2.   Philosopher Herbert Spencer, not Charles Darwin, coined the term.

3.   Of course, a few mutations here and there along the way probably helped.

4.   For the mathematically inclined, the probability of any outcome follows a binomial distribution for this example.

5.   Some regard sexual selection as different from natural selection, but the distinction is semantic and depends on how one defines "environment." If the female peacock's preference is considered part of the environment to which male peacocks

must adapt, then sexual selection may be viewed as a variant of natural selection, albeit with slightly different mathematical consequences. If one does not accept this definition of the male peacock's environment, then sexual selection may be considered a different phenomenon from natural selection.

6. The spousal correlation for intelligence and cognitive ability in industrialized countries is also influenced by the social propinquity created by the educational system. For example, the social milieu of college makes it easier for college students to meet, date, and eventually marry other college students.

7. Human culture has also profoundly influenced the evolution of species other than our own. Unfortunately, an all too frequent consequence of us humans being in an environment has been the extinction of other species.

8. An exception would be mutational effects from X rays, atomic energy, and certain chemicals.

● REFERENCES

Buss, D. M. (1994). *The evolution of desire: Strategies of human mating.* New York: Basic Books.

Dawkins, R. (1989). *The selfish gene* (New ed.). New York: Oxford University Press.

DeFries, J. C., Gervais, M. C., & Thomas, E. A. (1978). Response to 30 generations of selection for open-field activity in laboratory mice. *Behavior Genetics, 8,* 3-11.

Wright, S. (1968-1978). *Evolution and the genetics of populations: A treatise in four volumes.* Chicago: University of Chicago Press.

CHAPTER 14

HUMAN EVOLUTION

Protohuman Evolution

Anyone reading this section 50 years from now will laugh at its naïvete, and his or her bemused state will be justified. The discovery of new fossils, the sequencing of the human genome, and the completion of the Human Genome Diversity Project will provide new insights that will alter currently cherished beliefs. This has been the history of science in human evolution, so there is no reason to suspect that the trend will change. Still, we are stuck in the present and must do the best we can with the available data.

Most biologists suspect that humans and chimpanzees (our closest genetic relatives) split off from a common ancestor as recently as 4 to 5 million years ago (mya).[1] The split occurred in Africa. One of the first evolutionary developments that distinguished human ancestors from chimps was upright posture. One of the earliest of the human genera (plural of genus), the *Australopithecines* (a Latin term for "southern ape"), walked upright and had modified hands but in many other ways resembled a chimp. They were small (between 3 and 4 feet tall) and had curved fingers, a skull with a protruding jaw, a recessed cranium, and heavy ridges behind what are now the eyebrows.

The reason for the development of upright posture is unknown, but it certainly permitted the *Australopithecines* to travel long distances, freed their hands to carry objects, and may even have allowed more efficient thermoregulation. Because of these advantages conferred by upright posture, many anthropologists suspect that the early *Australopithecines* were adapting to life on the savanna[2] (the open places on the African plains) while the ancestors of today's chimps remained in the forested areas of central Africa. Over the course of 2 million years, several varieties and species of *Australopithecines* may have cohabited together and possibly even competed with one another in the savanna and woodlands that border the savanna. Little is known about the behavior of the *Australopithecines* other than that they probably used tools and were a highly social species, as chimps and humans are today.

About 2 mya, fossils begin to appear from our own genus, *Homo*. Although several species of *Homo* are recognized, we will lump them all together for didactic purposes and refer to them as *Homo erectus*. The most striking feature of evolution in *H. erectus* (i.e., striking for this book's purpose) is the change in the brain. Instead of the skull increasing in size as a function of increased body size, the very *form* of the skull changed. The upper cranium of the skull expanded and assumed a more rounded shape, permitting brain size to increase from about 450 cc to between 800 and 1200 cc. Other evolutionary trends continued—the protruding jaw receded a bit, teeth became smaller, and height increased. Two behavioral phenomena are striking—(a) tool use is now well documented in the form of flint and stone deliberately fashioned to act as chopping, scraping, and cutting tools; and (b) *Homo erectus* migrated out of Africa. Fossils of *erectus* have been found in China, Southeast Asia, and southern Eurasia. It is assumed that *erectus* retained the sociality of their ancestors.

As time progressed, these trends in skeletal evolution continued—the cranium and brain size increased, the jaw receded, the thick brow ridges shrank, and teeth became smaller. In more recent times (c. 100,000 or more years ago) anatomical variants[3] are evident in the fossil record. One of these, the Neanderthals,[4] were a heavy-boned hominid whose fossil remains stretch from Western Europe to the Middle East. A second variant, with a more gracile (i.e., slender) skeletal form, also appeared between 100,000 and 200,000 years ago. By 50,000 years ago, the gracile form lived side by side with Neanderthals in some areas.

Who were these variants, and how did they relate to anatomically modern humans (amh) and *Homo erectus*? This is a matter of considerable debate among anthropologists and evolutionary geneticists. Two main theories (along with numerous offshoots) have been proposed.

Theories of Recent Human Evolution

The first theory is termed the *multiregional hypothesis* (aka *regional continuity hypothesis*) and is espoused by some physical anthropologists (Wolpoff & Caspari, 1997). This view holds that *Homo erectus* populations in Africa, Europe, and Asia underwent convergent evolution and, with sufficient gene flow among the geographically separated populations, jointly evolved into amh. Convergent evolution occurs when different populations face similar selection pressures that lead to the same adaptive response. Development of the fin in fishes and in whales is a classic example in which two very different types of organisms evolved a similar mechanism for swimming through water. Applied to humans, the need to seek shelter from temperature extremes is the same the world over and could—in theory at least—lead to selection for the increased cognitive skills to build those shelters.

Few, if any, advocates of the multiregional hypothesis hold that convergent evolution alone is responsible for the worldwide anatomical similarity of modern humans. Some gene flow is required among geographically separated populations. Theorists posit that there was a sufficient amount of human migrations and mate exchanges between adjacent populations to permit *H. erectus* populations to evolve in similar directions. In this way, mutant but beneficial alleles that originated in, say, Africa could eventually spread to other regions of the Old World.

The multiregional hypothesis holds that the descendants of *Homo erectus* are our direct ancestors. Anatomically modern humans are the result of some beneficial mutations that caused an increase in population size. Subsequent migrations and interbreeding with extant groups of *Homo erectus* in different regions of the world spread these mutations. According to this view, Neanderthals were not a different species of hominids that became extinct. Instead, generations of matings between the Neanderthals and the more gracile variant, coupled with a selective advantage for the genes of the gracile variant, resulted in a change in the mean of a continuous distribution of skeletal dimensions.

The second theory has been dubbed the *Garden of Eden* or GOE hypothesis (Harpending & Rogers, 2000). The name of this theory has little to do with the accounts of creation given in the Judeo-Christian tradition. Instead, the term is a slightly perverse—but humorous—extension of early reports from the genetic literature of a "mitochondrial Eve" (Cann, Stoneking, & Wilson, 1987) and later a "Y-chromosome Adam" (see Cavalli-Sforza, 2000). Mitochondrial DNA and the Y chromosome are in many ways ideal for studying human evolution because they are passed intact from mother to child (mitochondria) or from father to son (Y chromosome) and do not recombine as the DNA on the autosomal chromosomes do.[5] This form of transmission has the mathematical implication that in some very ancient ancestral population, all but one of the mitochondrial variants (or Y chromosome variations) will eventually die out. After all, the mitochondria of a mother who has only sons will die out, as will the Y chromosome of a male who has only daughters. By examining today's mtDNA and today's Y chromosome, one can work backward to arrive at an approximate date for these ancestral populations.

Today's estimates are between 100,000 and 200,000 years ago. Somewhere in this time period, a single woman lived from whom all current mtDNA is derived. A man who also lived during this time gave rise to all variants of the Y chromosome seen today. Contrary to popular misconception, this Eve and Adam are *not* the ancestors of all modern humans. (In fact, they may not have been anatomically modern humans at all.) They are the ancestors of *only* our mitochondrial DNA and the DNA on the Y chromosome. Many other individuals contributed to the DNA in our autosomal chromosomes.

According to the GOE hypothesis, amh originated somewhere in Africa between 50,000 and 150,000 years ago. The African origin is suggested by the observation that genetic variation is greatest in contemporary African populations. This ancestral population was possibly a new species of *Homo* that grew in size and migrated—possibly more than once—out of Africa and into the Middle East.

One hallmark of the GOE theory is *population replacement*. Advocates of this speculate that early *Homo sapiens* was a completely different species that did not interbreed with the populations of *H. erectus* and Neanderthals with whom it came into contact. Instead, it competed with those populations and eventually replaced them.[6]

Two types of data are used in support of the GOE theory. First, archaeological investigations show noticeable skeletal differences between Neanderthals, recent *Homo erectus* populations, and the gracile form that is assumed to be our direct ancestor. In parts of Eurasia, the emergence of these fossils also coincides with a marked advance in technology stretching from Europe to Siberia. The second line of evidence consists of molecular genetic data. Estimates of the time frame for human origins from these data fit very well with the archaeological data.

Human Evolution Into the Historical Era

Irrespective of whether amh replaced and/or interbred with *Homo erectus* and Neanderthals, there is considerable agreement on the particulars of very recent human evolution (i.e., evolution from 100,000 to 50,000 years ago). The slanted forehead of *H. erectus* gave way to the large, vertical forehead of modern humans, permitting the brain to increase in size. The skeletal structure attained a gracile form very close to that of modern humans. Tool use—or at least the evidence of tool use—suggests that it developed into an art. Spearheads were invented, bone instruments were fashioned to sew, pictorial drawings appear in caves, and some implements show evidence of engraving. But human evolution was not finished by 50,000 years ago. The skeleton continued its gracile development, and cranium capacity increased further to give its present-day range of 1,000 to 2,000 cc, the average today being somewhere between 1,300 and 1,400 cc.

Most scientists believe that early amh were foraging hunter-gatherers. They lived in small, cooperative groups that would settle in a single location and hunt, dig roots, pick fruit, and possibly harvest grain until the immediate resources were depleted. Then they would move on. Many hypothesize strong sex-role differences during this period—the guys hunted, the gals gathered. The small human groups—like groups of virtually every other mammalian omnivore—adapted to seasonal change, migrating to areas of optimal foraging and hunting at the appropriate time of year. Somewhere in the history of this—and whether it started 2 mya or 20,000 years ago is anybody's guess—the mating structure changed. Some form of *Homo* eventually recognized a relative permanence in mating that said something to the effect that this guy (or these guys) has a recognized relationship with this gal (or these gals) that permits them to mate, call them "their own," and transfer property and prestige to their offspring. Early *Homo* also became cognizant of genealogy. Barak was not just Barak. He was also Thrug and Amalog's son.

Everyone agrees that the increasing human cranial capacity was accompanied by an increase in intellect—memory, symbolic manipulation, learning capacity, etc. The largest anatomical differences between human and chimp brains are in the frontal lobes—those areas associated with executive functioning, evaluation, and reason. The increase in frontal material permitted our hominid ancestors to develop culture beyond the simple social learning cultures of macaques, chimps, and bonobos. Our monkey and ape cousins have only the "monkey see—monkey do" cultural transmission. *Homo*'s ability to transmit culture includes simple imitation but expands into symbolic instruction. At some point *Homo* could communicate the idea "don't do it that way, do it like XYZ" without ever physically demonstrating the "XYZ" behavior. Barak is no longer just Barak and is no longer just Thrug and Amalog's son. He is also Gortog's grandchild, even though Gortog, dead for several years, is a person unknown to the listener.

The reasons behind the evolutionary increase in brain size are not known, although there is no shortage of speculation. The need to fashion better tools, the requirements for sophisticated social interaction with conspecifics, and the benefits of symbolic thought and language for competition between human groups have all been postulated as reasons for the intelligence of hominids. It is also possible that the causes for increased brain size shifted over time, say from social communication to symbolic and rational thought to competition. Whatever the reason(s), they must have been quite important. Metabolically, the brain is a very expensive organ. Although it comprises only 2% of body weight, it consumes about 20% of the body's metabolic resources. Such an expense does not come without important evolutionary trade-offs. Also, the increased brain size posed (and still does pose) difficult problems for mothers who must squeeze such a large structure through the pelvis and vagina during childbirth.

Two cultural inventions altered the environment for amh. The first (i.e., the first to be explained here, not necessarily the first temporally) was the domestication of certain animal species. A few human populations no longer had to hunt for meat. They could simply tame the "meat," lead it to green pastures, slaughter it at will, and use its milk, wool, and other products. The second invention was agriculture. It is thought that agriculture was developed sometime around 10,000 years ago, probably independently in several different areas of the world. The pattern of its discovery and diffusion is unclear, but that is of relatively little importance. The end result was the same—agriculture limited the nomadic wandering of some human populations. They had to stay in a single geographical area to plant, tend, and harvest crops.

It is assumed that agricultural populations increased in number. This had two important effects. First, some agricultural populations migrated into the adjacent areas occupied by hunter-gatherer societies. Because the agriculturists grew in size while the population size of their hunter-gatherer neighbors remained stable, the number of agriculturists would eventually overwhelm that of the hunter-gatherers. Through interbreeding, population growth, cultural assimilation, and/or competition, the agricultural societies would become dominant in many fertile areas of the world.

The second effect of population growth under agriculture was an elaboration of social roles. As the technology of raising crops improved, it was no longer necessary for everyone to toil in the fields. Some people could become what today's economists call service and manufacturing employees, while others became supervisors. The result was an integrated web of codependent roles and occupations, leading to the development of cities and what we now call civilization,[7] the first evidence of which appeared 5,000 years ago.

The archaeological record clearly shows that civilization did not start in one place and then spread unchecked throughout the world. Civilization appeared here and there in a series of starts and stops, and not from a slow, inexorable diffusion from a single central origin. In a manner still obscure to science, civilizations develop in an area, flourish, and disappear. To the best of our knowledge, the actual humans do not change, at least in any dramatic way—the cranial capacity of those who start and develop a civilization appears to be no different from that of those who disperse and engage in less sophisticated social, political, and occupational roles after the civilization's demise. Indeed, the reasons for change in civilizations are some of the greatest mysteries facing social science.

GENETICS AND HUMAN RACES ●

So far, we have examined humanity as a whole. Yet it is quite clear that over the course of history, humans have lived in different groups that have evolved different languages, cultures, and physical traits. What does genetics tell us about how individuals relate to a group and how different groups relate to one another? We begin the discussion by considering orangutans and jaguars.

Orangutans live on two large islands in Southeastern Asia, Borneo and Sumatra. By visual inspection, the orangs inhabiting Sumatra are indistinguishable from their cousins on Borneo, yet genetically, the two populations are quite different. They are two different races of orangutan.

Most jaguars have conspicuous orange, tan, and black spots, yet occasionally a jaguar is born with a dark, black coat that makes the spots impossible to see from a distance. Despite the glaring visual differences, these two types of jaguars are *not* different races.

To the geneticist, race need not imply visual morphological differences, and visual morphological differences need not imply race. Clearly, there are important differences between how geneticists define race and how societies define race. The social definition is *absolute* and *categorical*. It is the type of box that we check when filling out a form; it is how demographic statistics are broken down; it is often how we think of someone whom we have seen but never met, simply on the basis of that person's appearance; and it is based on clear, visual morphological differences.

Geneticists define a race as a population with a characteristic set of allele frequencies and whose ancestors have tended to mate among themselves for an appreciable amount of time (Goldsby, 1971). Geographical separation prevented the orangs on Borneo from freely mating with those on Sumatra, and evolutionary forces resulted in different allele frequencies on the two islands. The orangs qualify as genetic races. Only a few genes are responsible for the differences between black and spotted jaguars. The ancestors of spotted jaguars have freely mated with those of black jaguars. They fail to meet the genetic definition of race.

The genetic definition is *relative*, not absolute.[8] For this reason, some geneticists eschew the term *race* in favor of the term *genetic population*.[9] The Irish, Scots, and Welsh could be considered three different "races" of Celts, or they could be combined into a Celtic "race" if they were being compared to Greeks. The Zulus in South Africa, the !Kung in the Kalahari Desert, and Ibo in Nigeria could legitimately be compared as three different "races."

The genetic definition can also be dimensional. Genetically, human populations do not fall neatly into categories. Instead, they tend to blend into one another, often as a function of geographical proximity. The gradual expansion of humans throughout the Old World resulted in *some* geographical isolation, but many populations grew, expanded, and migrated to merge with other populations. As a result, when one color codes populations according to allele frequencies and then paints them onto a map of the Old World, the result resembles subtle changes in hue as one moves from one area to another. It does *not* resemble an Impressionist painting, with dabs of quite different colors placed adjacent to one another. The majority of human populations—or "races," if you prefer that term—genetically resemble the people geographically closest to them.

Note how the genetic definition of race mentions nothing about those visual and morphological characteristics that highlight the social definition. Genes for skin color, hair texture, and other observable physical characteristics are only a small part of the tens of thousands of loci in the human genome. Furthermore, population geneticist Mashitoshi Nei suspects that genes for external morphology can give misleading impressions of genetic distance because they change at a different evolutionary tempo than the rest of the genome (Nei, 1987). This is an important point, so let us further explore it.

Consider the following. The proverbial Martian biological anthropologist visits Earth and is asked to pick the "odd ape out" from the following collection of great apes—gibbons, orangutans, gorillas, chimps, and humans. Which would you pick? Now answer the following multiple-choice question:

The chimpanzees in the Bronx Zoo most closely resemble

(a) gorillas.
(b) orangutans.

(c) gibbons.

(d) the author of this book.

If the criteria for similarity were based on genes, then the odd ape out is the gibbon and the answer to the multiple-choice question is (d)—the author of this book. Despite all the obvious morphological differences between humans and the other great apes—density of hair, gracile skeleton, upright posture—we are genetically more similar to an orangutan than an orangutan is to a gibbon. Our closest genetic cousins are chimpanzees. Hence, a chimp is genetically more similar to us humans than to a gorilla or an orangutan. In short, external morphology is not always a good indicator of genetic distance among closely related populations or species.

The phenotype of human skin color follows the same lesson that we learned in discussing sickle-cell anemia. The primary correlate of gene frequency differences for sickle-cell anemia is malarial ecology, not race. Similarly, the primary correlate of skin pigmentation differences is *distance from the equator*. Dark skin is an evolutionary adaptation that has something to do with exposure to the sun and is found among the majority of Old World populations living in equatorial areas.[10] Many people in southern India and Sri Lanka are more darkly pigmented than some African populations, yet they are genetically closer to Scandinavians than they are to sub-Saharan Africans. Similarly, some populations in Papua New Guinea are visually indistinguishable from equatorial Africans but are genetically closer to current-day Japanese and Chinese than they are to Africans.

In summary, geneticists define "race" quite differently from social scientists and stress *all* genes, not simply those for skin color and other visible morphological differences. Because the vast majority of human genes result in "invisible" phenotypes (blood groups, kidney functioning, etc.), they are much more important for defining concepts like race or population than are loci for visible phenotypes. The old phrase "you can't judge a book by its cover" describes very well geneticists' view of human population differences. Concepts like "black," "white," and "people of color" are very useful and valid for the social scientist studying prejudice, but they are not particularly helpful to the geneticist.

In fact, the differences between the genetic and the social definitions of race become even more striking when one examines the types of data used by population geneticists to measure similarities and differences among populations. The simplest way to measure genetic distance between two individuals is to sequence a section of their DNA and then count the number of nucleotides that differ between the two.[11] However, to avoid the problem that natural selection may have created these differences, scientists prefer to study *neutral* genes. Neutral genes are those that have no selective advantage or disadvantage and are most often found among the "junk" part of the human genome.[12] We can corrupt the English language—and logic—by saying that these are the most invisible of the invisible phenotypes.

● GENETIC DIFFERENCES AMONG HUMAN POPULATIONS

Just how genetically different are human populations from one another? The short but correct answer is "Not very much." The same types of genetic studies that pointed to our recent African origins also imply that we are a very new species that has not had time for strong genetic divergence. Templeton (1999) compared genetic diversity among human populations to that of other large mammals and showed that coyotes, wolves, deer, gazelles, and elephants have anywhere from three to nine times the genetic diversity between their respective populations than we humans do among ours. He went on to argue that the term *race* should not be applied to human populations because no population is sufficiently different from any other one as to warrant the use of the word as it is typically used in population biology.

A full accounting of human genetic differences must await the results from the Human Genetic Diversity Project, a massive but troubled research project with two major aims: (a) the detection and cataloging of allelic differences among the quickly disappearing indigenous populations of the world and (b) using these data to reconstruct human evolution and migration. Nevertheless, smaller studies over the past 50 years have been so consistent in their findings that the broad conclusions are known (e.g., Cavalli-Sforza, Menozzi, & Piazza, 1994; Hartl & Clark, 1997; Nei, 1987; Nei & Roychoudhury, 1974). Somewhere between 10% and 15% of all human genetic variation differs between populations. The vast majority of human genetic variation—fully 85% to 90%—is found *within* human populations.[13]

The statistical jargon of between- and within-group differences is very abstract, so let us try to depict it in a picture. Figure 14.1 gives three normal curves with the same mean but different variances. The curve with the solid line has a variance of 1. This is analogous to the genetic diversity in the whole species. The curve with the short dashes gives the within-population genetic variance when it accounts for 85% of all genetic diversity. The curve with the longer dashes denotes the between-population genetic variance. Notice how similar the "total" curve is to the "within-population" curve. This demonstrates how the genetic variation *within* any human population—or "race," if you prefer that term—captures almost *all* the genetic diversity of our species.

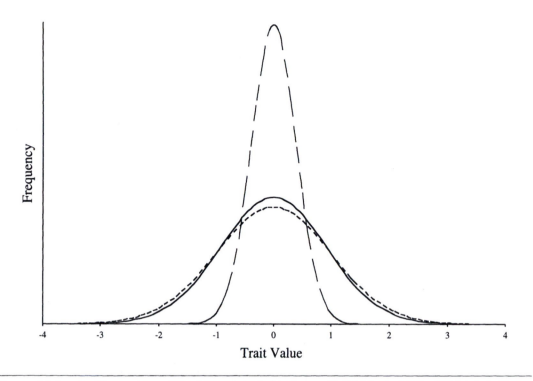

Figure 14.1   An Illustration of Total Phenotypic Variance (Solid Line), 15% of Which Is Due to Between-Group Variance (Long-Dashed Line Giving the Curve With the Highest Peak) and 85% to Within-Population Variance (Short-Dashed Curve).

A second way of picturing genetic diversity is to assume that we had the nucleotide sequence for a large stretch of human DNA and tabulated all the nucleotide differences in the human species. Let us scale these differences so that the total variance is 100 units, and let 15% of these differences be due to between-population (or between-race) differences. Now let us pick two individuals at random from the whole human species (regardless of race) and count the number of nucleotides at which they differ in this DNA stretch. Suppose that we repeat this an infinite number of times—selecting two random people and counting the number of nucleotide differences. We then tabulate the percentage of our pairs who have no differences, the percentage with one or fewer differences, the percentage with two or fewer differences, and so on. The solid line in Figure 14.2 gives a plot of these hypothetical data.[14] To interpret these data, pick a figure on the horizontal axis—say five, for example—and then read the value on the vertical axis for the solid curve. For five nucleotide differences, the value on the vertical axis is 30.3. This means

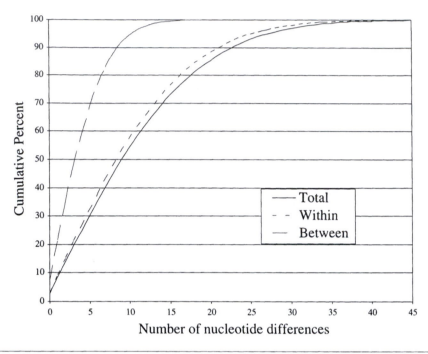

Figure 14.2   The Relationships Among Total Phenotypic Variance, Between-Group Variance, and Within-Group Variance.

that 30.3% of the pairs of randomly chosen individuals differed by five or fewer nucleotides. Hence, 69.7% of them differed by more than five nucleotides.

Suppose we now select two individuals *within the same population* (or *race*, if you prefer) and count their differences. Again, we repeat this an infinite number of times and tabulate the percentage of pairs who have a certain number of nucleotides (or fewer) different. This curve is depicted in the short-dashed line in Figure 14.2. Notice how this curve differs very little from the one from two randomly selected people from the entire species. This implies that two individuals within the same race are almost—but not quite—as different from each other as two individuals selected from the whole species. Most of human genetic diversity is found *within* a race.

The long-dashed curve in Figure 14.2 depicts what would happen if we calculated the *mean* nucleotide sequence for each race. We picked two races at random and then compared the *mean* nucleotide sequence of the first race with the *mean* nucleotide sequence of the second race. Again, by repeating the sampling a very large number of times and tabulating the differences, we would arrive at a curve similar to the long-dashed one in

Figure 14.2. Notice how this curve departs markedly from the other two. More than two-thirds of the racial means differ by five nucleotides or fewer, and about one third of the comparisons within a race differ by five or fewer nucleotides, while 30.3% of the comparisons made at the species level differ by five or fewer nucleotides. Of the racial means, 99.9% differ by 17 nucleotides or fewer, whereas this cutoff captures 82% of the within-race comparisons and 79% of the species comparisons.

If this hypothetical example were applied to, say, the ABO gene, the results would suggest that the majority of human populations have the A allele, the B allele, and the O allele in them. Although the populations differ in the *frequency* of the A, B, and O alleles, these differences in frequency are usually relatively minor compared to the fact that almost all human populations have the three alleles in them.

A final thought experiment could also illustrate the concept of between- and within-population genetic diversity. Suppose a grand catastrophe occurred (e.g., a large asteroid struck Earth) that resulted in the extinction of all of humanity except for a population of Eskimos living on the Arctic Circle. After many years, this population expands and migrates to eventually resettle the entire planet. From such limited origins, humanity would now have fully 85% to 95% of its pre-cataclysmic genetic diversity. That is, we would go from the solid-line normal curve in Figure 14.1 to the short-dashed curve in Figure 14.1. Or, if we wanted to select two randomly chosen survivors and compare them to randomly chosen people before the event, then the differences would be in the range of the short-dashed curve and the solid curve in Figure 14.2. People on different corners of the planet may *look* more similar to one another than they did before the calamity, but the genes for visible morphology are only a very small—and inconsequential—part of the totality of human genetic diversity.

NOTES ●

1.   In terms of biological classification, the split resulted in the development of the family Hominidae; hence, the term *hominid* refers to all of our ancient ancestors from this split onward.

2.   Preoccupation with the savanna environment may be a classic case of looking for the keys under the lamppost because the light is better there. Bones in humid, forested areas decay rapidly, whereas those in drier climates fossilize much easier.

3.   I use the term *variant* loosely. It does not necessarily imply a different species, although that might indeed be the case.

4.   Named after the Neander Valley in Germany where their fossils were first discovered. Although the term Neanderthal today carries the connotation of a brutish and stupid barbarian, Neanderthals had the noble qualities of aesthetics and respect for the dead, evident in their careful burials. Why they disappeared has not been

clearly established. They may have interbred with a more numerous variant of *Homo* and lost their distinctive anatomy and/or been driven toward extinction by competition with anatomically modern humans (amh).

5. There is, however, a small section of the Y chromosome, called the pseudoautosomal region, that recombines with a homologous region on the X chromosome.

6. Note that the ideas of replacement versus interbreeding are *not* mutually exclusive. Both phenomena may have occurred.

7. The term *civilization* has several meanings. Here, it is meant as an elaborate system of interacting social, political, and occupational roles that coincides with the development of cities. It is not meant to imply "cultural refinement" in either a moral or an aesthetic sense, nor is it meant to imply that nonagricultural societies are "uncivilized." *All* human populations have a culture, but not all human populations have a culture that involves cities.

8. A relative term has meaning only when it is compared to something else. Philadelphia is north of Baltimore, and Boston is north of Philadelphia; hence, Philadelphia can be north and south at the same time—it all depends on which city Philadelphia is compared to.

9. Be careful not to confuse the term *population* as used in genetics with the same term used in statistics.

10. The reason(s) for differences in human pigmentation are not completely known. The best guess is that our very early ancestors were lightly pigmented and had a dense covering of hair, much like today's chimps. Loss of hair was accompanied by darkening of the skin to prevent damage from ultraviolet (UV) radiation. As humans migrated from equatorial regions, selection pressure for UV protection diminished and was replaced by a greater need for UV light to assist in the synthesis of vitamin D, something better accomplished by lighter pigmentation.

11. Naturally, there are other ways in addition to this oversimplified example. For repeated nucleotide sequences, one could compare the number of repeats in person 1 and person 2 and then take the absolute value of the difference.

12. Neutral alleles are also helpful in constructing evolutionary clocks. Because mutations that cause nucleotide substitutions occur at a fixed rate, one can obtain crude estimates of the time of population divergence by studying neutral alleles. Alleles subject to selection cannot perform this task as easily as neutral alleles can.

13. Technically, 5% to 15% of all genetic variance is due to mean differences in allele frequencies between populations. The remaining 85% to 95% is within-population genetic variance.

14. The hypothetical curves in the figure were generated from Monte Carlo simulations assuming that the original distribution was normal.

● REFERENCES

Cann, R. L., Stoneking, M., & Wilson, A. C. (1987). Mitochondrial DNA and human evolution. *Nature, 325*, 31-36.

Cavalli-Sforza, L. L. (2000). *Genes, peoples, and languages.* New York: North Point Press.

Cavalli-Sforza, L. L., Menozzi, P., & Piazza, A. (1994). *The history and geography of human genes.* Princeton, NJ: Princeton University Press.

Goldsby, R. A. (1971). *Race and races*. New York: Macmillan.

Harpending, H., & Rogers, A. (2000). Genetic perspectives on human origins and differentiation. *Annual Review of Genomics and Human Genetics, 1*, 361-385.

Hartl, D. L., & Clark, A. G. (1997). *Principles of population genetics* (3rd ed.). Sunderland, MA: Sinauer Associates.

Nei, M. (1987). *Molecular evolutionary genetics*. New York: Columbia University Press.

Nei, M., & Roychoudhury, A. K. (1974). Genetic variation within and between the three major races of man, Caucasoids, Negroids, and Mongoloids. *American Journal of Human Genetics, 26*, 421-443.

Templeton, A. R. (1999). Human races: A genetic and evolutionary perspective. *American Anthropologist, 100*, 632-650.

Wolpoff, M., & Caspari, R. (1997). *Race and human evolution*. New York: Simon & Schuster.

CHAPTER **15**

INTRODUCTION TO EVOLUTIONARY PSYCHOLOGY

Imagine yourself and your partner alone on a camping trip far from civilization. In the middle of a dark night, you see a bright light several hundred meters away. What do you do? You would probably talk with your partner about several different options: (a) staying where you are, (b) walking and introducing yourselves to the unknown campers, (c) waiting until morning and then playing it by ear, or (d) finding a different campsite the next day to be away from other people. You would arrive at some mutual agreement and then execute that action. There is one behavior that neither of you would do—stand upright and, without communicating to each other, walk in a zombie-like trance toward the light.

Now imagine that you and your partner are moths instead of humans. Faced with a bright light on a dark night, both of you would orient and then proceed to the light quite oblivious of the other. There would be no social discourse or give-and-take maneuvering to achieve consensus. There is only a built-in stimulus response connection.

So why do humans and moths behave differently? Among the several levels at which this question can be answered is an evolutionary level. Moths have a hardwired response to light because at some point in their evolutionary history, moths that oriented and flew toward light reproduced more often than those who did not. We humans followed a different evolutionary path.

This example highlights an essential feature of evolutionary psychology—evolution predisposes the members of a species to engage in certain responses and at the same time constrains them from performing other responses. In the moth, DNA assists in the construction of a biological system that mechanically responds to light. Moth cognition—to the extent that there is any cognition at all—does not play a part in this behavior. In humans, DNA assists in the construction of a biology that permits enormous learning, the ability to think and plan ahead, symbolic communication with conspecifics, and cognitive appraisal of the likely outcomes of situations that we have never experienced. We are predisposed toward flexibility and constrained from developing a fixed and rigid response to light.

● SOCIAL ORGANIZATION, AGGRESSION, AND MATING OF THREE GREAT APES

Evolutionary psychology is ripe with examples from the animal world. Usually, a number of species are used, many of them quite distant to us humans, and each species illustrates a basic principle (e.g., the parental behavior of the male sea horse is an example of parental investment theory). Let us depart from this formula by first examining thumbnail sketches of the social organization, mating styles, and aggression of the three great apes that are our genetically closest relatives—gorillas, chimpanzees, and bonobos. By comparing and contrasting the behavior of these three species, we can illustrate many of the major issues of evolutionary psychology.

Gorillas

A gorilla community is dominated by a single adult male silverback, although sometimes the silverback will allow a good buddy or two to share his reign. The rest of the group consists of several adult females and their juvenile and adolescent offspring. The silverback(s) vigorously defend their harem against the attempts of single males to entice away one or more of the breeding females. Young adult males almost always leave their natal group and try to gather a harem of their own. Life is tough for the bachelor. He will either wander alone or join several other bachelors to form a group of their own. Gathering a harem is not easy. By dumb luck, an old silverback may die and the closest bachelor, after fending off attempts by rival males, may claim most of the harem. More typically, however, the male collects one female at a time by challenging a silverback in an established group and luring a female away. As a result, most males do not mate, and the lucky few who do sire a large number of offspring (Harcourt, Fossey, Stewart, & Watts, 1980).

Gorilla mating—like that in chimps and bonobos—begins when a female enters *estrus*.[1] In response to hormones, the female will "present" her bottom to the adult male(s) of the group. Because of the social structure, the female gorilla mates only with the silverback(s) in the group. In such a system, paternity is assured—if the father is not the dominant male, then it is his best buddy.

Although gorillas are remarkably peaceful in general, males engage in infanticide in two situations (Wrangham & Peterson, 1996). The first is when a male gains a new female or takes over a whole troop. In this situation, he will often kill all the infants of his new mate(s). The second situation is more insidious. A male may invade an established harem and kill an infant, despite an aggressive defense from the silverback and the infant's mother. When this occurs, a strange phenomenon takes place: Within a few days, the infant's mother will abandon her group and take up with the strange male who killed her offspring! A human mother might plot murderous revenge, but the gorilla mother prefers to desert a male who proved incapable of defending her infant in favor of another male who is more likely to protect her future infants. For the killer, this type of infanticide is a tactic to gain a mating female.

Chimpanzees

Chimps are organized into communities centered on a cadre of adult males. Males remain within the troop into which they are born and forge strong social bonds with one another. They will travel together, groom one another, and aggregate into opportunistic hunting parties. Although power politics and alliances are a way of life among the males within a chimp community, the males of a group unite against the males in neighboring communities. They actively patrol their own group's territory to prevent incursion, and they form "party gangs" to raid a neighboring chimp community to kill a male or abduct a female (Goodall, 1986; Wrangham & Peterson, 1996).

Females emigrate from their natal community and become associated with another group of males. Females do not bond with other females or with males as strongly as the males of a troop bond to one another, and they live in home ranges that overlap the troop's territory. In the dominance hierarchy within the group, all the adult males are invariably dominant to the females. According to Wrangham and Peterson (1996), a young male "enters the world of adult males by being systematically brutal toward each female in turn (when adult males aren't close enough to take sides) until he has dominated all of them. . . . In a typical interaction, he might charge at the female, hit her, kick her, pull her off balance, jump on top of her huddled and screaming form, slap her, lift her and slam her to the ground, and charge off again" (p. 143).

As for gorillas, chimp mating begins with estrus and has three forms (Tutin, 1980). The first and most typical form is for the female to mate promiscuously and frequently with virtually every male in her group. In the second form, which often occurs close to ovulation, one of the high-ranking males may form a short-term, possessive bond with the female. Here, the male will remain close to the female and use combinations of threats and aggression to discourage her from leaving and to prevent subordinate males from copulating. Both the promiscuous and possessive forms can take place within a single estrous period. The third and rarest form is the consortship. Here, the female and a single male depart from the group, often surreptitiously, and remain together for an extended period during which they actively avoid contact with other chimps. Because of the highly promiscuous nature of chimp sex, paternity is seldom certain.

Chimp mating can involve considerable aggression. Males, especially lower ranking ones, will intimidate a female by threat and physical beating, eventually coercing her into copulating with him. A female in heat attracts the attention of numerous males who, particularly close to ovulation, chase her and fight among themselves over the right to have sex. If a male can isolate the female from the other males, he will sometimes force her into a consortship.

Like gorillas, male chimps may practice infanticide when a new female joins their group with an infant. Males will gang up on the new female and, despite her defense, eventually rip the infant away from her, take it to a secluded area, and kill it.

The vicious side of chimps is matched by their ability to make peace (de Waal, 1989). One group of chimps does not sit down with its neighbors to make peace, but individual chimps within a group deliberately go out of their way to reconcile conflict. A subtle touch and a glance might be sufficient to appease an aggressor. Grooming calms an upset colleague and promotes friendship.

Bonobos

Many scientists and most lay people are unaware of the pygmy chimpanzee or bonobo.[2] If they see one at a zoo, they will mistake it as a common chimpanzee. Indeed, although there are striking similarities in appearance between the bonobo and the chimp,[3] the two are separate species whose territories do not overlap. The bonobo (or *Pan paniscus*) lives in the dense rain forests south of the Congo river, while the chimp (*Pan troglodytes*) lives north of the river, often in more open and drier regions.

Like chimps, bonobos are social primates. Males remain with their natal group, while females typically emigrate to a neighboring group. However, the structure of a bonobo community is quite different from that of a chimp community. In contrast to the strong male–oriented chimp society, the adult bonobo female is either codominant or has a moderate dominance advantage over her male counterpart, even though she is physically smaller than he is (Kano, 1992; Wrangham & Peterson, 1996). Among bonobos, who you are counts more than what sex you are. The strongest social bonds are among females and between a male and his mother. The weakest bonds are among males. The strong power politics of chimp males takes a decidedly softer tone in male bonobos. In fact, an adult bonobo male often relies on his mother and her close female friends to intervene and mute aggression from another male (de Waal, 1989, 1995).

As for chimps, heterosexual sex in bonobos is associated with estrus, but a bonobo female spends more of her cycle in sexually receptive mode than her chimpanzee cousin. Bonobo mating is largely promiscuous, so paternity is rarely assured.

The techniques of bonobo sex give the impression that some ancient bonobo had memorized a human sex manual and tried out everything in it. In the bonobo's life, sex begins long before puberty and involves a number of different positions (among them, the infamous missionary position), genital stimulation by hands, and overt oral sex. And bonobo sex is not strictly of the hetero variety. Two female bonobos will engage in *hoka-hoka*, the local African phrase for genito-genital rubbing. The two lie together in the missionary position, bring their clitorises together, and move their hips quickly from side to side. Hoka-hoka ends, as Wrangham and Peterson (1996), state, "with mutual screams, clutching limbs, muscular contractions, and a tense, still moment. It looks like orgasm" (p. 210).

Bonobos engage in sex for a much wider range of reasons than do chimps—and possibly even humans. It is not uncommon for a female chimp to offer sex in exchange for a favored food item, but among bonobos it is a regular occurrence. Sex is used for reconciliation after a disagreement (de Waal, 1989), for establishing friendships, for calming down an emotional friend, and for greeting someone who has been away for a while. It also may be done just for fun. Sex is frequent: A bonobo can mate several dozen times in a single day. It should come as little surprise that, after hearing this lecture in class, one student turned his eyes skyward, clasped his hands in prayer, and muttered, "God, if there is reincarnation, then next time please make me a bonobo."

Compared to chimps, almost every species is peaceful, but bonobo males are especially so. Intermale aggression does occur among bonobos, but not at nearly the rate it does among chimps. Male aggression against a female, almost a daily occurrence in chimps, is much less frequent in bonobos. Any bonobo male with sufficient temerity to threaten and attack a female is likely to find himself driven off by a gang of her female friends. Infanticide, if it takes place at all, is rare. There have been no documented cases of bonobos forming party gangs to invade a neighboring territory in order to kill a male. To the contrary: Two adjacent bonobo communities have been known to meet, socialize, and, of course, have sex with each other's members. This is something unheard of in chimp society.[4]

● ARE HUMAN SOCIAL ORGANIZATION AND MATING BIOLOGICALLY CONSTRAINED?

To illustrate predispositions and constraints shaped by evolution, let us compare human social organization, mating patterns, and aggression to those of gorillas, chimps, and bonobos. Imagine, for the moment, the college-aged men and women belonging to a human culture that follows the pattern of gorillas. There could be sororities and fraternities, of course, but they would take a decidedly different form. Each sorority would be small and headed by a mature adult male[5] who would jealously guard his harem and their offspring from contact with any other college male. To keep his females under eye, the male probably would demand that they all take the same classes that he takes. Perhaps two or three different harem groups may share the same classroom, but there probably would be physical barriers in the room to prevent them from interacting. Otherwise, the males would disrupt the class by their displays, posturing, games of one-upmanship, and even overt aggression to prevent any female in their harem from leaving and/or to entice another female into joining their harem.

Each coed would feel that it is quite natural to have sex with the male and have him as the father of her children. Although there may be squabbles among the women, there would be no possessiveness or jealousy about sharing him with the others. Both the male and the females may feel physical and perhaps even emotional attraction to one another; however, the concept of casually dating someone else would never even cross anyone's mind.

Males without a harem would either live solitary lives or join together into an all-male fraternity. Bachelor males could easily take classes with other bachelor males, but to maintain order, the college would prohibit bachelors from taking courses with harems. If a harem master gets a bit long in the tooth, a bachelor will engage in repeated displays of dominance and aggression with him (and with other bachelors) in order to drive him away and take over the women. If the bachelor succeeds, the females will not follow their former mate and father of their children. They will placidly go with the victor, have sex with him, and have his children.

There would be continual games of dominance between the bachelors and a harem male as he leads his harem and children across campus. Sometimes a bachelor might find a female and her infant isolated from the main group. In this situation, he might grab and kill the infant despite vigorous protests and attacks from the mother. It may take a few days for the female to get over this event, but soon she would find herself attracted to her child's killer and would leave her own harem group to join him. There would be no charges of murder, nor would there be any disciplinary action from the university. The bachelor did what any reasonable unattached male would do to try to get a mate.

Now imagine a different scenario. Again, let us consider collegiate life, but this time, one organized on the basis of the chimpanzee culture. Here, there are no dominant males with their harems. Instead, there would be very strong fraternities with fierce—perhaps even murderous—rivalries among them. Sororities, if there were any, would have poor internal organization compared to that of the fraternities. In general, the women would act a bit more as loners, while the males would almost always be found with their buddies. Each sorority would be strongly associated with a fraternity. The guys might play politics and power games among themselves, but each fellow would act bossy toward the women, who, in turn, would submit to his authority.

A coed would go through cycles of heat and sexual abstinence. As she enters heat, the guys will pay closer attention to her and quarrel among themselves to get near her. Although she might prefer some males to others, she would find it very natural to have sex repeatedly with all the frat boys. She must be careful in spurning someone's advances; if she protests too much, she may be beaten and raped. As ovulation nears, one of the more dominant males might try to sequester her for himself by challenging any subordinate who tries to mate with her. He may be successful for a while, but he usually will fail to inhibit her promiscuity—after all, he cannot guard her 24 hours a day. If she becomes pregnant, she will not know who the father is.

Finally, let us imagine what a bonobo college might be like. There would be no harems like those of the gorilla; neither would there be the fraternity-dominated social structure of the chimp. There would still be fraternities and sororities, each fraternity being associated with a sorority, but if there were any dominance, the sororities would have the edge. There would indeed be disagreements and aggression, but they would be very muted compared to those at "Chimpanzee U." Frat boys would soon learn that it was inadvisable to get too uppity with a lady—her friends would get together and chastise them for such rude behavior.

As it is for chimps, sex would be promiscuous, but in stark contrast to chimps and gorillas, sex would be used for much more than simple procreation, and it would not be strictly heterosexual. Are you with someone you care for? Then bond and have sex. Did you and friend just ace a difficult exam? Celebrate by having sex! Did you have harsh words with a friend? Don't just kiss and make up, have sex. Just run into a sorority lady that you haven't seen in a while? Run up to her and have sex! Is a friend distraught over a bad grade? Before you help him study, make certain that you calm him down by having sex. Did someone just bring a pizza into the frat house? Polite manners dictate that you have sex with the delivery person before you ask for a slice. Can you imagine your college winning the championship football game in the last few seconds? It would be perfectly natural for the TV camera to pan over the victorious Bonobo U fans having wild sex in the bleachers.

What is wrong with the gorilla, chimp, and bonobo scenarios? Why do they appear frightening or amusing? If we humans are extraordinarily open to cultural influences, they why have we never evolved societies that have the organization and mating structure of gorillas? Certainly there are polygynous societies in which a male can have a harem, but even these societies differ dramatically from those of the gorilla. One male with his harem can live peacefully alongside other males. Although there may be challenges to a male, there would not be constant aggression on the part of bachelors to usurp another's harem. If a bachelor were to kill a woman's infant, we humans would forgive her if she retaliated in a murderous rage but consider it pathological for her to fall in love with him because of his action.

Many societies have the chimp's ethos of male dominance, even to the point of tacitly condoning male battery of women. But has there ever been a society with the promiscuous mating structure of the chimp? Promiscuity does occur in individuals, and it does vary in degree from one culture to another. But has it ever been the *modus vivendi* of a whole culture?

Finally, we humans are like bonobos in using sex for bonding and friend-ship. We may spend a few hours acting like our primate cousins, as, for example, descriptions of the banquets hosted by the Roman emperor Caligula suggest. But has there ever been a society with morals that match that of the bonobo? Do we know of any culture in which proper etiquette dictates that you should have indiscriminate sex with all your male and female friends in all the different circumstances of the bonobo?

Exactly why are we different from gorillas, chimps, and bonobos? Students can easily develop a litany of possible reasons, ranging from human language through human logic to human morals. An evolutionary psychologist, however, would trace all these mechanisms back to a single source: Our evolutionary history has biologically predisposed us to act in certain ways and has biologically constrained us from acting in other ways. In short, we do not organize and mate like gorillas, chimps, and bonobos because our genes make it difficult for us to adopt these patterns at a social level.

HOW ARE HUMANS DIFFERENT FROM OTHER APES? •

Humans definitely do not have the social organization of gorillas. All human societies are multimale, in the sense that several adult males live together, form bonds, and cooperate among themselves. Neither do we have the organization of chimps. In stark contrast to chimps, human females form strong bonds with one another and human males can have strong bonds with human females. Bonobos also have flexible bonding, but our social structure differs from that of bonobos in terms of our flexibility. Human cultures can have the male-dominated social structure of chimps, an egalitarian structure, or possibly even strong matriarchies.

Our mating behavior differs from that of our ape relatives in two important ways. The first is our flexibility. Our cultures can be monogamous, polygamous, or polyandrous.[6] They can either permit or strongly proscribe promiscuity. The second difference between apes and us is marriage. All human societies that have ever been described recognize marriage, although the form of marriage may differ from our Western view of the institution. Anthropologists disagree about the universals in marriage, but the following characteristics typically are present:

- Marriage is socially recognized; that is, the members of a village, tribe, or state recognize the union.
- Marriage has the expectation of generating offspring.
- Marriage is associated with kinship. Although kinship ties can happen outside marriage, marriage always involves the right of the offspring to be socially recognized as the kin of the parents and of the parents' kin.

- Marriage has relative permanence. The marital state is entered into for a long, as opposed to a short, time period (i.e., a brief sexual encounter, a night, a week, or a breeding season). The length of the time period is, of course, variable.
- Marriage involves some degree of sexual exclusivity. The partners in a marriage have the right to have sex with each other. In addition, one of or both the partners are often socially admonished not to have sex with certain others. The degree of sexual exclusivity is variable across cultures.
- Marriage involves the transfer of property and/or title. Again, exactly what is transferred and the degree to which it is transferred varies, but most societies that have personal property recognize that it can be bestowed on offspring.

Affective bonding is a reason for marriage. Love and romance may be the most variable characteristic of marriage. Many cultures condone arranged marriages between people who may have never even met. Typically, such marriages are entered into for the purpose of establishing kinship and/or property ties. However, every culture either overtly recognizes romance as a legitimate reason for marriage or has myths or stories about couples in love who want to enter the state of marriage and consider it tragic if they cannot fulfill their desires.

Although there are legitimate reasons to disagree with this list or to argue that other factors should be added to it, it is obvious that gorillas, chimps, and bonobos do not have the institution of marriage that we humans do. Humans can and do mate without marriage and can even have children, the recognition of kinship, and the transference of property outside the institution. Virtually every human culture, however, recognizes a special union between one (or more) male(s) and one (or more) female(s) that gives them the right to have sex, bear children, and so on.

● QUESTIONS ABOUT HUMAN BEHAVIOR

Many of our evolutionary predispositions are so commonplace that they are taken for granted. The behaviors are so much a part of common sense and everyday action that we perform them and engage in them oblivious to their adaptive significance. It just seems natural to take a rock-hard peach and place it on the counter for a few days to let it ripen. How many of us are conscious of the possibility that this simple action is a result of adaptation of our taste buds and pleasure centers to bias us toward eating fruit at a stage of optimal nutritional value? Even though I teach this example year after year, I almost never think of it when shopping at the produce stand.

Because many adapted behaviors appear so "natural," the only way to guess at their evolutionary significance is to ask questions that appear dumb and bizarre because everyone knows the answer in the first place. But it is not the *answer* to these questions that is important. The critical questions to ask are "*Why* is this the answer?" and "*Why* are other logical possibilities *not* the answer?" Do we humans mate like the praying mantis? Of course not! It is perfectly obvious that we do not! But now ask yourself, "*Why* don't we mate like the praying mantis?"

Below is a sampling of such questions. We lack a time machine that can transport us backward for many millennia to observe whether the evolutionary psychologist's answers to these questions are correct, but the questions themselves do provide food for thought.

Why Are There Human Societies in the First Place?

Several animal species are solitary and do not form groups. Individual tigers, for example, keep to their own territory and come together only for mating purposes. Gibbons live in solitary nuclear family groups and deliberately hoot and call so that other gibbon families keep their distance. We humans are very strong social animals, so much so that we regard a hermit who desires no human contact as odd and eccentric. Are we biologically predisposed toward living in groups, interacting with others, and developing social codes of conduct? Perhaps the fact that humans have societies in the first place derived through evolutionary adaptations.

Why Are Small Children Cute?

Imagine a public park with a playground for preschool children. Suppose that the day is so nice and warm that the residents of a local Alzheimer's center are sitting on park benches watching the children play. Why do passersby look at the children, smile, laugh gently when a youngster emits flatulence and messes his diaper, and strike up conversations with the children's caretakers about how "cute" and "precious" the little ones are? Why do people react so differently to the Alzheimer's patients? Only some extraordinary humans would regard them as cute and precious. Incontinence often accompanies the advanced stages of Alzheimer's disease, but laughing at an elderly patient defecating in his diaper is regarded more as a sign of sarcastic disdain than as an expression of mild bemusement.

Why do people adopt children and not Alzheimer's patients? Certainly both types of people are in equal need of care, succor, and nurturance, yet in Western societies there is great demand for babies to adopt but little demand for Alzheimer's patients. Our preference for the young often extends beyond humans. How many families prefer to adopt a young puppy, and how many prefer an elderly dog? Evolutionary psychologists have pointed out that the physical features of "cuteness" in young children are shared with many other young in the mammalian world—rounded heads that are large relative to body length, large eyes, and small noses. This is why puppies all have pug snouts. Are these characteristics some types of physical cues that we are biologically predisposed to respond to with a feeling of love and caring?

Why Go Through Childbirth?

Until recently, childbirth was one of the most physically risky events for a young woman. Contrary to popular opinion, genealogies reveal a startling amount of serial marriages in the 1700s and 1800s. Marriages did not dissolve through divorce. Instead, they dissolved through death of a spouse, and the hemorrhages and infections associated with childbirth were a major contributor to mortality. Women knew this at the time, yet they still had babies. Logically, this was irrational. At the time, there was such a surplus of parentless infants and children that the orphanage was a stable institution in every large community. Why risk death when you can adopt a child?

Even today, most husbands and wives desire a child of their own, despite all the inconvenience and risk of pregnancy and childbirth. Why would a woman put up with months of nausea, vomiting, weight gain, possible edema, and hypertension when she could avoid all that and adopt a child? Couples will even spend tens of thousands of dollars in attempts to overcome fertility problems before considering adoption, which itself could add more thousands of dollars to their debt. And why do we want to adopt babies rather than the elderly?

Every parent acknowledges that children require enormous investments of money and time. Career paths can be compromised, social life can be curtailed, and exotic vacations can be sacrificed, all for the purpose of having and raising one's own children. Yet the majority of partnered couples eventually eschews the safety of birth control and deliberately tries to reproduce. Perhaps our genes and biology have predisposed us humans to want children of our own, and the hidden evolutionary urges and motivations are so strong that we humans will defy logic and reason to act on those urges.

Why Have Sex?

To most of us humans, this is a dumb question. Sex with the right person is fun and pleasurable. It initiates and preserves close bonds. It is something that we seek and will go out of our way to have. Why? The evolutionary psychologist's answer to this question is best investigated by imagining what sex would be like if it were as interesting and pleasurable as flossing your cat's teeth. How many people would reproduce if sex were a boring and onerous activity? Very few, one might guess. And what would happen to any species biologically predisposed to experience sex as a burden? Surely, extinction.

Why is sex pleasurable, and why do we humans go out of our way to have sex? An evolutionary psychologist might respond that sex is pleasurable because the pleasure we experience is one of nature's tricks to ensure that we reproduce. What better way is there to guarantee reproduction than to make the very acts and behavior of reproduction rewarding and pleasurable? According to this line of thought, the phenomenal experience of enjoyment and pleasure in sex is the *proximal* evolutionary mechanism to achieve the *distal* evolutionary goal of guaranteeing reproduction. We humans are soft-wired to follow the proximal goal of pleasure regardless of the distal goal of reproduction. A surreptitious, Saturday-night visit to the apartments and dorms on any college campus would surely provide data that agree with this view. Sexual activity would be going on behind closed doors, but the majority of encounters would be for the purpose of mutual pleasure, while very few would be directed at reproduction. Indeed, the possibility of sex leading to pregnancy is usually a cause for concern and anxiety—not celebration—among single young adults.

Once again, the perspective of the evolutionary psychologist is best revealed by considering the logical and rational alternatives to what we humans would "just like to do." With contemporary medical technology, it is not necessary to have sex to reproduce. A couple desiring a baby could easily visit the local sperm bank and have the woman artificially inseminated. There are considerable advantages to this. There is no problem with contracting sexually transmitted diseases, sperm donors can be screened against medical and psychological problems, and donors can be selected for desirable traits such as high intelligence, ambition, athletic ability, good looks, and even-tempered personality. If we humans were designed to have reproduction as our major, proximal goal, then sperm and egg banks are the logical choice. Yet we regard that option (save, of course, for problems of infertility) as sterile, cold, unromantic, and passionless. Most of us would prefer to generate offspring in the old-fashioned way—having passionate and pleasurable sex with another fallible human being whom we care about.

Why Have Sex With Other People?

The next time that you find yourself in a conversation about relationships, ask your friends these questions: "What would you really like in a mate?" "Which of these qualities would be essential, and which would just be nice to have?" and "What type of mate would you settle for?" You will receive many responses, virtually all of them describing positive traits such as kind, nice, intelligent, good looking, and outgoing. There is one response that you will never hear—"I want my mate to be another human being."

How many people fall in love with a rock or spend a Saturday night playing romantic music to a fir tree? We have fondness and love for our pets, yet how many of your friends responded to your question that they would accept nothing less than a golden retriever as their ideal mate? Most people find these questions humorous, but to an evolutionary psychologist, the answers are obvious. We humans—like every other sexual species that has intercourse—are softwired to want to mate with conspecifics. We do not capriciously develop a fondness for mating objects depending on what is happening to us at the time. Sometime long ago in evolution—probably long before we mammals developed—mechanisms for mating with conspecifics and not other objects were firmly established in the nervous system, and they have continued to be transmitted to this day.

Why Don't We Just Smell Other Humans?

We all know what dogs do when they meet. They see each other at a distance, approach, and then smell each other's behinds for a while. How many times have you watched two humans wave at a distance, come together, and then bend down to smell each other before shaking hands? We humans recognize each other through vision and sometimes through sound. According to the evolutionary psychologist, we are biologically biased toward experiencing the world in terms of sight and sound. Smells occur. We can sense them, differentiate them, and act and behave differently because of odors. But the olfactory sense is not our primary mode of interfacing with the environment.

Many species behave in quite the opposite way. Mice and rats recognize their colony mates through a characteristic "colony smell." If one extracts a male rat from a colony, washes him sufficiently to remove the characteristic odor, and replaces him, then other males—sometimes his own sibling littermates—can attack him as an intruder and even kill him. How many times have you read of people killing their brothers because they did not smell right?

Our biological predisposition toward vision and hearing over olfaction has influenced medical institutions. There are hearing clinics and hearing aids for folks with auditory problems, and we are all aware of friends who wear glasses or contact lenses to correct their vision. Have you ever heard of an MD specializing in "olfactorology," an olfactory clinic, or a "smelling aid" that people place in their noses to help them smell better? If rats and mice have evolved the equivalent of human intelligence and human technology, they probably would have invented the "smelling aid" long before they ever designed gizmos to correct vision.

WRAPPING IT UP ●

We have questioned the source of many simple human characteristics and behaviors ranging from the cuteness of babies to the pleasure of sex. The interrogatory form of exposition was deliberate. That is, the text is continually asking questions of the form "Why do we humans behave this way and not this other way?" instead of declaring this or that as scientific fact. The reason for the interrogatory form is that it is almost impossible to prove many evolutionary explanations. Scientists do not have a time machine that can transport them backward in time to observe and objectively report human evolution. Instead, scientists operate as Sherlock Holmes did in solving a mystery— gathering current facts and using deduction to find a simple explanation for those facts. Holmes and Dr. Watson, however, had an advantage over us. A putative culprit could always confess to the crime and remove lingering doubts. The "culprits" in evolutionary psychology are long dead and buried.

Consequently, many hypotheses and theories in evolutionary psychology are speculative, but so are many of the arguments *against* evolutionary psychology. How does one prove that we humans are *not* biologically predisposed toward viewing certain physical features as "cute" without crawling into the hypothetical time machine and observing that evolution progressed in a different direction? Society and culture may indeed influence our perceptions of sex as pleasurable, but are social and cultural norms the *only* reason for sex's hedonistic quality? Once again, we must climb into the time machine to disprove the evolutionary hypothesis.

Perhaps at some future date, we may identify genes and biological mechanisms that underlie our phenomenal sense of "cuteness." Or maybe we will identify neuronal circuits and chemicals associated with the pleasure in sex. Such information together with future data on the genetic similarities and differences among primate species may help to untangle the different hypotheses about the evolutionary origins of these behaviors. Until such data are available, however, it is best to phrase the issue in terms of questions that, with our current technology, cannot be fully answered. We must also treat our personal answers to these questions with a healthy dose of skepticism. After all, many theories in the behavioral sciences that seemed "perfectly reasonable" at the time have had to be abandoned when the technology to disconfirm those "perfectly reasonable" hypotheses became available.

● NOTES

1. Estrus (adjectival form = *estrous*) is a cyclical phenomenon among mammals in which a female becomes sexually excited and will either initiate or accept mating. It occurs around ovulation and often involves physical change in the sex organs.

2. Bonobos are also called pygmy chimpanzees. They do not, however, differ greatly in size from the common chimp.

3. The easiest way to distinguish a bonobo from a chimp is to look at the hair on top of its head. Chimps have short hair with no "style" to it. Bonobos have long hair that is neatly parted right down the middle, with the appearance of being combed out to each side.

4. The picture of bonobos as the "make love, not war" species of *Pan* is tempered by the fact that bonobos have not been studied in their wild habitats as intensively as chimps. Hence, certain types of aggression, like infanticide and murder, may occur, but at such low rates that they have yet to be observed.

5. Or, in some cases, two or more adult males.

6. Polygamy is the generic term for multiple mates. In polygyny, one male has more than one female mate, and in polyandry, one female has more than one male mate.

● REFERENCES

de Waal, F. (1989). *Peacemaking among primates*. Cambridge, MA: Harvard University Press.

de Waal, F. B. (1995). Bonobo sex and society. *Scientific American, 272*, 82-88.

Goodall, J. (1986). *The chimpanzees of Gombe: Patterns of behavior*. Cambridge, MA: Harvard University Press.

Harcourt, A. H., Fossey, D., Stewart, K. J., & Watts, D. P. (1980). Reproduction in wild gorillas and some comparisons with chimpanzees. *Journal of Reproduction and Fertility* (Suppl. 28), 59-70.

Kano, T. (1992). *The last ape: Pygmy chimpanzee behavior and ecology*. Stanford, CA: Stanford University Press.

Tutin, C. E. (1980). Reproductive behaviour of wild chimpanzees in the Gombe National Park, Tanzania. *Journal of Reproduction and Fertility* (Suppl. 28), 43-57.

Wrangham, R., & Peterson, D. (1996). *Demonic males: Apes and the origins of human violence*. Boston: Houghton Mifflin.

CHAPTER 16

PRINCIPLES OF EVOLUTIONARY PSYCHOLOGY

INTRODUCTION ●

The previous chapter posed a number of simple questions about human behavior and explained how evolutionary psychology might answer those questions. At the end, the reader was admonished to maintain an attitude somewhere between skepticism and open-mindedness toward the answers provided by both evolutionary psychologists and their critics.

If that chapter gave you some interesting questions to think about, then it succeeded in its purpose. But it could also give the misleading impression that evolutionary psychologists are a breed of armchair speculators. This is definitely not the case. There are well-developed principles and theories within evolutionary psychology that have sparked considerable empirical research. In this chapter, four major theories are explored—(a) prepared learning, (b) inclusive fitness and kin selection, (c) reciprocity and cooperation, and (d) parental investment.

● PREPARED LEARNING

Several decades ago, American psychology held several laws of learning as sacred. The law of *equipotentiality* stated that an organism could learn to associate any stimulus to any response with equal ease. The classic example is Pavlov's dog, who, according to this law, could have learned to associate a bright light with food as easily as it learned to associate the bell with food. The two stimuli, light and bell, are equipotent in the sense that given the same learning parameters, both eventually could lead the dog to salivate. A second law was *temporal contiguity*. This law stated that the presentation of a novel stimulus with a learned stimulus must occur at nearly the same time. In Pavlov's case, the food must be presented shortly after the bell is rung for learning to occur. The dog never would learn to salivate in response to the bell if the food were presented 3 days after the bell. A third law was *practice*—it took many trials before the behavior was fully learned.

These laws begin to crumble after a series of fortuitous studies in the 1950s and 1960s by psychologist John Garcia and his colleagues. Garcia's initial interest centered on the behavioral effects of low doses of radiation. In the experimental paradigm, rats were placed into a special chamber for a relatively long time while they were exposed to a constant amount of low-level X-ray radiation. To keep the rats healthy, the chamber was equipped with water bottles containing saccharin-flavored water. Garcia and his colleagues noticed three important things: (a) as expected, the rats became sick from the doses of X rays; (b) quite unexpectedly, the rats stopped drinking the sweetened water; and (c) the rats needed no practice to avoid the water—they learned after one and only one trial.

Garcia's genius consisted of asking one simple question: "Why should these rats avoid drinking the water when the learning situation violated the accepted laws of learning?" According to the Pavlovian tradition, the unconditioned response (sickness) occurred several hours after the conditioned stimulus (sweetened water).[1] This clearly violated the law of temporal contiguity because the pairing of sweetened water and sickness did not occur within a short time interval. In addition, there was no need for practice: Most rats learned to avoid the water after a single trial.

Garcia abandoned his initial interest in radiation poisoning to focus on this peculiar phenomenon of learning. His general results and conclusions are illustrated by the study of Garcia and Koelling (1966). Rats were assigned to one of four groups in a 2 × 2 factorial design. The first factor was the sensory quality of water given to the rats—it could be either colored with a food dye and oxygenated with bubbles (colored, bubbly water) or mixed with saccharin (sweetened water). The second factor consisted of the consequences

Table 16.1 Results of the Garcia and Koelling Study on Conditioned Avoidance

	Aversive Stimulus	
Type of Water	**Shock**	**Lithium**
Colored, bubbly	High avoidance	Low avoidance
Sweetened	Low avoidance	High avoidance

Results are taken from Garcia and Koelling (1966).

of drinking the water: Half the rats in each group were given an electrical shock upon drinking, whereas the other half were made to become sick several hours later by lacing their water with lithium.[2] The results of this experiment are presented in Table 16.1.

The rats in the colored, bubbly water/shock group eventually learned to avoid drinking the water, albeit after a number of trials. This accords well with the laws of learning current at the time. Rats shocked after drinking sweetened water, however, failed to learn avoidance within the time limit of the study. This fact clearly violated the established law of equipotentiality, under which sweetness should lead to just as much avoidance as did the colored water.

Curiously, the effect of making the rats sick showed the opposite pattern. Rats made sick by the colored water had a difficult time learning to avoid it, whereas rats sickened by lithium in sweetened water learned to avoid the water after one trial. The colored-water/lithium group followed the established laws of learning because sickness did not occur in temporal contiguity with the water. The sweetened-water/lithium group, on the other hand, violated the laws just as much as did the rats made sick by X rays in the earlier experiment.

The current explanation for these surprising results is that the laws of learning depend in important ways on the biological predisposition of a species. The rat has evolved into a highly olfactory creature that perceives the world in terms of smell and taste. Indeed, rat colonies develop a characteristic smell that is used to recognize colony mates and identify intruders.[3] Rats are also scavengers who dine on a surprisingly wide variety of organic material. Because they locate food through smell, they are especially attracted to rotting fruit, vegetable, and animal matter because of its pungent odor. Rotting food, however, poses a problem for digestion because it can create sickness when it is too far gone.

Rats react to their food in a peculiar way. When a rat locates a novel food source, he seldom gobbles it all up. Instead, he will nibble a little bit of it, go away for several hours, and then return. The rat may repeat this another time or two—a quick taste, a lengthy departure, and then a return—but soon he will return and gorge on the food. If an experimenter laces the original food source with enough poison to make the rat sick but not enough to kill him, the rat may return but will not eat the food anymore. It is usually a quick, one-trial learning experience.

Evolutionary psychologists speculate that rats evolved a biological predisposition and a behavioral repertoire to avoid rotting foods that may make them ill. At some point, rats who nibbled at a novel food source outreproduced those who gobbled large amounts, presumably because the gobbling strategy had a high probability of incapacitation or even death through sickness. Similarly, rats who nibbled and quickly learned outreproduced those who nibbled but took a long time to learn. And what sensory cues would the rat use to tell bad food from good food? Most likely, they would be olfactory cues.

In this way, rats in the Garcia and Koelling study would easily learn to associate an olfactory cue (water sweetness) with eventual sickness but would have a harder time associating a visual cue (colored, bubbly water) with sickness. Rats who learned to avoid sweetened water when they became sick were biologically predisposed to learn this and to learn it quickly. If a rat drinking the bright, bubbly water were able to cogitate about his situation, he might think, "Every time that guy puts me into this box, I get sick, but it can't be the water because it tastes perfectly OK." Rats are not biologically prepared to associate a visual cue with sickness.

Similarly, electric shock is not a natural event in the ecology of the rat. The cogitating rodent given sweetened water would be quite perplexed— "The water tastes good and did not make me sick. Nothing wrong with that stuff." Again, this is a biological constraint. Finally, the rats given two stimuli that are quite arbitrary from the perspective of their natural habitats—bright, bubbly water and shock—followed all the rules of avoidance learning that had been established early in the century, that is, the paradigms using arbitrary stimuli and shock.

Proponents of this interpretation of the data are quick to point out the role reversal that happens in different species. Birds, who are highly visual like us humans, associate visual cues with sickness with the ease that rats learn about olfactory cues and illness. Birds will readily learn to avoid, say, blue food pellets (which make them sick) and eat red pellets. When presented with a novel pellet that is half blue and half red, the bird will peck at the middle, break the pellet in two, and then eat the red half.

The general phenomenon has come to be called *prepared learning* (Seligman & Hager, 1972) or *biological constraints on learning*, a hypothesis initially proposed in 1911 by the famous learning theorist E. L. Thorndike but ignored by later researchers.[4] The prepared or constrained part of the learning process is due to the biology that has been evolutionarily bequeathed to a species, an evolutionary procedure discussed in the previous chapter. Preparedness consists of all those biological factors that make it easy for the members of a species to learn certain responses but make it difficult for them to acquire other responses. In terms of human behavior, the most often touted example is fear and phobia.

Human Fears and Phobias[5]

From the perspective of evolutionary psychology, fear and panic—like most human emotions—should be viewed as adaptive responses (Nesse, 1990). They may be unpleasant to experience, but they serve the useful function of prompting us to avoid dangerous situations and/or to energize our bodies for fight or flight. The relationship between fear and adaptiveness resembles the inverted U-shaped function of stabilizing selection (see Figure 13.2). In general, it is good to be in the middle of distribution. Too little fear could lead to maladaptive risk taking, whereas too much fear might incapacitate a person.

To understand biological and evolutionary factors in human fears and phobias, we must first recognize three salient empirical findings about them—(a) the types of fears and phobias, (b) the age of onset of fears, and (c) precipitating events. The first salient aspect of these stimuli is that they are not a random sample of the stimuli with which humans tend to have noxious experiences. Surveys about the types of stimuli that humans fear have been very consistent. The majority of fears and phobias[6] involve spatial stimuli (heights, enclosed places), specific animals (snakes, bats, spiders, rats), and public speaking. Many of us have received a punishing electrical shock while trying to extract an obstreperous bagel from the toaster with a fork, but no clinician has ever reported treating a toaster phobia, a bagel phobia, or a fork phobia. Neither are mental health professionals overwhelmed by clients complaining of electrical outlet or extension cord phobias. A person seriously injured in a car crash in a red Volkswagen may develop strong fears of driving or riding in a car, but hardly any of them panic at the sight of a red Volkswagen parked at a curb. Children sometimes develop strong fears and phobias of darkness, but few, if any, develop fears of all the other stimuli associated with going to sleep—pillows, pajamas, sheets, bedtime stories, or even the light bulb. How many of us know someone who panics at the sight of a bowl of chili, even though the person may have had a highly unpleasant experience eating chili that was too spicy for his taste? Most of us have been burned by touching a hot stove or cooking pan. Do you know anyone with a stove phobia, a double-boiler phobia, or a frying pan phobia? Why is it easy to acquire a fear of snakes but hard to acquire one of toasters?

A second salient aspect of human fears and phobias is the age of onset. Fears and phobias of specific animals usually have an onset in childhood. More than 95% of them develop before the age of 12. Phobias of heights, on the other hand, increase with age. It is not unusual for someone unafraid of heights in their teens and twenties to acquire a fear of heights in middle or late adulthood. Agoraphobia—a serious multiphobic condition that involves fears of many spatial situations, crowds, and being alone—has an onset in the teens and early twenties. It is unusual for it to appear in early childhood or after age 40. Why should fears develop at different ages?

Finally, we must recognize that a large number of phobias develop in the absence of an adverse experience with the object or situation. Most people phobic of specific animals report that they have had this fear as long as they can remember and can recall no specific event that initiated the fear. Very few people develop a fear of heights because they have fallen from a great height. Why should someone develop a phobia in the absence of an adverse learning experience?

Evolutionary psychologists posit that we are biologically prepared to acquire certain types of fears at certain times in the life span. Even before our own species evolved, hominid youngsters had to learn very quickly what types of animals to avoid. Perhaps the nervous system of an ancient primate ancestor evolved a sensitive period for the acquisition of fear responses to dangerous animals, and we inherited that mechanism. In addition, we may be sensitized to acquire these fears through social learning. Seeing someone shout and run away from a snake or being admonished by elders to avoid snakes might generate just as much fear as having a bad personal encounter with one. Indeed, we humans may follow the pattern of rhesus monkeys, who, when raised in a laboratory, show no congenital fear of snakes. In a single trial, however, they will develop an intense fear of snakes when they are exposed to another monkey who exhibits fear in the presence of a snake (Mineka, Davidson, Cook, & Keir, 1984).

It should come as no surprise, then, that people placed in experimental situations develop fear responses and even cognitive appraisals of fear differently for biologically prepared stimuli than for biologically neutral stimuli. Ohman, Erixon, and Lofberg (1975) developed autonomic fear responses[7] in subjects to pictures of either a snake or a house. The fear rapidly extinguished for the picture of a house but was maintained at a high level for the picture of the snake. Tomarken, Mineka, and Cook (1989) presented pictures of both prepared stimuli (snake or spider) and neutral stimuli (mushroom or flower) to subjects and then randomly shocked subjects one-third of the time after a picture was shown. Despite the fact that the subjects were shocked just as much with the snake/spider pictures as with the mushroom/flower pictures, they reported that they were shocked more after the snake/spider pictures than after the pictures of the neutral stimuli. Somehow, prepared stimuli influence cognitive estimation of probabilities.

With the example of prepared learning, we can see how evolutionary psychology moves away from speculation and into the laboratory. The hypothesis of preparedness explains the learning studies on rats as well as the epidemiological data on human phobias (types of phobias, age of onset, etc.). It is also a good explanation for the considerable amount of laboratory data from humans (see Marks, 1987). Hence, it is a useful construct that serves to put a number of different puzzle pieces together.

Prepared learning also illustrates the lemonade quality of human experience. Too often, learning has been cast as a purely environmental phenomenon completely antithetical to genetics. Learning definitely involves the environment, but it equally occurs within the context of a nervous system that experiences the environmental events. As shown in the first module of this book, all the enzymes, receptors, peptide hormones, and so on operating in this system have their blueprints encoded in genes. Learning is as much lemonade as is the body's reaction to stress.

INCLUSIVE FITNESS AND KIN SELECTION ●

Sometimes, mothering ringneck pheasants perform a marvelous act of self-sacrifice. If a large animal treads too close to her nest, she will make a great deal of noise and run through the field, flapping her wings. The safest course of action for her is to be silent, run a few steps to build up the momentum for flight, and then soar away. Yet she makes herself deliberately conspicuous to a potential predator and is sometimes caught in the process. Prairie dogs show similar behavior. When a raptor soars overhead or a land-based predator approaches the colony, the prairie dogs who initially spot the threat stand upright on their hind legs and issue a series of loud barks that act as alarm codes for their colony mates to run posthaste to their burrows. This behavior assists the colony as a whole, but at the expense of making the signaler conspicuous to the predator.

These are examples of *altruism*, a behavior that can reduce the reproductive fitness of the altruist but increase the fitness of conspecifics. Ever since Darwin's time, altruism posed a problem for natural selection. Any heritable behavior that reduced fitness should decrease over time. Consider a prairie dog colony that consists of 50% altruists and 50% cheats.[8] When a cheater spots a predator, he hightails it to the nearest burrow. The odds that the predator eats an altruist are slightly increased because the cheater has just removed one of his own kind from the denominator of vulnerable prairie dogs. When the altruist spies the threat, she announces her position to the predator and places herself in danger. Both the other altruists and the cheaters benefit, but if anyone is to be devoured, it is once again more likely to be the altruist than the cheater.

A solution for this had to wait until 1964, when W. D. Hamilton published a classic paper (Hamilton 1964a, 1964b). Using mathematical models, Hamilton showed that altruism could evolve when altruistic genotypes preferentially benefit other altruistic genotypes over cheater genotypes. The clearest way for an altruistic genotype to do this is to have mechanisms that bias it to work altruistically for *close genetic relatives*. If I have an altruistic genotype, then the most likely individuals in the world to share this genotype will be my parents, siblings, and children. When this concept was presented to the famous geneticist J.B.S. Haldane, he quipped that he would never give his life for his brother, but he would for two brothers or eight first cousins.[9]

Hamilton's work presented the twin ideas of *inclusive fitness* and *kin selection*. Inclusive fitness is defined as the *fitness of an individual along with the fitness of close relatives*.[10] Your inclusive fitness would be a weighted sum of your own reproductive fitness and that of your first-degree relatives, second-degree relatives, and so on. Kin selection refers to an implication of inclusive fitness that *natural selection can work on the close genetic relatives of the organism actually performing the behavior*. In a loose sense, fitness can be expressed in terms of kinships, just as we have seen it being expressed in terms of genotypes, phenotypes, and individuals.

Inclusive fitness and kin selection have been used to explain many different human behaviors. The very fact that we humans recognize and pay close attention to genealogy may reflect a cognitive mechanism, developed through evolution, that helps in kin recognition. The phrase "blood is thicker than water" has been interpreted as a realistic description of human emotions and behaviors that preferentially benefit kin over others. Several aspects of altruistic parental behavior may have evolved through kin selection. Continual themes in fiction portray noble parents shielding their young children from potential harm, but evil stepparents threatening their stepchildren.

Daly and Wilson (1988) have pointed out how familial homicide patterns agree quite well with kin selection. Although it is rare, parents do murder their children, but the perpetrator of such a heinous act is much more likely to be a stepparent than a biological parent. Despite the hyperbolic threat "do that again and I'll kill you" echoed by many a frustrated parent, very, very few parents ever even contemplate homicide when it comes to their offspring. The inhibition against homicide is not restricted to parents and their offspring. Ask yourself the following two questions: "In your whole lifetime, which person has shouted at you and hit you the most?" and "Which person have you yelled at and fought with the most?" If you respond like most people, then you will nominate a brother or sister, yet fratricide (the killing of a sibling) is very rare. Humans are much more likely to kill a spouse than an offspring or sibling.

RECIPROCITY AND COOPERATION ●

A close cousin to inclusive fitness is the concept of reciprocity and cooperation, sometimes called reciprocal altruism. Traditionally, inclusive fitness and kin selection have been used to refer to altruism toward genetic relatives. Reciprocity and cooperation deal with *behavior that requires some "sacrifice" but also has beneficial consequences between conspecifics who are not necessarily genetic relatives*. Hence, the target of the behavior—a genetic relative versus another conspecific—distinguishes inclusive fitness from reciprocity/cooperation. Robert Trivers (1971) developed the concept in a seminal paper.

To understand reciprocity and the problem it posed for evolutionists, we must once again consider cheaters. Lions and wolves hunt large prey cooperatively. Although the fact is mentioned infrequently on nature shows, chasing, grabbing, and killing large prey is not a safe enterprise. Zebras kick and bite, wildebeests have horns, and caribou have antlers, so predators can be hurt, sometimes even mortally so, in the hunt. Imagine a cheating lioness who approaches the prey only after it is dead. Would not her behavior be advantageous? She can participate in the feast but avoids the risk of injury. If cheating has a selective advantage, then would it not eventually result in the extinction of cooperative hunting? Another problem is how cooperative hunting ever got started in the first place. Most feline predators, such as the lynx, tiger, cheetah, leopard, and jaguar, make a perfectly fine living at solitary hunting. Why did lions ever develop cooperation?

According to Trivers (and others including John Mayard Smith and Axelrod who developed mathematical models of the evolution of reciprocity), cooperation cannot evolve alone. It must be accompanied by mechanisms that detect and reward mutual cooperators and detect and punish cheaters. Consider grooming in primates. It serves the very useful function of eliminating large parasites (fleas, lice, etc.) from a hairy monkey or ape. Imagine that you are a chimp and that a fellow chimp, Clyde, continually presents himself to you to be groomed. Being the nice chimp that you are, you groom Clyde every time that he requests it. After a while, however, you notice something peculiar. Whenever you present yourself to Clyde for grooming, he refuses. Ask yourself how you truly feel about this situation and how you are likely to respond to Clyde's future presentations. Again, if you are like most people, when Clyde presents to you, you would feel some form of negative emotion that could range from mild exasperation to downright contempt, depending on the type of chimp you are. At some point, you are also likely to refuse to groom Clyde. Evolutionary psychologists would say that this is your "cheat detection and punishment" mechanism in action.

Reciprocity evolves when reciprocity and cheating can be recognized or anticipated and then acted upon. If your roommate, Mary, is cramming for her physics exam, you are likely to bake some banana bread for her when you suspect that Mary will do something nice for you on the eve of your big chemistry exam next week. But if Mary were the type of roommate who clutters and trashes the place, leaving you to do all the cleaning up, then you are likely to feel irritated and aggravated at her. No banana bread tonight! We feel that it is right and just that everyone does his or her fair share, and as parents, we spend considerable time and effort inculcating this ethos into our children.[11]

One of the strengths of the modern evolutionists is their ability to uncover subtle and non-obvious phenomena that fit better with evolutionary theory than with other theory. You were correct to express skepticism of the Mary example—after all, there really is no way to determine the relative influences of a biologically softwired "cheat detector" and your upbringing on the behavior. But consider the following example, taken from Pinker (1997, pp. 336 ff)[12].

Figure 16.1 shows three sets of four cards. Consider for a moment the set in panel (a). Each of the four cards has a letter on one side and a number on the other side. Which cards would you turn over to test whether you could falsify the following statement: "If a card had a D, then it must have a 3 on the other side?"

Panel (b) has a similar problem. Suppose that you have a job checking on whether bars are obeying the state law and serving alcohol only to people age 21 and over. You go into Jack's bar and find four patrons represented by the cards in panel (b). The patron's age is on one side, and his or her beverage is on the other. Which cards in panel (b) would you turn over to check if Jack's bar is following the law?

Finally, suppose that you are in Jill's deli chatting with one of the servers, a situation represented in panel (c). The server says that everyone who eats

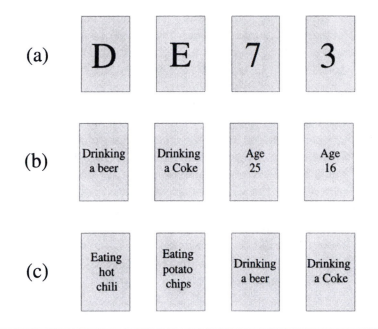

Figure 16.1 Three Different Problems With the Same Logical Pattern.

hot chili peppers here always drinks a cold beer. Again, there are four patrons, and their food is on one side of a card and their beverage on the other side. Which cards would you turn over to check out the server's statement?

All three of these problems have the *same* logical form. Pinker points out, however, that most people get the letter/number and the chili problem *wrong* but get the bar problem *correct*! If we humans were really using the formal rules of logic to solve these problems, we should solve each problem equally well.

Consider the bar problem. The correct solution is to turn over the "Drinking a beer" and the "Age 16" cards. If the "Drinking a beer" card has someone under age 21, then Jack's bar is not obeying the law. Similarly, if the "Age 16" card reveals that the person is drinking alcohol, then Jack's bar is not obeying the law. Turning over the "Drinking a Coke" and the "Age 25" cards do not help to solve the problem. Someone drinking a Coke can be any age, and a 25-year-old can drink anything.

In the letter/number problem, the correct solution is the D and the 7 cards. Pinker states that most people pick either the D card or the D and the 3 cards. If the proposition holds, then the D card *must* have a 3 on the other side and the 7 card *must not* have a D on the other side. Turning over the

3 card does not help solve the problem because 3 could be paired with any letter. A similar logic holds for the chili problem, for which the correct solution is turning over the "Eating hot chili" card (which, if the proposition holds, should have a "Drinking beer" on the other side) and the "Drinking Coke" card (which must *not* have "Eating hot chili" on the other side).

This example is based on a number of studies summarized by Leda Cosmides and John Tooby (1992, 1994), who conclude that our cheater detector is elicited in the bar problem but not in the letter/number problem or the chili problem.[13] Jack's bar is disobeying the rules ("cheating") if alcohol is being served to someone under 21. There is no morality associated with a D card or with the beverage one drinks while eating chili peppers. These data do not agree with the idea that the mind learns formal rules and then applies these rules to specific cases. It does agree with the evolutionary theory of reciprocity. We humans are biologically sensitized to detect cheating, so a logical problem with a content based on cheating is easier to solve than an identical logical problem with arbitrary content.

● PARENTAL INVESTMENT

Robert Trivers, who first explicated reciprocity and cooperation, also gave us parental investment theory (Trivers, 1972). This theory states that *in any species, the parent (male or female) that invests the most time, energy, and resources on its offspring will be the choosier mate.* The theory begins by asking the fundamental question of why many species act finicky in choosing mates. Most evolutionists explain mate preferences as mechanisms that genes have developed in organisms to assist in their own (i.e., the genes' own) replication. If I am a gene in an organism of a sexual species, not only do I want "my" organism to reproduce, but I also want "my" organism to reproduce with a mate who has good genes.[14] Hence, if mechanisms develop to recognize good mates, then natural selection will increase their frequency.

Trivers's theory maintains that the fastidiousness of mate preferences will be stronger in the sex that expends the most resources in producing offspring. Ordinarily, this will be the female, because biologists define a female as the sex of a species that produces the larger gamete. (Hence, human women are females because eggs are many, many times the size of sperm.) The sex that produces the larger gamete produces fewer of those gametes. Hence, each gamete is more "precious" in a reproductive sense.[15]

In mammals, the female expends more resources on offspring than the male. Fertilization in mammals is internal to the female, offspring development takes place in the female's uterus, and the female must suckle the infant for a significant period of time. Hence, female mammals should be choosier mates than male mammals. Indeed, this is always the case. In species where one sex competes for mating, males compete with other males for the opportunity of having sex with females. Females do not butt heads with each other for the opportunity of mating with any random guy in the herd. Even in chimps and bonobos, for which mating is largely promiscuous, every male in a troop tries quite hard to have a go at any female in estrus. Whenever one sex shuns a mating attempt, it is the female shunning a male and not a male shunning a female.[16]

Parental investment theory, along with the concept of certainty of parenthood, has been used to explain many different types of human mate preferences. Females must commit 9 months to pregnancy and then, unless manufactured baby formula is used, more than a year to feeding a single offspring. Even if a woman conceived after her first menstruation, she could bear one child per year until menopause, and the most likely number of offspring for a female during most of human evolution was probably no more than five (Nesse & Williams, 1994). A human male, on the other hand, has the potential of fathering a baby every single day after puberty. Female humans are biologically constrained to devote considerable resources to a single offspring; human males lack such constraints.[17] Hence, human females should have more discriminating mate preferences than do males.

A litany of empirical observations is used to support this conclusion. Certainly in Western cultures, anecdotal observations agree with it. Males are more ready than females to engage in anonymous sex, even to the point of paying for it. Women report more sexual advances made on them by men than men report sexual advances initiated by women. Personal ads written by women request males for relationships more often than those authored by men; men's personal ads stress sex (Deaux & Hanna, 1984). Consider the following questions: How long would you have to know someone before feeling comfortable going out on a date with that person? and How long would you have to know someone before getting married? Both males and females have similar time frames—a short time frame for dating and a longer one for matrimony. Now consider this question: How long would you have to know someone before having sex? The average woman picks a time frame somewhere between dating and marriage. Males pick a time frame *shorter* than dating (Buss & Schmitt, 1993).

This account of human parental investment, however, faces a real problem—why should men ever stick around at all? If sleeping around with as many women as possible maximizes the reproductive fitness of the genes in a male organism, why would these genes ever develop mechanisms that predispose a man to settle down with a woman? The evolutionists' answer to this is that it effectively "takes two to tango." Just like the peacock's tail, men's behavior is influenced by women's mate preferences. If mutations arose that influenced women to prefer men who stuck around, and if there were men who actually did stick around, and if the pairing between this type of woman and this type of man had high reproductive fitness, then females who prefer stable males would increase in frequency, as would males who actually remain stable.

● OVERVIEW

The large growth in evolutionary approaches to behavior has made inroads into conventional thinking in psychology, anthropology, and criminology, yet the field is not without its critics. The kindest critics acknowledge that the enterprise resembles a discipline like astronomy that also lacks a time machine and the ability to perform true experiments. However, they lament that evolutionary psychologists do not have a well-developed science against which to gauge their predictions—as astronomy has physics. The most strident critics dismiss the field outright, largely because of philosophical convictions that biology does not play a major role in human behavior.

The very brief overview of evolutionary psychology provided here should not lead to an overly dismissive attitude nor to an overly accepting view of the field. As the principles of evolution give different insights into problems of cognitive psychology, social psychology, clinical work, and criminology, we should welcome these ideas as testable hypotheses. The extent to which the predictions of the hypotheses are realized in empirical data eventually will determine the usefulness of this approach.

● NOTES

1.   It takes several hours before the effects of radiation produce sickness.
2.   Lithium cannot be tasted, but when given in sufficient amounts, it is poisonous. Curiously, small doses of lithium help in stabilizing the marked mood swings of manic-depressives.
3.   If an adult male rat is taken from his colony and given a bath sufficient to remove the colony smell, he will be attacked or even killed when he is reintroduced to the group. Even his littermates will attack him.
4.   Thorndike (1911) proposed both primary and secondary laws of learning. His primary laws received considerable attention, much to the detriment of one of his secondary laws that stated that for learning to occur, the organism must be prepared to learn.

5. See Isaac Marks (1987) for a thorough overview of this topic.

6. A phobia is an intense fear that the person cognitively realizes is too extreme for the situation but cannot avoid feeling. Phobias usually lead to avoidance of the object or situation. Phobias can lead to phobic disorder, in which the person suffers from some personal or social incapacitation because of the phobia.

7. Autonomic responses are sweating, increased heart rate, and irregular respiration—the types of phenomena measured by polygraphs.

8. Most people would use the word "selfish" as the appropriate antonym for altruism. In *The Selfish Gene*, however, Richard Dawkins (1989) points out that from a gene's perceptive, altruism is actually a selfish action to help the gene replicate itself. Hence, most evolutionists prefer the word "cheat" to "selfish."

9. I have found several different texts that quote Haldane, all differing slightly from one another, but the substance of his comment remains that given in this text.

10. In terms of the concept of fitness given in the chapter on the five forces of evolution (Chapter 13), inclusive fitness may be more broadly defined as *the fitness of an individual plus others with the same genotype*. In this case, it simply equals the fitness of genotypes irrespective of the individuals carrying those genotypes.

11. Because biological tendencies and learning are not mutually exclusive, parental reminders and admonitions can serve to reinforce behavioral patterns to which we are already genetically predisposed.

12. Almost every introductory text in cognitive psychology will have an example similar to this one.

13. Technically, Cosmides and colleagues conclude that the logical problem is easier to solve whenever it involves a social "contract."

14. Again, recognize the anthropomorphism here. In reality, the genes that increased in frequency were those that developed mechanisms in their organisms for recognizing and mating with others that possessed beneficial genes.

15. Even in insects, the female is almost always the choosier of the sexes. In several insect species, the males present "nuptial gifts" to the female by offering her another dead insect (usually killed by the male) to consume. When the gift is small, stale, or unpalatable, the female effectively says "Goodbye, Charlie" and flits away in search of a better offer. Once she finds a satisfactory present, she begins consuming the carcass. The male moves behind her and copulates while she is munching away in gustatory delight.

16. Advocates of parental investment theory are fond of pointing out discrepancies to the "female is choosier" rule, although to my knowledge, the rule has no contradiction among mammals. In the sea horse and the jacuna bird, the male invests more in the offspring than the female. In the sea horse, the female deposits her eggs into a male's pouch, where they are fertilized, incubated, and cared for after hatching by their father. The female jacuna bird maintains a large territory containing several males. She is fertilized by one male, lays her eggs, and leaves the male to tend the nest and feed the chicks while she moves on to another male and conceives. In both cases, the male apparently is choosier than the female in mating.

17. The constraints referred to here are purely physical. Human males may have *behavioral* constraints that are also biologically influenced and may limit their reproductive potential.

● REFERENCES

Buss, D. M., & Schmitt, D. P. (1993). Sexual strategies theory: An evolutionary perspective on human mating. *Psychological Review, 100*, 204-232.

Cosmides, L., & Tooby, J. (1992). Cognitive adaptations for social exchange. In J. Barkow, L. Cosmides, & J. Tooby (Eds.), *The adapted mind* (pp. 163-228). New York: Oxford University Press.

Cosmides, L., & Tooby, J. (1994). Beyond intuition and instinct blindness: Toward an evolutionarily rigid cognitive science. *Cognition and Emotion, 50*, 41-77.

Daly, M., & Wilson, M. (1988). *Homicide*. Hawthorne, NY: Aldine.

Dawkins, R. (1989). *The selfish gene* (New ed.). New York: Oxford University Press.

Deaux, K., & Hanna, R. (1984). Courtship in the personal column: The influence of gender and sexual orientation. *Sex Roles, 11*, 363-375.

Garcia, J., & Koelling, R. A. (1966). Relationship of cue to consequence in avoidance learning. *Psychonomic Science, 4*, 123-124.

Hamilton, W. D. (1964a). The genetic evolution of social behavior: I. *Journal of Theoretical Biology, 7*, 1-16.

Hamilton, W. D. (1964b). The genetic evolution of social behavior: II. *Journal of Theoretical Biology, 7*, 17-52.

Marks, I. M. (1987). *Fears, phobias, and rituals: Panic, anxiety, and their disorders*. New York: Oxford University Press.

Mineka, S., Davidson, M., Cook, M., & Keir, R. (1984). Observational conditioning of snake fear in rhesus monkeys. *Journal of Abnormal Psychology, 93*, 355-372.

Nesse, R. M. (1990). Evolutionary explanations of emotions. *Human Nature, 1*, 261-289.

Nesse, R. M., & Williams, G. C. (1994). *Why we get sick: The new science of Darwinian medicine*. New York: Times Books.

Ohman, A., Erixon, G., & Lofberg, I. (1975). Phobias and preparedness: Phobic versus neutral pictures and conditioned stimuli for human autonomic responses. *Journal of Abnormal Psychology, 84*, 41-45.

Pinker, S. (1997). *How the mind works*. New York: W. W. Norton & Company.

Seligman, M. E. P., & Hager, J. L. (1972). *Biological boundaries on learning*. New York: Appleton-Century-Crofts.

Thorndike, E. L. (1911). *Animal intelligence*. New York: Macmillan.

Tomarken, A. J., Mineka, S., & Cook, M. (1989). Fear-relevant selective associations and covariation bias. *Journal of Abnormal Psychology, 98*, 381-394.

Trivers, R. L. (1971). The evolution of reciprocal altruism. *Quarterly Review of Biology, 46*, 35-57.

Trivers, R. L. (1972). Parental investment and sexual selection. In B. Campbell (Ed.), *Sexual selection and the descent of man: 1871-1971* (pp. 136-179). Chicago: Aldine.

MODULE III

BEHAVIORAL GENETICS OF INDIVIDUAL DIFFERENCES

CHAPTER 17

INTRODUCTION TO MODULE III

Individual Differences

INTRODUCTION ●

Despite the fact that we humans have a certain sameness in our behavior, we also show important individual differences. We all acquire and use language. This is a *sameness* that interests the evolutionary psychologist. But it is also clear that there are marked individual differences in the way we use language. Shakespeare and Goethe displayed eloquence with language that most of us lack. Module III of this book treats individual differences and, hence, presents the literature on *behavioral genetics*.[1]

Behavioral genetics ask questions such as "Why do some people like stinky cheeses that other people find offensive?" and "Why are some people content to sit at home alone while other people prefer to socialize?" Evolutionary psychology and behavioral genetics often treat the same phenotypes but

276 ● HUMAN GENETICS FOR THE SOCIAL SCIENCES

approach them from different directions. Take, for example, intellect and cognition. Evolutionary psychologists, for example, John Tooby and Leda Cosmides, research cognitive modules such as the ability for us humans to detect cheaters. Behavioral geneticists such as Thomas Bouchard ask why some people are smarter than others. Phobias are another area of interest to both disciplines. Evolutionary psychologists wonder why we easily develop phobias of snakes but hardly ever acquire phobias of electrical outlets. Behavioral geneticists ask why Wilbur developed a phobia of heights while his brother, Waldo, never acquired that fear.

● QUICKIE STATISTICS

To understand individual differences, it is important to understand several quantitative principles that will pop up from time to time throughout the rest of the book. This section presents some basic statistics that will be necessary for an understanding of these quantitative models.

Distributions

The first important concept is that of a distribution. A distribution is a mathematical function that gives the frequency of various trait values.[2] Typically, the trait value is plotted on the horizontal axis and the frequency of that trait value is on the vertical axis. Figure 17.1 illustrates two common distributions. The solid line gives the bell-shaped curve of a *normal distribution*, the most important distribution that we will deal with in this text. Phenotypic scores in the middle of the distribution are the most frequent. As one moves away from the middle in either direction, the frequencies of the phenotypes become smaller and smaller. Intelligence, most personality traits—indeed, most behavioral phenotypes—show a frequency distribution similar to the normal.

The dashed line is an example of an exponential distribution. Here, low phenotypic values are the most frequent; the higher the phenotypic score, the less frequent it is. A few traits, such as number of felony convictions, resemble an exponential more than a normal distribution.

The Mean

The *mean* of a distribution is the arithmetic average. It is computed by adding all the scores together and dividing by the number of observations.

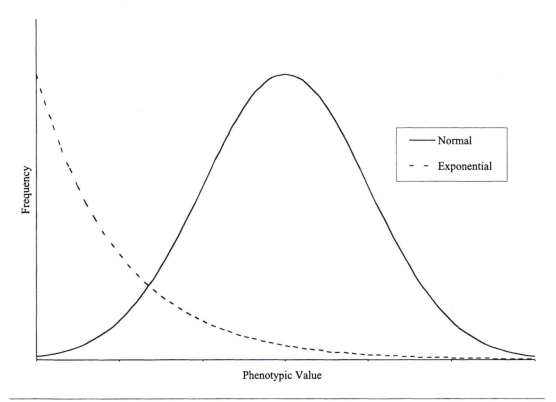

Figure 17.1 Examples of a Normal Distribution (Solid Line) and an Exponential Distribution (Dashed Line).

The mean is a *measure of central tendency or location* and answers the question, "Around which number do the scores tend to cluster?"

The Variance and Standard Deviation

The *variance* of a distribution is a measure of *individual differences around the mean*. It is a measure of the degree to which scores are dispersed away from the mean. A variance can range from 0 to a large positive number. A variance of 0 signifies that there is no dispersion around the mean—every score is the same, equal to the mean. For example, the number of eyes for normal individuals in the human species has a variance of 0. We all have two eyes; it is not the case that some humans have one eye, others have two, and yet others have three. The larger the variance, the more the scores are

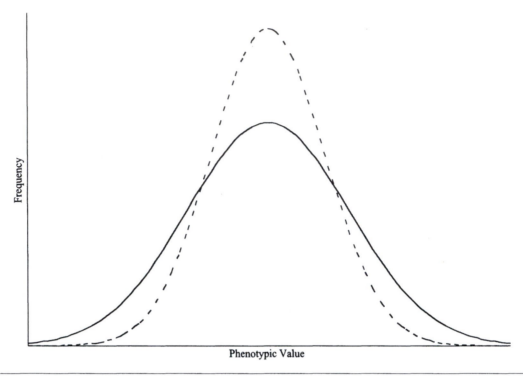

Figure 17.2   Two Normal Distributions With the Same Mean but Different Variances. The variance of the distribution with the solid line is greater than the variance of the distribution with the dashed line.

scattered around the mean. Figure 17.2 shows two normal distributions with the same mean but with different variances.

The solid line in Figure 17.2 is a normal distribution with a larger variance than the normal distribution depicted by the dashed line. The scores for the solid-line distribution are spread out more around the mean than they are for the dashed-line distribution. Hence, there are more phenotypic individual differences for the solid-line distribution than there are for the dashed-line one.[3]

A statistic closely related to the variance is the standard deviation. Mathematically, the standard deviation is the square root of the variance, so it too must range from 0 to a large positive number. The standard deviation has the same interpretation as the variance. It is a measure of the spread of scores around the mean, and the larger the standard deviation, the greater the individual differences.

An important feature of variance is that it can be partitioned. As we will see, the variance in the phenotype can be partitioned into a portion due to genetic variance and another portion due to environmental variance. This partitioning helps geneticists to answer two important questions—to what extent are observable individual differences due to individual differences in genotype, and to what extent are observable individual differences due to individual differences in the environment?

The Correlation Coefficient

Correlation coefficients are the most common statistic used to quantify the similarity of relatives for a continuous trait. A correlation coefficient is a measure of *the extent to which scores on one variable can predict scores on a second variable*. Mathematically, a correlation coefficient can range from −1.0 to 1.0. The correlation coefficient has two important attributes. The first is the *sign* of the correlation. A positive sign (i.e., a correlation between 0 and 1.0) denotes a direct relationship. Here, high scores on the first variable predict high scores on the second variable, and, conversely, low scores on the first variable predict low scores on the second variable. The correlation between height and weight, for example, is positive. People who are taller than average tend to (but do not necessary *have* to) weigh more than the average person, and people smaller than average in height tend to weigh less than the average person. A negative sign (i.e., a correlation coefficient less than 0) denotes an inverse relationship. In this case, high scores on one variable predict low scores on the second variable, and, conversely, low scores on the first variable predict high scores on the second variable. The correlation between the amount of time spent partying and studying, for example, is negative. Students who spend a very large amount of time partying tend to get lower than average grades, whereas students who spend little time at parties tend to receive higher grades.

One way to visualize the sign of a correlation is to create a *scatterplot*. The first step in constructing a scatterplot is to draw a horizontal axis for one variable (usually called the X variable) and a perpendicular vertical axis for the second (or Y) variable. The next step is to plot all the data points on this graph. Suppose that the first observation in the data has a score of 1.2 on the X variable and 0.6 on the Y variable. Go to 1.2 on the *x*-axis and then move straight up until you reach 0.6 on the *y*-axis. Make a dot at that spot. Repeat this procedure with each observation in the data set. In behavioral genetics research, one relative's phenotypic score is used as the X variable, and the other relative's phenotypic score is used as the Y variable. Figure 17.3 depicts two scatterplots, one for a positive correlation and the other for a negative correlation, for the case when the two variables are the phenotypic scores of a pair of sibs.

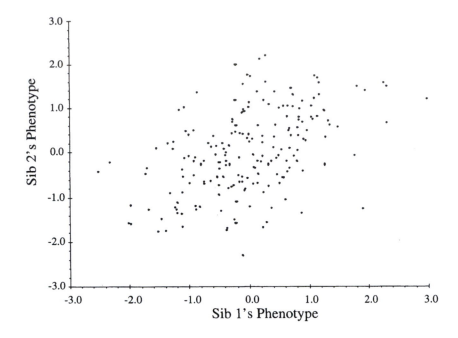

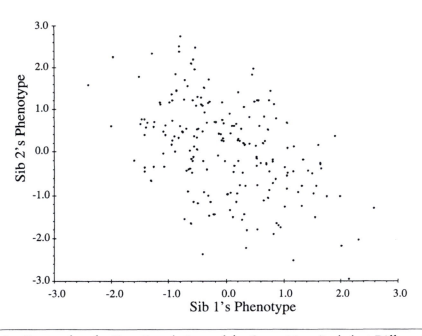

Figure 17.3 Scatterplots for Two Correlations of the Same Magnitude but Different Signs. Top panel = positive correlation; bottom panel = negative correlation.

For a positive correlation, the points take a southwest to northeast orientation (e.g., Los Angeles to Boston). The orientation for a negative correlation is from northwest (Seattle) to southeast (Miami). Negative correlations for pairs of relatives are rare.

The second important attribute of the correlation is the square of the correlation coefficient. Because a correlation can range between −1.0 and 1.0, the square of the correlation must range between 0 and 1.0. The square of the correlation is a measure of the *amount of predictability* between the two variables. Statistically speaking, the correlation squared gives *the proportion of variance in one variable that is predictable from the other variable*. Because variance is a measure of individual differences, another way of stating the previous statement is that the correlation squared is a measure of the extent to which *individual differences in one variable are predictable from individual differences in the second variable*. If the correlation squared is 0, then there is no predictability—the two variables are not related to each other. If the squared correlation is 1.0, then we can perfectly predict scores on one variable by knowing scores on the second variable.

The strength of the relationship is apparent by the shape of the scatterplot. When the correlation is 0, then the dots look as if a circle could enclose them. As the correlation increases, the dots take on an elliptical appearance. As the correlation gets larger and larger, the area enclosing the dots becomes more and more elliptical. When the correlation is at its maximum of 1.0, the dots all fall on a straight line. Figure 17.4 depicts four different values of the correlation coefficient when the X variable is sib 1's phenotypic score and the Y variable is sib 2's phenotypic score.

Correlations very close to 0 are sometimes encountered in behavioral genetic research for distant relatives. Correlations of .25 are typical of those reported for first-degree relatives (parent-offspring and sibs) for personality traits. Inspection of panel (b) in Figure 17.4 suggests that correlations of this magnitude imply *some* similarity among relatives, but not a particularly large degree of similarity. Correlations near .50 are seldom encountered for first-degree relatives but are not unusual for identical twins. Correlations of .75 and above are found only for identical twins and for relatives on some traits that are strongly influenced by the family environment, such as religious preference.

Later, we shall see how the correlations computed for specific types of relatives (twins and adoptees) are used to estimate the proportion of phenotypic variance that is attributable to genetic individual differences and the proportion that is due to environmental influences.

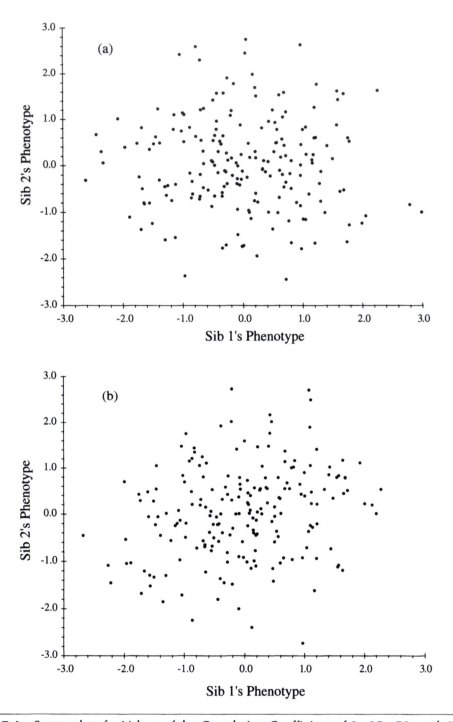

Figure 17.4 Scatterplots for Values of the Correlation Coefficient of 0, .25, .50, and .75 (for Panels a Through d, Respectively).

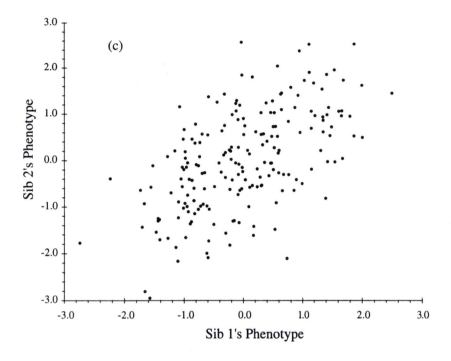

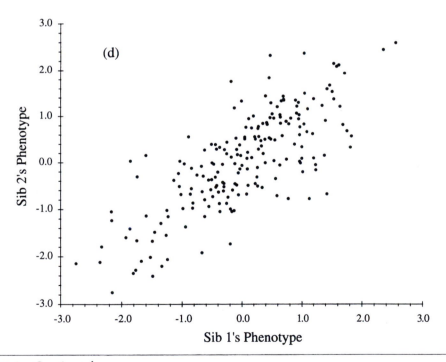

Figure 17.4 Continued

● QUANTITATIVE THINKING

Finally, I offer a word of advice in interpreting etiological statements—*think quantitatively*. It is not informative to ask, "Is this difference in mate preference due to biology or to culture?" Instead, ask "How much of this difference is biological?" and "How much is cultural?" It is most important to ask, "How do biology and culture combine to produce this difference?" You can always answer "Zero" or "Not at all" to these quantitative questions, but arriving at a numerical estimate—even a very rough one—guides science much better than a black-or-white, all-or-none answer. To give a concrete example, later in this module we will show that genes influence IQ scores and IQ influences eventual social status, leading to the inference that there is social stratification for IQ genes. That indeed may be true, but asking "*How much* do genes influence IQ scores" and "*How much* do differences in IQ predict social status" is much more revealing. The amount of social stratification by genes for IQ turns out to be quite small.

● A DISCLAIMER

The amount of published research in behavioral genetics is voluminous. It is not possible to synopsize this information even in an entire book devoted solely to the topic. I have been selective—rather than catholic—in the material covered in this module. We will learn about personality, intelligence, and social status, and two deviant phenotypes—schizophrenia and antisocial behavior. In reading this module, treat these phenotypes as "models" for the much larger body of phenotypes that behavioral geneticists have researched.

● NOTES

1. Behavioral genetics is a misnomer because evolutionary psychology is also very interested in genetics and behavior. However, the term historically has been used to refer to the study of genetic individual differences in behavior.

2. The distribution in this sense is technically called a probability density function in mathematical statistics.

3. This assumes that the two distributions are on the same measurement scale. Many measurement scales for behavioral traits (e.g., IQ, personality scales) are arbitrary, so the statement in the text does not apply to them.

CHAPTER 18

QUANTITATIVE GENETICS I

Important Concepts

INTRODUCTION ●

The chapters on Mendel and Morgan (Chapters 9 and 10) showed how the transmission of genes from one generation to another follows a precise mathematical formula. The traits discussed in that chapter, however, were discrete traits—peas are either yellow or green, and someone either has a disorder or does not have a disorder. Many behavioral traits are not like these clear-cut, have-it-or-don't-have-it phenotypes. For example, people vary from being quite shy to very outgoing. But is shyness a discrete trait or merely a descriptive adjective for one end of a continuous distribution? This chapter will discuss the genetics of quantitative, continuously distributed phenotypes.

Let us note first that genetics has made important—albeit not widely recognized—contributions to quantitative methodology in the social sciences.

The concept of regression was initially developed by Sir Francis Galton in his attempt to predict offspring phenotypes from parental phenotypes; it was later expanded and systematized by his colleague, Karl Pearson,[1] in the context of evolutionary theory. The analysis of variance was formulated by Sir Ronald A. Fisher[2] to solve genetic problems in agriculture. Finally, the famous American geneticist Sewell Wright developed the technique of path analysis, which is now used widely in psychology, sociology, anthropology, economics, and other social sciences.

● CONTINUOUS VARIATION

Continuous Variation and a Single Locus

Let us begin the development of a quantitative model by considering a single gene with two alleles, *a* and *A*. Define the *genotypic value* (aka *genetic value*) for a genotype as *the average phenotypic value for all individuals with that genotype*. For example, suppose that the phenotype was IQ, and we measured IQ on a very large number of individuals. Suppose that we also genotyped these individuals for the locus. The genotypic value for genotype *aa* would be the average IQ of all individuals who had genotype *aa*. Hence, the means for genotypes *aa*, *Aa*, and *AA* would be different from one another, but there would still be variation around each genotype. This situation is depicted in Figure 18.1.

The first point to notice about Figure 18.1 is the variation in IQ around each of the three genotypes, *aa*, *Aa*, and *AA*. Not everyone with genotype *aa*, for instance, has the same IQ. The reasons for this variation within each genotype include environmental variation as well as the effects of loci other than the one genotyped.

A second important feature about Figure 18.1 is that the means of the distributions for the three genotypes differ. The mean IQ (i.e., the genotypic value) for *aa* is 94, that for *Aa* is 96, and that for *AA* is 108. This implies that the locus has some influence on individual differences in IQ.

A third feature of note in Figure 18.1 is that the genotypic value of the heterozygote is not equal to the average of the genotypic values of the two homozygotes. The average value of genotypes *aa* and *AA* is (94 + 108)/2 = 101, but the actual genotypic value of *Aa* is 96. This indicates a certain degree of *dominant gene action* for allele *a*. Allele *a* is not completely dominant; otherwise, the genotype value for *Aa* would equal that of *aa*. Hence, the degree of dominance is incomplete.

A fourth feature of importance is that the curves for the three genotypes do not achieve the same height. This is due to the fact that the three genotypes

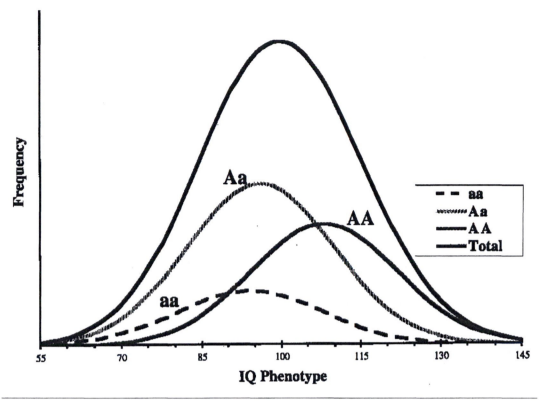

Figure 18.1   Distributions for Three Genotypes at a Single Locus and the Resulting Phenotypic Distribution (Total).

have different frequencies. In the calculations used to generate the figure, it was assumed that the allele frequency for *a* was .4 and the frequency for *A* was .6, giving the genotypic frequencies as .16 (*aa*), .48 (*Aa*), and .36 (*AA*). Consequently, the curve for *Aa* has the highest peak, the one for *AA* has the second highest peak, and that for *aa* has the lowest peak.

A final feature of note is that the phenotypic distribution of IQ in the general population (the solid line in Figure 18.1) looks very much like a normal distribution. The phenotypic distribution is simply the sum of the distributions for the three genotypes. For example, the height of the curve labeled "Total" when IQ equals 90 is the distance from the horizontal axis at 90 to the curve for genotype *aa* plus the distance from the horizontal axis at 90 to the curve for genotype *Aa* plus the distance from the horizontal axis at 90 to the curve for genotype *AA*. Social scientists often mistakenly conclude that the phenotypic distribution must be trimodal because it is the sum of three different distributions.[3]

Table 18.1   Genotypes and Genotypic Values for Two Loci That Contribute to Individual Differences in a Continuous Trait

	bb		Bb		BB		Mean
AA	AAbb	101	AABb	106	AABB	111	108
Aa	Aabb	89	AaBb	94	AaBB	99	96
aa	aabb	87	aaBb	92	aaBB	97	94
Mean		93		98		103	100

The gene depicted in Figure 18.1 is currently termed a *QTL* for *Q*uantitative *T*rait *L*ocus. Behavioral genetic research devotes considerable effort toward uncovering QTLs for many different traits—intelligence, reading disability, various personality traits, and psychopathology. The mathematical models that quantify the extent to which a QTL contributes to trait variance are not necessary for us to know.

Continuous Variation and Multiple Loci

It is unlikely that one and only one gene contributes to individual differences in IQ, so let us examine the influence of a second gene. Suppose that we could genotype people at another locus for IQ, say the *B* locus with its two alleles, *b* and *B*. We would now have nine genotypic values, as illustrated in Table 18.1. Once again, we would compute the mean IQ score for all those with a genotype of *aabb* and then enter this mean into the appropriate cell of the table. Next we could compute the genetic value for all those with genotype *Aabb* and enter this value into the table, and so on. The results—hypothetically at least—would be similar to the data given in Table 18.1.

We could also draw curves for each genotype analogous to the curves depicted in Figure 18.1. This time, however, there would be nine normal curves, one for each genotype. We could continue by adding a third locus with two alleles. This would give 27 different genotypes and 27 curves. If we could identify each and every locus that contributes to IQ, then we would probably have a very large number of curves. The variation within each curve would be due to the environment.

This model is equivalent to the polygenic model introduced in Chapter 6 during the discussion of DCG. At the present time, we cannot identify all the genes for a polygenic phenotype, calculate the types of data in Table 18.1, or plot the data à la Figure 18.1. Hence, these tables and figures are useful for *understanding* quantitative genetics, but they cannot be used for any *practical application* of quantitative genetics to IQ.

IMPORTANT QUANTITATIVE CONCEPTS ●

Introduction

The following sections are the core of this chapter. They explain in English the six important concepts in quantitative behavioral genetics: (a) heritability, (b) environmentability, (c) genetic correlation, (d) environmental correlation, (e) gene-environment interaction, and (f) gene-environment correlation. Although these six are described at a conceptual level, it is important to recognize that behavioral geneticists try to quantify each of them—that is, arrive at an actual number to estimate these six quantities and then judge how important this quantity is for a behavioral phenotype. The next chapter presents an introduction to the estimation and testing of these quantities. What follows is an introduction to the concepts behind these six quantities.

I. Heritability and Environmentability

The concepts of heritability and environmentability of polygenic traits are central to quantitative analysis in behavioral genetics. Instead of providing formal definitions of these terms, let us begin with a simple thought experiment and then discover the definitions through induction.

Imagine that scores on the behavioral trait of impulsivity are gathered on a population of individuals. These observed scores will be called the *phenotypic values* of the individuals. Assume that there was a futuristic genetic technology that could genotype all the individuals in this population for all the loci that contribute to impulsivity. One could then construct a *genotypic value* for each individual. Just as with one or two loci, the genotypic value for a polygenic trait is defined as the mean phenotypic value of all those individuals with that genotype in the population. For example, if Wilbur Waterschmeltzer's genotype for impulsivity is *AaBBCCddEeff* and the mean impulsivity score for all individuals in the population who have genotype *AaBBCCddEeff* is 43.27, then Wilbur's genotypic value is 43.27.

Imagine another technical advance that would permit us to calculate and quantify all the environmental experiences in a person's life that could contribute to the person's level of impulsivity. This would be the *environmental*

Table 18.2   Hypothetical Data Set Containing the Genetic, Environmental, and Phenotypic Values for Individuals

	Genetic Value = G	Environmental Value = E	Phenotypic Value = P
Abernathy Abercrombie	113	96	107
Beulah Bellwacker	92	74	77
. . .	. . .	. . .	. . .
Zelda Zwackelbee	118	104	118

value for an individual. We would now have a very large set of data, part of which is illustrated in Table 18.2.

From the data in this hypothetical table, we would compute a correlation coefficient between the genotypic values and the phenotypic values. Recall that the square of the correlation coefficient between two variables gives the proportion of variance in one variable attributable to (i.e., predicted by) the other variable. Consequently, if we square the correlation coefficient between the genotypic values and the phenotypic values, we would arrive at the proportion of phenotypic variance predicted by (or attributable to) genetic variance. This quantity, the square of the correlation coefficient between genotypic values and phenotypic values, is called *heritability*.[4]

Thus, heritability is a quantitative index of the importance of genetics for individual differences in a phenotype. Strictly defined, heritability is *the proportion of phenotypic variance attributable to or predicted by genetic variance*. Because heritability is a proportion, it will range from 0 to 1.0. A heritability of 0 means that genes do not contribute to individual differences in the trait, whereas a heritability of 1.0 means that trait variance is due solely to heredity. A less technical view would define heritability as *a measure, ranging from 0 to 1.0, of the extent to which observed individual differences can be traced in any way to genetic individual differences*. Heritability is usually denoted as h^2, a convention that we will adopt from now on.

Just as we could compute a correlation between genetic values and phenotypic values, we could also compute correlations between environmental values and phenotypic values. Squaring this correlation would give us the *environmentability* of the trait. Environmentability has the same logical meaning as heritability but applies to the environment instead of the genes. Environmentability is *the proportion of phenotypic variance attributable or predicted by environmental variance*. It is also a *quantitative index, ranging from 0 to 1.0, of the extent to which environmental individual*

Table 18.3 Hypothetical Data Set Containing the Genetic, Environmental, and Phenotypic Values for Individuals on Two Traits

	Verbal			Quantitative		
	Genetic Value = G_V	*Environ-mental Value = E_V*	*Phenotypic Value = P_V*	*Genetic Value = G_Q*	*Environ-mental Value = E_Q*	*Phenotypic Value = P_Q*
Abernathy Abercrombie	590	620	610	630	620	620
Beulah Bellwacker	410	380	400	510	470	490
. . .	. . .	. . .	. . .	. . .	. . .	. . .
Zelda Zwackelbee	630	540	580	520	590	540

differences underlie observable, phenotypic individual differences. We will denote environmentability as e^2.

II. Genetic Correlations and Environmental Correlations

You probably took the SAT or the ACT to enter college, and you received two subscale scores, one for verbal and the other for quantitative abilities. If a behavioral geneticist were performing a twin study of the SAT or ACT, he or she could report heritability (h^2) and environmentability (e^2) for the verbal section and heritability (h^2) and environmentability (e^2) for the verbal section. There is nothing the matter with that, but much more information can be gained by analyzing both phenotypes simultaneously. When more than one phenotype is analyzed at the same time—it is termed *multivariate genetic analysis*.

The extra information from multivariate genetic analysis consists of the *genetic correlation* and the *environmental correlation* among the traits. To discover the meaning of these quantities, examine Table 18.3, which updates Table 18.2 to depict two phenotypes—SAT verbal and SAT quantitative.

Once again, we can compute the correlation between the genetic values for verbal and phenotype values for verbal ability (i.e., h_V) and square this quantity to estimate the heritability for verbal scores (h_V^2). Or, we could square the correlation between the environmental values for quantitative ability and the phenotypic scores for quantitative ability to arrive at the environmentability of quantitative ability (e_Q^2). The genetic correlation, usually denoted by r_g, consists of the *correlation between the genotypic values for two traits*. That is, for the present example,

$$r_g = \text{corr}(G_V, G_Q).$$

The genetic correlation tells us the extent to which the genotypic values for one trait predict the genotypic values for the second trait. It has the same meaning as any correlation; the only difference is that it applies to genotypic values. Hence, a genetic correlation of 0 implies that the two sets of genotypic values are statistically independent of each other; one cannot predict the genetic values of one trait by knowing the genetic values of the other trait. A genetic correlation approaching 1.0 implies strong predictability; in this case, knowing the genotypic values of one trait perfectly predicts the genotypic values of the other trait.[5]

The environmental correlation, or r_e, has an analogous definition—it is the *correlation between the environmental values of the two traits*, or, in terms of the current example,

$$r_e = \text{corr}(E_V, E_Q).$$

The environmental correlation informs us how well environmental values for one trait predict environmental values for the other trait.

III. Gene-Environment Interaction

In nonscientific discussions about the importance of genes in human behavior, behavioral geneticists often encounter an attitude best described in something said to the author at a party—"It is not the gene and it is not the environment that is important. It is the *interaction* between the gene and the environment that is crucial." Indeed, the notion of interactionism has been raised almost to the status of dogma in many circles. This is not necessarily bad. But neither is it good, because the simple phrase "gene-environment interaction" has equivocal meetings, and the usefulness of interactionism depends on which meaning is being used.

The first and the generic meaning of gene-environment interaction—and the one most often used in the nonscientific literature—defines it as *the fact that both genes and environment contribute to behavior*. This is the *lemonade* concept, the theme of which is central to this book. The second meaning of the term is found most often in the scientific literature within behavioral genetics. It interprets the term "interaction" in a statistical sense.

This meaning implies that the *actual relationship between the environment and a phenotype depends on the genotype, or equivalently, the actual relationship between a genotype and a phenotype depends on the environment.* The first definition (i.e., lemonade) will be referred to as the *loose* definition and the second as the *strict* or *statistical* definition. For those of you aware of the concept of interaction in the analysis of variance (ANOVA), these definitions are meaningful. For those of you who suspect that ANOVA is a committee devoted to abolishing the *Nova* series on PBS, these definitions will be vague and vacuous, so perhaps an example will help.

An Example of Gene-Environment Interaction

Asian Americans in both California (Klatsky, Siegelaub, Landy, & Friedman, 1983) and Hawaii (Johnson et al., 1984) who were born in Asia drink much less alcohol than their sons and daughters who were born and raised in the United States. The difference in alcohol consumption between the parental and offspring generations must be the result of culture and environment because drinking in most Asian countries follows the same abstemious quality brought over by the immigrants.

We have also learned how the polymorphism for a form of the enzyme aldehyde dehydrogenase (ALDH-2) influences individual differences in alcohol consumption among Asians, even those raised in the United States (see Chapter 5). Those with a deficient DNA blueprint for ALDH-2 become ill after consuming alcohol, so their risk of exhibiting alcohol abuse and developing alcohol dependence is diminished.

Hence, there is good evidence that both a known gene and a known environmental factor (enculturation in Western society) influence individual differences in alcohol consumption among Asian Americans. Clearly, this is an example of gene-environment interaction in the loose sense of the term—in *lemonadish* terms, both the ALDH polymorphism and growing up in the United States contribute to phenotypic differences in alcohol consumption.

Whether this involves a *statistical* gene-environmental interaction cannot be resolved from these data. To illustrate the point, consider a study that would measure alcohol consumption and ALDH genotypes in both the immigrant and U.S.-born generations of an Asian American community. The results would look like either of the two graphs depicted in Figure 18.2.

The graph on the left-hand side portrays gene-environment interaction in the loose sense. In both the older and the younger generations, ALDH-2 genotypes predict alcohol use: Those with the active enzyme drink more than those with the inactive (deficient) form do. Culture has also influenced alcohol use: The younger generation drinks more on average than their parents do. In ANOVA terms, this graph suggests a main effect for ALDH

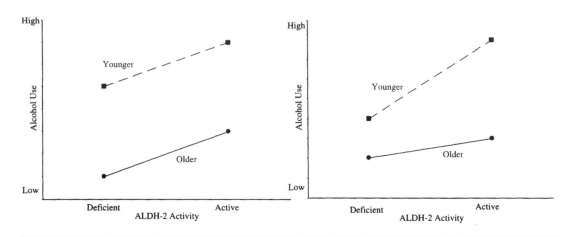

Figure 18.2 Illustration of Gene-Environment Interaction. Both the left and right panels illustrate gene-environment interaction in the loose sense. Only the right panel illustrates gene-environment interaction in the statistical sense.

genotype and a main effect for generation. However, the two lines in the left-hand panel of Figure 18.2 are parallel. Hence, there is no *statistical* interaction between genotype and generation, and hence no gene-environment interaction in the *statistical* sense of the term.

The graph on the right illustrates gene-environment interaction in the strict sense. There, the two lines are no longer parallel. (Indeed, any statistical interaction involves testing whether the lines are parallel or not. If the two lines are within sampling error of being parallel, then there is no statistical interaction. When they are not parallel, then there is a statistical interaction.) In the older generation, ALDH weakly predicts alcohol use; the line is close to being flat, and there is not much difference in drinking between those with and those without the active enzyme. In the younger generation, however, ALDH is a much stronger predictor of alcohol use. This illustrates the phrase "the actual relationship between a genotype and a phenotype depends on the environment" in the definition of a statistical gene-environment interaction. In this case, the relationship between ALDH and drinking depends on whether the person was a recent immigrant from Asia (the older generation) or a person raised in a Western environment (the younger generation).

How Important Is Gene-Environment Interaction?

The answer to this question depends on which definition of gene-environment interaction is used. As demonstrated in Chapter 1, gene-environment interaction in the loose, lemonade sense of the phrase is *always* important for human behavior. Monozygote twins always correlate less than 1.0, so there must always be an important environmental contribution to human behavior. Also, almost all human behaviors demonstrate some degree of heritability, so genes are important. Hence, the lemonadish concept that genes and environment *both* contribute to individual differences in human behavior is as close to a universal statement as one can get in the behavioral sciences.

Unfortunately, we have no real idea of how important gene-environment interaction in the statistical sense is for human behavior. The reason is not a lack of efforts to find an answer or of theory to explain interactions. The biggest problem is a lack of technology to gather adequate empirical data to examine interactions. To test for an interaction, it is necessary to directly measure genotypes or environments (preferably both). However, the ability to do extensive human genotyping was acquired relatively recently. Also, the environment, especially aspects of family life, is not nearly as easy to measure as one might suspect. Many putative environmental aspects of a household may be more reflections of parental phenotypes than causal environmental inputs into a child's behavior. The classic example of the number of books in a house—often found to correlate with a child's academic achievement—may be a better index of parental intelligence and interest in reading than a direct and causal environmental influence on the children.

IV. Gene-Environment Correlation

Gene-environment correlation occurs when people with high genetic values for a trait experience environments with high values for the trait. The converse, of course, is also true—people with low genetic values experience environments with low values.[6] The effect of such a gene-environment (GE) correlation is to increase phenotypic variance, that is, to create a wider range of individual differences.

Several different mechanisms can produce GE correlation, two of which will be described here. The first is the joint transmission of genes and environments within families. For example, consider a husband and wife who are quite intelligent themselves and also have considerable intellectual interests. In addition to providing their offspring with favorable genes for intelligence, they may also foster reading skills, curiosity, inquisitiveness, and a host of other factors that environmentally promote high intelligence in their offspring. Couples with lower than average intelligence may provide less favorable environments to their offspring. The result would be GE correlation that Plomin, DeFries, and Loehlin (1978) have termed *passive* GE correlation.

A second mechanism is self-selection of environments (Scarr & McCartney, 1983), and it generates what Lindon Eaves (personal communication) has dubbed the *smorgasbord model* of GE correlation.[7] A smorgasbord is a buffet of different breads, cheeses, vegetables, fishes, meats, and other foodstuffs. On the first pass, most people sample a little of everything, but on the second pass, they return for those dishes that they found most tasty. In the course of our development, most of us experience a wide variety of different people, academic subjects, work activities, pastimes, hobbies, and other environmental influences. These are equivalent to the first pass through the buffet. Those people whom we enjoy associating with become our friends, those academic subjects that perked our interest become our majors, those work activities we found enjoyable become our careers, and so on. This is the behavioral equivalent of the second pass through the smorgasbord. If genes influence the type of people we find rewarding to be around (and if being around these people alters our behavior), if genes influence the type of academic subjects we find interesting (and if pursuit of those topics alters our subsequent behavior), and if genes influence the work we find enjoyable (and if that work causes subsequent changes in our behavior), then GE correlation will be induced.[8]

How Important Is GE Correlation?

Many of the statements about the effects of GE interaction apply to GE correlation. There is considerably more theoretical writing about GE correlation than there are empirical data on the issue. Once again, the lack of data does not reflect a lack of effort. Rather, there are two major problems in gathering data on GE correlation. The first is that longitudinal data are required during the active phase of a mechanism that induces GE correlation. For example, the association between adolescent peer groups and delinquency is a ripe area for exploring the extent to which such peer groups are self-selected by teenagers already predisposed toward antisocial behavior versus the extent to which the peer groups themselves foster problem behavior. The longitudinal twin data that could help to answer this question are just being gathered. The second and more difficult problem is the one shared with gene-environment interaction—finding good measures of the environment.

In a highly underreferenced paper,[9] Eaves, Last, Martin, and Jinks. (1977) noted that the *existence* of both GE interaction and GE correlation is less important than the specific mechanism that generates the interaction or correlation and the parameters of the situation before that mechanism entered the picture. For example, if the correlation between the environments of relatives (η, in the model developed in Chapter 19) is very low to begin with, then GE interaction can lower the correlation among relatives and lead to an underappreciation of genetic influences. On the other hand, if η is low and the smorgasbord model of GE correlation applies, then GE correlation is included in the estimate of heritability. Here, one may underestimate the importance of the environment. Finally, if η is low and both GE interaction and the smorgasbord GE correlation mechanisms begin, then perhaps their statistical impacts will cancel each other out. Confusing? It should be to the novice in behavioral genetics. The real challenge of GE interaction and GE correlation does not lie in finding numerical values that estimate these concepts. Rather, it resides in identifying the *mechanisms* that generate these statistical quantities in the first place.

THE TWIN AND ADOPTION METHODS ●

Family Correlations

Even with the marvelous technology of modern genetics, it is not possible to directly measure genotypic values for polygenic traits, and it stretches the imagination to suppose that we can measure environmental values for all those varying factors that influence a trait. Instead, we observe only phenotypes in relatives.

Table 18.4 illustrates the type of data that behavioral geneticists gather. The family is the unit of observation, and the phenotypic scores for the different classes of relatives are the variables. For the data in Table 18.4, we would compute the correlation between the variables "parental IQ" and "child IQ," giving a parent-offspring correlation.[10]

But correlations among the relationships in ordinary nuclear families cannot be used to estimate heritability. Behavioral similarity between, say, parents and offspring may be due to any of three factors: (a) shared genes, (b) shared environments, and (c) some combination of shared genes and shared environments. Consequently, behavioral scientists usually study two special types of relatives to tease apart the influence of shared genes from that of shared environment. These two special populations are twins and adoptees. Each is discussed in turn.

The Twin Method: Rationale

Monozygotic (MZ) or *identical* twins are the result of the fertilization of a single egg. The cells from this zygote[11] divide and divide over and over again, but early in the course of development, some cells physically separate

Table 18.4 Organization of Data for Computing the Correlation Between Parent and Offspring

Family	Parent IQ	Child IQ
Athabaska	107	104
Bottomwinger	77	98
. . .	. . .	. . .
Zakmeister	118	102

and begin development as an independent embryo. The reasons for the separation are currently unknown. Because the two individuals start out with the same genes, they are effectively genetic clones of each other, and any differences between the members of an identical twin pair must be due to the environment. Included in the environment is the fact that one twin may have developed from more cells than the other, because it is suspected that the original separation is seldom an equal 50-50 split. MZ twins look so much alike that people who do not know them well often confuse them.

Dizygotic (DZ) or *fraternal* twins result when a woman double ovulates and each egg is fertilized independently. Genetically, DZ twins are as alike as ordinary siblings, sharing on average 50% of their genes, and they look as much alike as ordinary brothers and sisters. Differences between the members of a fraternal twin pair will be due both to the environment and to the different alleles that each member inherits.

Consequently, the logic of the twin method is quite simple. If genes contribute to a trait, then MZ twins should be more similar to each other than are DZ twins. Thus, the striking physical similarity of MZ twins in terms of height, facial features, body shape, hair color, eye color, and other physical characteristics suggests that genes influence individual differences in these traits because fraternal twins are no more alike in their physical features as are ordinary siblings.

The Twin Method: Assumptions

The central assumption of the twin method is often called the *equal environments assumption*. This assumption states that *environmental factors do not make MZ twins more similar than they make DZ twins similar.* To violate this assumption, two very important phenomena must *both* occur: (a) environmental factors must treat MZ twins more similarly than DZ twins and (b) similarity in treatment *must* make a difference in the *phenotype under study*. An example can help to illustrate. Parents often dress identical twin children in similar outfits. All of us have seen a pair of identical twin girls outfitted in the same dress or a pair of young MZ boys both wearing a sailor suit. Parents frequently dress their DZ twins in identical attire, but not nearly with the frequency of parents with MZ twins. Consequently, if the phenotype under study were "fashion in young children," then the equal environments assumption would be violated and we should not use the twin method to estimate heritability.

Let us take this example a bit further. Suppose that the phenotype under study was adult shyness. The first facet of the equal environments is violated because the MZ twins in the sample will have been dressed more alike as children than the DZ twins. However, the second facet of the equal environments assumption—that similarity in treatment makes a difference in the phenotype under study—probably would not be true. If it were true, then being dressed as a child in, say, a cowboy outfit as opposed to a sailor suit would have an important influence on adult shyness. Hence, for the phenotype of childhood fashion, the equal environments assumption would be violated, but for the phenotype of adult shyness, the assumption may be valid.

Potential difficulties with the equal environments assumption begin shortly after fertilization (see Segal, 1999, for an excellent discussion concerning twins and the origins of twinning). Because they result from independent fertilizations, DZ twins develop separate umbilical cords, amniotic sacs, chorions,[12] and placentas. (In a significant proportion of DZ twins, particularly those where each member implants close to the other, the placentas will fuse together during development, leading to a single afterbirth.) Consequently, DZ twins are always dichorionic and diamniotic. Although they may be crowded in the womb, they usually have independent blood supplies from the mother.

The intrauterine status of MZ twins, however, depends on the time of the splitting of the blastomere. When the split is very early, the twins may implant separately in the uterus and follow the same developmental pattern of DZ twins—separate amniotic sacs, chorions, and placentas.[13] This pattern occurs in about 25% to 35% of MZ twins. When the split occurs later, then the two twins develop within a single chorion and are called *monochorionic*. The remaining 65% to 75% of MZ twins follow this pattern. When the split is very late, then the monochorionic twins may actually share a single amniotic sac.[14]

The result of these intrauterine differences between MZ and DZ twins is poorly understood. At first glance, it may appear that development within the same chorion might lead to greater MZ twin similarity, but some twin experts argue that it might also increase differences between MZ twins.

Often, development within a single chorion leads to crowding and unequal distribution of blood to the twins. Unfortunately, there are few empirical data on this topic. Sokol et al. (1995) reported that monochorionic MZ twins were more similar than MZ dichorionic twins on some childhood personality measures but not on measures of cognitive ability. Perhaps intrauterine effects are trait-dependent.

The second major way in which the assumption may be violated is in parental and peer treatment of MZ and DZ twins. Here, empirical data on the equal environments assumption suggests that the assumption is very robust. That is, for most substantive studies thus far on human behaviors studies, the effects of violating the assumption are very minor. It is quite true that as children, MZ twins are often called by rhyming or alliterative names (e.g., Johnnie and Donnie), that they are dressed alike more frequently than DZ twins, and that in general parents treat them more as a unit than they do fraternal twins (Segal, 1999). However, several different types of data suggest that this treatment does not influence substantive phenotypic traits later in life.

The first line of evidence is that *actual* zygosity predicts behavioral similarity better than *perceived* zygosity (Scarr, 1968; Scarr & Carter-Saltzman, 1979). In the past, many parents of twins were misinformed or made erroneous conclusions on their own part about the zygosity of their offspring.[15] Consequently some parents raised their DZ twins as MZ twins, whereas others treated their MZ offspring as DZ pairs. Their biological zygosity rather than their rearing zygosity better predicted the behavioral similarity of these twins.

A second line of evidence relies on the fact that even though *on average* parents of MZ children treat them more alike than parents treat their DZ children, there is still strong variability in the way parents of MZ pairs treat their children. Some parents accentuate their MZ offsprings' similarity by making certain that they have the same hairstyle, clothing, brand of bicycle, and so on. Other parents will actually go out of their way to avoid treating their MZ children as a unit and deliberately try to "individualize" them. However, those MZ twins treated as a unit were no more similar in their adolescent and adult behavior than those who were deliberately individualized (Kendler, Neale, Kessler, Heath, & Eaves, 1993; Loehlin & Nichols, 1976).

The final and best line of evidence comes from studies of twins raised apart. These twins are not raised in completely random environments, but they are certainly not subject to the subtle treatments of being dressed alike, as are many twins who are raised day in and day out in the same household for all their childhood and early adolescence. As one scholar of twins raised apart, James Shields, put it, "The importance of studying separated twins is to demonstrate that the microenvironment of daily living in the same household is not solely responsible for the great similarity observed in twins raised together" (James Shields, personal communication, 1976).

If sibling resemblance were due mainly to the environment and if violation of the equal environments assumption were the major reason why MZ twins raised together correlated higher than DZ twins raised together, then two predictions can be made about separated twins. First, the correlation for separated twins should be small and close to 0; it should certainly be less than the correlation for siblings raised together. Second, the correlation for MZ twins raised apart should not be different from the correlation for DZ twins raised apart. The available data on twins raised apart are inconsistent with both of these predictions (Bouchard, Lykken, McGue, Segal, & Tellegen, 1990). First, for almost all traits that have been studied, the correlations for twins raised apart have been substantial and significant. Second, MZ twins raised apart are consistently *more* similar than biological siblings and DZ twins who are raised together. Finally, MZ twins raised apart correlate higher than DZ twins raised apart.

Taken together, all these lines of evidence suggest that the equal environments assumption meets the definition of a robust assumption. A *robust assumption* is one that might actually be violated, but the effect of violating the assumption is so small that the estimates and substantive conclusions are not altered. For example, Newtonian physics is incorrect, but one can use Newtonian principles to build a bridge or design a skyscraper. In these situations, the assumptions of Newtonian physics are robust even though they are technically wrong.

The Adoption Method: Rationale

The logic of the adoption method is as simple as the logic of the twin method, provided that nonfamilial adoptions are used. When parents adopt and raise a child to whom they are not genetically related, any similarity between the parents and child must have something to do with the environment. Similarly, when there are two adoptive children raised in the same family, then sibling resemblance between the two must also be environmental in nature.

When children are adopted shortly after their birth, then shared genes are the only reason they would show similarity with their biological relatives. Thus, correlations between adoptees and their genetic relatives give evidence for heritability.

The Adoption Method: Assumptions

Two critical assumptions about the adoption method are the absence of selective placement and the representativeness of the adoptive families. Selective placement occurs most often when adoption agencies deliberately try to place adoptees with adoptive parents who resemble the adoptee's genetic parents. Like the equal environments assumption in the twin method, the critical issue is not whether selective placement occurs—it does—but whether the selective placement influences the trait in question.

Some contemporary adoption studies report strong selective placement for race/ethnicity and for religion. Placement for religion is seldom done deliberately; it is mostly a secondary consequence of different religious denominations supporting their own adoption agencies. Catholic Social Services, for example, deals mostly with Catholic unwed mothers and place children into Catholic homes. Similar venues exist for other religiously affiliated agencies. Hence, one must be cautious in interpreting adoption data on phenotypes that may correlate strongly with religious affiliation (e.g., attitudes toward abortion).

There is moderate selective placement for physical characteristics, especially height. The rationale here is to avoid placing a child into a home where the child might "stick out like a sore thumb." For behavioral traits, the empirical evidence suggests that selective placement is usually—but not always—small or nonexistent. It is hard to make generalizations about selective placement for behavioral traits because different adoption studies work with different adoption agencies. For example, selective placement on parental education was weak in two recent studies, one from Texas (Horn, Loehlin, & Willerman, 1979) and the other from Colorado (Plomin & DeFries, 1985), yet was significant in a third study, from Minnesota (Scarr & Weinberg, 1978, 1994). Typically, adoption researchers test for selective placement and, if it is present, adjust their statistical methods to account for it.

The second assumption about the adoption method concerns the representativeness of the adoptive families. Adoptive parents are screened—sometimes intensively—on issues of positive mental and physical health, the ability to financially support a child, and the probability of providing a safe and secure home for the child. Researchers mistakenly assume that the screening process is *for* wealth, *for* positive mental health, and so on. Instead, the process is *against* extreme poverty and *against* serious psychopathology. As a result, mean income of adoptive families is not very different from average income in the general population—it is just that the lower tail of the income distribution is missing.

Selection against psychopathology is a more serious matter. Parental alcoholism, criminal behavior, psychosis, drug abuse, and several other factors can exclude a family from adopting a child. As a result, there may be a restriction in range in the environments provided by adoptive parents, making it very difficult to detect a correlation between adoptees and their adoptive relatives. Hence, one should be cautious in interpreting low correlations among adoptive relatives as evidence for a lack of family environmental influence on the trait. Once again, one must consider restriction in range on a trait-by-trait basis. It may be very important for phenotypes like antisocial behavior but rather weak for personality traits.

THE FAMILY ENVIRONMENT ●

The behavioral genetic definition of "family environment" sows untold confusion among social scientists, so it is important to discuss it. According to almost all social science research, the term *family environment* refers to the physical, psychological, and social state of the household and the members within it. Physical attributes include the physical area of the house, the number of books or computers, and adequacy of provisions. Psychological variables tap such constructs as parental warmth, psychopathology, and sibling interactions, while social variables measure such contracts as parental education and religion. This definition of family environment is termed the *substantive* definition.

In contrast, the definition of family environment used in behavioral genetic research is a *statistical* definition.[16] According to this definition, the family environment consists of *all those factors that make relatives similar on a phenotype*. The phrases "all those factors" and "make relatives similar" are very important. *Both* of these must be present for a causal factor to be considered part of the statistical family environment.

Literally, the phrase "all those factors" does not restrict causal variables from physically occurring inside the family unit. If living in the same neighborhood makes siblings similar to one another, then the factor of "living in the same neighborhood" is part of the statistical family environment. Other factors relevant for siblings might include going to the same (or very similar) schools, having overlapping groups of friends, and sharing a religion.

Likewise, the phrase "make relatives similar" is crucial for understanding the statistical family environment. If siblings share a religion but religion does not make siblings similar on the personality trait of sociability, then "sharing a religion" is *not* part of the statistical family environment for sociability.

Hence, if some factor physically occurs within the family household but does not make siblings similar, then it is *not* part of the statistical family environment. For example, consider Papa Smith, a rather authoritarian and argumentative chap whose in-your-face style and rigid views of right and wrong influence both of his sons. Aaron Smith, something of a chip off the old block, argues right back, and the continual verbal interactions between him and Papa reinforce Aaron's tendency to express his views openly. Zeke Smith, on the other hand, is very intimidated by Papa and becomes submissive in his public persona. In this scenario, Papa Smith is definitely part of the family environment (in the substantive use of the term) of the Smith brothers.

However, Papa is not part of the statistical family environment for Aaron and Zeke because his influence is to make them phenotypically different from each other. Although Papa is a shared experience for Aaron and Zeke, he does not make them similar.

For some phenotypes—most notably personality traits—the effects of the statistical family environment for siblings are very small. This finding has often been interpreted as implying that parents have no effect on their children's personality. Although this conclusion *may* be true, the data are not sufficient to prove it. All the data say is that the net effect of being raised in the same family does not, on average, make siblings similar to one another in personality. For each Papa Smith in a population, there may be a corresponding Papa Jones whose influence on his children is to make them similar. The differences induced by the Papa Smiths may cancel out the similarities created by the Papa Joneses, resulting in a negligible statistical family environment. The effect of the *substantive* family environment, on the other hand, may be quite important for personality development.

Just as social scientists sometimes use the term *nonfamily environment* to refer to factors outside the household and its members, behavioral geneticists will use that term but again in a statistical sense. The statistical non-familial environment is defined as *all those factors that make relatives different from one another*. Papa Smith is part of the statistical nonfamily environment. If the neighborhood peer group makes siblings similar for juvenile delinquency, then they are part of the statistical family environment but the substantive nonfamily environment.

At this point, the insightful reader might ask why behavioral geneticists have not developed a new vocabulary to avoid the equivocation and all the resulting confusion. The short answer is that behavioral geneticists have indeed used different terminology and have tried to be explicit about their definitions, but the subtle differences in meaning have not caught on in the broader social science literature. Table 18.5 presents the statistical concepts, their definitions, and the terms used most often in behavioral genetic research to refer to these statistical quantities. It is important to commit them to memory. Both the general literature in behavioral genetics and the remaining chapters in this book will use these terms.

● COMMENTS ON HERITABILITY AND ENVIRONMENTABILITY ESTIMATION

The next chapter will describe simple methods for obtaining numerical estimates of the concepts described above as well as the assumptions behind the

Table 18.5   Terminology Used in the Behavioral Genetics Literature to Refer to the Statistical Quantities of Between-Family Environmental Variance and Within-Family Environmental Variance

Statistical Quantity	*Definition*	*Terms Used in the Behavioral Genetics Literature*
Between-family environmental variance (the statistical family environment)	All factors that make relatives similar to one another on a phenotype = the extent to which being raised together makes relatives similar	Family environment Shared environment Common environment Shared, family environment
Within-family environmental variance (the statistical nonfamily environment)	All factors that make relatives different from one another on a phenotype = the extent to which idiosyncratic experiences make relatives different	Nonfamily environment Nonshared environment Unique environment Idiosyncratic environment

estimation process. Before embarking on that, we must gain insight into the accuracy of these quantitative estimates and the various factors that influence them. The important points about heritability and environmentability are listed below.

With humans, h^2 and e^2 are measured with some accuracy, but not with complete accuracy. Temperature can be measured accurately with a thermometer. Estimations of h^2 and e^2 have the accuracy of going outside in the middle of the day and guesstimating the temperature without a thermometer. On a frigid winter day, you may be hard pressed to distinguish a temperature of 0 degrees Fahrenheit from 10 degrees or even −10 degrees, but you know darn well that it is not 40 degrees, 70 degrees, or 100 degrees. On a blistering summer day, you may not be able to tell 95 degrees from 105 degrees, but you can estimate with confidence that it is not 70 degrees, 40 degrees, or 0 degrees. Heritability and environmentability cannot be estimated well to the second digit, but they can be placed into categories of low (arbitrarily taken here as 0 to .30), moderate (.30 to .60), and high (.60 to 1.0).

Heritability and environmentability are population concepts and statistics that apply only weakly to individuals. An h^2 of .40 for achievement motivation does *not* mean that 40% of your achievement motivation is due to your genes and the remaining 60% is generated by your environment. Your own level of achievement motivation could be determined almost completely by your genes or almost completely by your environment and yet be totally consistent with an h^2 of .40. The heritability simply means that *averaged over an entire population*, 40% of observed individual differences in achievement motivation are attributable to genetic individual differences. For similar reasons, an extremely deviant score for a heritable trait does not necessarily imply that a person is a genetic "deviant." Antisocial behavior has a moderate heritability, but that fact alone does not imply that a chronic felon has an extreme genotype for antisocial behavior.[17]

Heritability depends on the range of environments, and environmentability depends upon the range of genotypes. A simple example can illustrate this principle. Farmer Jones buys corn seed that consists of a wide variety of different genotypes. She plants each seed in the same soil, gives it the same amount of fertilizer and water, and makes certain that each plant receives an identical amount of sunlight. At the end of the growing season, some corn plants are taller than others. All differences in height must be differences in the genotypes of the corn because each seed and plant received the same environmental treatment. The heritability of height for Farmer Jones's corn plants would be 1.0. If Farmer Smith bought corn seeds that were genetically identical but then planted them at different depths in different soils and provided them with differing amounts of water, fertilizer, and sunlight, then the environmentability for height in her crop would be 1.0. Thus, h^2 and e^2 have a yin-yang relationship. Decrease one and the other increases; increase one and the other decreases. This can lead to some counterintuitive conclusions. Providing equal schooling for all children is a laudable social goal, but it could increase the heritability of academic achievement.

Heritability and environmentability within populations are uninformative about differences between populations. In the above example, suppose that Farmer Smith's plants were on average 4 inches taller than Farmer Jones's. To what extent is this due to the genotypes of the seeds or to the environments of the corn plants? There is no way to tell. Hence, even under conditions of perfect heritability and environmentability within populations, it is not possible to determine the reasons why one population differs from another. There was significant heritability for contracting tuberculosis (TB) in the late 1800s and early 1900s, and there may well be heritability for it today. That is, heritability of TB may be significant in past years and may also be significant today. Does that imply that the difference in TB prevalence between the initial and terminal years of the 20th century is due to genetic differences? Of course not. The great reduction in TB prevalence over the century is better explained by improved antibiotics and public health measures than by the death of most genetically susceptible people in the interim. To give concrete applications of this general principle, we would conclude that (a) the fact that a trait is heritable in both males and females does not imply that genes contribute to mean sex differences, and (b) heritability of a trait within ethnic groups does not imply that mean ethnic differences are due to genes.

NOTES ●

1. After whom is named the Pearson product-moment correlation.

2. After whom the *F* statistic is named.

3. The phenotypic distribution *may* be trimodal, but it will be so only when the means for the three genotypes are very, very different. When single genes exert only a small influence on a phenotype, then the phenotypic distribution can appear quite smooth, as the present example suggests.

4. Two assumptions are necessary to define heritability (and later, environmentability) this way. First, it is assumed that the genotypic values are uncorrelated with the environmental values. Second, there is no statistical interaction between genotypic values and environmental values. These assumptions will be discussed later in the chapter.

5. It is tempting to interpret genetic correlations in terms of the number of genes that two traits have in common; however, the situation is more complicated than that (see Carey, 1988).

6. Logically, it is possible to have a negative gene-environment correlation, but few researchers concern themselves with this.

7. The exact origin of the phrase "smorgasbord model" is obscure. It first came into this author's awareness in casual conversation when Lindon Eaves graciously provided him with a ride home, but the concept had been extensively bantered about in teatime conversations involving Lindon Eaves, Nick Martin, Andrew Heath, Jeffrey Long, and this author.

8. Self-selection mechanisms are termed "active" GE correlation by Plomin et al. (1978).

9. Underreferenced in the sense that few contemporary researchers refer to that paper any more, not in the sense that it contains few references.

10. Readers familiar with data analysis should realize that because families do not have the same number of offspring, family data usually are not "rectangular." There are methods to take care of such data sets, but they are too advanced for this text. The interested reader should consult Neale and Cardon (1992).

11. A *zygote* is "scientificese" for a fertilized egg.

12. Two separate "sacs" enclose a fetus. The first of these is the amniotic sac, containing the amniotic fluid, and the second is the chorionic sac, surrounded by a layer of cells referred to as the chorion.

13. As for DZ twins, the two placentas may fuse during development.

14. The fact that the DZ twins are always dichorionic leads to the erroneous conclusion among many obstetricians that fraternal twins always have two afterbirths while identical twins have only a single afterbirth. Not long ago, I interviewed a mother of

an opposite-sex DZ pair who swore that her son and daughter were identical twins because the doctor told her so on the basis of a single afterbirth.

15. A persistent myth, held even by some MDs, was that identical twins have one afterbirth while fraternal twins have two afterbirths. What is true is that DZ twins always have two chorions (a sac enclosing the amnion and amniotic fluid), whereas MZ twins may have either one or two chorions. Either type of twins can have one or two afterbirths.

16. The statistical definition has its origin in ANOVA techniques developed for genetic analysis in agronomy. As applied to humans, each human family would be a single cell in a very large one-way ANOVA. The scores for the individuals within a family are the within-group numbers for a cell in the ANOVA. Hence, the within-family variance component reflects all those factors that make relatives of a family different from one another. The between-group variance component taps factors that make members of a family similar to one another but different from members of other families. With genetically informative designs (twins, adoptees), one can estimate a within-family environmental variance component and a between-family environmental variance component (see Jinks & Fulker, 1970). The between-family environmental variance is the quantity that behavioral geneticists have taken to calling the "family environment."

17. The difference between population statistics and predictability of a trait for an individual may be problematic for those without a strong quantitative background, so perhaps an analogy will help. Suppose that I gathered a random sample of 500 adult males and 500 adult females and measured their height. How much would you wager that the average height of the males was significantly greater than the average height of the females? If you had no personal scruples about betting and if you knew about statistics, you should beg or borrow—but not steal—as much money as you could for your wager. The odds that you will win are greater than a billion to one. Now suppose that I picked a random male from this sample. How much would you bet that he is taller than the average for the whole sample of 1,000 people? Would you bet the farm on this? Of course not! There is much more uncertainty guessing about an individual than there is in guessing about population statistics (the mean heights of males and females).

● REFERENCES

Bouchard, T. J. J., Lykken, D. T., McGue, M., Segal, N. L., & Tellegen, A. (1990). Sources of human psychological differences: The Minnesota study of twins reared apart. *Science, 250*, 223-250.

Carey, G. (1988). Inference about genetic correlations. *Behavior Genetics, 18*, 329-338.

Eaves, L. J., Last, K., Martin, N. G., & Jinks, J. L. (1977). A progressive approach to non-additivity and genotype-environmental covariance in the analysis of human differences. *British Journal of Mathematical and Statistical Psychology, 30*, 1-42.

Horn, J. M., Loehlin, J. C., & Willerman, L. (1979). Intellectual resemblance among adoptive and biological relatives: The Texas Adoption Project. *Behavior Genetics, 9*, 117-207.

Jinks, J. L., & Fulker, D. W. (1970). Comparison of biometrical, genetical, MAVA, and classical approaches to the analysis of human behavior. *Psychological Bulletin, 73*, 311-349.

Johnson, R. C., Nagoshi, C. T., Schwitters, S. Y., Bowman, K. S., Ahern, F. M., & Wilson, J. R. (1984). Further investigation of racial/ethnic differences and of familial resemblances in flushing in response to alcohol. *Behavior Genetics, 14,* 171-178.

Kendler, K. S., Neale, M. C., Kessler, R. C., Heath, A. C., & Eaves, L. J. (1993). A test of the equal-environment assumption in twin studies of psychiatric illness. *Behavior Genetics, 23,* 21-27.

Klatsky, A. L., Siegelaub, A. B., Landy, C., & Friedman, G. (1983). Racial patterns of alcohol beverage use. *Alcoholism: Clinical and Experimental Research, 7,* 372-377.

Loehlin, J. C., & Nichols, R. C. (1976). *Heredity, environment, and personality: A study of 850 sets of twins.* Austin: University of Texas Press.

Neale, M. C., & Cardon, L. R. (1992). *Methodology for genetic studies of twins and families.* Dordrecht, The Netherlands: Kluwer.

Plomin, R., & DeFries, J. C. (1985). *Origins of individual differences in infancy: The Colorado adoption project.* Orlando, FL: Academic Press.

Plomin, R., DeFries, J. C., & Loehlin, J. C. (1978). Gene-environment interaction and correlation in the analysis of human behavior. *Psychological Bulletin, 84,* 309-322.

Scarr, S. (1968). Environmental bias in twin studies. *Eugenics Quarterly, 15,* 34-40.

Scarr, S., & Carter-Saltzman, L. (1979). Twin method: Defense of a critical assumption. *Behavior Genetics, 9,* 527-542.

Scarr, S., & McCartney, K. (1983). How people make their own environments: A theory of genotype environment effects. *Child Development, 54,* 424-435.

Scarr, S., & Weinberg, R. A. (1978). The influence of "family background" on intellectual attainment. *American Sociological Review, 43,* 674-692.

Scarr, S., & Weinberg, R. A. (1994). Educational and occupational achievements of brothers and sisters in adoptive and biologically related families. *Behavior Genetics, 24,* 301-325.

Segal, N. L. (1999). *Entwined lives: Twins and what they tell us about human behavior.* New York: Dutton.

Sokol, D. K., Moore, C. A., Rose, R. J., Williams, C. J., Reed, T., & Christian, J. C. (1995). Intrapair differences in personality and cognitive ability among young monozygotic twins distinguished by chorion type. *Behavior Genetics, 25,* 457-466.

CHAPTER **19**

QUANTITATIVE GENETICS II

Estimation and Testing

INTRODUCTION ●

The previous chapter presented quantitative genetics from a conceptual view.
We learned about heritability, environmentability, the behavioral-geneticist's
definition of family environment, and other concepts. This chapter will show
how to estimate these quantities from actual data.

ESTIMATING HERITABILITY AND ●
ENVIRONMENTABILITY: A QUANTITATIVE MODEL

This section will develop a mathematical model for twin and adoption
data that permits the estimation of heritability and environmentability. The
overall logic behind estimation is not difficult to grasp and consists of the
following steps:

311

1. We have observed numbers in the form of correlation coefficients for different types of relatives (MZ twins, DZ twins, adoptive sibs, etc.). Using the principles of quantitative genetics, write an equation for each of these correlations in terms of the unknown quantities of heritability and environmentability. The form of these equations will be observed correlation = algebraic formula.

2. There will also be an equation for the phenotypic variance. Write down this equation.

3. We now have a series of simultaneous equations, but usually there are more unknown algebraic quantities than there are equations. Hence, it is necessary to make assumptions about the unknowns.

4. Once there are as many unknowns as there are equations, use the techniques learned in high school algebra to solve for the unknowns.

The most difficult part of this section is the notation. Because there are several different types of relationships (e.g., MZ twins and DZ twins), it is necessary to use subscripts to keep track of them. Hence, the equations look intimidating, but if you "sound them out," it becomes easy to understand them.

The Model

The model for the similarity for any pair of relatives is depicted in Figure 19.1. In this figure, G denotes genotypic value, E denotes environmental value, and P stands for phenotypic value.[1] Subscripts 1 and 2 denote, respectively, the first and the second relative. If the relatives were siblings, then G_1 denotes the genotypic value for sib 1, E_2 stands for the environmental value of sib 2, and so on. If the relatives were parent and offspring, then E_1 could represent the environmental values of parents, P_2 could denote the phenotypic values of the offspring, and so on.

The model in Figure 19.1 is one of several different models used to analyze genetic data. As the aphorism "all roads lead to Rome" implies, the various models will all generate the same substantive conclusions. The only advantage of the model in Figure 19.1—and the reason that it is used here— is that it avoids the equivocal use of the term "family environment" that has impeded communication between behavioral geneticists and other social scientists (see Chapter 18).

In this figure, the straight, single-headed arrows (or *paths*) originating in the Gs and entering the Ps denote the possibility that genotypic values predict phenotypic values. The hs on these two arrows quantify this effect. Strictly

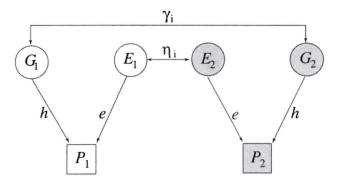

Figure 19.1 A Model for the Correlation Between the Phenotypes of Two Relatives.

NOTE: Subscripts 1 and 2 denote the two relatives, G denotes the genotype, E denotes the environmental value, and P denotes the phenotypic values of the relative.

speaking, h is the correlation between genotypic and phenotypic values.[2] Similarly, the paths from the Es to the Ps denote the prediction of phenotypic values from environmental values, and e is the correlation between E and P.

The double-headed arrow connecting G_1 to G_2 denotes the fact that the genotypic values of relatives may be correlated. The quantity γ_i (Greek lowercase gamma) gives this correlation. Similarly, the double-headed arrow connecting E_1 to E_2 allows for the possibility that the environmental values of the two relatives are correlated, and η (Greek lowercase eta) denotes this correlation. Both γ and η have the subscript attached to them to denote the type of relationship. For example, if the relationship of immediate interest were DZ twins, then i = DZ and the equation would contain the algebraic quantities γ_{DZ} (read "gamma sub DZ"—the correlation between the genotypes for DZ twins) and η_{DZ} (read "eta sub DZ"—the correlation between the environmental values for DZ twins). The values of γ and η for different types of relationships are given in the columns labeled "General" in Table 19.1.

The Two Central Equations of the Model and How to Write Them

We can now use the rules of path analysis developed by Sewall Wright to derive two central equations for the quantitative model. The first important equation is that for the phenotypic variance. Because the quantitative model

Table 19.1   Values of γ and η for Different Types of Genetic and Adoptive Relationships Under a General Model and Under a Simple Model That Assumes Only Additive Genetic Action, Random Mating, and Random Placement of Adoptees

Relationship	Notation	γ General	γ Simple	η General	η Simple
MZ twins together	mzt	1.0	1.0	η_{mzt}	η_{twin}
MZ twins apart	mza	1.0	1.0	η_{mza}	0
DZ twins together	dzt	γ_{sibs}	.50	η_{dzt}	η_{twin}
DZ twins apart	dza	γ_{sibs}	.50	η_{dza}	0
Siblings together	sibst	γ_{sibs}	.50	η_{sibst}	η_{sib}
Siblings apart	sibsa	γ_{sibs}	.50	η_{sibsa}	0
Parent-offspring together	pot	γ_{pot}	.50	η_{pot}	η_{po}
Parent-offspring apart	poa	γ_{poa}	.50	η_{poa}	0
Grandparent-grandchild	gg	γ_{gg}	.25	η_{ggt}	η_{gg}
Uncle/aunt-nephew/niece	uann	γ_{uann}	.25	η_{uannt}	η_{uann}
Half sibs, together	hst	γ_{hst}	.25	η_{hst}	η_{sib}
Half sibs, apart	hsa	γ_{hsa}	.25	η_{hsa}	0
Cousins	cous	γ_{cous}	.125	η_{cous}	η_{cous}
Adoptive parent-offspring	apo	γ_{apo}	0	η_{apo}	η_{po}
Adoptive sibs	asibs	γ_{asibs}	0	η_{asibs}	η_{sib}

is expressed in terms of standardized variables,[3] the variance of the phenotype will equal 1.0. The equation for this variance is

$$1.0 = b^2 + e^2. \tag{1}$$

The second equation expresses the correlation for any type of relative pair in terms of the unknowns in Figure 19.1 (i.e., γ_i, η_i, b, and e). Let R_i denote the correlation for the ith type of relationship. Then

$$R_i = \gamma_i b^2 + \eta_i e^2. \tag{2}$$

For this equation, read "R sub i equals gamma sub i times h squared plus eta sub i times e squared." In substantive terms, the equation states "The correlation for the ith relationship (R_i) equals the correlation between the genotypic values of the ith relationship times the heritability ($\gamma_i b^2$) plus the correlation between the environmental values for the ith relationship times the environmentability ($\eta_i e^2$)."

To write an equation for a specific type of relationship, go to Table 19.1, look up the relationship, and then substitute the appropriate subscript for the subscript i in equation (2). For example, if the relationship were identical twins raised together, the subscript is mzt, so we would substitute γ_{mzt} for γ_i and η_{mzt} for η_i in equation (2). Hence, the equation would be

$$R_{mzt} = \gamma_{mzt}b^2 + \eta_{mzt}e^2.$$

This equation states, "The correlation for MZ twins raised together (R_{mzt}) equals the correlation between the genotypic values of MZ twins raised together (γ_{mzt}) times the heritability (b^2) plus the correlation between the environmental values for MZ twins raised together (η_{mzt}) times the environmentability (e^2)." In any concrete application, we would substitute the observed numerical value for R_{mzt} in this equation.

Equations (1) and (2) are very important, so you should devote time to memorizing them. This cumbersome notation has been used deliberately because later it will reveal to us some important assumptions about the twin method and the adoption method.

A Numerical Example

Now that we have learned the important equations and how to write them, let us go through the four steps mentioned earlier with a specific example. Suppose that we collected data on twins raised together and found that $R_{mzt} = .60$ and $R_{dzt} = .45$. Using Step 1, we would write the equation for identical twins as

$$.60 = \gamma_{mzt}b^2 + \eta_{mzt}e^2$$

and the equation for fraternal twins as

$$.45 = \gamma_{dzt}b^2 + \eta_{dzt}e^2.$$

Writing the equation for the phenotypic variance in Step 2 gives

$$1.0 = b^2 + e^2.$$

Although there are three equations, there are six unknowns—b^2, e^2, γ_{mzt}, γ_{dzt}, η_{mzt}, and η_{dzt} (the unknowns, or *parameters* as statisticians call them, will always be the algebraic quantities on the right-hand side of the equation when you follow these rules). From high school algebra, recall that it is not possible to find estimates of the six unknowns because there are more unknowns than there are equations, a situation that mathematicians call *underidentification*. To overcome this problem, behavioral geneticists typically make assumptions (Step 3 in the process). There are two sets of assumptions, the first dealing with γ_{mzt} and γ_{dzt} and the second dealing with η_{mzt} and η_{dzt}.

The first set of assumptions derives from genetic theory and is presented in Text Box 19.1. The value of γ for identical twins, irrespective of whether they are raised apart or together, will always be 1.0. For all other types of genetic relationships, however, γ depends on unknown quantities about gene action and the form of assortative mating when assortative mating is present. The typical assumptions are that all gene action is additive and that there is no assortative mating. If these assumptions are robust, then $\gamma = .50$ for first-degree relatives (parent-offspring, siblings), $\gamma = .25$ for second-degree relatives (grandparent-grandchild, uncle/aunt-nephew/niece, half siblings), $\gamma = .125$ for third-degree relatives, and so on. At each degree of genetic relationship, the value of γ is halved; hence, for nth-degree relatives, $\gamma = .5^n$. Genetic models that use these assumptions are termed *simple, additive genetic* models, and the values of γ under this model are given under the column for γ labeled "Simple" in Table 19.1. If we make these assumptions, then the three equations for the problem can be written as

$$.60 = b^2 + \eta_{mzt}e^2,$$

$$.45 = .5b^2 + \eta_{dzt}e^2,$$

and

$$1.0 = b^2 + e^2.$$

There are now three equations, but because of the assumptions about γ, the number of unknowns has been reduced from six to four. Those unknowns are b^2, e^2, η_{mzt}, and η_{dzt}.

The second set of assumptions—those involving η—depend on two assumptions: (a) selective placement of adoptees into their adoptive environment and (b) the equal environments assumption in twin studies. These assumptions are discussed in Text Box 19.2. When placement is random with respect to phenotypes (i.e., no selective placement), then the values of η for all genetic relatives raised apart from one another is 0. When the equal environments assumption in twin studies is robust, then the η for MZ twins raised together equals the η for DZ twins raised together. The value for η under random placement of adoptees and the equal environments assumption is

Text Box 19.1

THE PROBLEM WITH γ

Here, a small digression is in order because the quantity γ in the path model requires some explanation. This quantity is the correlation between the genotypic values of relatives. If the relatives are identical twins, then γ = 1.0 because the twins have identical genotypes. For fraternal twins and for ordinary siblings, the precise mathematical value of γ is not known. If the world of genetics were a simple place where each allele merely added or subtracted a small value from the phenotype and there were no assortative mating for the trait, then γ would equal .50. This value of γ is often assumed in the analysis of actual data, more for the sake of mathematical convenience than for substantive research demonstrating that the assumptions for choosing this value are valid.

If gene action is not simple and additive, then the value of γ will be something less than .50. The two classic types of nonadditive gene action are *dominance* and *epistasis*. Dominance occurs when the phenotypic value for a heterozygote is not exactly halfway between the phenotypic values of the two homozygotes. Epistasis occurs when there is a statistical interaction between genotypes. Both dominance and epistasis create what is termed *nonadditive genetic variance*. For technical reasons, nonadditive genetic variance reduces the correlation between first-degree relatives to something less than .50. The extent of the reduction depends on the type of relatives.

Assortative mating, on the other hand, will tend to increase the value of γ. When parents are phenotypically similar and when there is some heritability, then the genotypes of parents will be correlated. The effect of this is to increase the genetic resemblance of their offspring over and above what it would be under random mating.

What should be done under such complexities? The typical strategy of setting γ equal to .50 is not a bad place to start. If a trait shows strong assortative mating, then more elaborate mathematical models can be developed to account for the effects of nonrandom mating. The real problem occurs with nonadditive genetic variance. When this is present, the techniques described in the text overestimate heritability. This is another reason why heritability estimates should not be interpreted as precise, mathematical quantities.

Text Box 19.2

THE PROBLEM WITH η

A small digression is useful here to explore the meaning of η. This parameter is usually interpreted as a measure of *family environment*, but the term "family environment" has the rather strange and esoteric meaning explicated in the previous chapter. In this context, the family environment is defined *as all those factors, both inside and outside the physical household, that make relatives similar on the phenotype being studied*. Repetition is good for learning, so let us reinforce the discussion of the family environment in Chapter 18 in this text box.

Suppose that relatives in question were pairs of young sibs. Such siblings live in the same neighborhood, usually attend the same schools, and often have friends in common. If neighborhood, quality of school, and peers influence a phenotype such as achievement motivation, then they are part of the "family environment" for siblings, even though these variables do not originate within the physical household of the sibs.

Suppose that future research found that parents treat their children differently in subtle ways, for example, by encouraging the sib with the higher grades in school to study more and take academics more seriously. This parental action will make pairs of siblings *different*, not similar. Hence, it would *not* be considered a family environmental factor even though from a psychological perspective it involves social interaction between parents and their offspring.

An astute reader may question why anyone would regard η as a measure of "family environment" when family environment is defined in such an odd way. This perspective has considerable merit, but the sad fact is that this definition of η and the family environment has been used so much in the literature that it is almost carved in stone. At the risk of offending many colleagues, I suggest a vigorous sandblasting of that stone. Let us begin to view η for what it really is—the correlation between the environments of relatives. It is an index of the environmental similarity of relatives and measures the extent to which relatives are correlated because they have some environmental factors in common. Family factors— defined in the substantive sense outlined in Chapter 18—can make η high or can make η low, just as factors outside the family can influence η. In short, η is a statistical concept that overlaps with—but does not completely define—the substantive meaning of "family environment" as the term is used in social science research.

given in the column for η labeled "Simple" in Table 19.1. If we now substitute the values for η in this column into the equations, we have

$$.60 = b^2 + \eta_{\text{twin}}e^2,$$

$$.45 = .5b^2 + \eta_{\text{twin}}e^2,$$

and

$$1.0 = b^2 + e^2.$$

We now have three equations in three unknowns (or parameters)—b^2, e^2, and η_{twin}—so we can estimate the unknowns. The last step (Step 4) is to use high school algebra to solve for the unknowns. The easiest way to start this is to subtract the second equation from the first equation,

$$.60 - .45 = b^2 + \eta_{\text{twin}}e^2 - .5b^2 - \eta_{\text{twin}}e^2,$$

or

$$.15 = .5b^2.$$

Multiplying both sides of this equation by 2 (which, of course, is equal to dividing both sides by .5) gives the estimate for heritability,

$$.30 = b^2.$$

Substitute this numeric value for b^2 into the third equation,

$$1.0 = .30 + e^2,$$

so

$$e^2 = .70.$$

We have now estimated the environmentability.

To estimate the correlation between twin environments (η_{twin}), substitute the numerical values for b^2 and e^2 into either of the two equations for the twin correlations. It makes no difference in this case whether we select the one for MZ twins or DZ twins—we will arrive at the same estimate. Arbitrarily taking the correlation for MZ twins and substituting the numeric values of heritability and environmentability gives

$$.60 = .30 + \eta_{\text{twin}}(.70).$$

Now use algebra to solve for η_{twin}:

$$\eta_{twin} = \frac{.60 - .30}{.70} = .43.$$

Suppose that the trait that we were studying in this example were sociability. We would conclude that 30% of the observed individual differences in sociability are attributable to genetic individual differences (because $h^2 = .30$) and that 70% of the observed individual differences in sociability are attributable to the environment (because $e^2 = .70$). To repeat this statement using statistical jargon, we conclude that 30% of the phenotypic variance is due to genetic sources and the remaining 70% of phenotypic variance arises in some way from the environment. We would also conclude that the correlation between twin environments is .43. This suggests that something about being raised in the same family makes twins similar, although it is not possible to pinpoint the specific factors responsible for producing this similarity.

Making Life Simple

More examples of how to estimate parameters can be found on the Web site for this book. First, let us examine the traditional equations for the twin and the adoption methods when the simplifying assumptions mentioned above are made. They are presented in Tables 19.2 and 19.3, respectively.

In practice, the tortuous route of the four steps mentioned above is seldom applied in behavioral genetics research. The four steps are useful here for the student because they illustrate the types of assumptions usually made and the exact places where those assumptions are made. Typically, behavioral geneticists collect data in accord with a specific design, make the assumptions necessary for that design, and then use the equations in Tables 19.2 and 19.3 to estimate the parameters.

To illustrate, let us return to the example of sociability. We have used a design of twins raised together, so we automatically make the assumptions of a simple, additive genetic model, no assortative mating, and equal twin environments. This places us squarely into the row labeled "Twins raised together" in Table 19.2. To refresh our memories, the correlation that we observed to MZ twins raised together (R_{mzt}) was .60 and the correlation for

Table 19.2 Estimation of Heritability, Environmentability, and the Correlation Between Twins' Environments Using the Twin Method and the Assumptions of Equal Environments for MZ and DZ Twins Raised Together and No Selective Placement of Adoptees

Design	h^2	e^2	η_{twin}
Twins raised together	$= 2(R_{mzt} - R_{dzt})$	$1 - h^2$	$\eta_{twin} = \dfrac{R_{mzt} - h^2}{e^2}$
Twins raised apart	$= R_{mza}$ $= .5R_{dza}$	$1 - h^2$ $1 - h^2$	. .

NOTE: Notation follows that in Table 19.1. A dot (.) denotes that a quantity cannot be estimated using that design.

Table 19.3 Estimation of Heritability, Environmentability, and the Correlation Between Relatives' Environments Using the Adoption Method and Assumption of No Selective Placement of Adoptees

Design	h^2	e^2	η
Sibs apart and together	$= .5R_{sibsa}$	$1 - h^2$	$\eta_{sibs} = \dfrac{R_{sibst} - .5h^2}{e^2}$
Sibs together and adoptive sibs	$= 2(R_{sibst} - R_{sibsa})$	$1 - h^2$	$\eta_{sibs} = \dfrac{\overline{R}asibs}{e^2}$
Parent-offspring together and apart	$= 2R_{poa}$	$1 - h^2$	$\eta_{po} = \dfrac{R_{apo}}{e^2}$

NOTE: Notation follows that in Table 19.1.

DZ twins raised together (R_{dzt}) was .45. Plugging these values into the equations for the row labeled "Twins raised together" gives

$$h^2 = 2(.60 - .45) = 2(.15) = .30,$$

$$e^2 = 1 - h^2 = 1 - .30 = .70,$$

and

$$\eta_{twin} = \frac{.60 - h^2}{e^2} = \frac{.60 - .30}{.70} = .43.$$

Note that these are the same values that we arrived at using the long, tortuous method of going through Steps 1 through 4.

● A SECOND MATHEMATICAL MODEL

The Model

The model described above has been used in behavioral genetic research, but a slightly different model has gained prominence in recent years. Both models arrive at the same substantive conclusions; they just express the information in different terms. Because this model and its terminology are used so often, it is important to understand the concepts behind it in order to understand the behavioral genetic literature.

The model is depicted in Figure 19.2. It differs from the model in Figure 19.1 in that it subdivides the environment into two parts, the *common environment* (the latent variables denoted as *C* in the figure) and the *unique environment* (the two *U*s in the figure). The common environment is defined as *all those environmental factors that make relatives raised together similar on the trait of interest*. (Note that the common environment is equal to the statistical concept of between-family environmental variance discussed in Table 18.5.)

The unique environment is defined as *all those environmental factors that make relatives different from each other on the trait of interest*. Individual learning experiences, having different friends, and being treated differently by parents are all aspects of the unique environment of a phenotype, provided that they influence that phenotype. (Once again, review the discussion of Table 18.5.

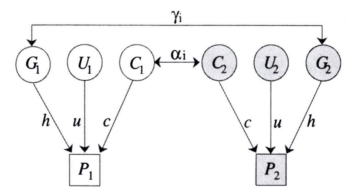

Figure 19.2   An Alternative Model for the Correlation Between Two Relatives Denoted as Subscripts 1 and 2.

NOTE: *G* is the genotypic value, *C* is the common environmental value, *U* is the unique environmental value, and *P* is the phenotypic value of the relative.

Also note that when phenotypes are not measured with perfect accuracy—a fact that applies to virtually every behavioral phenotype—then measurement error is included in the unique environment.)

In this model, b remains the correlation between genotypic values and phenotypic values, c is the correlation between common environmental values and phenotypic values, and u is the correlation between unique environmental values and phenotypic values. The meaning of γ_i remains the same—the correlation between the genotypes of the relatives. The quantity α_i is the correlation between the common environments of genetic relatives. For relatives raised together, $\alpha_i = 1.0$, but for relatives raised apart, $\alpha_i = 0$ under the assumption of random placement of adoptees.

The Two Central Equations for This Model (and How They Relate to the Previous Model)

In this model, the total environmentability (that is, e^2 in the first model) is subdivided into the common environmentability (c^2) and the unique environmentability (u^2). Hence,

$$e^2 = c_i^2 + u_i^2$$

and the equation for the phenotypic variance becomes

$$1 = b^2 + c_i^2 + u_i^2.$$

The generic correlation for the relatives is

$$R_i = \gamma_i b^2 + \alpha_i c_i^2$$

where the subscript i denotes the type of relationship (i = mz, dz, poa, etc., depending on the data).

The quantity c^2 in this model equals the correlation between the relatives' environments in the first model (η) times the total environmentability (e^2), or

$$c_i^2 = \eta_i e^2.$$

A Numerical Example

The same four steps used to solve for b^2, e^2, and η_i in the first model may be used to solve for b^2, c_i^2, and u_i^2 in this model. Let us take the previous example, in which we obtained a correlation for identical twins raised together (mzt) of .60 and a correlation of fraternal twins raised together (dzt) of .45. Under the assumption of a simple, additive genetic model and equal environments for twins, the two twin equations can be written as

$$.60 = h^2 + c^2_{twin}$$

and

$$.45 = .5h^2 + c^2_{twin}.$$

The equation for the variance is

$$1 = h^2 + c^2_{twin} + u^2_{twin}.$$

There are three simultaneous equations in three unknowns—h^2, c^2_{twin}, and u^2_{twin}.

Once again, algebra must be used to find numerical values for these unknowns. Subtracting the second twin equation from the first gives

$$.60 - .45 = h^2 + c^2_{twin} - .5h^2 - c^2_{twin},$$

so

$$.15 = .5h^2.$$

Multiplying both sides by 2 gives the value of h^2 as .30, just what we found in the first model. If we substitute this quantity into the equation for MZ twins, we have

$$.60 = .30 + c^2_{twin},$$

so c^2_{twin} is also equal to .30. Note how this figure is within rounding error of the quantity $\eta_{twin}e^2$ (.43 × .70 = .301) reported by the first model. Finally, substituting the values of h^2 and c^2_{twin} into the equation for the phenotypic variance, we have

$$1 = .30 + .30 + u^2_{twin},$$

so

$$u^2_{twin} = .40.$$

Table 19.4 Estimation of Heritability, Common Environmentability, and Unique Environmentability in Twin Studies Using the Assumptions of Equal Environments for MZ and DZ Twins Raised Together and No Selective Placement of Adoptees

Design	h^2	c_i^2	u_i^2
Twins raised together	$= 2(R_{mzt} - R_{dzt})$	$= 2R_{dzt} - R_{mzt}$	$= 1 - h^2 - c^2$
Twins raised apart	$= R_{mza}$	.	.
	$= .5R_{dza}$	.	.

NOTE: Notation follows that in Figure 19.2. A dot (.) denotes that a quantity cannot be estimated using a particular design.

Table 19.5 Estimation of Heritability, Environmentability, and the Correlation Between Relatives' Environments Using the Adoption Method and Assumption of No Selective Placement

Design	h^2	c_i^2	u_i^2
Sibs apart and together	$= .5R_{sibsa}$	$= R_{sibst} - .5h^2$	$= 1 - h^2 - c^2$
Sibs together and adoptive sibs	$= 2(R_{sibst} - R_{sibsa})$	$= R_{sibst} - .5h^2$	$= 1 - h^2 - c^2$
Parent-offspring together and apart	$= 2R_{poa}$	$= R_{apo}$	$= 1 - h^2 - c^2$

The substantive conclusions from this analysis are as follows. First, genetic individual differences contribute to 30% of phenotypic individual differences in sociability—a conclusion identical to that arrived at in the first model. In total, the environment (i.e., $c^2 + u^2$) contributes to the remaining 70% of phenotypic individual differences—again, just what we found in the first study. Thirty percent of all phenotypic differences are attributable to the common environment of twins (i.e., c^2 or all those environmental factors that make twins similar in sociability), while 40% of phenotypic individual differences are due to idiosyncratic experience unique to an individual (i.e., u^2).

Making Life Simple

Tables 19.4 and 19.5 give shortcuts for estimating the parameters for this model when the simplifying assumptions are made. Note that the quantities c^2 and u^2 in these tables contain the subscript i. This denotes the possibility that the common and unique environmental effects for, say, parent and offspring are not the same quantities as those for, say, siblings.

● ESTIMATING GENETIC CORRELATIONS AND ENVIRONMENTAL CORRELATIONS

The previous chapter showed that we cannot calculate heritability directly by calculating the correlation between genotypic values and phenotypic values and squaring the result. Nor could we estimate environmentability by calculating the correlation between environmental values and phenotypic values and squaring the result. The reason for this is simple—we lack the technology to arrive at numerical estimates of genotypic values or environmental values for continuous traits. The same logic applies to the estimation of genetic and environmental correlations. We cannot calculate them directly. Instead, we must use data on twins or adoptees and—with some simplifying assumptions—obtain rough estimates of their values.

One very important point to recognize is that the phenotypic correlation between two traits is a function of the genetic and environmental correlations and the heritabilities and environmentabilities of the two traits. Specifically, for the traits of verbal ability (subscript V) and quantitative ability (subscript Q), the extent to which an individual's verbal score predicts his or her quantitative score can be written as

$$r_p = r_g h_V h_Q + r_e e_V e_Q. \tag{3}$$

In terms of the notation given in the previous chapter, this ghastly looking equation states that the correlation between phenotypic verbal and phenotypic quantitative scores (r_p) equals the genetic correlation times the square root of the two heritabilities ($r_g h_V h_Q$) plus the environmental correlation times the square root of the two environmentabilities ($r_e e_V e_Q$). In actual data analysis, we observe r_p and with twins or adoptees can arrive at estimates of r_g, r_e, h_V, h_Q, e_V, and e_Q. Hence, we can estimate the *extent to which the phenotypic correlation is attributable to genetic sources* as well as *the extent to which environmental factors contribute to the phenotypic correlation*. The quantity

$$\frac{r_g h_V h_Q}{r_p} \tag{4}$$

Table 19.6 Twin Correlations for the English and Mathematics Subtests of
the National Merit Scholarship Qualifying Test

Correlation		Zygosity	
		MZ (N = 509 pairs)	DZ (N = 330 pairs)
Within individuals		.61	.59
Cross-twin			
	Twin 1 English to Twin 2 English	.75	.56
	Twin 1 English to Twin 2 math	.56	.37
	Twin 1 math to Twin 2 math	.72	.44

SOURCE: Data are from Loehlin and Nichols (1976).

gives the proportion of phenotypic correlation between verbal and quantitative scores attributable to genetic sources. Similarly, the quantity

$$\frac{r_e e_V e_Q}{r_p} \tag{5}$$

gives the proportion of the phenotypic correlation attributable to environmental sources. A numerical example can assist in understanding these quantities.

A Numerical Example

Table 19.6 presents twin correlations for the English and Mathematics subtests of the National Merit Scholarship Qualifying Test (NMSQT) on a sample of more than 800 twin pairs (Loehlin & Nichols, 1976).[4] Note that these are real data, not hypothetical numbers that were made up as in Table 18.3.

Let us begin by stating the assumptions. We will assume that there is no dominance, no epistasis, and no assortative mating.[5] Hence, γ will be .50 for DZ twins. We will also assume that η is equal for MZ and DZ twins, that there is no gene-environment interaction, and that there is no gene-environment correlation.

We begin by calculating h^2, e^2, and η for the English subtest. Using the equations in Table 19.2 and the English test as a phenotype, we can calculate that

$$h_E^2 = 2(R_{\text{mzt-E}} - R_{\text{dzt-E}}) = 2(.75 - .56) = 2(.19) = .38,$$

$$e_E^2 = 1 - h_E^2 = 1 - .38 = .62,$$

and

$$\eta_E = \frac{R_{\text{mz-E}} - h_E^2}{e_E^2} = \frac{75 - .38}{.62} = \frac{.37}{.62} = .60.$$

The subscript E in these equations means that the observed correlations (e.g., $R_{\text{mzt-E}}$) and the parameter estimates (e.g., h_E^2) pertain to the English subtest. Hence, 38% of the individual differences in English scores are attributable in some way to genetic individual differences, while the other 62% of differences are due to the environment. The correlation of .60 between twin environments is substantial, suggesting that being raised in the same family contributes to individual differences in English test scores.

For the mathematics subtest, the equations in Table 19.2 give

$$h_M^2 = 2(R_{\text{mzt-M}} - R_{\text{dzt-M}}) = 2(.72 - .44) = 2(.28) = .56,$$

$$e_M^2 = 1 - h_M^2 = 1 - .56 = .44,$$

and

$$\eta_M = \frac{R_{\text{MZT-M}} - h_M^2}{e_M^2} = \frac{.72 - .56}{.44} = \frac{.16}{.44} = .36.$$

For the mathematics phenotype, genetic individual differences are responsible for 56% of phenotypic individual differences, and environmental differences contribute to the remaining 44%. The correlation between twin environments is .36, suggesting an important role for factors associated with being raised in the same family.

Given the assumptions, we can write the correlation for the English test in one MZ twin and the math test in the other MZ twin as

$$R_{mZt-E,M} = r_g b_E b_M + \eta_{twin-E,M} e_E e_M.$$

Again, subscripts E and M refer to English and math, respectively. The quantity $\eta_{twin-E,M}$ represents the correlation between one twin's environmental values for English and his or her cotwin's environmental values for math. Because the heritability of English was .38, the quantity b_E will be $\sqrt{b_E^2} = \sqrt{.38} = .6164$. Similarly, e_E equals $\sqrt{e_E^2} = \sqrt{.62} = .7874$, b_M equals $\sqrt{b_M^2} = \sqrt{.56} = .7483$, and e_M equals $\sqrt{e_M^2} = \sqrt{.44} = .6633$. Substituting these four quantities into the above equation for identical twins raised together gives

$$R_{mZt-E,M} = r_g (.6164)(.7483) + \eta_{twin-E,M} (.7874)(.6633)$$
$$= .4613 r_g + .5223 \eta_{twin-E,M}.$$

From Table 19.6, the observed correlation between the English test score of one MZ twin and the mathematics score of the other twin (i.e., $R_{mzt-E,M}$) is .56. Substituting this quantity into the above equation gives

$$.56 = .4613 r_g + .5223 \eta_{twin-E,M}.$$

The general equation for fraternal twins is

$$R_{dzt-E,M} = .5 r_g b_E b_M + \eta_{twin-E,M} e_E e_M.$$

Again, substitute the observed correlation for the English score of one fraternal twin and the math score of the other fraternal twin into this equation (i.e., put the value of .37 from Table 19.6 into the equation in place of the algebraic quantity $R_{dzt-E,M}$). Then replace b_E, b_M, e_E, and e_M with their numerical values. The correlation for fraternal twins is now

$$.37 = .5 r_g (.6164)(.7483) + \eta_{twin-E,M} (.7874)(.6633)$$
$$= .2037 r_g + .5223 \eta_{twin-E,M}.$$

Now subtract this equation for DZ twins from the equation for MZ twins:

$$.56 - .37 = .4613 r_g + .5223 \eta_{twin-E,M} - .2307 r_g - .5223 \eta_{twin-E,M}$$

$$.19 = .2306 r_g$$

so

$$r_g = \frac{.19}{.2306} = .8239.$$

In words, this equation states that the estimated correlation between genotypic values for the English subtest and the genotypic values for the mathematics subtest (r_g) is .82. Genetic values for one subtest strongly predict those for the other subtest. Substituting this numeric value for r_g into the equation for MZ twins gives

$$.56 = .4163 \, (.8239) + .5233 \eta_{twin\text{-}E,M}.$$

Hence,

$$\eta_{twin\text{-}E,M} = \frac{.56 - (.4163)\,(.8239)}{.5223} = \frac{.2170}{.5223} = .4155.$$

This is a moderate correlation for most social science research. In substantive terms, it means that those environmental factors that make one twin score high in English moderately predict the environmental factors that make the other twin proficient in math.

Finally, we want to obtain an estimate of r_e, the extent to which an individual person's environment for English test scores predicts his or her own environment for math scores. To do this, we substitute the numerical values for r_p, r_g, b_V, b_M e_E, and e_M that we have already calculated in equation (3), the one for the phenotypic correlation between English and math scores. There are two difference values for r_p, the value of .61 for MZ twins and .59 for DZ twins (see Table 19.6). Let us take the average of these and estimate the value of r_p as .60. Substituting these values into equation (3) gives

$$.60 = .8239 \, (.6164) \, (.7483) + r_e \, (.7874) \, (.6633)$$

so

$$r_e = \frac{.60 - .8239\,(.6164)\,(.7483)}{.7874\,(.6633)} = \frac{.2200}{.5223} = .4212.$$

The environmental correlation of .42 suggests that there is a moderate relationship between the environmental values for the English score and those for the math score.

How much of the phenotypic correlation between English and math scores (i.e., $r_p = .60$) is attributable to genetic differences, and how much of this correlation is influenced by environmental individual differences? These questions can be answered by substituting the quantities that we have estimated into equations (4) and (5). The percentage of the correlation due to genetic individual differences is

$$\frac{r_g h_V h_Q}{r_p} = \frac{.8239\ (.6164)\ (.7483)}{.60} = .63.$$

The percentage of the correlation due to environmental individual differences is

$$\frac{r_c e_V e_Q}{r_p} = \frac{.4212\ (.7874)\ (.6633)}{.60} = .37.$$

That is, about 60% of the correlation (to be exact, 63%) is attributable to genetic individual differences, and the other 40% (to be exact again, 37%) derives from environmental differences. So why do people who score well on English also tend to score well on math? About 60% of the reasons can be traced to genes and the other 40% to the environment.

TESTING ESTIMATES OF HERITABILITY, ● ENVIRONMENTABILITY, AND GENETIC AND ENVIRONMENTAL CORRELATIONS

Suppose that we went through the exercise outlined above for our precious twin data gathered on, say, bird watching and arrived at an estimate of h^2 of .28. Is this sufficient to convince our fellow scientists that genes contribute to individual differences in bird watching? Certainly, our estimate of the heritability is greater than 0, but most social scientists would ask whether this estimate is *significantly* greater than 0. We have now moved beyond simple estimation and into the realm of *hypothesis testing*—do our estimates of heritability (or environmentability, or genetic correlation, or environmental correlation) really differ from a hypothesized value?

The most frequently hypothesized value of heritability is 0. That is, behavioral geneticists are challenged to demonstrate that the estimates of heritability are really different from 0 or, in substantive terms, that genetic individual differences really contribute to phenotypic individual differences. The method for doing this is to fit two different models to observed correlations. The first model is the one described above—that is, we use the equations to estimate h^2. The second model assumes that h^2 is really 0 and then estimates e^2 (which will always be 1.0 when $h^2 = 0$) and the η for the relationship in question. Using advanced statistics that involve the comparison of the two models, one can arrive at statistical decisions about which model gives the better fit for the data. The mechanics of this process are too complicated for us to consider here, so the interested reader is referred to Eaves, Eysenck, and Martin (1989), Neale and Cardon (1992), and Loehlin (1998). The important point is that there are well-established statistical principles that guide behavioral genetic research. These principles follow the same logic as ordinary social science research would in, say, assessing whether an observed correlation differs significantly from a hypothesized correlation of 0.

From a conceptual viewpoint, the techniques in behavioral genetics fit two different models to the data. The first is a *general* model that fits as many unknowns (i.e., parameters) to the data as possible. The second is a *constrained* model that sets one or more parameters to a specific, numerical, hypothesized value. Then statistical decision rules are used to assess the relative merit of the general versus the constrained model in predicting the observed data. If the statistical decision rules tell us that the constrained model fits the data poorly, then we reject the constrained model and prefer the general model. If the statistical decision rules tell us that the constrained model fits the data almost as well as the general model, then we give preference to the constrained model because it is more parsimonious than the general model.[6] That is, the constrained model uses fewer parameters than the general model but statistically fits the data almost as well as the general model.

A Numerical Example

Suppose that the fictitious data on bird watching reported a correlation of .41 for 387 pairs of MZ twins raised together and a correlation of .27 for 404 pairs of DZ twins raised together. The general model fits three parameters—h^2, e^2, and η_{twin}—to these two correlations, plus the equation for the phenotypic variance. Because there are three simultaneous equations (one for R_{mzt}, the second for R_{dzt}, and the third for the phenotypic variance) and three unknowns, the general model will give a perfect fit to the data. That is, the predicted correlations derived from the estimates of h^2, e^2, and η_{twin} will equal the observed correlations.

Table 19.7   Testing Mathematical Models

			Model	
Quantity	Observed	General	$h^2 = 0$	$\eta_{twin} = 0$
R_{mzt}	.41	.41	.34	.43
R_{dzt}	.27	.27	.34	.17
χ^2		0.00	4.94	1.60

Suppose that we wanted to compare this general model to a constrained model that hypothesized that there was no heritability for bird watching. In this case, we would set h^2 to 0 and the three equations would be written as

$$R_{mZt} = .41 = \eta_{twin} e^2,$$

$$R_{dzt} = .27 = \eta_{twin} e^2,$$

and

$$1 = e^2.$$

We still have three equations, but there are now only two unknowns—e^2 and η_{twin}. This is a situation that mathematicians call *overdetermination*. Special techniques—too advanced for us to consider here—must be used to estimate the two unknowns. I applied one of these techniques to these data[7] and obtained estimates of $e^2 = 1.0$ and $\eta_{twin} = .34$. Table 19.7 gives the observed and the predicted correlations from this model along with a statistic (χ^2 with 1 degree of freedom) that measures the discrepancy between the observed and predicted correlations. Note how the value for χ^2 is 0.00 for the general model. This indicates that there are no differences between the observed and predicted correlation for the general model. The larger the value of χ^2, the more the predicted correlations deviate from their observed counterparts.

With $h^2 = 0$ and $\eta_{twin} = .34$, the predicted correlation between both MZ and DZ twins is .34. The χ^2 is 4.94, and its associated p value (not shown in the table) is less than .05. Hence, it is rather improbable that this model could explain the data. According to scientific convention, we reject this model and conclude that h^2 is significantly different from 0.

Table 19.7 also gives the predicted correlation correlations and χ^2 from a different model that estimated h^2 but sets η_{twin} to 0. In English, this model says that there is no correlation between the environments of twins. The estimate of h^2 for this model is .43, giving a predicted correlation of .43 for MZ twins and .165 for DZ twins. The χ^2 of 1.60 is not significant (i.e., its p value is greater than .05). Hence, we would conclude that the correlation between twin environments is small and close to 0.

● AN OVERALL PERSPECTIVE ON ESTIMATION AND TESTING

If I had a hat, I would take it off in honor of you persevering readers who have gone through all this material and made it to this point. Chances are that most of you who are reading these words right now have started this chapter, given up because of frustration or boredom, and flipped to the end in hope of finding a quick bottom line. The material in this chapter is dull—very, very dull, in fact—but also difficult and challenging. It goes far beyond undergraduate statistics and gives a taste—more of a small nibble than a salacious gulp—of the way that the scholastic descendants of Mendel and Darwin now approach problems in genetics.

This is a classic situation in which knowing the *logic* behind the method is much more important than knowing the *mechanics* of implementing the method. The quick bottom line (i.e., logic) is given in the following steps:

- Develop a mathematical model of the way the genes and environment work for a specific phenotype. This mathematical model will contain certain unknowns called parameters.
- Use established mathematical techniques to estimate these unknowns or parameters. The techniques outlined above involve simultaneous linear equations, but more advanced mathematical strategies may be employed for other problems.
- After the parameters have been estimated, compare the observed data to the predictions of the model. In the examples, the observed data are correlations, so the observed correlations are compared to the predicted correlations of the mathematical model.
- Using statistical techniques and established scientific guidelines, assess how well the predictions of the model (i.e., the predicted correlations) fit the observed data (i.e., the observed correlations). If the fit is poor, then reject the mathematical model as a plausible explanation of the observed data. The specific statistical techniques employed in this step are beyond the scope of this book, so one can think of them as a "black box."

NOTES ●

1. Technically, this figure is a path diagram. Observed variables are denoted by rectangles. Because we measure phenotypes, the two *P*s are encased in rectangles. Circles or ellipses denote unobserved or latent variables. Because we cannot measure genotypic values and environmental values, the *G*s and *E*s are enclosed in circles.

2. In general, *b* is the standardized regression coefficient when phenotypic values are regressed on genotypic values. This equals the correlation in the present case because it is assumed that *G* is not correlated with *E*.

3. In this case, standardized variables have means of 0 and standard deviations of 1. Because the variance is the square of the standard deviation, the variance of standardized variables will also be 1.

4. The correlations here were calculated directly from the data in the form of intraclass correlation matrices and hence will differ slightly from the numerical estimates in Loehlin and Nichols (1976).

5. Although there are no data on the spousal correlation for NMSQT scores, it is likely that there will be some assortative mating because mates have moderate resemblance on IQ scores and years of education. We will see the effect of violating this assumption in a later section.

6. The phrase "almost as well" is important. For technical reasons, a constrained model can never fit the data as well as a general model. The key decision is whether the constrained model is statistically "much worse" than the general model or is "only a tiny bit worse" than the general model.

7. The technique minimized the chi-square (χ^2) in the function $\chi^2 = \Sigma_i (N_i - 3)$ $(Zobs_i - Zpre_i)^2$, where *N* is the number of pairs for the ith zygosity and $Zobs_i$ and $Zpre_i$ are, respectively, the Z transforms of the observed and predicted correlation for the ith zygosity. See Neale and Cardon (1992) for further details.

REFERENCES ●

Eaves, L. J., Eysenck, H. J., & Martin, N. G. (1989). *Genes, culture and personality: An empirical approach.* San Diego: Academic Press.

Loehlin, J. C. (1998). *Latent variable models: An introduction to factor, path, and structural analysis* (3rd ed.). Mahwah, NJ: Lawrence Erlbaum.

Loehlin, J. C., & Nichols, R. C. (1976). *Heredity, environment, and personality: A study of 850 sets of twins.* Austin: University of Texas Press.

Neale, M. C., & Cardon, L. R. (1992). *Methodology for genetic studies of twins and families.* Dordrecht, The Netherlands: Kluwer.

CHAPTER 20

GENES, IQ SCORES, AND SOCIAL STATUS I

The Phenotype of IQ

INTRODUCTION ●

Nothing in behavioral genetics has sparked more acerbic and acrimonious debate than the issues surrounding the genetics of intelligence and social class. Science requires debate and argument, so differing opinions about heredity, intelligence, and social structure should be healthy signs. Instead, opinions are often stated with such a rhetorical voracity that personal and political agendas drown out sound empirical data. The sad consequence is that a chapter like this one is required in this book—there is simply too much misinformation about IQ test scores within the social sciences to proceed directly into a discussion of genetics.

   The purpose of the chapter is simple and can be gleaned by rereading the chapter's title. I deliberately chose the phrase "IQ scores" over the word "Intelligence." At the end of this chapter, you should have an appreciation for what an IQ score means. That does not imply that you will know what Intelligence (with a capital "I") is. All the data on the genetics of "Intelligence" and on the extent to which the genes for "Intelligence" contribute to eventual social status are based on concrete numbers derived from an IQ test. In short, the empirical data are all predicated on IQ test scores, not on various definitions of "Intelligence." Hence, to appreciate and interpret the empirical data, it is much more important to recognize what an IQ score measures than what any theoretician in psychology, sociology, or anthropology says an IQ score *should* measure.

We will first explore the history of intelligence tests. Thereafter we will examine items typically found on contemporary intelligence tests, review data on the stability of IQ scores, survey the empirical data on the variables correlated with scores on intelligence tests, and discuss the issue of multiple intelligences.

● THE HISTORY OF THE PSYCHOLOGICAL CONSTRUCT OF INTELLIGENCE

The end of the 19th century saw two different schools of thought about mental processes and the best ways to measure them. Early psychologists such as Francis Galton exemplify the first school. To oversimplify matters, Galton viewed mental processes as what today would be call a "black box" that interfaces between sensory input and motor output. The mental processes themselves could not be observed directly. Instead, the task of the psychologist was to vary the complexity of the sensory inputs and then observe individual differences in output. Lawful relationships between the complexity of the sensory input and the speed and/or accuracy of the respondent would be crude measures of intelligence or some allied mental processes.

A major paradigm developed by these investigators was *reaction time*, an example of which is illustrated in Figure 20.1. A subject is seated in front of an apparatus that has three lights, all turned off at the moment. The research participant places the index finger of his or her dominant hand on the solid button at the bottom of Figure 20.1. At a time set by the investigator but unknown to the subject, one of the three lights flashes on. The participant must then remove his or her index finger from the solid button and press the dotted button below the light that had flashed. Two very simple quantitative measures can be derived from this test: (a) the amount of time it takes the subject to release pressure on the solid button and (b) after the solid button's release, the amount of time elapsed until the correct dotted button is pressed.

Figure 20.1   An Example of a Reaction-Time Paradigm. The participant places a finger on the solid-colored button and, when a light flashes, must move the finger and press the dotted button below the light.

Mastery of this task requires little cognitive skill. All but those with severe cognitive deficits will continually press the correct button as soon as they receive the verbal instructions about the task. The major variable of individual differences c is the *time* it takes to process the sensory stimulus and then react to it by removing a finger from the fixed button and pressing on the correct button.

There are enormous variations of reaction time tests. Instead of lights, one could flash an integer number on a computer screen. One could have two buttons, and the subject could be instructed to press the left one if the number is even and the right one if the number is odd. Perhaps two integers would be presented and the research participant required to press the left button if the sum of the two is odd but the right button if the sum is even.

Despite all the variations, the paradigm has the following two salient points: (a) the task is "easy" in the sense that everyone can understand it and come up with the correct solution and (b) the individual differences thought to underlie mental processes consist of the time it takes to process the sensory information and perform the motor response.[1] "Intelligence" defined this way is largely a variable associated with the speed of information processing.

The second tradition of intelligence and intelligence testing had its origin in the public school system of France. In the 1890s, Alfred Binet was commissioned by the French government to arrive at a simple and expedient way to distinguish those children who would profit from a public education from those who would not benefit from schooling. Binet's eventual answer to his charge differed strikingly from Galton's in two ways: (a) instead of measuring responses to purely sensory stimuli, Binet measured responses to *practical, real-life problems*; and (b) instead of presenting problems that all schoolchildren could solve easily, Binet administered tasks of *varying difficulty*—some children could perform the task correctly but other children would fail to execute it appropriately. (Galton, of course, used tasks that all schoolchildren, barring of course those with the most severe cognitive problems, could easily grasp and perform correctly). According to Binet, those children who got a lot of the tasks correct would "profit" from public schooling. whereas those who failed most of the tasks would not be suitable for education.

It is the Binet tradition that gave rise to modern intelligence testing. Owing greatly to the historical context of their development, most modern IQ tests have three salient features that define the modern construct of intelligence. First, the content of the items involves problems that tap a broad range of academic skills—vocabulary, reading comprehension, verbal analogies, syllogisms, mathematics, symbolic processing, etc.—all topics that are taught and tested in a school setting. There are not tests of sensory thresholds or reaction time. Neither are there items about practical, real-life social problems (e.g., who to invite to a birthday party), emotional problems (e.g., how to react to rejection from a peer), or occupational, vocational, or interest problems (e.g., the best way to catch trout).

Second, the items on the IQ test have definite right and wrong answers that can be agreed upon by the majority of people in the culture or by expert knowledge.[2] The answers to a question are not simply arbitrary responses like the typical true or false response to an item on a personality inventory.

Third, items have a variety of difficulty levels. They are not akin to Galton's tasks, with nearly everyone able to easily "pass" all the items. For subjects of a given age, some items are easy while others are difficult. In short, items on an IQ test can discriminate among subjects just as Binet's simple tasks could discriminate among French children.

Table 20.1 Examples of Vocabulary Items on a Multiple-Choice
Intelligence Test

Gaudy means	*Succor means*	*Garrulous means*
gangly	foolish	inquisitive
clever	nurture	unrepentant
flashy	breathe	obnoxious
attractive	sense	unruly
unrefined	impale	talkative

CONTEMPORARY INTELLIGENCE TESTS ●

Items on Intelligence Tests: Content Validity

In psychometric terms, an item in a test or questionnaire has *content validity* when there is a clear and reasonable connection between what the item asks and the construct or variable that it purports to measure. For example, the item "I am a sociable person" has good content validity for extraversion but poor content validity if it were to measure interests in architecture.

One of the best ways of assessing what contemporary intelligence tests measure is to turn content validity on its head—just read the items on any test and ask the question, "How would I describe people who get most of these items wrong, and how would I describe people who get most of these items correct?" Because of copyright laws, actual items from an IQ test cannot be reproduced herein, but the following examples are good illustrations of the types of items that might be found on tests such as the Wechsler Adult Intelligence Scale (WAIS) that measure several different facets of intelligence.[3]

Most comprehensive measures of intelligence include a measure of vocabulary. Examples of items that measure vocabulary are given in Table 20.1. For an adult, a simple item might ask for the meaning of the word "clarity," while a slightly more difficult item might ask for the meaning of the word "maudlin."

Verbal analogies are often found in IQ tests. In these items, the task is less to know the meaning of words as to deduce logical relationships between pairs of words. Two examples are given in Table 20.2.

Other types of measures tap the ability to construct complete and coherent ideas from words. One classic example is word rearrangements, three examples of which are provided in Table 20.3. Here the task is to arrange the words to make a complete sentence.

Table 20.2   Examples of Verbal Analogy Items

Dog is to god as rat is to	Cantaloupe is to melon as maple is to
tar	hockey
dog	leaf
goddess	tree
mouse	walnut
dirty	shrub

Table 20.3   Rearranging Words to Form a Complete Sentence

Rearrange the words in each item to form a complete sentence

1) dawn moving the at got party.
2) time stitch nine a saves in.
3) exam the very was final hard.

Another example is syntactic reasoning. Here, a series of nonsense words is presented, but the ordering of the words along with their prefixes and suffixes resembles a syntactically correct English sentence—the sentence simply has no meaning. The task is to recognize which words are nouns, verbs, adjectives, and so on. Examples are given in Table 20.4.

Many items on IQ tests relate to quantitative skills. One skill consists of correctly recognizing the relationship between a series of numbers and then predicting the next number in the sequence. Table 20.5 gives examples.

A second quantitative skill consists of elementary mathematics problems, some examples of which appear in Table 20.6.

Notice how many of the items above depend not only on knowledge of the English language but also on familiarity with certain cultures.[4] Rearranging the words "time stitch nine a saves in" in Table 20.3 gives an aphorism from the English-speaking world that may not be familiar to other cultures. It is reasonable to hypothesize that Americans might more easily recognize this sentence than would other native English speakers such as Australians or New Zealanders.. For this reason, there have been several attempts to develop measures of intelligence that are culture-free.[5]

Examples of this kind of testing include Cattell's Culture Free Test (Cattell, 1940) and the Raven's Progressive Matrices (Raven, 1960, 2000). This type of test typically presents visual or geometric objects that have a certain logic to them, and the respondent is required to complete a series or to pick out a discrepant object among a group. Examples appear in Figures 20.2 and 20.3.

Table 20.4   Syntactic Inference Problems

A globish trop belloped wolpingly. She twangdly gumished the _____.

After the bargper srabaved in Osterham, he wobgobled a grat. I took the grat and frampaged it back to the _____.

Dwabble froboshinly sarfed over a schnaffle. Then Wigham also _____.

Table 20.5   Examples of Series Completions

2, 4, 8, 16, ___.
1, 1, 2, 4, ___.
25, 5, 36, 6, ___.

NOTE: The person is given the series of numbers and is asked to give the next number in the sequence.

Table 20.6   Arithmetic Problems

You purchase $4.65 worth of fruit and hand the clerk a $5 bill. What is the least number of coins that you can receive as change?

Your friend lives 32 miles from your house. On a visit, you average 45 miles per hour traveling to your friend's home but 36 mph on the return leg. What was your total travel time going and coming from your friend's home?

What is the length of the largest straight stick that you could place completely inside a circle with a 50-inch circumference?

At the beginning of this section, the reader was asked to read the items and ask the following question: "How would I describe people who get most of these items wrong, and how would I describe people who get most of these items correct?" If you are like many others who answered this question, you would describe high scorers as "smart" and "clever" and low scorers as "dull," "poorly educated," or "educationally disadvantaged." If asked to give an abstract definition to the major dimension tapped by these items, most people come up with one or more of the following descriptors: (a) ability to reason abstractly, (b) ability to manipulate symbols, (c) ability to learn, (d) ability to absorb cultural teachings, and (e) exposure to traditional culture. Your own answers to the question probably are similar to some of these responses. But before you prematurely decide on a definition of intelligence, read the next section on the correlates of IQ tests.

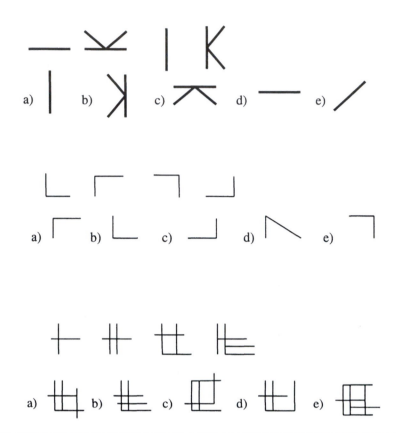

Figure 20.2   Examples of IQ Test Items That Do Not Depend Strongly on Vocabulary. Four geometric figures are given in a series, and the task is to select which alternative—a through e—completes the series.

Correlates of IQ Scores: Construct Validity

A classic concept in the behavioral sciences is *construct validity* (Cronbach & Meehl, 1955). Applied to intelligence, the extent to which an IQ test has construct validity depends on its correlations with other variables that should, in commonsense terms, correlate with intelligence. This section reviews the important correlations of IQ test scores. In reading this section, it is crucial to have a firm grasp of the quantitative meaning of a correlation coefficient.[6] The relationship between any two social science variables should never be viewed in either-or terms—that is, that a relationship is either present or absent. Instead, the relationship should be viewed as a point along

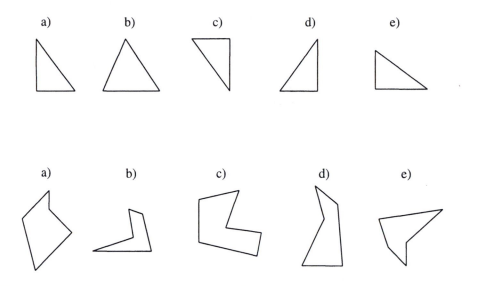

Figure 20.3 Two Examples of Items That Do Not Depend on Strongly Verbal Culture. The task is to pick the item that does not share the characteristics of the others.

a continuum that has as its extreme ends the absence of any predictability (a correlation of 0.0) and perfect predictability (a correlation of 1.0). "How strong is the relationship between IQ and variable X?" is a more informative question than "Is there a relationship between IQ and X?"

A major portion of construct validity is the agreement among IQ tests. If there are several different IQ tests, all of which purport to measure the same construct of intelligence, then any one of the tests should predict scores on the other tests. Does this happen? Yes. The correlations between scores on one measure of intelligence and others are usually around .70 to .80 (Jensen, 1980, p. 315).[7]

A second prediction stems from the results of your own answer about high and low scorers on the items in tests of cognitive ability. Should people who (are smart, are clever, have good abstract reasoning, are educationally advantaged, are exposed to conventional culture—feel free to insert your own phrase here) do better in school than people who (are dull, have problems manipulating symbols, have difficulties seeing logical relationships, are educationally disadvantaged, lack exposure to traditional culture—again, insert your own phrase)? All but the most obstinate would answer yes to this question. So what are the correlations between IQ tests and school performance?

There are two answers to this question, depending on how one measures school performance. One classic measure of school performance is a score (or scores) on standardized tests. Here, the results from decades of empirical research have been strikingly consistent (see Snow & Yallow, 1982, for a comprehensive review). Correlations between IQ test scores and measures of general scholastic knowledge (e.g., scores on the verbal and quantitative sections of the SAT or ACT) are in the range of .60 to .80—quite high coefficients for the behavioral sciences. Correlations between IQ scores and measures of more specific scholastic knowledge—such as standardized tests on history, geography, literature, and science—are only slightly lower.

A second measure of school performance is simply grades. They could be measured, for example, by grade point average (GPA) in high school or instructor ratings of course performance in the armed services. The type of measurement of school performance may make a statistical difference but not a great practical difference. Correlations between IQ test scores and grades are usually lower than those between IQ scores and scores on standardized achievement tests, but they are still quite high. They typically range between .40 and .60.

Now, combine the history of IQ tests, the items on IQ tests, and the empirical correlates of IQ tests and ask yourself what IQ tests measure.

Reliability and Stability of IQ Scores

Psychometrically, the reliability of a test consists of the extent to which one gets the same results when the test is administered on two occasions.[8] The time interval between testing depends on the nature of the trait being measured. For traits that change rapidly (e.g., mood), the interval may be minutes or hours; for traits that should be relatively constant (e.g., educational level of your grandparents), the interval could be measured in years. Several twists and variations of testing are used to avoid memory effects (e.g., giving the odd items at Time 1 and the even items at Time 2).

One of the most persistent myths in some social science circles is that IQ tests are unreliable. In fact, IQ tests are among the most reliable of all measures in psychology. Reliabilities of individually administered adult IQ tests consistently exceed .90 for the total IQ scores that are the topic of this chapter and the next. Reliabilities are slightly lower for infants, but not by much. They are usually in the high .80s. Jensen (1980, Table 7.4) compiled reliabilities from the manuals of 33 different group tests of intelligence or general mental abilities. They averaged around .90. Hence, an IQ score is measured with high reliability.

Table 20.7 Stability Correlations for IQ as a Function of Years Between Testing in Infants and Children

	Correlation		
Years Between Testing	**Study 1**	**Study 2**	**Study 3**
1	.87	.83	.90
2	.82	.79	.86
3	.79	.74	.84
4	.81	.70	.81
5	.79	.65	.78
6		.61	.75
7		.57	.72
8		.47	.69
9			.66
10			.64

NOTE: Data for Study 1 are from Hirsch (1930) as cited in Jensen (1980, Table 7.7, p. 129); data for Study 2 are from the Louisville Twin Project, cited in Humphreys (1989); and data for Study 3 are from the Fels Longitudinal Project, cited in Jensen (1980, Table 7.6, p. 129).

The stability of IQ scores is measured by the correlation of test scores on two or more occasions that are relatively far apart.[9] The stability of IQ scores depends on two different factors, the age at which the individuals are tested and the time interval between tests. Testings 1 year apart have correlations that range between .85 and .95, almost as high as the reliability of IQ scores permits. As the time interval increases, the correlation decreases, but the amount of decrease depends on the age of initial testing. Correlations between IQ scores measured in infancy/early childhood and those in adulthood are small, on the order of .30 to .45. As children get older, the correlation increases (Bloom, 1964; Jensen, 1980) but does not seem to approach the correlation between testings 1 year apart. Table 20.7 presents stability correlations as a function of years between testing from three different studies. Compared to many psychological traits, IQ scores show a high degree of stability.

The same data also illustrate another feature about IQ—it is *not* immutable. If IQ were as immutable as height during the early to middle adult years, then the correlation between testings at *any* two time points should equal the reliability of the IQ test. The observed correlations are lower, although there has not been much data gathered during the middle adult period on this issue. The situation is analogous to the stability of batting averages among major league baseball players. Those with high averages in any one year tend to—but do not necessarily *have* to—have high averages in other years. Batting ability is stable but not immutable.

● INTELLIGENCE AND INTELLIGENCES

Is intelligence "one thing"? Or are there a number of intelligences, each adapted and honed to a specific cognitive task? Our examination of IQ test items above cannot answer this question. Clearly, items that tap one and only one cognitive ability (e.g., number series) have an obvious and logical relationship to one another. But do people who score high on the number series items also get the vocabulary items correct? As is true for many questions in psychology, one can argue long into the night about the answer, but scientifically speaking, any answer must be based on empirical data—just what is the correlation between scores on number series and scores on vocabulary?

If we consider only those types of items found on traditional IQ tests, we can find a consistent empirical finding that has been replicated over the past century: People who do well on one set of items listed above also do well on the other types of items. In short, there are moderate to high positive correlations among all subtests of mental ability (Carroll, 1993; Jensen, 1998). Theorists who place a heavy emphasis on this observation argue for a construct of *general intelligence*, most commonly abbreviated as g, and posit that individual differences in g are a major reason behind the positive correlation among specific mental abilities. The IQ scores that have been discussed in this chapter and that will be discussed in the next one are all measures of g.

The same theorists using the same data also convincingly demonstrate that human intelligence cannot be captured completely by this single number. There are some unknown aspects of any concrete cognitive ability that are specific to that cognitive ability and are not tapped by g. For example, a person's score on a vocabulary measure taps more than that person's g—it also includes attributes of that person that are specific to verbal ability and others that are specific to vocabulary.

A suitable analogy of the relationship between different cognitive abilities comes from the physical morphology of human body parts. Suppose that we dissected a number of human cadavers and measured the length, breadth, girth, and weight of each body part. Each number that we write down for a corpse would be analogous to an item on an IQ test. Common sense dictates that there will be positive correlations among these measures

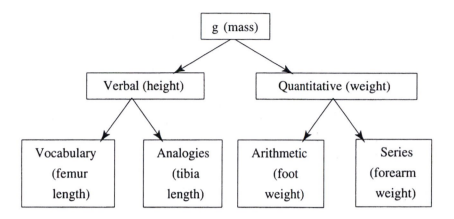

Figure 20.4   A Model of the Hierarchical Organization of IQ Test Scores Along With Analogous Constructs From Anthropometric Measures

of body parts. People who have long feet will—all other things being equal—have a long tibia, femur, and head length. Long feet will also tend to be broader, have a greater girth, and weigh more than short feet. Hence, people with long feet will tend to have broader and wider calves, as well as arms and heads that weigh more than those of folks with smaller feet. The theorists who emphasize *g* place a premium on the physical equivalent of *body mass*—one can measure the space that a cadaver occupies as well as the weight of the dead body and arrive at a single numerical estimate of mass.

At the same time, it is obvious that different cadavers can allocate the same quantitative measure of mass in different ways—a tall but lean body structure can achieve the same body mass as a short, squat morphology. In short, there are real individual differences specific to, say, height that are not completely tapped by mass, just as there are real individual differences in, say, ability in arithmetic that are not completely captured by *g*.

One favored model used to explain individual differences in both cognitive ability and morphology is the *hierarchical model* depicted in Figure 20.4. Mass is a physical variable used to explain why tall people tend to weigh more than short people, and *g* is a psychological variable used to explain why people who score high on verbal tasks also tend to score high on quantitative problems. Just as height is a physical variable composed of several different more fine-grained variables, so is verbal ability a psychological variable used to explain why vocabulary scores correlate with verbal analogies apart from the influence of *g*.

The precise mathematics behind this model need not concern us,[10] but they give a clear quantitative meaning to an IQ score. Suppose that we administered a large number of traditional IQ items to a large sample of people. Now ask the following question: If we had to select one and only one dimension that would best capture the individual differences in correct and incorrect responding to all those items, what dimension would that be? Mathematically, that answer reduces to g, and the best estimate of a person's score on g is the person's IQ score. From this perspective, an IQ score is that single number that best captures the information contained in a series of responses to IQ test items. Analogously, mass is the number that best captures individual differences in physical measurement of body parts. Mind you, just as mass cannot perfectly predict height and weight, the IQ score does *not* capture *all* the information in the items. The IQ score is just the best single number that can be picked.

A very different question is whether we *should* reduce all these item responses to a single dimension. On this question, a fierce debate within psychology and education was ignited early in the 20th century and still burns unchecked today.[11] The issues surrounding this debate deserve attention, but they need not concern us here for one simple, pragmatic reason: almost all the genetic data on intelligence and the relationship of intelligence to social status use a single IQ score or some other measure of g. There is simply not a large empirical database gathered on twins and adoptees that relates vectors of scores on specific cognitive abilities to education, occupational status, and income. We simply lack sufficient empirical data to judge whether other approaches to measuring human intelligence are superior. Like it or not, we are stuck with g.

● CONCLUSIONS ABOUT IQ SCORES

Let us review for a moment. We have seen the items that compose an IQ score, the reliability of IQ test scores, the stability of this measure, the correlates of IQ scores, and the extent to which a single number called "an IQ score" captures a range of cognitive abilities. So what is the phenotype captured by a single number—the total number of items correct (or culturally considered as correct) on an IQ test?

As stated in the introduction to this chapter, the ultimate decision is left to the reader. But if asked for an opinion, I would suggest the following: An IQ test score is a measure of the current industrialized world's concept of "bookish/academic smarts." The contemporary intelligence tests that began with Henri Binet were deliberately constructed to predict scholastic outcome in the French public school system. Items on the tests have been refined by psychometric knowledge and their content expanded far beyond the initial Binet scales. Still, the basic philosophy has remained intact—the content of the items and the aim of prediction are to gauge how well one will do in school, not necessarily in life itself. Items related to catching trout, comforting sick friends, deciding on a mate, strategies for appeasing friends and foes, selecting an occupation, deciding whether or not to emigrate, and maximizing the enjoyment of life do not appear on today's IQ tests. Critics of IQ test scores delight in pointing out these logical shortcomings, while IQ aficionados highlight the correlations of IQ test scores with real-life variables present in industrialized societies. Irrespective of your own opinion on the issue, all the content in the next chapter involves IQ test scores. To interpret these data, you must have some concept of what an IQ test score measures, so decide that now and then proceed to the next chapter.

NOTES ●

1. Early psychologists such as Galton emphasized simple tasks and speed of reaction. Today's cognitive psychologists have expanded these types of tasks much further than can be described in this text.

2. There may indeed be gradations of right and wrong in an answer, but not all answers to an item are equally acceptable. The degree to which culture consensus as opposed to expert opinion defines the correctness of a response is, of course, highly dependent upon the item. Cultural consensus is paramount for the meaning of vocabulary, whereas expert opinion rules in mathematics.

3. A wide variety of sample test items may be found in Jensen (1980, pp. 125-167).

4. Indeed, some of the items in this text were deliberately constructed to illustrate cultural loading. Some tests of intelligence would eliminate these types of items while others might include them.

5. I use the phrase "culture-free" because that is the term used in the literature. A more appropriate phrase would be the intelligence tests that have "diminished cultural influence."

6. A brief overview of the correlation coefficient is given in Chapter 17.

7. Adjusting these correlations for measurement error would bring them into the .80 to .90 range.

8. Psychometricians have developed several different models for reliability; hence, the model presented here is not the only one.

9. The time interval that distinguishes reliability from stability depends on the trait being assessed. Also note that a trait can be measured with high reliability but have little stability over long periods of time.

10. The mathematical model is principal components analysis. The first principal component in such an analysis finds the linear combination of variables that maximizes the variance along a single dimension.

11. For different positions on this issue, see Gardner (1983, 1993), Jensen (1998), and Sternberg (1988).

● REFERENCES

Bloom, B. S. (1964). *Stability and change in human characteristics*. New York: Wiley.

Carroll, J. B. (1993). *Human cognitive abilities: A survey of factor-analytic studies*. New York: Cambridge University Press.

Cattell, R. B. (1940). A culture-free intelligence test, Part 1. *Journal of Educational Psychology, 31*, 161-179.

Cronbach, L. J., & Meehl, P. M. (1955). Construct validity in psychological tests. *Psychological Bulletin, 52*, 281-302.

Gardner, H. (1983). *Frames of mind: The theory of multiple intelligences*. New York: Basic Books.

Gardner, H. (1993). *Multiple intelligences: The theory in practice*. New York: Basic Books.

Humphreys, L. (1989). Intelligence: Three kinds of instability and the consequences for policy. In R. L. Linn (Ed.), *Intelligence: Measurement, theory, and public policy* (pp. 193-216). Urbana: University of Illinois Press.

Jensen, A. R. (1980). *Bias in mental testing*. New York: Free Press.

Jensen, A. R. (1998). *The g factor: The science of mental ability*. Westport, CT: Praeger.

Raven, J. (2000). Raven's progressive matrices: Change and stability over culture and time. *Cognition, 41*, 1-48.

Raven, J. C. (1960). *Guide to the standard progressive matrices*. London: H. K. Lewis.

Snow, R. E., & Yallow, E. (1982). Education and intelligence. In R. J. Sternberg (Ed.), *Handbook of human intelligence* (pp. 493-585). Cambridge, UK: Cambridge University Press.

Sternberg, R. J. (1988). *The triarchic mind: A new theory of human intelligence*. New York: Penguin.

CHAPTER 21

GENES, IQ SCORES, AND SOCIAL STATUS II

Genetic Epidemiology

INTRODUCTION ●

This chapter will initially examine the genetic epidemiology of IQ scores, the definition of the social status phenotype, and the genetic epidemiology of social status. The most important section follows these three topics—it treats the relationship between IQ scores and social status variables.

GENES AND IQ SCORES: GENETIC EPIDEMIOLOGY ●

Kinship Correlations From Older Studies

Table 21.1 presents a portion of the world literature on kinship correlations for IQ that was compiled by Thomas Bouchard and Matt McGue in

Table 21.1 Kinship Correlations for Intelligence

Kinship	Number of Studies	Number of Pairings	Correlation
MZ apart	3	65	.72
Sibs apart	2	203	.24
Biological parent-offspring apart	4	814	.22
MZ together	34	4,672	.86
DZ together	41	5,546	.60
Sibs together	69	26,473	.47
Biological parent-offspring together	32	8,433	.42
Half sibs together	2	200	.31
Cousins	4	1,176	.15
Adoptive sibs	6	369	.34
Adoptive parent-offspring	6	1,397	.19
Husband-wife	16	3,817	.33

SOURCE: Data are from "Familial Studies of Intelligence: A Review," Bouchard & McGue, *Science*, *212*, pp. 1055-1059.

1981. Studies appearing after that publication will be discussed later. For the moment, examine the table, the number of different studies that have been done, and the average correlations for relatives with various degrees of genetic and environmental relationships.

First, examine the correlations for genetic relatives who have not been raised in the same household. The pooled correlation for MZ twins raised apart is .72, and the correlations for first-degree relatives (sibs and parent-offspring) are slightly above .20. This gives strong evidence for a genetic influence on IQ. Otherwise, why would relatives who have not shared any environmental similarity correlate greater than 0.0?

Next, examine the correlations for kinships of different degrees of genetic relationship for those who have been exposed to the same family environment. MZ twins raised together correlate .86; DZ twins, .60; sibs, .47; parents and offspring, .42; and half sibs, .31. Notice how the correlations decline according to genetic relatedness. Another salient point about these correlations comes from a comparison of them with those for genetic relatives raised apart. For MZ twins, the correlations are apart = .72 and together = .86; for sibs, apart = .24 and together = .47; and for parent-offspring, apart = .22 and together = .42. Clearly living (or being raised) in the same family increases the similarity among relatives. This is a key point that differentiates the genetics of cognitive abilities from those of personality—family environment does not make relatives very similar for personality traits, but it does make relatives similar for intelligence.

Examining the correlations for genetically unrelated individuals who live in the same family reinforces this point. The correlation for adoptive parents and offspring is .19, and the correlation for adoptive siblings is .34. Clearly, this similarity must be due to the effects of family environment.

Heritability can be computed in several ways from these data. The correlation for MZ twins raised apart gives a direct estimate of around .70. Using twins raised together, one gets an estimate of .52. From data on parent-offspring and siblings raised apart, the estimate is slightly above .40. Once again, we find that heritability falls into the moderate range. It is neither large (i.e., .80 or greater) nor small (i.e., .20 or smaller).

The correlation for genetically unrelated individuals living in the same families gives a direct estimate of the family environment effect on intelligence (i.e., the quantity ηe^2). Because these correlations lie between .19 and .34, we can conclude that somewhere between 20% and 35% of the observed individual differences in IQ are attributable to the family environment.

The idiosyncratic environment (i.e., all those environmental factors unique to an individual and not shared by relatives) constitutes the rest of the pie. This can be estimated as 1.0 less the correlation for MZ twins raised together, or 1.0 − .86 = .14. Hence, around 15% of the observed individual differences in IQ scores are attributable to the idiosyncratic environment.

Kinship Correlations for New Studies

Do the correlations from studies published since 1981 agree with these earlier studies? Several major (and many minor) studies have appeared since that time, and the results are generally—although not always—consistent. The first of these studies comes from the Minnesota study of twins raised apart (Bouchard, Lykken, McGue, M., Segal, & Tellegen, 1990), which to date is the largest series in the world literature of twins who have been raised in different households. For the five different measures of IQ scores, the correlations for 42 to 48 pairs of MZ twins raised apart ranged from .64 (verbal scores on the WAIS) to .78 (first principal component of special mental abilities). The second study was of data from a smaller series of Swedish twins raised apart, in which the MZ apart correlation was .78 (Finkel, Pedersen,

McGue, & McClearn, 1995; Pedersen, Plomin, Nesselroade, & McClearn, 1992). These correlations fit well within the pooled estimate of .72 previously presented in Table 21.1.

Newer studies include longitudinal twin data from both the United States (Cherny et al., 1994) and the Netherlands (Rijsdijk, Vernon, & Boomsma, in press). The other major works include adoption studies from Denmark (Teasdale & Owen, 1984) and Colorado (Cardon & Fulker, 1994; Plomin, Fulker, Corley, & DeFries, 1997), as well as follow-ups of an early adoption series from Minnesota (Scarr, Weinberg, & Waldman, 1993; Weinberg, Scarr, & Waldman, 1992) and from Texas (Loehlin, Horn, & Willerman, 1994, 1997). A major new finding emerged from these data: The IQ correlation for nongenetic relatives raised in the same family depends on the ages of the relatives. All the adoption correlations in Table 21.1 involved *young children*. These correlations, along with those from the more recent studies, suggest that there is an important shared environment influence on IQ in younger children. When these young children become older and leave the home, this family environmental influence seems to dissipate. The pooled correlation for *adult* adoptive relatives is −.01 (Bouchard, 1998; McGue, Bouchard, Iacono, & Lykken, 1993). In short, when nongenetic relatives become adults, they do not seem to resemble each other on IQ scores any more than two randomly selected adults from the general population.

To summarize, IQ scores are highly familial, in the sense that they show strong family resemblance. Like personality, genes are an important source for this familial resemblance, and heritability of IQ scores is in the moderate range. Unlike personality, for which genes are the major source of familial similarity, shared family environment is important for the resemblance of IQ scores among relatives. This common environmental influence appears important for young children but seems to diminish in adults. The salient features of the family environment responsible for this effect are unknown.

The Flynn Effect: A Shared Family Environment Influence on IQ

The entry of the United States into World War I was accompanied by the first group-administered IQ tests—the Army Alpha test for recruits with English language skills and the Army Beta tests for those recruits (mostly recent immigrants) with linguistic skills in languages other than English. At the time of induction of the National Guard into the Armed Forces shortly preceding the attack on Pearl Harbor, it was noticed that the mean score of recruits on these tests greatly exceeded those of the inductees in WWI (Tuddenham, 1948). At the same time, psychologists such as Cattell (1936, 1951) noted that the mean

IQ scores of the general population were rising despite the demographic "dysgenic" trends that will be discussed later in this chapter.

Such data were of largely academic importance until a series of publications by Flynn (1984, 1987) gave convincing documentation that IQ scores in Western industrialized societies were rising over time. Small European countries such as the Netherlands and Denmark have universal conscription among males. Except for those with gross physical or mental anomalies, all males in these countries are required to register for the armed forces and to take a series of standardized tests. Because the standardized tests included a measure of IQ used year after year, the data effectively constituted a whole population (i.e., males) who were administered the same test year after year. Flynn's data demonstrated that the mean scores on this test increased year after year. Thus, the Flynn effect was born—IQ scores are increasing over time and appear to be doing so in the entire industrialized world.

The current controversy over the Flynn effect does not involve its existence—with few exceptions, everyone acknowledges that raw IQ scores are increasing over time. The big debate is over *why* scores are increasing. Many, including Flynn (1998) himself, suspect that there has been no real change in the anatomical and physiological substrates of IQ. Instead, they argue that variables including increasing familiarity with test taking have driven the secular trend. This may indeed be true, but it poses a strong challenge to the interpretation of the genetic data on IQ—to what extent does the similarity among relatives measure real similarity in IQ as opposed to sophistication in test-taking?

Whatever the ultimate causes of the Flynn effect, the rise in IQ scores has been so strong that it cannot plausibly be caused by any known genetic mechanism of evolution. Population size is much too large for genetic drift to influence the change. Neither have any reasonable data over the past 50 years suggested increased reproductive fitness for high IQ scores. In fact, much of the data suggested that low IQ is associated with increased fitness. Hence, almost everyone believes that the source of the Flynn effect is in the common family environment for siblings.[1] Just what aspects of the common environment are responsible for the effect? Nutrition, test-taking acumen, and schooling are likely suspects, but to date there are no convincing data to pick out the real culprit(s) from the innocents (Neisser, 1998).

Genes, *g*, and Multiple Intelligences

The previous chapter discussed the controversy about intelligence as a single construct, as opposed to the notion of multiple intelligences. Do the genetic data shed any light on this problem? The answer is a qualified "yes."

The data on genetics give insight into the problem, but given the large number of twin and adoption studies on IQ, relatively few have taken the extra time and effort to perform the difficult analyses that could help answer this question.

The types of data necessary for these analyses consist of cross-twin, cross-trait correlations. A cross-twin, cross-trait correlation is best understood by taking a simple example. Under ordinary circumstances, we could compute the correlation between, say, the vocabulary score of Twin 1 and the vocabulary score of Twin 2. The result would be a quantitative index of the extent to which the twins resemble each other in their vocabulary scores. This is a cross-twin, *same*-trait correlation. A cross-twin, cross-trait correlation is computed as the correlation between one trait in Twin 1 and a *different* trait in Twin 2. An example would be the correlation between Twin 1's vocabulary score and Twin 2's arithmetic score.

In real life, researchers compute two cross-twin, cross-trait correlations, one for MZ twins and the other for DZ twins. Comparison of the MZ with the DZ correlation informs us of the genetic influence on the reasons behind the phenotypic correlation between vocabulary and arithmetic. To phrase the problem slightly differently, we could first ask the question of why individuals who score high on vocabulary also tend to score high on arithmetic. Some of this relationship may be due to genes and some of it to environment. When the MZ cross-twin, cross-trait correlation is higher than the DZ cross-twin, cross trait correlation, then genes must be an important reason for the correlation. Sophisticated statistical analysis—beyond the scope of this book—may be used to arrive at an actual quantitative measure of how important the genes are for the correlation between vocabulary and arithmetic.

The data from several twin (e.g., Alarcon et al., 1998; Petrill et al., 1998) and adoption projects (e.g., Rice, Carey, Fulker, & DeFries, 1989) have given a very consistent answer to this question—there is a genetic *g*. In the previous discussion of intelligence and multiple intelligences, we found that scores on any one mental ability test predict scores on any other mental ability. We also learned that because of this, *g* is a legitimate concept—a single number that captures as much variability as possible among the diverse measures of cognitive talent. The data show that these two statements describing the *phenotype* also apply to the *genotype*. Multivariate genetic analysis has continually shown that hypothetical genetic values for any one cognitive ability predict those genetic values for any other mental trait. There is also a genetic *g*.

Table 21.2 illustrates these two points using published twin data on the scales of the proportion of phenotypic variance in a WAIS (Wechsler Adult Intelligence Scale) attributable to genetic individual differences (i.e., the heritabilities). The numbers above the diagonal give the proportion of the phenotypic correlation between two different scales that is due to genotypic

Table 21.2 Genetic Correlations (Below the Diagonal) and the Genetic Correlation Divided by the Phenotypic Correlation (Above the Diagonal) for Subscales of the Wechsler Adult Intelligence Scale

Subscale	IN	CO	AR	SI	DS	VO	DY	PC	BD	PA	OA
Information (IN)		.65	.56	.66	.61	.74	.92	.51	.55	.90	.70
Comprehension (CO)	.82		.81	.70	.76	.76	.75	.58	.56	.99	.72
Arithmetic (AR)	.54	.72		.77	.90	.85	.99	.89	.86	.92	.99
Similarities (SI)	.92	.92	.75		.62	.72	.59	.58	.59	.99	.72
Digit span (DS)	.34	.32	.62	.39		.76	.62	.30	.94	.99	.54
Vocabulary (VO)	.91	.92	.79	.96	.44		.82	.74	.74	.92	.76
Digit symbol (DY)	.59	.53	.72	.55	.49	.68		.47	.50	.57	.04
Picture completion (PC)	.60	.79	.77	.79	.13	.83	.45		.52	.58	.56
Block design (BD)	.55	.62	.89	.75	.72	.74	.46	.71		.77	.61
Picture arrangement (PA)	.79	.86	.65	.93	.34	.79	.30	.65	.70		.86
Object assembly (OA)	.56	.69	.60	.78	.21	.69	.03	.81	.77	.82	

SOURCE: Calculated from data in Tambs, Sundet, and Magnus (1986).

factors. For example, the number .65 for the Information and Comprehension scales means that 65% of the phenotypic correlation between these two scales is attributable to genetic factors. (The nature of these genetic factors, of course, cannot be determined by these figures.) If you visually inspect the 55 different estimates above the diagonal, you will find that only 3 of them are lower than .50 (i.e., half of the phenotypic correlation). This means that genes are the major source behind all the reasons why one cognitive ability correlates with another mental talent.

The numbers below the diagonal are genetic correlations. They are estimates of the extent to which hypothetical genetic values on a WAIS scale predict genotypic values on another WAIS scale. Inspection of these numbers also shows overall strong relationships among most of the WAIS scales—the genes influencing scores on one trait also affect scores on other traits. Statistically, these results point to a genetic g, although the biochemical nature of the genetic g is unknown.

Genes and the Development of IQ

Suppose that I have two beakers, both of which contain 2 ounces of water. I pour the first beaker into a tall, thin container and the second beaker into a short, squat container. Which of the two containers—the tall, thin one or the short, squat one—has more water? To you and me, the answer is simple. Both have the same amount of water, exactly 2 ounces. But young children more often than not identify the tall, thin container as having more water than the short, squat container.

Reflect on this for a minute. You are an adult and are fully aware of all the symbolic processing and abstract reasoning that goes into giving a correct answer to this question. But as young children, both you and I were quite likely to have arrived at an erroneous conclusion. Our genes and our prenatal environment have not changed in the interim, but obviously our intelligence has. The general problem that this example addresses is the following—is intelligence an "innate" quality or does it develop over time?

Both common sense and research data suggest that the degree of symbolic encoding, processing, and reasoning increases over time. Four-year-olds can solve more difficult problems than 2-year-olds, and 8-year-olds can solve more difficult problems than 4-year-olds. To what extent is this difference due to accumulated experience with the real world, and to what extent is it due to developmental and maturational effects of the human nervous system? At this time, there is not enough empirical data to answer this question, but from a genetic perspective, one point is clear—humans are not just "born" with intelligence. Intelligence develops over time, although the reasons behind this development are obscure. In short, there really is no such thing as "innate intelligence." Intelligence is lemonade.

The problem outlined above focuses on differences in *mean* levels of intelligence over time. A completely different problem consists of the *consistency of individual differences* over time. That is, irrespective of the increase in intelligence from years 2 to 4, why do children who score high at age 2 also tend to score high at age 4? Here, the emerging data suggest that genes contribute to the stability of individual differences in intelligence over time.

The types of data are analogous to the cross-twin, cross-trait correlations outlined above, but instead consist of cross-twin, cross-time correlations. To what extent does the IQ score of Twin 1 at Time 1 predict the IQ score of Twin 2 at Time 2? If these correlations are higher for MZ than DZ twins, then we have good evidence that genes contribute to the stability of individual differences in IQ over time. Three major empirical studies that have data related to this issue—the Louisville Twin Project (Wilson, 1983, 1986), the Colorado Adoption Project (Plomin & DeFries, 1985; Plomin, DeFries & Fulker, 1988; DeFries, Plomin, & Fulker, 1994), and the McArthur Longitudinal Twin Project (Chambers, 1999; Cherny et al., 1994)—are consistent in their results: Genes are major contributors to the stability of IQ over time.

Table 21.3 presents data from the McArthur Twin Project, which measured IQ from 14 months through 7 years of age.[2] Figures above the diagonal estimate the percentage of a phenotypic correlation between two time points attributable to the shared, family environment while the numbers below the diagonal estimate the contribution of the genes to this correlation. For example, the phenotypic correlation between IQ measured at 14 months and IQ measured at 20 months is .64. Of this correlation, 41% appears to be due to the common family environment and 52% is attributable to genetic sources. In total, then, 93% of the correlation is due to familial factors—shared genes and shared environment.

There is an intriguing pattern to these correlations. Genes contribute to the stability of IQ scores at all ages. The common environment, on the other hand, may have age-dependent effects on IQ stability. Examine the figures for the row involving 14-month IQ. There is an important contribution to stability at 20 months (41%) that diminishes slightly at 24 months but then drops close to zero at 36, 48, and 84 months. The row for stability starting at 20 months shows a similar pattern. At later ages, common environment seems to contribute importantly to IQ stability. Hence, the common environment does not appear to be a strong reason for IQ stability from infancy to early childhood, although it does seem to contribute to stability for

Table 21.3   Approximate Percentage of the Stability of IQ Attributable to Genes (Below the Diagonal) and to the Family Environment (Above the Diagonal)

Age in Months	Age in Months					
	14	*20*	*24*	*36*	*48*	*84*
14		41	21	08	00	00
20	52		61	70	38	31
24	81	43		36	44	50
36	95	28	72		29	50
48	100	71	65	74		47
84	100	77	54	40	51	

SOURCE: Computed from data in Chambers (1999).

adjacent testings in infancy and to stability during early childhood. Genes, on the other hand, contribute to stability at all ages.

Surprisingly, there are no modern genetic studies of IQ stability in the transition from adolescence to adulthood and during the early and middle adult years. Research in later adult years suggests that the stability of cognitive talent in the elderly is due mostly to genes (Plomin, Pedersen, Lichtenstein, & McClearn, 1994). There is also evidence that genes contribute to some patterning of decline in cognitive ability in older adults (Swan, Carmelli, et al., 1990; Swan, LaRue, et al., 1992).

In summary then, genes are important contributors to IQ stability in infancy and early childhood and are the major source of stability in later life.

● SOCIAL STATUS: THE PHENOTYPE

The concept of social status (aka socioeconomic status) has had a long history in the social sciences, particularly sociology and psychology. It is a composite variable that is the sum of three separate phenotypes—education, occupational status, and income. Education typically is measured as the highest educational level completed and not simply the number of years spent in school. That is, a college graduate with a bachelor's degree is awarded 16 years of education even though the person may have spent 5 years in college to complete the degree.

Occupational status consists of an arbitrary—but well agreed on—scale of job prestige. If one takes a large group of occupations and has people rank them on their prominence, then one finds a strong amount of agreement. An electrician is more prestigious than a full-time burger-flipper, an electrical engineer has more status than an electrician, and a neurosurgeon has higher prominence than an electrical engineer. Low-status occupations are generally unskilled or semiskilled labor. Next on the hierarchy lies skilled labor, such as shop attendants and the trades (plumber, carpenter, electrician), followed by low- and then middle-level management positions. At the top are medical doctors, lawyers, business owners, and high-level managers.

The third variable composing social status deals with money. Economists distinguish three facets of monetary differences between families—earnings, income, and wealth. Earnings are the amount of money that one makes from a job or profession, usually measured over the course of a year or so to avoid seasonal phenomena that might influence weekly or monthly earnings. Income includes earnings but adds to them all other sources of money that one regularly receives, such as investment dividends. Wealth includes income but adds to it all accrued monetary resources, such as home equity and capital investments. The behavioral genetics literature almost always deals with earnings and/or income.[3] There appears to be no twin or adoption data related directly to wealth.

Let us call this version of social status the "traditional" measure. There are indeed critics of the construct of social status and others who extend the construct to include psychological variables such as orientation to achievement and. Once again—just like the IQ score—the majority of the literature deals with the traditional three measures of social status. Hence, we are stuck with this definition just as we were stuck with the definition of an IQ score.

SOCIAL STATUS: GENETIC EPIDEMIOLOGY ●

This section will review the twin and adoption data on education, occupational status, and income. Table 21.4 presents the results of the major recent twin studies on the issue.[4] To interpret these data, focus on the comparison of MZ and DZ correlations within a study and within a phenotype. Because the studies come from different countries and some have data from different generations, it is unwise to compare the correlations of one study with those of another.

There are more data on educational level than on occupational status and income combined. In all five studies, the MZ correlation is significantly higher than the DZ correlation, and as is true for most behavioral phenotypes, heritability is in the moderate range. Even though the data come from different countries, each of the five twin studies t reports a significant effect for shared, family environment, effect size ranging between one quarter and

Table 21.4   Twin Correlations for the Three Variables That Define Social Status

Sample	Location	Education		Occupational Status		Income	
		MZ	DZ	MZ	DZ	MZ	DZ
1[a]	United States	.76	.54			.54	.30
2[b]	Norway	.87	.65				
3[c]	Norway	.72	.49	.47	.27		
4[d]	United States	.75[e]	.62[e]			.56	.36
5[f]	Australia	.85[e]	.58[e]			.68	.32

a. From Behrman and Taubman (1989) and Taubman (1976).
b. Pooled estimates from Heath et al. (1985).
c. Calculated from the variance components presented in Tambs, Sundet, Magnus, and Berg (1989); note that this sample partly overlaps with that of Heath et al. (1985).
d. From Aus and Krueger (1994).
e. Corrected for measurement error.
f. Miller, Mulvey, and Martin (1995); see also Baker, Treloar, Reynolds, Heath, and Martin (1996).

one half of the phenotypic variance.[5] The genetics of education, however, are not as simple as calculating parameter estimates. Using virtually the whole population of twins in Norway, Heath et al. (1985) demonstrated that both heritability and common environment were influenced by year of birth and sex. Similar influences were absent in a very large sample of Australian twins (Baker et al., 1996). These results suggest that the cultural background must always be considered in the interpretation of genetic data.

Interestingly, there are few sets of twin data on occupational status. Still, the one study from Table 21.4 and the results of other studies that did not report twin correlations (Lichtenstein & Pedersen, 1997) suggest moderate heritability for this phenotype. Finally, the three twin studies with data on income also suggest a genetic effect.

There are few sets of adoption data on social status. Only one study—and one with very modest sample sizes at that—examined the similarity between adopted siblings and genetically related siblings raised apart. The correlations are presented in Table 21.5 (Study 1) along with the results of a second adoption study (Scarr & Weinberg, 1994)[6] and a third study (Rowe, Vesterdal, & Rodgers, 1998) that compared the similarity of full sibs to half siblings raised in the same family.

All studies suggest heritability for education, and Study 3 replicates the genetic effect from the twin data on income. There is suggestive evidence for a shared environment influence on education because adoptive siblings

Table 21.5 Correlations for Siblings and Half Siblings Raised Together and Apart for Traditional Measures of Social Status

		Education			Occupational Status	Income
Genetic Relationship	Rearing Status	Study 1[a]	Study 2[b]	Study 3[c]	Study 2[b]	Study 3[c]
Full sibs	Together	.67	.32	.52	.01	.31
Half sibs	Together			.42		.16
Unrelated	Together	.43	.13		.29	
Full sibs	Apart	.38				
Half sibs	Apart	.00				

a. From Teasdale and Owen (1981, 1984, 1986).
b. From Scarr and Weinberg (1994).
c. From Rowe, Vesterdal, and Rodgers (1998).

365

resemble each other more than chance. This common environment influence is also evidenced by the significant correlation between the adoptive family background and the educational level of the adoptee reported in both adoption studies. The data on occupational status are confusing because the correlation for unrelated sibs (.29) exceeds that for full sibs (.01).

● GENES, IQ SCORES, AND SOCIAL STATUS: THE QUESTION OF "HOW"

For those readers who have taken the introductory chapter to heart, the genetic epidemiology of IQ scores, education, occupational status, and income should be boring. In that chapter, we learned that there is moderate heritability for almost all behavioral phenotypes, so IQ and social status are more likely to follow this rule than be exceptions to it. We also learned that behavioral genetic research is more interested in the question of "how" genes influence phenotypes than in estimating heritability. Data from the past century have been unequivocal in demonstrating that people with above-average IQ scores tend to achieve higher levels of education, obtain more prestigious jobs, and make more money than those with lower IQ scores (see Hunt, 1995, and Neisser et al., 1996, for general reviews). But how do genes for IQ scores influence social status?

Two Extreme Views

Let us start this discussion by contrasting two radically different views of the situation, both of them deliberately set up as "straw people" herein in order to help the student understand the issues. The first straw person starts with Herrnstein and Murray's (1994) view of IQ and social structure. IQ, according to them, is quite heritable and a powerful, independent predictor of education, occupational status, income, and a host of other variables such as job performance, welfare dependency, and crime. Over the past century, society has been moving more and more toward a *meritocracy*, a social system in which movement up and down the ladder of social status depends more on an individual's own talents and abilities than on the family into which the person was born.[7] The talent and ability that matters most to social movement is IQ. Both the educational system and the labor marketplace are becoming increasingly more efficient in selecting for IQ. It no longer takes an average level of IQ to become a physician or to move up the corporate staircase into a vice presidency.

Because genes influence IQ, because IQ has a causal influence on eventual social status, and because society is becoming ever more efficient in selecting for IQ, society is becoming increasingly more stratified on the basis of the genes for IQ. Because families at the bottom of this heap tend to have more children than those at the top, the United States gradually will evolve from a largely middle class society into one resembling a capitalistic Third World culture. A few genetically talented and/or wealthy families will form a quasi-aristocracy at the top; the large, impoverished majority at the bottom will have declining advantage; and the broad-based middle class will almost disappear. To recognize that this is an oversimplification of Herrnstein and Murray's (1994) position, I will call this the Murrnstein hypothesis.

To complete the straw man at the opposite end of the spectrum, consider the work of Lewontin, Rose, and Kamin (1984). These critics of behavioral genetics argue that IQ is a very narrowly defined phenotype that has little direct relevance for social status and that all the genetic data presented in this chapter are seriously flawed. At the very least, they are agnostics. If the definition of intelligence could be expanded, if we could reliably and validly measure this expanded construct (or constructs), and if new genetic data could be gathered that overcome the methodological problems, then—in theory at least—the results might actually validate the Murrnstein hypothesis. Instead, I will develop a new straw person and term it the Rosemintin hypothesis, based on imagined conversations with these critics.

According to Rosemintin, society has not moved very far away from medieval "heritocracies" in which social status is determined mainly by parental status. Those families that accrue a sufficient amount of wealth will move into desirable neighborhoods, where their children attend upscale schools. Better education in these schools, along with the advantage of encyclopedias and computers at home, increases IQ scores. The children will also associate with wealthy peers and role models who stress the importance of education and well-paying occupations in accumulating wealth. The children are encouraged not only to attend college but to attend elite colleges, where they develop networks of social contacts that "grease the wheels" for them to move into better jobs. (After all, their parents can afford a private college.) In short, parental advantage "jump starts" their social status, and when they themselves become part of the wealthy, they can "jump start" their own children's careers.

The Murrnstein and Rosemintin hypotheses have the same view of social status, and both accept the fact that IQ scores are correlated with social status. What they differ in is *how* this correlation comes about. Murrnstein suggests that genes for IQ are a major causal factor. IQ scores are highly heritable and IQ drives the social status train. It is true that some individuals will

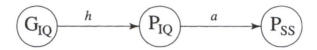

Figure 21.1 The Murrnstein Model: Genes for IQ (G_{IQ}) Influence Phenotypic IQ (P_{IQ}), Which Then Influences Eventual Social Status (P_{SS})

obtain great wealth by inheriting fortunes, but for each trust-funder there are a hundred people who obtain their social status from merit. Rosemintin, on the other hand, views the correlation between IQ scores and social status as noncausal and mediated by parental advantage. Family wealth and social status perpetuate themselves. Economic advantage leads to good schooling and higher IQ scores, and impoverishment leads to a deprived education and lower IQ scores. It is true that there are rags-to-riches stories, but these are few and far between compared to the majority of people who start out life with different degrees of advantage.

Sadly, it is now time to dispel both the Murrnstein and Rosemintin positions as myths by examining data. The "sadly" modifier comes about because within academia there are still small minorities—albeit very vocal ones that receive more attention in the popular press than among scholars in the field—who come close to these extreme positions.

The biggest argument against the Murrnstein hypothesis comes from quantitative considerations of the very data that adherents cite to support it. Consider the mathematical implications of the Murrnstein model depicted in Figure 21.1. Individual differences in the genotype for IQ (G_{IQ} in the figure) contribute to phenotypic individual differences in IQ (P_{IQ}). These phenotypic IQ differences, in turn, have a direct causal effect on a person's phenotypic social status (P_{SS}).

The quantity b in Figure 21.1 gives the causal effect of genetic individual differences on phenotypic individual differences in IQ. This quantity is simply the square root of the heritability for IQ. The quantity a marking the arrow from P_{IQ} to P_{SS} measures the strength at which IQ causes social status. From this model, the extent to which genes for IQ result in social stratification is given by the quantity a^2b^2—the square of the causal relationship between IQ and social status times the heritability for IQ. Now let us plug numbers into this equation and view the results.

One can obtain an upper bound estimate of a^2b^2 by substituting the *correlation* between IQ and social status for the quantity a. This is an upper bound estimate because the correlation coefficient is the sum of two effects—the actual causal effect of IQ on social status plus all the indirect, but

Table 21.6 Phenotypic Correlations Between IQ Scores and Traditional Measures of Social Status From Five Large Population Surveys

Study	Correlation Between IQ and		
	Education	*Occupation*	*Income*
1[a]	.55	.43	.35
2[b]	.47	.36	.35
3[c]	.56	.47	.20
4[d]	.58	.45	.36
5[e]	.60		.31

a. Veterans data from Jencks et al. (1979, Table A2.7).
b. PSID data set from Jencks et al. (1979, Table A2.5).
c. Project Talent data from Jencks et al. (1979, Table A2.9).
d. Olneck Brothers data from Jencks et al. (1979, Table A2.11).
e. NLSY data from Rowe, Jacobson, and Van den Oord (1999).

noncausal, effects that influence the correlation. By accepting the larger estimates of heritability, we can then calculate the *maximal* value of the extent to which IQ genes result in social stratification. The largest estimate of heritability for IQ in the literature comes from the correlation for MZ twins raised apart—it is about .70. The correlation between IQ and social status depends on the individual variable for social status; it is largest for education and smallest for income. Table 21.6 provides estimates of these correlations from five large studies of the general U.S. population.

The average correlation between IQ and education in Table 21.6 is around .55. Hence, the maximal estimate of a^2b^2 is $.55^2(.70) = .21$. This figure means that genetic differences for IQ account for—at a maximum—21% of the phenotypic variance in education. The average correlation for IQ and occupational status is about .43, giving the estimate of a^2b^2 as $.43^2(.70) = .13$. Finally, the average correlation between IQ and income is .31, giving a^2b^2 as $.31^2(.70) = .07$. These estimates are not trivial when compared to the effect sizes in most social science research areas, but they are certainly not huge in any absolute sense. I leave it to the reader to enter his or her own preferred values for heritability and the correlations between IQ and social status, then come to his or her own conclusions about whether we are about to develop something close to a "caste system" (Herrnstein & Murray, 1994) based on the genetics of IQ.

Mathematical predictions from the Rosemintin hypothesis are presented in Figure 21.2. Parental social status (Parental$_{ss}$) influences offspring IQ (P_{IQ}) via the path marked *b*. Parental social status also directly influences offspring

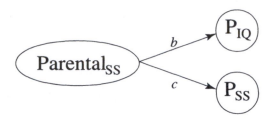

Figure 21.2   The Rosemintin Model: Parental Social Status (Parental$_{SS}$) Jointly Influences Offspring IQ (P$_{IQ}$) and Offspring Social Status (P$_{SS}$)

social status (P$_{SS}$) through path c. According to this model, the predicted correlation between an individual's own IQ and social status should be the product of these two quantities, or bc. Once again, we can obtain the maximal estimate of this correlation by substituting the observed correlation between parental social status and offspring IQ for b and the observed correlation between parental and offspring social status for c. We can then compare this maximal estimate to the observed correlation between an individual's IQ and social status to examine how well the model explains the data.

Again, the estimates of b and c depend on the specific social status variable. Mulligan (1999), as cited by Bowles and Gintis (2001), reviewed these data and arrived at average estimates of c ranging from .29 (parental education with offspring education) to .43 (parental income with offspring income). Estimates of b are a bit harder to obtain because many studies do not subdivide parental social status into education, occupational status, and income in computing the correlation. A review by White (1982) places the correlation in the .30 to .40 range. Let us accept the highest value, .40. Hence, the predicted value for IQ and any social status variable should range between .29(.40) = .12 and .43(.40) = .17. Compare this range with the observed correlations given in Table 21.6. The observed correlations are always *higher*—often substantially higher—than the ones predicted by the Rosemintin model.

That there is something fundamentally wrong with this model can be seen by recognizing that the product of two fractions must always be less than either of the two fractions themselves. Because b and c are fractions, the product bc must always be less than b and less than c. To say this in English, the Rosemintin model implies that the correlation between IQ and social status (bc) must *always* be less than the correlation between parental social status and offspring IQ (b). The empirical evidence over the past century says just the opposite—an individual's IQ is a better predictor of his or her eventual social status than the social status of the family in which he or she was raised. There must be factors in addition to family advantage that are responsible for the correlation between IQ and social status.

To the bleary-eyed student dazed by the "correlations between this, that, and the other thing" tone of this prose, I offer a quick—but very important—synopsis. The simpleminded notion that "(a) genes influence IQ and (b) IQ influences social status, so therefore (c) genes for IQ strongly stratify society" is wrong. Social stratification by genes for IQ is *not zero*, but the effect is *not large* either. To provide an analogy, we all agree that rain causes slippery roads and slippery roads cause accidents. But this does not imply that every person—or even the majority of people—driving on a rainy day will have an automobile accident.

Similarly, the simpleminded notion that "(a) parental social status influences offspring IQ, and (b) parental social status also influences an off-spring's eventual social status, so therefore (c) the correlation between IQ and social status is due to parental social status" is equally incorrect. *Some* of the correlation between IQ and social status may be due to parental social status, but *not all* of the correlation is due to it. Consider another analogy: Rain causes the roads to be slippery and rain causes automobile accidents. But obviously rain is not *the only* reason why slippery roads are correlated with accidents. The day could be bright and shiny, but a patch of ice, oil, or even gravel could result in a fender bender.

If you are beginning to think that the relationship between genes, IQ scores, and social status is complicated, then you are on the right track. Human behavior is complicated and multifactorial, so phenotypes such as IQ and social status are probably the result of a convoluted network of causal factors. Simple explanations of human behavior, such as the Murrnstein and Rosemintin views, are usually simpleminded as well.

A Complete View: Emerging Patterns in a Puzzle

The data necessary to acquire a complete view on genes, IQ scores, and social status would include genetically informative kinship correlations gathered with the types of designs used in large population surveys. Social status of the family of origin must be closely indexed, IQ should be measured during childhood and adolescence (and preferably again, later in life), and data on education, occupational status, and income should be gathered throughout the life span. There are simply no such data that meet all these requirements. Instead, we have only a few studies—almost all of which are cross-sectional and/or retrospective—that have analyzed how genes, IQ scores, and social status are related to one another. The situation is similar to that of working on a giant picture puzzle without the picture available and with little more than the edgework and a few small sections completed. It is still too early to guess what the whole picture look like—although there is no shortage of speculation on this issue. More time is needed to expand the small sections and piece some of them together before we make any firm conclusions about the subject composition of the whole picture. The following paragraphs give results on how those few semi-completed sections of the puzzle appear right now.

The first section of the puzzle nearing completion is fairly clear and tells us that *there is more to the genetics of social class than simply the genes for IQ scores*. The small amount of multivariate genetic data point to this conclusion (Lichtenstein & Pedersen, 1997; Rowe et al., 1999), but they are much too complicated to present here. Instead, we can view the topic through a simplified example. We have seen that both IQ and educational level are heritable, so let us hypothesize that the only reason for the heritability of education is the genetic effect for IQ. Specifically assume that the only reasons for heritability for education are that (a) genes influence phenotypic IQ and (b) phenotypic IQ permits one to move further through the educational system. We are back to the model depicted in Figure 21.1, but this time we can obtain a maximum estimate for the heritability for education. From the model, the heritability for education should be a^2b^2—the same figure for the genetic effect on social stratification for education we arrived at in discussing the Murrnstein model. Rounding off, that figure was .20, so we should expect that heritability for education should be no higher than .20.

Now compare this predicted number with the observed estimates from the twin data on education given in Table 21.4. Here, heritability can be estimated as $2(R_{mz} - R_{dz})$ or twice the difference between the MZ and DZ correlations. Most of these estimates are in the intermediate range of .40 to .50, well above the predicted value of .20. Something is the matter with this model. Exactly what is wrong?

There are too many possibilities to discuss each one in turn, but most scholars speculate that genes other than those for IQ also influence education. We all know that there are many different reasons why some people go far in the educational system while others drop out early. Some of the reasons include motivation, achievement drive, interest patterns, and personality. Examples abound. Someone with the intellectual capacity to succeed in medical school may have an intense interest in working outdoors with nature. She might forgo postgraduate education to become a forest ranger. We all know of people who do well in the educational system (a prerequisite for entering college and graduate school) because they study all the time. We also know others with considerable intellectual talents who receive average grades because they do not study very much. If the genetics of these traits are similar to those of other behaviors—that is, they have moderate heritability—and if these traits have a causal influence, however moderate, on eventual educational attainment, then there is more to the genetics of education than simply the genes for IQ.

A similar argument can be made for income. The estimate of a^2h^2 for income is .07, so the maximal heritability for income according to the model should be .07. The observed data from Table 21.4 give observed heritability estimates in the .40 to .50 range, similar to those for education but far greater than that predicted by the model. Once again, genes for personality, interests, and motivation may influence income independently of IQ. Our forest ranger is unlikely to have the same earnings as a physician. Religious clergy usually are well educated and have higher-than-average occupational status, but those types of vocations are seldom tickets to great wealth.

In summary, observed heritabilities for the social status variables of education, occupational status, and income are too large to be explained solely by the genetic effects for IQ. Most researchers suspect that personality, interest patterns, and motivational factors influence social status variables, but like unconnected puzzle pieces, these factors remain isolated from the larger section of knowledge because there have been no empirical data to join them.

The second major section of the emerging puzzle suggests that *IQ works as an "indolent gatekeeper" for eventual social status*. That is, IQ permits the gates to higher education to be open but does not provide a rigid system of entry (the *indolent* or *lazy* part of the gatekeeping). Think for a minute of the major factors that influence the majority of college admissions. They are high school grades, scores on standardized tests such as the ACT and SAT, and references. Coming from a rich family that generously contributes to the alumni fund does not hurt. Neither do unique individual achievements such as outstanding athletic or musical talent. But these exceptions are infrequent compared to the three criteria outlined above. Now reflect on what we have learned about the major correlates of IQ scores—they are school grades and scores on standardized achievement tests. Hence, to the extent that intelligence has any causal role on individual differences in school grades and standardized test scores, it is likely to also influence admissions to institutes of higher education.

But recall the indolence of the IQ gatekeeper: It *assists* but does not *guarantee* opening of the gate to college. Variables such as studiousness, achievement-motivation, and interests are also likely to have their own roles in the complicated causal decisions behind college admission. One thing is certain: Few, if any, colleges require only an IQ score for admission. Freshmen are admitted on the basis of *scholastic achievement* in high school, not directly on the basis of an IQ test score. We will review data on this after we examine the third emerging section of the puzzle.

The third puzzle section is that some social status variables operate as gatekeepers for other social status variables; in particular, education works as a major gatekeeper for occupational status. Once again, the gatekeeping role is more on the indolent and perfunctory side and not a rigid slave to rules carved in stone. The arguments for this are similar to those made above for intelligence. For example, there was no government edict that required Bill Gates to have a PhD. before founding and becoming the CEO of Microsoft. Instead of belaboring the issue, let us examine the pertinent data.

The data presented come from four longitudinal studies previously analyzed by Jencks et al. (1979).[8] Longitudinal studies have the advantage that certain causal arrows can be eliminated. In a cross-sectional study of IQ and education in, say, 40-year-olds, interpretation of the correlation between IQ and education in terms of causal paths is problematic. IQ may influence education, education may increase IQ, other variables may influence both IQ and education, and some combination of all three of these possibilities may be operating. Longitudinal data, although they cannot completely resolve the causal pathways, can eliminate some of the alternatives and give a clearer picture of what *might* be going on. Consider the correlation between IQ measured in the early high school years and educational level at age 40. Unless something is dramatically wrong with our understanding of the physics of space and time, educational level at age 40 cannot be a causal influence on adolescent IQ. Hence, the correlation between high school IQ and adult education probably reflects some combination of IQ causing education and of the influence of other variables such as parental social status on both IQ and education.

The first temporal variable in these types of data is parental social status, measured by father's educational level and occupational status. (Data on parental income were not available in all four of these studies.) The second is adolescent IQ score of the offspring, the third is educational level, the next is occupational status, and the final one is earnings or income. Through the statistical technique of multiple regression, we can predict any one variable from all those other variables that *precede* it in time.[9] Table 21.7 presents an example of this type of analysis, in which we try to predict IQ score from the two parental social status variables.

In this table, the numbers are coefficients from the multiple regression that mathematically controls for one variable when examining the influence of the other variables.[10] They are analogous—but not identical—to correlations. Numbers close to 0 suggest that a variable aids very little in making predictions when other variables are controlled for. The larger the number, the

Table 21.7 The Best Predictors of a Person's Adolescent/Young Adult IQ Score[a]

	Predictor Variables	
Data Set[b]	*Father's Education*	*Father's Occupational Status*
Veterans	.15	.17
Panel Study of Income Dynamics	.16	.17
Talent	.16	.24
Olneck	.18	.18

a. Standardized regression coefficients predicting offspring IQ from father's education and occupational status.
b. See Jencks et al. (1979) for the meaning of the data sets.

more predictive ability a variable offers. Consider the entry of .17 from the veterans study, in which adolescent/young adult IQ is predicted from father's occupational status. The control for father's education has the following interpretation. If we took all those fathers with, say, a high school education—no more and no less—then how well do differences in father's occupational status predict offspring IQ? The answer is .17. Similarly, the values for father's education control for occupational status. For example, suppose we examined only those fathers with a status of skilled workers, such as plumbers, carpenters, and electricians. To what degree do educational differences among these fathers predict offspring IQ? The answer would be .15 in the veterans data and .16 in the data from the Panel Study of Income Dynamics (PSID).

In interpreting the data in this and the subsequent tables, it is important to compare the numbers across a *row* and ask yourself the question, "which variable(s) are the better predictors in this study?" For Table 21.7, father's occupational status is a better predictor in three of the four studies, but not by very much. Most professional statisticians who examine the data would be struck by how similar these numbers are. Their basic conclusion would be that father's education and father's occupational status are equally good predictors of offspring IQ.

Table 21.8 presents the predictability of educational level from the two parental social status variables *and* a person's own IQ. A very clear picture emerges from all four studies: IQ is definitely the best predictor. The two parental social status variables still contribute significantly to prediction, but their influence is much smaller than that of IQ. These data illustrate a point

Table 21.8   The Best Predictors of a Person's Educational Level[a]

Data Set[b]	Father's Education	Father's Occupational Status	Own Test
		Predictor Variables	
Veterans	.13	.14	.49
Panel Study of Income Dynamics	.20	.18	.38
Talent	.15	.11	.49
Olneck	.20	.16	.49

a. Standardized regression coefficients predicting offspring education from father's education and occupational status and offspring IQ.
b. See Jencks et al. (1979) for the meaning of the data sets.

Table 21.9   The Best Predictors of a Person's Occupational Status[a]

Data Set[b]	Father's Education	Father's Occupational Status	Own Test	Own Education
		Predictor Variables		
Veterans	.04	.10	.12	.49
Panel Study of Income Dynamics	.00	.06	.08	.56
Talent	.03	.02	.16	.54
Olneck	−.02	−.00	.16	.51

a. Standardized regression coefficients predicting offspring occupational status from father's education and occupational status, offspring IQ, and offspring education.
b. See Jencks et al. (1979) for the meaning of the data sets.

made above in discussion of the Rosemintin hypothesis: A person's own IQ is a better predictor of his or her eventual social status than is the social status of the family that raised him or her. These data illustrate IQ's role as a somewhat inattentive gatekeeper. High IQ is one of many different assets that can assist in movement up the educational ladder, but no one is standing at the base of the ladder demanding to see an IQ score before allowing a person to start climbing.

Table 21.9 gives the most interesting data. Here, we predict occupational status from the four variables that precede it. Once again, a very clear picture emerges from all four studies. The best predictor is *education*, not IQ or family background. In fact, father's social status in these studies ceases to be

Table 21.10 The Best Predictors of a Person's Income[a]

Data Set[b]	Father's Education	Father's Occupational Status	Own Test	Own Education	Own Occupational Status
			Predictor Variables		
Veterans	−.05	.17	.21	.01	.25
Panel Study of Income Dynamics	−.01	−.01	.17	.24	.20
Talent	.07	−.02	.07	.08	.15
Olneck	−.01	.05	.14	.17	.23

a. Standardized regression coefficients predicting offspring income from father's education and occupational status, offspring IQ, offspring education, and offspring occupational status.
b. See Jencks et al. (1979) for the meaning of the data sets.

a significant predictor at all—the values for father's education and occupational status are all close to 0. With an average value of .14, IQ has only modest predictive value. It is education that best predicts differences in occupational prestige, illustrating the gatekeeping role for education on other aspects of social status.

What has happened to IQ? If we place causal interpretations on these results, IQ would still be one of the causal factors for occupational status. It is just that its role is mainly *indirect*. The major causal pathway is that IQ influences education, and then education influences occupational status; the direct effect of IQ on occupational status is small. To say the same thing in a different way, consider only those people whose highest educational attainment is a bachelor's degree. As a group, their average occupational status will exceed that of the general population. Among them, differences in IQ also predict occupational status—those with higher IQ scores will have slightly better jobs than those with lower scores—but the effect is not very large. The biggest impact of IQ in this group is to *help them get their sheepskins to begin with*.

The final data (Table 21.10) predict income from all the variables that occur before it in time. Here the numbers do not show the clear pattern that the previous ones did. Family background—at least in terms of paternal education and occupational status—is not a significant predictor. IQ has some predictive power; its average value is .15, so it has as much of a residual effect on income as it did for occupational status. The effect of educational level varies among the studies. Its average value of .13 is similar to that of IQ, but coefficients are more variable. The best predictor in three of the four studies is occupational status, but it does not play the dominant role that education did in Table 21.9 or IQ did in Table 21.8. Hence, if there is a gatekeeper for income, it is likely to be occupational status, but its role is not as strong as that of IQ for education or education for occupational status.

A Complete View: Areas of Uncertainty

In completing a puzzle for which the final picture is unknown, it is possible to make startling errors. Part of the puzzle that seems to be a large polka-dotted balloon may turn out to be a clown's tunic. Hence, it becomes important to describe the limitations and uncertainties of the puzzle.

We have only incomplete and fuzzy estimates of the extent to which genes for IQ are correlated with genes for educational attainment, occupational status, and income. Granted, there are good data using large samples for *some* of these correlations (Taubman, 1976) and data on small samples for others (e.g., Lichtenstein & Pedersen, 1997), but we lack a large body of evidence using large samples for all the genetic correlations that we would like to estimate with confidence. To complicate matters, data come from all over the industrialized world. There may be important differences between nations that influence genetic estimates.

One of the largest areas of uncertainty lies in the definition of the IQ score. Although it is the best single number to describe the results of many different intellectual and cognitive tasks, it is not the *only* way to summarize a large number of responses. One could measure specific aspects of intelligence—vocabulary, reading comprehension, mathematical reasoning, spatial ability, and memory, among others—and then do a genetic analysis of social status using all these scores instead of a single number. The available data suggest that these specific cognitive abilities (as they are often called) are heritable, but we simply do not know how the genes for these traits relate to eventual social status. It could very well turn out that we have *underestimated* the influence of genes for cognition on social stratification because we interpreted data based on the single number measuring g.

Many cognitive psychologists, while recognizing the predictive power of the IQ score, favor studying cognition using more refined variables such as executive functioning and working memory. Other scholars criticize the IQ score because—logically at least—it does not include practical intelligence or social intelligence. Once again, there are no twin or adoption data on using these approaches to measure cognition and intelligence. Many scholars hypothesize that the additional variables will add to the predictability of social status variables and/or be better predictors themselves than a single IQ score. If this is the case and if these other variables—like virtually all behavioral traits—have a moderate heritability, then we are likely to have once again underestimated the extent to which genes for intelligence also influence individual differences in social status.

We also lack twin and adoption data on how well genes for that unknown conglomeration of vocational goals, interests, personality, and motivational differences are associated with social status. These are not cognitive variables per se, but they may be very important for understanding the heritability of education, occupation, and income.

One glaring lack of research is that on the heritability of school grades, one of the direct criteria used for admission to colleges and then to graduate and professional schools. Grades have an important genetic correlation to IQ scores (Thompson, Detterman, & Plomin, 1991; Wadsworth, DeFries, Fulker, & Plomin, 1995), but admission (or lack of it) is based on GPA and not an IQ score. If grades and scores on the SAT or ACT were directly entered into the equation predicting educational level for Table 21.8, then the predictive effect of IQ score might be greatly diminished.

GENES, IQ SCORES, AND SOCIAL POLICY ●

An acerbic debate over genes, intelligence, and the very social fabric of society has persisted from Galton's time to the present. In Victorian England, cries echoed about the demise of the English population because the lower classes—presumably of lower intelligence—were having more offspring than the advantaged classes. Today, such a phenomenon has been termed "dysgenesis" (Herrnstein & Murray, 1994), with the tacit assumption that, if the phenomenon is left unchecked, the very pillars of modern social structure may crumble. It is not the province of a book like this one to advocate one social policy over another; however, it is important to bring up issues that a thoughtful reader must mull over in coming to his or her own conclusions.

First consider the term "dysgenesis." The prefix "dys" means bad or ill. Combined with "genesis," the term implies an ill, bad, or less-than-optimal genetic trend. Applied to intelligence, dysgenesis carries the implicit assumption that high intelligence is good (eugenic) and low intelligence is bad (dysgenic). This is clearly an issue of *values*. All things being equal, a majority of us wish for high intelligence in our children, but that majority quickly becomes a minority when the "all things being equal clause" is violated. If given a choice, which type of child would you prefer—a highly intelligent one who goes through life as a very unhappy person or a very happy one with less than average intelligence?

Human intelligence has advanced medicine, energy resources, transportation, commerce, and communication in ways unimagined centuries ago. Has this been good for our species? Balance for a moment the advances in modern medicine with the problems of increased population growth and utilization of resources that accompany those same advances. Our "intelligent" societies may be burning enough fossil fuels to change the ecology of the planet. Is this "better" or "superior" to a simple hunter-gatherer society that travels here and there to live off the land? Maybe "dys-genesis" involves high symbolic reasoning and its associated technocracy while "eugenesis" implies a more ecological melding of human behavior within planetary limitations. Which is really "good"?

In addition to the issue of values, there are good scientific reasons to question issues of differential reproduction as a function of IQ. Predictions often take current reproductive trends and extrapolate them well into the future. Empirically, however, reproductive trends can change quite quickly, negating long-term predictions. Examine the past century: the high birth rate among immigrant families at the turn of the 20th century, the reduction in birth rates accompanying the Great Depression, the post–World War II baby boom, and the rise in childless career women toward the end of the century. If there is one thing to be learned, it is that major social factors are associated with increases and decreases in fertility. How well, then, can one extrapolate from cross-sectional data to broad evolutionary trends that can be measured only over tens of generations?

To give a concrete example, in the middle of the 20th century, Higgins, Reed, and Reed (1962) demonstrated a slightly positive fitness effect for IQ—just the opposite of "dysgenesis." They report that previous studies in this area (see Anastasi, 1956, for a review) never counted individuals with low IQ who did not reproduce at all. Individuals with lower IQ, when they do indeed reproduce, have more children than individuals with higher IQs. The confounding factor is that individuals with low IQs simply do not reproduce as often as those with higher IQs. To give a hypothetical example, consider 100 individuals with low IQ and 100 individuals with high IQ. Half of the low-IQ folks actually reproduce, and those low-IQ individuals who do in fact reproduce have an average of three offspring. Hence, of the 100 low-IQ people, the next generation gets $100 \times .5 \times 3 = 150$ gene copies. Of the 100 individuals with high IQs, 90% reproduce, but on average they have only two children (one less than the low-IQ folks who reproduce). Their contribution to the next generation is $100 \times .9 \times 2 = 180$ gene copies. Obviously, the number of gene copies left by the high-IQ folks (180) is greater than those left by the low-IQ people (150). Is the same trend going on today? Only sound empirical data can answer that question.

Another crucial scientific observation that must always enter policy debates is the Flynn effect, described earlier in this chapter. Even if there is a selective advantage for low IQ, the mean population IQ has been *increasing*, not decreasing, over the past 100 years. Passionate argument accompanies speculation about the source behind the Flynn effect. Some, including Flynn himself, suspect that there has really been no change in the physiology behind intelligence. Instead, they argue that the rise in mean IQ scores is due to increasing sophistication in test-taking. Assume for the moment that this is true. Then how much of the observed IQ difference between people of low and high social status is due to test-taking sophistication? Certainly, any projections about "dysgenesis" must take into account differences in test-taking ability.

On the other hand, there are well-documented, long-term secular trends that definitely involve physiological changes. The increase in average height and the decrease in age of menarche are two examples. Perhaps some of the Flynn effect includes poorly understood changes in anatomy and/or physiology over time. Nutrition is one obvious candidate, but most studies have not reported significant effects for nutrition, save for extreme starvation. With the advent of radio and later television, children may have been exposed to a wider variety of problem-solving tasks as the century progressed. And two very definite results have come out of the neuroscience literature—human brains mature long after birth and, in rodents at least, experience does change the brain.

Lastly, we must recognize that industrialized societies have not in fact collapsed, as the Victorian doomsayers predicted they would, because of excessive population growth at the bottom of the IQ curve.

Many readers who reflect on these issues will conclude that the scientific terrain relevant for social policy includes large deserts and swamps bereft of data. There are vast areas of the puzzle where theoreticians enthusiastically claim the puzzle pieces fit but the observer applying simple common sense raises an eyebrow. One last question—How confident would you be in constructing social policy based on something that you really do not yet understand?

NOTES

1. The reason why the data on adult adoptive siblings have not shown the effect may be that all samples are severely restricted in range for the age of the adoptees. It would probably take a series of adult adoptees ranging in age from 20 to 80 to demonstrate the Flynn effect.

2. The McArthur project is still under way, and the twins are being followed up.

3. Technically, the natural logarithm of income is used in data analysis to make the distribution more normal. I will refer only to income, with the implicit assumption that the natural logarithm of income is the actual variable used in data analysis.

4. A few studies that contain relevant data are omitted from this table because they did not present twin correlations or results that permitted the estimation of twin correlations.

5. As with intelligence, interpretation of the common environmental influence is confounded by the high spousal correlation for educational levels. The difficulty is not the *size* of the marital correlation. One can measure that and place it into a mathematical model. The problem is the *source* of the correlation. The mathematical consequences for *mate attraction* (people are attracted to mates with similar amounts of education) are different from those on *mate propinquity* (college students associate largely with other college students and hence generate assortment for intelligence). The precise blend of propinquity and attraction that generated the marital correlations for education is unknown.

6. The offspring in this study, by Scarr and Weinberg (1994), ranged in age from 22 to 30. Hence, many of them have not completed their education or career paths.

7. The opposite of a meritocracy is a *heritocracy*, taken to an extreme in feudal society in which social status (wealthy nobility versus impoverished serf) is mostly determined by the status of one's parents. Naturally, meritocracy and heritocracy are not categories but opposite poles of a continuum on which different societies can be ranked.

8. See the notes to Table 21.6 for the references to these four data sets.

9. Once again, this technique is an approximation. For example, it does not account for the causal influence of parents with a smart offspring who take on extra jobs so that their child can attend college. Here, child IQ plays some causal role in parental income.

10. Technically, these quantities are called standardized partial regression coefficients.

● REFERENCES

Alarcon, M., Plomin, R., Fulker, D. W., Corley, R., & DeFries, J. C. (1998). Multivariate path analysis of specific cognitive abilities data at 12 years of age in the Colorado Adoption Project. *Behavior Genetics, 28,* 255-264. [Published erratum appears in *Behavior Genetics, 29,* 77]

Anastasi, A. (1956). Intelligence and family size. *Psychological Bulletin, 53,* 187-209.

Baker, L. A., Treloar, S. A., Reynolds, C. A., Heath, A. C., & Martin, N. G. (1996). Genetics of educational attainment in Australian twins: Sex differences and secular changes. *Behavior Genetics, 26,* 89-102.

Behrman, J. R., & Taubman, P. (1989). Is schooling "mostly in the genes"? *Journal of Political Economy, 97,* 1425-1446.

Bouchard, T. J., Jr. (1998). Genetic and environmental influences on adult intelligence and special mental abilities. *Human Biology, 70,* 257-279.

Bouchard, T. J., Jr., Lykken, D. T., McGue, M., Segal, N. L., & Tellegen, A. (1990). Sources of human psychological differences: The Minnesota Study of Twins Reared Apart. *Science, 250,* 223-228.

Bouchard, T. J., Jr., & McGue, M. (1981). Familial studies of intelligence: A review. *Science, 212,* 1055-1059.

Bowles, S., & Gintis, H. (2001). The inheritance of economic status: Education, class and genetics (Working Paper 01-01-005). Santa Fe, NM: Santa Fe Institute.

Cardon, L. R., & Fulker, D. W. (1994). A model of developmental change in hierarchical phenotypes with application to specific cognitive abilities. *Behavior Genetics, 24,* 1-16.

Cattell, R. B. (1936). Is our national intelligence declining? *Eugenics Review, 28,* 181.

Cattell, R. B. (1951). The fate of national intelligence: Test of a thirteen-year prediction. *Eugenics Review, 42,* 136-148.

Chambers, M. (1999). *Academic achievement and IQ: A longitudinal genetic analysis.* Unpublished doctoral dissertation, University of Colorado.

Cherny, S. S., Fulker, D. W., Emde, R. N., Robinson, J., Corley, R. P., Reznick, J. S., et al. (1994). A developmental-genetic analysis of continuity and change in the Bayley Mental Development Index from 14 to 24 months: The MacArthur Longitudinal Twin Study. *Psychological Science, 5,* 354-360.

DeFries, J. C., Plomin, R., & Fulker, D. W. (Eds.). (1994). *Nature and nurture during middle childhood.* Cambridge, MA: Blackwell.

Finkel, D., Pedersen, N. L., McGue, M., & McClearn, G. E. (1995). Heritability of cognitive abilities in adult twins: Comparison of Minnesota and Swedish data. *Behavior Genetics, 25,* 421-431.

Flynn, J. R. (1984). The mean IQ of Americans: Massive gains 1932 to 1978. *Psychological Bulletin, 95,* 29-51.

Flynn, J. R. (1987). Massive IQ gains in 14 nations: What IQ tests really measure. *Psychological Bulletin, 101,* 171-191.

Flynn, J. R. (1998). IQ gains over time: Toward finding the causes. In U. Neisser (Ed.), *The rising curve: Long-term gains in IQ and related measures* (pp. 25-66). Washington, DC: American Psychological Association.

Heath, A. C., Berg, K., Eaves, L. J., Solaas, M. H., Corey, L., Sundet, J., et al. (1985). Educational policy and the heritability of educational attainment. *Nature, 314,* 734-736.

Herrnstein, R. J., & Murray, C. (1994). *The bell curve: Intelligence and class structure in American life.* New York: Free Press.

Higgins, J. V., Reed, E. W., & Reed, S. C. (1962). Intelligence and family size: A paradox resolved. *Social Biology, 9,* 84-90.

Hunt, E. (1995). The role of intelligence in modern society. *American Scientist, 83,* 356-368.

Jencks, C., Bartlett, S., Corcoran, M., Crouse, J., Eaglesfield, D., Jackson, G., et al. (1979). *Who gets ahead? The determinants of economic success in America.* New York: Basic Books.

Lewontin, R. C., Rose, S., & Kamin, L. J. (1984). *Not in our genes: Biology, ideology, and human nature.* New York: Pantheon.

Lichtenstein, P., & Pedersen, N. L. (1997). Does genetic variance for cognitive abilities account for genetic variance in educational achievement and occupational status? A study of twins reared apart and twins reared together. *Social Biology, 44,* 77-90.

Loehlin, J. C., Horn, J. M., & Willerman, L. (1994). Differential inheritance of mental abilities in the Texas Adoption Project. *Intelligence, 19,* 325-336.

Loehlin, J. C., Horn, J. M., & Willerman, L. (1997). Heredity, environment and IQ in the Texas Adoption Project. In R. J. Sternberg & E. L. Grigorenko (Eds.), *Intelligence, heredity, and environment* (pp. 105-125). New York: Cambridge University Press.

McGue, M., Bouchard, T. J., Jr., Iacono, W. G., & Lykken, D. T. (1993). Behavior genetics of cognitive ability: A life-span perspective. In R. Plomin & G. E. McClearn (Eds.),

Nature, nurture & psychology (pp. 59-76). Washington, DC: American Psychological Association.

Miller, P., Mulvey, C., & Martin, N. G. (1995). What do twin studies reveal about the economic returns to education? A comparison of Australian and U.S. findings. *American Economic Review, 85*, 586-599.

Neisser, U. (Ed.). (1998). *The rising curve: Long-term gains in IQ and related measures*. Washington, DC: American Psychological Association.

Neisser, U., Boodoo, G., Bouchard, T. J. J., Boykin,. A. W., Brody, N., Ceci, S. J., et al. (1996). Intelligence: Knowns and unknowns. *American Psychologist, 51*, 77-101.

Pedersen, N. L., Plomin, R., Nesselroade, J. R., & McClearn, G. E. (1992). A quantitative genetic analysis of cognitive abilities during the second half of the life span. *Psychological Science, 3*, 346-353.

Petrill, S. A., Plomin, R., Berg, S., Johansson, B., Pedersen, N. L., Ahern, F., et al. (1998). The genetic and environmental relationship between general and specific cognitive abilities in twins age 80 and older. *Psychological Science, 9*, 183-189.

Plomin, R. (1999). Genetics and general cognitive ability. *Nature, 402*, C25-C29.

Plomin, R., & DeFries, J. C. (1985). *Origins of individual differences in infancy: The Colorado adoption project*. Orlando, FL: Academic Press.

Plomin, R., DeFries, J. C., & Fulker, D. W. (1988). *Nature and nurture during infancy and early childhood*. New York: Cambridge University Press.

Plomin, R., Fulker, D. W., Corley, R., & DeFries, J. C. (1997). Nature, nurture, and cognitive development from 1 to 16 years: A parent-offspring adoption study. *Psychological Science, 8*, 442-447.

Plomin, R., Pedersen, N. L., Lichtenstein, P., & McClearn, G. E. (1994). Variability and stability in cognitive abilities are largely genetic later in life. *Behavior Genetics, 24*, 207-215.

Rice, T., Carey, G., Fulker, D. W., & DeFries, J. C. (1989). Multivariate path analysis of specific cognitive abilities in the Colorado Adoption Project: Conditional path model of assortative mating. *Behavior Genetics, 19*, 195-207.

Rijsdijk, F. V., Vernon, P. A., & Boomsma, D. I. (2002). Application of hierarchical genetic models to Raven and Wais subtests: A Dutch twin study. *Behavior Genetics, 32*, 199-210.

Rowe, D. C., Jacobson, K. C., & Van den Oord, E. J. (1999). Genetic and environmental influences on vocabulary IQ: Parental education level as moderator. *Child Development, 70*, 1151-1162.

Rowe, D. C., Vesterdal, W. J., & Rodgers, J. L. (1998). Herrnstein's syllogism: Genetic and shared environmental influences on IQ, education, and income. *Intelligence, 26*, 405-423.

Scarr, S., & Weinberg, R. A. (1994). Educational and occupational achievements of brothers and sisters in adoptive and biologically related families. *Behavior Genetics, 24*, 301-325.

Scarr, S., Weinberg, R. A., & Waldman, I. D. (1993). IQ correlations in transracial adoptive families. *Intelligence, 17*, 541-555.

Swan, G. E., Carmelli, D., Reed, T., Harshfield, G. A., Fabsitz, R. R., & Eslinger, P. J. (1990). Heritability of cognitive performance in aging twins: The National Heart, Lung, and Blood Institute Twin Study. *Archives of Neurology, 47*, 259-262.

Swan, G. E., LaRue, A., Carmelli, D., Reed, T. E., & Fabsitz, R. R. (1992). Decline in cognitive performance in aging twins: Heritability and biobehavioral predictors from the National Heart, Lung, and Blood Institute Twin Study. *Archives of Neurology, 49,* 476-481.

Tambs, K., Sundet, J. M., & Magnus, P. (1986). Genetic and environmental contributions to the covariation between the Wechsler Adult Intelligence Scale (WAIS) subtests: A study of twins. *Behavior Genetics, 16*, 475-491.

Tambs, K., Sundet, J. M., Magnus, P., & Berg, K. (1989). Genetic and environment contributions to the covariation between occupational status, educational attainment, and IQ: A study of twins. *Behavior Genetics, 19*, 209-221.

Taubman, P. (1976). The determinants of earnings: Genetic, family and other environments: A study of white male twins. *American Economic Review, 66*, 858-870.

Teasdale, T. W., & Owen, D. R. (1981). Social class correlations among separately adopted siblings and unrelated individuals adopted together. *Behavior Genetics, 11*, 577-588.

Teasdale, T. W., & Owen, D. R. (1984). Heredity and familial environment in intelligence and educational level: A sibling study. *Nature, 309*, 620-622.

Teasdale, T. W., & Owen, D. R. (1986). The influence of paternal social class on intelligence and educational level in male adoptees and non-adoptees. *British Journal of Educational Psychology, 56*, 3-12.

Thompson, L. A., Detterman, D. K., & Plomin, R. (1991). Associations between cognitive abilities and scholastic achievement: Genetic overlap but environmental differences. *Psychological Science, 2*, 158-165.

Tuddenham, R. D. (1948). Soldier intelligence in World Wars I and II. *American Psychologist, 3*, 54-56.

Vogler, G. P., & Fulker, D. W. (1983). Familial resemblance for educational attainment. *Behavior Genetics, 13*, 341-354.

Wadsworth, S. J., DeFries, J. C., Fulker, D. W., & Plomin, R. (1995). Cognitive ability and academic achievement in the Colorado Adoption Project: A multivariate genetic analysis of parent-offspring and sibling data. *Behavior Genetics, 25*, 1-15.

Weinberg, R. A., Scarr, S., & Waldman, I. D. (1992). The Minnesota Transracial Adoption Study: A follow-up of IQ test performance at adolescence. *Intelligence, 16*, 117-135.

White, K. R. (1982). The relation between socioeconomic status and academic achievement. *Psychological Bulletin, 91*, 461-481.

Wilson, R. S. (1983). The Louisville twin study: Developmental synchronies in behavior. *Child Development, 54*, 298-316.

Wilson, R. S. (1986). Continuity and change in cognitive ability profile. *Behavior Genetics, 16*, 45-60.

CHAPTER **22**

PERSONALITY

PERSONALITY: THE PHENOTYPE ●
AND ITS MEASUREMENT

The word "personality" has various meanings that range from the qualities of an individual person to evaluative judgments about those qualities (e.g., "She has a great personality."). Genetics has studied personality almost exclusively in terms of psychological trait theory. Trait theory dissects personality into a series of variables called traits and then measures individual differences in those traits. To illustrate, consider the trait of Social Closeness measured in the Multidimensional Personality Questionnaire or MPQ[1] developed by Auke Tellegen (1985; Tellegen et al., 1988). People low on this trait are content to be by themselves and do not go out of their way to seek social interactions; people high on the trait would rather be with other people than be alone and actively pursue social situations. It is assumed that knowledge of the level of a person's Social Closeness can make predictions about the person. For example, if Sam is low on Social Closeness, then he is likely to enjoy solitary leisure habits like reading. If Betty is high on Social Closeness but also enjoys reading, then she is more apt to join a reading group than is Sam.

There are various ways to rank order individuals on Social Closeness. *Behavioral assessment* focuses on the actual behavior of people like Sam and

Betty. It would measure such behaviors as the number of social groups that Sam and Betty belong to, the percentage of their leisure time spent in solitary versus social activities, and the extent to which they engage strangers in conversation. Behavioral assessments of personality are often done in laboratory situations—for example, place Sam and Betty alone together in a room and measure the amount of conversation initiated by each one. Because of the large commitment of time and money to behavioral assessment, there are few data sets on the genetics of personality measured by this technique.

A second generic way of measuring a trait like Social Closeness taps *opinions* and *perceptions* about Sam's and Betty's behavior instead of the behavior itself. One example of this measurement mode is the *rating scale*. Here, a friend of Sam is presented with a description of Social Closeness, is asked to think about Sam with relation to all the other people she or he knows, and then is requested to rate Sam on, say, a 5-point scale—well below average, below average, average, above average, or well above average. By far the most common technique is to have the person rate himself or herself, in which case the technique is most often called *self-report*.

A second version of the self-report, the opinion/perception mode of measurement, involves presenting the person with a simple statement and then asking the person to indicate whether the statement is true or false in relation to that person. An example statement (or *item*, as they are more commonly referred to) is "I find it hard to think of things to say when I meet a new person." People answering true to this item are assumed to be lower on Social Closeness than those answering false. Typically, a personality questionnaire will contain a number of items relating to Social Closeness, and a person's score will consist of the sum of responses over all the relevant items. If Betty scores higher on this sum than Sam, then she is said to be higher on the trait of Social Closeness than is Sam.

The majority of personality data on adult twins and adoptees have been gathered using self-report questionnaires or rating scales. The reason for this is simple—cost. It is much less expensive to have a person complete a questionnaire and then optically scan the answer sheet than to bring the person into a laboratory and pay for a trained research assistant to record the person's behavior.

Finally, personality measurement and assessment depends on the age of the person being assessed. All the above techniques apply to adolescent and adult personality for the simple reason that young children lack the reading and interpretive skills to complete a contemporary, standardized personality inventory. Assessment of a child's personality must rely on the reports of informants such as the parents or teachers of the child. This type of assessment has problems of its own. The review of the literature that follows will focus first on the adult personality (i.e., assessment in the late teens and

Table 22.1   Lower-Order Personality Traits Measured by the Multidimensional Personality Questionnaire

Trait	Low Scorers Say True to the Items	High Scorers Say True to the Items
Well-Being	I am seldom "really happy."	I am a happy person.
Social Potency	On social occasions, I like to stay in the background.	I like to take charge of things.
Achievement	I usually work hard enough to just get by.	I like to put in long hours to accomplish something.
Social Closeness	I would be happy to live alone.	I prefer living with other people than living alone.
Stress Reaction	I seldom get worried.	I easily get upset.
Alienation	People treat me fairly.	Life has given me a raw deal.
Aggression	I prefer to turn the other cheek.	If someone crosses me, I will let them know about it.
Control vs. Impulsivity	I usually act before thinking.	I like to have detailed plans before doing something.
Harm Avoidance vs. Danger Seeking	I like to do something dangerous just for the thrill of it.	I prefer to remain safe and sound in most things.
Traditionalism	Traditional values of obedience and morality need to be rethought.	People should have more respect for authority than they do.
Absorption	Music never reminds me of colors, smells, or sights.	I can lose contact with reality watching a beautiful sunset.

beyond) and then discuss the issue of continuity (both of assessment and of substantive issues) between childhood and adulthood.

THE ORGANIZATION OF ADULT PERSONALITY ●

All omnibus personality inventories measure several different traits. For example, the MPQ measures the 11 traits listed in Table 22.1. How do these different traits relate to one another? This has been a matter of considerable—and still unresolved—debate among psychologists. Current thinking views traits as being *hierarchically organized*. The items from a single scale of a personality questionnaire (e.g., Well-Being in Table 22.1) are summed to form a score on a *lower-order trait*. Because the scores on some lower-order traits correlate with the scores on other lower-order traits, a *higher-order trait* is postulated.

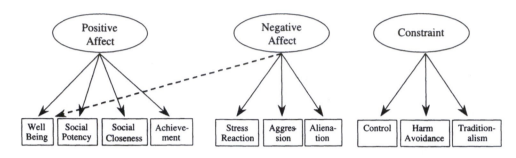

Figure 22.1   An Example of the Hierarchical Organization of Personality According to Tellegen's Multidimensional Personality Questionnaire

Figure 22.1 illustrates the hierarchical model as applied to the MPQ. Auke Tellegen, the developer of the MPQ, noted that there were positive correlations among the traits of Well-Being, Social Potency, Social Closeness, and Achievement. That is, someone who scored high on any one of these four lower-order traits had a small tendency to score above the mean on the other three traits. Using a statistical procedure called factor analysis, Tellegen postulated the existence of a higher-order trait to account for this observation. He called the trait Positive Affect. Similar observations and statistical analysis led him to postulate two other higher-order traits, Negative Affect and Constraint, that accounted for the correlations among the remaining scales.

It is essential to recognize two features of the hierarchical model. First, there is not always a simple correspondence between lower- and higher-order traits. This is illustrated by the dashed arrow from Negative Affect to Well-Being. This represents the fact that the lower-order trait of Well-Being measures aspects of two higher-order traits, Positive Affect and Negative Affect.

A second important point concerning the hierarchical model is an admonition against thinking of lower-order traits as being nothing more than manifestations of higher-order traits. For example, Social Potency has very important attributes that are specific to it and quite different from its relationship with Positive Affect. Similarly, the relationship among the higher-order trait of Negative Affect and its lower-order traits of Stress Reaction, Alienation, and Aggression is not akin to the relationship between the H_2O molecule and its appearance as a liquid (water), a solid (ice), and a gas (vapor). There are aspects of, say, Stress Reaction that are unique to this lower-order trait. A better analogy is to think of the higher-order traits as a genus and the lower-order traits as the various species belonging to that genus. Each species has characteristics that are unique to that species and make it different from the other species in the genus.

In the discussion of adult personality, we rely on two different theoretical systems, both of which use trait theory and self-report personality inventories. The first is the MPQ, which is used to illustrate the genetics of personality for lower-order traits. The second is the personality system evolved by the late Hans Eysenck that focuses on the higher-order traits of Extraversion (which is equivalent to Positive Affect in Tellegen's MPQ) and Neuroticism (which is equivalent to Negative Affect). Finally, the term "adult personality" refers to data collected on people from their mid- to late teenage years onward. It is used to avoid the cumbersome—but more exact—phrase "adult and/or late adolescent personality."

GENETICS OF ADULT PERSONALITY TRAITS ●

The Empirical Data

First let us examine data on the higher-order dimensions of Extraversion (or Positive Affect) and Neuroticism (Negative Affect) to get a generic impression of how similar relatives are for personality. Also, because there are more genetic data on these two personality traits than on any others, we can examine the consistency of the data across studies.

Table 22.2 presents the correlations originally compiled by Loehlin (1992) and updated for this book from several large studies around the world using adult twins raised together. First, examine the sample sizes (i.e., number of twin pairs). They are all quite large. Next, for each study compare the correlation for MZ pairs with the correlation for DZ pairs for Extraversion. For each study, the correlation for MZs is higher than the correlation for DZs. Do the same for Neuroticism. Again, the MZ twins consistently resemble each other more than the DZ twins. Finally, examine the consistency of the correlations across studies. Despite the fact that the studies come from different countries and use different personality inventories to measure Extraversion and Neuroticism, the correlations are remarkably consistent. With three exceptions, identical twins have correlations that range from .40 to .60, while those for fraternal twins usually range from about .10 to .25. Remember these figures.

The data in Table 22.2 lead to two of the consistent findings in the personality literature. First, note that all the correlations for identical twins are significantly less than 1.0. This leads to the major conclusion that *identical twins are not identical in personality*. They are *similar* to each other, but they are far from carbon copies when it comes to their degree of shyness, forcefulness, and sociability (for Extraversion) or worrisomeness, irritability, and affective lability (for Neuroticism). The second conclusion is that

Table 22.2 Studies of Extraversion and Neuroticism in Twins Raised Together

| | Sample Size | | Correlations | | | |
| | | | Extraversion | | Neuroticism | |
Study	MZ	DZ	MZ	DZ	MZ	DZ
1[a]	303	172	.51	.20	.46	.07
2[b]	481	312	.60	.24	.52	.24
3[c]	4987	7790	.51	.21	.50	.23
4[d]	1799	1103	.52	.17	.50	.23
5[e]	2320	4824	.48	.14	.39	.15
6[f]	453	362	.39	−.04	.35	.10
7[g]	123	127	.55	.23	.41	.18
8[h]	600	304	.56	.28	.53	.13

a. Data are from Eaves, Eysenck, and Martin (1989).
b. Data are from Loehlin and Nichols (1976).
c. Data are from Floderus-Myrhed, Pederson, and Rasmuson (1980).
d. Data are from Martin and Jardine (1986).
e. Data are from Rose, Koskenvuo, Kaprio, Sarna, and Langinvainio (1988).
f. Data are from Heath, Neale, Kessler, Eaves, and Kendler (1992).
g. Data are from Jang, Livesley, Vernon, and Jackson (1996).
h. Data are from Riemann, Angleitner, and Strelau (1997).

identical twins are more similar than fraternal twins despite the fact that both types of twins have been raised together, day in and day out, for all of their childhood, adolescence, and early adulthood.

Although the second conclusion is consistent with a genetic influence on personality, an informed critic could raise several objections before concluding that the patterning of correlation does indeed imply a genetic influence. Identical twins are often treated as a unit and often share the same friends, and the sheer fact that they physically resemble each other so much may induce some behavioral similarity. Could these factors contribute to the greater similarity within MZ pairs than within DZ pairs?

One answer to this question is to examine the data on twins raised apart. Table 22.3 presents the correlations for Extraversion and Neuroticism for studies of twins raised apart and together. For a single trait and for a single zygosity, compare the two columns of correlations for twins raised together and apart. For both Extraversion and Neuroticism, there is a slight—but only slight—tendency for twins raised together to be more similar than twins raised apart. The difference in correlations between twins raised together and apart does not reach overall statistical significance. This leads to a quite

Table 22.3   Studies of Extraversion and Neuroticism in Twins Raised Apart

| | Extraversion | | | | Neuroticism | | | |
| | MZ | | DZ | | MZ | | DZ | |
Study	Together	Apart	Together	Apart	Together	Apart	Together	Apart
1	.33	.38	.13	.12	.32	.25	.10	.11
2	.54	.30	.06	.04	.41	.25	.24	.28
3	.63	.34	.18	−.07	.54	.61	.41	.29
4	.42	.61			.38	.53		

This table is adapted from Loehlin (1992).

startling conclusion—*twins who are raised together in the same household for the better part of 20 years are no more or only slightly more similar to each other than twins who are raised in different households!* This has very important implications for the role of the family environment in making relatives similar in personality, a topic that will be dealt with later.

Is there any independent way to verify this striking and unexpected conclusion? The clearest and most salient way is to examine the similarity of genetically unrelated individuals who live in the same family. If the rearing environment has little influence on making relatives similar, then the correlations for adoptive relatives should be small and close to 0.0. Of course, there is seldom a real-world equivalent to adoptive twins, but it is possible to examine the correlations for adoptive parents and their adopted children and the correlations for adoptive siblings. Table 22.4 presents these data.

For extraversion, there is virtually no resemblance between adoptive parents and their adopted children—all three correlations differ only trivially from 0.0. Statistically, none of the three correlations for adoptive siblings is significantly different from 0.0. All of the correlations for neuroticism are positive—something that one would not expect if the true correlation were really 0.0. However, none of these correlations differs significantly from 0.0. (The correlation of .23 for adoptive sibs in Study 1 shows a trend toward significance but because of small sample size fails to reach it.) The conclusion from the adoption data verifies the data on twins raised apart: *If the family environment does make relatives similar to one another for personality, the effect is very, very small.*

Perhaps the level at which personality is studied contributes to these conclusions. After all, extraversion and neuroticism are two higher-order traits, each composed of several lower-order traits. Perhaps there is considerable variability in the lower-order traits. Some lower-order traits may be highly

Table 22.4   Studies of Extraversion and Neuroticism in Adoptive Families

Study	Number of Pairings	Correlations Extraversion	Correlations Neuroticism
Adoptive parents/ adopted siblings			
1[a]	220	−.02	.07
2[b]	369	.01	.02
3[b]	504	.01	.06
Adopted siblings			
1[a]	58	−.11	.23
2[b]	75	.07	.05
3[b]	125	−.13	.09

SOURCE: This table is adapted from Loehlin (1992).
a. Data are from Eaves, Eysenck, and Martin (1989).
b. Data are from Loehlin (1992), Tables 2.4 and 3.5.

heritable; others may have little heritability. Maybe the family environment influences a few of—but not all—the lower-order traits. Some of these influences could cancel each other out when looking at higher-order traits and lead to data such as that in Tables 22.2, 22.3, and 22.4.

We can examine this possibility by concentrating on the lower-order traits of the MPQ, data for which are presented in Table 22.5. Several salient aspects of Table 22.5 are obvious from eyeball inspection of the correlations. First, note that the correlation between spouses is effectively 0.0 for every trait except for Alienation and Traditionalism. This pattern was independently replicated in a much larger study (Finkel & McGue, 1997) and reinforces the conclusion given in an earlier chapter that there is little assortative mating for personality.

Second, compare the column for MZ apart to the column for DZ apart. In all cases except Social Closeness, for which the difference is trivial, the correlations for identical twins raised apart exceed those for fraternal twins raised apart. This suggests that genetics play some part in twin resemblance; otherwise, the two columns should have similar numbers. Third, compare the column for the correlations for identical twins raised together) (MZ together) to the column of fraternal twins raised together (DZ together). Once again, the correlations for identical twins exceed those for fraternal twins. This is an independent argument for the heritability of personality traits. Fourth, compare the correlations between twins raised apart and twins raised together (i.e., the column for MZ apart versus MZ together and the

Table 22.5 Kinship Correlations for the Lower-Order Scales of the Multidimensional Personality Questionnaire

Trait	Spouses (N = 103)	Together				Apart	
		Parent-Offspring (N = 168)	Sibs (N = 194)	DZ Twins (N = 114)	MZ Twins (N = 217)	DZ Twins (N = 27)	MZ Twins (N = 44)
Well-Being	−.02	.16	.19	.23	.58	.18	.48
Social Potency	−.20	.19	.21	.08	.65	.27	.56
Achievement	−.02	.11	.05	.13	.51	.07	.36
Social Closeness	.12	.14	.07	.24	.57	.30	.29
Stress Reaction	−.04	.24	.23	.24	.52	.27	.61
Alienation	.54	.27	.16	.38	.55	.18	.48
Aggression	.01	.18	.28	.14	.43	.06	.46
Control	.05	.13	.08	−.06	.41	.03	.50
Harm Avoidance	.06	.15	.19	.17	.55	.24	.49
Traditionalism	.42	.27	.37	.47	.50	.39	.53
Absorption	.08	.13	.19	.41	.49	.21	.61

SOURCE: Family data are from Carey (unpublished) and Carey and Rice (1983). Twin data are from Tellegen et al. (1988).

column for DZ apart versus DZ together). How different are these estimates? A simple eyeball inspection of these figures suggests that overall, there is not much difference—the correlations for twins raised apart are quite similar to those for twins raised together. These data, along with other twin data on lower-order personality traits, suggest that the pattern for the higher-order traits is not the result of "cancellation." The genetics of lower-order traits parallel those for higher-order traits—identical twin correlations are in the .40 to .60 range; fraternal twin correlations are in the .10 to .50 area; and correlations for twins raised apart are similar to those for twins raised together.

Before discussing the implications of these results, it is important to comment on the lower-order MPQ trait of traditionalism. The post–World War II era witnessed considerable interest in this trait when psychologists researched the question of why so many people in Germany and German-occupied territories became ardent followers of Nazism. What emerged from the research was a personality trait—termed Authoritarianism at that time (Adorno, Frenkel-Brunswick, Levinson, & Sanford, 1950)—which is tapped by the traditionalism scale of the MPQ. People high on the trait place important emphasis on established morality, religion, and obedience to authority. Low scorers are not amoral and unreligious; rather, they tend to be more freethinking about social issues and obedience to established authority. The key point here is that personality dimensions that tap social attitudes are still heritable, but unlike most other lower-order traits, they are influenced by family environment. It also should be realized that this is a replicable finding reported in other samples using other inventories (Beer, Arnold, & Loehlin, 1998; Eaves et al., 1989; Eaves et al., 1999; Truett, Eaves, Meyer, Heath, & Martin, 1992).

The Loehlin and Nichols Observations

The generalizations made above about the genetics of adult personality are not new. A quarter of a century ago, John Loehlin and Robert Nichols (1976) published the results of a study on 850 pairs of twins. In summarizing their findings, they stated

The differences between identical and fraternal twin correlations did not appear to be consistently greater for some traits than for others. . . . the body of data we have surveyed is substantial enough so that it becomes difficult to defend the proposition that large and consistent trait-to-trait differences in the resemblance of identical- and fraternal-twin pairs are characteristic of traits in the personality . . . domain. (p. 86)

Because heritability is a function of the difference between identical and fraternal twin correlations, the Loehlin and Nichols hypothesis may be restated succinctly in the following form: *There is little differential heritability across personality traits.* That is, personality traits have heritabilities in the moderate range of .40 to .60. It is simply *not* the case that some personality traits have very high heritabilities (i.e., .80 or above), whereas others have low heritabilities (i.e., .20 or less).

In the same work, Loehlin and Nichols also commented on the role of family environment:

Thus, a consistent—though perplexing—pattern is emerging from the data (and it is not purely idiosyncratic to our study). Environment carries substantial weight in determining personality—it appears to account for at least half the variance—but that environment is one for which twin pairs are correlated close to zero. (Loehlin & Nichols, 1976, p. 92)

This conclusion—offered 25 years ago—implies that there is little influence of family environment on personality traits. Otherwise, the correlation between the environments of twins would be substantial. We witnessed the lack of evidence for family environment in creating similarity among relatives for extraversion and neuroticism. Although this theme has been echoed continually throughout the behavioral genetics literature (e.g., Rowe, 1994; Rowe & Plomin, 1981; Scarr & McCartney, 1983), it has only recently gained attention from the wider audience of behavioral scientists (Harris, 1995, 1998). Arguably, it is one of the most important findings of behavioral genetics, and we will discuss it later.

As we examine other issues about personality, it is important to keep in mind both of these observations from Loehlin and Nichols—little differential heritability and the lack of evidence for strong family-environment effects for making relatives similar in their personalities.

Sex Differences in the Heritability of Personality

It is obvious that young boys and girls are treated differently simply because of their gender. Does this differential treatment result in some traits being more heritable in males than in females? The discussion of heritability in Chapter 18 stressed the importance of environmental variation. If everyone is treated the same environmentally, then individual differences are mostly genetic and heritability will be large. But if individuals receive very different environmental treatments, then heritability will be smaller. It is perfectly plausible that young girls may be treated more similarly than young boys for one personality trait, but the opposite may happen for a different trait.

The literature is very consistent in finding that males and females can have different heritabilities for personality traits (Carey & Rice, 1983; Eaves, D'Onofrio, & Russell, 1999; Eaves et al., 1989; Finkel & McGue, 1997). But this is only part of the story. Table 22.6 presents estimates of broad-sense heritability for males and females along with the results of statistical tests of differences in heritability (the data are from Finkel & McGue, 1997). Of the 11 lower-order traits, 3 have significant differences in heritability. On two of the traits, Alienation and Control, males have a greater heritability than females. For the third trait, Absorption, heritability is greater in women than in men.

But examine the magnitude of the differences in heritability. The largest difference is for Alienation, for which the heritabilities are .39 (females) and .61 (males). Both of these numbers are within the limits of the Loehlin and Nichols observations. In short, although these differences are statistically significant, heritabilities for both males and females fall into the moderate range.

We can now summarize the issue of differential heritability in a single statement: Males and females are much more similar in terms of the magnitude of genetic influences for personality than they are different. The Loehlin

Table 22.6   Sex Differences in Heritability for the Multidimensional Personality Questionnaire

	Heritability		Significant Sex Differences?
	Females	*Males*	
Well-Being	.40	.40	No
Social Potency	.54	.53	No
Achievement	.38	.32	No
Social Closeness	.47	.44	No
Stress Reaction	.45	.43	No
Alienation	.39	.61	Yes
Aggression	.39	.35	No
Control	.33	.47	Yes
Harm Avoidance	.45	.46	No
Traditionalism	.55	.52	No
Absorption	.44	.26	Yes

SOURCE: Data are from Finkel and McGue (1997).

and Nichols hypothesis holds equally well for males and females. Whatever sex differences have been found and reported, albeit statistically significant, are not large. It is certainly not the case that one personality trait has a very large heritability in males and an insignificant heritability in females.

Continuity and Change in Adult Personality

The Empirical Data

Consider Sam and Steve, a pair of siblings close in age who have recently moved out of their parents' home and begun their adult lives in separate households. As they develop their own circle of friends, embark on different occupations, marry, and have children, will their personalities diverge? Or might age and the absence of their intense sibling rivalry in childhood and adolescence make Sam and Steve more similar to each other? Or maybe the two effects cancel each other out, so that with a large number of Sams and Steves there is no change in similarity over time.

From a scientific perspective, we should ask whether the correlation for relatives changes with age. A small but rather convincing literature suggests that there is indeed change, but that during the adult years the magnitude of change is relatively small. Studies of large samples have been able to find statistically significant effects in the form that DZ twins become less similar over time, but the magnitude of the change is small and of little practical value (Eaves & Eysenck, 1976; Martin & Jardine, 1986). Twins past their retirement age have correlations that are not appreciably different from those of younger twins (Pedersen & Reynolds, 1998).

A second related issue is the extent to which Sam's and Steve's individual personalities stay the same or change with time. Do the "slings and arrows of outrageous fortune" change personality, or do we remain fundamentally the same? The answer to this question varies according to the age of maturity of the individuals in the study, the type of personality inventory used, the time period between observations, and other factors. In general, however, studies of adults about age 30 and older show rather strong contiguity in personality, in the sense that correlations between time points varying from 5 to 10 years are often .60 or higher (Costa & McCrae, 1988; Pedersen & Reynolds, 1998).[1] Stability from the late teens to early adulthood may be somewhat lower, but not much (McGue, Bacon, & Lykken, 1993).

A more pertinent question explores the reasons for the continuity and change in adult personality. To what extent do genes contribute to continuity and change? Perhaps early experiences act as a glue that "cements" personality early on, so that most of the adult continuity is due to the environment. On the other hand, perhaps genes are a major source of continuity and the immediate environment induces small changes in personality. There is no overwhelming body of empirical data that addresses this important issue, but the results of the few available studies are consistent (McGue et al., 1993; Pedersen & Reynolds, 1998; Viken, Rose, Kaprio, & Koskenvuo, 1994)—the long-term stability of personality is due mostly to genes.

Table 22.7 illustrates the type of data used to make this conclusion. The sample is a small number of twins who initially took the MPQ between ages 17 and 30 and were then tested 10 years later. The correlations in the column labeled "Stability" treat each twin pair as two separate individuals; the numbers indicate how well we can predict adult personality over a 10-year period. The two columns labeled "Same Time" give the correlations for MZ and DZ twins when both twins are measured at the same time. Notice that the MZ and the DZ correlations are on the same order as the respective columns in Table 22.5, although the DZ correlations tend to vary a bit more because of small sample size. The columns labeled "Different Time" give the correlation between one twin's score at the first testing and his or her twin partner's score 10 years later—that is, the data indicate how well Sam's score at a given time predicts Steve's score measured 10 years later.

Run your eyes over the first three correlations of a row—the stability correlation, the MZ (Same Time) correlation, and the MZ (Different Time)

Table 22.7   Twin Correlations in Adult Personality When Traits Are Measured at the Same Time and at Different Times

	Stability	MZ (N = 79)		DZ (N = 48)	
		Same Time	Different Time	Same Time	Different Time
Well-Being	.50	.42	.40	.15	.07
Social Potency	.62	.64	.54	.09	.09
Achievement	.48	.40	.24	−.08	−.03
Social Closeness	.55	.53	.47	.20	.10
Stress Reaction	.53	.46	.41	.03	.01
Alienation	.40	.48	.27	.34	.06
Aggression	.54	.60	.43	−.11	−.11
Control	.55	.49	.45	.10	.01
Harm Avoidance	.64	.54	.43	.30	.30
Traditionalism	.47	.45	.30	.32	.12
Absorption	.69	.60	.53	.46	.40

SOURCE: Adapted from McGue and Lykken (1993).

correlations. Do you notice a pattern as you move from one lower-order trait to another? Generally, the Stability coefficient is the highest and the Different Time correlation is the lowest of the three entries. Although this pattern stands out, the fundamental observation is that the three values *do not differ very much*. This tells us that MZ twins are almost as similar when they are measured 10 years apart as when they are measured at the same time. Sam's personality right now can predict Steve's personality 10 years later almost as well as it can predict Steve's personality right now. Furthermore, the extent to which the characteristics of members of MZ twin pairs can predict each other's personalities over time is lower than—but not *much* lower than—the extent to which an individual's own score can predict his or her own score 10 years later. That is, Sam's score predicts Steve's score 10 years later only slightly worse than Sam's score predicts his own later score.

The correlations for DZ twins are lower than those for MZ twins, and both sets of DZ correlations (Same Time and Different Time) are considerably lower than the Stability coefficients. Perhaps because of the small sample size, the correlations for DZ twins tested at the same time are not significantly higher than the correlations over the 10-year interval, but there is a faint patterning similar to that of the MZ twins. If Sam and Steve were fraternal twins, then Sam's score at a given time could predict Steve's score 10 years later almost as well at it could predict Steve's score at the same time that Sam's was measured.

Table 22.8   Hypothetical Correlations for Longitudinal Twin Data Under Different Models
of Stability

		Correlations			
		MZ		DZ	
Stability Due Solely to	Stability	Same Time	Different Time	Same Time	Different Time
Family environment	.60	.60	.60	.60	.60
Nonfamily environment	.60	.40	.00	.20	.00
Genes	.60	.60	.60	.30	.30

What do these patterns mean? The meaning is best illustrated by making
up correlation coefficients under different models for the source of stability
in personality. Examine Table 22.8, which does just that. If the stability of
adult personality were due exclusively to the factors involved with the early
family environment, then the twin correlations should equal the stability
coefficients and the MZ correlations should equal the DZ correlations. If the
stability came from the environment, but *not* the *family* environment, then
the pattern should be a high stability coefficient but twin correlations at different times that are close to zero. Finally, if stability were a matter of genes,
then the patterning of the last row of Table 22.8 would be· evident in the
empirical data.

Because the patterning of the data is closest to the last row, the data suggest that the major source of personality stability resides in genes, with a
small contribution from the environment (but not the family environment).
This result is not peculiar to this study. Both Viken et al. (1994) and Pedersen
and Reynolds (1998) replicated this finding, using much larger samples of
twins on the traits of extraversion and neuroticism.

Before we discuss theories that can account for these findings, a cautionary word is necessary.[2] There is a great deal of difference between the
phrase "genes are the major source of personality stability" and its frequent
misinterpretation as "genes fix one's personality." Although it is true that
genes are the principal reason for stability, it is equally true that adult personality is *not* 100% stable over long periods. The stability coefficients in
Table 22.7 are on the order of .50; if personality were stable within the
limits of measurement error, then these correlations would be on the order
of .85 (see McGue et al., 1993). Environmental factors definitely influence
personality, but they appear largely responsible for personality *change*
over time.

The Set Point Model

The set point model (SPM) is an attempt to explain the empirical results concerning genetics and the continuity and change in adult personality. Like most such models, it has been informally bandied about by behavioral geneticists for many years and claims multiple authorship. The account of the model here is illustrated using Lykken and Tellegen's (1996) work on the MPQ trait of well-being.

The SPM assumes that genes contribute very strongly to a person's "set point" for a personality trait such as well-being and that fluctuations in the environment produce short-term changes in the phenotype of well-being. To illustrate this model, suppose that we had the equivalent of a psychometric thermometer to measure well-being every day for a very long period of time. The SPM holds that a single person's phenotypic well-being will fluctuate over the time period because of positive and negative environmental experiences. For example, getting an A on an exam that you were worried over could increase well-being, whereas getting a speeding ticket might decrease it. If the effect of the environmental experience is large—as might be true for getting dumped in a significant relationship—then a person's phenotype could be altered for a considerable period of time. Depending on factors like the length and intensity of the original relationship, a person's well-being phenotype could be lowered for a few days, a few weeks, or maybe even several months. The key feature of the SMP is that *after these positive and negative experiences, a person will tend to regress back to his or her original set point*.

The model is illustrated in Figure 22.2 for two hypothetical people, Abel and Zed. Abel's set point is one standard deviation above the mean and is denoted in the figure by the straight, solid horizontal line at that value. Zed's set point is one standard deviation below the mean and is depicted by the straight dashed line. The fluctuating solid and dashed lines give Abel's and Zed's respective phenotypes over time. It is assumed that Abel and Zed have the same positive and negative experiences every day—an implausible situation, but one that helps to explain the model.

Both Abel and Zed start out the time period very close to their respective set points. For the first 30 days, the typical fluctuation of "good days" and "bad days" changes their state of well-being. Note that there are some days when Zed is happier than Abel is on other days. For example, Zed's well-being scores on Days 11 and 14 exceed Abel's scores on days 17 and 18. On Day 30, something extraordinarily positive happens to Abel and Zed. Zed's phenotype now exceeds Abel's set point. Because the event is so important, its effects carry over for a number of days afterward; however, by Day 45,

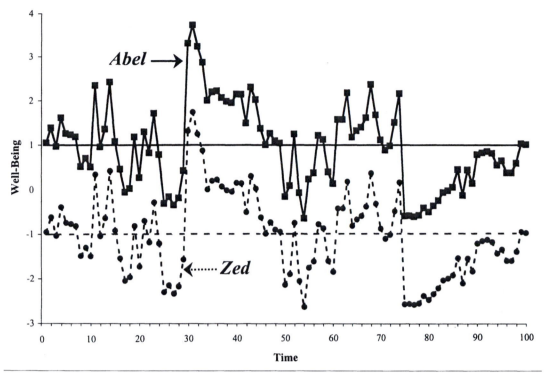

Figure 22.2   An Example of the Set Point Model for Hypothetical Individuals Abel and Zed

both Abel and Zed have returned to their respective set points. Thereafter, day-to-day fluctuations occur until Day 75, when very negative events occur for both Abel and Zed. Once again, these events are so salient that they alter mood for a number of days afterward, but slowly, both Abel and Zed recover and eventually reach their respective set points by Day 99.

Now imagine Abel and Zed both completing the Well-Being scale of the MPQ. Both read a question similar to "Basically, I am a happy person." Both are likely to look over their past experiences and mentally take an average of their level of happiness, ignoring the extremely high and low points. Abel is more likely to answer "true" to this item than Zed. For an item like "I am not as optimistic as most people I know," both are again likely to average their mood. This time, Zed is more likely to answer "true" than Abel. Hence, if Zed and Abel are given the Well-Being measure twice over a long period of time, Zed's score is likely to be lower than Abel's on both occasions. They are both responding in terms of their average behavior or something close to their set point.

The SPM is quite useful and explains the genetic data on the stability of personality. It also explains many other attributes of self-reported happiness such as the tendency for lottery winners to report that being an unexpected recipient of a financial fortune increases happiness but after a year or so, they are just as happy as they were before winning the lottery (Myers & Diener, 1995). However, much more data need to be gathered before the SPM is verified. For example, no one has taken daily measures of MZ and DZ twins over a long time to see if the predictions of the model hold.

● WHAT HAPPENED TO THE FAMILY ENVIRONMENT?

One of the most surprising results from genetic research on personality is the lack of correlated environments among relatives. Genetic relatives raised in different households with little or no contact during what are assumed to be the formative years are just about as similar as relatives who have spent years living together. Furthermore, genetically unrelated people who live together resemble one another little more than do random collections of individuals. These results cannot be attributed to a fatal flaw in behavioral genetic designs because we can indeed detect the effects of family environment for traits such as IQ scores in infants and children. It simply appears that being raised in the same family does not make relatives very similar regarding personality. Relatives have similar personalities only because they share genes. So what has happened to the role of parents in shaping their children's extraversion, fearfulness, emotionality, integrity, and all the other traits that constitute personality?

These observations have led some psychologists to challenge the cherished belief that family members influence one another's behavior (Harris, 1995, 1998; Rowe, 1994). To be fair, the data on personality are consistent with this interpretation, but they do not *prove* it. The data say that parents do not make their children behave *similar to one another*. They do not necessarily imply that parents have no effect on their children.

Consider the following scenario in the family of our trusted duo, Sam and Steve, whom we will call the Smiths. Papa Smith is an assertive and domineering chap, and his son, Sam, is a chip off the old block. If Sam does something that displeases Dad, he is certain to hear about it, and the tone of the communication is likely to be confrontational. Sam, however, is unlikely to acquiesce in such circumstances, so he and Papa frequently get into purposeless arguments. As a result of such behavior, Sam becomes more assertive than he otherwise would be.

Sam's brother, Steve, is considerably more submissive. Faced with Papa's bluster, Steve probably will accede to his demands and act demurely to avoid further confrontation. As a result, Steve becomes more submissive than he otherwise would have been.

Does Papa influence his sons' behavior? Yes. He has an effect on both Sam and Steve. But is Papa Smith making his children behave *similarly*? No! In fact, his behavior has the opposite effect because he is making Sam and Steve more different than they otherwise would be.

Now think of what happens if there are a large number of different families. Some parents make their children's personalities similar, so we give them a plus. Families like the Smiths, however, make their children's personality more different, so we give them a minus. In calculating a correlation coefficient, we sum over all families, so perhaps the pluses and minuses cancel each other out and we end up with a number close to 0. According to this hypothetical scenario, parents do indeed influence their children. It is just that the net effect over all families is not to make siblings *similar* to one another.

We can call these phenomena *idiosyncratic parent effects*. Parents do influence their children's personality, but the influence is so idiosyncratic that, over the whole population, it does not make siblings similar to each other. Note that this view is purely theoretical. There are no empirical data to either support or refute this view; in fact, it would be quite difficult to gather such data.

To recapitulate, the data on genes and personality suggest that being raised in the same family does not make relatives similar and that genes are the major—and perhaps only—reason why relatives have similar personalities. Do parents have no lasting effect on their children? We do not know. It could be that we humans have not evolved an "imitate your parents and only your parents" mechanism, so our parents become just two among the large number of conspecifics that we observe, imitate, and adapt to. Indeed, both Rowe (1994) and Harris (1995, 1998) accent the role of peers over parents in influencing personality. On the other hand, parents may indeed have a lasting influence—it is just not one that makes their offspring similar to one another.

DEVELOPMENT AND PERSONALITY ●

Thus far, the discussion of personality has been restricted to the adult years. But what about infants, children, and young adolescents? What is called personality in adults is often called *temperament* in infants and young children (Goldsmith, Buss, & Lemery, 1997; Plomin & Caspi, 1999), with the precise age at which temperament changes to personality deliberately left vague.

Table 22.9 presents kinship correlations for various types of genetic and environmental relatives on the EASI questionnaire (Buss & Plomin, 1975); its updated version, the EAS Temperament Survey (Buss & Plomin, 1984); or its clone, the Colorado Child Temperament Inventory (Rowe & Plomin, 1977). These instruments measure the higher-order dimensions of emotionality (a construct almost identical to neuroticism), sociability (very similar to extraversion), and activity. Although there are a considerable number of correlations in this table, many of them have been gathered on the same sample but at different ages.

First examine the MZ correlations. They are not terribly different from those for adults. The problem in childhood personality comes when one examines the correlations for all other types of relationships. Simply put, they do not make any sense. Look at the correlations for DZ twins, then compare them with those for adult DZ twins given in Table 22.2. With the odd exception, the correlations for adult DZ twins are significantly greater than 0. On the other hand, the correlations for DZ children are all over the place. Some are significantly positive (e.g., those for Emotionality and Activity in Study 5), many are close to 0, but others are significantly negative (i.e., Activity in Study 1). Correlations for siblings appear more in agreement with a simple genetic model than those for DZ twins.

Parent-offspring correlations also are confusing. If there is something genetic to childhood personality, and if that something genetic follows a simple model, then we should expect that the correlations for biological parents who give their children up for adoption and their genetic offspring should be significant. Instead, the observed correlations (Biological parent-offspring apart, Table 22.9) are very close to 0. Again, if a simple genetic model holds, then correlations for genetic parents who raise their own children (Biological parent-offspring together) should be higher than those for adoptive parents and their adopted offspring (Adoptive parent-offspring). They are not.

So how should these data be interpreted? The answer is that there is no way to know, although there is little shortage of speculation. Let us list the potential difficulties that might contribute to this pattern of data.

1. *Sample size.* Data on adults are easy and relatively inexpensive to collect because one can mail out questionnaires. Much of the childhood data, on the other hand, involves bringing families into a laboratory, greatly increasing the cost of and the time to complete the research. Compare the sample sizes in Table 22.2 with those in Table 22.9. Correlations based on smaller-sized samples will be more variable and "bounce around" more than those calculated from larger Ns.

Table 22.9 Kinship Correlations for the Higher-Order Traits of Emotionality (Neuroticism), Activity, and Sociability (Extraversion) Involving Children

| | | | Age in | | | Correlation | | |
Relationship	Study[a]	Sample[b]	Months	Rater	N	Emotionality	Activity	Sociability
MZ twins	1	1	14	Parents	100	.35	.50	.35
	1	1	20	Parents	100	.51	.59	.53
	2	2	42	Parents	100	.54	.61	.57
	5	4	164	Parents	86	.58	.73	.52
DZ twins	1	1	14	Parents	100	−.02	−.25	.03
	1	1	20	Parents	100	−.05	−.24	.11
	2	2	42	Parents	97	.15	−.01	.15
	5	4	164	Parents	91	.27	.20	.05
Full sibs	6	3	30	Parent	77	.13	.11	.09
	3	3	84	Teacher	70	.18	.37	.03
	3	3	84	Tester	86	−.06	.27	.32
	4	3	140	Self	101	.04	.05	.11
	5	4	164	Parent	154	.14	−.07	.08
Biological parent-offspring together	6	3	48	Parent	470	.11	.07	.15
	4	3	140	Self	184	.03	.06	.13
Biological parent-offspring apart	6	3	48	Parent	267	.02	.01	.09
	4	3	140	Self	162	−.04	.05	.02
Half sibs	5	4	164	Parent	105	.16	−.02	.06
Adoptive parent-offspring	6	3	48	Parent	444	.11	.07	.17
	4	3	140	Self	162	.04	−.03	.06
Adoptive sibs	6	3	30	Parent	68	.15	−.04	.02
	3	3	84	Teacher	63	−.15	−.10	−.10
	3	3	84	Tester	73	.15	.08	−.06
	4	3	140	Self	92	.08	−.04	.05
	5	4	164	Parents	124	.00	−.19	−.26

NOTE: Age may be either exact age or average age of the sample. Sample sizes (Ns) have been interpolated or averaged when exact sizes were not given in the original publication.

a. Code for study: 1 = Plomin et al. (1993); 2 = Neale and Stevenson (1989); 3 = Schmitz, Saudino, Plomin, Fulker, and DeFries (1996); 4 = Plomin, Corley, Caspi, Fulker, and DeFries (1998); 5 = Saudino, McGuire, Reiss, Hetherington, and Plomin (1995); 6 = Plomin, Coon, Carey, DeFries, and Fulker (1991).

b. Code for sample: 1 = McArthur Longitudinal Twin Study; 2 = Stevenson's English twins; 3 = Colorado Adoption Project; 4 = Nonshared Environment in Adolescent Development Project.

2. *Problems in measuring childhood personality.* Assessment for infants and young children is almost always done through a second party, most often a parent, teacher, or tester involved in the research fieldwork. Agreement among these three different sources is often poor, and the limited available evidence (Phillips & Matheny, 1997) suggests that the poor agreement is due to some combination of rater bias and the simple fact that children act differently in different situations.

3. *Age-dependent genetic effects.* It is clear that genes are regulated over the course of development. Perhaps this also applies to some of the genes for individual differences in personality. If the genetic effects in young children are not the same as those in adults, then correlations between genetic parents and their offspring will be reduced. This may contribute to some of the low parent-offspring correlations in Table 22.9, but it cannot account for the low correlations for DZ twins or for some of the full sib data in the table.

4. *Nonadditive genetic effects.* In the simple genetic model, all gene action is assumed to be additive. To the extent that there is dominant and epistatic gene action, the resulting dominance and epistatic variance may lower correlations for first-degree relatives (see Chapters 18 and 19). Plomin et al. (1998) have proposed this as a major culprit for the confusing childhood data. However, none of the quantitative experts in the field has ever been able to develop a plausible biological model in which the majority of the variance is due to dominance and epistatic variance. Nonadditive genetic effects certainly occur, but they are not likely to explain the whole pattern of these data.

5. *Contrast effects.* There are two different types of contrast effects, which will be called *sibling contrast effects* and *rater contrast effects*. Sibling contrast effects are the opposite of imitation. Sibling imitation is just what it sounds like—siblings imitate each other's behavior, increasing their similarity. Sibling contrast occurs when one sib does just the opposite of the other, resulting in decreased sibling similarity. Rater contrast effects involve the raters of children, not the actual behavior of the children. Imagine two mothers who are rating their twin children on sociability. Mama number 1 looks at her two MZ girls, says to herself that there is not much difference between them, and gives them an identical rating. Mama 2 looks at her two DZ girls and recalls that Susie is more talkative and outgoing than Sally. Hence, she rates Susie as higher than average on sociability and Sally as lower than average on the trait. This subtly illustrates a rater contrast effect. Instead of rating Sally relative to all other girls her age, Mama 2 is comparing her with her twin sister to arrive at a rating. Statistically, the effects of sibling contrast are identical to those of rater contrast. Hence, there is no practical way to distinguish

the two from the data in Table 22.9. Regardless of their source, contrast effects will lower correlations among siblings.

To give an example, suppose that sociability had a heritability in infants of .40, giving an MZ correlation of .40 and a DZ correlation of .20. As the twins get a bit older, a small contrast effect of –.10 occurs. Using a mathematical model of contrast, the resulting correlation in MZ twins becomes .22 while the correlation in DZ twins reduces to 0.

There is convincing evidence that contrast effects are present in some studies (e.g., Saudino et al., 1995), although they are just as convincingly absent in others (e.g., Neale & Stevenson, 1989). Perhaps the contrast is mostly of the rater variety, and the care of the researcher in instructing raters on how to complete a questionnaire is an important issue. The problem with contrast effects is that they cannot explain the low correlations between genetic parents and their adopted-away offspring. In the hypothetical example, that correlation should be close to .20.

The preceding discussion has been tedious, so let us end by giving three quick "bottom lines" to the genetics of personality development in children. First, the empirical literature is very messy and confusing because of the inconsistent patterning of the correlations for first-degree and adoptive relatives. Second, no single explanation can account for this pattern; the answer is likely to reside in some combination of the five difficulties mentioned above and undoubtedly other problems that have not been mentioned. Third, the genetics of temperament and personality development will remain mysterious until the measurement problems can be identified and corrected. It is sad to see so much data being collected in this important area and so little effort devoted to sorting out the measurement issues.[3]

NOTES

1. Current personality theory favors the *five-factor model* (McCrae & Costa, 1999), but relatively little genetic data has been gathered using this model compared to other—albeit related—models and measuring instruments. This review will focus on data from Hans Eysenck's system (which has the most genetic data) and from the MPQ (which illustrates the relationship between higher- and lower-order traits).

2. It is important not to confuse stability in a trait's mean with stability in individual differences. The average value of a trait may change over time, but the rank-ordering of people at the different time points may remain quite stable (e.g., height measured at age 15 and again at age 25). Also, the mean may remain stable over time, but the rank-ordering of individuals could change. The discussion herein involves stability only in terms of the rank-ordering of individuals over time.

3. Some of the measurement problems can be addressed with much of the data already collected. Examples include the following. Insight into contrast effects might be gained by comparing data from single-child families (where there is no opportunity for contrast) to multichild families. Better description of the methods of data collection might help to examine why some studies find contrast while other studies do not. The approaches utilized by Neale and Stevenson (1989) and Phillips and Matheny (1997) could be applied to examine rater bias.

● REFERENCES

Adorno, T. W., Frenkel-Brunswick, E., Levinson, D. J., & Sanford, R. N. (1950). *The authoritarian personality*. New York: Harper.

Beer, J. M., Arnold, R. D., & Loehlin, J. C. (1998). Genetic and environmental influences on MMPI factor scales: Joint model fitting to twin and adoption data. *Journal of Personality and Social Psychology, 74*, 818-827.

Buss, A. H., & Plomin, R. (1975). *A temperament theory of personality development*. New York: Wiley.

Buss, A. H., & Plomin, R. (1984). *Temperament: Early developing personality traits*. Hillsdale, NJ: Lawrence Erlbaum.

Carey, G., & Rice, J. (1983). Genetics of personality temperament: Simplicity or complexity? *Behavior Genetics, 13*, 43-83.

Costa, P. T., Jr., & McCrae, R. R. (1988). Personality in adulthood: A six-year longitudinal study of self-reports and spouse ratings on the NEO Personality Inventory. *Journal of Personality and Social Psychology, 54*, 853-863.

Eaves, L., D'Onofrio, B., & Russell, R. (1999). Transmission of religion and attitudes. *Twin Research, 2*, 59-61.

Eaves, L. J., & Eysenck, H. J. (1976). Genotype × age interaction for neuroticism. *Behavior Genetics, 6*, 359-362.

Eaves, L. J., Eysenck, H. J., & Martin, N. G. (1989). *Genes, culture and personality: An empirical approach*. San Diego: Academic Press.

Finkel, D., & McGue, M. (1997). Sex differences and nonadditivity in heritability of the Multidimensional Personality Questionnaire Scales. *Journal of Personality and Social Psychology, 72*, 929-938.

Floderus-Myrhed, B., Pederson, N., & Rasmuson, I. (1980). Assessment of heritability for personality, based on a short form of the Eysenck Personality Inventory. *Behavior Genetics, 10*, 153-162.

Goldsmith, H. H., Buss, K. A., & Lemery, K. S. (1997). Toddler and childhood temperament: Expanded content, stronger genetic evidence, new evidence for the importance of environment. *Developmental Psychology, 33*, 891-905.

Harris, J. R. (1995). Where is the child's environment? A group socialization theory of development. *Psychological Review, 102*, 458-489.

Harris, J. R. (1998). *The nurture assumption: Why children turn out the way they do*. New York: Touchstone.

Heath, A. C., Neale, M. C., Kessler, R. C., Eaves, L. J., & Kendler, K. S. (1992). Evidence for genetic influences on personality from self-reports and informant ratings. *Journal of Personality and Social Psychology, 63*, 85-96.

Jang, K. L., Livesley, W. J., Vernon, P. A., & Jackson, D. N. (1996). Heritability of personality disorder traits: A twin study. *Acta Psychiatrica Scandinavica, 94*, 438-444.

Loehlin, J. C. (1992). *Genes and environment in personality development*. Newbury Park, CA: Sage.

Loehlin, J. C., & Nichols, R. C. (1976). *Heredity, environment, and personality.* Austin: University of Texas Press.

Lykken, D., & Tellegen, A. (1996). Happiness is a stochastic phenomenon. *Psychological Science, 7,* 186-189.

Martin, N. G., & Jardine, R. (1986). Eysenck's contributions to behavior genetics. In S. Modgil & C. Modgil (Eds.), *Hans Eysenck: Consensus and controversy* (pp. 13-62). Lewes, Sussex, UK: Falmer Press.

McCrae, R. R., & Costa, P.T.J. (1999). A five-factor theory of personality. In L. A. Pervin & O. P. John (Eds.), *Handbook of personality research* (2nd ed., pp. 139-153). New York: Guilford.

McGue, M., Bacon, S., & Lykken, D. T. (1993). Personality stability and change in early adulthood: A behavioral genetic analysis. *Developmental Psychology, 29,* 96-109.

Myers, D. G., & Diener, E. (1995). Who is happy? *Psychological Science, 6,* 10-19.

Neale, M. C., & Stevenson, J. (1989). Rater bias in the EASI temperament scales: A twin study. *Journal of Personality and Social Psychology, 56,* 446-455.

Pedersen, N. L., & Reynolds, C. A. (1998). Stability and change in adult personality: Genetic and environmental components. *European Journal of Personality, 12,* 365-386.

Phillips, K., & Matheny, A. P., Jr. (1997). Evidence for genetic influence on both cross-situation and situation-specific components of behavior. *Journal of Personality and Social Psychology, 73,* 129-138.

Plomin, R., & Caspi, A. (1999). Behavioral genetics and personality. In L. A. Pervin & O. P. John (Eds.), *Handbook of personality: Theory and research* (2nd ed., pp. 251-276). New York: Guilford.

Plomin, R., Coon, H., Carey, G., DeFries, J. C., & Fulker, D. W. (1991). Parent-offspring and sibling adoption analyses of parental ratings of temperament in infancy and childhood. *Journal of Personality, 59,* 705-732.

Plomin, R., Corley, R., Caspi, A., Fulker, D. W., & DeFries, J. (1998). Adoption results for self-reported personality: Evidence for nonadditive genetic effects? *Journal of Personality and Social Psychology, 75,* 211-218.

Plomin, R., Emde, R. N., Braungart, J. M., Campos, J., Corley, R., Fulker, D., et al. (1993). Genetic change and continuity from fourteen to twenty months: The MacArthur Longitudinal Twin Study. *Child Development, 64,* 1354-1376.

Riemann, R., Angleitner, A., & Strelau, J. (1997). Genetic and environmental influences on personality: A study of twins reared together using the self- and peer-report NEO-FFI scales. *Journal of Personality, 65,* 449-475.

Rose, R. J., Koskenvuo, M., Kaprio, J., Sarna, S., & Langinvainio, H. (1988). Shared genes, shared experiences, and similarity of personality: Data from 14,288 adult Finnish co-twins. *Journal of Personality & Social Psychology, 54,* 161-171.

Rowe, D. C. (1994). *The limits of family influence: Genes, experience, and behavior.* New York: Guilford.

Rowe, D. C., & Plomin, R. (1977). Temperament in early childhood. *Journal of Personality Assessment, 41,* 150-156.

Rowe, D. C., & Plomin, R. (1981). The importance of nonshared (E1) environmental influence in behavioral development. *Developmental Psychology, 17,* 517-531.

Saudino, K. J., McGuire, S., Reiss, D., Hetherington, E. M., & Plomin, R. (1995). Parent ratings of EAS temperaments in twins, full siblings, half siblings, and step siblings. *Journal of Personality and Social Psychology, 68,* 723-733.

Scarr, S., & McCartney, K. (1983). How people make their own environments: A theory of genotype × environment effects. *Child Development, 54,* 424-435.

Schmitz, S., Saudino, K. J., Plomin, R., Fulker, D. W., & DeFries, J. C. (1996). Genetic and environmental influences on temperament in middle childhood: Analyses of teacher and tester ratings. *Child Development, 67,* 409-422.

Tellegen, A. (1985). Structures of mood and personality and their relevance to assessing anxiety, with an emphasis on self-report. In A. H. Tuma & J. Maser (Eds.), *Anxiety and the anxiety disorders* (pp. 681-706). Hillsdale, NJ: Lawrence Erlbaum.

Tellegen, A., Lykken, D. T., Bouchard, T. J., Jr., Wilcox, K. J., Segal, N. L., & Rich, S. (1988). Personality similarity in twins reared apart and together. *Journal of Personality and Social Psychology, 54*, 1031-1039.

Truett, K. R., Eaves, L. J., Meyer, J. M., Heath, A. C., & Martin, N. G. (1992). Religion and education as mediators of attitudes: A multivariate analysis. *Behavior Genetics, 22*, 43-62.

Viken, R. J., Rose, R. J., Kaprio, J., & Koskenvuo, M. (1994). A developmental genetic analysis of adult personality: Extraversion and neuroticism from 18 to 59. *Journal of Personality and Social Psychology, 66*, 722-730.

CHAPTER 23

SCHIZOPHRENIA

INTRODUCTION ●

In 1971, Eliot Slater (at that time, the foremost psychiatric geneticist in the world) and Valerie Cowie published *The Genetics of Mental Disorders*. The book was encyclopedic—it synopsized all the world's empirical literature on schizophrenia, the affective disorders, the neuroses (as they were called then), mental retardation, seizure disorders, and personality disorders. Today, such an undertaking would surpass the capabilities of even the most talented scholarly duo and would require a volume each for every major form of psychopathology. Because of the enormous advances in research, a single chapter cannot summarize a single disorder. To avoid diluting knowledge by discussing a number of disorders, I focus exclusively in this chapter on schizophrenia. It serves as a good model for the genetics of psychopathology in general.

SCHIZOPHRENIA: THE PHENOTYPE ●

No one is born with schizophrenia. Instead, the psychopathology develops over time—sometimes slowly and mysteriously, but other times abruptly.

Onset before puberty and after age 50 are rare but deserving of attention when encountered. Most cases appear between the ages of 15 and 35. For males, the average age of first symptoms is around 22 years, with first admission at 28. Females have a delayed onset for reasons that are not understood. The respective figures for women are 25 and 32. Despite the age difference in onset, schizophrenia is not a sexist disorder—males and females are affected equally. About 1% of the general population will develop schizophrenia at some point in their lives, making it a "common" disorder. Prognosis can be grim, including a very high risk of death from suicide. Although there are well-documented cases of social recoveries, many schizophrenics are so changed by the illness that they require extensive mental health assistance to function in society. Hence, schizophrenia places a deep burden on health resources, not to mention the families of victims.

The behavior of schizophrenics before their onset is statistically different from that of their normal peers (Cornblatt, Obuchowski, Roberts, Pollack, & Erlenmeyer-Kimling, 1999; Erlenmeyer-Kimling et al., 2000), but the differences are so small and so diffuse that there is no practical way as yet of predicting who will and will not develop the disorder in the general population. Sometimes the disorder develops insidiously. Gradually, normal positive and negative affect may give way to a lack of any affect, the ability to experience pleasure slowly diminishes, the person could experience feelings of unreality, and problems with concentration and attention emerge. Thereafter, he or she may develop overvalued ideas (e.g., extreme preoccupation with a health food fad or joining a cult) and become socially isolated. To the friend or relative, the person seems to be developing eccentricities. Eventually, overt delusions and hallucinations[1] appear. They can take many different forms, but friends and relatives now recognize that something serious is the matter and take the schizophrenic into treatment.

Other cases may have a more abrupt onset with little of the gradual deterioration marking the hypothetical case given above. Rather, an otherwise normal person becomes convinced that he or she is receiving personal messages from the television, is being spied on by the government, or has been given a special mission to count all the books in the local library. Irving Gottesman (1991), an erudite scholar of schizophrenia, has highlighted the extraordinary variability in the clinical signs and symptoms of the disorder. Schizophrenia affects cognition (memory and executive functioning), attention, affect (which can range from its total absence to episodes of silly and inappropriate laughter), motivation, personality, and even motor behavior (e.g., stereotyped movements). Still, there is no single symptom that is found in all schizophrenics, and a single person may show different constellations of symptoms at different times during the illness.

Neither is there a single biological marker that can be used to diagnose schizophrenia. Despite a century of research on the brains of schizophrenics, there is no visible pathology such as the neuronal plaques and tangles that characterize Alzheimer's disorder or the death of glial cells that mark other neurodegenerative disorders.[2] Within the schizophrenic brain, the ventricles (fluid-filled sacs deep within the brain) are larger on average than those of normal brains,[3] but there is so much overlap between the two types of brains that ventricle size cannot be used as a diagnostic measure. The absence of detectable neuropathology has led many to posit that schizophrenia is a neurodevelopmental disorder and not a neurodegenerative one.

A large number of biochemical (e.g., amino acid levels in certain brain regions), physiological (e.g., eye tracking, reaction time, certain evoked potentials from the brain), and psychological (e.g., attention span, language functioning) variables have been researched, resulting in many replicable findings. Invariably, schizophrenics lie toward the "bad" end of the variables (e.g., aberrant eye tracking, short attention span, poor communication skills). However, none of these biochemical, physiological, or psychological variables is powerful enough to be used to diagnose schizophrenia.

Many, but not all, experts suspect that schizophrenia is a collection of heterogeneous disorders. In this sense, one should speak of "the schizophrenias" instead of schizophrenia. If this view is correct, then presently there is no way to differentiate any one of the disorders from the others by simply examining the phenotype. Researchers who hold this view try to find subsets of schizophrenics who might show one or more specific abnormalities that might distinguish them from other schizophrenics. To date, identification of subtypes has not been successful.

A considerable amount has been learned in the past century of schizophrenia research, but much of this knowledge reduces to a simple aphorism—if one can measure a physiological variable related to the nervous system, a cognitive trait, or anything that has to do with human affect, personality, or social interaction, then schizophrenics tend to score on the abnormal end of the variable. Separating potential *causes* of schizophrenia from the *consequences* of such a devastating and complicated illness still remains difficult. In many ways, the disorder remains almost as mysterious today as it did to those who first described it in the late 1800s.

GENETIC EPIDEMIOLOGY OF ●
SCHIZOPHRENIA I: HERITABILITY

Shortly after the disorder was first classified by Emil Kraeplin as *dementia praecox* and given the name schizophrenia[4] by Eugen Bleuler in 1908, it was observed that schizophrenia would often run in families. Table 23.1 gives the

Table 23.1   Risks for Schizophrenia in Genetic Relatives of Schizophrenics

Genetic Relation	Type of Relation	Risk (%)
General population		1
Third-degree	Cousins	2
Second-degree	Uncles/aunts	2
	Nieces/nephews	3
	Grandchildren	4
	Half siblings	6
First degree	Children	13
	Parents	6
	Siblings	9
	DZ twins	17
Identical	MZ twins	48

SOURCE: Adapted from Gottesman (1991), Figure 10.

risk for schizophrenia in different types of genetic relatives of a schizophrenic as compiled by Gottesman (1991) from the best Western European studies reported over the past century. Risk for cousins (2%) is only slightly greater than for the general population. Second-degree relatives have a risk of around 5%, whereas first-degree relatives have a risk close to 10%. These figures clearly indicate that schizophrenia is not a simple, fully penetrant recessive (e.g., PKU) or dominant disorder (e.g., Huntington's disease).

Several of the risk figures deserve comment. The risk to children (13%) is significantly higher than the risk for parents (6%). This discrepancy is attributed to the well-documented fact that schizophrenics have a lower reproductive fitness than normals, producing only half the children of normals. In addition, it is usually the less severe schizophrenics who marry and have children. A second noteworthy discrepancy is the fact that DZ twins have a higher risk than full siblings (17% versus 9%), despite the fact that DZ twins and sibs have the same degree of genetic relatedness. The reasons for this are unknown but are likely to include the fact that the DZ cotwins have been studied more intensively than sibs and the possibility of pre- and/or perinatal effects on schizophrenia. Finally, the fact that risk for parents is about 6% carries the necessary implication that most schizophrenics—in fact, more than 90%—will be born to nonschizophrenic parents.

Risk for MZ cotwins is almost 50%, suggesting that genes play an important role in the familial aggregation of schizophrenia. Adoption studies confirm the genetic influence. Schizophrenia in biological relatives—not in adoptive relatives—predicts schizophrenia in adoptees (Heston, 1966; Ingraham & Kety, 2000).

The strength of the genetic influence is difficult to quantify because estimation of heritability depends on the mode of transmission for schizophrenia, and we simply do not know the mode of transmission. Working on the assumption of the polygenic-threshold model described in Chapter 7, McGue, Gottesman, and Rao (1983) estimated heritability at close to .70, with negligible influence from the shared family environment. However, if there is marked heterogeneity in schizophrenia, this figure could be misleading.[5]

GENETIC EPIDEMIOLOGY OF SCHIZOPHRENIA II: ● BEYOND HERITABILITY

Family and twin studies provide much more important information about schizophrenia than simple numerical estimates of heritability (see Gottesman & Erlenmeyer-Kimling, 2001). Concordant MZ twins have similar ages of onset, similar profiles of clinical signs and symptoms, and similar courses of illness (Abe, 1969; Cardno et al., 1999; Gottesman & Shields, 1972). Some family studies also report familial clustering of signs and symptoms. These observations are consistent with the hypothesis that schizophrenia is a heterogeneous collection of disorders. However, there are so many *differences* in clinical manifestation among concordant sibs, DZ twins, and MZ twins that no one has been able to conclusively subdivide schizophrenia into separate familial disorders based exclusively on symptoms. In addition, a familial correlation for symptoms is also consistent with the hypothesis of modifying loci—that is, that genes might not contribute to schizophrenia per se but may influence the form it takes.

A second important finding is that 5% to 10% of first-degree relatives exhibit eccentricities, peculiar ideas, suspiciousness, and/or odd social behavior but never seem to develop the full-blown delusions and hallucinations of the full psychosis (Asarnow et al., 2001; Kendler et al., 1993). Various names—schizoid, schizophreniform, schizophrenic spectrum—have been used over the years to describe this subclinical phenomenon, the currently favored phrase being schizotypal personality disorder (SPD). The available data suggest that SPD is familially and genetically related to full-blown schizophrenia. The reasons why someone with SPD does not decompensate into schizophrenia are unknown.

Severity of schizophrenia in a proband is associated with familial risk: The relatives of severely affected schizophrenics are at higher risk than relatives of less severe probands. The situation is best illustrated in the Maudsley twin series (Gottesman, 1991; Gottesman & Shields, 1972). No matter how severity was measured—number of hospitalizations, length of treatment, outcome, or global ratings of psychopathology—there was a consistent tendency for twin concordance to be associated with proband severity. The reason for the severity-concordance relationship is not understood, but it may come from some combination of three different factors. First, if there is marked heterogeneity in schizophrenia, the less severe cases may contain more phenocopies than severe schizophrenics may. Second, to the extent that there is multifactorial, polygenic transmission, the more severe cases may have a greater genetic loading than the mild cases. Finally, difficulties in diagnosis could influence the relationship. Severely affected schizophrenics have longer and more detailed case history information that might increase accuracy in diagnosis. Mild cases, on the other hand, may include more false positive diagnoses.

One of the most intriguing aspects of the genetic epidemiological literature has been the study of MZ twins discordant for schizophrenia. Indeed, this type of research highlights how genetic studies can be used for much more than simply calculating heritability. Differences between the well and the ill twin reflect facets of the idiosyncratic environment that play a causal role in schizophrenia, or they can tap the consequences of the illness itself. Variables that occur long before the onset of illness are more likely to be causal than those measured after the illness. An example of each type of variable is given below.

Early twin researchers reported an association between laterality and discordance—MZ twins discordant for schizophrenia also tend to be discordant for handedness (Gottesman & Shields, 1972). A recent study reported that fingerprint (aka dermatoglyphic) differences are greater in discordant MZ twins than in concordant MZ twins (Davis & Bracha, 1996). Because fingerprints develop before birth and handedness develops in late infancy, these variables are probably manifestations of unknown, but early, developmental processes that may play a role in schizophrenia.

Differences in personality and some cognitive variables in discordant pairs probably measure the effects of the illness. The ill twin of the pair shows more deviance in traditional personality measures than the well twin (DiLalla & Gottesman, 1995). More important, the moderate to strong personality resemblance found among ordinary twin pairs is missing in discordant MZ twins. A very similar pattern occurs for neuropsychological functioning (Goldberg et al., 1995). These findings suggest that the personality aberrations and some aspects of unusual cognitive functioning may be consequences of the disease.

The causal versus consequential role for many other variables that differentiate the well from the ill MZ twin is unclear. Ill twins tend to have larger brain ventricles (those fluid-filled "lakes" within the brain) than well twins. They also show more EEG abnormalities (Stassen et al., 1999), abnormal auditory information processing (Weisbrod, Hill, Niethammer, & Sauer, 1999), and neurological soft signs (Cantor-Graae et al., 1994). Are these parts in the causal network of schizophrenia, or are they consequences of the illness? Currently, there is no unambiguous answer. Instead, these factors must be pieced together with the results from other research to develop hypotheses that guide future research. To give an example, McNeil, Cantor-Graae, and Weinberger (2000) report that enlarged ventricles were associated with birth trauma and prolonged labor. Given that pregnancy and birth complications are weakly associated with schizophrenia, the McNeil et al. results support the notion that ventricle size may be a facet of idiosyncratic environmental experiences (birth complications) that play an etiological role in the disorder.

A final important result from discordant MZ twins comes from the risk for schizophrenia in their offspring. If the ill twins are largely environmental phenocopies, then the risk to the offspring of the *well* twin should be close to the population base rate. On the other hand, if both members of the twin pair have elevated genetic loadings on schizophrenia but the ill twin experienced some adverse unique environmental events to make him or her break down, then *both* twins should transmit the same above-average genetic liability to their offspring. In this case, the offspring of both the well and the ill twins would have the same, elevated risk of developing schizophrenia. A study of a series of Danish discordant twins suggests that the latter hypothesis fits the data better than the former (Gottesman & Bertelsen, 1989).

THE MULTIFACTORIAL THRESHOLD ● MODEL REVISITED: DIATHESIS-STRESS

Let us revisit the multifactorial threshold model that we briefly examined in the discussion of disorders with complex genetics and examine its application to schizophrenia. Figure 23.1 is an adaptation of the original threshold model proposed by Gottesman and Shields (1967, 1972). It depicts four different components of liability. According to Gottesman and Shields, *specific* genetic liability is a quantitative scale that measures the propensity to develop schizophrenia per se. That is, the genes for this liability dimension make a person vulnerable to *schizophrenia*—not necessarily to anxiety disorders, general stress susceptibility, emotional instability, or any other of a large number of traits that might influence the probability that someone develops psychopathology. The central empirical evidence for specific genetic liability is that the most common form of psychopathology seen

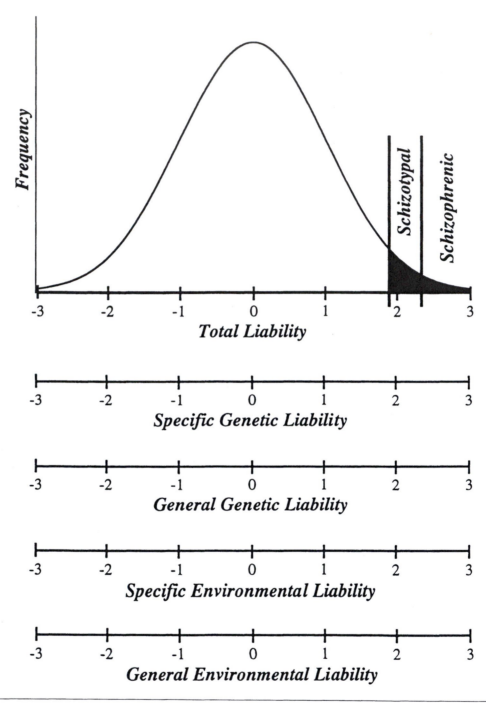

Figure 23.1 The Multifactorial Threshold Model for Liability to Schizophrenia and Schizotypal Personality Disorder

in the MZ cotwins of schizophrenic probands (allowing for base rates of other psychopathology) is schizophrenia or schizophrenic-like disorders such as SPD.

The mean of the general population for specific genetic liability is 0. Individuals with negative values are protected from developing schizophrenia, although they may have little protection from developing other forms of psychopathology. Those with high positive scores are at high risk for breaking down with schizophrenia, but not necessarily with manic-depressive disorder, antisocial personality, or other disorders.

The genes in the specific genetic liability dimension do not operate in a vacuum. Their biological activity works in concert with the "background music" provided by the rest of the genome and the environment. Several of those other loci may contribute to the development of schizophrenia but not in a direct way. The quantitative effects of these genes form the scale of *general* genetic liability. Gottesman and Shields hypothesized that a number of different background traits influence the development of many different forms of psychopathology. As an example, take the personality dimension of neuroticism. People high on this trait may be at risk for many different disorders—panic disorder, generalized anxiety disorder, obsessive compulsive disorder, depression, and even schizophrenia. The particular *form* of the disorder in any given person, however, depends on the *specific* liabilities of that person. Again, the population mean for general genetic liability is 0. Those with strong genetic assets will score on the negative (i.e., less vulnerable) end of the scale, and those with genetic liability factors will have positive scores.

Specific and general environmental liabilities work in analogous ways to the genetic liabilities but apply to environmental factors. There is not the strong empirical evidence for specific environmental liability as there is for specific genetic liability. It is included here to allow for the possibility that factors like a virus may influence schizophrenia per se. Many researchers speculate that most of the environmental influences on schizophrenia fall under the general environmental liability dimension. One of the most salient variables contributing to this dimension is environmental stress. Hence, the multifactorial threshold model is often referred to as the *diathesis-stress model* in psychopathology, the word *diathesis* being a fancy synonym for liability.

In its simplest form, the diathesis-stress or polygenic threshold model assumes that everyone has a latent phenotype (called total liability) that is a combination of all the specific and general liabilities mentioned above. That is, total liability = $\beta_1 \times$ specific genetic liability + $\beta_2 \times$ general genetic liability + $\beta_3 \times$ specific environmental liability + $\beta_4 \times$ general environmental liability. The subscripted βs are unknown weights that specify how important one of the liabilities is in its contribution to total liability.[6] Once the total liability exceeds a certain point (the first threshold), a process begins, and the person develops some signs and symptoms of schizophrenia and SPD becomes apparent. When the liability is very large, the person crosses a second threshold and the overt hallucinations and delusions of schizophrenia become apparent. This is an example of a *two-threshold* model in which passing the first threshold leads to the development of a mild form of the disorder but passing the second threshold results in a more severe form. One could generalize this principle to a *multiple-threshold* model that may have more than two thresholds.

The diathesis-stress model has two important uses in psychopathology. First, the mathematics of the model can be used to calculate the *correlation in liability* for relatives. When data on twins and/or adoptees are available, these correlations can be used to calculate heritability in a manner identical to calculating heritability for personality or intelligence. In this case, the heritability is termed the *heritability of liability*. It is not strictly the heritability of schizophrenia per se. Instead, it is the heritability of *all* those multifactorial factors that go into the predisposition for developing schizophrenia. In terms of the model in Figure 23.1, heritability of liability includes both the specific genetic liability and the general genetic liability. Analogously, one could compute the environmentability of liability (or e^2) as well as the correlation in environmental liability for relatives (η).

The second importance of the diathesis-stress model as outlined above is that it guides scientific research. Thinking in a multifactorial mode requires discipline because according to this train of thought, there is no such critter as *the* cause of schizophrenia. Instead, there are several causes—perhaps as few as three or maybe as many as 300—that work together. The same may be said about the consequences of the disorder. Hence, cognitive psychologists are not backing a different horse than biochemists in researching schizophrenia. They are likely to be exploring different pathways of the complicated etiology and/or symptomatology of the disorder.

Diathesis-Stress and Lemonade

Stress takes many forms. Negative life events such as the death of a loved one are one type of stress. Other life events may be pleasurable or aversive, depending on their context and the individual affected by them. For example, leaving home to attend a distant college involves trials as well as rewards. In terms of the diathesis-stress model, separation from family and friends in this case could be a specific environmental stressor for depression, a general environmental stressor for schizophrenia, or perhaps even an environmental asset.

Other types of stress may be self-imposed rather than external events. Negative life events themselves show some heritability, suggesting that we can assist in the creation of our own stressors. Poor job performance can result in a person being fired that itself can lead to anxiety about money and worries over self-worth. Furthermore, general genetic and general environmental liabilities may have influenced the poor job performance in the first place.

Lastly, environmental stress must be evaluated with consideration for its biological and even genetic influence on the organism. One consequence of stress is the excretion of large amounts of cortisol. As we saw in Chapter 4, on genetic regulation, cortisol has the effect of enhancing and inhibiting transcription. Hence, all those genetic and environmental factors that influenced job performance will also influence the probability of getting fired. Once fired, the stresses about money, finding a new job, self-esteem, and so on can increase cortisol excretion that, in turn, regulates expression of a number of different genes in different bodily tissues. Thus, the genes and environmental factors for job performance can assist in creating a cascade of events that ultimately influence many other genes. Once again, it is lemonade.

MOLECULAR GENETIC STUDIES OF SCHIZOPHRENIA ●

The best way to introduce this topic is to quote directly from the abstracts of recent journal articles on the molecular genetics of schizophrenia.

> Studies of schizophrenia kindreds have yielded robust evidence for susceptibility at 18p11.2 and 22q11-13. . . . Similarly, confirmed schizophrenia vulnerability loci have been mapped, too, for 6p24, 8p, and 13q32. (Berrettini, 2000, p. 245)

> As with most complex inheritance diseases, there are at this time no identified susceptibility genes for schizophrenia. . . . Nonetheless, progress has occurred. . . . Genetic linkages and associations have been reported and replicated, although there have been inconsistencies between studies. (Gershon, 2000, p. 240)

> In the last decade, a new wave of molecular genetic studies of families with schizophrenia has yielded unconvincing evidence for the involvement of multiple putative loci. (DeLisi, 2000, p. 187)

Figure 23.2   A Schematic of Chromosome 6 Giving Two Areas of Purported Linkage to Schizophrenia

Pretty confusing, isn't it? Opinion ranges from "confirmed loci" to "unconvincing evidence," with many more researchers occupying various intermediate positions. To illustrate the current state of molecular-genetic studies of schizophrenia, let us examine one chromosome (number 6) and review the empirical findings.

The interest in exploring chromosome 6 for genes in schizophrenia began with the report of a single pedigree where a chromosomal translocation between chromosomes 6 and 11 segregated with a vaguely defined psychotic illness (Holland & Gosden, 1990). Five years later, Wang et al. (1995) and then Straub et al. (1995) reported positive findings of linkage for a schizophrenia susceptibility locus in the *p* (short) arm of chromosome 6. Figure 23.2 depicts chromosome 6 and the region of the *p* arm where this gene may lie. (Also depicted is a region of the *q* arm that is currently being investigated for another susceptibility gene.)

Soon thereafter, a flurry of results on chromosome 6 hit the journals, some of which supported the original finding to various degrees (e.g., Lindholm et al., 1999; Moises et al., 1995; Schwab et al., 1995), while others failed to detect linkage (e.g., Daniels et al., 1997; Garner et al., 1996; Gurling et al., 1995). The most recently published overview of all the linkage results to chromosome 6 (Nurnberger & Foroud, 1999) concluded that there is tentative but not conclusive evidence for linkage and that the results need to be pursued with more vigor.

What might be the possible reasons for the inconsistency in the literature? One answer may simply be sample size. Several of the studies that failed to replicate the finding involved a small number of families (e.g., Daniels et al., 1997).[7] Secondly, the actual effect of the locus on chromosome 6 may be very small. Most researchers regard this as a "susceptibility" gene—one that increases risk, but only slightly. A third possibility is an association of the schizophrenia susceptibility locus on chromosome 6 with ethnicity. The strongest evidence for linkage comes from the initial reports of Straub et al. (1995) and Wang et al. (1995) that were dominated by a large number of Irish pedigrees. Perhaps the susceptibility allele has a higher frequency among Celtic peoples than in other populations.

Whatever the cause, the overall story of chromosome 6 is not a one-of-a-kind tale. Almost all reported linkages have followed the same pattern. Sobering failures to replicate dampen the enthusiasm following an initial positive report. It is tempting for the novice scientist to dismiss this line of research entirely, but that is a serious error. These results may be telling us something very, very important—*there may not be single genes of very large effect for schizophrenia and possibly for most other forms of psychopathology.* Most geneticists in the field interpret the data as supporting a polygenic mode of inheritance—several genes contribute to the liability of developing schizophrenia, and the effect size for each locus is relatively small. Thus, linkage studies require a very large number of pedigrees to detect these loci. To overcome this problem, research groups have joined into consortiums in which data are pooled and analyzed in the same manner. For example, Levinson et al. (2000) recently published results suggesting that linkage results to a gene on the other arm of chromosome 6 (6q) are robust.

The biggest advantage of these confusing results is that they can guide future research based on emerging genetic knowledge and technologies. As more and more human genes are identified and characterized at the molecular level, the strategy to detect vulnerability loci will switch from the linkage design to the more powerful association design. Instead of blindly assessing the tens of thousands of human loci for their relevance for schizophrenia, the linkage results point to areas of the genome that should first be explored. The 6p or 6q regions in Figure 23.2 potentially implicated in schizophrenia contain several hundreds of genes to perhaps a thousand or so, not many thousands. Searching for one needle in one haystack is much easier than searching for that needle in a hundred different haystacks.

● OTHER FORMS OF PSYCHOPATHOLOGY

Although schizophrenia is the most studied disorder in the genetics of psychopathology, there have been twin and (a few) adoption studies on other disorders. With the exceptions noted below, the results are similar to those for schizophrenia in the following ways:

1. MZ twins are never 100% concordant for a disorder. This clearly implicates the environment for all forms of psychopathology studied thus far. Hence, statements like "alcoholism is a genetic disorder" or "bipolar manic-depression is due to heredity" are very misleading.

2. The risks to relatives do not follow the pattern of simple Mendelian inheritance, even if that pattern is "souped up" by espousing incomplete penetrance and variable expressivity. The results of almost all forms of segregation analysis (a statistical attempt to find major Mendelian loci for disorders with complex genetics) have been mixed (Carey, 1987).

3. Hence, all forms of psychopathology studies thus far are DCGs (disorders with complex genetics).

4. Although many researchers—perhaps even the majority of them—suspect heterogeneity, no subdivision of any disorder into "types" has been so compelling as to put them into a textbook. The best example is depression. Despite attempts to classify depression into "exogenous versus endogenous," "reactive versus nonreactive," and "neurotic versus psychotic," the data suggest that they do not run true to type within families.

5. To date, no genes of very large effect have been reported by a large and replicated body of linkage or association results. To be sure, there are interesting leads here and there, but no single result has passed the crucial test of replication in a large number of independent labs.

The reasons for this state of affairs are unclear, but the empirical data have certainly dampened the initial enthusiasm of investigators who hoped to detect such phenomenon as a "chromosome 13 form of schizophrenia." On the other hand, the confusing results should not lead to a state of despair in which linkage and association studies are abandoned as being unproductive. The puzzling results are telling us *something important*—it is just that we have not been clever enough to figure out what that important something is. Currently, the most favored hypothesis is that polygenic transmission is responsible for the lion's share of the genetic diathesis. Hence, the effect of any single locus will be on the small side and hard to detect in studies that lack very large numbers of pedigrees.

Here and there, we do find exceptions to these (over)generalizations. MZ twins are not 100% concordant for severe forms of agoraphobia and social phobia, but careful clinical study of the well cotwins suggest that most—perhaps even all—of them show subclinical features similar to the full-blown syndrome (Carey & Gottesman, 1981). These cotwins may be fearful enough to shun subway trains or avoid open places, but their anxiety fails to cause sufficient interference in ordinary behavior to merit the diagnosis of a "disorder." The discussion of ALDH deficiency in the chapter on Mendelian traits (Chapter 5) is a clear example of a major locus influencing the susceptibility to alcohol problems; it is the best-documented exception to item 5 above. Also, there is a body of consistent linkage results suggesting that an important gene on chromosome 6 contributes to reading disability (Gayan et al., 1999).

As we learn more about the human genome, eventually we will develop more and more exceptions to these generalizations. What we cannot anticipate, however, is *how long* it might take to develop a large body of well-replicated genetic associations with psychopathology.

● NOTES

1. Delusions are ideas and feelings that are highly incongruent with reality (e.g., feeling that there is a vast governmental conspiracy specifically directed at oneself). Hallucinations are sensory perceptions that do not arise from a physical stimulus (e.g., hearing voices).

2. Glial cells (also known as neuroglia) are connective tissues that bind and support neurons in the central nervous system.

3. There is also a concomitant decrease in the volume of the cortical matter and certain other structures in the brains of schizophrenics.

4. Previously, the disorder was called dementia praecox (premature dementia). Bleuler, noting that the course of the illness was not always consistent with dementia (a chronic and irreversible deterioration of cognitive functioning), renamed it schizophrenia from the Greek roots *schizo* (split) and *phrenos* (mind). In the popular mind, schizophrenia is often equated with "split personality," a concept that is not justified scientifically.

5. In fact, if there is marked heterogeneity, an argument could be made that heritability should not be calculated in the first place. A more important goal would be to identify the sources of heterogeneity.

6. The model described is a simple additive one. In principle, it can be expanded to account for other factors such as an interaction between specific genetic liability and some environmental factor.

7. Small samples reduce the statistical power of linkage analysis. That is, they make it more difficult to detect a linkage when in fact the linkage is present.

● REFERENCES

Abe, K. (1969). The morbidity rate and environmental influence in monozygotic co-twins of schizophrenics. *British Journal of Psychiatry, 115*, 519-531.

Asarnow, R. F., Nuechterlein, K. H., Fogelson, D., Subotnik, K. L., Payne, D. A., Russell, A. T., et al. (2001). Schizophrenia and schizophrenia-spectrum personality disorders in the first-degree relatives of children with schizophrenia: The UCLA family study. *Archives of General Psychiatry, 58*, 581-588.

Berrettini, W. H. (2000). Susceptibility loci for bipolar disorder: overlap with inherited vulnerability to schizophrenia. *Biological Psychiatry, 47*, 245-251.

Cantor-Graae, E., McNeil, T. F., Rickler, K. C., Sjostrom, K., Rawlings, R., Higgins, E. S., et al. (1994). Are neurological abnormalities in well discordant monozygotic co-twins of schizophrenic subjects the result of perinatal trauma? *American Journal of Psychiatry, 151*, 1194-1199.

Cardno, A. G., Marshall, E. J., Coid, B., Macdonald, A. M., Ribchester, T. R., Davies, N. J., et al. (1999). Heritability estimates for psychotic disorders: The Maudsley twin psychosis series. *Archives of General Psychiatry, 56*, 162-168.

Carey, G. (1987). Big genes, little genes, affective disorder, and anxiety: A commentary. *Archives of General Psychiatry, 44*, 486-491.

Carey, G., & Gottesman, I. I. (1981). Twin and family studies of anxiety, phobic, and obsessive disorders. In D. F. Klein & E. Rabkin (Eds.), *Anxiety: New research and changing concepts* (pp. 117-136). New York: Raven Press.

Cornblatt, B., Obuchowski, M., Roberts, S., Pollack, S., & Erlenmeyer-Kimling, L. (1999). Cognitive and behavioral precursors of schizophrenia. *Development and Psychopathology, 11*, 487-508.

Daniels, J. K., Spurlock, G., Williams, N. M., Cardno, A. G., Jones, L. A., Murphy, K. C., et al. (1997). Linkage study of chromosome 6p in sib-pairs with schizophrenia. *American Journal of Medical Genetics, 74*, 319-323.

Davis, J. O., & Bracha, H. S. (1996). Prenatal growth markers in schizophrenia: A monozygotic co-twin control study. *American Journal of Psychiatry, 153*, 1166-1172.

DeLisi, L. E. (2000). Critical overview of current approaches to genetic mechanisms in schizophrenia research. *Brain Research Review, 31*, 187-192.

DiLalla, D. L., & Gottesman, I. I. (1995). Normal personality characteristics in identical twins discordant for schizophrenia. *Journal of Abnormal Psychology, 104*, 490-499.

Erlenmeyer-Kimling, L., Rock, D., Roberts, S. A., Janal, M., Kestenbaum, C., Cornblatt, B., et al. (2000). Attention, memory, and motor skills as childhood predictors of schizophrenia-related psychoses: The New York High-Risk Project. *American Journal of Psychiatry, 157*, 1416-1422.

Garner, C., Kelly, M., Cardon, L., Joslyn, G., Carey, A., LeDuc, C., et al. (1996). Linkage analyses of schizophrenia to chromosome 6p24-p22: An attempt to replicate. *American Journal of Medical Genetics, 67*, 595-610.

Gayan, J., Smith, S. D., Cherny, S. S., Cardon, L. R., Fulker, D. W., Brower, A., et al. (1999). Quantitative-trait locus for specific language and reading deficits on chromosome 6p. *American Journal of Human Genetics, 64*, 157-164.

Gershon, E. S. (2000). Bipolar illness and schizophrenia as oligogenic diseases: Implications for the future. *Biological Psychiatry, 47*, 240-244.

Goldberg, T. E., Torrey, E. F., Gold, J. M., Bigelow, L. B., Ragland, R. D., Taylor, E., et al. (1995). Genetic risk of neuropsychological impairment in schizophrenia: A study of monozygotic twins discordant and concordant for the disorder. *Schizophrenia Research, 17*, 77-84.

Gottesman, I. I. (1991). *Schizophrenia genesis: The origins of madness*. New York: Freeman.

Gottesman, I. I., & Bertelsen, A. (1989). Confirming unexpressed genotypes for schizophrenia: Risks in the offspring of Fischer's Danish identical and fraternal discordant twins. *Archives of General Psychiatry, 46*, 867-872.

Gottesman, I. I., & Erlenmeyer-Kimling, L. (2001). Family and twin strategies as a head start in defining prodromes and endophenotypes for hypothetical early-interventions in schizophrenia. *Schizophrenia Research, 51*, 93-102.

Gottesman, I. I., & Shields, J. (1967). A polygenic theory of schizophrenia. *Proceedings of the National Academy of Sciences of the United States of America, 58*, 199-205.

Gottesman, I. I., & Shields, J. (1972). *Schizophrenia and genetics: A twin study vantage point*. New York: Academic Press.

Gurling, H., Kalsi, G., Chih-Hui Chen, A., Green, M., Butler, R., Read, T., et al. (1995). Schizophrenia susceptibility and chromosome 6p24-22 [Letter and comment]. *Nature Genetics, 11*, 234-235. [Erratum appears in *Nature Genetics, 13*, 129]

Heston, L. L. (1966). Psychiatric disorders in foster home reared children of schizophrenic mothers. *British Journal of Psychiatry, 112*, 819-825.

Holland, T., & Gosden, C. (1990). A balanced chromosomal translocation partially co-segregating with psychotic illness in a family. *Psychiatry Research, 32*, 1-8.

Ingraham, L. J., & Kety, S. S. (2000). Adoption studies of schizophrenia. *American Journal of Medical Genetics, 97*, 18-22.

Kendler, K. S., McGuire, M., Gruenberg, A. M., O'Hare, A., Spellman, M., & Walsh, D. (1993). The Roscommon Family Study: III. Schizophrenia-related personality disorders in relatives. *Archives of General Psychiatry, 50*, 781-788.

Levinson, D. F., Holmans, P., Straub, R. E., Owen, M. J., Wildenauer, D. B., Gejman, P. V., et al. (2000). Multicenter linkage study of schizophrenia candidate regions on chromosomes 5q, 6q, 10p, and 13q: Schizophrenia linkage collaborative group III. *American Journal of Human Genetics, 67,* 652-663.

Lindholm, E., Ekholm, B., Balciuniene, J., Johansson, G., Castensson, A., Koisti, M., et al. (1999). Linkage analysis of a large Swedish kindred provides further support for a susceptibility locus for schizophrenia on chromosome 6p23. *American Journal of Medical Genetics, 88,* 369-377.

McGue, M., Gottesman, I. I., & Rao, D. C. (1983). The transmission of schizophrenia under a multifactorial threshold model. *American Journal of Human Genetics, 35,* 1161-1178.

McNeil, T. F., Cantor-Graae, E., & Weinberger, D. R. (2000). Relationship of obstetric complications and differences in size of brain structures in monozygotic twin pairs discordant for schizophrenia. *American Journal of Psychiatry, 157,* 203-212.

Moises, H. W., Yang, L., Kristbjarnarson, H., Wiese, C., Byerley, W., Macciardi, F., et al. (1995). An international two-stage genome-wide search for schizophrenia susceptibility genes. *Nature Genetics, 11,* 321-324.

Nurnberger, J. I., Jr., & Foroud, T. (1999). Chromosome 6 workshop report. *American Journal of Medical Genetics, 88,* 233-238.

Schwab, S. G., Albus, M., Hallmayer, J., Honig, S., Borrmann, M., Lichtermann, D., et al. (1995). Evaluation of a susceptibility gene for schizophrenia on chromosome 6p by multipoint affected sib-pair linkage analysis. *Nature Genetics, 11,* 325-327.

Slater, E., & Cowie, V. (1971). *The genetics of mental disorders.* Oxford, UK: Oxford University Press.

Stassen, H. H., Coppola, R., Gottesman, I. I., Torrey, E. F., Kuny, S., Rickler, K. C., et al. (1999). EEG differences in monozygotic twins discordant and concordant for schizophrenia. *Psychophysiology, 36,* 109-117.

Straub, R. E., MacLean, C. J., O'Neill, F. A., Burke, J., Murphy, B., Duke, F., et al. (1995). A potential vulnerability locus for schizophrenia on chromosome 6p24-22: Evidence for genetic heterogeneity. *Nature Genetics, 11,* 287-293.

Wang, S., Sun, C. E., Walczak, C. A., Ziegle, J. S., Kipps, B. R., Goldin, L. R., et al. (1995). Evidence for a susceptibility locus for schizophrenia on chromosome 6p24-22. *Nature Genetics, 10,* 41-46.

Weisbrod, M., Hill, H., Niethammer, R., & Sauer, H. (1999). Genetic influence on auditory information processing in schizophrenia: P300 in monozygotic twins. *Biological Psychiatry, 46,* 721-725.

CHAPTER 24

ANTISOCIAL BEHAVIOR AND VIOLENCE

INTRODUCTION ●

Are the Ted Bundys, John Wayne Gacys, and Jeffrey Dahmers of this world genetic freaks? More than one media reporter has contacted behavioral geneticists with that question, and contemporary films such as *The Bad Seed* and *Natural Born Killers* prey on this theme. The topic is not a new one. In *The Tempest*, Shakespeare described Caliban as "a born devil on whose nature nurture can never stick."

Since Darwin's time—and likely before—the evolutionary significance of and the genetics of prosocial and antisocial behavior have been controversial topics. From the perspective of the 21st-century social scientist, the state of affairs can be succinctly stated by paraphrasing Winston Churchill: "Never has so much been written by so many based on so few [data]."

This chapter is a busy one. After explicating the phenotype, it examines the empirical data on the genetic epidemiology of antisocial behavior (ASB). It then returns to the major theme of Chapter 1 of this text—lemonade and the "how" of behavior. We will examine the "how" of genes and ASB from one

431

perspective of contemporary behavioral genetics by examining the degree to which the heritability of ordinary personality traits might explain some of the genetic influence on ASB. Then, we will integrate some of the ways in which evolutionary psychologists view ASB. Once again, the purpose of the exercise is to explore the various ways in which psychologists, anthropologists, sociologists, and other social scientists are applying the techniques of genetics to help further the understanding of a very complicated group of behaviors.

● ANTISOCIAL BEHAVIOR: THE PHENOTYPE

Three Definitions

The empirical genetic literature defines antisocial behavior (ASB) in three different but interrelated ways. The first type of definition might be called the *criminal records* definition because the phenotype is defined in terms of arrests and/or convictions for serious offenses as recorded by the police or courts. This definition is used most often in the large population-based twin and adoption studies from Scandinavia, where centralized criminal records can be searched easily. It is most often encountered in the fields of sociology and criminology.

The second definition, termed here the *psychiatric* definition, treats antisocial behavior in terms of a *DSM-IV*[1] diagnosis of *conduct disorder* and/or *antisocial personality disorder*. Conduct disorder is diagnosed when a person exhibits a certain number of behavioral symptoms during childhood. Examples of the symptoms include persistent, serious lying; stealing; chronic violation of age-appropriate rules at home or at school; persistent running away from home; vandalism; and physical violence. Antisocial personality disorder is diagnosed only in adults (defined by *DSM-IV* as persons age 18 and older). A positive diagnosis of conduct disorder is a *sine qua non* for antisocial personality disorder, but in addition, the person must exhibit a series of other persistent antisocial behaviors that extend beyond childhood. These behaviors include inconsistent employment history; inadequate parenting; financial irresponsibility; disregard for the truth; persistent criminality; and physical violence. Assessment of these diagnoses is done through either self-report questionnaires or (most often) interview responses.

The third definition is more psychological in nature and is called *psychopathy* (aka *sociopathy*). This type of definition relies more heavily on a constellation of personality traits (and less on an overt history of antisocial actions) than either the criminal records or the psychiatric definition. The hallmark personality trait is lack of conscience. Other traits include failure to feel guilt and remorse after an antisocial action and inability to form warm and lasting interpersonal relationships (Hare, Hart, & Harpur, 1991; Lykken, 1995).

The three definitions overlap more than they compete with one another. Most—but not all—felons in resident prison populations quality for a diagnosis of antisocial personality disorder (Guze, 1976). Many psychiatrists working in the field make this diagnosis but in reality treat diagnosis as the end of a continuously distributed trait in the population rather than a "disease." In addition, many adults who exhibit the personality traits of the psychopath also have criminal records or merit a diagnosis of antisocial personality disorder (Widiger et al., 1996). Sadly, no twin or adoption study has reported a complete multivariate analysis of these three definitions.

Violence

Many criminologists distinguish between property crimes (examples of which are theft, embezzlement, and selling drugs) and violent crimes (examples of which are murder, rape, assault, and robbery). Here, violence may be defined as any act (or threat of such an act) that adversely affects the physical and psychological well-being of another person. This definition of violence will become important later in the chapter.

Natural History of Antisocial Behavior

A considerable number of both retrospective (e.g., Robins, 1974) and prospective (e.g., Huizinga, Loeber, & Thornberry, 1993; Loeber & Farrington, 2000; Loeber, Stouthamer-Loeber, & White, 1999) studies have converged upon a modal profile of people who engage in persistent antisocial behavior. Precursors are usually—but not always—evident in early childhood and take the form of unruliness, impulsivity, disobedience, and aggression. Such early behavior shows a moderate degree of stability over time and across situations—the unruly child at home often gets into trouble at school. What tends to change with age is the nature of the antisocial behavior. Disobedience at school develops into truancy, petty thievery of mom and dad's loose change gives way to stealing, and sibling aggression morphs into bullying. In the transition to adolescence, there is often precocious (and promiscuous) sexual behavior and early experimentation with cigarettes, alcohol, and illicit drugs. More serious delinquent behavior develops and many—but not all—youth who engage in such behavior start to come to the attention of the legal system. In years past, they were called juvenile delinquents. ASB persists into adulthood and is manifest in many different areas of life. Frequently observed are failure to sustain long-term relationships, particularly sexual ones; flitting from job to job with long periods of unemployment; failure to meet financial obligations and defaulting on debts; and engagement in overt criminal activity. Dependence on alcohol and drugs, along with depressive disorders, is not untypical in adults with significant ASB.

It is crucial to recognize that this is a *modal* (i.e., most frequent) profile and that there are many exceptions to it. Many, probably the majority, of adolescents who get into trouble with the law cease antisocial behavior when they become adults. Conversely, model children can develop persistent antisocial behavior as adults (e.g., Ted Bundy). There is speculation that there may be genetic differences associated with the age course of ASB, with a heavier genetic loading being found in life-course-persistent ASB than in ASB limited to adolescence (DiLalla & Gottesman, 1989; Moffitt, 1993).

It is important to point out the role of violence in the natural history of ASB. People who specialize in violence or a particular form of violence—like serial killers and serial rapists—are surprisingly rare. The deservedly intense press coverage given to such individuals probably misleads us into believing that they are more common than they actually are. In the majority of cases, violence occurs as scattered events within the life-course of someone with a long history of ASB, mostly of the nonviolent variety (Blumstein, Cohen, Roth, & Visher, 1986).

● GENETIC EPIDEMIOLOGY

Basic Findings

Table 24.1 presents an overview of the recent (post-1970) twin studies dealing with ASB. Despite the fact that the studies come from a variety of different countries and use different definitions of ASB, there is a surprising degree of consistency in their results. All but two studies—one on adults (Dalgard & Kringlen, 1976) and the other on children and adolescents (Thapar & McGuffin, 1996)—failed to find a statistically significant difference in concordance or correlation between MZ and DZ twins. One of the studies in Table 24.1 (Grove et al., 1990) dealt with MZ twins raised apart, so it is unlikely that methodological problems with the twin study are responsible for these consistent results.

A number of studies also suggest that there is a significant correlation between the environments of twins (i.e., η), but here a word of caution is

Table 24.1 A Summary of the Major Twin Studies on Antisocial Behavior

Place	Age	Phenotype	Sample References	$h2 > 0$?	$\eta > 0$?
Norway	Adults	Criminal records	Dalgard & Kringlen (1976)	No	Yes
Denmark	Adults	Criminal records	Carey (1992); Christiansen (1968); Cloninger & Gottesman (1987)	Yes	?/Yes
United States and United Kingdom	Adults (raised apart)	Psychiatric (CD & ASP)	Grove et al. (1990)	Yes	
United States	Adults (male veterans)	Psychiatric (CD & ASP)	Lyons et al. (1995)	Yes	Yes
United States	Adults (psychiatric patients)	Psychiatric (CD & ASP)	Carey (1993)	Yes	?/Yes
Canada	Adult	Psychiatric	Jang, Vernon, & Livesley (2000)	Yes	
United States	Adolescents	Psychiatric	Rowe (1983, 1985, 1986)	Yes	
United States	Children and adolescents	Psychiatric (CD)	Eaves et al. (1993); Meyer et al. (2000); Pickles et al. (1994)	Yes	Yes
United Kingdom	Children	Psychiatric	Graham & Stevenson (1985)	Yes	
United States	Children and adolescents	Psychiatric	Edelbrock et al. (1995)	Yes	Yes
United Kingdom	Children and adolescents	Psychiatric	Thapar & McGuffin (1996)	No	Yes
Australia	Adults	Psychiatric (CD)	Slutske et al. (1997, 1998)	Yes	
United Kingdom and Sweden	Children and adolescents	Psychiatric	Eley, Lichtenstein, & Stevenson (1999)	Yes	
United States	Children and adolescents	Psychiatric	Neiderhiser et al. (1999)	Yes	
United States	Children and adolescents	Psychiatric (CD)	Taylor, Iacono, & McGue (2000)	Yes	
United States	Children and adolescents	Psychiatric(CD)	Young et al. (2000)	Yes	Yes

435

advised. The situation for ASB parallels that for intelligence, in the sense that this environmental correlation is most important during childhood and adolescence and decreases in the adult years. Indeed, as for IQ scores, the heritability of ASB and allied traits such as aggression appears to increase with age, whereas the influence of the common family environment declines (Mason & Frick, 1994; Miles & Carey, 1997; Rhee & Waldman, 2002).

The adoption data presented in Table 24.2 paint a similar picture. ASB in adoptees is predicted by ASB (or some close correlate of ASB) in their biological relatives. The results are not *completely* unanimous in this regard, but the overall trend certainly suggests a genetic effect. For the reasons outlined in the Chapter 18 on quantitative genetics, it is unwise to use adoption data to arrive at conclusions about lack of a common, family environmental effect on ASB, but the data clearly implicate a genetic reason for the similarity among relatives.

Expanded Findings

The literature is also fairly consistent about several other issues of ASB. The age issue was mentioned earlier. In childhood and early adolescence, familial resemblance for ASB is due to both genes and the family environment; sometime during the transition into adulthood, the influence of the family environment diminishes, whereas the effect of genes increases. Some studies have reported sex differences in heritability (Eley, Lichtenstein, & Stevenson, 1999; Graham & Stevenson, 1985) for symptoms of conduct disorder, whereas other studies report no sex differences (e.g., Rhee & Waldman, 2002; Slutske et al., 1997). It is likely that the situation for sex differences in ASB is similar to that for personality. That is, there may indeed be statistically detectable differences in heritability for males and females, but the actual differences probably are small and secondary to the fact that ASB has moderate heritability in both males and females throughout most of the life span.

A further finding in the literature is that there may be a bona fide statistical gene-environment interaction in the genesis of ASB. This interaction involves the antisocial genotype and the rearing environment during childhood and adolescence, and it takes the form depicted in Figure 24.1. In reality, there are no such things as an "antisocial genotype" and a "prosocial genotype" as shown in this figure. Instead, there is a continuum of genotypes that quantitatively vary in their susceptibility to engage in ASB. However, it is convenient to take the top 50% of these genotypes and arbitrarily call them the "antisocial genotype," and to label the lower 50% as being the prosocial

Table 24.2 A Summary of the Major Adoption Studies on Antisocial Behavior

Place	Age	Phenotype	Sample References	h2 > 0 ?	η > 0?
United States	Adults	Criminal records	Crowe (1972, 1974)	Yes	
Denmark	Adults	Criminal records	Hutchings (1972); Hutchings & Mednick (1975, 1977)	Yes	
Denmark	Adults	Criminal records	Baker (1986); Baker et al. (1989); Gabrielli & Mednick (1983, 1984); Mednick, Gabrielli, & Hutchings (1984); Moffitt (1987)	Yes	
Sweden	Adults	Criminal records	Bohman (1978); Bohman et al. (1982); Cloninger et al. (1982); Sigvardsson et al. (1982)	Partly	
United States	Older teenagers and adults	Psychiatric	Cadoret & Cain (1980); Cadoret, Cain, & Crowe (1983); Cadoret, O'Gorman, et al. (1985); Cadoret, Troughton, et al. (1986); Cadoret, Yates, et al. (1995)	Yes	Yes
United States	Children and adolescents	Psychiatric	O'Connor, Deater-Deckard, et al. (1998); O'Connor, Neiderhiser, et al. (1998)	Yes	

437

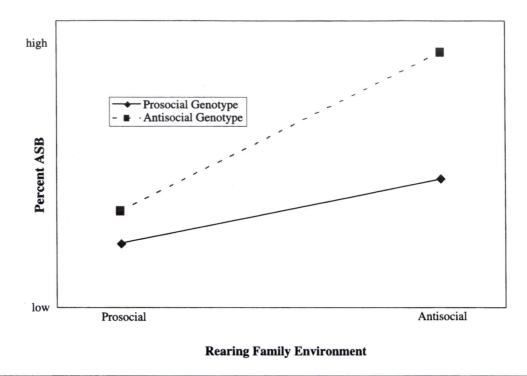

Figure 24.1   The Form of Possible Genotype-Environment Interaction in Antisocial Behavior

genotype. A similar categorization is used for the home environment in Figure 24.1.

The form of this interaction suggests that antisocial genotypes are more sensitive to the environment than prosocial genotypes. As a group, those with prosocial genotypes develop into prosocial adults, with the rearing environment playing only a small effect (i.e., a *small* effect relative to the environment's effect on the antisocial genotype). Antisocial genotypes, on the other hand, respond more to the family environment than do prosocial genotypes. That is, a change from a good to a poor family environment produces a greater phenotypic change in the antisocial genotype than in the prosocial genotype. Hence, antisocial genotypes are more sensitive to the rearing environment than antisocial genotypes.

The gene-environment interaction has been reported most strongly in the adoption studies undertaken by Remi Cadoret (Cadoret, 1982; Cadoret, Yates, Troughton, Woodworth, & Stewart, 1995). Both of the large adoption studies in Scandinavia report a similar type of interaction, although the actual interaction term does not always reach statistical significance (Cloninger,

Sigvardsson, Bohman, & von Knorring, 1982; Hutchings & Mednick, 1975). Clearly, this area deserves more research.

Violence

A final issue in genetic epidemiology concerns violent offending. Here, the literature is confusing and contradictory. The large Danish adoption study (Mednick, Gabrielli, & Hutchings, 1984) reports no resemblance between adoptees and either their biological or adoptive relatives for violent crime. All the genetic effect, it appears, occurred for property offenses. Taken at face value, these results imply that there is no familial resemblance for violence. However, the very large study on Danish twins reported large and significant correlations for violent offending in both MZ and DZ twins, although the difference between the MZ and the DZ correlations failed to reach statistical significance (Cloninger & Gottesman, 1987; see Carey, 1994). These twin data say that violence is really familial but not strongly heritable. Hence, violent offending seems to run in families according to one study (the twins) but not in the other (the adoptees). Unfortunately, none of the other studies analyzed their data separately for violent and property crimes. Until we can ascertain whether or not violence runs in families, we cannot make any conclusions one way or the other about genes and violence.

Summary

We are now in a position to address the questions raised in the introduction to this chapter. Is the genetic effect on ASB being driven by a small number of Calibans whose nature prevents them from being swayed by nurture? Are an extremely deviant and violent subset of criminals (the Bundys, Gacys, and Dahmers of the world) responsible for the heritability of ASB? The available evidence suggests just the opposite. Specialists in violent offending are rare (Blumstein et al., 1986), and the extent to which genes contribute at all to violence is unknown. Hence, if there are genetic Calibans, they are likely to be very, very rare and will not alter statistics like heritability that apply to whole populations.[2]

A second argument against the "Caliban hypothesis" lies in the form of the gene-environment interaction depicted in Figure 24.1. If the world's Calibans were responsible for the association between genes and ASB, then we would expect that antisocial genotypes should be insensitive to the rearing environment. Instead, we found just the opposite.

In sum, the data suggest that heritability for antisocial behavior probably occurs over the whole range of antisocial behaviors, with the possible (and questionable) exception of violence. Most researchers suspect that ASB is a continuously distributed trait, quite akin to a personality trait, that acts as a susceptibility dimension with inputs from biology and from the social and interpersonal environment. Presently, we have no good evidence for the existence of genetic natural-born killers.

● GENES AND ANTISOCIAL BEHAVIOR: THE HOW

This section will use the phenotype of ASB to illustrate how genetic research in behavior is moving away from establishing the fact that genes contribute to ASB and toward explaining the "how" of genes, environment, and ASB. It will illustrate the "how" from three different but complementary perspectives—the study of individual differences, evolutionary psychology, and molecular biology.

The Individual Differences Perspective

Imagine the following scenario. You are back in your senior year of high school. After school lets out one day, you and several of your friends walk down a nearby street, where you encounter something unexpected—a brand-new BMW convertible parked by the curb with the top down, the keys in the ignition, and the likely owner nowhere in sight. Of the many choices facing you and your comrades, I list four:

- *Very antisocial*: You steal the car with the intent of finding someone to sell it to and split the profits.
- *Moderately antisocial*: You spend the rest of the day and evening joyriding in the car. You have no intention of selling it and making money—you just want to have fun. After you are finished joyriding, you park the car somewhere and leave it.
- *Neutral*: You and your friends comment on the [expletive deleted] stupidity of the owner and walk on.
- *Prosocial*: Concerned that someone may steal the car and create considerable anguish for the owner, you remove the keys, write down the license number, and drop the keys and license number at the nearest police station.

If this situation were encountered by numerous groups of high school seniors, one fact is certain—the groups would not universally make the same choice. A few would opt for theft, some would hand in the keys to the police, and most would settle on some intermediate decision.

The key point is this: If this decision process is like any other substantive human behavior or trait (intelligence, any personality trait, any interest pattern, divorce, combat exposure, etc.), there will be some heritability to the response. In short, the phenotype of "decisions about encountering a new BMW with the keys in the ignition" probably would have an intermediate degree of genetic influence on it.

Now reflect for a minute on the issue of *how* genes might contribute to the individual differences in decisions for this situation. We can quickly discount several genetic mechanisms. It is completely implausible that eons of hominoid evolution resulted in sensory and cognitive mechanisms that made humans respond to the stimulus of "keys in a BMW" in the same way as herring gull chicks respond to a red dot on their parents' beaks.[3] Virtually all the stimuli, both perceived and imagined, are of such recent origin that evolution has not had sufficient time to orchestrate DNA sequences specifically encoded for "BMW perception," "implications of keys in ignition switches," or "neuronal pleasure circuits for joyriding." In short, it is unlikely that genes have any *direct* influence on any of the decisions listed above. Heredity may, however, have many *indirect* influences on a single behavior.

One indirect influence may come from personality traits. Consider impulsivity. People high on this trait tend to act without thinking, whereas those low on the trait tend to cogitate over the pros and cons of an action before behaving in any concrete way. All things being equal, would people high on impulsivity tend to drive the car away or hand the keys to the police? Impulsivity is heritable (see the data in Chapter 22 on the MPQ variable of Control—the opposite of impulsivity). If genes influence a basic personality dimension such as impulsivity, and if impulsivity is a causal factor (even though it may be a weak causal factor) in auto theft, then genes will have some nonzero influence on auto theft.

Other heritable personality traits may also have weak causal effects on the BMW situation. An example is thrill-seeking (see the MPQ variable of Harm Avoidance—the opposite end of thrill-seeking—in Chapter 22). People high on thrill-seeking like to engage in exciting—and potentially dangerous—situations, and this dimension has consistently been shown to correlate with antisocial behavior. All things being equal, would someone with a high thrill-seeking temperament be more likely to ride off in the BMW than someone low on this dimension?

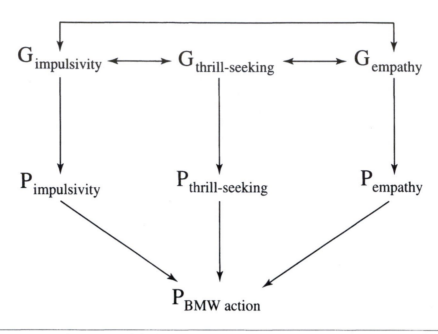

Figure 24.2   A Mediation Model of Gene Action for Antisocial Behavior

Another pertinent trait is empathy. High empathy requires a person to put him- or herself in the place of another human and act with consideration given to the other person's feelings. The high school senior with a great degree of empathy would think about the owner of the BMW and say to him- or herself, "If this were my BMW, what would I want the passers-by to do?" Would high empathizers have a tendency to make different decisions than low empathizers? At this stage, we could take the three variables mentioned thus far—impulsivity, thrill-seeking, and empathy—and begin to construct a causal model of the antisocial BMW response. Figure 24.2 illustrates this model.

In the figure, no genetic influences *directly* influence theft of the BMW. Instead, the genetic influences impinge on personality traits that in turn increase or decrease the probability of theft. This type of model is called a *mediational model*—the personality traits of impulsivity, thrill-seeking, and empathy *mediate* the genetic influence on BMW theft. Mediational models are commonly encountered in psychology (Baron & Kenny, 1986) and are a subset of the direction-of-causality models developed in behavioral genetics (Carey & DiLalla, 1994; Heath et al., 1993; Neale et al., 1994).

The model in Figure 24.2 may be "souped up" by including other variables. Consider the trait of independence versus susceptibility to peer pressure. If you are truly insightful about your own behavior, you will readily admit that any decision about the BMW convertible is a function of your *friends'* impulsivity, thrill-seeking, empathy, and perhaps other traits as well as of your own traits. Imagine that you were walking down the street with Bonnie and Clyde. Would your response be different in the company of this nefarious duo than if your companions were Mother Teresa and the Flying Nun? In short, through the mediating variable of your susceptibility to peer pressure (and perhaps other variables), your friends' genes for impulsivity, thrill-seeking, and empathy could be weak causal factors of *your own* behavior.

At this point, we can introduce an important distinction among the variables involved in ASB. The first class of variables deals with *proximal* phenotypes. These are the individual differences on traits that one is ultimately interested in—for example, BMW theft in the present example. In terms of antisocial behaviors, proximal variables might include murder, rape, assault, theft, embezzlement, and other crimes, as well as behaviors that are antisocial, though not criminal. The second type of variables falls under the rubric of *distal* traits. These are phenotypes that—in theory at least—genes influence directly and in turn directly influence individual differences in the distal phenotype. According to Figure 24.2, impulsivity, thrill-seeking, and empathy are distal phenotypes, whereas "BMW action" is a proximal phenotype.

To summarize, a mediational model may have a large number of variables that influence the probability of any specific antisocial action. Even though there may be no genetic effects that *directly* influence the specific ASB, the sum of all the *indirect* (i.e., *mediational*) effects could result in significant heritability for an ASB.

The biggest advantage of the mediational model is that it is *testable*. Researchers can gather data on relatives and then test whether the correlations between relatives for a specific ASB show that propensity to commit the ASB is indeed mediated by such factors as impulsivity, thrill-seeking, empathy, and peer attitudes. (The specifics of how to perform such testing are too advanced for this text; the interested reader can find them in Heath et al., 1993, and Neale et al., 1994). Because this is a cutting-edge technique, few published studies test these models. Hence, we cannot yet survey the literature and come to substantive conclusions about the empirical merits of these models.

ASB and Evolutionary Psychology: Homicide

Much of evolutionary psychology consists of examining behaviors that are performed in such an oblivious and perfunctory fashion that they appear

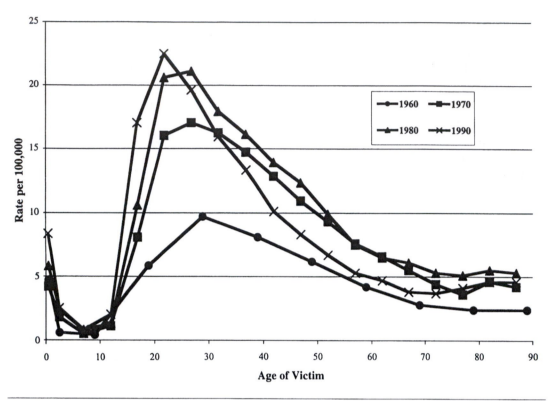

Figure 24.3   U.S. Homicide Victimization Rates by Age Over Four Decades.
SOURCE: U.S. Vital Statistics.

to be "second nature." Following the organization used in previous chapters, let us question the obvious to see how evolutionary psychology might help us to understand ASB. We will take homicide as an example and ask three relevant questions.

To prepare the stage, examine Figure 24.3, which provides U.S. homicide rates from 1960 to 1990 as a function of age of the victim. Note how there is a "spike" in rates that starts right after birth. The homicide rate then drops dramatically, so that infancy and childhood are the age periods of least risk for being killed by another human. Rates increase at adolescence, reach their maximum during the early adult years, and then steadily decrease into old age.

Question 1: Why Don't Genetic Relatives Kill One Another?

Martin Daly and Margo Wilson (1988a, 1988b), two evolutionary psychologists who have extensively studied homicide and homicide patterns, hypothesize that many of the attributes of homicide in Western industrialized societies fit well into theories of evolutionary psychology. Consider the following observations Daly and Wilson make about genetic relatedness and homicide among people living together.

- Unrelated people living together are 11 times as likely to be homicide victims than cohabiting genetic relatives.
- Studies in England, Australia, Canada, and the United States demonstrate that a child's probability of being a victim of fatal child abuse is much greater when living with stepparents or other substitute parents than when residing with genetic parents.
- In cases in which a genetic parent does kill a child (aka *genetic filicide*), the most vulnerable time is within the first year of the child's life. Thereafter, genetic filicide rates decline rapidly, until by age 6 the rate is less than five per million; it then remains steady at that level (Canadian data).
- Although general homicide rates start increasing in the early teens, rates of genetic filicide continue to be low and may even decrease in teenage children.

Daly and Wilson invoke parental investment theory, kinship theory, and inclusive fitness (see Chapter 16) to help explain these phenomena. Their argument goes something like this. Being mammals, we humans invest considerable resources in our offspring, and evolution has left us with a series of neurobiological mechanisms that enable us to recognize genetic relatives (including offspring, of course) and act protectively toward them. One central parameter of parental investment is simply the time already invested in an offspring. All things being equal, we have put more time and effort into raising and protecting a 5-year-old child than a 5-month-old baby. Hence, a mechanism that inhibits parents from damaging the reproductive potential of their children may have evolved and is likely to be engaged in much greater force for older offspring than for young neonates. In short, people with genes that inhibited serious aggression to their children left more copies of those genes than people with genes that failed to inhibit such aggression. That frequent refrain of the ever-frustrated parent—"do that again and I'll kill you"—is a hackneyed smokescreen. Although frustration may be frequent and deeply felt, the predicted dire consequences rarely occur.

Question 2: Why Don't Children Kill One Another?

To be sure, there are documented cases of homicide that involve children, but they are exceptionally rare. In fact, of the whole life span, childhood is the age of lowest homicide risk (see Figure 24.3). Why?

One obvious candidate for the nonlethal nature of childhood aggression is the physical strength and coordination of children. Perhaps they simply do not have the physical ability to commit homicide. This is certainly a factor during early infancy and childhood, but during the early grade school years, children develop sufficient strength to strangle someone or club someone to death with a baseball bat, for example.

Another possible candidate is inundation of media violence. Again, this probably plays a role, but it is unlikely to be a major factor. Statistics on homicide victimization before the advent of cinema and before the introduction of television document the relationship well before the current debate about media violence was even thought of.

Perhaps children are simply nonaggressive to begin with. Although we consider childhood a time of innocence in terms of moral culpability, it is definitely not a time of innocence in terms of physical aggression. Aggression does not increase in frequency from early childhood to middle childhood to adolescence. Instead, it occurs with its highest frequency as soon as infants are mobile enough to interact with one another, remains high throughout childhood, and decreases in early adolescence (Tremblay et al., 1999). What changes during adolescence is the *seriousness and lethality* of aggression, not the frequency of hitting, kicking, biting, and other aggressive behaviors.

Adolescence marks the start of the transition from high to low frequency of aggressive acts but low to high lethality of the same actions. The fact that this transition occurs during the period when the organism is beginning to develop reproductive capabilities has prompted several evolutionary psychologists to suspect that the two are associated. In fact, the peak ages for homicide risk are the early adult years, coinciding closely with the peak time of fertility (see Figure 24.2). We will discuss the implications of this after we consider the next question.

Question 3: Why Males as Victims and Perpetrators?

Most homicides involve males killing other males. Indeed, depending on age and ethnicity, a male is anywhere from 8 to 12 times as likely to commit murder than a female. Why?

In most societies, with only a handful of documented exceptions, aggression that leads to injury and death is a male enterprise. In contemporary industrialized societies, males are about 10 times as likely as females to be perpetrators of murder (Zimring & Hawkings, 1997).The ratio becomes even more extreme when one includes homicides that occur in the context of organized warfare. It is foolhardy to discount the importance of social roles and expectations in such a gender difference, but it may be just as silly to attribute *all* the sex difference to socialization.

Rowe (2001) points out that no sociological theory of crime considers the overt physical differences between females and males, yet to evolutionary psychologists, these same physical differences demand explanation. Two of the major differences—height and upper body strength—are certainly correlated with success in using threat and/or overt physical aggression. Hence, at some point in evolution—and whether the relevant time was before or after the human-chimp split is unknown—there *may have been* sexual selection favoring height, upper body strength, and aggression in males.

According to this view, male aggression is an adaptation to the environment (Rowe, 1996). Was such aggression directed at males within the same group, as it might be if there were active, within-group competition for mates? Or did the aggression develop largely to protect the group from males in other groups? Or did both factors—within-group competition and between-group protection—each play a salient role in the adaptation? The answers to these questions may well have been lost over time, but we modern humans are the inheritors of the legacy. In the past, men who used threats and lethal aggression left more gene copies than their contemporaries who employed different strategies.

Homicide: An Evolutionary Perspective

We have set the stage to examine the overall view of homicide from an evolutionary perspective. There is a popular social science notion, perhaps derived from the *tabula rasa* view, that we are born innocent and must acquire the wherewithal to become tainted by aggression. Evolutionary psychology turns this view on its head: We humans may be born with all the cognitive mechanisms to produce threats and to act aggressively, but we actually learn *not* to use these techniques in our day-to-day lives. This is why young children show very high rates of nonlethal aggression. It is also why you and I, if asked to identify the one person whom we hit, kicked, and bit the most during our lifetime, would probably nominate a sibling and would definitely pick childhood as the time of maximal occurrence of violence. Yet for some reason, children rarely exhibit lethality in their aggression.

Starting in late childhood and early adolescence, the rate of physical aggression decreases, while the seriousness of the consequences for a given aggressive act also increases. The reason for this is not clear, even within evolutionary psychology. Daly and Wilson (1988a, 1988b) emphasize that this is the time during a male's life history when he first has the physical capacity to reproduce and is beginning to engage in mate-acquiring behavior. Such a young male competes not only with older, established males, but also with the males within his own cohort. Perhaps threats, aggression, and even more general antisocial behavior at this stage of life help one to acquire the skills and resources for competing with other males for status and mating opportunities.

An alternative view—but not a mutually exclusive one—is that this is also the age at which skills for group defense are learned in preparation for actually defending the group. Perhaps lethality is required either to successfully aggress against another group or to defend one's own group against the lethal consequences of aggression. Through some complex interaction between evolutionary legacy and societal expectations, males assumed (and/or were assigned) the roles of aggressor and defender. Once mechanisms are in place that permit lethal aggression in the first place, they can easily be co-opted to apply to other situations such as acquiring a mate (or mates) within a group. Hence, lethal violence within groups is more likely to be directed against males than females.

Still, amid all this, we humans inhibit the lethality of our aggression (though not necessarily the aggression itself) when the target is a genetic relative. If we ignored genetics, then the dyad that would be at highest risk of involving a homicide would be a pair of young adult male sibs living together. Both are of the higher-risk sex (male). Both are likely to have had a history of aggressive acts directed at each other (a known risk factor for homicide). Both are cohabiting (another risk factor). And both are young. Yet fratricide (the killing of a sibling) is very rare (Daly & Wilson, 1988a, 1988b).

The How: Molecular Genetics

The Most Replicable Molecular Genetic Association in Psychiatry and Psychology

There is a surprising amount of molecular genetic work that touches on ASB, but little of it is directed explicitly at crime or other antisocial actions. Instead, these studies involve individuals and/or families with other traits (most noticeably alcoholism), with the participants subdivided by the presence or absence of antisocial behavior (e.g., Goldman, Lappalainen, & Ozaki, 1996; Hill, Zezza, Wipprecht, & Neiswanger, 1999; Lappalainen et al., 1998).[4] Hence, one will encounter studies of alcoholics with antisocial personality and alcoholics without antisocial personality. Much of this work explores the serotonin system,[5] a major neurotransmitter system in the brain, because there has been some empirical and theoretical evidence suggesting that inactivity in this system may be associated with impulsivity, aggression, and other antisocial behavior (see Lesch & Merschdorf, 2000). To date, the evidence is

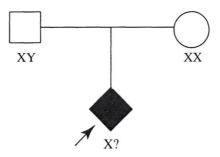

Figure 24.4 Schematic for a Transmission Disequilibrium Test for the Effect of the Y Chromosome on Antisocial Behavior.

mixed, and, as for most other molecular genetic work on behavior, it is necessary to postpone making strong conclusions until a large body of empirical work has been published and carefully analyzed.

This is a curious phenomenon because ASB and alcoholism are the two behavioral phenotypes with the most replicable molecular marker in all of psychiatry and psychology! This molecular marker is the very best example of lemonade and the *how* of genes, environment, and behavior that was the topic of Chapter 1 of this text. Let us take some time to explore it inductively.

The discussion of the association design (Chapter 11) pointed out that family-based association designs are the "gold standard" in genetics. Let us take one family-based design, the transmission disequilibrium test (TDT), and apply it to a diagnosis of antisocial personality (ASP) and alcohol abuse/dependence. The TDT design depicted in Figure 24.4, one should note, is identical in form to that presented in Figure 11.1. The affected offspring has a diagnosis of, say, ASP, and the informative parent is the father. The question is whether the father has a tendency to transmit his X or his Y chromosome to the affected offspring.

If there is no association between the sex chromosomes and ASP, then the father's probability of transmitting his Y chromosome should be .50. On the other hand, if there is a real association, then the probability should be different from .50. This TDT, of course, is nothing more than asking whether there are more males with ASP than females. The same could be said of a diagnosis of alcohol abuse or dependence. Table 24.3 gives actual results of this TDT from a twin sample gathered to study psychopathology (Gynther, Carey, Gottesman, & Vogler, 1995). For both ASP and alcohol, there is a significant difference in transmission from the 50/50 split predicted by the null hypothesis. The presence of a Y chromosome increases the risk that a person receives a diagnosis of ASP and a diagnosis of alcohol abuse/dependence.

Table 24.3 Transmission Disequilibrium Test for the X and Y Chromosomes for Diagnoses of Antisocial Personality Disorder and Alcohol Abuse/Dependence

| | Consensus Diagnosis | | | | | |
| | Antisocial Personality (ASP) (N = 82) | | Alcohol Abuse or Dependence (N = 206) | | Both ASP and Alcohol (N = 67) | |
	X	Y	X	Y	X	Y
Expected	41	41	103	103	33.5	33.5
Observed	27	55	72	130	19	48
χ^2	9.56		18.66		12.55	
$p <$	.001		.0001		.001	

SOURCE: Data are from Gynther, Carey, Gottesman, and Vogler (1995) and from unpublished data sources of Gottesman and Carey.

These results are of no surprise to anyone familiar with criminality and psychopathology—the facts that more men than women engage in antisocial behavior and that men are more susceptible to problems with alcohol were established long ago. Presenting the same results in the guise of a genetic test adds absolutely nothing to scientific knowledge, but it does have major lessons for both the geneticist and the social scientist.

Is This Association "Spurious"?

Two major criticisms are always made when these TDT results (or the results of other family-based designs) are presented to a scientific audience. The first criticism, voiced most frequently by social scientists, is that the results are flawed because they fail to consider socialization. This line of thinking thoroughly confuses descriptive statements with etiological inferences (see Chapter 12). All the TDT results state is that a 46,XY karyotype is at higher risk than a 46,XX karyotype for receiving a diagnosis of antisocial personality and/or alcohol abuse/dependence. The results tell us nothing about *how* these karyotypes come to predict the phenotypes. Differential socialization is a perfectly reasonable hypothesis for explaining the *how*. It is just that socialization responds to something that is genetic to begin with. Would anyone care to call the DNA and associated protein scaffolding of the X and the Y chromosomes "social constructions?"

The second criticism of these TDT results comes from geneticists who claim that there is something "fundamentally different" between the X and Y chromosomes and, say, a polymorphism in the serotonin transporter gene.[6] To my knowledge, no molecular biologist has ever reported a "fundamental difference" between loci on the X and Y chromosomes and loci on any auto-somal chromosome other than the number of and ordering of the four nucleotides. Yet this "fundamental difference"—which, by the way, no critic has ever been able to put into words—must exist. These critics seems to imply that the relationship between sex chromosomes and behavior permits more environmental effects than one involving, say, an enzyme polymor-phism on an autosomal chromosome.

Let us term this view the "endogenous engine theory" of genes and behavior in the sense that a single gene or its polypeptide product is viewed as a little machine that "drives" a behavior. So, the serotonin transporter pro-tein may be an "aggression" molecule that is central in some "aggression cir-cuits" in the brain, irrespective of whatever the environment is doing. The X and Y chromosomes, on the other hand, may "drive" physical differences in genitalia (among other things) but then indirectly influence phenotypes such as ASB because of society's treatment and expectations of behavior associ-ated with those physical differences. It's as if serotonin genes can have only direct impacts on aggression, whereas loci on the X and Y chromosomes can have direct and/or indirect effects.

The problem with the endogenous engine theory is that there is no sci-entific or logical reason to assume that the serotonin transporter locus *must* have a direct and only a direct influence on aggression. Consider! Low levels of serotonin are thought to "cause" ASB, but there is a long tradition associat-ing low levels of serotonin with depression and suicide (e.g., Asberg, Traskman, & Thoren, 1976; Coppen, 1972). So is the serotonin transporter locus an "aggression engine" or a "depression engine"? Perhaps it is neither. Perhaps the "serotonin system" in the brain—and hence the serotonin trans-porter locus—has no direct effect on either aggression or depression. Perhaps some of the structures in the brain in which serotonin plays a principal role as a neurotransmitter influence individual differences in sensitivity to cues from the social environment. Low serotonin neurotransmission may be associated with insensitivity to the social environment. Sociopaths fail to respond to the social feedback that their behavior is inappropriate, just as depressives respond poorly to the social feedback that they are really worthwhile and cherished human beings. In this hypothetical scenario, the serotonin trans-porter locus is not an "engine" for aggression or depression. Instead, it inhibits both sociopaths and depressives from profiting from the social envi-ronment around them and worsens their condition. If the gene is an "engine," it is an "engine" for *severity* that is not specific to either ASB or depression.

● LEMONADE REDUX

Let us recapitulate. The presence of a Y chromosome is a real, causal factor in the development of ASB and problems with excessive intake of alcohol. Some people bristle at this statement because they think it implies that the Y chromosome is only an "endogenous engine" that fuels breach of conduct, wanton licentiousness, and inebriety irrespective of social influences. NOT! The lesson from Chapter 1, reinforced, I hope, in many of the ensuing chapters, is that the Y chromosome is one of many constituents of ASB, much as sugar, water, and lemon juice are constituents of lemonade. The evolutionary legacy of vertebrates, mammals, primates, great apes, and finally our own human line forged physical differences between males and females that extend beyond the shape of external genitalia. Similarly, social expectations and reinforcements for behavior of 46,XY karyotypes that vary from human culture to human culture (and from time to time within a culture) also have direct causal influences on male behavior.

Antisocial behavior is lemonade. The replicable and definitive association relationship between the Y chromosome and ASB is the best illustration of lemonade that empirical data can provide. But lemonade means much, much more than the platitudinous aphorism that "both genes and environment contribute to human behavior." Consider the following two statements:

- Poverty has a causal influence on antisocial behavior.
- The reason that poverty has a causal influence on antisocial behavior relates to genes.

These two statements are entirely consistent from a lemonade perspective.[7] Now consider the following two statements:

- Among males, differences in testosterone levels have a causal influence on antisocial behavior.
- The reason that differences in male testosterone levels cause antisocial behavior relates to stereotyped sex-role expectations.

Again, these statements are entirely consistent from a lemonade perspective.[8]

Confused? If you are indeed confused, then it is time for you—the committed social scientist or the committed biologist—to start thinking "outside the box." We know that environments influence gene expression—the HPA axis example in Chapter 4 clearly illustrates this phenomenon. We also know that genotype influences societal response—otherwise, at formal events men would wear gowns as frequently as women. Human behavior is a complex compound. Just as the problem of lemonade asks us how sugar, water, and lemon juice combine to form this compound, the question of human behavior asks how genetic legacy and environmental contingencies combine to generate a phenotype.

NOTES ●

1. *DSM* stands for the *Diagnostic and Statistical Manual of the American Psychiatric Association*. The current version is version four; hence the term *DSM-IV*.

2. The rarity of such individuals should not detract from their importance for research. Logically, it is possible that a few rare pedophiles may be rare genetic variants with miswired nervous systems that respond sexually to young children instead of mature adults. Studying the genetics of these rare individuals may provide clues to the etiology of pedophilia.

3. In ethology, the herring gull example is a classic case of an innate releasing mechanism—a biologically "hard-wired" response to a stimulus. Herring gull chicks respond to the stimulus of a red dot by pecking at it. The parents, who have a red dot on their beaks, respond to the pecking by feeding the chicks.

4. The reason for this is partly the nature of research funding. Three large national institutes are devoted to mental health and addiction research—the NIAAA (National Institute on Alcohol Abuse and Alcoholism), NIDA (National Institute on Drug Abuse), and NIMH (National Institutes of Mental Health). The single institute devoted to ASB, the NIJ (National Institute of Justice), is considerably smaller and has a budget that is only a small fraction of the budgets of the other three institutes.

5. The major genetic polymorphisms involve the serotonin transporter gene, genes for serotonin receptors 1A and 2B, and genes for two enzymes that break down serotonin—monoamine oxidase A and catechol-*O*-methyltransferase.

6. There is a real polymorphism in the serotonin transporter locus, but it is much too soon to conclude that it definitely is associated with ASB. For that reason, treat this example as hypothetical.

7. There is no empirical justification for these two statements, but they are consistent with what is known about genes, environment, and antisocial behavior. As a hackneyed example, suppose that poverty induces stress in the people immersed in it. Such stress will influence the HPA hormonal response described in Chapter 4. Perhaps there are individual differences in such a response that then contribute to antisocial behavior. Hence, the causal chain is this: Poverty causes stress, which then causes ASB. But the correlation between stress and ASB in this context may be due entirely to genes.

8. Again, there is no empirical evidence supporting or refuting these statements. Hypothetically, one could imagine that higher testosterone levels are associated with a number of physical characteristics (increased height, muscle mass, body hair) that females respond to. Males with these characteristics are reinforced by females for engaging in selfish, antisocial behavior through which they are better able to provide the females with resources.

● REFERENCES

American Psychiatric Association. (1994). *Diagnostic and statistical manual of mental disorders: DSM-IV.* Washington, DC: Author.

Asberg, M., Traskman, L., & Thoren, P. (1976). 5-HIAA in the cerebrospinal fluid. A biochemical suicide predictor? *Archives of General Psychiatry, 33,* 1193-1197.

Baker, L. A. (1986). Estimating genetic correlations among discontinuous phenotypes: An analysis of criminal convictions and psychiatric hospital diagnoses in Danish adoptees. *Behavior Genetics, 16,* 127-142.

Baker, L. A., Mack, W., Moffitt, T. E., & Mednick, S. (1989). Sex differences in property crime in a Danish adoption cohort. *Behavior Genetics, 19,* 355-370.

Baron, R. M., & Kenny, D. A. (1986). The moderator-mediator variable distinction in social psychological research: Conceptual, strategic, and statistical considerations. *Journal of Personality & Social Psychology, 51,* 1173-1182.

Blumstein, A., Cohen, J., Roth, J. A., & Visher, C. A. (1986). *Criminal careers and "career criminals."* Washington, DC: National Academy Press.

Bohman, M. (1978). Some genetic aspects of alcoholism and criminality: A population of adoptees. *Archives of General Psychiatry, 35,* 269-276.

Bohman, M., Cloninger, C. R., Sigvardsson, S., & von Knorring, A. L. (1982). Predisposition to petty criminality in Swedish adoptees: I. Genetic and environmental heterogeneity. *Archives of General Psychiatry, 39,* 1233-1241.

Cadoret, R. J. (1982). Genotype-environment interaction in antisocial behaviour. *Psychological Medicine, 12,* 235-239.

Cadoret, R. J., & Cain, C. (1980). Sex differences in predictors of antisocial behavior in adoptees. *Archives of General Psychiatry, 37,* 1171-1175.

Cadoret, R. J., Cain, C. A., & Crowe, R. R. (1983). Evidence for gene-environment interaction in the development of adolescent antisocial behavior. *Behavior Genetics, 13,* 301-310.

Cadoret, R. J., O'Gorman, T. W., Troughton, E., & Heywood, E. (1985). Alcoholism and antisocial personality. Interrelationships, genetic and environmental factors. *Archives of General Psychiatry, 42,* 161-167.

Cadoret, R. J., Troughton, E., O'Gorman, T. W., & Heywood, E. (1986). An adoption study of genetic and environmental factors in drug abuse. *Archives of General Psychiatry, 43,* 1131-1136.

Cadoret, R. J., Yates, W. R., Troughton, E., Woodworth, G., & Stewart, M. A. (1995). Genetic-environmental interaction in the genesis of aggressivity and conduct disorders. *Archives of General Psychiatry, 52,* 916-924.

Carey, G. (1992). Twin imitation for antisocial behavior: Implications for genetic and family environment research. *Journal of Abnormal Psychology, 101,* 18-25.

Carey, G. (1993). Multivariate genetic relationships among drug abuse, alcohol abuse, and antisocial personality. *Psychiatric Genetics, 3,* 141.

Carey, G. (1994). Genetics and violence. In A. J. Reiss, Jr., K. A. Miczek, & J. A. Roth (Eds.), *Understanding and preventing violence: Vol. 2. Biobehavioral influences* (pp. 21-58). Washington, DC: National Academy Press.

Carey, G., & DiLalla, D. L. (1994). Personality and psychopathology: Genetic perspectives. *Journal of Abnormal Psychology, 103,* 32-43.

Christiansen, K. O. (1968). Threshold of tolerance in various population groups illustrated by results from Danish criminological twin study. In A.V.S. de Reuck & R. Porter (Eds.), *CIBA Foundation symposium on the mentally abnormal offender* (pp. 107-116). London: Churchill.

Cloninger, C. R., & Gottesman, I. I. (1987). Genetic and environmental factors in antisocial behavior disorders. In S. A. Mednick, T. E. Moffitt, & A. Stack (Eds.), *The causes of crime: New biological approaches* (pp. 92-109). New York: Cambridge University Press.

Cloninger, C. R., Sigvardsson, S., Bohman, M., & von Knorring, A. L. (1982). Predisposition to petty criminality in Swedish adoptees: II. Cross-fostering analysis of gene-environment interaction. *Archives of General Psychiatry, 39*, 1242-1247.

Coppen, A. (1972). Indoleamines and affective disorders. *Journal of Psychiatric Research, 9*, 163-171.

Crowe, R. R. (1972). The adopted offspring of women criminal offenders: A study of their arrest records. *Archives of General Psychiatry, 27*, 600-603.

Crowe, R. R. (1974). An adoption study of antisocial personality. *Archives of General Psychiatry, 31*, 785-791.

Dalgard, O. S., & Kringlen, E. (1976). A Norwegian twin study of criminality. *British Journal of Criminality, 16*, 213-232.

Daly, M., & Wilson, M. (1988a). Evolutionary social psychology and family homicide. *Science, 242*, 519-524.

Daly, M., & Wilson, M. (1988b). *Homicide*. New York: A. de Gruyter.

DiLalla, L. F., & Gottesman, I. I. (1989). Heterogenetity of causes for delinquency and criminality: Lifespan perspectives. *Development and Psychopathology, 1*, 339-349.

Eaves, L. J., Silberg, J. L., Hewitt, J. K., Rutter, M., Meyer, J. M., Neale, M. C., et al. (1993). Analyzing twin resemblance in multisymptom data: Genetic applications of a latent class model for symptoms of conduct disorder in juvenile boys. *Behavior Genetics, 23*, 5-19. [Erratum appears in *Behavior Genetics, 23*(5), 423]

Edelbrock, C., Rende, R., Plomin, R., & Thompson, L. A. (1995). A twin study of competence and problem behavior in childhood and early adolescence. *Journal of Child Psychology and Psychiatry and Allied Disciplines, 36*, 775-785.

Eley, T. C., Lichtenstein, P., & Stevenson, J. (1999). Sex differences in the etiology of aggressive and nonaggressive antisocial behavior: Results from two twin studies. *Child Development, 70*, 155-168.

Gabrielli, W. F., Jr., & Mednick, S. A. (1983). Genetic correlates of criminal behavior: Implications for research, attribution, and prevention. *American Behavioral Scientist, 27*, 59-74.

Gabrielli, W. F., Jr., & Mednick, S. A. (1984). Urban environment, genetics, and crime. *Criminology, 22*, 645-652.

Goldman, D., Lappalainen, J., & Ozaki, N. (1996). Direct analysis of candidate genes in impulsive behaviours. *CIBA Foundation Symposium, 194*, 139-152.

Graham, P., & Stevenson, J. (1985). A twin study of genetic influences on behavioral deviance. *Journal of the American Academy of Child Psychiatry, 24*, 33-41.

Grove, W. M., Eckert, E. D., Heston, L., Bouchard, T. J., Jr., Segal, N., & Lykken, D. T. (1990). Heritability of substance abuse and antisocial behavior: A study of monozygotic twins reared apart. *Biological Psychiatry, 27*, 1293-1304.

Guze, S. B. (1976). *Criminality and psychiatric disorders*. New York: Oxford University Press.

Gynther, L., Carey, G., Gottesman, I. I., & Vogler, G. (1995). A twin study of substance abuse. *Psychiatry Research, 56*, 213-220.

Hare, R. D., Hart, S. D., & Harpur, T. J. (1991). Psychopathy and the DSM-IV criteria for antisocial personality disorder. *Journal of Abnormal Psychology, 100*, 391-398.

Heath, A. C., Kessler, R. C., Neale, M. C., Hewitt, J. K., Eaves, L. J., & Kendler, K. S. (1993). Testing hypotheses about direction of causation using cross-sectional family data. *Behavior Genetics, 23*, 29-50.

Hill, S. Y., Zezza, N., Wipprecht, G., Xu, J., & Neiswanger, K. (1999). Linkage studies of D2 and D4 receptor genes and alcoholism. *American Journal of Medical Genetics, 88*, 676-685.

Huizinga, D., Loeber, R., & Thornberry, T. P. (1993). Longitudinal study of delinquency, drug use, sexual activity, and pregnancy among children and youth in three cities. *Public Health Reports, 108*, 90-96.

Hutchings, B. (1972). *Environmental and genetics factors in psychopathology and criminality.* Unpublished master's thesis, University of London.

Hutchings, B., & Mednick, S. A. (1975). Registered criminality in the adoptive and biological parents of registered male criminal adoptees. *Proceedings of the Annual Meeting of the American Psychopathological Association, 63*, 105-116.

Hutchings, B., & Mednick, S. A. (1977). Criminality in adoptees and their adoptive and biological parents: A pilot study. In S. A. Mednick (Ed.), *Christiansen, K. O.* (pp. 127-141). New York: Gardner.

Jang, K. L., Vernon, P. A., & Livesley, W. J. (2000). Personality disorder traits, family environment, and alcohol misuse: A multivariate behavioural genetic analysis. *Addiction, 95*, 873-888.

Lappalainen, J., Long, J. C., Eggert, M., Ozaki, N., Robin, R. W., Brown, G. L., et al. (1998). Linkage of antisocial alcoholism to the serotonin 5-HT1B receptor gene in 2 populations. *Archives of General Psychiatry, 55*, 989-994.

Lesch, K. P., & Merschdorf, U. (2000). Impulsivity, aggression, and serotonin: A molecular psychobiological perspective. *Behavioral Sciences and the Law, 18*, 581-604.

Loeber, R., & Farrington, D. P. (2000). Young children who commit crime: Epidemiology, developmental origins, risk factors, early interventions, and policy implications. *Development and Psychopathology, 12*, 737-762.

Loeber, R., Stouthamer-Loeber, M., & White, H. R. (1999). Developmental aspects of delinquency and internalizing problems and their association with persistent juvenile substance use between ages 7 and 18. *Journal of Clinical Child Psychology, 28*, 322-332.

Lykken, D. T. (1995). *The antisocial personalities.* Hillsdale, NJ: Lawrence Erlbaum Associates.

Lyons, M. J., True, W. R., Eisen, S. A., Goldberg, J., Meyer, J. M., Faraone, S. V., et al. (1995). Differential heritability of adult and juvenile antisocial traits. *Archives of General Psychiatry, 52*, 906-915.

Mason, D. A., & Frick, P. J. (1994). The heritability of antisocial behavior: A meta-analysis of twin and adoption studies. *Journal of Psychopathology & Behavioral Assessment, 16*, 301-323.

Mednick, S. A., Gabrielli, W. F., Jr., & Hutchings, B. (1984). Genetic influences in criminal convictions: Evidence from an adoption cohort. *Science, 224*, 891-894.

Meyer, J. M., Rutter, M., Silberg, J. L., Maes, H. H., Simonoff, E., Shillady, L. L., et al. (2000). Familial aggregation for conduct disorder symptomatology: The role of genes, marital discord and family adaptability. *Psychological Medicine, 30*, 759-774.

Miles, D. R., & Carey, G. (1997). Genetic and environmental architecture on human aggresssion. *Journal of Personality & Social Psychology, 72*, 207-217.

Moffitt, T. E. (1987). Parental mental disorder and offspring criminal behavior: An adoption study. *Psychiatry, 50*, 346-360.

Moffitt, T. E. (1993). "Life-course persistent" and "adolescence-limited" antisocial behavior: A developmental taxonomy. *Psychological Review, 100*, 674-701.

Neale, M. C., Walters, E., Heath, A. C., Kessler, R. C., Perusse, D., Eaves, L. J., et al. (1994). Depression and parental bonding: Cause, consequence, or genetic covariance? *Genetic Epidemiology, 11*, 503-522.

Neiderhiser, J. M., Reiss, D., Hetherington, E. M., & Plomin, R. (1999). Relationships between parenting and adolescent adjustment over time: Genetic and environmental contributions. *Developmental Psychology, 35*, 680-692.

O'Connor, T. G., Deater-Deckard, K., Fulker, D., Rutter, M., & Plomin, R. (1998). Genotype-environment correlations in late childhood and early adolescence: Antisocial behavioral problems and coercive parenting. *Developmental Psychology, 34,* 970-981.

O'Connor, T. G., Neiderhiser, J. M., Reiss, D., Hetherington, E. M., & Plomin, R. (1998). Genetic contributions to continuity, change, and co-occurrence of antisocial and depressive symptoms in adolescence. *Journal of Child Psychology & Psychiatry & Allied Disciplines, 39,* 323-336.

Pickles, A., Crouchley, R., Simonoff, E., Eaves, L., Meyer, J., Rutter, M., et al. (1994). Survival models for developmental genetic data: Age of onset of puberty and antisocial behavior in twins. *Genetic Epidemiology, 11,* 155-170.

Rhee, S. H., & Waldman, I. D. (2002). Genetic and environmental influences on antisocial behavior: A meta-analysis of twin and adoption studies. *Psychological Bulletin, 128,* 490-529.

Robins, L. N. (1974). *Deviant children grow up.* Huntington, NY: Krieger.

Rowe, D. C. (1983). Biometrical genetic models of self-reported delinquent behavior: A twin study. *Behavior Genetics, 13,* 473-489.

Rowe, D. C. (1985). Sibling interaction and self-reported delinquent behavior: A study of 265 twin pairs. *Criminology, 23,* 223-240.

Rowe, D. C. (1986). Genetic and environmental components of antisocial behavior: A study of 265 twin pairs. *Criminology, 24,* 512-532.

Rowe, D. C. (1996). An adaptive strategy theory of crime and delinquency. In J. D. Hawkins (Ed.), *Delinquency and crime: Current theories.* Cambridge, UK: Cambridge University Press.

Rowe, D. C. (2001). *Biology and crime.* Los Angeles: Roxbury.

Sigvardsson, S., Cloninger, C. R., Bohman, M., & von Knorring, A. L. (1982). Predisposition to petty criminality in Swedish adoptees: III. Sex differences and validation of the male typology. *Archives of General Psychiatry, 39,* 1248-1253.

Slutske, W. S., Heath, A. C., Dinwiddie, S. H., Madden, P. A., Bucholz, K. K., Dunne, M. P., et al. (1997). Modeling genetic and environmental influences in the etiology of conduct disorder: A study of 2,682 adult twin pairs. *Journal of Abnormal Psychology, 106,* 266-279.

Slutske, W. S., Heath, A. C., Dinwiddie, S. H., Madden, P. A., Bucholz, K. K., Dunne, M. P., et al. (1998). Common genetic risk factors for conduct disorder and alcohol dependence. *Journal of Abnormal Psychology, 107,* 363-374.

Taylor, J., Iacono, W. G., & McGue, M. (2000). Evidence for a genetic etiology of early-onset delinquency. *Journal of Abnormal Psychology, 109,* 634-643.

Thapar, A., & McGuffin, P. (1996). A twin study of antisocial and neurotic symptoms in childhood. *Psychological Medicine, 26,* 1111-1118.

Tremblay, R. E., Japel, C., Perusse, D., McDuff, P., Boivin, M., Zoccolillo, M., et al. (1999). The search for the age of "onset" of physical aggression: Rousseau and Bandura revisited. *Criminal Behavior and Mental Health, 9,* 8-23.

Widiger, T. A., Cadoret, R., Hare, R., Robins, L., Rutherford, M., Zanarini, M., et al. (1996). DSM-IV antisocial personality disorder field trial. *Journal of Abnormal Psychology, 105,* 3-16.

Young, S. E., Stallings, M. C., Corley, R. P., Krauter, K. S., & Hewitt, J. K. (2000). Genetic and environmental influences on behavioral disinhibition. *American Journal of Medical Genetics, 96,* 684-695.

Zimring, F. E., & Hawkings, G. (1997). *Crime is not the problem: Lethal violence in America.* New York: Oxford University Press.

REFERENCES

Abe, K. (1969). The morbidity rate and environmental influence in monozygotic co-twins of schizophrenics. *British Journal of Psychiatry, 115,* 519-531.

Adorno, T. W., Frenkel-Brunswick, E., Levinson, D. J., & Sanford, R. N. (1950). *The authoritarian personality.* New York: Harper.

Alarcon, M., Plomin, R., Fulker, D. W., Corley, R., & DeFries, J. C. (1998). Multivariate path analysis of specific cognitive abilities data at 12 years of age in the Colorado Adoption Project. *Behavior Genetics, 28,* 255-264. [Published erratum appears in *Behavior Genetics, 29,* 77]

American Psychiatric Association. (1994). *Diagnostic and statistical manual of mental disorders: DSM-IV.* Washington, DC: Author.

Anastasi, A. (1956). Intelligence and family size. *Psychological Bulletin, 53,* 187-209.

Anastasi, A. (1958). Heredity, environment, and the question "How?" *Psychological Review, 65,* 197-208.

Aran, O., Galatzer, A., Kauli, R., Nagelberg, N., Robicsek, Y., & Laron, Z. (1992). Social, educational and vocational status of 48 young adult females with gonadal dysgenesis. *Clinical Endocrinology, 36,* 405-410.

Armstrong, F. D., Thompson, R. J., Jr., Wang, W., Zimmerman, R., Pegelow, C. H., Miller, S., Moser, F., Bello, J., Hurtig, A., & Vass, K., for the Neuropsychology Committee of the Cooperative Study of Sickle Cell Disease. (1996). Cognitive functioning and brain magnetic resonance imaging in children with sickle cell disease. *Pediatrics, 97,* 864-870.

Asarnow, R. F., Nuechterlein, K. H., Fogelson, D., Subotnik, K. L., Payne, D. A., Russell, A. T., et al. (2001). Schizophrenia and schizophrenia-spectrum personality disorders in the first-degree relatives of children with schizophrenia: The UCLA family study. *Archives of General Psychiatry, 58,* 581-588.

Asberg, M., Traskman, L., & Thoren, P. (1976). 5-HIAA in the cerebrospinal fluid. A biochemical suicide predictor? *Archives of General Psychiatry, 33,* 1193-1197.

Azen, C., Koch, R., Friedman, E., Wenz, E., & Fishler, K. (1996). Summary of findings from the United States Collaborative Study of children treated for phenylketonuria. *European Journal of Pediatrics, 155*(Suppl. 1), S29-S32.

Bailey, D. B., Jr., Hatton, D. D., & Skinner, M. (1998). Early developmental trajectories of males with fragile X syndrome. *American Journal on Mental Retardation, 103,* 29-39.

Baker, L. A. (1986). Estimating genetic correlations among discontinuous phenotypes: An analysis of criminal convictions and psychiatric hospital diagnoses in Danish adoptees. *Behavior Genetics, 16,* 127-142.

Baker, L. A., Mack, W., Moffitt, T. E., & Mednick, S. (1989). Sex differences in property crime in a Danish adoption cohort. *Behavior Genetics, 19,* 355-370.

Baker, L. A., Treloar, S. A., Reynolds, C. A., Heath, A. C., & Martin, N. G. (1996). Genetics of educational attainment in Australian twins: Sex differences and secular changes. *Behavior Genetics, 26,* 89-102.

Barash, D. P. (1982). *Sociobiology and behavior* (2nd ed.). New York: Elsevier.

Baron, R. M., & Kenny, D. A. (1986). The moderator-mediator variable distinction in social psychological research: Conceptual, strategic, and statistical considerations. *Journal of Personality & Social Psychology, 51,* 1173-1182.

Beer, J. M., Arnold, R. D., & Loehlin, J. C. (1998). Genetic and environmental influences on MMPI factor scales: Joint model fitting to twin and adoption data. *Journal of Personality and Social Psychology, 74,* 818-827.

Behrman, J. R., & Taubman, P. (1989). Is schooling "mostly in the genes"? *Journal of Political Economy, 97,* 1425-1446.

Bennetto, L., Pennington, B. F., Porter, D., Taylor, A. K., & Hagerman, R. J. (2001). Profile of cognitive functioning in women with the fragile X mutation. *Neuropsychology, 15,* 290-299.

Berenbaum, S. A., & Hines, M. (1992). Early androgens are related to childhood sex-typed toy preferences. *Psychological Science, 3,* 203-206.

Berenbaum, S. A., & Resnick, S. M. (1997). Early androgen effects on aggression in children and adults with congenital adrenal hyperplasia. *Psychoneuroendocrinology, 22,* 505-515.

Berrettini, W. H. (2000). Susceptibility loci for bipolar disorder: Overlap with inherited vulnerability to schizophrenia. *Biological Psychiatry, 47,* 245-251.

Blacker, D., & Tanzi, R. E. (1998). The genetics of Alzheimer disease: Current status and future prospects. *Archives of Neurology, 55,* 294-296.

Bloom, B. S. (1964). *Stability and change in human characteristics.* New York: Wiley.

Blumstein, A., Cohen, J., Roth, J. A., & Visher, C. A. (1986). *Criminal careers and "career criminals."* Washington, DC: National Academy Press.

Bohman, M. (1978). Some genetic aspects of alcoholism and criminality: A population of adoptees. *Archives of General Psychiatry, 35,* 269-276.

Bohman, M., Cloninger, C. R., Sigvardsson, S., & von Knorring, A. L. (1982). Predisposition to petty criminality in Swedish adoptees: I. Genetic and environmental heterogeneity. *Archives of General Psychiatry, 39,* 1233-1241.

Bouchard, T. J., Jr. (1998). Genetic and environmental influences on adult intelligence and special mental abilities. *Human Biology, 70,* 257-279.

Bouchard, T. J., Jr., Lykken, D. T., McGue, M., Segal, N. L., & Tellegen, A. (1990). Sources of human psychological differences: The Minnesota Study of Twins Reared Apart. *Science, 250,* 223-228.

Bouchard, T. J., Jr., & McGue, M. (1981). Familial studies of intelligence: A review. *Science, 212,* 1055-1059.

Bowles, S., & Gintis, H. (2001). The inheritance of economic status: Education, class and genetics (Working Paper 01-01-005). Santa Fe, NM: Santa Fe Institute.

Brunner, H. G., Nelen, M., Breakefield, X. O., Ropers, H. H., & van Oost, B. A. (1993). Abnormal behavior associated with a point mutation in the structural gene for monoamine oxidase A. *Science, 262,* 578-580.

Brunner, H. G., Nelen, M. R., van Zandvoort, P., Abeling, N. G., van Gennip, A. H., Wolters, E. C., et al. (1993). X-linked borderline mental retardation with prominent behavioral disturbance: Phenotype, genetic localization, and evidence for disturbed monoamine metabolism. *American Journal of Human Genetics, 52,* 1032-1039.

Burgard, P., Schmidt, E., Rupp, A., Schneider, W., & Bremer, H. J. (1996). Intellectual development of the patients of the German Collaborative Study of children treated for phenylketonuria. *European Journal of Pediatrics, 155*(Suppl. 1), S33-S38.

Buss, A. H., & Plomin, R. (1975). *A temperament theory of personality development.* New York: Wiley.

Buss, A. H., & Plomin, R. (1984). *Temperament: Early developing personality traits.* Hillsdale, NJ: Lawrence Erlbaum.

Buss, D. M. (1994). *The evolution of desire: Strategies of human mating.* New York: Basic Books.

Buss, D. M., & Schmitt, D. P. (1993). Sexual strategies theory: An evolutionary perspective on human mating. *Psychological Review, 100,* 204-232.

Cadoret, R. J. (1982). Genotype-environment interaction in antisocial behaviour. *Psychological Medicine, 12,* 235-239.

Cadoret, R. J., & Cain, C. (1980). Sex differences in predictors of antisocial behavior in adoptees. *Archives of General Psychiatry, 37,* 1171-1175.

Cadoret, R. J., Cain, C. A., & Crowe, R. R. (1983). Evidence for gene-environment interaction in the development of adolescent antisocial behavior. *Behavior Genetics, 13,* 301-310.

Cadoret, R. J., O'Gorman, T. W., Troughton, E., & Heywood, E. (1985). Alcoholism and antisocial personality. Interrelationships, genetic and environmental factors. *Archives of General Psychiatry, 42,* 161-167.

Cadoret, R. J., Troughton, E., O'Gorman, T. W., & Heywood, E. (1986). An adoption study of genetic and environmental factors in drug abuse. *Archives of General Psychiatry, 43,* 1131-1136.

Cadoret, R. J., Yates, W. R., Troughton, E., Woodworth, G., & Stewart, M. A. (1995). Genetic-environmental interaction in the genesis of aggressivity and conduct disorders. *Archives of General Psychiatry, 52,* 916-924.

Cann, R. L., Stoneking, M., & Wilson, A. C. (1987). Mitochondrial DNA and human evolution. *Nature, 325,* 31-36.

Cantor-Graae, E., McNeil, T. F., Rickler, K. C., Sjostrom, K., Rawlings, R., Higgins, E. S., et al. (1994). Are neurological abnormalities in well discordant monozygotic co-twins of schizophrenic subjects the result of perinatal trauma? *American Journal of Psychiatry, 151,* 1194-1199.

Cardno, A. G., Marshall, E. J., Coid, B., Macdonald, A. M., Ribchester, T. R., Davies, N. J., et al. (1999). Heritability estimates for psychotic disorders: The Maudsley twin psychosis series. *Archives of General Psychiatry, 56,* 162-168.

Cardon, L. R., & Fulker, D. W. (1994). A model of developmental change in hierarchical phenotypes with application to specific cognitive abilities. *Behavior Genetics, 24,* 1-16.

Cardon, L. R., Smith, S. D., Fulker, D. W., Kimberling, W. J., Pennington, B. F., & DeFries, J. C. (1994). Quantitative trait locus for reading disability on chromosome 6. *Science, 266,* 276-279.

Carey, G. (1987). Big genes, little genes, affective disorder, and anxiety: A commentary. *Archives of General Psychiatry, 44,* 486-491.

Carey, G. (1988). Inference about genetic correlations. *Behavior Genetics, 18,* 329-338.

Carey, G. (1992). Twin imitation for antisocial behavior: Implications for genetic and family environment research. *Journal of Abnormal Psychology, 101,* 18-25.

Carey, G. (1993). Multivariate genetic relationships among drug abuse, alcohol abuse, and antisocial personality. *Psychiatric Genetics, 3,* 141.

Carey, G. (1994). Genetics and violence. In A. J. Reiss, Jr,. K. A. Miczek, & J. A. Roth (Eds.), *Understanding and preventing violence: Vol. 2. Biobehavioral influences* (pp. 21-58). Washington, DC: National Academy Press.

Carey, G., & DiLalla, D. L. (1994). Personality and psychopathology: Genetic perspectives. *Journal of Abnormal Psychology, 103,* 32-43.

Carey, G., & Gottesman, I. I. (1981). Twin and family studies of anxiety, phobic, and obsessive disorders. In D. F. Klein & E. Rabkin (Eds.), *Anxiety: New research and changing concepts* (pp. 117-136). New York: Raven Press.

Carey, G., & Rice, J. (1983). Genetics of personality temperament: Simplicity or complexity? *Behavior Genetics, 13,* 43-83.

Carey, G., & Williamson, J. (1991). Linkage analysis of quantitative traits: Increased power by using selected samples. *American Journal of Human Genetics, 49,* 786-796.

Carroll, J. B. (1993). *Human cognitive abilities: A survey of factor-analytic studies.* New York: Cambridge University Press.

Cattell, R. B. (1936). Is our national intelligence declining? *Eugenics Review, 28,* 181.

Cattell, R. B. (1940). A culture-free intelligence test, Part 1. *Journal of Educational Psychology, 31,* 161-179.

Cattell, R. B. (1951). The fate of national intelligence: Test of a thirteen-year prediction. *Eugenics Review, 42,* 136-148.

Cavalli-Sforza, L. L. (2000). *Genes, peoples, and languages.* New York: North Point Press.

Cavalli-Sforza, L. L., Menozzi, P., & Piazza, A. (1994). *The history and geography of human genes.* Princeton, NJ: Princeton University Press.

Chambers, M. (1999). *Academic achievement and IQ: A longitudinal genetic analysis.* Unpublished doctoral dissertation, University of Colorado.

Chapman, R. S., & Hesketh, L. J. (2000). Behavioral phenotype of individuals with Down syndrome. *Mental Retardation and Developmental Disability Research Reviews, 6,* 84-95.

Cherny, S. S., Fulker, D. W., Emde, R. N., Robinson, J., Corley, R. P., Reznick, J. S., et al. (1994). A developmental-genetic analysis of continuity and change in the Bayley Mental Development Index from 14 to 24 months: The MacArthur Longitudinal Twin Study. *Psychological Science, 5,* 354-360.

Chiang, P. W., Carpenter, L. E., & Hagerman, P. J. (2001). The 5'-untranslated region of the fmr1 message facilitates translation by internal ribosome entry. *Journal of Biological Chemistry, 276,* 37916-37921.

Christiansen, K. O. (1968). Threshold of tolerance in various population groups illustrated by results from Danish criminological twin study. In A. V. S. de Reuck & R. Porter (Eds.), *CIBA Foundation symposium on the mentally abnormal offender* (pp. 107-116). London: Churchill.

Chu, C. E., Donaldson, M. D., Kelnar, C. J., Smail, P. J., Greene, S. A., Paterson, W. F., et al. (1994). Possible role of imprinting in the Turner phenotype. *Journal of Medical Genetics, 31,* 840-842.

Cicchetti, D. (1988). The organization and coherence of socioemotional, cognitive, and representational development: Illustrations through a developmental psychopathology perspective on Down syndrome and child maltreatment. *Nebraska Symposium on Motivation, 36,* 259-366.

Clarke, D. J., Boer, H., Chung, M. C., Sturmey, P., & Webb, T. (1996). Maladaptive behaviour in Prader-Willi syndrome in adult life. *Journal of Intellectual Disability Research, 40,* 159-165.

Cloninger, C. R., & Gottesman, I. I. (1987). Genetic and environmental factors in antisocial behavior disorders. In S. A. Mednick, T. E. Moffitt, & A. Stack (Eds.), *The causes of crime: New biological approaches* (pp. 92-109). New York: Cambridge University Press.

Cloninger, C. R., Sigvardsson, S., Bohman, M., & von Knorring, A. L. (1982). Predisposition to petty criminality in Swedish adoptees: II. Cross-fostering analysis of gene-environment interaction. *Archives of General Psychiatry, 39,* 1242-1247.

Coppen, A. (1972). Indoleamines and affective disorders. *Journal of Psychiatric Research, 9,* 163-171.

Cornblatt, B., Obuchowski, M., Roberts, S., Pollack, S., & Erlenmeyer-Kimling, L. (1999). Cognitive and behavioral precursors of schizophrenia. *Development and Psychopathology, 11,* 487-508.

Cosmides, L., & Tooby, J. (1992). Cognitive adaptations for social exchange. In J. Barkow, L. Cosmides, & J. Tooby (Eds.), *The adapted mind* (pp. 163-228). New York: Oxford University Press.

Cosmides, L., & Tooby, J. (1994). Beyond intuition and instinct blindness: Toward an evolutionarily rigid cognitive science. *Cognition and Emotion, 50*, 41-77.

Costa, P. T., Jr., & McCrae, R. R. (1988). Personality in adulthood: A six-year longitudinal study of self-reports and spouse ratings on the NEO Personality Inventory. *Journal of Personality and Social Psychology, 54*, 853-863.

Cronbach, L. J., & Meehl, P. M. (1955). Construct validity in psychological tests. *Psychological Bulletin, 52*, 281-302.

Crowe, R. R. (1972). The adopted offspring of women criminal offenders: A study of their arrest records. *Archives of General Psychiatry, 27*, 600-603.

Crowe, R. R. (1974). An adoption study of antisocial personality. *Archives of General Psychiatry, 31*, 785-791.

Dalgard, O. S., & Kringlen, E. (1976). A Norwegian twin study of criminality. *British Journal of Criminality, 16*, 213-232.

Daly, M., & Wilson, M. (1988a). Evolutionary social psychology and family homicide. *Science, 242*, 519-524.

Daly, M., & Wilson, M. (1988b). *Homicide*. New York: A. de Gruyter.

Daniels, J. K., Spurlock, G., Williams, N. M., Cardno, A. G., Jones, L. A., Murphy, K. C., et al. (1997). Linkage study of chromosome 6p in sib-pairs with schizophrenia. *American Journal of Medical Genetics, 74*, 319-323.

Davis, J. O., & Bracha, H. S. (1996). Prenatal growth markers in schizophrenia: A monozygotic co-twin control study. *American Journal of Psychiatry, 153*, 1166-1172.

Dawkins, R. (1989). *The selfish gene* (New ed.). New York: Oxford University Press.

de Vries, B. B., Halley, D. J., Oostra, B. A., & Niermeijer, M. F. (1998). The fragile X syndrome. *Journal of Medical Genetics, 35*, 579-589.

de Waal, F. (1989). *Peacemaking among primates*. Cambridge, MA: Harvard University Press.

de Waal, F. B. (1995). Bonobo sex and society. *Scientific American, 272*, 82-88.

Deaux, K., & Hanna, R. (1984). Courtship in the personal column: The influence of gender and sexual orientation. *Sex Roles, 11*, 363-375.

DeFries, J. C., Gervais, M. C., & Thomas, E. A. (1978). Response to 30 generations of selection for open-field activity in laboratory mice. *Behavior Genetics, 8*, 3-11.

DeFries, J. C., Plomin, R., & Fulker, D. W. (Eds.). (1994). *Nature and nurture during middle childhood*. Cambridge, MA: Blackwell.

DeLisi, L. E. (2000). Critical overview of current approaches to genetic mechanisms in schizophrenia research. *Brain Research Review, 31*, 187-192.

Delooz, J., Van den Berghe, H., Swillen, A., Kleczkowska, A., & Fryns, J. P. (1993). Turner syndrome patients as adults: A study of their cognitive profile, psychosocial functioning and psychopathological findings. *Genetic Counseling, 4*, 169-179.

Diamond, A. (1994). Phenylalanine levels of 6-10 mg/dl may not be as benign as once thought. *Acta Paediatrica, 83*, (Suppl. 407), 89-91.

Diamond, A. (1996). Evidence for the importance of dopamine for prefrontal cortex functions early in life. *Philosophical Transactions of the Royal Society of London. Series B: Biological Sciences, 351*, 1483-1493.

DiLalla, D. L., & Gottesman, I. I. (1995). Normal personality characteristics in identical twins discordant for schizophrenia. *Journal of Abnormal Psychology, 104*, 490-499.

DiLalla, L. F., & Gottesman, I. I. (1989). Heterogenetity of causes for delinquency and criminality: Lifespan perspectives. *Development and Psychopathology, 1*, 339-349.

Dittmann, R. W., Kappes, M. E., & Kappes, M. H. (1992). Sexual behavior in adolescent and adult females with congenital adrenal hyperplasia. *Psychoneuroendocrinology, 17*, 153-170.

Dittmann, R. W., Kappes, M. H., Kappes, M. E., Borger, D., Meyer-Bahlburg, H. F., Stegner, H., Willig, R. H., & Wallis, H. (1990). Congenital adrenal hyperplasia. II:

Gender-related behavior and attitudes in female salt-wasting and simple-virilizing patients. *Psychoneuroendocrinology, 15,* 421-434.

Dittmann, R. W., Kappes, M. H., Kappes, M. E., Borger, D., Stegner, H., Willig, R. H., & Wallis, H. (1990b). Congenital adrenal hyperplasia. I: Gender-related behavior and attitudes in female patients and sisters. *Psychoneuroendocrinology, 15,* 401-420. (Published erratum appears in *Psychoneuroendocrinology, 16,* 369-371)

Dunne, M. P., Martin, N. G., Statham, D. J., Slutske, W. S., Dinwiddie, S. H., Bucholz, K. K., et al. (1997). Genetic and environmental contributions to variance in age at first sexual intercourse. *Psychological Science, 8,* 211-216.

Dykens, E. M., & Kasari, C. (1997). Maladaptive behavior in children with Prader-Willi syndrome, Down syndrome, and nonspecific mental retardation. *American Journal of Mental Retardation, 102,* 228-237.

Eaves, L., D'Onofrio, B., & Russell, R. (1999). Transmission of religion and attitudes. *Twin Research, 2,* 59-61.

Eaves, L. J., & Eysenck, H. J. (1976). Genotype × age interaction for neuroticism. *Behavior Genetics, 6,* 359-362.

Eaves, L. J., Eysenck, H. J., & Martin, N. G. (1989). *Genes, culture, and personality: An empirical approach.* San Diego: Academic Press.

Eaves, L. J., Last, K., Martin, N. G., & Jinks, J. L. (1977). A progressive approach to non-additivity and genotype-environmental covariance in the analysis of human differences. *British Journal of Mathematical and Statistical Psychology, 30,* 1-42.

Eaves, L. J., Silberg, J. L., Hewitt, J. K., Rutter, M., Meyer, J. M., Neale, M. C., et al. (1993). Analyzing twin resemblance in multisymptom data: Genetic applications of a latent class model for symptoms of conduct disorder in juvenile boys. *Behavior Genetics, 23,* 5-19. [Erratum appears in *Behavior Genetics, 23*(5), 423]

Edelbrock, C., Rende, R., Plomin, R., & Thompson, L. A. (1995). A twin study of competence and problem behavior in childhood and early adolescence. *Journal of Child Psychology and Psychiatry and Allied Disciplines, 36,* 775-785.

Eley, T. C., Lichtenstein, P., & Stevenson, J. (1999). Sex differences in the etiology of aggressive and nonaggressive antisocial behavior: Results from two twin studies. *Child Development, 70,* 155-168.

el-Hazmi, M. A., Warsy, A. S., al-Swailem, A. R., al-Swailem, A. M., & Bahakim, H. M. (1996). Sickle cell gene in the population of Saudi Arabia. *Hemoglobin, 20,* 187-198.

Erlenmeyer-Kimling, L., Rock, D., Roberts, S. A., Janal, M., Kestenbaum, C., Cornblatt, B., et al. (2000). Attention, memory, and motor skills as childhood predictors of schizophrenia-related psychoses: The New York High-Risk Project. *American Journal of Psychiatry, 157,* 1416-1422.

Falconer, D. S. (1965). The inheritance of liability to certain diseases, estimated from the incidence among relatives. *Annals of Human Genetics, 31,* 1-20.

Falk, C. T., & Rubenstein, P. (1987). Haplotype relative risk: An easy reliable way to construct a proper control sample for risk calculations. *Annals of Human Genetics, 51,* 227-233.

Faraone, S. V., Doyle, A. E., Mick, E., & Biederman, J. (2001). Meta-analysis of the association between the 7-repeat allele of the dopamine D(4) receptor gene and attention deficit hyperactivity disorder. *American Journal of Psychiatry, 158,* 1052-1057.

Farrer, L. A., Cupples, L. A., Haines, J. L., Hyman, B., Kukull, W. A., Mayeux, R., et al. (1997). Effects of age, sex, and ethnicity on the association between apolipoprotein E genotype and Alzheimer disease. A meta-analysis. *JAMA, 278,* 1349-1356.

Fine, R. E. (1999). The biochemistry of Alzheimer disease. *Alzheimer Disease and Associated Disorders, 13*(Suppl. 1), S82-S87.

Finkel, D., & McGue, M. (1997). Sex differences and nonadditivity in heritability of the Multidimensional Personality Questionnaire Scales. *Journal of Personality and Social Psychology, 72,* 929-938.

Finkel, D., Pedersen, N. L., McGue, M., & McClearn, G. E. (1995). Heritability of cognitive abilities in adult twins: Comparison of Minnesota and Swedish data. *Behavior Genetics, 25,* 421-431.

Floderus-Myrhed, B., Pederson, N., & Rasmuson, I. (1980). Assessment of heritability for personality, based on a short form of the Eysenck Personality Inventory. *Behavior Genetics, 10,* 153-162.

Flynn, J. R. (1984). The mean IQ of Americans: Massive gains 1932 to 1978. *Psychological Bulletin, 95,* 29-51.

Flynn, J. R. (1987). Massive IQ gains in 14 nations: What IQ tests really measure. *Psychological Bulletin, 101,* 171-191.

Flynn, J. R. (1998). IQ gains over time: Toward finding the causes. In U. Neisser (Ed.), *The rising curve: Long-term gains in IQ and related measures* (pp. 25-66). Washington, DC: American Psychological Association.

Gabrielli, W. F., Jr., & Mednick, S. A. (1983). Genetic correlates of criminal behavior: Implications for research, attribution, and prevention. *American Behavioral Scientist, 27,* 59-74.

Gabrielli, W. F., Jr., & Mednick, S. A. (1984). Urban environment, genetics, and crime. *Criminology, 22,* 645-652.

Ganguli, M., Chandra, V., Kamboh, M. I., Johnston, J. M., Dodge, H. H., Thelma, B. K., et al. (2000). Apolipoprotein E polymorphism and Alzheimer disease: The Indo-US Cross-National Dementia Study. *Archives of Neurology, 57,* 824-830.

Garcia, J., & Koelling, R. A. (1966). Relationship of cue to consequence in avoidance learning. *Psychonomic Science, 4,* 123-124.

Gardner, H. (1983). *Frames of mind: The theory of multiple intelligences.* New York: Basic Books.

Gardner, H. (1993). *Multiple intelligences: The theory in practice.* New York: Basic Books.

Garner, C., Kelly, M., Cardon, L., Joslyn, G., Carey, A., LeDuc, C., et al. (1996). Linkage analyses of schizophrenia to chromosome 6p24-p22: An attempt to replicate. *American Journal of Medical Genetics, 67,* 595-610.

Gayan, J., Smith, S. D., Cherny, S. S., Cardon, L. R., Fulker, D. W., Brower, A., et al. (1999). Quantitative-trait locus for specific language and reading deficits on chromosome 6p. *American Journal of Human Genetics, 64,* 157-164.

Gerdes, L. U., Klausen, I. C., Sihm, I., & Faergeman, O. (1992). Apolipoprotein E polymorphism in a Danish population compared to findings in 45 other study populations around the world. *Genetic Epidemiology, 9,* 155-167.

Gershon, E. S. (2000). Bipolar illness and schizophrenia as oligogenic diseases: Implications for the future. *Biological Psychiatry, 47,* 240-244.

Goedde, H. W., Agarwal, D. P., & Harada, S. (1983). Pharmacogenetics of alcohol sensitivity. *Pharmacology, Biochemistry and Behavior, 18,* 161-166.

Goldberg, T. E., Torrey, E. F., Gold, J. M., Bigelow, L. B., Ragland, R. D., Taylor, E., et al. (1995). Genetic risk of neuropsychological impairment in schizophrenia: A study of monozygotic twins discordant and concordant for the disorder. *Schizophrenia Research, 17,* 77-84.

Goldman, D., Lappalainen, J., & Ozaki, N. (1996). Direct analysis of candidate genes in impulsive behaviours. *CIBA Foundation Symposium, 194,* 139-152.

Goldsby, R. A. (1971). *Race and races.* New York: Macmillan.

Goldsmith, H. H., Buss, K. A., & Lemery, K. S. (1997). Toddler and childhood temperament: Expanded content, stronger genetic evidence, new evidence for the importance of environment. *Developmental Psychology, 33,* 891-905.

Goodall, J. (1986). *The chimpanzees of Gombe: Patterns of behavior*. Cambridge, MA: Harvard University Press.

Gottesman, I. I. (1991). *Schizophrenia genesis: The origins of madness*. San Francisco: W. H. Freeman.

Gottesman, I. I., & Bertelsen, A. (1989). Confirming unexpressed genotypes for schizophrenia: Risks in the offspring of Fischer's Danish identical and fraternal discordant twins. *Archives of General Psychiatry, 46*, 867-872.

Gottesman, I. I., & Erlenmeyer-Kimling, L. (2001). Family and twin strategies as a head start in defining prodromes and endophenotypes for hypothetical early-interventions in schizophrenia. *Schizophrenia Research, 51*, 93-102.

Gottesman, I. I., & Shields, J. (1967). A polygenic theory of schizophrenia. *Proceedings of the National Academy of Sciences of the United States of America, 58*, 199-205.

Gottesman, I. I., & Shields, J. (1972). *Schizophrenia and genetics: A twin study vantage point*. New York: Academic Press.

Gotz, M. J., Johnstone, E. C., & Ratcliffe, S. G. (1999). Criminality and antisocial behaviour in unselected men with sex chromosome abnormalities. *Psychological Medicine, 29*, 953-962.

Graham, P., & Stevenson, J. (1985). A twin study of genetic influences on behavioral deviance. *Journal of the American Academy of Child Psychiatry, 24*, 33-41.

Griffiths, P., Paterson, L., & Harvie, A. (1995). Neuropsychological effect of subsequent exposure to phenylalanine in adolescents and young adults with early-treated phenylketonuria. *Journal of Intellectual Disability Research, 39*, 365-372.

Grove, W. M., Eckert, E. D., Heston, L., Bouchard, T. J., Jr., Segal, N., & Lykken, D. T. (1990). Heritability of substance abuse and antisocial behavior: A study of monozygotic twins reared apart. *Biological Psychiatry, 27*, 1293-1304.

Gurling, H., Kalsi, G., Chih-Hui Chen, A., Green, M., Butler, R., Read, T., et al. (1995). Schizophrenia susceptibility and chromosome 6p24-22 [Letter and comment]. *Nature Genetics, 11*, 234-235. [Erratum appears in *Nature Genetics, 13*, 129]

Gusella, J. F., Wexler, N. S., Conneally, P. M., Naylor, S. L., Anderson, M. A., Tanzi, R. E., et al. (1983). A polymorphic DNA marker genetically linked to Huntington's disease. *Nature, 306*, 234-238.

Guze, S. B. (1976). *Criminality and psychiatric disorders*. New York: Oxford University Press.

Gynther, L., Carey, G., Gottesman, I. I., & Vogler, G. (1995). A twin study of substance abuse. *Psychiatry Research, 56*, 213-220.

Hagerman, R. (1997). Fragile X: Treatment of hyperactivity. *Pediatrics, 99*, 753.

Hagerman, R. J., & Hagerman, P. J. (2001). Fragile X syndrome: A model of gene-brain-behavior relationships. *Molecular Genetics and Metabolism, 74*, 89-97.

Hamilton, W. D. (1964a). The genetical evolution of social behavior: I. *Journal of Theoretical Biology, 7*, 1-16.

Hamilton, W. D. (1964b). The genetical evolution of social behavior: II. *Journal of Theoretical Biology, 7*, 17-52.

Harcourt, A. H., Fossey, D., Stewart, K. J., & Watts, D. P. (1980). Reproduction in wild gorillas and some comparisons with chimpanzees. *Journal of Reproduction and Fertility* (Suppl. 28), 59-70.

Hare, R. D., Hart, S. D., & Harpur, T. J. (1991). Psychopathy and the DSM-IV criteria for antisocial personality disorder. *Journal of Abnormal Psychology, 100*, 391-398.

Harpending, H., & Rogers, A. (2000). Genetic perspectives on human origins and differentiation. *Annual Review of Genomics and Human Genetics, 1*, 361-385.

Harris, J. R. (1995). Where is the child's environment? A group socialization theory of development. *Psychological Review, 102*, 458-489.

Harris, J. R. (1998). *The nurture assumption: Why children turn out the way they do*. New York: Touchstone.

Hartl, D. L., & Clark, A. G. (1997). *Principles of population genetics* (3rd ed.). Sunderland, MA: Sinauer Associates.

Haseman, J. K., & Elston, R. C. (1972). The investigation of linkage between a quantitative trait and a marker locus. *Behavior Genetics, 2*, 3-19.

Hauser-Cram, P., Warfield, M. E., Shonkoff, J. P., Krauss, M. W., Sayer, A., & Upshur, C. C. (2001). Children with disabilities: A longitudinal study of child development and parent well-being. *Monographs of the Society for Research in Child Development, 66*, 1-114.

Hay, D. A. (1985). *Essentials of behavior genetics.* London: Blackwell.

Heath, A. C., Berg, K., Eaves, L. J., Solaas, M. H., Corey, L., Sundet, J., et al. (1985). Educational policy and the heritability of educational attainment. *Nature, 314*, 734-736.

Heath, A. C., Kessler, R. C., Neale, M. C., Hewitt, J. K., Eaves, L. J., & Kendler, K. S. (1993). Testing hypotheses about direction of causation using cross-sectional family data. *Behavior Genetics, 23*, 29-50.

Heath, A. C., Neale, M. C., Kessler, R. C., Eaves, L. J., & Kendler, K. S. (1992). Evidence for genetic influences on personality from self-reports and informant ratings. *Journal of Personality and Social Psychology, 63*, 85-96.

Helleday, J., Edman, G., Ritzen, E. M., & Siwers, B. (1993). Personality characteristics and platelet MAO activity in women with congenital adrenal hyperplasia (CAH). *Psychoneuroendocrinology, 18*, 343-354.

Herrnstein, R. J., & Murray, C. (1994). *The bell curve: Intelligence and class structure in American life.* New York: Free Press.

Heston, L. L. (1966). Psychiatric disorders in foster home reared children of schizophrenic mothers. *British Journal of Psychiatry, 112*, 819-825.

Higgins, J. V., Reed, E. W., & Reed, S. C. (1962). Intelligence and family size: A paradox resolved. *Social Biology, 9*, 84-90.

Higuchi, S., Matsushita, S., Muramatsu, T., Murayama, M., & Hayashida, M. (1996). Alcohol and aldehyde dehydrogenase genotypes and drinking behavior in Japanese. *Alcoholism: Clinical and Experimental Research, 20*, 493-497.

Hill, S. Y., Zezza, N., Wipprecht, G., Xu, J., & Neiswanger, K. (1999). Linkage studies of D2 and D4 receptor genes and alcoholism. *American Journal of Medical Genetics, 88*, 676-685.

Hilton, C., Osborn, M., Knight, S., Singhal, A., & Serjeant, G. (1997). Psychiatric complications of homozygous sickle cell disease among young adults in the Jamaican Cohort Study. *British Journal of Psychiatry, 170*, 69-76.

Holland, T., & Gosden, C. (1990). A balanced chromosomal translocation partially co-segregating with psychotic illness in a family. *Psychiatry Research, 32*, 1-8.

Hoogeveen, A. T., & Oostra, B. A. (1997). The fragile X syndrome. *Journal of Inherited Metabolic Disease, 20*, 139-151.

Hook, E. B. (1973). Behavioral implications of the human XYY genotype. *Science, 179*, 139-150.

Horn, J. M., Loehlin, J. C., & Willerman, L. (1979). Intellectual resemblance among adoptive and biological relatives: The Texas Adoption Project. *Behavior Genetics, 9*, 117-207.

Huisman, J., Slijper, F. M., Sinnema, G., Akkerhuis, G. W., Brugman-Boezeman, A., Feenstra, J., et al. (1993). Psychosocial effects of two years of human growth hormone treatment in Turner syndrome. *Hormone Research, 39*, 56-59.

Huizinga, D., Loeber, R., & Thornberry, T. P. (1993). Longitudinal study of delinquency, drug use, sexual activity, and pregnancy among children and youth in three cities. *Public Health Reports, 108*, 90-96.

Humphreys, L. (1989). Intelligence: Three kinds of instability and the consequences for policy. In R. L. Linn (Ed.), *Intelligence: Measurement, theory, and public policy* (pp. 193-216). Urbana: University of Illinois Press.

Hunt, E. (1995). The role of intelligence in modern society. *American Scientist, 83,* 356-368.

Huntington's Disease Collaborative Research Group. (1993). A novel gene containing a trinucleotide repeat that is expanded and unstable on Huntington's disease chromosomes. *Cell, 72,* 971-983.

Hutchings, B. (1972). *Environmental and genetics factors in psychopathology and criminality.* Unpublished master's thesis, University of London.

Hutchings, B., & Mednick, S. A. (1975). Registered criminality in the adoptive and biological parents of registered male criminal adoptees. *Proceedings of the Annual Meeting of the American Psychopathological Association, 63,* 105-116.

Hutchings, B., & Mednick, S. A. (1977). Criminality in adoptees and their adoptive and biological parents: A pilot study. In S. A. Mednick (Ed.), *Christiansen, K. O.* (pp. 127-141). New York: Gardner.

Huxley, A. (1936). *Brave new world.* Garden City, NY: Sun Dial Press.

Ingraham, L. J., & Kety, S. S. (2000). Adoption studies of schizophrenia. *American Journal of Medical Genetics, 97,* 18-22.

Isles, A. R., & Wilkinson, L. S. (2000). Imprinted genes, cognition and behaviour. *Trends in Cognitive Science, 4,* 309-318.

Jacobs, P. A., Betts, P. R., Cockwell, A. E., Crolla, J. A., Mackenzie, M. J., Robinson, D. O., et al. (1990). A cytogenetic and molecular reappraisal of a series of patients with Turner's syndrome. *Annals of Human Genetics, 54,* 209-223.

Jacobs, P. A., Brunton, M., Melville, M. M., Brittain, R. P., & McClemont, W. F. (1965). Aggressive behavior, mental sub-normality and the XYY male. *Nature, 208,* 1351-1352.

Jang, K. L., Livesley, W. J., & Vernon, P. A. (1996). Heritability of the big five personality dimensions and their facets: A twin study. *Journal of Personality, 64,* 577-591.

Jang, K. L., Livesley, W. J., Vernon, P. A., & Jackson, D. N. (1996). Heritability of personality disorder traits: A twin study. *Acta Psychiatrica Scandinavica, 94,* 438-444.

Jang, K. L., Vernon, P. A., & Livesley, W. J. (2000). Personality disorder traits, family environment, and alcohol misuse: A multivariate behavioural genetic analysis. *Addiction, 95,* 873-888.

Janus, C., & Westaway, D. (2001). Transgenic mouse models of Alzheimer's disease. *Physiology and Behavior, 73,* 873-886.

Jencks, C., Bartlett, S., Corcoran, M., Crouse, J., Eaglesfield, D., Jackson, G., et al. (1979). *Who gets ahead? The determinants of economic success in America.* New York: Basic Books.

Jensen, A. R. (1980). *Bias in mental testing.* New York: Free Press.

Jensen, A. R. (1998). *The g factor: The science of mental ability.* Westport, CT: Praeger.

Jinks, J. L., & Fulker, D. W. (1970). Comparison of biometrical, genetical, MAVA, and classical approaches to the analysis of human behavior. *Psychological Bulletin, 73,* 311-349.

Johnson, R. C., Nagoshi, C. T., Schwitters, S. Y., Bowman, K. S., Ahern, F. M., & Wilson, J. R. (1984). Further investigation of racial/ethnic differences and of familial resemblances in flushing in response to alcohol. *Behavior Genetics, 14,* 171-178.

Kano, T. (1992). *The last ape: Pygmy chimpanzee behavior and ecology.* Stanford, CA: Stanford University Press.

Kendler, K. S., McGuire, M., Gruenberg, A. M., O'Hare, A., Spellman, M., & Walsh, D. (1993). The Roscommon Family Study: III. Schizophrenia-related personality disorders in relatives. *Archives of General Psychiatry, 50,* 781-788.

Kendler, K. S., Neale, M. C., Kessler, R. C., Heath, A. C., & Eaves, L. J. (1993). A test of the equal-environment assumption in twin studies of psychiatric illness. *Behavior Genetics, 23,* 21-27.

Kessler, S., & Moos, R. H. (1973). Behavioral aspects of chromosomal disorders. *Annual Review of Medicine, 24,* 89-102.

Klatsky, A. L., Siegelaub, A. B., Landy, C., & Friedman, G. (1983). Racial patterns of alcohol beverage use. *Alcoholism: Clinical and Experimental Research, 7,* 372-377.

Koch, R., Fishler, K., Azen, C., Guldberg, P., & Guttler, F. (1997). The relationship of genotype to phenotype in phenylalanine hydroxylase deficiency. *Biochemical and Molecular Medicine, 60,* 92-101.

Kotler, M., Manor, I., Sever, Y., Eisenberg, J., Cohen, H., Ebstein, R. P., et al. (2000). Failure to replicate an excess of the long dopamine D4 exon III repeat polymorphism in ADHD in a family-based study. *American Journal of Medical Genetics, 96,* 278-281.

LaHoste, G. J., Swanson, J. M., Wigal, S. B., Glabe, C., Wigal, T., King, N., et al. (1996). Dopamine D4 receptor gene polymorphism is associated with attention deficit hyperactivity disorder. *Molecular Psychiatry, 1,* 121-124.

Lappalainen, J., Long, J. C., Eggert, M., Ozaki, N., Robin, R. W., Brown, G. L., et al. (1998). Linkage of antisocial alcoholism to the serotonin 5-HT1B receptor gene in 2 populations. *Archives of General Psychiatry, 55,* 989-994.

Lesch, K. P., & Merschdorf, U. (2000). Impulsivity, aggression, and serotonin: A molecular psychobiological perspective. *Behavioral Sciences and the Law, 18,* 581-604.

Levinson, D. F., Holmans, P., Straub, R. E., Owen, M. J., Wildenauer, D. B., Gejman, P. V., et al. (2000). Multicenter linkage study of schizophrenia candidate regions on chromosomes 5q, 6q, 10p, and 13q: Schizophrenia linkage collaborative group III. *American Journal of Human Genetics, 67,* 652-663.

Lewontin, R. C., Rose, S., & Kamin, L. J. (1984). *Not in our genes: Biology, ideology, and human nature.* New York: Pantheon.

Lichtenstein, P., & Pedersen, N. L. (1997). Does genetic variance for cognitive abilities account for genetic variance in educational achievement and occupational status? A study of twins reared apart and twins reared together. *Social Biology, 44,* 77-90.

Lichter, J. B., Barr, C. L., Kennedy, J. L., Van Tol, H. H., Kidd, K. K., & Livak, K. J. (1993). A hypervariable segment in the human dopamine receptor D4 (DRD4) gene. *Human Molecular Genetics, 2,* 767-773.

Lindholm, E., Ekholm, B., Balciuniene, J., Johansson, G., Castensson, A., Koisti, M., et al. (1999). Linkage analysis of a large Swedish kindred provides further support for a susceptibility locus for schizophrenia on chromosome 6p23. *American Journal of Medical Genetics, 88,* 369-377.

Loeber, R., & Farrington, D. P. (2000). Young children who commit crime: Epidemiology, developmental origins, risk factors, early interventions, and policy implications. *Development and Psychopathology, 12,* 737-762.

Loeber, R., Stouthamer-Loeber, M., & White, H. R. (1999). Developmental aspects of delinquency and internalizing problems and their association with persistent juvenile substance use between ages 7 and 18. *Journal of Clinical Child Psychology, 28,* 322-332.

Loehlin, J. C. (1992). *Genes and environment in personality development.* Newbury Park, CA: Sage.

Loehlin, J. C. (1998). *Latent variable models: An introduction to factor, path, and structural analysis* (3rd ed.). Mahwah, NJ: Lawrence Erlbaum.

Loehlin, J. C., Horn, J. M., & Willerman, L. (1994). Differential inheritance of mental abilities in the Texas Adoption Project. *Intelligence, 19,* 325-336.

Loehlin, J. C., Horn, J. M., & Willerman, L. (1997). Heredity, environment and IQ in the Texas Adoption Project. In R. J. Sternberg & E. L. Grigorenko (Eds.), *Intelligence, heredity, and environment* (pp. 105-125). New York: Cambridge University Press.

Loehlin, J. C., & Nichols, R. C. (1976). *Heredity, environment, and personality: A study of 850 sets of twins.* Austin: University of Texas Press.

Lorey, F. W., Arnopp, J., & Cunningham, G. C. (1996). Distribution of hemoglobinopathy variants by ethnicity in a multiethnic state. *Genetic Epidemiology, 13,* 501-512.

Lykken, D. T. (1995). *The antisocial personalities.* Hillsdale, NJ: Lawrence Erlbaum Associates.

Lykken, D., & Tellegen, A. (1996). Happiness is a stochastic phenomenon. *Psychological Science, 7,* 186-189.

Lyons, M. J., Goldberg, J., Eisen, S. A., True, W., Tsuang, M. T., Meyer, J. M., et al. (1993). Do genes influence exposure to trauma? A twin study of combat. *Am J Med Genet, 48,* 22-27.

Lyons, M. J., True, W. R., Eisen, S. A., Goldberg, J., Meyer, J. M., Faraone, S. V., et al. (1995). Differential heritability of adult and juvenile antisocial traits. *Archives of General Psychiatry, 52,* 906-915.

Mannens, M., & Alders, M. (1999). Genomic imprinting: Concept and clinical consequences. *Annals of Medicine, 31,* 4-11.

Marks, I. M. (1987). *Fears, phobias, and rituals: Panic, anxiety, and their disorders.* New York: Oxford University Press.

Martin, N. G., & Jardine, R. (1986). Eysenck's contributions to behavior genetics. In S. Modgil & C. Modgil (Eds.), *Hans Eysenck: Consensus and controversy* (pp. 13-62). Lewes, Sussex, UK: Falmer Press.

Mason, D. A., & Frick, P. J. (1994). The heritability of antisocial behavior: A meta-analysis of twin and adoption studies. *Journal of Psychopathology & Behavioral Assessment, 16,* 301-323.

McCauley, E., Ross, J. L., Kushner, H., & Cutler, G., Jr. (1995). Self-esteem and behavior in girls with Turner syndrome. *Journal of Developmental and Behavioral Pediatrics, 16,* 82-88.

McCrae, R. R., & Costa, P. T. J. (1999). A five-factor theory of personality. In L. A. Pervin & O. P. John (Eds.), *Handbook of personality research* (2nd ed., pp. 139-153). New York: Guilford.

McGue, M., Bacon, S., & Lykken, D. T. (1993). Personality stability and change in early adulthood: A behavioral genetic analysis. *Developmental Psychology, 29,* 96-109.

McGue, M., Bouchard, T. J., Jr., Iacono, W. G., & Lykken, D. T. (1993). Behavior genetics of cognitive ability: A life-span perspective. In R. Plomin & G. E. McClearn (Eds.), *Nature, nurture & psychology* (pp. 59-76). Washington, DC: American Psychological Association.

McGue, M., Gottesman, I. I., & Rao, D. C. (1983). The transmission of schizophrenia under a multifactorial threshold model. *American Journal of Human Genetics, 35,* 1161-1178.

McGue, M., & Lykken, D. T. (1992). Genetic influence on risk of divorce. *Psychological Science, 3,* 368-373.

McNeil, T. F., Cantor-Graae, E., & Weinberger, D. R. (2000). Relationship of obstetric complications and differences in size of brain structures in monozygotic twin pairs discordant for schizophrenia. *American Journal of Psychiatry, 157,* 203-212.

Mears, J. G., Lachman, H. M., Cabannes, R., Amegnizin, K. P., Labie, D., & Nagel, R. L. (1981). Sickle gene: Its origin and diffusion from West Africa. *Journal of Clinical Investigation, 68,* 606-610.

Mednick, S. A., Gabrielli, W. F., Jr., & Hutchings, B. (1984). Genetic influences in criminal convictions: Evidence from an adoption cohort. *Science, 224,* 891-894.

Meyer, J. M., Rutter, M., Silberg, J. L., Maes, H. H., Simonoff, E., Shillady, L. L., et al. (2000). Familial aggregation for conduct disorder symptomatology: The role of genes, marital discord and family adaptability. *Psychological Medicine, 30,* 759-774.

Miles, D. R., & Carey, G. (1997). Genetic and environmental architecture on human aggresssion. *Journal of Personality & Social Psychology, 72*, 207-217.

Miller, P., Mulvey, C., & Martin, N. G. (1995). What do twin studies reveal about the economic returns to education? A comparison of Australian and U.S. findings. *American Economic Review, 85*, 586-599.

Mineka, S., Davidson, M., Cook, M., & Keir, R. (1984). Observational conditioning of snake fear in rhesus monkeys. *Journal of Abnormal Psychology, 93*, 355-372.

Mirchev, R., & Ferrone, F. A. (1997). The structural link between polymerization and sickle cell disease. *Journal of Molecular Biology, 265*, 475-479.

Moffitt, T. E. (1987). Parental mental disorder and offspring criminal behavior: An adoption study. *Psychiatry, 50*, 346-360.

Moffitt, T. E. (1993). "Life-course persistent" and "adolescence-limited" antisocial behavior: A developmental taxonomy. *Psychological Review, 100*, 674-701.

Moises, H. W., Yang, L., Kristbjarnarson, H., Wiese, C., Byerley, W., Macciardi, F., et al. (1995). An international two-stage genome-wide search for schizophrenia susceptibility genes. *Nature Genetics, 11*, 321-324.

Money, J. (1970). Behavior genetics: Principles, methods and examples from XO, XXY and XYY syndromes. *Seminars in Psychiatry, 2*, 11-29.

Muramatsu, T., Wang, Z. C., Fang, Y. R., Hu, K. B., Yan, H., Yamada, K., Higuchi, S., Harada, S., & Kono, H. (1995). Alcohol and aldehyde dehydrogenase geno-types and drinking behavior of Chinese living in Shanghai. *Human Genetics, 96*, 151-154.

Murayama, M., Matsushita, S., Muramatsu, T., & Higuchi, S. (1998). Clinical character-istics and disease course of alcoholics with inactive aldehyde dehydrogenase-2. *Alcoholism: Clinical and Experimental Research, 22*, 524-527.

Myers, D. G., & Diener, E. (1995). Who is happy? *Psychological Science, 6*, 10-19.

Nakawatase, T. V., Yamamoto, J., & Sasao, T. (1993). The association between fast-flushing response and alcohol use among Japanese Americans. *Journal of Studies on Alcohol, 54*, 48-53.

Nance, W. E., & Neale, M. C. (1989). Partitioned twin analysis: A power study. *Behavior Genetics, 19*, 143-150.

Neale, M. C., & Cardon, L. R. (1992). *Methodology for genetic studies of twins and families.* Dordrecht, The Netherlands: Kluwer.

Neale, M. C., & Stevenson, J. (1989). Rater bias in the EASI temperament scales: A twin study. *Journal of Personality and Social Psychology, 56*, 446-455.

Neale, M. C., Walters, E., Heath, A. C., Kessler, R. C., Perusse, D., Eaves, L. J., et al. (1994). Depression and parental bonding: Cause, consequence, or genetic covariance? *Genetic Epidemiology, 11*, 503-522.

Nei, M. (1987). *Molecular evolutionary genetics.* New York: Columbia University Press.

Nei, M., & Roychoudhury, A. K. (1974). Genetic variation within and between the three major races of man, Caucasoids, Negroids, and Mongoloids. *American Journal of Human Genetics, 26*, 421-443.

Neiderhiser, J. M., Reiss, D., Hetherington, E. M., & Plomin, R. (1999). Relationships between parenting and adolescent adjustment over time: Genetic and environ-mental contributions. *Developmental Psychology, 35*, 680-692.

Neisser, U. (Ed.). (1998). *The rising curve: Long-term gains in IQ and related mea-sures.* Washington, DC: American Psychological Association.

Neisser, U., Boodoo, G., Bouchard, T.J.J., Boykin,. A. W., Brody, N., Ceci, S. J., et al. (1996). Intelligence: Knowns and unknowns. *American Psychologist, 51*, 77-101.

Nesse, R. M. (1990). Evolutionary explanations of emotions. *Human Nature, 1*, 261-289.

Nesse, R. M., & Williams, G. C. (1994). *Why we get sick: The new science of Darwinian medicine.* New York: Times Books.

Neve, R. L., & Robakis, N. K. (1998). Alzheimer's disease: A re-examination of the amyloid hypothesis. *Trends in Neurosciences, 21*, 15-19.

Nicholls, R. D., & Knepper, J. L. (2001). Genome organization, function, and imprinting in Prader-Willi and Angelman syndromes. *Annual Review of Genomics and Human Genetics, 2*, 153-175.

Nurnberger, J. I., Jr., & Foroud, T. (1999). Chromosome 6 workshop report. *American Journal of Medical Genetics, 88*, 233-238.

O'Connor, T. G., Deater-Deckard, K., Fulker, D., Rutter, M., & Plomin, R. (1998). Genotype-environment correlations in late childhood and early adolescence: Antisocial behavioral problems and coercive parenting. *Developmental Psychology, 34*, 970-981.

O'Connor, T. G., Neiderhiser, J. M., Reiss, D., Hetherington, E. M., & Plomin, R. (1998). Genetic contributions to continuity, change, and co-occurrence of antisocial and depressive symptoms in adolescence. *Journal of Child Psychology & Psychiatry & Allied Disciplines, 39*, 323-336.

Ohman, A., Erixon, G., & Lofberg, I. (1975). Phobias and preparedness: Phobic versus neutral pictures and conditioned stimuli for human autonomic responses. *Journal of Abnormal Psychology, 84*, 41-45.

Pedersen, N. L., Plomin, R., Nesselroade, J. R., & McClearn, G. E. (1992). A quantitative genetic analysis of cognitive abilities during the second half of the life span. *Psychological Science, 3*, 346-353.

Pedersen, N. L., & Reynolds, C. A. (1998). Stability and change in adult personality: Genetic and environmental components. *European Journal of Personality, 12*, 365-386.

Penner, K. A., Johnston, J., Faircloth, B. H., Irish, P., & Williams, C. A. (1993). Communication, cognition, and social interaction in the Angelman syndrome. *American Journal of Medical Genetics, 46*, 34-39.

Pericak-Vance, M. A., Grubber, J., Bailey, L. R., Hedges, D., West, S., Santoro, L., et al. (2000). Identification of novel genes in late-onset Alzheimer's disease. *Experimental Gerontology, 35*, 1343-1352.

Petrill, S. A., Plomin, R., Berg, S., Johansson, B., Pedersen, N. L., Ahern, F., et al. (1998). The genetic and environmental relationship between general and specific cognitive abilities in twins age 80 and older. *Psychological Science, 9*, 183-189.

Phillips, K., & Matheny, A. P., Jr. (1997). Evidence for genetic influence on both cross-situation and situation-specific components of behavior. *Journal of Personality and Social Psychology, 73*, 129-138.

Pickles, A., Crouchley, R., Simonoff, E., Eaves, L., Meyer, J., Rutter, M., et al. (1994). Survival models for developmental genetic data: Age of onset of puberty and antisocial behavior in twins. *Genetic Epidemiology, 11*, 155-170.

Pinker, S. (1997). *How the mind works*. New York: W. W. Norton & Company.

Plomin, R. (1999). Genetics and general cognitive ability. *Nature, 402*, C25-C29.

Plomin, R., & Caspi, A. (1999). Behavioral genetics and personality. In L. A. Pervin & O. P. John (Eds.), *Handbook of personality: Theory and research* (2nd ed., pp. 251-276). New York: Guilford.

Plomin, R., Coon, H., Carey, G., DeFries, J. C., & Fulker, D. W. (1991). Parent-offspring and sibling adoption analyses of parental ratings of temperament in infancy and childhood. *Journal of Personality, 59*, 705-732.

Plomin, R., Corley, R., Caspi, A., Fulker, D. W., & DeFries, J. (1998). Adoption results for self-reported personality: Evidence for nonadditive genetic effects? *Journal of Personality and Social Psychology, 75*, 211-218.

Plomin, R., Corley, R., DeFries, J. C., & Fulker, D. W. (1990). Individual differences in television viewing in early childhood: Nature as well as nurture. *Psychological Science, 1*, 371-377.

Plomin, R., & DeFries, J. C. (1985). *Origins of individual differences in infancy: The Colorado adoption project.* Orlando, FL: Academic Press.

Plomin, R., DeFries, J. C., & Fulker, D. W. (1988). *Nature and nurture during infancy and early childhood.* New York: Cambridge University Press.

Plomin, R., DeFries, J. C., & Loehlin, J. C. (1978). Gene-environment interaction and correlation in the analysis of human behavior. *Psychological Bulletin, 84,* 309-322.

Plomin, R., Emde, R. N., Braungart, J. M., Campos, J., Corley, R., Fulker, D., et al. (1993). Genetic change and continuity from fourteen to twenty months: The MacArthur Longitudinal Twin Study. *Child Development, 64,* 1354-1376.

Plomin, R., Fulker, D. W., Corley, R., & DeFries, J. C. (1997). Nature, nurture, and cognitive development from 1 to 16 years: A parent-offspring adoption study. *Psychological Science, 8,* 442-447.

Plomin, R., Pedersen, N. L., Lichtenstein, P., & McClearn, G. E. (1994). Variability and stability in cognitive abilities are largely genetic later in life. *Behavior Genetics, 24,* 207-215.

Ramus, S. J., Forrest, S. M., Pitt, D. B., Saleeba, J. A., & Cotton, R. G. (1993). Comparison of genotype and intellectual phenotype in untreated PKU patients. *Journal of Medical Genetics, 30,* 401-405.

Raven, J. (2000). The Raven's Progressive Matrices: Change and stability over culture and time. *Cognition, 41,* 1-48.

Raven, J. C. (1960). *Guide to the Standard Progressive Matrices.* London: H. K. Lewis.

Reed, W., & Vichinsky, E. P. (1998). New considerations in the treatment of sickle cell disease. *Annual Review of Medicine, 49,* 461-474.

Repetto, G. M. (2001). Genomic imprinting and human chromosome 15. *Biological Research, 34,* 141-145.

Rhee, S. H., & Waldman, I. D. (2002). Genetic and environmental influences on antisocial behavior: A meta-analysis of twin and adoption studies. *Psychological Bulletin, 128,* 490-529.

Rice, T., Carey, G., Fulker, D. W., & DeFries, J. C. (1989). Multivariate path analysis of specific cognitive abilities in the Colorado Adoption Project: Conditional path model of assortative mating. *Behavior Genetics, 19,* 195-207.

Riemann, R., Angleitner, A., & Strelau, J. (1997). Genetic and environmental influences on personality: A study of twins reared together using the self- and peer-report NEO-FFI scales. *Journal of Personality, 65,* 449-475.

Rijsdijk, F. V., Vernon, P. A., & Boomsma, D. I. (2002). Application of hierarchical genetic models to Raven and Wais subtests: A Dutch twin study. *Behavior Genetics, 32,* 199-210.

Robins, L. N. (1974). *Deviant children grow up.* Huntington, NY: Krieger.

Robinson, A., Bender, B. G., & Linden, M. G. (1990). Summary of clinical findings in children and young adults with sex chromosome anomalies. *Birth Defects Original Article Series, 26,* 225-228.

Rose, R. J., Koskenvuo, M., Kaprio, J., Sarna, S., & Langinvainio, H. (1988). Shared genes, shared experiences, and similarity of personality: Data from 14,288 adult Finnish co-twins. *Journal of Personality & Social Psychology, 54,* 161-171.

Ross, J., Zinn, A., & McCauley, E. (2000). Neurodevelopmental and psychosocial aspects of Turner syndrome. *Mental Retardation and Developmental Disabilities Research Reviews, 6,* 135-141.

Rowe, D. C. (1983). Biometrical genetic models of self-reported delinquent behavior: A twin study. *Behavior Genetics, 13,* 473-489.

Rowe, D. C. (1985). Sibling interaction and self-reported delinquent behavior: A study of 265 twin pairs. *Criminology, 23,* 223-240.

Rowe, D. C. (1986). Genetic and environmental components of antisocial behavior: A study of 265 twin pairs. *Criminology, 24,* 512-532.

Rowe, D. C. (1994). *The limits of family influence: Genes, experience, and behavior.* New York: Guilford.

Rowe, D. C. (1996). An adaptive strategy theory of crime and delinquency. In J. D. Hawkins (Ed.), *Delinquency and crime: Current theories.* Cambridge, UK: Cambridge University Press.

Rowe, D. C. (2001). *Biology and crime.* Los Angeles: Roxbury.

Rowe, D. C., Jacobson, K. C., & Van den Oord, E. J. (1999). Genetic and environmental influences on vocabulary IQ: Parental education level as moderator. *Child Development, 70,* 1151-1162.

Rowe, D. C., & Plomin, R. (1977). Temperament in early childhood. *Journal of Personality Assessment, 41,* 150-156.

Rowe, D. C., & Plomin, R. (1981). The importance of nonshared (E1) environmental influence in behavioral development. *Developmental Psychology, 17,* 517-531.

Rowe, D. C., Stever, C., Giedinghagen, L. N., Gard, J. M., Cleveland, H. H., Terris, S. T., et al. (1998). Dopamine DRD4 receptor polymorphism and attention deficit hyperactivity disorder. *Molecular Psychiatry, 3,* 419-426.

Rowe, D. C., Vesterdal, W. J., & Rodgers, J. L. (1998). Herrnstein's syllogism: Genetic and shared environmental influences on IQ, education, and income. *Intelligence, 26,* 405-423.

Rubinsztein, D. C., & Easton, D. F. (1999). Apolipoprotein E genetic variation and Alzheimer's disease: A meta-analysis. *Dementia and Geriatric Cognitive Disorders, 10,* 199-209.

Saudino, K. J., McGuire, S., Reiss, D., Hetherington, E. M., & Plomin, R. (1995). Parent ratings of EAS temperaments in twins, full siblings, half siblings, and step siblings. *Journal of Personality and Social Psychology, 68,* 723-733.

Scarr, S. (1968). Environmental bias in twin studies. *Eugenics Quarterly, 15,* 34-40.

Scarr, S., & Carter-Saltzman, L. (1979). Twin method: Defense of a critical assumption. *Behavior Genetics, 9,* 527-542.

Scarr, S., & McCartney, K. (1983). How people make their own environments: A theory of genotype environment effects. *Child Development, 54,* 424-435.

Scarr, S., & Weinberg, R. A. (1978). The influence of "family background" on intellectual attainment. *American Sociological Review, 43,* 674-692.

Scarr, S., & Weinberg, R. A. (1994). Educational and occupational achievements of brothers and sisters in adoptive and biologically related families. *Behavior Genetics, 24,* 301-325.

Scarr, S., Weinberg, R. A., & Waldman, I. D. (1993). IQ correlations in transracial adoptive families. *Intelligence, 17,* 541-555.

Schmitz, S., Saudino, K. J., Plomin, R., Fulker, D. W., & DeFries, J. C. (1996). Genetic and environmental influences on temperament in middle childhood: Analyses of teacher and tester ratings. *Child Development, 67,* 409-422.

Schwab, S. G., Albus, M., Hallmayer, J., Honig, S., Borrmann, M., Lichtermann, D., et al. (1995). Evaluation of a susceptibility gene for schizophrenia on chromosome 6p by multipoint affected sib-pair linkage analysis. *Nature Genetics, 11,* 325-327.

Segal, N. L. (1999). *Entwined lives: Twins and what they tell us about human behavior.* New York: Dutton.

Seligman, M.E.P., & Hager, J. L. (1972). *Biological boundaries on learning.* New York: Appleton-Century-Crofts.

Sharman, A.C., & Brand, M. (1998). Evolution and homology of the nervous system: Cross-phylum rescues of *otd/Otx* genes. *Trends in Genetics, 14,* 211-214.

Sherman, S. L., Jacobs, P. A., Morton, N. E., Froster-Iskenius, U., Howard-Peebles, P. N., Nielsen, K. B., Partington, M. W., Sutherland, G. R., Turner, G., & Watson, M. (1985). Further segregation analysis of the fragile X syndrome with special reference to transmitting males. *Human Genetics, 69,* 289-299.

Sherman, S. L., Morton, N. E., Jacobs, P. A., & Turner, G. (1984). The marker (X) syndrome: A cytogenetic and genetic analysis. *Annals of Human Genetics, 48*, 21-37.

Siegel, P. T., Clopper, R., & Stabler, B. (1998). The psychological consequences of Turner syndrome and review of the National Cooperative Growth Study psychological substudy. *Pediatrics, 102*, 488-491.

Sigvardsson, S., Cloninger, C. R., Bohman, M., & von Knorring, A. L. (1982). Predisposition to petty criminality in Swedish adoptees: III. Sex differences and validation of the male typology. *Archives of General Psychiatry, 39*, 1248-1253.

Skuse, D. H., James, R. S., Bishop, D. V., Coppin, B., Dalton, P., Aamodt-Leeper, G., et al. (1997). Evidence from Turner's syndrome of an imprinted X-linked locus affecting cognitive function. *Nature, 387*, 705-708.

Slater, E., & Cowie, V. (1971). *The genetics of mental disorders*. Oxford, UK: Oxford University Press.

Slutske, W. S., Heath, A. C., Dinwiddie, S. H., Madden, P. A., Bucholz, K. K., Dunne, M. P., et al. (1997). Modeling genetic and environmental influences in the etiology of conduct disorder: A study of 2,682 adult twin pairs. *Journal of Abnormal Psychology, 106*, 266-279.

Slutske, W. S., Heath, A. C., Dinwiddie, S. H., Madden, P. A., Bucholz, K. K., Dunne, M. P., et al. (1998). Common genetic risk factors for conduct disorder and alcohol dependence. *Journal of Abnormal Psychology, 107*, 363-374.

Small, G. W. (1998). The pathogenesis of Alzheimer's disease. *Journal of Clinical Psychiatry, 59*, 7-14.

Smalley, S. L., Bailey, J. N., Palmer, C. G., Cantwell, D. P., McGough, J. J., Del'Homme, M. A., et al. (1998). Evidence that the dopamine D4 receptor is a susceptibility gene in attention deficit hyperactivity disorder. *Molecular Psychiatry, 3*, 427-430.

Snow, R. E., & Yallow, E. (1982). Education and intelligence. In R. J. Sternberg (Ed.), *Handbook of human intelligence* (pp. 493-585). Cambridge, UK: Cambridge University Press.

Sokol, D. K., Moore, C. A., Rose, R. J., Williams, C. J., Reed, T., & Christian, J. C. (1995). Intrapair differences in personality and cognitive ability among young monozygotic twins distinguished by chorion type. *Behavior Genetics, 25*, 457-466.

Solomon, E., & Bodmer, W. F. (1979). Evolution of sickle variant gene. *Lancet, 1*, 923.

St. George-Hyslop, P. H. (2000). Molecular genetics of Alzheimer's disease. *Biological Psychiatry, 47*, 183-199.

Stassen, H. H., Coppola, R., Gottesman, I.I., Torrey, E. F., Kuny, S., Rickler, K. C., et al. (1999). EEG differences in monozygotic twins discordant and concordant for schizophrenia. *Psychophysiology, 36*, 109-117.

Steinmetz, C. G., Xie, P., Weiner, H., & Hurley, T. D. (1997). Structure of mitochondrial aldehyde dehydrogenase: The genetic component of ethanol aversion. *Structure, 5*, 701-711.

Sternberg, R. J. (1988). *The triarchic mind: A new theory of human intelligence*. New York: Penguin.

Straub, R. E., MacLean, C. J., O'Neill, F. A., Burke, J., Murphy, B., Duke, F., et al. (1995). A potential vulnerability locus for schizophrenia on chromosome 6p24- 22: Evidence for genetic heterogeneity. *Nature Genetics, 11*, 287-293.

Swan, G. E., Carmelli, D., Reed, T., Harshfield, G. A., Fabsitz, R. R., & Eslinger, P. J. (1990). Heritability of cognitive performance in aging twins: The National Heart, Lung, and Blood Institute Twin Study. *Archives of Neurology, 47*, 259-262.

Swan, G. E., LaRue, A., Carmelli, D., Reed, T. E., & Fabsitz, R. R.. (1992). Decline in cognitive performance in aging twins: Heritability and biobehavioral predictors from the National Heart, Lung, and Blood Institute Twin Study. *Archives of Neurology, 49*, 476-481.

Takeshita, T., Maruyama, S., & Morimoto, K. (1998). Relevance of both daily hassles and the ALDH2 genotype to problem drinking among Japanese male workers. *Alcoholism: Clinical and Experimental Research, 22*, 115-120.

Tambs, K., Sundet, J. M., & Magnus, P. (1986). Genetic and environmental contributions to the covariation between the Wechsler Adult Intelligence Scale (WAIS) subtests: A study of twins. *Behavior Genetics, 16*, 475-491.

Tambs, K., Sundet, J. M., Magnus, P., & Berg, K. (1989). Genetic and environment contributions to the covariation between occupational status, educational attainment, and IQ: A study of twins. *Behavior Genetics, 19*, 209-221.

Tanaka, F., Shiratori, Y., Yokosuka, O., Imazeki, F., Tsukada, Y., & Omata, M. (1997). Polymorphism of alcohol-metabolizing genes affects drinking behavior and alcoholic liver disease in Japanese men. *Alcoholism: Clinical and Experimental Research, 21*, 596-601.

Tang, M. X., Maestre, G., Tsai, W. Y., Liu, X. H., Feng, L., Chung, W. Y., et al. (1996). Effect of age, ethnicity, and head injury on the association between APOE genotypes and Alzheimer's disease. *Annals of the New York Academy of Sciences, 802*, 6-15.

Tassone, F., Hagerman, R. J., Chamberlain, W. D., & Hagerman, P. J. (2000). Transcription of the FMR1 gene in individuals with fragile X syndrome. *American Journal of Medical Genetics, 97*, 195-203.

Taubman, P. (1976). The determinants of earnings: Genetic, family and other environments: A study of white male twins. *American Economic Review, 66*, 858-870.

Taylor, J., Iacono, W. G., & McGue, M. (2000). Evidence for a genetic etiology of early-onset delinquency. *Journal of Abnormal Psychology, 109*, 634-643.

Teasdale, T. W., & Owen, D. R. (1981). Social class correlations among separately adopted siblings and unrelated individuals adopted together. *Behavior Genetics, 11*, 577-588.

Teasdale, T. W., & Owen, D. R. (1984). Heredity and familial environment in intelligence and educational level: A sibling study. *Nature, 309*, 620-622.

Teasdale, T. W., & Owen, D. R. (1986). The influence of paternal social class on intelligence and educational level in male adoptees and non-adoptees. *British Journal of Educational Psychology, 56*, 3-12.

Tellegen, A. (1985). Structures of mood and personality and their relevance to assessing anxiety, with an emphasis on self-report. In A. H. Tuma & J. Maser (Eds.), *Anxiety and the anxiety disorders* (pp. 681-706). Hillsdale, NJ: Lawrence Erlbaum.

Tellegen, A., Lykken, D. T., Bouchard, T. J., Jr., Wilcox, K. J., Segal, N. L., & Rich, S. (1988). Personality similarity in twins reared apart and together. *Journal of Personality and Social Psychology, 54*, 1031-1039.

Templeton, A. R. (1999). Human races: A genetic and evolutionary perspective. *American Anthropologist, 100*, 632-650.

Thapar, A., & McGuffin, P. (1996). A twin study of antisocial and neurotic symptoms in childhood. *Psychological Medicine, 26*, 1111-1118.

Theilgaard, A. (1984). A psychological study of the personalities of XYY- and XXY-men. *Acta Psychiatrica Scandinavica, 315*(Suppl.), 1-133.

Thomas, P. W., Higgs, D. R., & Serjeant, G. R. (1997). Benign clinical course in homozygous sickle cell disease: A search for predictors. *Journal of Clinical Epidemiology, 50*, 121-126.

Thomasson, H. R., Edenberg, H. J., Crabb, D. W., Mai, X. L., Jerome, R. E., Li, T. K., Wang, S. P., Lin, Y. T., Lu, R. B., & Yin, S. J. (1991). Alcohol and aldehyde dehydrogenase genotypes and alcoholism in Chinese men. *American Journal of Human Genetics, 48*, 677-681.

Thompson, L. A., Detterman, D. K., & Plomin, R. (1991). Associations between cognitive abilities and scholastic achievement: Genetic overlap but environmental differences. *Psychological Science, 2*, 158-165.

Thorndike, E. L. (1911). *Animal intelligence*. New York: Macmillan.

Tomarken, A. J., Mineka, S., & Cook, M. (1989). Fear-relevant selective associations and covariation bias. *Journal of Abnormal Psychology, 98*, 381-394.

Trefz, F. K., Burgard, P., Konig, T., Goebel-Schreiner, B., Lichter-Konecki, U., Konecki, D., Schmidt, E., Schmidt, H., & Bickel, H. (1993). Genotype-phenotype correlations in phenylketonuria. *Clinica Chimica Acta, 217*, 15-21.

Tremblay, R. E., Japel, C., Perusse, D., McDuff, P., Boivin, M., Zoccolillo, M., et al. (1999). The search for the age of "onset" of physical aggression: Rousseau and Bandura revisited. *Criminal Behavior and Mental Health, 9*, 8-23.

Trivers, R. L. (1971). The evolution of reciprocal altruism. *Quarterly Review of Biology, 46*, 35-57.

Trivers, R. L. (1972). Parental investment and sexual selection. In B. Campbell (Ed.), *Sexual selection and the descent of man: 1871-1971* (pp. 136-179). Chicago: Aldine.

Truett, K. R., Eaves, L. J., Meyer, J. M., Heath, A. C., & Martin, N. G. (1992). Religion and education as mediators of attitudes: A multivariate analysis. *Behavior Genetics, 22*, 43-62.

Tu, G.-C., & Israel, Y. (1995). Alcohol consumption by Orientals in North America is predicted largely by a single gene. *Behavior Genetics, 25*, 59-65.

Tuddenham, R. D. (1948). Soldier intelligence in World Wars I and II. *American Psychologist, 3*, 54-56.

Turkheimer, E. (2000). Three laws of behavioral genetics and what they mean. *Current Directions in Psychological Science, 9*, 160-164.

Tutin, C. E. (1980). Reproductive behaviour of wild chimpanzees in the Gombe National Park, Tanzania. *Journal of Reproduction and Fertility* (Suppl. 28), 43-57.

van Lieshout, C. F., De Meyer, R. E., Curfs, L. M., & Fryns, J. P. (1998a). Family contexts, parental behaviour, and personality profiles of children and adolescents with Prader-Willi, Fragile-X, or Williams syndrome *Journal of Child Psychology and Psychiatry and Allied Disciplines, 39*, 699-710.

van Lieshout, C. F., De Meyer, R. E., Curfs, L. M., Koot, H. M., & Fryns, J. P. (1998b). Problem behaviors and personality of children and adolescents with Prader-Willi syndrome. *Journal of Pediatric Psychology, 23*, 111-120.

Van Tol, H.H.M., Wu, C. M., Guan, H.-C., Ohara, K., Bunzow, J. R., Civelli, O., et al. (1992). Multiple dopamine D4 receptor variants in the human population. *Nature, 358*, 149-152.

Viken, R. J., Rose, R. J., Kaprio, J., & Koskenvuo, M. (1994). A developmental genetic analysis of adult personality: Extraversion and neuroticism from 18 to 59. *Journal of Personality and Social Psychology, 66*, 722-730.

Vogler, G. P., & Fulker, D. W. (1983). Familial resemblance for educational attainment. *Behavior Genetics, 13*, 341-354.

Wadsworth, S. J., DeFries, J. C., Fulker, D. W., & Plomin, R. (1995). Cognitive ability and academic achievement in the Colorado Adoption Project: A multivariate genetic analysis of parent-offspring and sibling data. *Behavior Genetics, 25*, 1-15.

Wainscoat, J. S., Bell, J. I., Thein, S. L., Higgs, D. R., Sarjeant, G. R., Peto, T. E., & Weatherall, D. J. (1983). Multiple origins of the sickle mutation: Evidence from beta S globin gene cluster polymorphisms. *Molecular Biology and Medicine, 1*, 191-197.

Wang, S., Sun, C. E., Walczak, C. A., Ziegle, J. S., Kipps, B. R., Goldin, L. R., et al. (1995). Evidence for a susceptibility locus for schizophrenia on chromosome 6pter-p22. *Nature Genetics, 10*, 41-46.

Weinberg, R. A., Scarr, S., & Waldman, I. D. (1992). The Minnesota Transracial Adoption Study: A follow-up of IQ test performance at adolescence. *Intelligence, 16*, 117-135.

Weisbrod, M., Hill, H., Niethammer, R., & Sauer, H. (1999). Genetic influence on auditory information processing in schizophrenia: P300 in monozygotic twins. *Biological Psychiatry, 46*, 721-725.

White, K. R. (1982). The relation between socioeconomic status and academic achievement. *Psychological Bulletin, 91*, 461-481.

Widiger, T. A., Cadoret, R., Hare, R., Robins, L., Rutherford, M., Zanarini, M., et al. (1996). DSM-IV antisocial personality disorder field trial. *Journal of Abnormal Psychology, 105*, 3-16.

Wilson, R. S. (1983). The Louisville twin study: Developmental synchronies in behavior. *Child Development, 54*, 298-316.

Wilson, R. S. (1986). Continuity and change in cognitive ability profile. *Behavior Genetics, 16*, 45-60.

Witkin, H. A., Mednick, S. A., Schulsinger, F., Bakkestrom, E., Christiansen, K. O., Goodenough, D. R., et al. (1976). Criminality in XYY and XXY men. *Science, 193*, 547-555.

Wolpoff, M., & Caspari, R. (1997). *Race and human evolution.* New York: Simon & Schuster.

Wrangham, R., & Peterson, D. (1996). *Demonic males: Apes and the origins of human violence.* Boston: Houghton Mifflin.

Wright, R. (1994). *The moral animal.* New York: Pantheon.

Wright, S. (1968-1978). *Evolution and the genetics of populations: A treatise in four volumes.* Chicago: University of Chicago Press.

Yin, S. J. (1994). Alcohol dehydrogenase: Enzymology and metabolism. *Alcohol and Alcoholism, 2*, 113-119.

Yoshida, A. (1992). Molecular genetics of human aldehyde dehydrogenase. *Pharmacogenetics, 2*, 139-147.

Young, S. E., Stallings, M. C., Corley, R. P., Krauter, K. S., & Hewitt, J. K. (2000). Genetic and environmental influences on behavioral disinhibition. *American Journal of Medical Genetics, 96*, 684-695.

Zimring, F. E., & Hawkings, G. (1997). *Crime is not the problem: Lethal violence in America.* New York: Oxford University Press.

Zori, R. T., Hendrickson, J., Woolven, S., Whidden, E. M., Gray, B., & Williams, C. A. (1992). Angelman syndrome: Clinical profile. *Journal of Child Neurology, 7*, 270-280.

Zucker, K. J., Bradley, S. J., Oliver, G., & Blake, J. (1996). Psychosexual development of women with congenital adrenal hyperplasia. *Hormones & Behavior, 30*, 300-318.

AUTHOR INDEX

SUBJECT INDEX

ABOUT THE AUTHOR

Gregory Carey is Associate Professor, Department of Psychology, and Faculty Fellow, Institute of Behavioral Genetics, both at the University of Colorado at Boulder.

CPSIA information can be obtained at www.ICGtesting.com
227852LV00001B/2/P

9 780761 923459